30

P9-CCO-179

# Mary Wollstonecraft

## A REVOLUTIONARY LIFE

By the same author

*Women's Friendship in Literature*

*The Sign of Angellica; Women, Writing and Fiction 1600–1800*

*Gender, Art and Death*

*The Secret Life of Aphra Behn*

# Mary Wollstonecraft

## A REVOLUTIONARY LIFE

Janet Todd

Columbia University Press
New York

For Elizabeth

First published in Great Britain in 2000
by Weidenfeld & Nicolson

© 2000 Janet Todd

**The Library of Congress Cataloging-in-Publication number is 00-027352.
A full CIP record is available.**

Printed in Great Britain

ISBN 0-231-12184-9

# CONTENTS

List of illustrations      vii
Preface      ix
List of principal characters      xiii

PART I      1

PART II      121

PART III      203

PART IV      365

Notes      459
Bibliography      497
Index      507

# ILLUSTRATIONS

*Between pages 266 and 267*
The earliest known portrait of Mary Wollstonecraft by an unknown artist, commissioned by William Roscoe, 1791

> *Bond of Trustees of the National Museums and Galleries on Merseyside (Walker Art Gallery, Liverpool)*

Richard Price by Thomas Holloway after Benjamin West

> *By courtesy of the National Portrait Gallery, London*

Robert and Caroline King, Lord and Lady Kingsborough, artist unknown

> *Private collection*

Joseph Johnson by W. Sharpe after Moses Haughton

> *By courtesy of the National Portrait Gallery, London*

Illustrations by William Blake to Mary Wollstonecraft's *Original Stories*, second edition, 1791

> *Private collection*

Henry Fuseli by John Opie, exhibited in 1794

> *By courtesy of the National Portrait Gallery, London*

Self-portrait by John Opie, 1785

> *By courtesy of the National Portrait Gallery, London*

Mary Wollstonecraft by John Opie, *c.* 1792

> *© Tate Gallery, London*

Helen Maria Williams by J. Singleton, published 1792

> *Courtesy David Alexander*

Mary Wollstonecraft by J. Chapman after an unknown artist, published 1798

> *Private collection*

William Godwin and Thomas Holcroft at the Treason Trials by Sir Thomas Lawrence, 1794

> *Kenneth Garlick collection*

Elizabeth Inchbald by George Dance, 1794

> *By courtesy of the National Portrait Gallery, London*

Amelia Alderson, from Religious Tract Society, 1855

> *Private collection*

William Godwin by J. W. Chandler, 1798

> *© Tate Gallery, London*

Mary Wollstonecraft by John Opie, *c.* 1797

> *By courtesy of the National Portrait Gallery, London*

# PREFACE

In 1796 Amelia Alderson met the famous feminist Mary Wollstonecraft. She had been disappointed by most things in life but 'You & the *Lakes of Cumberland* have exceeded my expectations,' she wrote. 'I am not born to tread in the beaten track,' said her new friend.

Virginia Woolf called Wollstonecraft's life 'an experiment'; in 1885 the *Athenaeum* breathlessly termed it 'one of the most thrilling romances'. It was also a scandal: she loved a woman and at least three men, bore an illegitimate child during the French Revolution and was vilified by the nation as a whore and an 'unsex'd Female'. Yet, despite being sexual and passionate, she was profoundly, often irritatingly, moral and puritanical. Her dilemmas remain unresolved: how to reconcile the individual and the community? How to adjust motherhood to intellectual life and sexual desire? Is the price a woman pays for indulged sex too high?

For most writers, their writings matter most; this is so with her contemporary, Jane Austen. But Wollstonecraft insists we attend to her life. In her first book, she declared, the 'chosen few wish to speak for themselves'; in the last work published in her lifetime, she confessed, 'I found I could not avoid being continually the first person – "the little hero of each tale." ' Her voice is most insistent in her letters, which she wrote as child, daughter, companion, friend, teacher, governess, sister, literary hack, author, lover and wife. She talks and thinks on paper, using it as therapy, occasionally for self-mastery. She writes on the move, in boats, in remote Swedish inns, in freezing revolutionary Paris, before plunging suicidally into the Thames, and after her rescue. She dedicates herself to expressing her Self.

In Wollstonecraft's writings a new female consciousness comes into being, one that valued and reflected endlessly on its own workings, refusing to acknowledge anything absurd in the stance. No one living before her moment in the late eighteenth century, either man or woman, so clearly conveys this consciousness, one so sure of its significance, individuality and authenticity, its self-absorbed right and need to display itself for the attention of others. The huge sense of the 'I' in Mary Wollstonecraft's work is often infuriating but it is undeniably modern.

There are many books on Wollstonecraft's thought alone; I have not tried to duplicate them because I see her ideas as inextricably linked to her experience. She is at her best and most original when her writing interacts with her life. The loves of Mary Wollstonecraft have often been written. Here I stress also her tortured relations with her family, especially her two sisters, whom she mothered and smothered. All are part of a network of dependence, a family which circulated its pounds and grumbled about the necessity. Because they shared her volatile, depressive and self-dramatising temperament and were caught up in her tumultuous life, the sisters' letters reveal what Mary might have been without her special zest, and how she might have lived had she not made much of herself and taken the momentous step of becoming the 'first of a new *genus*', a professional woman writer.

The absence or presence of letters has dictated what periods have been emphasised in the story. The girlhood relationship with Fanny Blood was intense and long-lasting, but no letters survive between the pair and the tie is shadowy. The letters she wrote to the Swiss artist Fuseli existed into the late nineteenth century when they were handed over to the Shelley family and disappeared. So this relationship too remains unclear. Her main lover, Gilbert Imlay, can be seen only through Wollstonecraft's demanding letters, while William Godwin, her first biographer, husband, and the publisher of her posthumous works, exists both in his own and in her words. Since this final one is the only relationship so thoroughly documented, it looms large in the story, but it lasted for just sixteen months of Wollstonecraft's thirty-eight-year life. The extant letters have survived with the approval of their owners: Godwin let the public have only those which he thought worthy, and her last living sister, Everina, censored and probably destroyed what was too revealing.

The posthumous life of Mary Wollstonecraft changes with fashion. In different decades different aspects seem important. I have depended a good deal on excellent past biographies, beginning with Godwin's *Memoirs of the Author of A Vindication of the Rights of Woman*, written in 1798, the year following his wife's death. Grieving and expecting others to grieve with him, he mistakenly thought the nation would welcome a candid view of the woman he had surprisingly come to love. In the late nineteenth century, after decades of abuse, partly arising from Godwin's unusual frankness, Charles Kegan Paul in 1878 and Elizabeth Robins Pennell in 1885 used their biographies largely for vindication.

With the twentieth century it was possible to describe Wollstonecraft without too obvious an agenda. Ralph Wardle's ground-breaking biography in 1951 provided the first full account of the life, writings and context. In 1979 Wardle also published an edition of the letters; I have made full use of this and of the few extra letters discovered in the Pforzheimer Collection, New York.

When Wardle wrote his book Mary Wollstonecraft was largely unknown. By the 1970s, however, she was being celebrated as the mother of feminism. In this decade several biographies appeared, all adding something to her picture: Margaret George (1970), Edna Nixon (1971), Eleanor Flexner (1972), Claire Tomalin (1974), Emily W. Sunstein (1975), and Margaret Tims (1976). All were eager to show the formation of the feminist and the genesis of the public works, especially, of course, *A Vindication of the Rights of Woman*, now coming into prominence through early feminist criticism. Adding to these, William St Clair treated Wollstonecraft within a quadruple biography of Godwin, Wollstonecraft, Mary and Percy Bysshe Shelley (1989).

I am indebted to all these past biographies and to the biographical and critical work of Kenneth Neill Cameron, Mary Favret, Moira Ferguson, Bridget Hill, Richard Holmes, Mary Jacobus, Vivien Jones, Elaine Jordan, Harriet Devine Jump, Gary Kelly, Roger Lonsdale, Jane Moore, Mitzi Myers, Jane Rendall, Virginia Sapiro, Ashley Tauchert, Barbara Taylor and Eleanor Ty, among others. I have a personal debt for help and advice to Bruce Barker-Benfield, Antje Blank, Katherine Bright-Holmes, Marilyn Butler, Robert Clark, Jon Cook, John Davies, Elizabeth Denlinger, Derek Hughes, Ruth Inglis, Tim O'Hagan, Rosie Palumbo, James Raven, Tom Lloyd, Miranda Seymour, William St Clair, Elizabeth Spearing, Emily Sunstein, Sylvana Tomaselli, Claire Tomalin, Gina Luria Walker, and John Windle.

I have appreciated receiving answers and documents from librarians and curators of the following institutions: the Bodleian Library, Oxford; the University Library, Cambridge; the British Library; the Public Record Office, Kew; the Guildhall Library, London; the Library of University College, London; the London Metropolitan Archives; the Library of the Royal Society of Medicine; the City of Westminster Archives Centre; the Family Records Centre, Islington; Holborn Local Studies and Archives; the Berkshire Record Office, Reading; the Norfolk Archives, Norwich; the East Riding Archive Center, Beverley; Beverley Public Library; the Carmarthen County Archives; Pembroke County Archives, Haverfordwest; Keele University Library; the National Portrait Gallery; the New York Public Library; the Walker Art Gallery, Liverpool; the Pforzheimer Library, New York; the Library of Congress, Washington. I am especially grateful to Lord Abinger for granting me permission through the Bodleian Library to quote material from his manuscripts.

My final thanks are to the University of East Anglia for a semester's leave to complete this project.

Cambridge 1999

# PRINCIPAL CHARACTERS

Alderson, Amelia (1769–1853), from Unitarian family in Norwich. Went to London 1794 and became friend of Godwin, Holcroft, Tooke, and Inchbald. Knew MW in 1796. In 1798 married John Opie. Wrote plays and novels, including *Adeline Mowbray* (1804) which addressed issues related to the life and opinions of MW; became pious; died a Quaker.

Allen, John Bartlett (1733–1803), Pembrokeshire squire of Cresselly; married Elizabeth Hensleigh (d. 1790), granddaughter of vicar of Laugharne. Among their ten children was Elizabeth, who in 1792 married Josiah Wedgwood II of Etruria.

Ann, an orphan, possibly niece or cousin of second Mrs Skeys. Adopted by MW when 11; subsequently in the charge of Everina Wollstonecraft and Ruth Barlow.

Arden, Jane (1758–1840), born in Beverley, daughter of John Arden. MW's childhood friend and correspondent. Became governess and opened a successful school in Beverley in 1784. She married in 1798 and wrote several books for young people.

Arden, John (d. 1791), scientist and teacher. Settled in Beverley in the 1750s. Gave public lectures and met MW in Beverley and Bath.

Backman, Elias (1760–1829), merchant, friend and business associate of Imlay in France; moved to Gothenburg in Sweden 1794; visited by MW in summer 1795.

Barbauld, Anna Laetitia (1743–1825) (née Aikin), educational writer, teacher, poet, and essayist; from Dissenting background; married Revd Rochemont Barbauld; no children; lived in Hampstead when MW was working in London.

Barlow, Joel (1754–1812), American chaplain, editor and author; married Ruth Baldwin in 1781; went to Paris to sell American land, then moved to London where met MW; went to Hamburg 1794; returned to America 1805 and died on mission to Napoleon in Poland.

Barlow, Ruth (1756–1818) (née Baldwin), daughter of Connecticut blacksmith; married Joel; moved with him between London and Paris; friend of MW; died on estate, Kalorama, near Washington; no children.

Bishop, Meredith (1753–1835), shipwright from Rotherhithe; married Elizabeth Wollstonecraft in October 1782 and settled in Bermondsey; daughter born August 1783; wife left him 1784.

Blake, William (1757–1827), poet and artist; in Johnson's circle; friend of Paine; illustrated MW's *Original Stories*.

Blood, Caroline (née Roe of Cragonboy, Co. Clare), married Matthew Blood; mother of Fanny, George and Caroline among other children; moved from Ireland to London and, with MW's help, back to Ireland.

Blood, Caroline, daughter of Caroline and Matthew, sister of Fanny and George; spent time in workhouse in London from at least 1787 to 1792.

Blood, Fanny or Frances (1757–86), daughter of Matthew and Caroline; lived in various places in and near London, as well as being sent to Ireland when family finances failed; MW's beloved friend and companion; opened school with her in Newington Green; travelled to Portugal to marry Hugh Skeys; died following childbirth.

Blood, George (1760–1840), son of Matthew and Caroline Blood, brother of Fanny and friend of Wollstonecraft sisters; 1777–80 at sea; returned to family home; worked at haberdasher's; fled to Dublin with MW's help, where worked at linen draper's; worked in wine merchant's in Dublin for eight years; proposed to Everina; correspondent of MW until she went to France; later married relative, Deborah Blood, had eight children, and became accountant to Associated Irish Mine Co. in Wicklow.

Blood, Matthew, improvident father of Fanny, George, and Caroline; married Caroline Roe; fled creditors in Ireland and settled in London; returned to Dublin with MW's help.

Bonnycastle, John (1750?–1821), mathematician and teacher; author of elementary books on mathematics; in 1780s professor of mathematics at the Royal Military Academy in Woolwich; friend of Fuseli; taught James Wollstonecraft.

Bregantz, Mrs, head teacher of Putney school; employed Eliza and, briefly, Everina; mother of Aline Fillietaz.

Brissot, Jacques Pierre (1754–93), French radical leader, pamphleteer and abolitionist; visited America; became leader of Girondin faction; from March 1793 involved with Imlay in Louisiana scheme; guillotined in October.

Brown, John (1735–88), doctor and medical writer; founder of the Brunonian system, a 'science of life'; author of *Elements of Medicine* (1788).

Burgh, James (1714–75), Scottish political and educational writer; set up academy in Stoke Newington in 1747, moving it to Newington Green 1750; author of *Thoughts on Education* (1747) and *Theophilus. Youth's Friendly Monitor* (1754). Campaigned for parliamentary reform in 1770s.

Burgh, Hannah (DNB lists Sarah) (formerly Harding) (d. 1788); in 1751 married as second husband James Burgh; befriended MW emotionally and financially during her time at Newington Green.

Burke, Edmund (1729–1850), Irish philosopher, politician, orator; MP for Bristol in 1774; supported the American colonists; associated with Whig reformers; wrote *A Philosophical Enquiry into the Sublime and Beautiful* (1756); then *Reflections on the Revolution in France* (1790) in which he attacked Richard Price; attacked by MW in *The Rights of Men* (1790).

Carlisle, Anthony, later Sir Anthony (1768–1840), surgeon and writer on science; knighted in 1821 after being surgeon extraordinary to the Prince Regent; friend of Godwin's; attended MW after childbirth.

Chapone, Hester (1727–1801) (née Mulso), poet and educational writer; in the circles of Samuel Richardson and Dr Johnson; wrote *Letters written on the Improvement of the Mind* (1773) for girls.

Christie, Rebecca (née Thomson) granddaughter of a wealthy carpet manufacturer in Finsbury Square, London; married Thomas Christie in 1792; friend of MW in Paris and London; nursed her after suicide attempt.

Christie, Thomas (1761–96), Scottish political writer and essayist; studied medicine; settled in London and founded *Analytical Review* with Johnson; to France 1789 after Revolution for six months; in 1792 married Rebecca Thomson and later returned to France where he worked on new constitution and became involved in commerce; went to Surinam on business 1796, died there. Friend of Imlay and MW.

Clare, Revd and Mrs, befriended MW in Hoxton near London between 1774 and 1776; Mrs Clare introduced MW to Fanny Blood and helped the Wollstonecraft sisters after Eliza Bishop's elopement in 1784.

Cristall, Anne (b. *c*.1768), from Cornwall, daughter of mariner John Cristall and wife Anne Batten; the family came to London and lived at Rotherhithe, then Blackheath; author of *Poetical Sketches* (1785); friend of Wollstonecraft sisters in 1780s and '90s.

Cristall, Joshua (1769–1847), from Cornwall, became china dealer in Rotherhithe; then painter of china in Potteries; probably met MW through sister, Anne; studied at Royal Academy and became notable watercolourist.

Darwin, Erasmus (1731–1802), physician, botanist, poet, freethinker; lived in Derby from 1781; published long poem on botany, *The Botanic Garden* (1789 and 1791) and prose work on evolution, *Zoonomia* (1794–6). Grandfather of Charles Darwin. Godwin tried to visit him in 1797.

Dawson, Sarah (d. 1812) (née Regis), widow of London merchant William Dawson, whose son owned the house in Milsom Street, Bath, where MW was employed as companion in 1779.

Dyson, George (d. 1822), hack writer, painter, translated *The Sorcerer* (1795); friend of Wollstonecraft and Godwin and initially admired by Godwin but later alienated him with quarrelsome ways and drunkenness.

Fenwick, Eliza (d. 1840), novelist and writer for children, married John Fenwick, radical editor and friend of Godwin, Hays, Robinson and MW, whom she nursed up to her death; endured difficult life after separated from impecunious husband in 1800; raised children and then orphaned grandchildren alone in England, Barbados and America.

Fillietaz, Aline (née Mercer), daughter of Eliza Wollstonecraft's headmistress in Putney; MW's landlady in early months in Paris in 1793.

FitzGerald, Mary (née Mercer), second wife, then widow, of Colonel Richard Fitz-Gerald and stepmother of Lady Kingsborough; 3 daughters: Maria, Harriet and Margaret; befriended MW in Ireland 1786–7.

Fordyce, Dr. George (1736–1802), Scottish physician at St Thomas' Hospital; Fellow of Royal Society and author of medical and philosophical texts; lectured on medical subjects; friend of Johnson, Godwin and MW, whom he attended in her final days.

Fuseli, Henry (1741–1825), Swiss painter, critic, born Johann Heinrich Füssli; with friend Lavater, studied theology in Zurich; arrived in London 1763 and became acquainted with Joseph Johnson; went to Italy in 1769 and returned to London ten years later; in 1782 exhibited *The Nightmare*; in 1788 married Sophia Rawlins; painted pictures based on Shakespeare and Milton; loved by MW; in 1799 became professor of painting at the Royal Academy.

Genlis, Madame de (1746–1830), educational writer and novelist, married comte de Genlis in 1762; governess to children of Duke of Orléans; published *Adelaide and Theodore* (1782); escaped France 1793 and lived by writing in England and Switzerland; returned to France 1802.

Godwin, Hannah (d. 1817), sister of William, lived in Guestwick, Norfolk, then London where found work as a seamstress; close to her brother William in early years in London; met MW; often visited Polygon after MW's death.

Godwin, Mary Wollstonecraft (1797–1851), daughter of MW and Godwin, author of *Frankenstein* and other novels; wife of poet Percy Bysshe Shelley; only one surviving child, Percy Florence Shelley, who died without issue.

Godwin, William (1756–1836), radical author and husband of MW; after her death, adopted Fanny Imlay; wrote *Memoirs*, published *Posthumous Works* (1798); and created character of Marguerite in *St Leon* as tribute to MW; in 1801 married second wife, Mary Jane Vial (Clairmont), mother of two illegitimate children, Charles and Claire; had one son, William.

Hays, Mary (1760–1843), novelist and polemical writer from Dissenting family; engaged to marry John Eccles, who died before wedding; in 1792 published pamphlet on public worship and met MW; published miscellaneous essays 1793; in love with Unitarian William Frend; published *Emma Courtney* (1796); wrote tribute to MW; much ridiculed for feminism; wrote *Appeal to the Men of Great Britain* and *Victim of Prejudice* (1799); suffered poverty; in later life came to know and admire Hannah More.

Hewlett, John (1762–1844), scholar, schoolteacher and cleric; kept school in Surrey; wrote on antiquities, mathematics and the Bible; published *An Introduction to Reading and Spelling*; knew MW in Newington Green and introduced her to Joseph Johnson.

Holcroft, John (1745–1809), son of shoemaker; became cobbler, teacher, actor and playwright; first play performed 1778 and first novel published 1780; close friend of Godwin; wrote *Anna St Ives* (1792); indicted for high treason in 1794; married four times; in financial trouble, went to Hamburg 1799, returning 1803; possibly at one time in love with MW.

Imlay, Fanny or Frances (1794–1816), daughter of MW and Gilbert Imlay; born in Le Havre; adopted by Godwin 1797; brought up with half-sister Mary, the family of the second Mrs Godwin and, later, half-brother William; absent when Mary and Claire Clairmont eloped with Shelley in 1814; wished to join aunts Eliza and Everina in Ireland as schoolteacher, but rejected after scandal of elopement; committed suicide in Swansea at age twenty-two, the body unclaimed by Godwin or Shelley.

Imlay, Gilbert (?1754–?1828), born in New Jersey; served in American war; involved in land speculation; came to London and Paris in 1790s; wrote *Topographical Description* (1792) and *The Emigrants* (1793); lover of MW in France and father of Fanny; probably died in Jersey.

Inchbald, Elizabeth (1753–1821), born in Suffolk; became actress, playwright, novelist; in 1772 married Joseph, seventeen years her senior; travelled around England and to Paris; in Liverpool met Siddons and Kemble, with whom she fell in love; widowed 1779; retired from stage 1789, lived from writing plays and novels; published *A Simple Story* (1791) and *Nature and Art* (1796); friend of Holcroft and Godwin; objected to marriage of Godwin and MW; died in establishment for Catholic ladies.

Johnson, Joseph (1738–1809), born near Liverpool, son of Baptist minister; became radical publisher working in St Paul's Churchyard, London. His bookshop formed a centre of literary and political activity; circle included Godwin, Blake, Paine, Fuseli among many others; employer and publisher of MW.

Johnson, Samuel (1709–84), most famous man of letters in mid-eighteenth-century England; from Lichfield; published *Dictionary* (1755) and *Lives of the English Poets* (1779–81); met MW in 1784.

Kemble, John Philip (1757–1823), actor, theatre manager, playwright and scholar; first played in Drury Lane in 1783; famous for leading roles in Shakespearean tragedy; often appeared with sister, Sarah Siddons; intimate with Inchbald; married in 1787.

King, Caroline, Viscountess Kingsborough (1754–1823), daughter of Col. Richard FitzGerald; married cousin Robert King 1769 and lived on her family estates in Mitchelstown; had seven sons and five daughters; separated from husband.

King, Margaret (1772–1835); had MW as governess 1786–7; married Lord Mount Cashell; held republican sentiments; left husband and lived with George Tighe in Italy, where she knew Mary and Percy Shelley.

King, Robert, Viscount Kingsborough (1754–99), MP for Cork, married cousin

Caroline; became second Earl of Kingston 1797; accused of murdering lover of his daughter Mary.

Macaulay, Catherine (1731–91) (née Sawbridge), historian and pamphleteer; published Whig *History of England from the Accession of James I to that of the Brunswick Line* from 1763 to 1783; supported American revolutionaries; in 1778 married as second husband William Graham twenty-six years her junior; visited America; published *Letters on Education* (1790) and *Observations on the Reflections of . . . Burke* (1791).

Marshall, James, studied with Godwin at Hoxton Academy; friend and sometimes fellow lodger with Godwin; acted as amanuensis; witnessed marriage of Godwin and MW.

Montagu, Basil (1770–1851), lawyer and miscellaneous writer, illegitimate son of Earl of Sandwich; came to London 1795; friend of Godwin; moved from early radical opinions but continued to support liberal causes like abolition of capital punishment.

Moore, Dr John (1729–1802), Scottish physician and writer; settled in London 1778; wrote novel *Zeluco* (1786) and many books on European countries, mainly revolutionary France; admirer of Helen Maria Williams.

More, Hannah (1745–1833), b. Bristol, educational writer, poet, playwright; knew Burke and Samuel Johnson; influential conservative voice on women's upbringing and education; refused to read MW's *Rights of Woman*; published *Strictures on the Modern System of Education* (1799).

Ogle, George (1742–1814), Irish MP and anthologised poet; favoured Irish independence but not Catholic emancipation; married Elizabeth Moore; knew MW in Ireland.

Opie, John (1761–1807), portrait painter from Cornwall; married Mary Bunn and divorced her in 1796 after she left him; painted MW; married Amelia Alderson in 1798.

Paine, Thomas (1737–1809), revolutionary writer and activist, son of staymaker from Thetford; propagandist in American Revolution; later part of Johnson's circle in London; published *The Rights of Man* (1791, 1792); in France; imprisoned during Reign of Terror; published *The Age of Reason* (1794, 1795); knew MW in London and Paris; returned to America where died poor.

Parr, Samuel (1747–1825), cleric and scholar, lived in Hatton, Warwickshire; engaged in philosophical controversy with many including Godwin; Godwin and Montagu visited him in 1797.

Parr, Sarah or Ann (d. 1810), daughter of Samuel, eloped with John Wynne 1797; bore three children; separated and sued for separate maintenance; returned to live with father.

Pinkerton, Ann or Nancy, upset MW with attentions to Godwin in 1797; saw Godwin after MW's death.

Price, Richard (1723–91), Welsh Presbyterian minister in Newington Green, reformer, writer, friend of Joseph Priestley and Benjamin Franklin; embraced Arian views; befriended MW when she worked on the Green; resigned pastorate 1783, left Green 1786 when wife died; delivered sermon to the Revolution Society at the Old Jewry, November 1789, and began Revolution controversy which Burke and Wollstonecraft joined.

Radcliffe, Ann (1764–1823) (née Ward), most famous and influential Gothic novelist; author of *The Mysteries of Udolpho* (1794) and *The Italian* (1797).

Reveley, Maria (1770–1836) (née James), spent part of childhood in Constantinople with her merchant father; studied painting in Rome; married Willey Reveley and came to England; two children born before she was twenty; much admired by Godwin; friend of MW in final year; widowed 1799 and Godwin proposed marriage, which she refused; married John Gisborne in 1800 and lived for a time in Italy, where met Mary and Percy Shelley.

Robinson, Mary, 'Perdita' (1758–1800) (née Darby), actress, poet, novelist; born in Bristol; educated at Hannah More's sisters' school and in Chelsea; at fifteen married a clerk, Thomas Robinson; bore daughter 1774; became actress and mistress of seventeen-year-old Prince of Wales, then of the politician Charles James Fox, then in 1782 of the soldier, politician and gambler, Banastre Tarleton; had miscarriage, became crippled with arthritis, and was deserted by Tarleton; friend of MW and Godwin. Wrote novels in 1790s, the first being *Vacenza* (1792).

Roland, Marie-Jeanne (1754–93), born in Paris, daughter of engraver; married Jean-Marie in 1780; involved in Girondin politics during Revolution; friend of Helen Maria Williams; guillotined by Jacobins; *Memoirs* published 1795.

Roscoe, William (1753–1831), Liverpool lawyer with interest in literature and the arts; married Jane Griffies in 1781 and had seven sons and three daughters; supporter of French Revolution and abolition of the slave trade; wrote life of Lorenzo de' Medici, printed at own expense in 1796; friend of MW and Fuseli; became Whig MP in 1806.

Rowan, Archibald Hamilton (1751–1834), wealthy Protestant Irishman, supporter of the Irish Volunteer Movement; born in London; married Sara Anne Dawson 1781; had ten children; involved in Irish politics from 1790; imprisoned but escaped to France 1794; met MW in Paris; to America where failed as calico printer; moderated liberal opinions and returned to Ireland.

Rousseau, Jean-Jacques (1712–78), influential philosopher and cultural analyst, born in Geneva; lifelong liaison with Thérèse Levasseur; sent their children to foundling hospital; published *Julie ou la Nouvelle Héloïse* (1761) and *Emile* (1762); in England 1766–7. *Confessions* published posthumously.

Schlabrendorf, Gustav, Graf von (1750–1824), Silesian nobleman; inherited fortune 1769 and began Grand Tour; spent six years in England and arrived in France during Revolution; met MW in 1793 when engaged to Jane Christie; imprisoned by Jacobins; after release remained in France despite expressed contempt for Napoleon; became reclusive in later life.

Seward, Anna (1742–1809), poet, daughter of canon of Lichfield; at first a supporter of French Revolution; then both denounced it and upbraided Helen Maria Williams for her continuing enthusiasm.

Siddons, Sarah (1755–1831) (née Kemble), actress, sister of John Philip Kemble; much acclaimed for roles in tragedy; married William Siddons, an actor.

Skeys, Hugh, Irish merchant with interests in Lisbon, Dublin and London; married Fanny Blood in Portugal in 1785; in same year she and their child died; returned to Ireland and married a second time; kept in touch with Wollstonecraft sisters.

Smith, Charlotte (1749–1806) (née Turner), poet and novelist, married 1765 to improvident Benjamin Smith, with whom she had twelve children; close to MW in radical opinions, but no evidence the two women ever met.

Southey, Robert (1774–1843), poet, friend of Coleridge; knew Godwin and MW at end of latter's life; became poet laureate 1813.

Stone, John Hurford (1763–1818), follower of Price; supported French Revolution; went to Paris 1792; involved in business and politics; friend of Paine; companion of Helen Maria Williams despite marriage to Rachel Coope (divorced 1794); briefly imprisoned; went to Switzerland with Williams; tried for treason *in absentia* 1796; became printer, died in France.

Tarleton, Banastre (1754–1833), MP, soldier (finally general) and politician from Liverpool; served in American War; returned to England 1782; became MP for Liverpool 1790 and held seat until 1806 when defeated by William Roscoe; lived with Mary Robinson whom he deserted; married 1798.

Taylor, Thomas (the Platonist) (1758–1835), translator, mathematician and scholar, met MW briefly in Walworth 1777; probably author of *Vindication of the Rights of Brutes*.

Tooke, John Horne (1736–1812), political agitator and linguistic theoretician; involved with radical John Wilkes in 1760s; tried for treason 1794 with Holcroft and others; entertained Godwin and MW.

Trimmer, Sarah (1741–1810) (née Kirkby), educational writer from Ipswich; married James Trimmer of Brentford where lived for rest of life; had nine surviving children whom she educated herself; published religious works for children and *Fabulous Histories* (1786), including the 'History of the Robins'; met MW in 1787.

Twiss, Francis (1750–1827), scholarly compiler; married 1786 Fanny or Frances Kemble, sister of Sarah Siddons; later he and Fanny kept a fashionable girls' school in Bath; friend of Inchbald and MW before marriage to Godwin.

Waterhouse, Joshua (d. 1827); fellow of St Catherine's College, Cambridge; met MW in Bath when she was a companion; involved in college scandal and lost fellowship; became recluse in last years and was murdered.

Wedgwood, Thomas (1771–1805), scientific investigator interested in radical ideas, one of three sons of the Staffordshire pottery master Josiah; admirer and patron of Godwin and Coleridge; knew MW in 1797; visited by Godwin in Etruria.

Williams, Helen Maria (1761/2–1827), poet, novelist and historian; from Berwick-on-Tweed; came to London and published poems and a novel; popular in liberal and Dissenting circles; to France 1790; published *Letters Written in France in the Summer of 1790*; after short visit to England, settled in France 1792 with mother and sisters; wrote further chronicles of the Revolution; relationship with John Hurford Stone; imprisoned during Terror; in Switzerland 1794 for six months; continued chronicles under Napoleon.

Wollstonecraft, Charles (1770–1817), born Beverley; MW's youngest and favourite brother; articled to Ned, quarrelled; dismissed by another lawyer; returned to father in Laugharne; to America 1792; failed in calico printing business with Rowan; in 1800 joined American army; married Sarah Garrison of New Orleans 1804, with whom had Jane Nelson; served in war of 1812; achieved rank of brevet major; divorced Sarah for adultery 1811; married Nancy 1813; after death, Nancy took stepdaughter to live in Cuba.

Wollstonecraft, Edward (1689–1765), wealthy master weaver of Spitalfields; married, first, Jane (d. 1732), their only surviving child in 1765 being Elizabeth Ann, married to Isaac Rutson; second, married Elizabeth (1716–46), mother of Edward John, MW's father.

Wollstonecraft, Edward Bland (Ned) (1757/8–1807), born in Spitalfields, eldest son of Edward John and Elizabeth, brother of MW; inherited part of grandfather's fortune; became lawyer in Tower Hill; married Elizabeth Munday 1778; two children: Edward and Elizabeth, both emigrated to Australia and died without issue; retired 1802.

Wollstonecraft, Edward Bland (d. 1795), probably relative of MW; first officer of the *Cruttendon*, part-owned by her grandfather and later brother Ned; married Lydia, had daughter Britania; possibly MW visited in Southampton.

Wollstonecraft, Edward John (1737?–1803), apprentice weaver, gentleman farmer, failed business man; born in Spitalfields; married, first, Elizabeth Dickson, with whom he had Edward Bland, MW, Henry Woodstock, Elizabeth, Everina, James and Charles; and, second, Lydia; died in Laugharne, leaving debts.

Wollstonecraft, Elizabeth (d. 1782) (née Dickson), from Ballyshannon in Co. Donegal; wife of Edward John and mother of seven children, including MW; died in Enfield after long illness.

Wollstonecraft, Elizabeth (called Eliza, Betsey, Bess) (b. 1763); sister of MW; married Meredith Bishop 1782; bore daughter, Elizabeth Mary Frances 1783; with MW left her husband and baby 1784; became schoolteacher and governess in Wales and Ireland; set up day school for girls in Dublin after MW's death; died in Dublin late 1820s or '30s.

Wollstonecraft, Everina or Averina (1765–1843), youngest sister of MW and Eliza; studied in Paris; became governess in Ireland; opened school for boys in Dublin; after Eliza's death to London and lived in Pentonville area till own death; disliked by niece Mary Shelley; occasionally helped financially by other niece Elizabeth in Australia.

Wollstonecraft, Henry Woodstock (1761–?), second brother of MW; apprenticed to apothecary-surgeon in Beverley; later life unknown.

Wollstonecraft, James (1768–1806), born in Essex; went to sea; studied at Woolwich 1788; back to sea on merchantman; to Paris, where suspected of being a spy and deported; joined Royal Navy; promoted to lieutenant; died of yellow fever.

# Part 1

*'I am a little singular in my thoughts of love and friendship;*
*I must have the first place or none'*

It began with the will. In 1765 the master silk-weaver Edward Wollstonecraft of Spitalfields died at the age of seventy-six and was buried with some ceremony in the elegant new church of St Botolph's, Bishopsgate. He had ignored babies just born and not necessarily intending to live, but had left legacies to all his other descendants – with the exception of a granddaughter, Mary. She was a child of five, old enough to have made some inroads into an old man's heart.

The omission was especially blatant when one third of the estate of some £10,000 went to her elder brother, only two years her senior. Seven-year-old Ned (Edward Bland) received a lease on land and a share in a merchant ship, the *Cruttendon*, on which a relative of the same name had been first officer. The boy 'who is to carry the empty family-name down to posterity', as his sister scornfully wrote, was also left his grandfather's portrait as symbol of his importance as 'deputy-tyrant of the house'.[1]

For old Edward Wollstonecraft women were weak and of little worth. He had a surviving daughter from a first union, Elizabeth, married to Isaac Rutson. He had worried how to leave her money without letting it fall, as it legally should from a wife, into the hands of her spouse. In the will he designated it specifically for her 'sole use' with no 'intermeddling' by her husband. Elizabeth had three living grown-up children; her father took so little interest in the girls he did not know the first name of his granddaughter's husband, but he did at least leave each grandchild £10, the same as he left to a servant and the local debtors. Elizabeth's Rutson stepdaughter had already 'shared sufficiently of my bounty' and he left her what he left each pauper in the St Botolph workhouse: 1s.[2]

The beginning of his detailed will of seven pages ordered a lavish funeral for a man whose money made him a 'gentleman'. It spoke much of his son, Edward John, product of his second marriage and father of Mary and Ned. He was the main legatee and would now have income from rents of thirty separate tenancies. He could if he chose be a 'gentleman' at once, though barely through his apprenticeship.

*

The family injustice would embitter and fuel Mary's life. She resented her eldest brother's privileges – he even had their mother's milk, unlike subsequent children. Much has been made of the effects on character of being the second-born, the child who must earn his or her place and is more outgoing, opinionated and unconventional than the eldest; Mary was a classic case. More can be made of the fact that she was a girl in a patriarchal world. In time she used this to form a general and justified reason for personal jealousy.

She was born on 27 April 1759, a year before the twenty-two-year-old George III ascended the throne proclaiming his intention to encourage 'piety and virtue' throughout his realm. The place was Primrose Street, Spitalfields, near where Liverpool Street Station now stands, a rather shoddy, overcrowded area of London noted for its shifting immigrant populations and its weavers, some of whom, like her grandfather, had grown rich. On 20 May, she was carried along busy Bishopsgate to St Botolph's to be christened into the Church of England, second child and first daughter of Elizabeth née Dickson, from a Protestant wine-merchant family in Ballyshannon, Ireland, and Edward John Wollstonecraft.[3]

Mary was the first of the children to be breast-fed by another woman, the usual practice in middle-class families who could afford the few shillings such service cost. Although maternal breast-feeding had been advocated by English authorities for the child's benefit from the late seventeenth century, women were unconvinced, remaining unsentimental about babies. By mid-century, the French were anxious about the number of infants dying – increasingly blamed on wet-nursing – and men started demanding that wives breast-feed. But in England infant mortality was decreasing and there was no cultural panic. Sometimes the wet-nurse came to the home but more often she took the child to her own poorer house, nursing it along with her own brood. So, for many infants such as Mary, the first experience of nurture came from a surrogate mother whilst their biological parent, when they were handed over to her, would be a relative stranger who had not seen their first steps or heard their first words. It was all conventional enough, but Mary later resented what she heard of her early life: '[A mother's] parental affection ... scarcely deserves the name, when it does not lead her to suckle her children.'[4]

Like most childhoods, Mary's was delivered to the public through adult memory. Later anger enveloped her infant rancour and gave form to grudges that inevitably arose from family life. Not long before her death she told William Godwin, her husband and first biographer, how harsh her early years now seemed. She was incensed that, of all the children born before and after her, she was not the favourite of mother or father. She hated the rigid discipline which she felt was imposed uniquely on her. Above her, the first-born Ned was coddled – below her the system dissolved with increasing numbers. Only she was restrained in trivial matters, made to sit silent for three or four hours in the company of disapproving parents.

Her parents filled her young vision. They were incompatible, unalike, similar only in indifference to herself. She felt enthralled by them and excluded. Her father was the first to impinge. He was bad-tempered then fond, veering erratically from kindness to cruelty. Such instability in the source of authority bred tension. Edward Wollstonecraft was a despot in his domestic kingdom, dominating the resentful childhood of his daughter, who would note her own mercurial moods and quick temper while never admitting the resemblance – though later she compared herself to Lear, that childish tyrant with three daughters. His first subject-victim was his wife.

Elizabeth Wollstonecraft's chosen response of submission did not pre-dispose her to appreciate other victims, and she and her eldest girl took no comfort in joint subjection. The pains of marriage were engraved on Mary's mind in this demeaning tie of father-tyrant and mother-slave, and the authority this mother naturally had over her was tainted by the vision of improper submission. Mary always declared her antipathy towards a relationship based on power: with much evidence to the contrary she asserted that women could not be gratified by dependence and that it must be called by its proper name of 'weakness'. She was further soured as she realised that Elizabeth was finding a substitute for her unloving spouse not in her eager self but in her eldest son, the fortunate and privileged Ned.[5]

That experiences of early childhood marked the adult was a firm belief of the eighteenth century, based on the theories of Locke, Hartley and others, that no knowledge was innate but came from the senses. As Amelia Alderson, a later friend of Mary, remarked, 'whatever [children] are in disposition and pursuit in the earliest dawn of existence, they will probably be in its meridian and its decline.'[6] This idea could lead in several directions. Although some progressive educators suggested that children might be encouraged to develop their own natures, the common view of child-rearing conformed pretty much to the Wollstonecraft practice, that parents' first duty was to control the child and teach it self-control.

Even their names divided mother and daughter. The eldest son had been named for his father, grandfather, and cousin or uncle, the second daughter would be given her mother's and grandmother's name, Elizabeth. Mary was called after a relative who might be generous in future, possibly her widowed aunt Mary, whose three children had died. But no generous aunt is men-tioned in her life, none becomes a surrogate mother. Indeed, although there were other Wollstonecrafts in the area – several sharing her name and no doubt second and third cousins – there was little sense of wider kin. It was the immediate nuclear family that dominated her early and later life; when this disappointed her she had no obvious place to turn.[7]

Mary's earliest years were spent with brother Ned and two younger children, Henry Woodstock and Elizabeth (Eliza), in the city amidst the bustle and din of crowded streets, trade, and manufacture. She lived in a brick merchant's house on Primrose Street, where the family's tenancies were located. Other silk-weavers were nearby, for the area was noted for fine materials, ever since the skilled Huguenots arrived as refugees from France after expulsion by Louis XIV.

The wealthy merchants' houses were many-storeyed, deep rather than wide, with gardens or courtyards behind. Like the narrow streets they fronted, they mixed business and living, the ground floors used for offices rather than manufacturing since much of the weaving was done in their homes by journeymen employing their masters' looms. The offices were constantly in use for buying and selling, paying wages and for stock. Outside thronged punks, coachmen, porters, wig- and mantua-makers, tanners, cobblers and shopkeepers; street vendors touted fruit and pies, wagons and carts took vegetables to the market of Spitalfields. The meat and poultry might arrive on foot, depositing filth only haphazardly swept into gutters. There were constant fights and brawls in the overcrowded streets and, in her grandfather's offices, the usual altercations between masters and men whose interests could never quite coincide.

A man of means wished sometimes to escape the vulgar bustle and live more genteelly in the country. Old Mr Wollstonecraft had felt this need and looked from the grime of London at the open fields of Essex close by. Since he wanted his family to rise in the world, he desired a country retreat even more for his privileged son than for himself. So, along with the city house in Primrose Street, he provided for Edward John's family a farm in Essex, 'an old mansion, with a court-yard before it, in Epping Forest, near the Whalebone', an area noted for dairy cattle. There Mary lived when she was four and five; it was the first place of which she was clearly conscious.[8] In Epping, another sister, more flamboyantly named Everina, was born. Perhaps Mrs Wollstonecraft read romantic novels.

The early experience of city and country was an important inheritance. However she grumbled about the place, Mary was always a Londoner, part of the three-quarters of a million people who inhabited the capital. With the fashionable and growing West End by Hyde Park and Buckingham House, soon to be Buckingham Palace, the royal parks and elegantly planned squares, as well as with the political centre of Westminster and Whitehall, she had little to do. Her London was the old walled commercial City to the east of the Strand. When she moved away as an adult it was to go no further than the new suburbs, still within walking distance of St Paul's, such as Islington or St Pancras. At the same time, a taste for the country fed her imagination and let her find green fields rejuvenating and rustics contented. 'God made the country, and man made the town,' wrote William Cowper, the nation's favourite poet when Mary was a young adult.[9] Along with thousands of other city-dwellers who would have groaned for boredom during a winter in Wales, she agreed.

When his father died, Edward John became moderately wealthy. He had inherited his parent's vanity of status and disliked the squalor and trade of Spitalfields; he yearned to define himself entirely by the title his father assumed in death: 'gentleman'. Despite the long years of apprenticeship, he determined at once to quit London. Weaving was in recession and masters reduced the rate they paid workers. This led to strikes and general unrest among the trading groups of London. In the late 1760s the unrest was harnessed by the radical populists John Wilkes and Horne Tooke, who used it to open up politics to the people and agitate for greater individual freedom.

The upheavals, only just contained by the City authorities, justified Edward's escape from a business he never liked. He had been given money without work and did not necessarily associate the two. To him it did not seem difficult to hold what had come easily. While keeping the Primrose Street houses for their rent, he would become a gentleman farmer, a more socially acceptable occupation than weaving handkerchiefs, but one for which he had no training. He found a property in Essex, in Ripple Ward, Barking, near the river Roding. There another son, James, was born.

In Barking, Edward was a substantial citizen, assessed expensively for poor rates and appointed overseer of the area's madmen and paupers. He hob-nobbed with gentry, such as the Gascoynes, who had also moved from London trade into county respectability some years before. Edward had sufficient means to succeed in farming in a fertile district of moderately sized properties. It was a time of agricultural change, however, and, although the area round Barking was as yet unaffected, farmers elsewhere were busy improving land by enclosing it and taking in nearby commons. The social result, the turning of cottagers into expatriate city workers or day-labourers without common rights, was painful to many, but the growth in food pro-duction was considerable and would support the steep rise in the English population in the next decades. Landowners had a chance to enrich them-selves if they took risks and invested wisely.

Much enjoying the new gentry life and society, Edward paid little attention to such capitalist activity and in less than four years his farm failed. His money was seeping away, but its psychological result in snobbery and contempt for its source in trade had already reached his children, along with shame at the family's decline. His eldest daughter, Mary, would always be concerned to establish her social significance in the world and mock those who gained theirs through trade.

The failure of the Barking farm began the zigzag of Edward's career across England and Wales. It made his children rootless and squandered his inheritance. Each farm he took was poorer and remoter than the last. Each time he left, he was more impecunious than when he had arrived. Such experiences would have soured the temper of a stabler man than Edward Wollstonecraft. As he grew drunken and violent, he circumscribed Mary's life more and more with his rages and remorse. She found him irritating, powerful, engrossing and appalling, and in time he would mark and mar her choice of lovers. In her public works he entered as tyrant, the embodiment of improper masculinity and weak despotic power, but also as a yearning for a complicated tainted love which had as much submission as sustenance within it. Perhaps the worst thing she wrote of him came in a private letter: 'I never had a father.'

From Barking the Wollstonecrafts moved in October 1768 to a farm near the village of Walkington, three to four miles from Beverley in the East Riding of Yorkshire. It is not known why they went so far or how they found the place. There seem to have been no close relatives in the area but Edward might have been attracted to lower farm rents and have come across an enticing newspaper advertisement. Those wanting to sell and rent out their properties to 'small genteel families' put notices in local papers, in this case the *York Courant*, chock-full of farms available in the area, or they could put a similar notice in newspapers from other farming regions. The land near Walkington was suitable for pasturing and Edward might have thought to succeed at the same sort of agriculture he had tried in Barking, if he had lower overheads.[10]

However similar in type, the open rolling countryside of the Yorkshire wolds seemed decidedly foreign to the southern family when they arrived. The climate was colder and windier, and some of the land flooded; more of it was needed to produce a good living than in the warmer south. Walkington was near enough for a quick horse-ride into Beverley or even, on a fine day, a brisk walk through fields, but in winter it must have felt remote from company and all forms of entertainment; Edward with his taste for high living cannot have been happy – nor can the children who depended on him.

There in Walkington in the summer of 1770 the seventh and last child, Charles, arrived.

Farming was of course no easier in Yorkshire than in Essex. Owners were enclosing their land in parts of the East Riding as well, although no application from Walkington was made until the 1790s. Since Edward Wollstonecraft's farm was presumably on a short lease, he would not have thought to enclose his land and thus improve his farming position, but he would have had the same trouble from the poor as more forward-thinking owners; labourers were responding to the removal of common rights by poaching and coursing without leave, both of which carried draconian penalties.

After three years Edward could stand no more. He quit the farm and moved his family into Beverley. It was probably a relief to all of them. Rainy days kept children indoors and it was not the sort of family that thrived on closeness and its own company. Gloomily contemplating his failing fortunes, Edward cannot much have enjoyed the clatter of children or taken pleasure in their clever sayings or sudden accomplishments.

No doubt the boys and girls slid on the frozen pond in the middle of Walkington village and went nutting in the hedgerows like others of their age, but such recollections did not loom large in their memories in later life. Mary's contemporary Thomas Holcroft thought that the anecdotes of childhood provided an onlooker with a guide to the character and temperament of the adult, and on his deathbed was at pains to record such moments: getting off a horse to pick up a dropped hat and being unable to get back on, a sister's thumb being sliced in half by a window shutter, his wonder at the relationship of sounds to letters.[11] When remembering her own childhood Mary described no such anecdotes, only the general sense that she despised dolls and liked hardy boys' sports. There are memories of feelings but few active tales. She gives little impression of the rough and tumble of families: despite her numerous siblings, she felt much like an only child or, rather, a far older daughter, too responsible too young.

In Beverley, the Wollstonecrafts took lodgings in the triangular Wednesday Market where there was a bustling trade in farm stuff and leather every week. The town, with about 5000 inhabitants, was small and neat, 'admirably built and paved'.[12] At the beginning of the century its society was dominated by county families who kept large detached mansions. Later it grew increasingly middle class, led less by gentry than clergymen, merchants, army officers and professional men, who built semi-detached and terraced houses. These were often leased to visitors who found the town relatively cheap, while being attracted to its cultured style and amenities.

One such house was probably the rented home of the Wollstonecrafts. Beverley Minster, built on cathedral-scale, was their nearest church and Mary took a short walk down Highgate to reach it. Contemplating it she could not have avoided gaining some taste for religious beauty. Its elegant late Gothic architecture had been recently restored and augmented by intricate lacy choir stalls carved above medieval misericords. These latter depicted town life and fabulous anecdotes: a man madly shoeing a goose, a cat playing the fiddle to her kittens. Mary was not a devotee of religious magnificence and she came to despise the 'childish routine' of 'slovenly' services in great cathedrals, but she found huge Gothic piles sublime and, after living so close to such a towering edifice, could never warm to Dissenting austerity in places of worship. She scorned the small, mean chapels of the Methodists being established in Beverley and the villages. True to her class, she found them and their worshippers inelegant and vulgar.

Apart from its Minster and restrained aesthetic, Beverley had the civic attractions burgeoning by mid-century in provincial towns; they appealed to a teenaged girl who had spent the previous three years in the country: a theatre, assembly rooms for concerts, meeting and dancing, a nearby poetry society, and a circulating library, an innovative system of lending books through subscription, paid yearly, quarterly, or even weekly by poor subscribers. Reading was an important part of life, especially for women whose literacy was increasing faster than men's, and the most famous contemporary man of letters, Dr Johnson, was right in his remark that 'General literature now pervades the nation through all its ranks.' London books by Goldsmith and Smollett could be purchased in York and Hull, while local authors offered sentimental romances and manuals on farming and cookery. Practical books on education were becoming popular, as well as the usual improving works for young persons such as *Youth's Faithful Monitor*, but it seems unlikely that Edward Wollstonecraft rushed to purchase these aids for his young brood. He himself probably avoided the *Complete English Farmer* advertised in the local paper, but might have taken one of the town-and-country magazines that kept provincials in touch with London, helped support a gentlemanly status, and provided tips on horse-racing along with national news.

Unhappily for his family, there was a race-course just outside the town on the Walkington side. Its grandstand was first erected in the year they arrived. Indeed its proximity might have influenced Edward in his initial choice of farm. The main races were in Whit week, and the newspapers carried descriptions of contestants. With a little travelling on the horse he so much enjoyed, he could attend race-weeks through much of the year. When Beverley was over, there were York, Richmond, Wakefield, and Doncaster. The rest of the time he could spend drinking and abusing his family. Sometimes he hit his eldest daughter, but he did not whip her.[13]

In the little provincial town where everybody knew everyone's business, Edward Wollstonecraft became a byword for foul temper and drunkenness. He upset his children and caused especial chagrin to Mary. Under the onslaught, his wife could do little but suffer and hug her favourite son. 'The good folks of Beverley (like those of most Country towns) were very ready to find out their Neighbours' faults, and to animadvert on them; – Many people did not scruple to prognosticate the ruin of the whole family, and the way he went on, justified them for so doing,' she wrote.[14]

In response to parental failings and neglect, she assumed a mother's role for the children that followed, especially the girls. Though too young for it, she yet found the role gratifying. Her bid for power even extended to her mother: she later told Godwin she had slept at nights on the landing near her mother's bedroom door to shield her from her drunken father's blows, not a situation Elizabeth Wollstonecraft can much have relished. The shielding might have answered Mary's desire to be useful, but the sight of a mother being beaten by an angry father must have troubled a sensitive girl: she felt hostile to the man who hit and the woman who succumbed. Marriage and tyranny were joined, as were love and power.

The experience of public and private shame strengthened and undermined Mary's character. In these Beverley days she became competitive, firm and determined, yet always threatened by an impulse towards abjection and self-disgust. To compensate, she later took fierce pride in her early struggles; towards the end of her life she wrote, 'strong Indignation in youth at injustice &c appears to me the constant attendant of superiority of understanding.' And, less complacently, 'A degree of exertion, produced by some want, more or less painful, is probably the price we must pay for knowledge.' Her knowledge included rejection of her inadequate parents and the resolution 'never to marry for interested motives, or endure a life of dependence'. In time she made her childhood unhappiness serve her purpose, but she never shed it.

Beverley had the advantage of allowing Mary some education. The eldest boys, destined for law and medicine, must have had formal training and, at some early affluent time, the parents planned a governess for the girls. But Edward's extravagance killed the scheme and they had to make do with occasional schooling, the sort which, according to the educationist Dr Gregory, would enable them 'to fill up, in a tolerably agreeable way, some of the many solitary hours [they] must necessarily pass at home'.[15] Presumably their mother taught them their letters with counters and cards and, as the eldest, Mary enforced the teaching on the younger siblings.

She herself attended a local day-school for girls, one of the many flourishing in the eighteenth century. A city like Chester had dozens, London far more. Beverley would have had at least two or three, none very expensive. Mrs Bine's boarding-school in nearby Hull taught girls for £15 a year and half a guinea entrance fee; day pupils could attend for half a guinea a quarter. Mrs Idle of York declared that her school discouraged 'too high Notions' and attended to housewifery and morals, but mostly the curriculum aimed at making a girl marriageable and ladylike – the nation's increased commercial wealth allowed men to enter new professions; for middle-class women it opened up the new role of 'lady'. For this a girl needed rudimentary French, needlework, music, dancing, writing, possibly some botany and accounts. Schools with more elevated pupils would stress deportment, fancy needlework and more French. Ann Hill of York made pupils converse in the language, so could charge over the going rate: fifteen guineas for boarders and 15s per quarter for day students.[16] Beverley is unlikely to have offered so much; the later trouble Mary had with French indicates little progress with the language as a child.

Latin was a staple subject of a boy's education: it opened up the classics and some science and philosophy, still available only in that language. Occasionally, Latin might be offered to a girl in school or at home from ambitious parents. But there was such cultural fear of the learned bluestocking as a byword for unmarriageability that few persevered. The clever Hester Chapone recoiled from a woman's 'exchanging the graces of imagination for the severity and preciseness of a scholar'. By Wollstonecraft's time a degree of learning might be part of ornamental accomplishments, useful for quieting a woman at home, but anything more was unnatural.

As a rigorously trained man, Godwin later described Mary's Beverley schooling condescendingly: 'it was not to any advantage of infant literature, that she was indebted for her subsequent eminence; her education in this respect was merely such, as was afforded by the day-schools of the place.' Yet, however short and inadequate, there is little doubt that she gained something: a knowledge of arithmetic perhaps, practice in writing and memorising quotations. Years later, when she considered national education, she praised the 'country day-school' for its inclusiveness and preparation for citizenship, in marked contrast to the great exclusive male public schools teaching vice and tyranny.

At home or with friends she read general books, magazines and newspapers, learning to consider social issues troubling the nation – and Beverley.

The growth of vagrancy, for example: one eighteen-strong gang afflicted the town and taxed its small House of Correction. Elsewhere, the poor responded violently to inflation and monopolies: market-women in Norwich over-turned traders' carts, believing their owners were keeping prices artificially high. Mary did not care for violence or mass action: she had a strong sense of the individual.

Trade was further interrupted by rumblings from America, the faraway continent which seemed a distant part of England. Already in 1771, the *York Courant*, excerpting news from London papers, described militant Boston patriots contemptuously returning a chest of millinery items to Bristol as 'unnecessary Gew-Gaws'. Over the next years the 'unhappy Differences with America' swelled into war. There was little jingoism in reports, more a sadness at a squabble among brothers that seemed to have gone tragically wrong. The later liberal sophistication of several Wollstonecraft children suggests that they read newspapers when young and possibly discussed politics at home or outside. Many thinking people sympathised with the American cause, despite its antagonism to England, and, when she later came to pronounce on past events, Mary echoed this sympathy.

The newspapers also printed comic anecdotes, often lightly misogynous; it was easy to gauge the culture's thinking on women. For example, they told of a London lady who, having ordered an elegant masquerade costume, went to boast to friends. While she was out, a creditor called and encountered the husband, a man of 'humorous Turn'. He bade him take and sell the costume in payment. On learning what had happened, the lady took 'to her Bed with Vexation'.[17] Yet, however trivially they were represented in papers, Mary could note how keenly women were solicited as readers. The *Lady's Magazine* had now become two rival periodicals each desperately touting for business.

Although so far from the London rulers, she could yet note the doings of the rich through the press. At Windsor, a ceremony of aristocratic installation was on so grand a scale that provincials could only gape. A hairdresser near St James's engaged ninety-four journeymen at half a guinea a day to decorate genteel heads, while the Duke of Grafton's robes cost 3000 guineas, excluding diamonds. In Windsor Castle 2000 beds were prepared; there were 2000 tables and 17 kitchens with 50 cooks in each. In one episode of the dinner, ladies were to swap places with the populace, but 'the *Canaille*', as the *York Courant* called them, 'were too impatient to wait ... the Moment the Desert was brought in, they rushed forward, & entirely cleared the tables in 2 minutes'. They also demolished in seconds a fountain of confectionery, while commandeering all the dinner of the King's Watermen and Gentlemen Pensioners. At the end of the festivities Windsor Castle had lost ten dozen spoons, much table linen and china, and suffered countless breakages. Velvet had been cut from chair backs, and tails of gowns ripped off ladies; one guest had her pearl ear-ring snatched by the 'rapacious' many. Still, the whole was a magnificent event and Drury Lane staged a representation in their next theatrical season.

The polarisation of rich and poor indicated in such incidents disturbed thinking people. They sensed a gulf that might violently be bridged between landowners and landless. Newspapers told of poachers punished with the 'utmost Rigour of the Law' and of press gangs coming up the nearby river Ouse to capture unwilling 'Hands' from villages, stealing them from poor families. On one such occasion Hannah Snell, the famous Amazon who had fought in campaigns, offered to defend a victim: she would fight anyone with fists, sticks or staffs – when she had 'put off her Stays, Gown, and Petticoats, and put on Breeches'. She had, she boasted, sailed the world, suffering more wounds than they had fingers: they should get back to sea and stop sneaking around like 'Kidnappers'. Then she snatched 'the poor Fellow from the Gang, and restored him to his Wife'. So the 'long Petticoats, headed by a Veteran Virago, overcame the short Trowsers.'[18] Edward Wollstonecraft probably thought this ridiculous. He kept his wife where she should be, under his control.

Beyond schooling and access to print, Beverley gave Mary cultured society. This included young Jane Arden, her especial friend. Jane made her declare the Beverley time a period of serenity as well as shame: 'I often recollect with pleasure the many agreeable days we spent together when we eagerly told every girlish secret of our hearts – Those were peaceful days.' Together the girls read, talked of books and shared secrets. Since the mid-teens were the median age for menstruation, they probably whispered about the troublesome effluence of the female body which, in popular belief, curdled milk, rotted meat and stopped bread rising.[19] They laughed 'from noon 'till night', gossiped about boys, and took rolling walks on the meadows and woods past windmills and ruins on Westwood common.

Mary had met Jane at her father's lectures. Poor but proudly terming himself a 'philosopher', John Arden was one of several itinerant lecturers who visited larger provincial towns responding to the new interest in experimental science. At this transitional point when science had entered general polite culture but not become professionalised it was accessible to laymen – and women. Arden had acquired a special portable laboratory of instruments, even inventing an electric orrery himself. The Catholic landowner William Constable from Burton Constable Hall in Hull, a great collector, used him as his agent, in one year spending the huge sum of £191; John Marshall, the maker, charged £12 for an instrument demonstrating electricity and £9 for another made of 7 lb of brass, with a further 15s for a covering of buckskin. High temperature thermometers were expensively obtained from the Staffordshire Wedgwoods, who shared the interest in science.[20] With his elaborate instruments Arden taught a course on electricity, gravitation, magnetism, astronomy, optics and the expansion of metals.[21] Students could use the cheaper microscopes and telescopes themselves; they would learn to read maps and globes showing the configuration of earth and planets.

Mary attended the lectures; later she visited the Ardens' home, finding it intellectual and harmonious beside her own turbulent one. Mr Arden encouraged her and taught her with Jane: she was proud to compete for praise.


When Jane went away Mary solaced herself by writing letters, desperate to keep herself in focus and impress with her sensitivity. They foreshadow a lifetime of prickly correspondence, in which she would assume postures alternately of neediness and lofty independence. They do more: they provide an extraordinary window on the mind of a fourteen-year-old girl with all her awkward yearnings and intellectual desires. They differ from the letters of the adult vindicator of women in style and vocabulary – but bear remarkable resemblances in mannerisms and tone.

The first extant letters come from 1773 or early 1774, when Jane was visiting a Miss C in Hull. Mary made a few spiteful remarks about other girls, including Miss R[udd?], who, she feared, was usurping her place as 'best friend'. Then she quoted some dire local verses:

> What nymph so fair as Dolly,
> Smart as Stanhope's polly,
> Should you be seen, with gout or spleen
> They'll cure your melancholy.

Nine stanzas of this mock-ballad were copied out for her friend, presumably rather admired by young Mary. If only she could be the object of poetry herself, she sighed, be numbered among the 'Beverley beauties'.

Having displayed her literary bent, she was eager to apologise for defects she might expose – she had had little schooling and was no calligrapher:

> I have just glanced over this letter and find it so ill written that I fear you cannot make out one line of this last page, but – you know, my dear, I have not the

advantage of a Master as you have, and it is with great difficulty to get my brother to mend my pens.

Jane answered from Hull, describing Miss C's impudence to her parents, as well as the absurd 'beau' plaguing her. Mary was delighted at the cattiness and replied, 'I cannot help pitying you; a girl of your delicacy must be disgusted with such nonsense.'

Then Jane returned to Beverley and Miss C came to stay. The intimacy of the letters diminished; Mary felt excluded. Jane argued that a person could have many equal friends; Mary doubted it, believing there was always a hierarchy – she needed to be on top. The girls quarrelled and refused to speak to each other. So Mary dashed off an aggrieved note:

> Your behaviour at Miss J—'s hurt me extremely, and your not answering my letter shews that you set little value on my friendship. – If you had sent to ask me, I should have gone to the play, but none of you seemed to want my company. – I have two favors to beg, the one is that you will send me all my letters; – the other that you will never mention some things which I have told you. – To avoid idle tell-tale, we may visit ceremoniously, and to keep up appearances, may whisper, when we have nothing to say: – The beaux whisper insignificantly, and nod without meaning. – I beg you will take the trouble to bring the letters yourself, or give them to my sister Betsy [Eliza].

The note produced no response, and Mary grew more frantic and self-revealing:

> Miss Arden. – Before I begin I beg pardon for the freedom of my style. – If I did not love you I should not write so; – I have a heart that scorns disguise, and a countenance which will not dissemble: – I have formed romantic notions of friendship. – I have been once disappointed: – I think if I am a second time I shall only want some infidelity in a love affair, to qualify me for an old maid, as then I shall have no idea of either of them. – I am a little singular in my thoughts of love and friendship; I must have the first place or none ... I would not have seen it, but your behaviour the other night I cannot pass over; – when I spoke of sitting with you at Church you made an objection, because I and your sister quarrelled; – I did not think a little raillery would have been taken in such a manner, or that you would have insinuated, that I dared to have prophaned so sacred a place with idle chit-chat.
>
> I once thought myself worthy of your friendship; – I thank you for bringing me to a right sense of myself. – When I have been at your house with Miss J— the greatest respect has been paid to her; every thing handed to her first; – in

short, as if she were a superior being: – Your Mama too behaved with more politeness to her.

... There is no accounting for the imbecillity of human nature – I might misconstrue your behaviour, but what I have written flows spontaneously from my pen and this I am sure, I only desire to be done by as I do; – I shall expect a written answer to this ...

The outpouring seems to have affected Jane, and Mary was slightly mollified; she needed to forgive her friend sufficiently to allow continued corresponding and talking. With little significance at home, she wanted consequence outside: for who she was, not just for what services she might fulfil.

The delicate manoeuvre of partial forgiveness was effected in the next letter through some popular lines of poetry. She had already displayed her enthusiasm for Beverley's verse, now she could show she also knew Gray, Pope and Dryden:

I have read some where that vulgar minds will never own they are in the wrong: – I am determined to be above such a prejudice, and give the lie to the poet who says –

'Forgiveness to the injured does belong
'But they ne'er pardon, who have done the wrong'

and hope my ingenuously owning myself partly in fault to a girl of your good nature will cancel the offence – I have a heart too susceptible for my own peace: – Till Miss C— came, I had very little of my own; I constantly felt for others; –

'I gave to misery all I had, a tear,
'I gained from heaven, 'twas all I wished a friend.' ...

As to the affair at Miss J—'s I am certain I can clear myself from imputation. – I spent part of the night in tears; (I would not meanly make a merit of it.) – I have not time to write fully on the subject, but this I am sure of, if I did not love you, I should not be angry. – I cannot bear a slight from those I love ...

A postscript told Jane that she kept her letters 'as a Memorial that you once loved me, but it will be of no consequence to keep mine as you have no regard for the writer.'[22] She returned an 'Essay upon friendship which your Papa lent me the other day ... Friendship founded upon virtue Truth and love; – it sweetens the cares, lessens the sorrows, and adds to the joys of life. – ... Happy beyond expression is that pair who are thus united ...' The essay was a blueprint for friendship and Jane was urged to live up to it.

Thereafter the girls settled down and recommended books to each other

again. Both continued lessons with Jane's father, Mary still (jokingly) competitive: 'Pray tell the worthy Philosopher, the next time he is so obliging as
to give me a lesson on the globes, I hope I shall convince him I am quicker
than his daughter at finding out a puzzle, tho' I can't equal her at solving a
problem.'[23]

In these letters to Jane Arden Mary sought to create herself as a literary
lady who would never write frivolously of her feelings: she had already
internalised a notion that her writing was authentic, expressing 'true'
emotion and that her raw articulation was superior to conventional polish.
The letters show that she found a partly nurturing, partly admonitory
authority in books, substituting for that of unacceptable parents. Apart from
the Beverley doggerel, she quotes the usual canon of male literature urged
on women in the conduct manuals of the day: she read anthologies that
excerpted their most serviceable and soothing lines and told genteel young
girls to store them up against future trials of the female life. Surprisingly, she
was not fascinated with romance, that staple of circulating libraries which
fed the imaginations of most literate girls and against which the culture
sternly warned. She did not even refer to Richardson's *Pamela* and its fable
of virtuous feminine power. Perhaps she was reacting to her mother. There
is no special evidence that Mrs Wollstonecraft liked novels, but, in her
fictional depiction of an inadequate mother, Mary portrays a reader of
romance.

However uncommon her avoidance of romance, Mary was a child of her
time in her fantasy of sentimental friendship.[24] In the *Lady's Magazine* of
1779 in a story called 'Matilda: or, the Female Recluse', the wealthy heroine,
finding her suitor desiring her money, retires with her friend to lead an
idyllic life of reading without men, sharing 'one house ... one purse ... one
heart', much as the real-life Ladies of Llangollen had done with éclat some
years before and the poet Anna Seward wanted to do with her adopted
sister.[25] In both her novels, *Mary, A Fiction* and *The Wrongs of Woman*, Mary
portrayed powerful female ties that improved on the unsatisfactory one of
mother and daughter. They were so intense they transformed friends into
family.

While seeking to define elevated friendship Mary made extreme emotional
demands on Jane. The letters display a mental masochism as Mary pursued
what must in the end cause misery: the demand for more significance than
Jane could grant. She wanted from her friend what literary romance allowed
the heterosexual couple: that the pair form a little island against the world,
each first with the other. It was a demanding notion, one never quite aban-

doned. Declaring herself desperate for independence throughout her life, she was never solely satisfied with pursuing autonomy; insufficiently loved, she competed relentlessly for affection and, lacking self-worth, desperately desired to be *first* with someone – anyone except her parents or herself. This power in longing, coupled with powerlessness in society, gave her mature writing its raw energy – as it gives these early letters.

Energy also came from her belief that she could change others with her words. At fourteen or fifteen Mary had little desire to change herself and did not wonder at her own attitudes or deviate from her tones of hurt, peevishness or apology. She took pride in her instability and especial sensitivity. Tossing out her letters to control her friend's attitudes, she did not stop to think whether they should be sent. As thoroughly as any American of the 1970s, Mary was caught in the sentimental myth that it was good to express every emotion, to let everything hang out. She had not the benefit of reading Jane Austen, born during these years, and of learning that sometimes one needed to keep quiet or not write. Neither young Mary nor the adult Wollstonecraft would have anything of this mannerly reticence. She must be taken as she was or feel rejected and bite back.

*'A friend whom I love better than all the world beside'*

The Beverley period ended abruptly in 1775. Edward decided he was unsuited to farming and would try business in London. With the move Mary's schooling ended. She had been in Yorkshire from nine to fifteen and a half, longer than she would live anywhere else and she always thought of herself as in part a Yorkshire woman, its dialect expressions on the tip of her tongue.

Just before they left, the family began to scatter. Her younger brother Henry was apprenticed on 16 January for seven years to an apothecary-surgeon, Marmaduke Hewitt, some time alderman and mayor of Beverley. Although in the lower rank of doctors, below the university-trained physician, the apothecary-surgeon could be a substantial citizen, acting as a sort of general practitioner able to dispense drugs. It was a good position for a second son and the apprenticeship cost the family a 'genteel' amount to purchase, probably about £200. John Arden made similar provision for his sons James and John.

Shortly afterwards, the Wollstonecrafts went south, a long, uncomfortable and hazardous journey taking at least two and a half days. The winter was harsh and carriages overturned on snowy roads. With so many children no method of transport was cheap. They may have hired a chaise or taken a public coach, sending household baggage by a Hull packet boat. There was no direct carriage route from Beverley to London and travellers had to go to York or Leeds to get places on the stage or to Sheffield to catch the London Old Fly. In winter children could not go as outside passengers and each would cost about £1 10s or more inside. There were lodgings at the stopovers made to avoid night highwaymen, and gin stops where travellers were urged to buy refreshments – indeed stage horses were often kept at inns to integrate services. Money was spent everywhere.

When they arrived in London Ned was articled to a lawyer. The rump of the family lodged in Queen's Row, Hoxton, an urbanised village taking city overspill. Edward Wollstonecraft tried 'a commercial speculation of some sort', which, like his farming, failed.

Hoxton was famous for its Dissenters who had founded an early academy there. This taught men excluded from Oxford and Cambridge for refusing to conform to the Church of England and provided a rigorous education in classics, philosophy, and theology, as well as modern languages and sciences. At this moment Mary's future husband, young William Godwin, not yet the famous atheist, was studying to become an Independent minister like his father and grandfather; he later wondered what would have happened if he, a youth of twenty, and she a girl of sixteen, had met. Would they have liked each other? Would they have surmounted their different backgrounds and family pressures to come together?

Perhaps Mary would not have wished any young man whose opinion she valued to know her family just then. Henry, apprenticed in Beverley, suddenly disappears from family letters. Since over the next years Mary obsessively kept tabs on all her siblings except the prosperous Ned, the silence is strange. Possibly Henry ran away from a harsh master. Newspapers advertised constantly for runaway apprentices, along with escaped horses and, occasionally, errant wives. But the complete silence suggests something more extreme, perhaps a breakdown or swerve into insanity. Melancholy afflicted the family, and an abandoned teenaged boy might have fallen over an acceptable line. He might have tried to kill himself, a common reason for incarceration.

A parliamentary act of 1742 had locked up the violent mad in houses of correction with criminals and paupers, the family paying upkeep if possible. After the mid-1770s all pauper lunatics from Yorkshire were supposed to go to the York Lunatic Asylum, with space for fifty-four patients. It was a filthy place; the male patients were beaten, even killed or 'lost', the women raped.[1] No family would want a relative there. The middle class made private arrangements, sometimes through advertising in the local press. One issue of the York Courant requested a home in a clergyman's family at the seaside for a genteel lady of about thirty-five: the notice was candid, 'to avoid unnecessary Trouble it is to be observed, that the Gentlewoman is not in her right Mind'. If less genteelly mad, a relative could be shut away in a private madhouse: both Hull and York had refuges where men and women of any age might be incarcerated for 'melancholia' or violence after drinking. Their treatment would be a mixture of bleeding, cupping, and purgatives. If they did not descend from their 'high' spirits, they were pronounced 'irre-coverable' and left alone.[2]

If such mental disaster had overtaken Henry and the Wollstonecrafts did not wish to leave him in Yorkshire, their destination of Hoxton was explained. It housed many of London's insane in three major lunatic asylums and over the years had grown synonymous with lunacy: clowns at Bartholomew Fair raised a laugh at its expense, fools were labelled 'fit for nothing but Bedlam or Hogsdon'. The Balmes House asylum had added the term 'barmy' to the language.[3] The huge Whitmore House was run by sadistic and grasping keepers, but this only became known later. In some cases the rich might pay as much as £1500 to incarcerate a relative, while pauper lunatics, housed in an appalling offshoot in Bethnal Green, were charged to the parish at 8s or 10s 6d a week. Both rich and poor could be cruelly treated, the former debauched into idiocy, the latter degraded into submission. Years later, when George III went mad, his callous attendants and his domineering doctor, Francis Willis, were both connected with the Whitmore Bedlam.

If Henry were insane, his absence from his siblings' lives was not unusual. Middle-class and gentry families usually disposed of the defective very thoroughly: Jane Austen's brother George and uncle Thomas were sent from home and hardly referred to. The only possible mention of the missing Henry Wollstonecraft comes from twelve years later in a letter of Mary's to her sister Everina: 'The account you sent about Henry has harried my spirits . . .'[4]

At sixteen in Hoxton Mary was restless and ambitious – or 'wild, but animated and aspiring' in Godwin's words – and she charmed a neighbouring clergyman, the Reverend Clare and his wife. They were her first surrogate family and she stayed with them for weeks on end. Deformed and sickly, Mr Clare was reclusive – allegedly he had needed only one pair of shoes in fourteen years. He had a discriminating passion for poetry, which he generously shared with Mary: later she described the Clares as a 'very amiable Couple' who 'took some pains to cultivate my understanding (which had been too much neglected) they not only recommended proper books to me, but made me read to them; – I should have lived very happily with them if it had not been for my domestic troubles, and some other painful circumstances, that I wish to bury in oblivion.' To Jane Arden she had already shown fear of marriage and spinsterhood, and the 'painful circumstances', which might have included Henry's fate, probably also included failed romance. Perhaps there was a suitor, ultimately frightened by her poverty and prickliness.

If so, Mrs Clare compensated by introducing Mary to a new friend, eighteen-year-old Fanny Blood from the straggling village of Newington Butts south of the Thames (where, incidentally, the redoubtable Hannah Snell had bested the press gang). Here was a girl infinitely more sophisticated than any Mary had met, uniting intellect with feminine charm and skill at painting and needlework. With this friend she could at last have the exclusive female relationship she craved, with no Miss R— to intervene. It was love at first sight and, before the initial visit ended, Mary 'had taken, in her heart, the vows of eternal friendship'.[5]

She began to fantasise life with Fanny without troublesome men or the female fear of rejection. As she put it,

> I enjoyed the society of a friend, whom I love better than all the world beside, a friend to whom I am bound by every tie of gratitude and inclination: To live with this friend is the height of my ambition ... her conversation is not more agreeable than improving ...

To Godwin, Mary later described it as 'a friendship so fervent, as for years to have constituted the ruling passion of [my] mind'.

Though better educated and more accomplished than Mary, Fanny came from an even poorer family, partly maintained by her sewing and painting. The Bloods as a group were genteel – in Ireland they owned land, some of which had been given by Charles II to a rogue ancestor, Colonel Thomas Blood. He had tried to steal the crown jewels, but, since he was a useful government spy, was rewarded rather than hanged. Whatever landed pretensions the Irish Bloods had, their London branch had sunk below the trading Wollstonecrafts. Fanny's mother, Caroline, had brought money into the marriage only to see it squandered by her irresponsible husband, Matthew, and they were now eking out a living trading in small sewn goods. Mary's family was contemptuous of the connection.

She was little concerned. With her new friend she read and talked, usually at the Clares' house where she was almost a fixture. They wrote letters for they lived far from each other, exchanging them whenever anyone travelled between the two places: postage was expensive and paid by the recipient. Fanny was fluent and wrote an elegant hand; so she 'undertook to be her [friend's] instructor' in writing. She must have been tactful since Mary was already sensitive about her style.

The relationship with Fanny Blood was close and for a time emotionally fulfilling. Perhaps it was erotic, even sexual, but this seems unlikely beyond the usual caresses of young girls. Years later Mary alluded in horror to 'nasty tricks' of boarding-school misses, but was vague whether she meant masturbation or lesbianism. 'Decent personal reserve' should exist between women who ought to avoid a 'gross degree of familiarity'.[6] Probably the girls corresponded fervently, but none of their letters has survived.

In the novel based on her friendship, Mary described a tie which ultimately failed her, but the clever and sensitive Fanny was not obviously unsatisfactory – perhaps Mary drew on the flightier Jane Arden for a friend who responded to love with 'involuntary indifference' and gave affection through pity. But, if Fanny *were* the model of this, then the problem might have been divided affection. She had been disappointed in love, possibly an early episode with Hugh Skeys, an Irish businessman with Portuguese interests, now half-heartedly wooing her. He had reason to hold back; none of Fanny's siblings seemed likely to flourish any more than their parents.[7]

Mary's dream of female community was interrupted in 1776 by Edward Wollstonecraft's need to quit London and appear a provincial gentleman again. This time he chose the pretty village of Laugharne in South Wales on the tidal river Taf close to the Towy estuary.

Consisting primarily of one long wide street, Laugharne had been a port (and site of piracy), and consequently had several good houses. In the early eighteenth century, its port had silted up, leaving its inhabitants to drink and depend penuriously on fishing and gathering the cockles that lay in thousands beneath the sandy riverbed. So the houses went for low rent and attracted English visitors from nearby Bristol, as well as residents from London desiring remoteness.[8] Its only access was from a winding road or small ferry.

Although Godwin declared that Edward went for 'agricultural pursuits', and the valley of the River Corran close to Laugharne had the kind of mixed crop and dairy farms he would have been used to, by now he had little capital and it is likely he chose the region to evade London creditors. Possibly he bought a house outright or took a long lease. He may have kept a cow or two, as most people did, but, if so, he tried to combine farming with business. The family would live on little: Wales was cheap.

The children were older than on the trek to Beverley and no doubt complained about the discomforts of an unwelcome trip spreading over days and stretching through the Gloucestershire Cotswolds, the Forest of Dean, across the Bristol Channel and along the South Wales coast. Given their father's volatile temper, they must have turned ill humour on each other. Their mother no longer had the comfort of her beloved Ned.

Once in Laugharne, Edward was restless, finding every excuse to make the long journey in reverse. He needed London for business, he declared, to attend to the Primrose Street houses, but also to carry on some hidden enterprise that must deliver fortune. Whatever called him he went without his troublesome family, which was left behind suspecting that it was London's pleasures that beckoned.

The removal 'answered no one good end' and the family resources dwindled further. Yet in Laugharne the Wollstonecrafts were not entirely despicable, and they came to know at least one well-placed family, that of John

Bartlett Allen at Cresselly, a Pembrokeshire Whig squire with interests in surrounding counties. He had nine daughters mostly too small to interest a young lady like Mary and contact was infrequent since they lived many miles away. Probably the Allens visited Laugharne where Allen's grandfather had been vicar and where he may have retained property. Edward Wollstonecraft and John Allen seem to have had little in common except for their irascible and domineering characters: Mr Allen was reputed to beat his daughters if they failed to provide clever conversation – if true, they retaliated later when they refused to let him bring home his mistress, a coalminer's daughter.

Infatuated with Fanny, Mary went reluctantly to Laugharne, swearing to return swiftly to her second home and friends. But while there she admired the wild, hilly Welsh scenery: the cliffs and clouds, the ruined twelfth-century castle grown with ivy and the gleaming tidal estuary with its screaming gulls and geese.

Yet always she preferred people; so it was fortunate that they remained there only a year. Edward returned from one of his 'business' trips to announce their removal east. As Mary summed up the adventure: 'a pretended scheme of economy induced my father to take us all into Wales ... Business or pleasure took him often to London, and at last obliged him once more to fix there.' The breathtaking detachment of this statement declares her alienation. She was judging as well as resenting her father.

This judgement derived from a serious misdemeanour, which, when it became clear, irrevocably diminished the family, making them no longer suitable acquaintances for the Gascoynes of Essex or the Allens of Pembroke. Edward's frequent trips had involved financial irregularity, perhaps something criminal – a fact which makes it likely that Laugharne was chosen for remoteness as well as economy. Now he was exposed and the Wollstonecrafts ruined. Even the rental money from Primrose Street was for a period swallowed up. Caught out, Edward for the first time attended to his long-suffering children. He had to for he proposed to plunder them.

Now practising law at 2 King Street, Tower Hill, Ned hoped to hear as little as possible from his feckless parent, but he had a large inheritance and, in the general chaos, his father looked longingly at it; he may even have managed to gain part since Ned went into debt now as well. Beyond Ned's money (and easier to purloin) there was the 'fortune' of the younger Wollstonecrafts, a small amount deriving from a source other than their grandfather's will: Everina later had a modest life annuity, while Mary referred to a lost legacy. Perhaps another member of the Wollstonecraft or, more likely, Dickson families, assessing Edward's character, had made this kindly provision for the younger children. Or possibly such annuities were part of her mother's marriage settlement.[9]

Whatever its source, Mary's legacy was demanded and given. Some of the younger siblings may also have been denuded but without having equivalent sense of loss. Then their father seems to have alienated the legacies to a Mr Roebuck, possibly the insurance broker in Nicholas Lane.[10] 'I very readily gave up my part,' wrote Mary later. 'I have therefore nothing to expect.' The money did not answer since Edward never recovered, but it was significant for Mary: had he not needed it, possibly her father might have left his wife and younger children in cheap Laugharne, returning to London alone.

The move and sacrifice gave her power, exploited to the full. Statuses shifted and, when she demanded as her price that she have her own room and that they live near Fanny Blood, her embarrassed father had to assent. So they moved to Walworth, south of London, close to Newington Butts, the Bloods' home, for Mary to be 'near her chosen friend'. It was a remarkable concession and one that bred resentment in the younger children.

The move brought little pleasure. By being in Walworth Mary could not make the Clares' Hoxton house her second home and she was thrown on her family – perhaps in their straitened circumstances the private room was not provided. She had had no wish to go to Wales, but had responded to the scenery and space; now they were cramped in poor lodgings in an undistinguished village, and the situation and diminished status lowered her spirits. She hated being bound to inadequate parents and loathed the need of them all to accept her father's masculine selfishness. She was sensitive to the damage of unearned privilege to owner and victims, desperate to escape from a family that harmed and shamed her. The complicated misery affected her health, as presumably it did Elizabeth's, and this joint debility was the nearest Mary came to an identification with her mother: 'my spirits were weak – in short, a lingering sickness was the consequence ... and if my constitution had not been very strong, I must have fallen a sacrifice long before this – as it is, my health is ruined, my spirits broken, and I have a constant pain in my side that is daily gaining ground on me.'[11]

At this uncomfortable time Ned married and went to live in St Katherine's Dock, a crowded area near the Tower and his office. Whatever he had given up to his father, over the next years he would distance himself from his family's declining fortunes; he did not offer to take his young sisters into his house as was often the custom. There was no such professional and emotional option for Mary, though she attempted several times to leave home, on each occasion prevented by 'intreaties and tears of her mother'. Mrs Wollstonecraft might not love her best but, without Ned, needed her dominant eldest daughter to help keep peace at home and manage her increasingly irascible spouse.

Meanwhile, the younger girls were packed off to one of the many boarding-schools in Chelsea, possibly paid for by Ned. Some years earlier, the actress, poet and novelist Mary Robinson, daughter of a speculating sea captain, had briefly attended a Chelsea school, which boasted a 'cultivated teacher' with an 'unfeminine propensity' to alcohol which ruined the school; then, still in her early teens, she helped her mother start their own establishment. Since her earlier school had been the very reputable More sisters' school in Bristol, she had had a good grounding in languages.[12] Like Mary Robinson the Wollstonecraft girls could expect no dowries, so it was hoped that some skill in drawing and sewing would make them marriageable. But they learnt little French, the pre-requisite for governessing in a good family; they were not being prepared for the most obvious independent life available to a lady.

In Walworth the family had taken lodgings with a young married bank clerk, Thomas Taylor, later named the 'Platonist' because he studied Greek philosophy. He conversed about Plato's writings with Mary, who took every opportunity of self-improvement. He spoke rapturously of the con-templative life he intended to follow. The effect of his thoughts on his manner impressed her: he seemed tranquil and his little study was an 'abode of peace'. Yet the passive route did not attract: she must be active or miserable.[13]

By spring 1778 she determined to leave home whatever the consequences. Living *near* to Fanny was no substitute for living *with* her and the friendship could not compensate for family gloom. To accept lodgings at the Bloods would have degraded them all. She would have to go away and earn her keep. Probably Fanny cautioned against a too impetuous launching into life. She herself was ailing and knew her limitations. Her suitor, Hugh Skeys, was still sustaining her hopes of marriage, but she felt certain of nothing, neither her abilities nor prospects. Mary was surer, more healthy, forthright and intolerant, and she was weary of other people's ineptitude. Seeing her aches, pains and low spirits, her mother may by now have accepted her need to escape and stopped tying her with tears. Mary is unlikely to have been silent about her irritation at her family, or, looking at her father, about the uselessness of sacrifice to such a cause.

# 3

*'I am averse to any matrimonial tie'*

Mary was just nineteen when, with her dream of life with Fanny intact, she became a lady's companion. She had grown into a tall young woman with auburn hair. She had light brown eyes, one lid of which was slightly paralysed, giving her sometimes a mocking, leering look. She was not conventionally pretty but, when stimulated by company, became vivacious and striking, and she was thought handsome enough.

In becoming a companion she was choosing one of the very few ill-paid options open to a middle-class woman. Her post could have been obtained through an agency or a newspaper advertisement; most likely it came through Mr Clare, who as an Anglican clergyman may have known her employer, Sarah Dawson, daughter of a Windsor canon and widow of a rich merchant. She was a lady 'of great peculiarity of temper' whose relatives did not care to live with her and she resided in the elegant new resort town of Bath, in Milsom Street, the best shopping area; the street included the Wedgwood china showrooms and the recently opened Octagon Chapel, known for its comfortable pews and used for fashionable worship and concerts. Mrs Dawson spent her summers at Windsor.

It was a courageous move for a girl who did not absolutely have to leave home. At such an age most genteel girls were hedged round by chaperones – although others kicked over the traces as thoroughly. Her contemporary Elizabeth Inchbald, later a playwright and novelist, absconded to London from East Anglia at eighteen to become an actress. Such young women knew themselves eccentric. Didactic fiction of the early nineteenth century showed the moral value of paid employment for females, but this was not so when Mary was growing up, and the novelists of her day routinely portrayed the horror of ladies earning bread outside the family.[1] Writing at about the time of Mary's departure, the young Frances Burney expressed the common attitude towards a woman exposing herself 'like a common Servant, to be Hired'; work was synonymous with 'servility' and 'abject dependance'.[2]

Later Mary bitterly described companioning:

Few are the modes of earning a subsistence, and those very humiliating. Perhaps to be an humble companion to some rich old cousin, or what is still worse, to live with strangers, who are so intolerably tyrannical, that none of their own relations can bear to live with them, though they should even expect a fortune in reversion ... If she cannot condescend to mean flattery, she has not a chance of being a favorite; and should any of the visitors take notice of her, and she for a moment forget her subordinate state, she is sure to be reminded of it ... The being dependant on the caprice of a fellow-creature, though certainly very necessary in this state of discipline, is yet a very bitter corrective, which we would fain shrink from.[3]

She had already shrunk from the 'caprice' of parents; family life must have been horrid for her to risk suffering it from a stranger.

In the late 1770s Bath was at the height of its fame as a watering-place, frequented alike by the young husband-hunting and the elderly sick. Its assemblies glittered with fashion, its shops bulged with luxuries. Lottery tickets were the rage, as were races and subscription balls. As 'an humble companion' Mary neither joined nor bought. Resentfully she gazed at the giddy, gay world she was not experiencing. A glance at the *Bath Chronicle* could confirm her worst fears about her status.[4]

Rank had to be policed in public if the 'quality' were not to be frightened away. Recently the master of ceremonies at the Assembly Rooms had received a complaint that servants, hairdressers and 'other improper persons' were attending the Monday balls, obliging ladies of rank and fashion to stand. They were also mixing with their betters in the tea- and card-rooms. From now on, no people in this station of life would be allowed to 'intrude themselves, where decency, propriety, and decorum, forbid their entrance'.[5]

Aware of her family's decline, Wollstonecraft felt her status within the 'servant' class – and after several months had only been twice to the Rooms with her employer. In the newspaper's personal columns she read her dismal future: a middle-aged person 'used to good company ... would be glad to wait on a lady as a companion, or housekeeper to a small but genteel family'. There were never enough 'small but genteel' families to go round needy ageing ladies used to good company.

Mary had one piece of luck in Bath: after two months she discovered Jane Arden's father and sisters. The previous year John had advertised in the *Bath Chronicle* that he was beginning his third course of experimental philosophy at an elegant lecture room at his house in St James's Street. There subscriptions and syllabuses could be obtained and, between twelve and one on non-lecture days, his extensive laboratory apparatus inspected.[6] She hurried to visit and learnt that Jane was 'well and agreeably situated' as a governess in the family of Sir Mortdant Martin in Burnham, Norfolk. After four and a half years she resumed contact: 'You will, my dear girl, be as much surprised at receiving a letter from me, as I was at hearing, that your family resided at Bath.' Her own life had been disturbed, she hinted, then awaited an answer before elaborating.

When it came, she poured out her life's misery between Beverley and Bath, solacing herself with self-dramatising and intended resignation. She had always attended church, though receiving scant instruction in doctrine. The Wollstonecrafts were not especially religious and little piety emerged in her earliest letters to Jane Arden, but now, probably influenced by the Revd Clare in Hoxton and the pious reading he encouraged, she felt she needed the otherwordly promises of Christianity. She accepted them selectively: like many Anglicans she doubted future punishment while confidently expecting future reward for earthly misery. God was a paternal figure, 'the kind parent' who compensated for failed earthly fathers; in this scheme she had little need for Jesus and his redemptive promise.

> I hinted to you in my last that I had not been very happy – indeed, I have been far otherwise: – Pain and disappointment have constantly attended me since I left Beverley. I do not however repine at the dispensations of Providence, for my philosophy, as well as my religion will ever teach me to look on misfortunes as blessings, which like a bitter potion is disagreeable to the palate tho' 'tis grateful to the Stomach – I hope mine have not been thrown away on me, but that I am both the wiser, and the better for them. – Tho' I talk so philosophically now, yet I must own, when under the pressure of afflictions, I did not think so rationally; my feelings were then too acute, and it was not till the Storm was in some measure blown over, that I could acknowledge the justness of it: – Young people generally set out with romantic and sanguine hopes of happiness, and must receive a great many stings before they are convinced of their mistake, and that they are pursuing a mere phantom; an empty name.

Then she turned to her consolation, Fanny Blood, on whose praises she could dwell an eternity. 'She has,' wrote Mary, 'a masculine understanding, and sound judgment, yet she has every feminine virtue.' Unhappily she was ailing and, if she recovered, might go abroad with Skeys: 'Tho' this change may probably restore her health, yet I cannot help grieving at it, as I shall then be deprived of my only comfort ...'

The remainder of the letter archly enquired whether Jane had met 'an agreeable Norfolk Swain ... you had I am sure a little spice of romance in your composition and must before this time have had a predilection in favor of some happy man'. The clichéd literary vocabulary marked her embarrassment, but she continued seriously, 'I should be glad to hear that you had met with a sensible worthy man, tho' they are hard to be found.'

The mingled condescension and envy with which she spoke of others' suitors make it likely that the 'painful circumstances' mentioned earlier included failed romantic hopes. In these early adult years Mary was quick to assume romance in others and displace her own desire.

It would be odd if she did not feel some yearning towards marriage. The old maid was stigmatised unless she had money. As a contemporary governess Agnes Porter lamented, 'I could not forbear partially and deeply reflecting on the ills that single women are exposed to, even at the hour of their death, from being the property of no-one.'[7] Yet Mary's expressed reluctance to marry was rational: for a person of her temperament its conventions of dependence could not have been emotionally satisfying and she could never quite see it as a contract rather than an enveloping institution. And there was always her parents' appalling example.

Roughly four months after her long synoptic letter to Jane Arden, in autumn 1779, she wrote to apologise for her silence. She had been to the resort town of Southampton, probably staying with Wollstonecraft relatives, Edward and Lydia, and their patriotically named daughter Britania. They had received her with 'so much civility that I left ... with regret'.[8] She had bathed in the sea, an activity much promoted for health in the 1770s, along with drinking sea-water. She felt better – but only in body. Now the sense of physical well-being had diminished and she was conveying to Jane both her gloom and the proper stance of Christian resignation, that some sickness and misery helped spiritual transcendence and worked against levity: 'I would not have you imagine that I repine at what has befallen me. – Reason, as well as religion convinces me all has happen'd for the best ... I am persuaded misfortunes are of the greatest service, as they set things in the light they ought to be view'd in and give those that are tried by them, a kind of early old age ...' (The sprightly Jane Arden must have smiled at this apparent change in her once demanding friend.) Mary would benefit by conversing with her much-travelled employer, Mrs Dawson, who had 'a very good understanding'; yet she could not help wailing that she had escaped one state of dependence only to find another: 'As to the vivacity you talk of, 'tis gone forever, and all I wish for, is a cheerful settled frame of mind, which I use all my endeavors to attain, and hope in time I shall.' Grimly she hoped that at least Jane was 'merry and well', untouched by 'the keen blast of adversity'.

A couple of months later Mary became more honest about her difficult life and her efforts to hold to female friendship over romance, clearer about her loneliness and dark moods. She clung to old friends and a past now bright beside her dismal present. She worked for 'prudential motives' and could not quit. 'I am among Strangers, far from all my former connexions.' Bath was packed with visitors enjoying balls and plays but she seldom went out: 'I am quite a piece of still life, not but that I am a friend to mirth and cheerfulness; – but I would move in a small circle; – I am fond of domestic pleasures and have not spirit sufficient to bustle about.'

Then Jane Arden left Norfolk to become a governess in Lord and Lady Ilchester's family in Redlynch, Somerset (incidentally as predecessor to Agnes Porter). The Ilchester family were cousins to the famous politician Charles James Fox and members of a great Whig dynasty. Although the daughters were very young – Lord Ilchester had only recently married his beautiful Irish bride – it was still a grand position for young Jane and argues her good education. Redlynch was near enough to Bath for visits to her family and no doubt she met her friend Mary again.

Perhaps, like Jane Austen a few years later, the young women walked down Pulteney Street to Sydney Gardens or made more ambitious excursions westwards to Beechen Cliff across the river Avon. Perhaps they walked to the corner of Mary's own Milsom Street to view Wedgwood's Queen's ware and vases, urns and cameos in porphyry, jasper and agate. It was not the sort of thing Mary would do alone.

They had little time, for soon Mrs Dawson removed her companion from the unused gaieties of Bath to Windsor. There Mary continued moody and unhappy, balefully looking from the margins, without even the occasional solace of Jane Arden.

She must have known the popular poem by John Armstrong, 'The Art of Preserving Health' (1744), and followed it in ascribing her ailments to the mind, which 'canker'd' the body. Since her melancholy was mentally caused she would not try the material remedies for 'lowness of spirits, horrors of mind, anxieties, confused thoughts, troublesome sleep and groundless fears' advertised in the newspapers. Vandour's Nervous Pills attacked nervous disorders affecting 'persons of relaxed fibres', substituting 'a severe chear-fulness of disposition, in the place of those horrors which so dreadfully oppress people of weak nerves'. Mary regarded potions as among the useless luxuries of life: she was not seeking physical relief but mental stamina.

Both poor and severe, she found female dress a problem in Windsor and Bath. In the 1770s it was at its most flamboyant. Satin pannier-style gowns were worn over striped taffeta underskirts over articulated hooped petticoats and laced corsets; the hair was backcombed and frizzed, surmounted by 'natural' and false curls, powdered with flour and topped with ostrich plumes or beribboned straw hats. This kind of showy fashion was beyond Mary's purse and desire: she took no pleasure in the new materials and her letters are unusually free of concern for gauze and muslin. No shop is mentioned, not even the less expensive near Walcot church in Bath, where millinery fashions were cheaply but elaborately made up. Of Windsor she moaned, 'This is the gayest of all gay places . . . nothing but dress and amusements are going forward.'

The frivolity seemed especially wrong when in June the country was lurching towards anarchy. The American War, now fully raging, was disrupting trade and the City of London was in volatile mood. At this moment the government proposed extending some tolerance to Roman Catholics and the measure ignited Protestant riots, stirred up by the young Lord George Gordon. Rapidly they became a looting and burning spree, which, since the City authorities acted slowly, raged for six days with hundreds dead and factories, shops, houses and prisons burnt. Breweries were targeted and streets for a time ran beer – killing a good many enthusiastic drinkers. It shocked the liberal middle-class, which saw that disorder and mob manipulation were dangerous weapons in any struggle.

Jane Arden now kept up the correspondence, giving family news and good wishes. When Mary replied in late spring or summer she assured Jane of what *she* wanted to be assured, that 'among the small number of my friends in whose memory I wish to live, you hold one of the first places'. Much had happened, she said, but she described little. Instead, like earlier ones, her letter revealed repressed yearning and insisted on divine comfort and early death. The sulky demanding girl of Beverley had become a scornful and depressive young lady, a 'spectator' of pleasure, an alienated being marginalised in an uncaring society: 'I wish to retire as much from [the world] as possible – I am particularly sick of genteel life, as it is called; – the unmeaning civilities that I see every day practiced don't agree with my temper; – I long for a little sincerity, and look forward with pleasure to the time when I shall lay aside all restraint.'

One reason for her alienation might have been romantic. Joshua Waterhouse, a clergyman don from St Catherine's College, Cambridge, unmentioned in her extant letters, was visiting fashionable places like Bath with his rich friend Sir John Danvers.[9] Thirteen years her senior, he may have known her employer, Mrs Dawson, daughter of a clergyman, or Mary might have met him while attending the Rooms. After his murder in 1827 letters both ardent and prudent were discovered among his numerous 'melting epistles'.[10]

Some came from the 'intellectual amazon' Mary Wollstonecraft.

When this sensational event happened, the elderly Waterhouse was miserly, reclusive and unkempt, but in early manhood he was spruce and fashionable. His education and ambition put him beyond Mary's reach for marriage, but he might have wanted a flirtation. He shared her background, being a farmer's son, and she was a vivacious, and reasonably attractive young woman eager to converse intelligently. Seemingly the pair enjoyed each other's company, then corresponded, then fell silent. The affair left a bitter taste, added to her depression, and made her wonder, not for the last time, whether it was better to live in pleasant hope than face uncomfortable reality. Her disappointment may have prompted fixation on her previously ignored appearance. She was dowdy, she realised glumly, an old maid at twenty-one: 'I have already got the wrinkles of old age, and so, like a true woman, rail at what I don't possess.'

Although Mary moaned and thought of death, Jane had inspirited her with a previous letter describing her plan of founding a small school with her sister Ann in Catherine Place, Bath. Such a project allowed young girls without resources to gain independence and avoid the loneliness of governessing. Or so many dreamed. Though disapproving the choice of Bath, Mary was enthusiastic. She lacked Jane's advantage of six years of governessing but she too might try this route, not with her sisters, but with Fanny Blood:

> I have ever approved of your plan, and it would give me great pleasure to find that you and your sister could contrive to live together; – let not some small difficulties intimidate you, I beseech you; – struggle with any obstacles rather than go into a state of dependance: – I speak feelingly. – I have felt the weight, and would have you by all means avoid it. – Your employment tho a troublesome one, is very necessary, and you have an opportunity of doing much good, by instilling good principles into the young and ignorant, and at the close of life you'll have the pleasure to think that you have not lived in vain, and, believe me, this reflection is worth a life of care.

Jane as governess was in as dependent a situation as her friend as companion, but Mary rarely imagined the difficulties of others being as intense as her own.

Ann and Jane Arden soon abandoned Bath finding it too competitive for, although spa towns and resorts were prime locations for schools since they could draw custom from seasonal visitors, Bath was especially well provided with schools and tutors. Mrs Wignall, for example, boarded and instructed up to twelve young ladies in the polite and useful branches of education;

Mrs Palmer taught morals, French, dancing and music with approved masters; Mrs Mainwaring and Miss Perks educated young ladies in St John's Court.[11] Given the oversupply, Jane and Ann decided to return with their father to Beverley. Ann's health was poor and Jane probably felt it best to be near her medical brothers, John and James. These were now notable in the town: John went on to be elected mayor nine times over the next thirty years, as well as becoming a partner in the main wine cellars, the Hengate Vaults. Meanwhile, their father continued to be patronised by the landowner Constable until his death in 1791.[12] Having such connections the sisters could soon advertise a 'Ladies Boarding School' in Eastgate off the Wednesday Market where the Wollstonecrafts had once lived.

Windsor had the advantage for Mary of being nearer than Bath to Fanny Blood's home. So without much expense or time she made a brief visit to her friend. It was an emotional oasis: Fanny received her 'in the most friendly manner' and they spent a comfortable week together, troubled only by knowing they would soon part. Hugh Skeys was absent and Mary mentioned the school plan as something to engross her and Fanny's future together. With no prospect of its coming into immediate being, her friend was gently encouraging: 'The next time we meet, it will be for a longer continuance, and to that period I look, as to the most important one of my life,' Mary told Jane. Then she added obscurely,

> this connexion must give the colour to my future days, for I have now given up every expectation and dependence that would interfere with my determination of spending my time with her. – I know this resolution may appear a little extraordinary, but in forming it I follow the dictates of reason as well as the bent of my inclination; for tho' I am willing to do what good I can in my generation, yet on many accounts I am averse to any matrimonial tie.

The abandoned 'expectation' was probably Joshua Waterhouse.

Back in Windsor she resumed companioning, feeling healthier than for some time. She could now see that Windsor had charms: the countryside was pleasing and she enjoyed forest rides. She listened to gossip about the amorous effect of the scandalous Prince of Wales on the town's women, visited with Mrs Dawson, and went to church. But still the untasted gaieties oppressed her, still she longed for a 'more retired situation' where people did not dress 'amazingly' and she was not thought 'a very poor creature'. Everywhere she condemned. Frivolity was morally wrong; Mrs Dawson's sister was improperly raising her daughters to be 'accomplished and fashionable' not 'good and sensible': 'In this she follows the crowd, and it is much to be lamented, that the Stream runs so rapidly that way.'[13]

Mary was proud of not following the 'crowd' herself. So she had no problem in disapproving the approved King George III because he killed horses in his haste at riding. She, on the other hand, had 'sometimes saved the life of a fly, and thought myself of consequence'. Indeed, despite the moaning of her letters, there was a decided sense of 'consequence' in Mary, the humble but haughty companion. It derived from both her puritanical austerity and her alienation among the trivial. When she wrote to Jane during one of Mrs Dawson's absences, the picture she painted of herself was a self-satisfied, self-absorbed one. In this trifling, luxurious town she excelled in abstemiousness, both in diet and dress, accepting with Armstrong that 'temperance is true luxury': 'I am just going to sup *solus* on a bunch of grapes, and a bread crust; – I'll drink your health in pure water'. Mrs Dawson had been through several companions in her life but only this formidable young woman managed to make her a little afraid.

# 4

*'A little patience, and all will be over!'*

Relationships with women like Jane and Fanny outside the home were more satisfactory to Mary than those within. She had left her family at a crucial time and, though her mother had in the end not prevented her going, she cannot have been pleased to see her daughter escaping duties that she believed a girl should assume, especially the eldest.

With Mary gone, the family slipped further down the social scale. They had moved to Walworth to humour her; now they went to the long, straggling village of Enfield in Middlesex about ten miles from London. The centre was an elegant square of early eighteenth-century houses rather like those in Beverley's Wednesday Market, but the Wollstonecrafts were more likely to have lodged in the newer rapidly built dwellings which were converting Enfield from a rural into an urban village. Money was tighter than ever, and Eliza and Everina had been removed from school. With no older sister, they had to fill Mary's place in the household and they resented her escape.

By now brother James had also left home. He had his sister's tendency to melancholy, not enhanced by his choice of career – or, most likely, his family's choice. At twelve he was dispatched to sea on board the *Carysfoot*. Since he had naval relatives on both sides, the family hoped for patronage in time, although by going straight to sea rather than through one of the naval academies, he was already disadvantaged. Many children chose seafaring for adventure or as an alternative to home, but James did not like the sea and tried often to escape over the next years. Without nautical inclination, existence on a damp and cramped ship with criminals and press-ganged men, smelling excrement and eating dry food, must have appalled a teenaged boy.

So there was only one son at home, eleven-year-old Charles, a surprisingly cheery youth. His parents wanted Ned to take him into articles when he was old enough. Charles probably hoped it would be soon.

The girls left behind continued to see Fanny Blood, who was always tactful in dealing with them, but they cared little for the rest of her family. Ned judged them all spongers. Eliza knew that Mary was writing often to Fanny, yet failed to keep in proper touch with her own family; she was annoyed to learn that, when she visited Fanny, Mary did not trouble to see them as well.

The sisters responded to Mary's neglect by neglecting her. Their mother did not write and neither of her younger daughters tried to mend the rift by sending good wishes in their own letters. It was Mary's turn to be hurt. It did not strike her that her mother, worn out from abuse and struggle, might be ailing and that the lowness of spirits from which she herself suffered might be felt by others. Indeed, her family thought that, altogether, she did not take sufficient notice of their miseries, while always descanting on her own. Everina had been seriously ill and Mary had not written to enquire. Eliza blamed her and Mary countered that none of them had seen fit to tell her the news.

When she wrote in August 1780 Eliza took an arch, facetious tone. She supposed that, in her new life, Mary seldom thought of them. Why should she? She had better things to occupy her. Mary was stung and dashed off a hurt reply. She had so internalised her family that she found it hard not to think of them always. Emphasising her own introspection, she assumed that constant anxiety could substitute for visits and letters, that somehow her sisters and mother should be grateful for her care and its malign bodily effect on herself: 'You don't do me justice in supposing I seldom think of you,' she retorted. 'The happiness of my family is nearer to my heart than you imagine perhaps too near for my own health or peace – For my anxiety preys on me, and is of no use to you.'

All three sisters suffered from self-pity, finding it hard to imagine another's response to what they wrote. They were all critical readers. Eliza had given pleasantries and Mary refused to let them pass: 'I should like to be remembered in a kinder manner,' she wrote. 'There is an air of irony through your whole epistle that hurts me exceedingly . . . it displeases me – I hate formality and compliments.' She had been especially upset by her mother's neglect, but could offer nothing to gain her affection except the veiled threat of her own death which would lead to a belated and proper understanding on her mother's part: 'of late she has not even desired to be remembered to me. – Some time or the other, in this world or a better she may be convinced of my regard – and then may think I deserve not to be thought so harshly of.'


Her mother had other things on her mind beyond her touchy daughter's feelings. For some time her health had been deteriorating. Her life had been hard and she had few resources and less resilience to help her fight bodily pain. She had withstood her husband's tantrums because that had seemed the best way to keep peace: she had not thereby earned his respect or inspired his care.

In autumn 1781 she was diagnosed with dropsy or edema, a fluid retention that could lead to swellings, ulcers, gangrene, lethargy and ultimately suffocation. Now at last the family had to send for Mary as eldest daughter. With a direct demand she could cope: *in extremis* her mother wanted her, that counted for much. She moved back home at once. It felt crowded and tense after the elegancies of Bath and Windsor, but she was of use and the novelty of her mother's gratitude sustained her through part of the winter. The illness would be fatal, they all saw.

Mary did what she could for the invalid, but, as the disease only slowly progressed, both mother and daughter became less patient. Confined for long weeks and months to a single room, the sick woman was not always thankful, while, tired and restricted, Mary was not consistently generous. As she deteriorated over the winter and into the spring, her mother became querulous and exacting, rather demanding the attentions than receiving them as gifts. It was not an easy illness to nurse and the sickroom must have stunk with decaying flesh and the messy paraphernalia of disease. Mary found herself hemmed in, dulled by tiredness, resentment, pity and disgust. She felt for her mother but did not judge her less harshly. She had not been a proper parent: 'To be a good mother – a woman must have sense, and that independence of mind which few women possess who are taught to depend entirely on their husbands,' she later wrote. 'Meek wives are, in general, foolish mothers.'

Edward Wollstonecraft had not been tender at the best of times and these were the worst. His wife's long illness tried his temper; often he believed her malingering and said as much. He was used to being served, not serving. For all their bouts of schooling, the girls had little domestic training and the household cannot have been smoothly run. None of them had much sense of managing and budgeting, and unpaid tradesmen easily became abusive. To keep the peace in the house and protect the dying woman, the daughters had to handle such matters, as well as their irascible father. Mary hated both duties. Later she wrote, 'Parental affection, indeed, in many minds, is but a pretext to tyrannise where it can be done with impunity, for only good and wise men are content with the respect that will bear discussion.'[1]

After months of pain and tedium, Elizabeth Wollstonecraft died. With so many sleepless nights Mary was worn out physically and emotionally. The attendance had not in the end brought the gratification she craved. For all Mary's dutifulness and care, her mother had not finally turned to her with fondness or insisted against a lifetime's habit that she loved her best. Instead, like her daughter, she concentrated on herself, murmuring before her death, 'A little patience, and all will be over!'

Or so Godwin recorded in his *Memoirs*. Although Mary did not mention the phrase at the time, she used it repeatedly in her published work, especially in her last novel, *The Wrongs of Woman*, where she added the imagined 'blessing' for the attending daughter: 'I shall not dwell on the deathbed scene, lively as is the remembrance, or on the emotion produced by the last grasp of my mother's cold hand; when blessing me, she added, "A little patience, and all will be over!" '[2]

In the same novel she described the callous amorousness of the husband with 'an artful kind of upper servant' whose new finery at church attracted gossip. Perhaps this was a fictional image of her father who was indeed attached to a woman called Lydia. Mary was appalled at the premature replacement of a worn-out mother.

When she wrote to Jane Arden she concentrated less on Elizabeth's death than on her own attenuated existence: was she herself alive or dead or just half alive? 'I am in the land of the living,' she concluded. She failed to assess the life of her mother as a being separate from herself. Yet a woman who had raised at least six 'vigorous and healthy' children, to use Godwin's words, in a disease-ridden age when over half of London infants died before they reached five, who had seen her brood through smallpox and chickenpox, measles and the chesty colds of childhood, was not negligible. For all her failings she had instilled in Mary an internal sense of right: 'when she felt she had done wrong,' she told Godwin, '[her mother's] chastisement [was] the only thing capable of reconciling her to herself'.[3] Whatever her effect on her daughter's opinions and cast of mind, Elizabeth Wollstonecraft would live for Mary mainly as a lamentable example. She gave her mother no eulogy when she was buried at Enfield on 19 April 1782.[4]

Despite her frailty and inadequacy, their mother had kept the remnant of the Wollstonecraft family together. With her death it disintegrated. Mary's sense of herself as a mother to the younger children could not overwhelm her desire to be free of them all again: mothering was never quite as fulfilling a role in practice as she imagined.

Her father did not urge her to stay or try to keep the family intact. Indeed, he was hardly functioning as a father. His finances were in such chaos that he fell entirely into the hard hands of his disapproving eldest son, who took over management of the Primrose Street houses and rationed out the rents. Probably he did so on condition that Edward went far away and lived as cheaply as possible. So, now a dependent not a patriarch, their father married

Lydia and took her and young Charles back to Laugharne. Mary felt a mixture of disgust and fury at this self-indulgent man. She had seen him again at close quarters and was glad he was going out of her sight. Years later she remained so antagonistic that her sisters feared what would happen if she ever encountered him in the flesh. None the less, when he lamented that Ned was starving him, she realised she loathed her grasping brother even more.

Laugharne was no place for marriageable daughters and Ned agreed to accommodate Eliza and Everina in his home in St Katherine's Street. His wife Elizabeth, now a mother, was reluctant, but probably he assured her that they would soon be married and off their hands – especially Eliza, who was remarkably pretty.

With the Wollstonecraft diaspora, Mary was freer than she had ever been. There was no question of going to Ned's and so she could work towards her goal of a life solely with Fanny. She thus moved into the crowded Bloods' home, now at 1 King's Row, in the busy suburban village of Walham Green, west of London. It was not quite what she had imagined. She had planned to take Fanny away not to arrive on her, depressed and homeless. Yet the family was welcoming: she was not bringing an injection of capital and had no skill at fancy needlework, but her energy and drive inspired them to hope that something might be done with her help. She believed in herself and made them believe.

She stayed with the Bloods for well over a year, seeing at first hand real poverty, although the admirable Fanny and her mother no doubt kept the small house 'furnished with peculiar neatness and propriety'. The pair were ruining their eyesight by sewing through the night to support themselves, the inadequate father and the younger children. Indeed, with less capacity and skill, Mary herself had to help with this chore. As Fanny later recorded:

> My mother used to sit at work, in summer, from *four* in the morning 'till she could not see at night, which with the assistance of one of her daughters did not bring her more than half a guinea a week, and often not quite that; and she was generally at least one third of the year without work, tho' her friends in that line were numerous ... [Mary] was almost *blinded* and sick to death after a job we did for Mrs Bensley...[5]

Mary must have seen the extent of Fanny's poor health and apprehended her inevitable limitations. For Fanny was no longer the 'instructor' and, now that they were together, dominance was shifting from the skilled friend to the assertive Mary who had already earned her own living outside the home.

With the Bloods Mary met visiting Irish friends and relatives: Betty Delane for example, the young daughter of a Dublin merchant, whose stolid temperament she rather condescendingly approved, and Neptune Blood, picturesquely named after an ancestor born at sea. She enjoyed flirting with him. Soon she began to be attached.[6]

In the beginning he answered her affections, perhaps even developing them in himself. But then he retreated. In Ireland the Bloods were a more substantial family than the London hangers-on, and Neptune Blood was snobbish and moved in fashionable circles. No more than Joshua Waterhouse would he consider marrying without money. He had come to visit Matthew Blood and his family but was shocked at their position in life. He would drop the connection when he returned to Dublin. Nothing had been promised; so the offended Mary reasoned that it was not really a withdrawal – perhaps the future might bring a change of heart and purpose.

She had compensations. Within the Blood ménage she could give free rein to her dominating personality and with the parents, Fanny's younger brother George and sister Caroline, she was soon 'first', as she had never been in her own better-placed family; each treated her with the most gratifying respect. She became their saviour, the 'Princess' in their midst, the title coined by George which she happily repeated. George was not as clever as Fanny but amiable and entertaining: though young he had been to sea and had extraordinary adventures, including being captured by a French privateer off the coast of America. She liked him. Despite Ned's warning of their sponging, Mary became responsible for the whole needy family who became so thoroughly her own that she often spoke of the parents as 'father' and 'our Mother'. The fecklessness that irritated her in the Wollstonecrafts only endeared the Bloods for it made them rely on her more. No event seemed to exclude her and now she could even contemplate going with Fanny to Lisbon to marry if the reluctant Hugh Skeys ever proposed.

She hoped he would do so soon. For, though loving the Bloods, she did not much like living with them. Walham Green was not unpleasant – it was a healthy place, noted for the surprising longevity of its inhabitants – but she was tired of it and poverty.[7] She envied Jane Arden a trip to Ireland and felt old and dull. She might accept that she was a 'singleton' to use Agnes Porter's word, but she could not bare stasis. She wanted the voyage to Lisbon even more for Fanny, whose health was deteriorating under the punishing regime. Only a warm climate could help her, some rest from the endless toil. But Skeys procrastinated.

Sometimes Mary felt desperate enough to move Fanny from the Bloods herself. Having been sensitised to tyranny and submission in her own dysfunctional family, she hated to see Mrs Blood manoeuvring to keep the peace by carefully handling a man who contributed nothing to the general welfare. Even Fanny was sometimes exasperated; then Mary urged her plan of their living alone. It was not quite clear what she herself could do, but Fanny could sew and draw and get good money for her work.

Heartened by encouragement at one such moment, Mary went to look for lodgings. She found a cheap, convenient place, moved in, then set about arranging for Fanny to come. But, as the time drew closer, Fanny demurred. She was overwhelmed by her friend when they were together, but felt scruples recur once the powerful presence was removed. She had an acute sense of responsibility for her family and was unwilling to leave her struggling if uncongenial mother.

So Mary had to abandon the scheme. She accused her friend of being 'irresolute' and the incident rankled. For her part, Fanny might well have been frightened at a temperament that impulsively translated vision into reality without considering all the factors or other people involved.

Mary's dissatisfaction did not break the friendship. Men might disappoint and her family alienate her, but Fanny remained her main emotional stay in the world. That she was involved with a man was no obstacle. They both regarded him more as a relative and prospective landlord than a lover. Hence the notion that they would *both* be travelling to Lisbon if the proposal came. So once more they waited in Walham Green for Skeys and rescue. It would be interesting to know if *he* realised that two women were attending to his words.

Now, however, a proposal of marriage came for Mary's pretty younger sister of nineteen. On 20 October 1782 Eliza married a well-to-do shipwright from Rotherhithe called Meredith Bishop, a friend of Skeys and owner of a business which built lighters to unload larger cargo ships. It was a good match – he and his father were listed in directories as 'eminent traders' – and Mary was pleased, although, closeted with the Bloods, she had little to do with arrangements at Ned's. From Wales, Edward Wollstonecraft sent his per-mission for the marriage of his underage daughter and Ned acted *in loco parentis*; the couple were married in his parish church of St Katherine's Near the Tower.[8]

In Mary's opinion Eliza was marrying too early. To marry before twenty meant that a girl had more than likely failed to discover a man of principle. Also marriage shut off her chance of developing her mind to its full potential: the young wife faced domestic duties and had to please another person too soon in life. She would have children when scarcely more than a child herself.[9]

The wedding, together with another recent one of a third Arden sister, raised again Mary's ambivalent sensations about marriage. She felt the power it had over all their minds. Did she want it desperately or not at all? Did it give significance to women or nullify them? Was the married woman or the spinster a blank and cipher? Caustically, she wrote to Jane about the two unions and her own uncomfortable but free state:

> I was just going to desire you to wish [your sister] joy (to use the common phrase) but I am afraid my good wishes might be unseasonable, as I find by the date of your letter that the honey moon, and the next moon too must be almost over. – The joy, and all that, is certainly over by this time, and all the raptures have subsided, and the dear hurry of visiting and figuring away as a bride, and all the rest of the delights of matrimony are past and gone and have left no traces behind them, except disgust: – I hope I am mistaken, but this is the fate of most married pairs. – Solomon says 'there is nothing new under the sun' for which reason I will not marry, for I dont want to be tied to this nasty world, and old maids are of so little consequence – that 'let them live or die, nobody will laugh or cry.' – It is a happy thing to be a mere blank, and to be able to pursue one's own whims, where they lead, without having a husband and half a hundred children at hand to teaze and controul a poor woman who wishes to be free. – Some may follow St Paul's advice 'in doing well', but I, like a true born Englishwoman, will endeavour to do better.

Then she told of Eliza, a 'mere child' in Beverley: 'she must now take place of us, being of the most honorable order of matrons'. Despite her need to downgrade marriage, she knew its cultural importance. Her depression in Hoxton, Bath and Windsor had had much to do with a dependence for which she was temperamentally unsuited, but, given the shadows of vanishing suitors in these years, it must also have concerned the romantic 'joy' and 'raptures' she loudly scorned but which she feared were passing her by.

# 5

Soon the new Eliza Bishop was pregnant. After a difficult labour, she gave birth to a girl in August 1783. The following month the baby was baptised at St Mary Magdalen in Bermondsey as Mary Elizabeth Frances, uniting her mother, her mother's eldest sister, and the sister's closest friend. She was a healthy child and all seemed well at first.[1]

Eliza did not recover from the birth trauma, however, instead falling into an acute post-natal depression. This was not a recognised medical condition, though records of insane asylums mentioned 'melancholia' following childbirth as a part cause of insanity, and many women recorded 'low spirits'. Bewildered, her husband and family sought reasons for her misery within her personality and marriage. Each blamed the other.

Meredith was a little older than Eliza and considered her emotional and moody. Now he suspected that the episode exaggerated her usual highly strung character. In medical manuals female hysteria was often ascribed to sexual fear or abstinence. Probably Meredith suggested he and his wife resume intercourse as a remedy for her low spirits. Given her state, Eliza is unlikely to have suckled her child. Old Galenic medicine told women to avoid intercourse during lactation but by the eighteenth century the injunction was medically discredited though sometimes remained popular with wives. Eliza had no such excuse.

Mary was sure that she knew the general cause of the depression. She may have had intense memories of a mad brother and of other young women who lost their wits or killed themselves after childbirth, but certainly she recollected her parents' unsatisfactory union, the 'lingering' illness of her mother and herself under the treatment of Edward Wollstonecraft. It was enough to make a woman mad – perhaps it ought to do so. She hated to see her sister heading into her mother's life. Depression was a sign of Eliza's superior sensibility: she was not her patient parent and should not be.

Mary acted at once. She interrupted her life with the penurious Bloods and moved into the Bishops' more comfortable house in Bermondsey, south of the river. She would look after her sister and see for herself exactly what was wrong. She did not wait to make her analysis but equated Meredith

Bishop with the dominating Edward Wollstonecraft – probably hearing of his sexual demands since she mentioned his need for 'gratification'. She took a dim view of recreative sex: men seemed to want it, while women only complied. Eliza would be better off without a husband and his unsavoury demands; she had made a huge mistake in marrying such a man so young.

By late autumn, in a time of biting cold, matters were desperate. Everina, still living with Ned and his wife, was rapidly being initiated into adulthood, treated one minute as a child to be sure, but at the next, addressed by her forceful sister in the tone only a sophisticated woman could interpret. To Everina, Mary painted a vivid portrait of the unstable and hallucinating Eliza:

> I cannot yet give any certain account of Bess or form a rational conjecture with respect to the termination of her disorder – She has not had a violent fit of phrensy since I saw you – but her mind is in a most unsettled state and attending to the constant fluctuation of it is far more harassing then the watching of those raving fits that had not the least tincture of reason – Her ideas are all disjointed and a number of wild whims float on her imagination and unconnected fall from her – something like strange dreams when judgement sleeps and fancy sports at a fine rate – Don't smile at my language – for I am so constantly forced to observe her (lest she runs into mischief) that my thought continual[ly] turn on the unaccountable wanderings of her mind – She seems to think she has been very ill used – and in short, till I see some more favorable symptoms I shall only suppose that her malady has assumed a new and more distressing appearance.

As with her mother's dying, so with Eliza's breakdown Mary placed herself centre stage. Indeed, she even feared her own madness. The only response for both of them was her mother's 'Patience'.

She could not sustain it. Miserable and fancying herself ill when inactive, Mary was always enlivened by activity. Now she cogitated a bold plan. With the continuing but fluctuating instability of her sister before her, the fear that her malady would settle into permanent madness, and her greater fear that Eliza would recover enough to accept the misery of an improper marriage and the distasteful regime of an unloved spouse, she determined to cut through the domestic distress of both partners now and for ever by simply rescuing her sister from her home, baby and husband. It was the most impudent and imprudent plan she could think up.

She gave no hint of what she expected for herself from the rescue, except its excitement. She had once tried to wean Fanny Blood from her family and failed. Then she would have gone with a skilled woman; the half-educated

Eliza was very different. When Mary herself left Bermondsey, she had nowhere to go except into dependence or the Bloods' cramped lodgings. Could it have been in the back of her mind that, if she had to make a home for her demented sister, she would also have one to offer Fanny? If she could lure one woman into her household, could she not lure another?

Mary broached the idea to young Everina. She wrote disjointedly, not quite saying what she meant but hoping her sister would fill in the gaps:

> I don't know what to do – Poor Eliza's situation almost turns my brain – I can't stay and see this continual misery – and to leave her to bear it by herself without any one to comfort her is still more distressing – I would do anything to rescue her from her present situation – My head is quite confused with thinking to so little purpose – I should have come over to you if I could have crossed the water – In this case something desperate must be determined on –

Once she had given it substance in her mind if not quite on paper, she relished the 'desperate' move and wondered if Ned would take in the absconding wife for a while. Could Everina ask him? Or should she talk to him herself? Whoever spoke must impress on him the need for absolute secrecy. If Bishop got wind of the plan they would have 'a storm to encounter that I tremble to think of'. Since Ned was already burdened with Everina and Charles, recently sent from Laugharne for articles, Mary must have strayed far from reality if she supposed for a moment that he would take in the errant Eliza.

In one description of Eliza's present state of mind, Mary quoted a most revealing statement. A sudden rescue was, she believed 'the only expedient to save Bess – and she declare[s] she had rather be a teacher than stay here.' The vision of teaching as an exit from matrimony sounds a great deal more like Mary than her helpless sister; much preaching of independence would be needed for any married woman to see it as a preferred option within the shame of a broken marriage. Years later Mary imagined a young woman saying after she chooses to be a teacher, 'When I am my own mistress, the crust I earn will be sweet.' This was not a general view. In Jane Austen's unfinished novel, *The Watsons*, the heroine, Emma, protests that she 'would rather be a Teacher at a school (and I can think of nothing worse) than marry a man I did not like'. To which her less refined sister replies, 'I would rather do anything than be a Teacher at a school.'[2] This was the usual opinion of the genteel young lady and Eliza probably mentioned the option as the *worst* she could think of. In reality she would have intended nothing of the sort.

Mary was resolved, however, justified by her understanding of Bishop's character: he was 'either a "lion or a spannial" . . . I can't help pitying B[ishop] but misery must be his portion at any rate until he alters himself'. Yet she could not accuse him of meanness. The Bloods were having one of their financial crises and, at the very moment when she was planning to steal his wife, she borrowed £20 from Bishop to rescue them from bankruptcy. He 'lent it very properly without any parade', she reported.

Everina felt left out of the drama going on south of the river. Her brother and sister-in-law did not want her and, to get out of the house, she may sometimes have been as keen on marriage as Eliza, though mostly she felt she did not know her own mind. She did not have Eliza's prettiness or Mary's forceful character. She hinted to Mary that she was miserable about something but did not say exactly what. Perhaps she had fallen in love and been rejected or not preferred; perhaps she was unhappy because she was not in love.

Without knowing why she was comforting her, Mary declared the only solution to Everina's problems to be time, maternal 'patience' – and a firm despairing character like her own. She set great store by her gloomy stoicism:

> I am really sorry to observe that you are not well – something I am persuaded preys on your mind besides our poor girl's illness – As you are so secret I leave you to time that sovereign alleviator of all griefs – have a little patience and some remedy will occur or you will cease to want it – I speak from experience – time has blunted the edge of many vexation[s] that I once thought I could never bear – I have no hope nor do I endeavour to attain any thing but composure of mind and that I expect to gain in some degree inspite of the storms and cross winds of life.

By the new year, stoicism was rejected as thoroughly as the Platonic Thomas Taylor's contemplation. Mary had forgotten her aim of 'composure' and her counselling of 'patience'. Melodramatically, she told Everina that 'misery haunts this house in one shape or other'. Bishop felt the tension and fell ill. He received no sympathy from his sister-in-law, who regarded his illness as an improper plea for understanding.

When he recovered, to Mary's disgust he began confiding in Fanny Blood's lover, Hugh Skeys.[3] She resented the male conspiracy even as she strengthened her female one. She wished she could get Skeys alone to put her side of the case. Then he could judge properly instead of succumbing to pity. She admired pity in herself but felt it might be manipulated in weaker people: 'As I can never speak to [Skeys] in private I suppose his pity may cloud his judgement – If it does I should not either wonder at it or blame him – For I that know and am fixed in my opinion cannot unwaveringly adhere to it – and when I reason am afraid of being unfeeling.' She did not think to use

Fanny as an envoy. Her friend was always on her side but Mary must have suspected that the events of these days were testing her loyalty and that she might not be the best solicitor for a recalcitrant wife and her dominating sister.

By now Bishop knew where the power lay and, having recovered from fever, he began addressing Mary; he did not care to be cast so entirely as the villain. But it was no good. The pair irritated each other with their mode of arguing. He thought her irrational and smug, right in her own mind whether she reasoned or emoted; Mary thought him over-logical, not attuned to the fluctuations of the heart. 'May my habitation never be fixed among the tribe that can't look beyond the present gratification – that draw fixed conclusions from general rules – that attend to the literal meaning only.' Bishop's reason had a sensual quality.

Then to everyone's surprise Eliza began to improve. Mary insisted that she would now become more melancholy since the saner she was the more she would understand her deplorable state. Bishop must have thought the worst over for, in her more peaceful mood, Eliza was wavering, wondering if she could not manage marriage and motherhood after all. She was afraid of escape and what it implied. Mary knew she must strengthen her limp sister to avoid her succumbing to pity for Bishop and the baby. Her mother had been malleable when she should have stood firm, leaving in the lurch those who tried to help her.

So, though Eliza dithered, Mary determined on rescue. The pair would abscond immediately; another day would persuade Eliza to stay. There was no suggestion of taking the baby, but the lack of any anxiety on Mary's part in separating mother and infant was extraordinary.[4] She knew she was acting against the feelings of both parents for the child, whose name she never mentioned in letters from the house. The fact that she had regarded herself as a motherless Mary seems not to have deterred her from creating a second.

Fanny had come to stay in Bermondsey for a few days and probably helped to arrange secret lodgings opposite the Mermaid in Church Street, Hackney. Then she and Mary packed Eliza's things; Fanny took some to a brushmaker's in the Strand to be collected later, while the remainder went to Ned's for Everina to lock up. Ned had, of course, refused to take in Eliza. Then, with only three guineas, Mary and Eliza left the Bermondsey house and crossed the Thames to Hackney, changing coaches so as to avoid detection by Bishop if he questioned drivers. Eliza was nearly demented and 'bit her *wedding* ring to pieces'.

From their 'comfortable' lodgings Mary scribbled her first note to Everina, noting her own 'trembling' hand. Eliza was now more composed and had assumed some of her sister's firmness: she would not return. 'When I can recollect myself I'll send you particulars,' Mary wrote, 'but, at present my heart beats time with every carriage that rolls by and a knocking at the door almost throws me into a fit.' Her main fear was that Bishop would appear in person 'panting for breath'; she would rather meet a lion. She was not sure of the law; Everina should ask Ned what they must do in a confrontation. '[C]an he force her ... I'll not suppose it,' she answered herself, knowing full well that he could. But it was, perhaps, the effect on Eliza of such a meeting that she most feared: 'Don't tell Charles or any creature – Oh! – let me entreat you to be careful – for Bess does not dread him now as much as I do.' She had taken on the burden of the enterprise: while Eliza slept, Mary, in maternal and husbandly role, was too 'agitated' to go to bed.

When Eliza awoke, Mary added a postscript to her first note. It gave a more disturbing picture of both young women: '[Eliza] looks now very wild – Heaven protect us – I almost wish for an husband – for I want some body to support me.' Despite the enthusiasm for female ties, Mary had little experience of women's help. She had wanted her mother's protection and not received it; she had admired Fanny Blood but now realised her own dominating spirit. The only being she could imagine as protector was the denied figure of the husband, from whom she was rescuing her sister. Inevitably she imagined him with irony.

Eliza sent a short note to Bishop, clarifying that she had left his home for good. It was enclosed in Mary's letter to Everina and may have been prompted by her sister. Bishop dashed round to Ned's to protest and discover where she had gone, though Ned had no more idea than he had.

His bewilderment was extreme. He had fulfilled the duties of a husband. He had not treated his wife cruelly in any legal sense; he had not beaten or humiliated her in public; he had not kept her in poverty or threatened her with the lunatic asylum or the workhouse, the usual grounds for petitions of separation. He had cherished her and the baby. He had provided a comfortable home and allowed her to bring her bossy sister into it; he had even played host to the sister's friend. Wives did sometimes go off with other men, without their babies; then they found themselves attacked in divorce courts while their lovers paid the wronged husbands for the pleasure of their company and the removal of a housekeeper. Not often did a woman elope with her sister.

No doubt Bishop wished he had shown that sister the door when he had the chance or never let her in. What could he do now but beg his wife to return and allow them to try the marriage again – without the intervention of her sister? To Ned he pleaded the needs of his motherless baby, already crying for its lost parent.

The scene of Bishop's appealing to Ned and his family was relayed to Mary; she received it grimly. She had expected this manoeuvre, seeing a cunning husband rather than a distraught father: 'The *plea* of the child occurred to me and it was the most rational thing he could complain of – I know he will tell a plausible tale and the generality will pity him and blame me – but however if we can snatch Bess from extreme wretchedness what reason shall we have to rejoice.' Eliza was less armoured. She sighed 'about little Mary who she tenderly loved' and her complaints moved her sister: 'on this score I both love and pity her – The poor brat it had got a little hold of my affections – some time or other I hope we shall get it.' This was indeed a forlorn notion, intended to salve Mary's conscience: a runaway wife had no claim on her child, as all of them knew.

As the intensity of the drama subsided, the two women realised they had little money and no changes of linen, not a handkerchief or apron between them. Their ailments burgeoned:

> Yesterday we were two languid Ladies – and even now we have pains in all our limbs and are as jaded as if we had taken a long journey – My legs are swelled and I have got a complaint in my stomach &c &c &c but all these disorders will give way to time if it brings a little tranquility with it – and, the thought of having assisted to bring about so desirable an event will ever give me pleasure to think of.

Lodged with their exasperated brother, Everina would not be outdone. Mary quite understood. 'I am sorry but not su[r]prised at your spirits being sunk,' she told her sister.

To keep them all to the mark, Mary needed to plan a future. A separate maintenance for Eliza was best but she had no legal title to one. Private arrangements were sometimes made between estranged spouses but they gave the wife no real security and technically she remained a married woman, whose future property could be claimed by a vindictive husband.[5] Since support was unlikely, Eliza would 'try to earn her own bread,' Mary told Everina with bravado. In an unguarded moment Fanny Blood agreed that 'bread' could easily be earned.

Her time with the Bloods and her recent need to borrow money for them from Bishop might have suggested to Mary the folly of ill-prepared women trying to keep themselves. Yet she believed herself capable of anything: 'with economy we can live on a guinea a week and that sum we can with ease earn – The Lady who gave Fanny five guineas for two drawings will assist us and we shall be independent.' They would sew and Fanny would teach them how to paint. There was also a Dr S— who promised help. Mary was ebullient and wrote to Ned that she, Fanny and Eliza would form an all-female establishment.

Fanny was horrified. Dr S— was already retreating and she could not see how women unaccustomed to tiresome work could succeed where she and her experienced mother had failed. Mary had been unequal to the task of fine needlework, while artistic skill was more difficult to acquire than her friend supposed. Indeed, Fanny might have felt a little piqued that ability such as hers, which allowed her to illustrate published books, could be picked up by anyone in a week or so. She admired Mary greatly but feared her impulsiveness. She had drawn back once before; now she suffered a sleepless night. In the morning she wrote agitatedly to Everina:

> The situation of our two poor girls grows ever more and more desperate – My mind is tortured about them, because I cannot see any possible resource they have for a maintenance . . . I find [Mary] wrote to her brother informing him that it was our intention to live all together, and earn our bread by painting and needle-work, which gives me great uneasiness, as I am convinced that he will be displeased at his sisters being connected with me; and the forfeiting his favour at this time is of the utmost consequence. – I believe it was I that first proposed the plan – and in my eagerness to enjoy the society of two so dear to me, I did not give myself time to consider that it is utterly impracticable. The very utmost I could earn, one week with another, supposing I had uninterrupted health, is half a guinea a week, which would just pay for furnished lodgings for *three* people to pig together. As for needle-work, it is utterly impossible they could earn more than half a guinea a week between them, supposing they had constant employment, which is of all things the most uncertain. This I can assert from experience . . . Mary's *sight* and health are so bad that I am sure she never could endure such drudgery . . . As for what assistance they could give me at the paints, we might be ruined before they could arrive at any proficiency at the art – I own, with sincere sorrow, that I was greatly to blame for ever mentioning such a plan before I had maturely considered it; but as those *who know me* will give me credit for a good intention, I trust they will pardon my *folly*, and inconsideration.

Something had to be done, however. Fanny had been talking to Mrs Clare from Hoxton, who doubted the wisdom of the escape but wanted to help now matters had gone so far. Together they concocted a scheme which might be a 'refuge from poverty'. Fanny knew the pride of the Wollstonecrafts. So she mentioned it with trepidation: 'this plan is no other than keeping a little shop of haberdashery and perfumery, in the neighbourhood of Hoxton, where they may be certain of meeting encouragement. Such a shop may be entirely furnished for fifty pounds, a sum which I should suppose might be raised for them, if it was mentioned to your brother.' Although Fanny was writing to Everina, she was glancing at the disapproving Ned, who might see her letter. He was pivotal, since without capital the shop idea would be impossible. He must be humoured:

> lest [Ned] should be averse from assisting them, from a notion that I should live with them, I solemnly declare that nothing is further from my intention; – and I wish you would take the earliest opportunity of assuring him, from me, *that on no account whatever will I ever live with them, unless fortune should make me quite independent* – which I never expect. – My health is so much impaired that I should be only a burden on them – and for my own part, I don't spend a thought on what may become of me. – All I wish is to see them provided for comfortably; but I will neither add to their distress, situated as they are now, nor meanly gain a subsistence by living with them hereafter, if fortune should smile on them. This is my fixed resolve . . .[6]

It was a clear, more practical letter that any Mary wrote during the crisis, laying out options that the Wollstonecraft sisters had never really contemplated; much like their father they expected money would come from somewhere as bounty or be lent by a kind undemanding benefactor. Without falling into the low spirits of Mary or Eliza, Fanny accepted a reduced life with a composure quite out of their reach. Her suggestion of a shop was reasonable, depressing, and probably, given the parties, as impracticable as painting and sewing. But her sense that much might be obtained by tact from Bishop and Ned could have been useful.

Mary was made of sterner stuff and, if she thought casually of the shop – perhaps it might be in Ireland she mused – she thought not at all of tact. However much she urged patience on others, she was far from Fanny Blood's self-denying resignation. Indeed, she was busy dramatising herself as *agent provocateur* in the scandal: 'I knew I should be the . . . *shameful incendiary* in this shocking affair of a woman's leaving her bed-fellow,' she crowed. Mrs Clare had made a useful suggestion, visited them in the rain, sent a pie and wine, and offered a loan, but Mary still mocked her cautious conventionality. She dared the world to censure her and felt pride at the notion of herself leading a band of independent, intrepid women. While her sisters continued melancholy and Fanny remained anxious, she was seized with pious elation: 'lost in sensual gratification many think of this world only,' she wrote, 'and tho' we declare in general terms that there is no such thing as happiness on Earth yet it requires severe disappointments to make us forbear to seek it and be contented with endeavoring to prepare for a better state.' Everina, who received these sentiments, probably winced at her sister's self-satisfied display at such a moment.

Mary was unstoppable; she swelled with the notion of herself as a Christian soul chosen for special penance: 'The mind of man is formed to admire perfection and perhaps our longing after it and the pleasure we take in observing a shadow of it is a *faint line* of that Image that was first stamped on the soul.' Religion was on her side, as in Bath. She was no 'enthusiast' – she had no liking for evangelical Methodism – but faith surpassed reason. It sounds as though she knew she had been bested by Bishop's rational arguments, his attention to 'literal meaning only'.

> Don't suppose I am preaching when I say uniformity of conduct cannot in any degree be expected from those whose first motive of action is not the pleasing the Supreme Being – and those who humbly rely on Providence will not only be supported in affliction but have a Peace imparted to them that is past all describing – This state is indeed a warfare and we learn little that we don't smart in the attaining – The cant of weak enthusiasts have made the consolations of Religion and the assistance of the Holy Spirit appear to them inconsiderate ridiculous – but it is the only solid foundation of comfort that the weak efforts of reason will be assisted and our hearts and minds corrected and improved till the time arrives when we shall not only see *perfection* but see every creature about us happy.

As with Jane Arden, here religion was less private piety than an assumption of priestly significance. Providence and she were in accord. She was no feminine soul relating to its 'masculine God' but a person with a direct apprehension of an ungendered Deity. Affliction educated and education led to perfection. She could take a smug satisfaction in her dramatic sufferings – though she had not as yet received the 'Peace . . . past all describing'.

Fanny had seen Eliza's agitation at leaving the baby and was anxious to gain information. She sent her brother George with a note to Skeys asking if he could get news from Bishop, but the answer was cool. He had seen his friend's grief and bewilderment and was not inclined to pander to the sentiment of these wrong-headed sisters. He wanted to help reconcile the parties and hoped that Fanny would convey Bishop's good will towards his wife. Perhaps, to keep the sisters from acting desperately through destitution, he sent them ten guineas: they 'came very opportunely . . . we are good oeconomists.'

They took Skeys's money but not his advice. Indeed Mary mimicked his pleading: 'He said *poor B[ishop]* was puzzling himself to "bring about a reconciliation" and that he "hoped" he might succeed as he thought he "would now endeavor to make Mrs B. happy".' She was impatient at his credulity: 'B. has told him a plausible tale and has not adhere[d] to truth – yet still 'tis wonderful he could be so deceived.' There was nothing to be done with men who believed each other. Mary was now caught in a power struggle with Bishop and Skeys, husband and husband-to-be of two women she controlled. Both recommended reconciliation. She knew she seemed a virago but there was no help for it.

Then Bishop changed tack: realising that his soft approach was failing, he stopped pleading the needs of the child and grew threatening. The new stance justified Mary's sternness: it was easier now to sustain her heroic posture and she grew elated again. 'I am cheered with the hope that our poor girl will never again be in this man's power – 'spite of the many vexation[s] that have and still occur – my spirits do not sink [–] supported by conscious rectitude I smile at B's malice and almost thank him for it as it give[s] me fresh strength to pursue what I have begun with vigor.'

The winter weather continued miserable, cold and rainy, and the need for firm action grew as the ten guineas diminished. Eliza had a little recovered from the hysteria of the flight, but both women were physically out of condition. Afraid to go out in case they were spotted by a spy of Bishop's, they huddled indoors where lack of exercise and stuffy rooms gave Eliza headaches. Mary had assumed her brother-in-law's fever; she joked that it kept her 'warm these cold nights'.

Ned was not coming forward with money for the shop, and without his help the plan was unviable – in any case it was not quite to Mary's taste. So she considered more carefully the cheaper option of opening a small school. She knew her sisters were ill-prepared, but times were desperate, and teaching was surely easier than sewing and painting or even shop-keeping. To have any chance of succeeding she needed the more educated and skilled Fanny Blood on board.

By now Mary was used to overcoming her friend's scruples and soon her resolve to make a female community triumphed. In February plans were firming up: the three would open a school. The Bloods cannot have been keen to see their main breadwinner leave home, but no doubt Mary dazzled them with the money they would make and the help she could soon provide.

For her venture she borrowed capital from someone, presumably outside the family – friends were surprisingly kind. Possibly the lender was Hannah Burgh, perhaps met through the Clares or through Dissenting friends from

Hoxton since her husband had been a schoolmaster in nearby Newington Green. She may have been the woman who bought Fanny Blood's drawings and who came to mind when Mary first considered her options. Mrs Burgh was a strong-minded older widow 'of excellent sense and character', whose marriage had been one of equality and joint benevolence.[7] She was attracted to the opinionated young woman who had so much to battle with in life and she became a great aid in Mary's schemes. Mary was now less fearful of encountering Bishop but it remained unwise to be too much abroad, and she did not like leaving Eliza too long. Reluctant Fanny, closer to Skeys and possibly Bishop than the rest of them, could not be relied on to move the project forward. So Mrs Burgh sought the suitable house and found it in Islington. Mary took it and installed Eliza. She then persuaded Fanny to join them and together they advertised for pupils by printing a prospectus or preparing handbills. But there were more schools and teachers than potential children, and, after a few months, the scheme collapsed. Fanny's fears were realised.

Mary refused to give up. A school was still the best option: it required only the rent of an unfurnished house, some furniture, fabric and needles for sewing, some books and hard work, where all others demanded more capital or skill. So she persevered and again consulted Mrs Burgh. As it happened, she had just seen the very house. It was large and empty and stood close to where she herself lived in leafy Newington Green, two miles north of London.

The Green was a square of substantial merchants' houses round a railed-in grass area with ancient elms. On the north side was a meeting house for Dissenters. Mary probably knew the place already since it was close to Hoxton and the prosperous Dissenting communities were linked. Pleasant flattish country stretched nearby, scattered with large forest trees through which the New River prettily undulated; the poet Samuel Rogers, a boy during these years, described a 'Green Lane', 'fern and flowers' and 'mingling elms'.[8]

Mary, Eliza, Fanny and their friends bustled round and at the end of two or three weeks had attracted nearly twenty pupils while augmenting their income by two families of lodgers. It was quite an achievement: three young women truly established as teachers in their own school in such a short time. If parents were paying at least half a guinea a quarter and lodgers paid their rent, they were solvent.[9]

Then, with mutual relief, Everina left Ned's and joined the trio, and Mary found herself in charge of her friend and two sisters. Finally the family of Bloods and Wollstonecrafts was completed by Fanny's brother George, always a favourite of Mary's. Through the Clares he found a job with a haberdasher and lodgings with an attorney called Palmer nearby. It was still not Mary's dream of life with Fanny – she had never managed to get her alone in all their time together – but her sister's disaster had propelled her into a daring action of independence which, without this stimulus, Fanny might have resisted. Perhaps, though, her resistance was lessened now, for it seems that Skeys had left for Lisbon without her.

The baby Mary never saw her mother again. She died the following year just days before her first birthday and was buried by her father in the Bermondsey church where she had been baptised. Bishop did not try to divorce Eliza. It was a costly business requiring an Act of Parliament and much discussion of one's personal life. Straight adultery might be uncomplicated, elopement with a sister would open a man to ridicule. Nor did he pursue his wife into her new life, as he was entitled to do. Bishop outlived all of them and Eliza never became a widow. If she wished to retain any remnants of reputation, there was no question of any further relationship with a man.[10]

# 6

No letters survive from Mary Wollstonecraft's early months in Newington Green – a pity since it was her first independent period near London. Although she may not have put on frippery to attend a concert in the Rotunda at Vauxhall or a masquerade in Ranelagh Gardens, she probably took conventional pleasures: walked along the pretty paths through corn-fields and woods of nightingales that linked the Green to the bigger village of Stoke Newington or occasionally attended the theatre in London two miles away. The only glimpses of her are serious, however.

The school had to be established and Mary was crucial. As usual, she enjoyed and repined at the responsibility of power. It was she who organised the venture, worked out a curriculum, hired a cook and maids, and energised the others. Eliza and Everina must have taught the accomplishments just learnt at their Chelsea boarding-school; Everina sketched well and could help Fanny instruct in art. Fanny could legitimately teach writing, sewing and painting. A fashionable school would need to offer French to a high standard, so theirs would never appeal to very highly placed parents, but there were sufficient children needing the rudiments to make the school viable. Mary was interested in education though she lacked much formal learning. Already in Windsor she had declared that morals should precede manners. This emphasis suited a community that emphasised the puritanical virtues of self-mastery, industry, sobriety and thrift.

Their own school was the goal of many genteel, poor young women humiliated as governesses in harsh vulgar families or despised as common teachers. The ratio of success to failure should have deterred them, but desperation was a spur. The cost of supplies which ate into profits was rarely anticipated, while failure of a single parent to pay could bankrupt them all. In the end, the Wollstonecraft school collapsed, for the multiple reasons that destroyed most schools, but it is an achievement that, with Mary's driving, it sustained four young women for two and a half years.[1] Mary never named particular pupils and stressed the pain over the pleasure of teaching, but the school established her as a pedagogue with her own theory of education.

Part of a long tradition of English radicalism stemming from the seventeenth-century Commonwealth period, the rationalist intellectual Dissenters of Newington Green were an established community who claimed to have purged religion of superstition, leaving only an essential creed. Starting from belief in freedom of conscience, they held the sort of reforming social views Mary was beginning to entertain from her own underprivileged experience. The American War had just ended in independence for the colonies and, for England, in the government of William Pitt the Younger, aged twenty-four – he would be in power for the rest of her life. He had become prime minister as a kind of non-party saviour to the nation, friend alike of the radical Horne Tooke and the conservative King George III. His father, Pitt the Elder, had hugely expanded Britain's colonial empire and revelled in foreign victories; now, after a shambolic period of military and political disasters, the son would win the peace and make necessary but gradual reforms by stopping the slave trade, extending religious liberty, and expanding the suffrage. Although mainly liberal Whigs, the Dissenters were ready to help and be helped. They took the national pride in Britain's constitution of commons, lords and king, theoretically balancing each other, but were acutely aware of flaws. They reverenced the settlement of 1688, the Glorious Revolution, while insisting it be developed – they were still excluded from full civil rights.

Although not vast in numbers, these Dissenters were articulate and confident, influencing the nation through newspapers and pamphlets. In Newington Green they held a weekly supper club which met in rotation in members' homes. Wollstonecraft could hone her skill at argument and allow them to help shape her concepts – though she sometimes judged they overindulged in deliberating and found their brand of rationalism cold. That people of such intellectual substance took her seriously bolstered her confidence. She was never convinced by Dissent and later she referred to the 'prim littleness' and habit of dissembling that the culture ascribed to Dissenters; yet she was always quick to point out 'how many ornaments to human nature have been enrolled amongst sectaries'.[2]

The acknowledged leader was Dr Richard Price. Small and staid in appearance, jolly and kindly in character, friend of Benjamin Franklin, Joseph Priestley and Horne Tooke, Price at sixty-two had huge intellectual stature as writer, politician and mathematician. Older than her father, he was a non-threatening patriarch who encouraged young people to question and analyse and, like John Arden, to experiment with microscopes and electricity. Unlike her father, who had had little sympathy for the ailing Elizabeth, Price devoted himself to his childless, invalid wife.

Mary listened to Price's occasional political sermons. Although she disapproved the 'Romish customs' of the Church of England, she found the austerity of Dissenting meeting-houses distasteful: thinking back to the soaring grandeur of Beverley Minster, she could not see why a noble pillar or arch should appear 'unhallowed'. Price was originally a Presbyterian but his staunch rationalism had led him towards Unitarianism, which embraced the ethics of Christianity while denying miracles and Christ's divinity. His final view, close to Unitarianism, might better be called Arian: he did not accept Christ as the guarantor of people's salvation, but he believed in his superiority. Sense impression created personality, he thought, but morality existed as a self-evident truth outside sensation. Through Price, Mary learnt that, while faith helped the individual soul, reason aided the individual in society, and that morality and liberty were welded together.[3] When he described this time in Mary's life, the apostate Godwin assured his readers that she never held Price's religious doctrines; yet parts of his rational Dissent and its emphasis on the individual's inner relationship with God confirmed her in her view that life was a probationary state in which moral character was developed for eternity. Price's brand of religion helped her on her road to an encouraging rational God who demanded that his creations be free to become moral. The Church of England would not entirely have disagreed but would have stressed the need for guidance from priest and doctrine.

The Dissenting views of Dr Price on the right of everyone to education, as well as his experience of discrimination, meant that he had sympathy for the aspirations of such a woman as Mary. In the eighteenth century the sympathetic male mentor role was popular: the often misogynous Samuel Johnson and the famous novelist Samuel Richardson had had coteries of bluestocking ladies for whom they became nurturing father figures. Also, many of the women writers who would dominate Wollstonecraft's era, Frances Burney, Maria Edgeworth, Hannah More, Germaine de Staël, and Jane Austen, had intellectual ties with fathers. Wollstonecraft yearned for something like this in surrogate form. She had found a little of it in Jane Arden's father and the Revd Clare; she found more in Dr Price.

Aside from Price, there was a friendly schoolmaster's widow, Mrs Cockburn, who took in lodgers, and of course Mrs Burgh, whose advice was invaluable since she had participated in her husband's school on the Green. James Burgh had advocated sensible education for both sexes, training that would prepare them for life rather than loading their minds with facts. In a utopian fantasy of 1764, he imagined a community where all sober men except Catholics would be citizens; property would be equally distributed; marriage be a civil matter and divorce with remarriage easily available. Although remaining the weaker sex rather than citizens and owners of property, women would be educated out of triviality and fondness for dress and all would parent children, so avoiding the cloying fondness of mothers which ruined the infant character. These sober, frugal and austere principles found an echo in Wollstonecraft's puritanical mind.[4]

With the school to run and Dr Price and Mrs Burgh at hand, Mary managed to play two roles for which she yearned: mother and daughter. She was the head of her all-female household, while acting the intellectual daughter outside.

Another fatherly intellectual (and perhaps religious) influence was Dr Johnson himself, whom she was taken to see in his lodgings shortly after her arrival. Now in his seventies, ill with asthma and dropsy, he had, like Fanny Blood, been advised to go south for health but, fearing the expense, lingered in London. He entertained his young guest kindly; when she left he invited her to come again.[5] Unhappily, he died the next September. His influence continued, however, for his depressive personality, melancholy realism and fear of the 'vacuities' of solitude agreed with her temperament. When his *Prayers and Meditations* were published posthumously, she was a reader, identifying with the pious uneasiness they portrayed, if not with their anxiety over personal worth and futurity. In time, she disagreed with his political conservatism, but turned to his writing in moments of personal crisis.

The meeting with Johnson had been arranged through a young school-teacher and Anglican clergyman, John Hewlett, whom Mary met in New-ington Green.[6] Hewlett had connections in the London literary world and was hoping to establish a second career as occasional writer on education and religion. Only a few years younger than she, he was clever and comely, and she wrote often of his generosity. Once she admitted to him that she was apt to get too fond of people and she always railed at his choice of wife – or rather his misfortune in being so 'yoked'.

Possibly she encountered other men who stirred her heart but did not respond; surviving letters, so open about her mental state, are reticent about emotional causes of her sinking moods. One such man might have been Mrs Burgh's nephew, the '*human*, rational Church', who had, like his aunt, lent her money; he visited but then found that 'business, and many other things prevent[ed] his calling often'. These, Wollstonecraft surmised, included her house full of 'tattling females'. One day Church told her she would never thrive in the world, and stopped visiting. Later she damned him with the epithet 'prudent': he had been too reticent either in money or emotion.

In the novel *Mary, A Fiction*, the wavering feelings of the heroine for her not quite adequate female friend are swept away in passionate affection when she realises how ill the friend has become. Always delicate in health, Fanny was clearly consumptive and the marriage to Skeys in Portugal, so long postponed that the partners had become strangers to each other, seemed especially desirable. Only through this could Fanny get to a warm healing climate, the sole remedy suggested for her state. So, it was with some relief that the call finally came – probably with Mary's prompting. She would not have hesitated to tell Skeys where his duty lay. Now that the offer had arrived, Fanny held back, but her friend urged her on.

In January 1785, Fanny left England for Portugal to be wed to a man whose appearance she now knew primarily from his portrait. As she wrote from Portugal, 'Skeys's picture was more like him than pictures in general are – but he is much fatter, and looks at least ten years older than it.' The long delay must have underlined her friend's fears about marriage: men did not readily take on intelligent females and they had less incentive to marry than impoverished women. Skeys had done the right thing in the end but his procrastination had caused unnecessary suffering: 'if he had had courage to have braved the worlds dread laugh, and ventured to have acted for himself he might have spared Fanny many griefs the *scars* of which will *never* be obliterated – nay more, if she had gone a year or two ago her health might have been perfectly restored.' Mary was angry at the half-heartedness:

> Before true passion, I am convinced, every thing but a sense of duty moves, True love is warmest when the object is absent – How Hugh could let Fanny languish in England while he was throwing money away in Lisbon, is to me inexplicable if he had a passion that did not require the *fuel* of seeing the object – I much fear he loved her not for the qualities that render her dear to my heart – Her tenderness and delicacy is not even conceived by a man who would be satisfied with the *fondness* of – (I mean one of the general run) of women.

If she knew something of why Skeys had delayed beyond the sense that he was marrying into a family beneath his own, she wanted to avoid being explicit. The pain of Fanny's life was acute enough without trivialising one of its causes. Again, however, the failures of Skeys put Mary where she had been with Bishop, defending women against men.

The school without Fanny was empty. Her sisters were uncongenial and Mary no doubt told them so. They were never able to meet her high standards and Godwin later admitted that she was resentful when disappointed. Eliza she thought vapourish and sneering, while the childish Everina was irresponsible. Both had been jealous of Fanny, who had engrossed their sister's love, and they felt sour towards Mary for being more popular on the Green.

Mary meanwhile was further depressed at losing Fanny's impetuous brother George who, with her help, had escaped to Dublin from bailiffs pursuing a paternity charge from a servant-girl. Mary had a low opinion of servants and believed George's denial. He left so hurriedly that he did not even secure his wages and, when she pursued them, she had been rudely received by the 'sweet wife' of his employer until she 'assumed the Princess'. The Clares, people of strict principles, had found him his post and were unamused by the affair: they 'were dreadfully afraid their *good* name should be *sullied* on account of their recommending a person who left his place so hastily'. Mary was contemptuous of such conventionality but the incident did the sisters' school no good.[7] It also led to a coolness between her and two of her most loyal friends.

George found work with a linen-draper in Dublin but did not flourish. He hoped his new brother-in-law would find him work in Portugal. Mary sensibly advised him to be quiet about his recent calamity: '[K]eep up your own dignity,' she urged. Skeys was a self-satisfied man with little tolerance.

For emotional comfort she turned again to letter-writing. She wrote often to Fanny, but neither her nor Fanny's letters have survived. Only one to Everina and Eliza signed 'Frances – (Heigh ho!) *Skeys*' and written five weeks after her arrival in Lisbon remains as witness to the sprightliness, even during low spirits, which Mary so much missed. Fanny had been ailing and, after a spell in the country with Skeys, had moved to be nearer physicians in town. There, she reported, 'the spitting of blood [is] quite stop'd, and my cough very trifling.' It did not sound overly encouraging – even when Fanny described new sociability: 'I shall remain in town ... a month or two, as I find it agrees with me, even tho' I play the rake here, and have a crowd of visitors almost every evening – I think, there is no end o'them and I shan't return the visits of half of them.'

The letter reveals that, whatever his past failings, Skeys was an attentive husband: he was, Fanny wrote affectionately, 'a good sort of a creature, and has sense enough to let his cat of a wife follow her own inclinations in *almost* everything – and is even delighted when he sees her in spirits enough to coquet with the men, whom to do them justice, are not backwards in that way.' She was pleased that he had made some stir in Portugal: 'He has been a dreadful flirt among the damsels here, some of whom I could easily perceive were disappointed by his marriage ... I am sorry to add, that he is too much enclined to pay more attention to his wife than any other woman – but 'tis a fault that a little time, no doubt, will cure.'

Whimsically, the letter hinted at past stresses among the young women at the school:

Depend on't I'll never attempt to make an apology to Bess for not writing sooner – she does not deserve it – a jealous Baggage! – for saying I would not value her love when she sent it. – As for Everina, she knew me better, and to her I will tell the whole truth – which was simply this – that it was always my wish, whenever I wrote to the two dear girls, to be as entertaining as *I* could possibly be – but which I found was not in my power, even in the smallest degree ever since my arrival at Lisbon, on account of an extreme depression of spirits ... So much by way of apology to you, Everina – and as for you, Eliza – come; we'll kiss and be friends again – for I know you love me a little bit, after all; and you ought to know that I love you too ...

She ended in sprightly style, 'Well, girls, are you almost tired? I knew you would – and now that you too are convinced of my inability to entertain you, will not I suppose desire – Yes, yes, I know you love me, and I will be sincerely glad to receive an epistle now and then.'

Apprehending more than Mary would ever admit, that all the young women were starved for male admiration, Fanny playfully sent them a series of interesting men from Portugal. The first came with the letter which needed 'no apology when conveyed to you by an agreeable young man, such as I hope the bearer of this will prove to be. I assure you I find him a tolerable *flirt*, tho' I have been but twice in his company; and, if such an animal as *I* am could engage a little of his attention, to what a degree of vivacity must he be animated by *the assemblage of irresistible charms* he will meet at N— Green.' She had another less handsome 'flirt' in store for dispatch in June, her doctor: 'if you are not carried away by prejudice on the first interview, he will afterwards probably steal into your favour, as he has done into mine. I have given a description of him to Mary; and she is, I hope, already prepared to love him – He leaves Lisbon in about a week ... I shall greatly regret his departure – and the more so, as he spends as much time with me as he possible can'.[8] When he arrived, the flirtatious physician was indeed a success and caused Mary once again to reveal a vicarious desire: 'He is such a man as my fancy has painted and my heart longed to meet with – his humane and tender treatment of Fanny made me warm to him and I behaved to him with the freedom of an old friend.'

If writing her own desire here, she was yet allowing Fanny to be its conduit. Whatever her romantic longings, she often dwelt on the friend who had long engrossed her. Despite the effort at lightness, the main message of Fanny's letter to Eliza and Everina was her ill health and unremitting low spirits. Mary would not have had far to look for a cause of the latter: Fanny too must have ached for her missing friend.

*

Letters to George began in July when he arrived in Dublin and were sent to him through Betty Delane in Brittain Street. They formed a catalogue of ladylike complaints. The headaches and morbid fancies suffered in Bath had returned as Mary felt the drudgery of the school without Fanny at its heart or George on its edge. The mindset resembled her dying mother's and she frequently echoed her final plea for 'patience':

> I have been very ill – and gone through the usual physical operations, have been bled and blistered – yet still I am not well – My harrassed mind will in time wear out my body – I have been so hunted down by cares – and see so many that I must encounter that my spirits are quite depressed – I have lost all relish for life and my broken heart is only chear[ed] by the prospect of death – I may be years a-dying tho' and so I ought to be patient – for at this time to wish myself away would be selfish.

In the mean time she allowed herself a rush of half-expressed erotic feeling for George, 'God Bless you and believe me sincerely and affectionately your friend – I feel that I love you more than I ever supposed that I did – Adieu to the village delights. I almost hate the Gre[en for it] seems the grave of all my comforts – S[hall I ne]ver again see your honest heart danc-[ing in] your eyes?' George was Fanny's brother and the mighty stock of feeling invested in her friend was momentarily bestowed on him. Her emotions disturbed her, as perhaps did George's warm response; after this expression she did not immediately write again. George grew anxious. Had her affection waned? When she replied, a couple of weeks later, it was in parental, nurturing, distancing mode, ascribing her unusual silence to low spirits and not hearing from Fanny. She might in future write joint letters to him and Betty Delane, she suggested, but never did. To help George overcome any untoward passions, she urged him into her own kind of piety:

> I value you on account of your goodness of heart, and other qualities that I give you credit for – your letters display them in the fairest point of view – and while I with pleasure observe your refinement of sentiment and am convinced that the very disappointments that gall you are improving you – can you, for a moment, believe that I am changed? – No, I am not a fair-weather friend – on the contrary, I think, I love most people best when they are in adversity – for pity is one of my prevailing passions – I am not fond of professions – yet once for all, let me assure you, that I have a motherly tenderness for you, and that my heart dances when I make any new discovery of *goodness* in you – It gives me the sincerest satisfaction to find, that you look for comfort where only it is to be met with – and that Being in whom you trust will not desert you! – Be not cast down, while we are struggling

with care life slips away, and through the assistance of Divine Grace, we are obtaining habits of virtue that will enable us to relish those joys that we cannot now form any idea of.

Her Christian faith did not endear her sisters to her. Having their undiluted company she felt utterly alien: she 'could as soon fly as open my heart to them', she told George. Eliza was satirical and contemptuous while Everina inspired nothing but indifference: 'I can neither *love* or *hate* her.' Sadly she catalogued the loss of her real family, the Bloods: 'Fanny first – and then you went over the hills and far away.' Resignation turned to despair: 'without some one to love This world is a desart to me'.

Fanny's silence bred anxiety. Then came alarming news. She was still in poor health and low spirits: now she was pregnant. Mary feared the outcome. For Eliza, marriage had resulted in too swift pregnancy and raving melancholia; in the more stable but sicklier Fanny the effect might be worse. She wished she could fly to Lisbon and cherish her friend in the dreadful time to come.

But the responsibilities she had assumed for her sisters detained her. When she had rescued them from their homes, she had not thought out their or her future or considered that Eliza and Everina lacked the energy to take further steps. She had supposed their helplessness transient; now she was stuck with two moping young women with whom she had nothing in common. She also had substantial debts to Mrs Burgh, her nephew and others, taken on when they had first begun teaching. She felt, she said, 'tied by the leg' to the school. In the wings remained the needy Blood parents. Not strictly her responsibility, they had lived with her and come to rely on her, especially with Fanny gone. All these burdens harrassed her and sometimes she even found writing to George too great a task: '[I] hate to write myself, when my spirits are low – you may perceive . . . how confused my thoughts are – I write one word for another.'

In early September, Mary heard that Skeys had found George a position in an English consulate at St Obes near Lisbon. The news unsettled her. The two people she loved most would be in Portugal; she wished even more acutely to escape the school and her dreary sisters' company. She tried again to mitigate depression with piety and pride in peculiar misery – she would be 'first' in affliction and believe with Milton that virtue needed adversity to create itself – but the posturing did not serve and impetuously she decided she too must leave. She was failing her sisters and condemning the school, she knew, but she could not exist without decisive action: once more, she chose flight. It was, perhaps, a response learnt from her peripatetic father, who had repeatedly run from trouble. Her experience with Eliza had reinforced it, teaching her the immediate headiness of escape and movement, however grave their results.

In this troubled and unsettled time, Mary spread gloom over all. She also conveyed incompetence. Pupils and lodgers fell off and neither of her sisters assumed responsibility for running the school. What they said when Mary announced her determination to abandon them and go to Portugal for Fanny's confinement is unrecorded.

The disapproval of others *is* on record however. Mrs Cockburn threatened to prevent the Wollstonecraft sisters taking any more lodgers if Mary left. But the 'good old woman', Mrs Burgh, came up trumps, possibly in response to Mary's unusual behaviour: 'I am grown quite meek and forbearing,' she told George. Mrs Burgh not only approved her plan but lent more money for the voyage – money which, Mary suspected, came from Dr Price. If approved by two such surrogate parents, she was ready for anything. Opposition from those she did not respect only made her more determined.

Yet, when she came to leave Newington Green, she must have had misgivings, knowing that the faltering school could hardly survive without her management. The sisters' future would then be one of lonely servitude as teachers and companions, the very fate she herself had abandoned with relief. Probably she would in time share their fate. But by now her confidence from conversations at the Green and her assertive letter-writing might have persuaded her that she could in time aim at a more exciting future; her friend Hewlett was planning to make money from writing advice and sermons and she might in part imitate him. Or perhaps she simply did not care what happened now Fanny was no longer with her.

# 7

Leaving the country was no easy task. Would-be passengers went to the relevant port, weighed the merits of boats touting for business, chose, booked their passage, then awaited events. There was, of course, wind and weather to consider but also the whim of the captain, whose estimate of the departure date was notoriously unreliable. Even when winds and tides were right, passengers could hang around a port for more than a week or, when once embarked, unceremoniously be disembarked to stand by for another moment. It was an expensive business, for seaside inns took advantage of delays.

Once she had found a boat and successfully stowed herself on it, she faced a long voyage for which nothing but George and her brother's stories could have prepared her. Sea life was unappealing, and the fastidious traveller was often nauseated by dirt and maggoty food. Sailors were either surly or over jocular and could make life gruesome for someone they found at all ridiculous.[1] Wollstonecraft discovered she was not especially prone to seasickness – a blessing since she was on board ship for thirteen stormy days, partly through the notorious Bay of Biscay. '[T]he sea was so rough – and we had such hard gales of wind the Capt. was afraid we should be dismasted,' she recorded. The ship rolled around and the sea washed in at the cabin windows. One of the passengers was continually seasick; another was an invalid, presumably travelling towards the sun as Fanny had done. He was so ill she feared he would not survive the voyage: 'I have supported him hours together gasping for breath, and at night if I had been inclined to sleep his dreadful cough would have kept me awake.' The experience bore fruit in her novel *Mary, A Fiction* where the sensitive heroine loves and nurtures just such an invalid man at sea.

Mary stepped off the boat in Lisbon in the nick of time. Indeed she came so much on cue she felt her arrival 'Providential'. Fanny was in labour and, four hours after her friend found her, was 'delivered of a boy'. Surprisingly, the child was alive and Fanny survived the ordeal, but she was in such a low state that Mary feared the worst. Day and night she sat by her, living a nightmare from which she could not wake. Were Fanny to survive, it would be more resurrection than recovery.

In these dreadful hours she tried to prepare her mind for the ultimate tragedy: 'I *labour* to be resigned,' she told her sisters, 'and by the time I am a little so some *faint* hope sets my thoughts again a float – and for a moment I look forward to days that will, alas! I fear, never come . . . I am almost afraid to look beyond the present moment.' Her own health had improved, as so often in active crises: 'I am tolerably well – and calmer than I could have expect[ed] to be.' As with Eliza in her breakdown, she felt sounder in the face of greater suffering. To her sisters she ascribed her health not to a good constitution but to the support of 'that Being – who alone can heal a wounded spirit'. Without the religious prop, she would 'have been mad before this'.

There was no question of Fanny's feeding the 'puny' child – whom they named William – and Mary obtained a wet-nurse. The mother deteriorated in spurts. At one moment she seemed so poorly that she was almost given up for dead, but Mary was afraid to ease her heart by writing to tell her sisters, in case, by stating what she knew, she would be 'signing her death warrant'. Then Fanny seemed to rally and the worst of her symptoms abated. She had a comfortable night and Mary dared to believe she might survive. '[Y]et,' she wrote to Eliza and Everina, 'I rejoice with trembling lips – and am afraid to indulge hope, she is very low – Her stomach is so weak it will scarce bear to receive the lightest nourishment – in short if I was to tell you all her complaints you would not wonder at my fears.'

Her fears were justified and, within a few days, mother and baby were both dead. As Portugal was a Catholic country, Protestant funerals had to be performed 'by stealth and in darkness'.

Death now hid Fanny's few frailties. Months after her death Mary cried out to George Blood, 'She was indeed . . . my best earthly comfort – and my poor heart still throbs with *selfish* anguish.' Over a decade later in her last completed book, *Letters from Sweden* she wrote: 'The grave has closed over a dear friend, the friend of my youth; still she is present with me, and I hear her soft voice warbling as I stray over the heath.'² At her own death she left a ring of Fanny's hair.

Thrown together, Wollstonecraft and the widower Skeys agreed tolerably well. She had always vacillated about him, unsure whether to see him as her rival with Fanny or a longed-for saviour for them both. She disapproved the shilly-shallying emotion, the embarrassed delays that had caused such grief and harm to her friend, but she could also acknowledge his generosity, his occasional sensitive response. She saw him as a crude, sensual man on the lines of Meredith Bishop, but sometimes she felt curiously disturbed by him. Often her criticism seemed to exceed her experience.

Curiously she hid from him her 'dismal' financial situation, though her secrecy did not prevent her disgust that he did not mitigate it. He should have known she was in debt and discreetly helped. In fact all he promised was some dress material from the custom house. Given her poverty, she welcomed even this modest present.

She stayed in Lisbon for several weeks, contemptuously regarding the alien Catholic culture. Its vicious sensuality appalled her, its baroque extremes of poverty and luxury; Portugal was, she judged, 'the most savage part of Europe, where superstition still reigns'.[3] She deplored the 'absurd' religion which encouraged incarceration of women in convents away from all that cheered her own life: congenial society and emotional ties. The good existence for her meant actively doing good; as she had told Thomas Taylor the Platonist in Walworth, she did not admire the contemplative way.

> In these abodes the unhappy individual, who in the first paroxysm of grief, flies to them for refuge, finds too late she took a wrong step. The same warmth which determined her will make her repent; and sorrow, the rust of the mind, will never have a chance of being rubbed off by sensible conversation, or new-born affections of the heart.[4]

Women who were not allowed to be wives and mothers became selfish and ambitious, desiring to obtain offices of trust and authority. Had she been less appalled by Portuguese Catholicism, she might have paused to consider why this was worse than marriage.

In late December she left Lisbon on an English ship. It was not the best time to travel, but she had probably worn out her welcome with Skeys and the school weighed on her mind. Since Fanny had died so promptly after her arrival, Eliza and Everina must have wondered why she delayed.

The voyage back was even more dramatic than the passage out and took a whole month. The drama was the more glamorous one of an incident at sea rather than weeks of seasickness and a dying passenger. Then she had shone as a comforter to the afflicted; now she was a heroine.

Some way out her ship encountered a French vessel in distress, so battered that the French captain and crew wanted to abandon it. So they hailed the English ship and, urging their predicament, begged the captain to take them onboard. The English captain refused: he had provisions enough for himself, his crew and passengers, but no more. His first duty was to the vessel under his command.

He had reckoned without Wollstonecraft. Listening to the shouted altercation, she was shocked at the lack of sympathy for the foreigners, as well as the neglect of basic sea duty, the helping of those in distress. She pleaded the Frenchmen's case and, when that failed, threatened the captain with a full account when they arrived home. This was persuasive and the French were taken on board. If the rations were thereby depleted, she could not grumble. In any case she had moral sustenance for 'she had the satisfaction to reflect that the persons in question possibly owed their lives to her interposition.'[5]

Mary was rapidly deflated when she reached Newington Green. It was the dead of winter, a time when she was often naturally gloomy, and her arrival from the more clement and lighter Portugal made the northern island all the darker. She had been away several months and during her absence Eliza and Everina -the 'girls' as she still called them – had let the school dwindle 'to nothing'. Not only had they not attracted new lodgers but some of their old ones were moving to Mrs Cockburn's.

Matters now demanded heroism quite equal to what she had revealed at sea but provided much less stimulus. The school might have been saved, but the small set-backs and disappointments she faced failed to rouse Mary as the ocean drama had done. Instead, over the next eight months, she sank into apathy, and the ailments that had afflicted her before the journey abroad renewed their attack. Presumably she borrowed more money from the accommodating Mrs Burgh and her nephew, thus increasing her debt and anxiety. The house with its 'enormous' rent, initially such a success, was now a millstone round her neck: it had to be paid for whether pupils came or not. She and her sisters must leave as soon as they could.

Some things improved, however. Fanny's death had made her father, Matthew Blood, 'an altered man'. Mary hoped he would continue so, that some good might come from his daughter's sufferings. Fanny's imprudent sister Caroline had left home; Mary trusted the absence would improve the moral tone of the others. Yet, however refined, the family remained impecunious. Skeys had sent no money. The Bloods had made him reluctant to propose to the worthy Fanny; now she was dead he cannot have relished an open-ended responsibility for this feckless group. Wearily Mary realised that, if anyone were to do anything, it would have to be herself. Their hook was in her flesh.

So it was with relief that she managed to put them on a boat for Ireland. They had come from there and always believed that, if they could return, they would flourish. Not having visited Ireland herself but incorporating her mother's nostalgia, she too trusted its magical powers and was overjoyed to see them go – it was 'a most Providential thing, and an answer to my fervent prayers'. She hoped that Mr Blood would continue his serious mood and she urged George to deepen it. For George too was back in Ireland. Things had not worked out in Portugal and he had, with the help of Betty Delane, found work in a Dublin wine merchant's shop. He would live with his parents again.

Once more Mary made him the recipient of her unstructured laments. She moaned of head and heart aches, debts, tedium and helpless sisters:

> I have lost all relish for pleasure – and life seems a burthen almost too heavy to be indured – My head is stupid, and my heart sick and exhausted – But why should I worry you? and yet if I don't tell you my vexations what can I write about ... Let me turn my eyes on which side I will, I can only anticipate misery – Are such prospects as these calculated to heal an almost broken heart – The loss of Fanny was sufficient of itself to have thrown a cloud over my brightest days – What effect then must it have, when I am bereft of every other comfort ... My eyes are very bad and my memory gone, I am not fit for any situation and as to Eliza I don't know what will become of her – My constitution is so impaired, I hope I shan't live long – yet I may be a tedious time dying ... I scarce know what I write ...

As with her mother's death, so Fanny's prompted thoughts of her own – she could not bear to be omitted from the drama or face the blank world alone. Her spirits sank under the emptiness that came after great strife and grief and she could not avoid welcoming death as a more active option than living misery. Her Anglican piety still gave structure to her moaning though it had little place for her troublesome body; this might express or impede the soul's workings but, in the more medically grounded and enlightened eighteenth century, was denied the significance it had achieved in medieval female mystics or seventeenth-century prophetesses, whose impressive displays of infirmity declared their spiritual state. From now onwards Wollstonecraft would be haunted by the insoluble, fundamental question of the relation of body and mind, and would try with conflicting vocabularies to address it. For the moment the problem seemed to make her faith more emotional, rapturous and urgent.

Meanwhile her debts haunted her like 'furies'. Fiercely independent yet never impervious to the world, she felt 'unprotected' when creditors were rude. Thoughts of another flight flashed across her mind but she suppressed them: she knew it a morally wrong way to solve problems. She owed money to friends like the local musician Hinxman who were not well off and who would be hurt by her defection.

To the less scrupulous George her fastidiousness seemed quixotic. She tried to explain that she needed to think well of herself: 'I am indeed very much distressed at present, and my future prospects are still more gloomy – yet nothing should induce me to fly from England – My creditors have a right to do what they please with me, should I not be able to satisfy their demands.' Providence had brought her in time to the dying Fanny and would see her through this crisis. Yet George urged her once more. Why did she not come to stay with his family? They were all so grateful to her that they would make her thoroughly welcome. Surely it was better than the dreary loneliness of England.

This time she answered with tactless honesty. Apart from her ethical scruples, her sense of superiority to the Bloods precluded this route. They had given her 'Princess' status; if she were a suppliant she would lose it. Also she deplored the need to please a domestic tyrant – she had had enough of this at home:

> I could not live with your father, or condescend to practise those *arts* which are *necessary* to keep him in temper – and as to being *under obligations to him* it would never do, perhaps, it is not in the power of any human creature to render such a situation easy – and a selfish person, I am sure could not – Besides, how you could think I could sit all day with the family, when you know we could not find conversation, surprises me ... I love your mother but she would not be a companion for me, any more than she was for Fanny.

What most weighed on her was the future of 'the girls'. She could not imagine Ned's taking them both again, certainly not the scarred Eliza. The school had been one of several options for her; for her sisters it seemed the only one, combining home, income and rationale for living. '[T]hey are not calculated to struggle with the world,' she told George. 'Eliza in particular is very helpless.' She wished she had considered this when making the dramatic escape and setting up her school with them ineradicably tied to it.

All through spring, well into May, Mary languished, complaining promiscuously, 'I am very far from being well, I have a pain in my side, and a whole train of nervous complaints, which render me very uncomfortable – My spirits are very very low, and am so opprest by continual anxiety 'tis a labour to me to [do] any thing – my former employments are quite irksome to me.' Desperately she wanted 'something decisive ... to happen ... 'tis this suspence, this dread of I cannot tell what, which harass[es] me.' She mused on death: 'I am only anxious to improve myself and so run my race that I may meet my poor girl where sorrow and sighing shall be no more.' She was haunted: 'I dreamt the other night I saw my poor Fanny, and she told me I should soon follow her.' Surely ailments, bad eyesight and confused thoughts, also foretold an early death: 'The prison walls are decaying – and the prisoner will ere long get free.'

One curious complaint she made at this time seems to refer to Fanny's death, which had left her emotionally alone in the world; yet it does not quite fit the case. Perhaps there was a secret added reason for her burgeoning depression: 'I am too apt to be attached with a degree of warmth that is not consistent with a probationary state, I have leaned on earth and have been *sorely hurt*.'[6] Probably this is Fanny, if the leaning is interpreted emotionally; probably not if also a matter of reliance and mental support. Could Skeys have disappointed in more ways than his reluctance to part with money?

Still nothing 'decisive' occurred and Mary drooped, her comforts being her letter-writing to George, her sense of peculiar and superior suffering, and her reiterated counsel of patience to anyone who would listen. She had thought so much in terms of a 'crisis', something dramatically awful, that it had assumed real substance. But there was only suspense bringing 'nervous complaints'. She could not energise herself whatever she preached to others: 'I can scarcely find a name for the apathy that has seized on me – I am sick of every thing under the sun – for verily every thing is grievous to me – all our pursuits are vain – only the end which they bring us to is of consequence.'

Incessantly she interrogated her state. Could there be a failing in temperament? Did it come from too great sensibility, too large a propensity to tenderness which flipped over into its opposite? She respected her response to others, as her attitude on board the English ship revealed, but how could she explain her occasional indifference, even coldness? 'I am often with myself at war – and forget the *shews* of love to other's – nay I cannot always feel alike – my heart sometimes overflows with kindness – and at others seems quite exhausted and incapable of being warmly interested about any one – my regards carried beyond the pitch which wisdom prescribes – often throw me into apathy.'

The extreme self-pity, the intense concentration on the self, was cultural as well as personal. Such introspection had some religious foundation in scrutiny of conscience, but the impression is far more of a secular sense of brooding subjectivity, a need to catalogue not necessarily explain each passing mood. In her descriptions she displayed the victim and aggressor. Writing of this time in his *Memoirs*, Godwin used the first label: 'she may be said to have been, in great degree, the *victim* of a desire to promote the benefit of others.' The aggressor was harder to express – it emerged in her flashes of contempt for the feckless or privileged.

Clearly a depressive, even manic depressive, tendency existed in the Wollstonecraft family, there already in the passive mother and volatile father, whose moods could swing violently from hatred to fondness. Henry Woodstock is unknown but the siblings Eliza, Everina and James revealed it as surely as Mary, and the bent continued in the few children in the next generation, Mary's and Ned's. But there was also a cultural component in their malady: the high esteem in which the middle classes held melancholy in the eighteenth century, an esteem that must sometimes have prevented the sufferer entirely from giving in to despair.[7]

In the seventeenth century melancholy seemed part of the human condition, the proper response of a thoughtful, pious man to life's inevitable sadness. In the eighteenth century religious melancholy fell out of fashion while secular melancholy achieved more of an elite status. Male melancholy in particular was much prized; in mid-century Thomas Warton's *The Pleasures of Melancholy* delivered it not as insanity or disease but as a kind of moody introspection, a sensitivity to oneself in nature and the world. 'Oh lead me,' he begged, 'to solemn glooms / Congenial with my soul; to cheerless shades ... ' James Boswell sighed, 'I do not regret that I am melancholy' for 'it is the temperament of tender hearts, of noble souls.'[8] Women followed the line and their commonplace books of favourite passages overwhelmingly concerned 'grief, disappointment, the fallen leaf, the faded flower, the broken heart and the early grave'. Mary's catalogue of miseries eased her heart and created her in the softened feminine character of the middle-class ideal, in her case still resolutely pious. A similar gloomy self-absorption appears in Charlotte Smith's popular *Elegiac Sonnets*.

Despite her reiterated intention of sinking slowly to death, Mary had in fact had one spurt of energy during these months. She was always telling people what to do, how to read and respond, how to raise their children and improve themselves. Friends like John Hewlett and Mrs Burgh encouraged her to put the pedagogic ideas she so copiously preached into print. The late prolific James Burgh had had success in this line and Mary could follow: she was as opinionated as any man.

Hewlett was immensely helpful. He obtained from her an outline of a short book of advice on educating girls and took it to a London publisher he knew near St Paul's, supporting the proposal with his personal testimonial. He did a good job, obtaining an advance of ten guineas despite the unknown author: '[Y]ou never saw a creature happier then he was when he returned to tell me the success of his commission,' she told George.[9] Despite her gloom, even she was pleased. She had not hesitated over what to do with the money: it was this that had shipped the Bloods to Dublin. Considering that she had so many debts and family responsibilities, so many needs herself, her action indicates how strongly she remained committed to anyone associated with her dead friend.

Her success owed much to the vogue for education, based on the prevailing but still new opinion, firmly held by the Newington Green Dissenters, that it could cure many of the ills of the individual and society. Female education especially fascinated a public seeking to define a role for the middle-class woman whose legal and economic importance was declining as her moral and social burgeoned. Conduct-books quarrelled among themselves about whether the nation would be advantaged by exaggerating or controlling delicate femininity in wives and daughters. Wollstonecraft knew exactly what she thought and inserted her work effortlessly into debates.

*Thoughts on the Education of Daughters* was speedily written for it grew from the homiletic letters to George Blood and her sisters. Echoing the title of James Burgh's influential *Thoughts on Education* of 1747 and Locke's founding *Some Thoughts Concerning Education* (1693), it accepted the prevailing Lockean view of the mind as a transparent entity which needed to be controlled and safeguarded from the passions for reason to function. Assuming the power of upbringing as supreme, prizing sincerity and scorning the deceptions of femininity, the book proceeded in robust censorious way, rather in the manner of Burgh, who believed in moral absolutes and felt that education must fit people to pass this life decently, while helping them ennoble their nature for the next. The twenty-seven-year-old Wollstonecraft disapproved baby talk, cosmetics, theatre, frivolity, and artificial manners and announced that it was 'sufficient for women to receive caresses, not to bestow them'; 'I am very far from thinking love irresistible.' In the current mode of exhortation and repressive religiosity, the book parroted some of her parents' opinions that had embittered her childhood – that a child should be shown who was master before becoming its parents' friend, that filial esteem always had a dash of fear in it and that feelings should be suppressed – but she was not as draconian in her views as Burgh or Hewlett and she had an acute (and personal) sense of what was owed to the child: 'It is only in the years of childhood that the happiness of a human being depends entirely on others – and to embitter those years by needless restraint is cruel.'[10]

Addressing the spinster and the miserably yoked as well as the marriageable miss, her book became prophetic of her later work by generalising her own misery into the cultural misery of 'unfortunate females who are left by inconsiderate parents to struggle with the world, and whose cultivation of mind renders the endeavor doubly painful – I felt what I wrote!'[11] The strain of melancholy echoed that in other women conduct-book authors, like Hester Chapone and Lady Sarah Pennington, an estranged wife writing for her absent daughters. Such writers sympathised more than their male counterparts with the lot of unhappy women who needed intellectual and moral improvement to withstand life's disappointments. As in her letters, the only comfort is the sense that 'Adversity is mercifully sent to force us to think' and a private feeling of spiritual and intellectual superiority.

In Wollstonecraft's view the genteel but poor girl could not expect love and friendship: 'The mind must then sink into meanness, and accommodate itself to its new state, or dare to be unhappy.' If such a girl anticipated happiness with men, she must be deceived. Few men would marry inferiors, however worthy, but they might from boredom flirt with them and so inflict deep and lasting wounds: 'Perhaps a delicate mind is not susceptible of a greater degree of misery, putting guilt out of the question, than what must arise from the consciousness of loving a person whom their reason does not approve.' Joshua Waterhouse perhaps or Neptune Blood prompted this bitter observation.

As in her letters, so here, Wollstonecraft rebelled against the common (usually male-authored) conduct-book morality that, seeing female education solely as preparation for marriage and dependence, preached self-control combined with deception. Dr Price had written 'to be *free* is to be guided by one's own will; and to be guided by the will of another is the characteristic of *Servitude*.'[12] Yet, while she promoted the independence that men like Burgh associated with the male merchant, she rebelled against the only methods through which it might reasonably be achieved by women. In one chapter, 'The Benefits which arise from Disappointments', she described the contempt meted out to the teacher, companion and governess, and gloomily anticipated her own future caught between vacuous, vain mothers and spoilt children.

*Thoughts* was published in early 1787 by the Dissenting and liberal bookseller and publisher Joseph Johnson, who worked from no. 72 St Paul's Churchyard. Swiftly it was excerpted in three parts in one of the nation's leading women's journals, the *Lady's Magazine*. It did not startle the world, but struck the editors as worthy of wider circulation; in their view it treated female virtue, knowledge and accomplishments in 'a sensible manner' while making 'many judicious observations'.[13]

In the midst of her quandary over the school and her own future options, the encouragement from Johnson, the *Lady's Magazine*, Hewlett and Mrs Burgh must have allowed Wollstonecraft to think further of an alternative career to teaching: an unconventional one of 'literary occupation'. In this she could use her strong-mindedness to preach to the public not simply her sisters and friends. If she had been excluded from a loving family she might make a community through generative words. She had been kindly received by Dr Johnson and impressed him: surely she could impress a less discriminating audience. She had much to say and her letter-writing had taught her to write quickly; something might be done to use her skills. *Thoughts* had taught her that one escape from dreary life was writing and that public expression could call on private grief.

Nothing would happen at once, however; even had she been quite sure of herself she could not now have embraced such a future. Instead, needing money desperately, she felt propelled along the conventional female path anticipated in *Thoughts*: 'I by no means like the proposal of being a governess – I should be shut out from society – and be debarred the *imperfect* pleasures of friendship – as I should on every side be surrounded by *unequals*.' But she need not be a governess for ever. Before she entered her subject life she visited Joseph Johnson to feed her dream of better things.

# 8

*'How my heart pants to be free'*

Mary decided that Everina should become a companion and Eliza a parlour-boarder, a fee-paying older pupil who would have her own room and socialise with the schoolmistress who would be expected to give her some training, probably in Eliza's case in French and needlework. She herself would wind up the school, sell the furniture, return the house to its owner, and negotiate repayment of debts. While this was happening she would move into cheap lodgings without a servant and keep herself through coaching the few remaining pupils. Such a life would not suit Eliza, for she 'could not give up the world or live in the style I intend to do'. Mary was proud of her austerity: 'I have done with all worldly pursuits, or wishes,' she told George. 'I *only* desire to subsist, without being dependant on the caprice of any fellow-creature.'

In early July she described her options to George. She could be a governess in Wales or Ireland. The latter seemed 'so advantageous' it became her duty to consider it 'and yet only duty would influence me if I accept of it.' The Irish offer came through Mrs Burgh, with the help of Dr Price, friends of Mr and Mrs Prior of Eton College. For £40 a year she would take charge of three of the five daughters of Robert and Caroline King, Lord and Lady Kingsborough; half the money would go to discharge her debts and settle Eliza.[1] A highly educated lady might have commanded twice her sum, but it was a good appointment for a woman of Mary's education. Indeed, at moments it seemed too good, more suitable for a French-speaking governess, which she assuredly was not. She hoped she had not been wrongly advertised by enthusiastic friends – and creditors.

It would be strange if, at so dismal a moment, marriage had not crossed her mind. But no one she wanted wanted her, including Neptune. She closed a letter to George, 'Give my love to your father and mother – and you may give the same to Neptune, I have done with all resentments – and perhaps I was as much to blame in expecting too much as he in doing too little – I looked for what was not to be found.' Yet possibly Ireland appealed over Wales because of a residual hope of this young man.

In August, debts still mounting, she formally accepted the Kingsborough offer. She was anxious about her poor French and fancy needlework but they would have to do. The sisters had been harder to place than anticipated, so Everina had had to be sent back to St Katherine's Street. Ned's wife was not pleased: she hoped she had seen the back of these troublesome girls. But even that disagreeable option was closed to Eliza, and the sale of the furniture and school effects at the Green had not raised enough money to allow her to be lodged in a genteel school. Perhaps too her strange marital status made her sometimes unacceptable. So Mary was grateful that Mrs Burgh could help her to a lowly teaching post in Mrs Sampel's boarding-school in Market Harborough, Leicestershire.

Market Harborough was in a pleasant, hilly place of scattered windmills and pretty cottages, which Eliza, with her liking for walks and keen eye for natural beauty, appreciated. Yet, as she had feared, the position was dire. Less pious than Mary, she was horrified to discover that her Presbyterian employers were not the cosmopolitan liberals of Newington Green but religious fanatics who damned books and plays and attended four services on a Sunday. She was stuck in a 'garret' at the top of the house, quite at odds with her ladylike status. Melodramatically she wrote to Everina, at times sounding remarkably like her eldest sister in her zestful self-pity, though she tended more towards literary cliché:

> Oh! How my heart pants to be free – I can no longer indulge the delusions of fancy, and the phantoms of hope are for ever, ever flown ... praying is their only amusement, not forgetting eating, and *Marr[y]ing*, and so on – The idea of parting from a *husband*, one could never make them *comprehend*, I could much sooner persuade them, that a stone might speak.[2]

Despite her anomalous state and contempt for the matrimonially obsessed, like Mary in moments of crisis, Eliza could still imagine no rescue beyond marriage. So she exclaimed to Everina, 'Ah! that you had a good *Husband*, to screen thee from those heart-breaking disagreeables.'

Left alone in Newington Green, Mary acutely felt the absence of Fanny and George. The break-up of the school seemed in part to erase friendship; from now onwards Fanny's image must live in her heart, sustained by rituals of remembrance. With George she would 'talk of our poor lost friend and cherish the melancholy pleasure'. Fanny inhabited her mind: '*even in my present hurrying life her image continually obtrudes itself* – and when I rejoice at her release – I cannot forget that I am a poor forlorn wretch without her.'

She began preparing for dependence by frantically practising her French and resentfully smartening her appearance, though she lacked money for clothes. The fading of her Green life accelerated as she heard of Mrs Price's death. Dr Price had long tended his wife and release determined him to move away. Saddened by the news, Mary thought fondly of her surrogate parents: Price 'has been uncommonly friendly to me' while 'Mrs Burgh has been as anxious about me as if I had been her daughter'. She wished she did not owe so much and that Mrs Burgh would not be so enthusiastic about her new post, but she was thankful to have inspired such affection in these good people.

Others also were kind: the once disapproving Mrs Cockburn made her a dashing new hat, but she still had to beg George, 'send me a few yards to match a gown, the pattern of which your mother has'; otherwise she would not be respectable enough for her new position. The material Skeys had promised in Portugal had never come, neither had any gift of money; she was disgusted: 'I will not dwell on his behaviour it has been *uniform* throughout'.

She needed more than hats and material. 'I owe near eighty or ninety pounds,' she wailed, that is, more than twice her future annual salary. '[S]ome of the debts I would give the world to pay.' The legacy to which the younger Wollstonecraft children were entitled had resurfaced and brother Ned was pursuing Roebuck in a lawsuit.[3] Mary had no firm hopes but the possible capital allowed her mentally to juggle debts and consider assuming new ones. She never suspected that Ned might have another agenda and consider the money some repayment for his unwilling keep of his sisters. With the legacy in mind and desperate to pay her most pressing or needy creditors, like the musician Hinxman, she now asked Mrs Burgh for a substantial loan, promising repayment when the lawsuit was settled.

Eliza had written a kind letter. When Mary left to go to Fanny, Eliza had been irritated and jealous, but now they were equal. She was a miserable teacher, her sister about to be a miserable governess. The letter warmed Mary, who appreciated Eliza at a distance, and she wrote back affectionately, if a touch condescendingly; it was her last letter from the Green: 'Indeed my dear girl I felt a glow of tenderness which I cannot describe – I could have clasped you to my breast as I did in days of yore, when I was your nurse – you know I doat on disinterested acts of kindness – and that it gives me the sincerest pleasure to receive favours from those I love.' She knew that Eliza was miserable but for once her sister had restrained her complaints; Mary was touched and grateful:

I was pleased to find you endeavor to make the best of your situation, and try to improve yourself – You have not many comforts it is true – yet you *might* have

been in a much more disagreeable predicament at present – but it is not the evils
that we escape which we dwell on – I *feel* the truth of this observation – and can
scarcely offer you a comfort which I do not lay-hold of myself – Life glides away –
and we should be careful not to let it pass without leaving some useful traces
behind it – I could go on moralizing for half an hour – and yet nature will prevail –
and reason cannot remove the oppression I feel at my heart . . .

However kindly she felt towards Mary at this moment, Eliza was probably
relieved that her sister had not taken another 'half an hour' for 'moralizing'.

In late September or early October Wollstonecraft stored her books at Mrs
Burgh's and set out for her new appointment as governess to the aristocracy.
She went via Eton, training-ground of its young men. She would stay with
the undermaster, John Prior, until she could meet up with the King sons and
travel to Ireland with them through Holyhead in North Wales, the shortest
crossing. She would have a day in Dublin with George Blood or Betty Delane,
'afterwards I have about a hundred and seventy miles to go before I reach
my destined home.' It could not be 'home' of course.

In Eton she was shocked by the public-school culture, regarding it much
as she had Catholic Portugal, with high-minded contempt: 'I could not live
the life they lead at Eton – nothing but dress and ridicule going forward'. In
its practice she perceived tyranny and slavery to convention.[4] Her experience
with the serious Dissenters had enhanced her sense of language as crucial
for understanding and morality: words should be as authentic as a speaker
could make them. Here they were trivialised and things that should be of
great moment were mocked. She hated the constant repartee of literary
nonsense passing for wit. It was worse than the society of Bath: pretentious
as well as frivolous. Once again she felt immeasurably superior, a nimble-
witted, middle-class woman confronting the barbarians: 'So much company
without any soci[a]bility, would be to me an insur[p]portable fatigue – I
am, 'tis true quite alone in a crowd – yet cannot help reflecting on the scene
around me, and my thoughts harrass me – Vanity in one shape or other
reigns triumphant – and has banished love in all its modifications – and
without it what is society?'

Her attitude was poor preparation for life with the upper orders, but she
could not help her thoughts. Indeed, she encouraged them. The Newington
Green Dissenters had a similar sense of aristocracy as the main perpetrators
of moral corruption in the nation, and she was secure in her prejudice. She
had already written an educational work, been applauded for it by friends,
and kept a school: she had a right to judge and generalise. She had no doubt

that she looked impartially and was correct in her censorious views:

> I am more than ever convinced that neither great virtues nor abilities will appear
> where refinement has gone beyond a certain pitch – selfishness gains ground and
> all the generous impulses, and warm affection are smothered – I like to see starts
> of affection and humanity – and on many occasions would have people consult
> their own heart only and if conscience does not check them act with vigor and
> dignity – as St Paul would advise, and not be conformed to the world.

The experience of this élite boarding-school confirmed her in one of her
educational principles: that children should not be sent away for training
but live at home and attend day schools. The aristocracy thought to slough
off responsibility on to these great establishments, which bred their sons to
vice, superficial manners and levity, unchecked by the presence of female
company; meanwhile, they themselves could pursue pleasures, fulfilling
none of the proper obligations and duties of parenthood.

Despite her moral self-satisfaction, Mary's ill health and depression continued and her mind often settled on Fanny. Her only comfort was otherworldly: 'My thoughts and wishes tend to that land where the God of love
will wipe away all tears from our eyes ... with what delight do I anticipate
the time – when neither death nor accidents of any kind will interpose to
separate me from those I love – A mind that has once felt the pleasure of
loving and being loved cannot rest satisfied with any inferior gratifications.'
Seeing her gloomy state and no doubt hearing her strictures, the Priors must
have wondered whom they had recommended to the high-born Kingsboroughs. Since she had not grasped that a degree of hypocrisy was necessary
in social life, especially when negotiating differences of class, how would she
and her employers do together in rural Ireland? Her book had not yet
been published, so her ladyship had not the opportunity of reading how
uncongenial her new governess expected to find her post and how thoroughly
she despised women who rouged and did not nurse their children. Still, the
division of Ireland into Protestant ascendancy and Catholic peasantry meant
that inequalities of birth among the former were less salient than distinctions
in England, and Mrs Prior may have hoped that the two women would in
time agree tolerably.

Mary moaned much to Everina, now miserable in St Katherine's Street
among the 'merest earth worms' as Mary called her brother and his wife.
Like Eliza, she had sent a soothing supportive letter, not blaming Mary as
she might have done in the wreck of all their hopes. Tenderness now
enveloped the youngest sister, to whom she had felt indifferent only a few
weeks before. Arguably Everina had drawn the shortest straw since she knew

what she had to face with Ned where the others had at least the excitement of change. '[H]ow grateful to me was your tender unaffected letter – I wept over it – for I am in a melting mood – and should have answered it directly; but I was so very unwell ... A whole train of nervous disorders have taken possession of me – and they appear to arise so much from the mind – I have little hopes of being better.' Renewed affection led to pain. Everina had promised to visit but had not been able to come: 'You will be surprised to hear that a disappointment with respect to your visit made me almost faint – last Friday ...' Yet, while she sympathised with Everina at Ned's, she could not forget her sister's failings: 'your image haunts me – and I could take my poor timid girl to my bosom and shield her from the keen winds – and if possible save her from the contagion of folly – or the inroads of sorrow!' There was often a sting in the tail of Mary's pity.

She had gleaned a little from the Priors about her new employers. They spent their winters at a Dublin townhouse, leaving the children and therefore their governess in the rural castle. While not liking the fashionable life Dublin implied, she dreaded country solitude: 'I find I shall be more alone in my new situation than I even supposed,' she wrote grimly. About Lady Kingsborough she knew nothing beyond gossip and some prepossessing views on education,

> From what I can gather – Lady K. must be a good kind of woman – and not a very happy one – for his Lordship has been very extravagant – and the children neglected and left to the management of servants – She says, in one of her letters to Mrs P[rior] that those who have hitherto had the care of them have neglected their minds and only attended to the ornamental part of their education, which she thinks ought ever to be a secondary consideration – These sentiments prejudice me in her favor – more than any thing I have heard of her – for I cannot venture to depend on the opinion of people who are dazzled by her superior station in life.

She herself seemed to know little of this 'station'. Lord and Lady Kingsborough were third cousins and now parents of twelve children though themselves only in their early thirties. They had wed at the ages of sixteen and fifteen, bringing such huge estates together that they became the largest landowners in Ireland. Protestant families like this were notorious for their indifference to Catholic tenants, but the Kings were relatively enlightened. When he had taken over as landlord, Lord Kingsborough had been appalled at the neglect of the estates, which had been abandoned to an Irish agent who visited once a year leaving a careless deputy to receive rents and cream off his share. To mend this state of affairs and also make the estates more lucrative, Lord Kingsborough hired the agricultural theorist Arthur Young to put the farms on a better footing. Young persuaded his employer to let the lands directly to the occupying farmers and cottagers, thus ridding himself of the vulture-like 'gombeen men' or middlemen.

In this plan he was opposed by a relative of Lady Kingsborough, who had been receiving profit rents and did not wish his income diminished. Castle intrigues followed and rumours were concocted to destroy the meddling Englishman: the married Young was said to be in love with Lady Kingsborough, with whom he played chess in the evening, while she was provoked into jealousy of a governess, Miss Crosby, allegedly involved with her husband. The upshot of these rumours was the dismissal of governess and agriculturist.[5] Lord Kingsborough continued the reforms of his sacked agent and was soon making the vast walled estates profitable without the usual exploitation. At the once disreputable Mitchelstown he built a sort of model town for his workers, with a library, schools and wide parallel roads, one for shops and trade and the other tree-lined and residential. Two squares contained a market and a college. Lady Kingsborough added a church, a Sunday school and an orphanage.

In due course, Wollstonecraft would be interested in land reform and tenancies, but for now she remained firmly self-obsessed. She did not enquire about the society into which she was travelling, concerned only with how she would relate to the principal castle inhabitants. Probably, Mrs Prior was discreet about the Miss Crosby affair. More likely, she told the new governess, an admirer of Milton, that the Kings were related to Edward King, whose death in the Irish Sea had inspired the famous elegy *Lycidas.*

Mary was eager to set off, but still there were delays. Then arrangements collapsed, the King boys took a different route, and, after a month of waiting, she departed without any family members. She was, however, escorted by a Kingsborough agent during part of her journey. He did not introduce himself clearly and, while enjoying his civility and attention, she was unsure who he was and what position he held. When she discovered on her arrival that he was the castle butler, she was glad she had not been over familiar. It was important for a governess to guard her status.

The boat trip to Ireland was delightful. The crossing could be fierce but, after the great voyage to Portugal, she was not apprehensive. Now the sea was smooth, the boat stable, and the weather fine, and there were wonderful views of the receding Welsh coast. Company always overtopped scenery for Mary and she recorded less of external nature than of the company on board.

Among the passengers was the Earl of Fingal and – more significantly since she was surfeited with noblemen – the tall, handsome Henry Gabell, a fellow of New College, Oxford: 'I had an agreeable companion – a young Clergyman, who was going to settle in Ireland, in the same capacity as myself,' she told Everina. After the superficialities of the last month, this earnest and affable young man thoroughly charmed her: 'He was intelligent and had that kind of politeness, which arises from sensibility.' Not quite enough to mention he was engaged to marry, but the pair agreed to correspond in Ireland.

Arriving in Dublin she saw Betty Delane, whom she and Fanny had always liked, as well as George and his parents. She reported that 'old Blood' was at last 'settled in a very eligible place'. It was almost too good to be true. Perhaps Ireland was a haven after all. Then she proceeded south to Mitchelstown Castle in County Cork, seat of Lord and Lady Kingsborough.

# 9

*'A state which is contrary to every feeling of my soul'*

Less attuned to externals than Eliza, Wollstonecraft failed to comment that Mitchelstown Castle was a smart square Palladian house with wings. It was built on the site of the old castle which the wealthy Lady Kingsborough had brought into her marriage. In keeping with Gothic taste, it incorporated two towers from the old structure, while Italian artisans had added plaster, mantels and elegant staircases. Classically designed gardens, statued terraces, conservatories, vineyards, and woods spread round it for 1,200 acres and above loomed the seven bluish mountains of the Galtees; through the grounds flowed the Funcheon River making red sandstone pools. Facing a life out of harmony with her ambitions, Wollstonecraft was determined to be miserable whatever scene she inhabited: 'There was such a solemn kind of stupidity about this place as froze my very blood – I entered the great gates with the same kind of feeling as I should have if I was going into the Bastille.'

Gossip had given her the failings of Viscount Kingsborough, and she was prepared to find in his wife a fellow victim. But the clever, talkative and dominating Lady Kingsborough disappointed her, and she realised the impossibility of their being fellows in anything. Wealth and power bred insolence and condescension. Wollstonecraft would brook neither.

So her distrust of the upper orders burgeoned, as did the inverse snobbery of the bourgeois before the aristocrat: 'Lady K. is a shrewd clever woman a great talker – I have not seen much of her as she is confined to her room by a sore throat – but I have seen half dozen of her companions – I mean not her children, but her dogs – To see a woman without any softness in her manners caressing animals and using infantine expressions – is as you may conceive very absurd and ludicrous – but a fine Lady is new species to me of animals.' It would be interesting to hear Lady Kingsborough's first impressions of this intimidating young woman who had come in the lowly position of governess. She had been chosen for her impeccable morality and intellect; no one had mentioned her formidable qualities.

The other women of the castle were simply '*Mrsus* and *Misses* without number'. Even the children were disagreeable on first sight: wild, uneducated and 'not very pleasing' – they did not intend to be since they were used to seeing governesses as the enemy. Yet, despite prickly attitudes on both sides, Wollstonecraft soon had to admit to Everina the 'civility', even 'kindness' of the castle inmates: 'I am ... treated like a gentlewoman by every part of the family.'

This was very important for a governess, who had to distance herself from the army of servants in such a great household, even the upper ones. Beside the eighty or so grooms, maids, cooks, and nursery maids, as well as house-keeper and butler – several receiving higher wages than herself – she remained exclusive and genteel, 'a something betwixt and between'. When she visited the steward's room, she envied the life securely below stairs but could not share it if she wished to maintain her status. Yet she would never be equal to the family, not even its lowliest members. It was a difficult position to negotiate – and a lonely one since the yearned-for privacy could become isolation. She wanted simultaneously to be the centre of attention to family and visitors and to retire to her room with her superiority. Similarly, castle guests and inhabitants wanted both to converse with so intelligent a woman and to avoid intimacy with a social inferior.

Mary did not write at once to Eliza, fearing her own misery contagious; also, given Eliza's admiration for genteel life, she might have been unsym-pathetic to the moanings of the governess in the foreign castle. When she did write she had taken further stock of her fellows. The mistress continued most engaging: 'Lady K. is a *clever* woman – and a well-meaning one; but not of the order of being, that I could love'; damningly she reminded Wollstonecraft of the despised wife of Hewlett, their old Newington Green friend. She was still incensed at her passion for dogs and dress: 'All her children have been ill – very disagreeable fevers – Her Ladyship visited them in a *formal* way – though their situation called forth my tenderness – and I endeavored to amuse them while she lavished awkward fondness on her dogs – I think now I hear her infantine lisp – She rouges – and in short is a fine Lady without fancy or sensibility. I am almost tormented to death by dogs.' Like Edward Wollstonecraft, Lady Kingsborough was tempestuous; for both Mary felt the contempt of those who have struggled for control. Lord Kingsborough, patrician landowner and Irish M.P. for Cork lived up to expectations: 'His Lordship, I have had little conversation with – but his countenace does not promise much more than good humour, and a little *fun* not refined.'

Happily there was refinement elsewhere: 'another face in the house appears to me more interesting – a pale one – no other than the author of 'Shepherds I have lost my love'. His wife is with him a gentle pleasing creature, and her sister, a beauty, and a sensible woman into the bargain.' George Ogle, a popular poet in his forties and MP for Wexford, was 'a *genius*, and *unhappy*'. Lady Kingsborough's stepmother, Mary FitzGerald, also seemed to offer equal friendship, though Wollstonecraft was on guard even against affability: 'I cannot easily forget my inferior station.' She had told Mrs FitzGerald of her book, recently published in London, and her acquaintance with Joseph Johnson. So Mrs FitzGerald consulted her on the education of her son, whom she wanted raised in a serious and suitable family; Wollstonecraft asked Johnson whether Anna Laetitia Barbauld or John Hewlett had actually set up their schools on the principles they advocated. At the same time she requested he send Charlotte Smith's elegiac sonnets, which had just reached a third edition, and some copies of 'my own little book' – he was notoriously slow at getting out his author's share. He duly sent them. He had already supplied her with Hewlett's sermons, as well as Cowper's poems, the former now lent to Betty Delane.

Her feelings towards the 'wild' children had by now improved. The tall, plain, fourteen-year-old Margaret was a 'sweet girl' on whom she made a strong impression. She welcomed it, having no fear of bonding, 'She has a wonderful capacity but she has such a multiplicity of employments it has not room to expand itself – and in all probability will be lost in a heap of rubbish miss-called accomplishments. I am grieved at being obliged to continue so wrong a system – She is very much afraid of her mother – that such a creature should be ruled with a rod of iron, when tenderness would lead her any where – She is to be always with me . . .'[1] The censorious blamed moral decay leading to elopement and disobedience on romantic novels and French governesses who taught only an elegant tongue. The King girls had avoided these evils: they had read '*cart*-loads of history' and understood 'several languages'. In Eton Wollstonecraft had supported high-minded intel-lect of the Newington Green sort against triviality; here she found herself valuing middle-class sentiment: 'I almost wish the girls were novel readers and romantic, I declare false refinement is better than none at all.' In contrast, Mrs FitzGerald's three daughters were mere commodities, 'fine girls, just going to market, as their brother says'.[2]

Her treatment as a 'gentlewoman' and the affection of Margaret did not diminish the depression carried from Newington Green through Eton to Ireland, and she continued to deposit her ailments on the dispirited Everina. Her letters are not dissimilar to those miserably penned to Jane Arden from Bath and Windsor in her first dependence – only now she was achieving a richer vocabulary of complaint. The next months in Mitchelstown cannot have been all dreadful – she read widely – one of the old castle towers had been turned into a large library – and enjoyed the entertainments in which she shared. But her letters invariably wailed and she said hardly a word of the glorious scenery or the local Irish beyond the castle walls. Only occasionally did she wonder about the root cause of her miseries beyond her yearning for Fanny: body, mind, heaven or circumstance:

> I must labor for content and try to reconcile myself to a state which is contrary to every feeling of my soul – I can scarcely persuade myself that I am awake – my whole life appears like a frightful vision and equally disjointed – I have been so very low spirited for some days passed, I could not write – all the moments I could spend in solitude were lost in sorrow – and unavailing tears ... the forms and parade of high life suit not my mind – I am in a land of strangers ... I must soon sink into a state of insensibility – and then shall awake to all the cares I have left behind. I hear a fiddle below [–] the servant[s] are dancing – and the rest of the family diverting themselves – I only am melancholy and alone – To tell the truth, I hope part of my misery arises from disordered nerves, for I would fain believe my mind is not so very weak ...
>
> oh! my Everina my heart is almost broken ... Life has lost its relish, all my faculties languish – I try to be patient; but only fatigue my spirits – and yet according to the general notion of things – I have no reason to complain – mine, at present, might be termed comparative rather than positive misery – let it be called what it will – I am grown a poor melancholy wretch ... I long for my eternal rest – My nerves are so impaired I suffer much more than I supposed I should do, I want the tender soothings of friendship – I want – but I will be resigned – if I was stronger; if my health was not so much impaired, I should have more power over myself, as it is I am quite unstrung – you must read my heart [in] my situation, to judge of it – it is not to be described – even the good humoured attention of the silly girls worry me – I am an exile – and in a new world – If my vanity could be flattered, by the respect of people, whose judgement I do not care a fig for – why in this place it has sufficient food – though rather of the grosser kind; but I hate to talk all myself, and only make the ignorant wonder and admire.[3]

Locked up with the inhospitable Ned and his wife, Everina yearned to be where people gave her flattery and respect.

Mary was so depressed, so deluged with hypochondria, that she even considered a material remedy: ass's milk. It did no good. Usually she was sure her 'distressing' disorders arose entirely from the mind. Only divine comfort would answer: she hoped her 'Heavenly Father' would have 'compassion on a poor *bruised reed*, & pity a miserable wretch whose sorrows he only knows! ... I almost wish my warfare was over.' Even the news that Ned's lawsuit with Roebuck had been settled in their favour failed to cheer; her only comment was that she could pay her debts to Mrs Burgh before dying.

Similar moaning went to George Blood. He too was informed how much she was valued: 'with respect to my situation I have no just cause for complaint. – the whole family make a point of paying me the greatest attention – and some part of it treat me with a degree of tenderness which I have seldom met with from strangers ...' Indeed she admitted that 'every thing which humanity dictates is thought of for me – and if I was not a strange being I should be contented from feeling satisfied – and not from reflecting that it is my duty in "whatsoever state I am, therewith to be contented".' But he was left in no doubt of her deep depression, quite unmoveable by any outside 'tenderness'. She 'vainly pant[ed] after happiness' and feared she had become over-refined, unable to 'relish the pleasures most people pursue'. Desperately she wanted 'any hope to gild my prospect – any thing to animate me in my race besides the desire of reaching the goal'. With George she had an added stimulus to misery: 'About this time last year I closed my poor Fanny's eyes – I have been reviewing my past life – and the ghost of my former joys, and vanished hopes, haunted me continually – pity me – and excuse my silence – do not reproach me – for at this time I require the most friendly treatment.'

Nearer Christmas Wollstonecraft was energised by nursing Margaret – 'my poor little favourite has had a violent fever'. In the intimacy which came from the child's physical danger, she fancied that she and Lady Kingsborough grew close; her ladyship even showed some interest in her family. Despite her determination to disapprove, Wollstonecraft was pleased. She began scheming again: with Lady Kingsborough's help, she would get her sisters to Dublin to teach. She even imagined them enjoying holidays at the castle. In her usual peremptory way, she conveyed the scheme to Eliza languishing in Market Harborough: 'This plan delights me, do not raise any objection – and try in the interim to perfect yourself in english and fancy works ... I am a GREAT favourite in this family – and am certain you would please them.'

Just after Christmas she wrote again to Everina, about to visit or be visited by her father and stepmother. She sent love to 'poor Charles', still lodging with Ned, and 'something civil' to her father and Lydia – though she feared it might 'blister' Everina's tongue to say it. She wanted Everina to find out what she could about the Roebuck money, which should surely have been coming their way by now. She had one last commission: 'tell Mrs Cockburn – if I make any conquests in Ireland it will be owing to the *blue hat* – which is the first phenomenon of the kind, that has made its appearance in this hemisphere.' This sprightly mode was so unusual that she drew attention to it: 'There is a period for you! – worthy of an author whose work is just ushered into the world.'

This new lighter mood dependent on Lady Kingsborough did not last. When the girl was out of danger her mother withdrew her maternal feeling and returned to her dogs. Wollstonecraft was appalled. With her sense of the mind's control of the body, she disapproved the medical treatment given to Margaret who, in her view, needed a lengthy natural convalescence after such a severe fever. Artificial remedies 'prematurely stopped' the illness, so allowing a 'remnant' to lurk in her blood. There was consumption in the family and Wollstonecraft knew the disease well, having watched its progress in Fanny Blood. She dreaded to see it appearing in young Margaret.

She was also miserable for herself. When Margaret was out of danger, the sudden intimacy between Lady Kingsborough and her governess dwindled and Wollstonecraft once more became 'a sojourner in a strange land', needing comfort from abroad. She had been gullible and fallen for aristocratic con-descension: she would not let it happen again. Years later when she was independent and famous, she still smarted from her remembered naïveté and lashed out at Lady Kingsborough, the 'very handsome woman' who 'takes her dogs to bed, and nurses them with a parade of sensibility, when sick' while suffering 'her babes to grow up crooked in a nursery ... The wife, mother, and human creature, were all swallowed up by the factitious character which an improper education and the selfish vanity of beauty had produced.'[4] The immediate result was her own access of fondness for the Kingsborough children and disgust with their distant mother:

> I go to the nursery – *something like* maternal fondness fills my bosom – The children cluster about me – one catches a kiss, another lisps my long name – while a sweet little boy, who is conscious that he is a favorite, calls himself my son – At the sight of their mother they tremble and run to me for protection – this renders them dear to me – and I discover the kind of happiness I was formed to enjoy.

Her letters reverted to the usual expression of misery and needs. Everina must write more punctually: 'I am here shut out from domestic society – my heart throbs when I see a hand written by any one to whom my affections are attracted.' The triviality appalled her: 'conversations which have nothing in them' and rituals of dress that consumed time: 'I see Ladies put on rouge without any mauvais honte – and make up their faces for the day – five hours, and who could do it less in – do many – I assure you, spend in dressing – without including preparations for bed washing with Milk of roses &c &c' The pride she had felt in her austerity amidst the fleshpots of Bath and Windsor was renewed as she watched the primping and painting, her contempt fed by the expense of cosmetics. Advertisements aimed at ladies of the nobility and gentry for milk of roses to cleanse, soften and preserve the skin cost 10s 6d for a large bottle. Her '&c' included other scorned potions such as Italian paste for whitening hands, neck and face and Lady Molyneux's liquid bloom that gave to the 'lovely white' the 'rose of nature' without the appearance of art.[5]

Lady Kingsborough used all this copiously. She was 'very *pretty*' Wollstonecraft noted, and '*always* pretty'.

*'[I] scarcely know what to do with myself'*

The Kingsboroughs planned to remove to Dublin in early February, 1787. Despite her initial fears, she found she was one of the party. Without her own horse or carriage she had usually been confined to Mitchelstown Castle, but in Dublin she could lead a metropolitan life, walking or using public hackney cabs or open 'sociables'. Never keen to make the best of things, she remained dismal: 'life is but a frightful dream – I long to go to sleep – with my friend in the house appointed for all living!'

Her debts from Newington Green preyed on her mind. The Roebuck money had been paid to Ned, to whom she refused to write directly, but she would be relieved only when a portion had gone to Mrs Burgh. If nothing happened soon, she would get Mrs Burgh to deal directly with her brother. In the mean time she asked her to give three of the stored books to Everina, one of which her sister could send by the Windsor stagecoach to Mrs Prior, perhaps to thank for her unexpectedly lengthy stay in Eton.

When she wrote to George she showed a different anxiety: was Neptune still in town? He was.

*En route* to Dublin she seems to have made a detour to visit her mother's kin in Cork. Then she called on the family of Archdeacon Baillie, of respectable but inelegant relatives of the Bloods in Tipperary, not far from Mitchelstown. Fanny had been dispatched there as a child during one of the financial crises and become attached to it; so it had poignancy for her friend. The Archdeacon was a 'rational man', who was *'coldly* correct in his behaviour, and style'; his wife was the image of Mrs Blood, which, Mary thought, said it all. A son tried to be agreeable and the daughter was quiet, her understanding 'such as it is – highly cultivated'. She reminded Mary a little of Fanny.

She arrived in Dublin with the children before the rest of the family and settled into the plain-fronted but spacious townhouse of Lord Kingsborough's father, the Earl of Kingston, 15–16 Henrietta Street, one of a group of palatial residences near the current Law Library in north Dublin. She was delighted with her elegant apartments: 'A fine school room – The use of one of the drawing rooms where the Harpsichord is – and a parlour to receive my *Male* visitors in – Here is no medium! – The last poor Governess – was treated like a servant.'[1]

Betty Delane came to call at once and was received in the new parlour; her sensible conversation was a treat after the superficialities of Mitchelstown and she charmed young Margaret King. She had her problems, especially money, and some time after she arrived Mary borrowed ten guineas for her from Lady Kingsborough's stepmother, Mrs FitzGerald. She also saw George Blood but was less impressed with his talk: he did not develop intellectually, she judged. Still she was happy to receive his welcoming gift: the new edition of Shakespeare's plays. George was planning to go to London and would meet Everina; he could bring back detailed news. Meanwhile, she *should* visit the Blood parents, but it rained on the planned day and she put off going. Neptune did not call on them either – more significantly he did not visit *her*, though he did ask after her.

George and Elizabeth Ogle lived close to the Kingston townhouse and she was pleased to receive them before the family arrived. Indeed they were attentive throughout her stay. At some point the 'agreeable companion' of her voyage from Wales, Henry Gabell, came round but not the returned Hugh Skeys for she had not told him her address. There were invitations as well. Elizabeth Ogle and her sister Mary invited her in the mornings, and sometimes she supped with them and George Ogle, finding 'the moments glided away enlivened by wit and rational conversation'. Then at midnight she returned to lie on her own sofa in her own parlour. People were all so pressing and kind that Dubliners became her standard for hospitality – only she thought it an overrated virtue.

Despite the continued faintings and palpitations duly recorded, Mary responded with better spirits to the more stimulating encounters of town, as well as to greater control over her own time. The rest of the family would soon come in a great '*hurly burly*' and new masters swarm in to teach the older children. Seeing the dissipations of Dublin, she hoped she might avoid her employer's company: 'The hours I have spent with L[ady] K[ingsborough] could not have been very pleasant – now she must visit – and my spirits are spared this weight.' She liked Mrs FitzGerald, but she and her daughters would not be living with the family in Dublin. In any case, when they arrived they were preoccupied in choosing materials and fitting clothes for presentation at the Lord Lieutenant's castle: 'I am then tranquil – I commune with my own spirit – and am detached from the world.'

When she wrote to Everina to tell her to address future letters to Lord

Kingsborough's in Dublin, her unusually 'tranquil' state did not prevent her lashing out at her sister's continuing failure to write: Eliza had done so, why hadn't Everina? 'Can I suppose that I am loved, when I am not *told* that I am *remembered*. I am not angry – but *hurt* and disappointed. Here I feel myself *alone* – dead to most pleasures ... it would cheer my heart to receive a little tokens of tenderness.' Everina might sometimes be ill, but mainly she lacked 'resolution' to exert herself. She was too trivial and selfish: otherwise she would understand that correspondence would '*improve*' her as well as comforting her sister.

She herself was bent on self-improvement. No more than before would she waste time on English novels, however refining of young girls. On first arrival in Ireland, she worried that her dismal French would be exposed and struggled to improve it through reading *Theodore and Adelaide* by Stephanie de Genlis, the most popular educational writer of the day; she thought it 'wonderfully clever'. She also tackled the popular romance, *Caroline de Lichtfield*, finding at 'one of the prettiest things I have ever read'; her unusual approbation perhaps stemmed from her satisfaction in being able to read the French. Later she added Italian and tackled serious English books of philosophy: 'I lately met with Blairs lectures on genius taste &c &c – and found them an intellectual feast.'

Though so admired, the very popular *Letters on Rhetoric* by the Scottish literary critic Hugh Blair had little effect on her epistolary style however. Blair had expressed the Augustan notion of letter-writing as good conversation, sprightly, witty and seemingly natural, above all entertaining, with a constant eye to the recipient. Mary had remarked in a letter to George Blood that he might dread hearing from her if she continued moaning; yet a few days later she regaled Everina with her sensitivity and morbid expectations, as she did her scarcely known publisher Joseph Johnson, informed grimly of her 'pleasure' at her 'declining health' – though her tying of it to the 'irksome' state of dependence might hint that he could help alleviate both. Perhaps her secret determination to become a writer gave all her communications worth in her eyes, however self-obsessed and repetitive. Just occasionally she sought to entertain as Fanny Blood had done. When she replied to Eliza, whom she knew to be gloomy, she tried 'fabricat[ing] a lively epistle'. However, most of the time she fell back on her preachy homiletic style or detailed her moods almost as if conversing with herself rather than another. She filled every inch of her paper with her personality and berated her correspondent for not doing the same. Everina was the most in need of censure and she wrote her a typical letter of stern advice, coupled with an indulgent exhibition of her own recurring symptoms:

your mind certainly requires great attention – you have seldom *resolution* to *think* or *exert* the talents nature, or to speak with more propriety, Providence has given you to be *improved* – our whole life is but an education for eternity – virtue is an *acquirement* – seek for the assistance of Heaven, to enable you *now* to be [taken]into Salvation, and regret not the time which is past, which, had others taken the greatest pains to form your mind could only have opened it to instruction – and made you capable of gaining experience – no creature is so situated but they may obtain His favor from whom *only* TRUE comfort flows if they seek it.

If she had taken her own advice, it had not much mitigated her state: 'I am not well – yet, repeat it, scarcely know what to do with myself.' She often felt nauseous and was close to fainting, she complained; she also had violent fits of trembling. But, she remarked sternly to Everina, 'I am . . . satisfied to bear these disorder – (though as they seem to attack the mind, they are doubly distressing) if I can fulfil the duties of my station.' At the same time she described outings to the theatre and asked Everina if she went much herself.

Such letters with their self-centred and divided messages irritated Everina, who found it hard to believe in Mary's posturing, her detachment from the world, and her continuing gloom amongst such gratification. Since Everina's own life produced rather less pleasure and she was only twenty-one, she wished her overbearing sister would keep her unctuous preaching for her books. She did not want to provoke further such letters, but, being less touchy than Eliza, replied with excuses. Unfortunately, she did not direct them to Viscount Kingsborough's house as instructed.

Hearing nothing, Mary wrote again at the beginning of March, descanting once more on Everina's shortcomings: 'I am a little surprised and disappointed at not receiving an answer to my two or three last letters; but I ought not to have expected from you that kind of affection, which only can gratify my heart, of course, my disappointment arises from myself – I too frequently, willing to indulge a delightful tenderness, forget the convictions of reason, and give way to chimerical hopes, which are as illusive as they are pleasant. I know very well friendship can only take root in a cultivated mind . . . You have a great many agreeable qualities – but I will have done with the subject.'

When Everina realised her mistake with Mary's address, she wrote directly to the Kingsboroughs, defending herself by describing her own miserable existence. Ned was unkind, his wife cruel; indeed, they so hated having her that they were sullying her reputation as excuse to be rid of her. What was she to do? She was desperate to move.

Such a sad letter after so long a silence abashed Mary and she wrote back immediately 'full of indignation' at Ned and his wife. She could think of no one to whom Everina could turn. Once she would have suggested Mrs Burgh, but now her surrogate mother was tarnished by her part in Mary's present servitude and was dismissed as conventional; she would be swayed by the gossip Ned had put about. It was back to Mary, but she could see no immediate solution: 'I have been thinking of you ever since I received your last – and am worried beyond measure.'

Then Mary received the wrongly-directed letters sent through George Blood and Hugh Skeys, who had not known her address. She was irritated with the circumstance and further annoyed by the contents. Unlike the latest letter, these ascribed Everina's neglect to low spirits, not Ned's unkindness. Mary grew impatient again. Persecution was excuse, not mere depression – at least for anyone else: 'If lowness of spirits were a sufficient apology for not writing I should very very seldom take up my pen,' she snapped. Her impatience let her scold and the scolding combined with self-satisfaction was more than Everina could bear. She retaliated and Mary promised, 'I shall never mention your writing again.' It was not a promise she could keep.

However irritated, she continued anxious about her sisters. Eliza's situation was dire and Mary felt miserable imagining 'her gloomy sing-song'. Although Lady Kingsborough had disappointed, Mrs FitzGerald had been looking out for the sort of situations two genteel, inexperienced, uneducated girls could fill. She was having little success: 'I am afraid it is not as easy, as I supposed, to get [Eliza] into a school in this country,' wrote Mary. Then she groaned, 'besides *what* could Eliza undertake?' Everina she thought might be placed as a governess, but she hated her own situation so much it was hard to recommend the life to another. Besides, if her own qualifications were inadequate, Everina's were worse, and the latter lacked the wit to hide her inadequacies. Ireland was no haven: 'The family pride which reigns here produces the worst effects – They are ingeneral proud and mean ... As a nation I do not *admire* the Irish, I never before felt what it was to love my country; but now I have a value for it built on rational grounds.' When she had paid her debts with her half year's stipend and the Roebuck money, she could perhaps borrow again to help her sisters to further training.

Then she learnt that brother Ned might be keeping at least part of the money. Mrs Burgh heard the same, probably from the indiscreet Everina, and advised Mary to write pleadingly to her brother. Mary was scornful: 'I do not intend to follow her advice, and suppose she will be displeased. I know she expected that I should make my fortunes here – and to pecuniary considerations, she thinks every thing ought to give way.' The Green was morally disintegrating. Dr Price had always been its centre and he had moved to Hackney; even Hewlett had sunk in her esteem.

Some weeks later she knew that Ned *had* purloined the money. Mrs Burgh would remain unpaid and Mary could take no '*active* step to make myself useful to those I am most interested in'. She was not over-anxious about her creditor, but something had to be done for her sisters. Everina had described Ned's treatment so graphically that Eliza refused to visit. As a result poor Everina became more desperate and was threatening to leave, whatever resulted. Mary approved, 'Let you go where you will,' she wrote. In the mean time she must rustle up money to get her to Eliza's and take the edge off grief, but Mrs Burgh must not hear of it. She would resent their using money that should be repaying her debt.

Now that she felt the rupture with Mrs Burgh, Mary disliked any tie: 'It is by no means pleasant to be under obligations to a person, with whose opinions I can so seldom coincide.' She was keener to excuse men than women and the mother figures Mrs Clare and Mrs Burgh were found wanting where their husbands or male friends were less blamed. Probably her relationship to her unsatisfactory parents, the one irritatingly weak and unloving, the other violently unpredictable and intermittently caressing, lay behind the recurrent attitude. Not writing off her generous loan, the once praised Mrs Burgh, who had treated her as a daughter, now appeared mercenary and manipulating.

Her other old friend, George Blood, also disappointed. Mary met him on his return from visiting Everina, who had been at her most vulnerable and confiding, and she discovered he had transferred his affections. The 'Princess' was out of his reach and he now fancied her sister: 'you have rivalled the princess – George talks continually of you and blushes when he mentions your name.'

Wollstonecraft's continuing vapourishness alarmed and bewildered Lady Kingsborough. She wanted her to consult her own doctor about the interminable symptoms; 'I am sure it would answer no good end,' her governess replied. She had disapproved of the treatment of young Margaret and did not trust the doctor and his potions.

Then she had a worse turn. She had been to church, probably St Ann's, the Kingsborough's usual place of worship, and had found the service discomposing. Lady Kingsborough took her out and made her sit down nearby. When she seemed a bit better they returned to Henrietta Street where Betty Delane was visiting. Wollstonecraft fell into a violent fit of trembling, which continued in varying degrees for the rest of the day. It terrified her friend.

The fit gave Lady Kingsborough ammunition and she reurged consultation with her doctor. Now Wollstonecraft agreed. She was rather pleased at the outcome, for he diagnosed the fashionable 'nervous fever' to which sensitive souls, especially women, were prey: 'I am not well, the Physician who attends this family thinks I have a constant nervous fever on me – and I am sure he is right.' Her symptoms validated by the medical profession, she was happy to accept some physiological psychology and took more comfort than before in the notion of the nervous body which sensitively displayed (and inspired) the miseries of the mind. As her depression continued, even worsened during the coming months, she became increasingly attuned to this ascription of mental states to the nervous system, while never abandoning her sense of suffering as the 'Will of Heaven'. The earlier diagnosis allowed more grumbling, for it made her largely blameless for her state, while physical symptoms demanded unqualified sympathy.[2] It was not all comfort, however, since, unlike special providence, nervous debility did not promise speedy death. 'Don't smile when I tell you that I am tormented with *spasms* – indeed it is impossible to enumerate the various complaints I am troubled with; and how much my mind is harrassed by them. I know they all arise from disordered nerves, that are injured beyond a *possibility* of receiving *any* aid from medicine – There is no cure for a broken heart!'

Her unease was exacerbated by growing obsession with Lady Kingsborough. She had hoped to see less of her in Dublin, to have more 'quietness in my own apartments', but instead she was caught up in the bustle and confusion of town life, the preparation of dresses and wreaths of roses for balls and masquerades which 'the whole house from the kitchen maid to the GOVERNESS are obliged to assist, and the children forced to neglect their employments.' The confounding of governess and kitchen maid was what a self-respecting lady had to fear. Happily she was managing to subvert young Margaret, who had 'a premature disgust to the follies of dress, equipage & the other usual objects of female vanity'.[3]

Not realising her governess's fury at the retreat from intimacy, Lady Kingsborough regarded herself as a good employer; she concerned herself with Wollstonecraft's health, was with her when possible, gave her her own parlour and invited her often into the drawing-room – this was especially kind since she was not one of those governesses who played foil to their mistress's wit and vivacity or comported herself with self-effacing discretion. But Wollstonecraft was unabashedly ungrateful for all her efforts:

You know, I never liked Lady K., but I find her still more haughty and disagreeable now she is not under Mrs FitzGerald's eye. Indeed, she behaved so improperly to me once, or twice, in the Drawing room, I determined never to go in to it again. I could not bear to stalk in to be stared at, and her proud condescension added to my embarrassment, I begged to be excused in a civil way – but she would not allow me to absent myself – I had too, another reason, the expence of hair dressing, and millinery, would have exceeded the sum I chuse to spend in those things. I was determined – just at this juncture she offered me a present, a poplin gown and petticoat, I refused it, and explained myself – she was very angry; but Mrs F, who was consulted on the occasion, took my part, and made her ask my pardon, and consent to let me stay always in my own room – Since that [time] she has endeavored to treat me with more propriety, and I believe she does do so to the best of her knowledge. She is very proud, and ready to take fire on the slightest occasion – her temper is violent, and anger intirely predominates in her mind – now, and then, I have seen a momentary start of tenderness – sufficient to convince me she might have been a more tolerable companion, had her temper been properly managed; as to her understanding, it could never have been made to rise above mediocrity. I pity her, but I am deprived of all society, and when I do sit with her, she worries me with prejudices, and complaints. I am very well persuaded that to make any great advance in morality genius is necessary – a peculiar kind of genius which is not to be described, and cannot be conceived by those who do not possess it – you might as well expect a man born blind to have just notions of the beauty arising from varied rays of light.

Did Wollstonecraft or Lady Kingsborough most excel in pride? On the evidence of this letter, one might answer, the governess. She lacked social status but not intellectual and moral self-esteem. It was not unusual for a mistress to offer a gown to a dependant, but Wollstonecraft's puritanical satisfaction in her plain style, as well as her antagonism to the relationship the gift implied, meant that she could not accept with grace.

Lady Kingsborough persevered, thinking to combat the prickliness and priggishness with more society. Wollstonecraft had mentioned her wish to go to a masquerade; Lady Kingsborough gave her two tickets, one for herself and one for Betty Delane. But Wollstonecraft refused them because the costume would be too expensive. Lady Kingsborough offered to lend her her own black domino, a large cape that disguised the whole person. It was no good, Wollstonecraft was 'out of spirit – and thought of another excuse' – that she was unused to such outings and would not know how to act. In some exasperation her employer then proposed that she herself accompany Wollstonecraft and Betty Delane, along with Mary Moore, George Ogle's sister-in-law. They would visit 'the houses of several people of fashion who saw masques'. Finally the governess agreed. What is more she had a good time – Thanks to her nervous fever – as she related to Everina:

> We ... were a tolerable, nay, a much admired group. Lady K. went in a domino, with a smart cockade. Miss Moore dressed in the habit of one of the females, of the new discovered Islands, Betty D. as a forsaken shepherdess – and your sister Mary in a black domino. As it was taken for granted the stranger who was just arrived, could not speak the language, I was to be her interpreter, which afforded me an ample field for satire. I happened to be very melancholy in the morning – as I am every morning almost, but at night my fever gives me *false* spirits – this night the lights the novelty of the scene, and every things together contributed to make me *more* than half mad – I gave full scope to a satirical vein –

After such studied reluctance, this kind of showing off must have infuriated Lady Kingsborough. In conduct books, women were repeatedly told to hide any knowledge and stifle any wit they might have, especially in front of men; a married aristocratic lady might indulge herself, but certainly not a hired governess.

Then Lady Kingsborough went away for a fortnight; Wollstonecraft felt relieved, yet the departure heralded an even deeper bout of depression. She spoke mournfully about Fanny Blood with Betty Delane and shut herself in her room to read Rousseau's educational novel *Émile*. Addressed to the 'tender, anxious mother', the book appealed to her in caring mode, excluding the cold aristocrat who passed as biological mother. In Rousseau's approach the (boy) child ought not to be oppressed into good behaviour but led to adult rational morality and goodness through his senses and needs: 'there must be no submission to authority if you would have no submission to convention [later]'.

Looking from the words to the author she found Rousseau a kindred spirit, 'a strange inconsistent unhappy creature', a lonely idealist who fell into despair at reality and was as self-absorbed as herself. Dr Johnson had detested him: 'Rousseau, Sir, is a very bad man ... I would rather sign a sentence for his transportation, than that of any felon who has gone from the Old Bailey these many years.' But in some areas of life she had moved on from Dr Johnson, and she was, she later said, half in love with Rousseau.

With her early pious complexion, she had arrived late at the Cult of Sensibility, its heyday being in the 1770s. Clearly in its agonised Rousseauian form it suited her temperamentally more than Christian piety or the Lockean stress on the mind alone. Other governesses without her literary hopes but with similar distaste for dependence, such as Agnes Porter, addressed their 'melancholy' with sturdy reading in *The Whole Duty of Man*, concluding that 'there are sun-shines and storms in the moral as in the natural world,' and praying God to make them 'thankful'. As the years passed Porter managed to esteem her work: 'seven years I have now seen in revolution, and the pretty child of ten years of age shoot up into the fine woman of seventeen. What is the florist's pride or pleasure compared to this!'⁴ But the sentimental heroine of Fanny Burney's 'The Witlings' was less resilient: her situation was cruel abjection and servility, and she hoped for a short life to terminate it, much as Wollstonecraft sometimes did.

Now, with the help of Rousseau (and the interesting Mr Ogle), Wollstonecraft embraced the individualist and self-gratifying values of sensibility, its preference for moral fineness over social rank and birth, its compensatory élitism of mind and exquisite physical feeling. Being a prey to melancholy and moodiness argued superiority, not just a misfortune to be combated, as Dr Johnson had suggested, or indeed a malaise due to solitude and 'sickly musings', as John Armstrong urged in *The Art of Preserving Health*. She was more sensitive than others, her body finely interacting with the social world; whatever her mental and nervous peculiarities, they were her glory as well as her pain. She was reading La Rochefoucauld and she selected maxims: 'That vivacity which increases with age is not far from madness,' she quoted, 'I then am mad'; it was not Armstrong's madness that came from excess imagination combined with 'delicate Self-Love' or Johnson's, the disease of subjectivity.

Her letters revealed more than intellectual development. *Émile* described the onset of male sexuality as a second birth. Now a yearning for love was shouting from her pages and, in the awkward literary quotations, sudden changes of topic, hiatuses, breaks, gaps, confused syntax and obscure connections, she seemed desperate to confide an erotic obsession to Everina but never quite did. Something resisted the passage into words and she wearily deflected emotion into the usual expectation of decline and death, negative of Rousseau's 'second birth'. The loss of the beloved Fanny had influenced her state, though something more seemed added, something not quite explained by her special sensitivity, a sense that the mind rarely knew all and that the body had desires imprinted from earliest times.

I am, at present, rather melancholy than unhappy – the things of this world appear *flat, stale* and *unprofitable* to me, and, sometimes, I am perhaps, too impatient to leave the *unweeded* garden. I do not now complain, a listless kind of dispair has taken possession of me, which I cannot shake off ... as to my heart, He only who made it can account for, and compassionate its numerous weaknesses, why then should I display them to those who would, perhaps, rather dispise than pity me – yet so frequently do they force themselves on my view – and so lively are the emotions I wish to analyze – they too often tincture my conversation and letters – These dark tinges occur continually – they want *relief* – I am only alive to *attendrissement* – Certainly I must be in love – for I am grown 'thin and lean, pale and wan'.

Then came a revealing postscript:

> I am like a *lilly* drooping – Is it not a sad pity that so sweet a flower should waste its sweetness on the *Desart* air, or that the Grave should receive its *untouched* charmes. Yours an Old Maid – ' 'Tis true a pity and 'tis pity tis true' – Alas!!!!!!!!

Less melodramatically she wrote, 'I sit up very late. 'Tis the only time I *live*, in the morning I am a poor melancholy wretch – and at night *half* mad, a p[re]tty account I give of myself.' George Blood's present of Shakespeare had borne fruit in this strong identification with *Hamlet*; she combined the sensitive prince and the mad Ophelia.

Neptune was in Dublin. Perhaps she wrote to him, perhaps he replied or did not and she was hurt again. Involuntarily she found herself looking out for him.[5] The odd hints of 'tenderness' from strangers, flattery of 'the grosser kind', and her own too great 'refinement' might imply that she had become the object of partly wanted, partly unwanted attentions in her hothouse society. Perhaps from the married but chastely flirtatious Mr Ogle or unrefined Lord Kingsborough. By now she probably knew he had allegedly seduced the earlier governess, presently receiving a generous pension.[6] Years later, when the third King girl had grown up to become as scandalous as her teacher, and Lord Kingsborough was accused of murdering his nephew, now his daughter's lover, the gossip was repeated that Wollstonecraft and his Lordship had been intimate. They say, wrote Bishop Percy of Dromore to his wife, that Wollstonecraft wanted 'to discharge the Marriage Duties, with [Lady Kingsborough's] husband'. Given her horror of sensuality, it seems unlikely, but attentions might have been paid and received, regretted for being too much and too little.[7] She might have taken seriously what Lord Kingsborough simply regarded as a 'little *fun*'. Once she admitted blushing redder than her Ladyship's rouge when he entered the drawing-room and saw her.

Dissenters holding to puritanical ideals were often appalled at the assaults of sexuality and revolted by their uncleanliness or weakness. Without this stern Calvinist background Wollstonecraft was not so clear; she had no access to the modern notion of sexuality as a primary root of human identity and was not ready with Rousseau to see it as natural but socially disruptive – perhaps she had not yet read his description of the lovesick young girl, tearful, dreamy and lethargic. Wollstonecraft was simply bewildered at her violent oscillations of mood, and, although she hinted at amorous feelings and disappointments, she never ascribed her state to properly or improperly repressed sexual longing.

When she returned home, Lady Kingsborough continued to feel challenged by her moody governess and determined to be even nicer. Probably she had been speaking to Mrs FitzGerald, who had a soft spot for Wollstonecraft and admired her care for her siblings. Lady Kingsborough had noticed how lively she had become in the masquerade. Perhaps she had been starved for elegant entertainment. So she carried her to fashionable plays in which the famous actors and actresses from the London stage were performing. She introduced her in the Rotunda and Green Room, where theatrical and society people mingled. But any effect gained was lost by Wollstonecraft's at last spying Neptune in the crowd.

She was, of course, in Lady Kingsborough's party. Neptune was snobbish and, when he observed her in the Rotunda in such elevated company, he desired to speak and began walking towards her. Offended by weeks of neglect, she refused to acknowledge his presence. Had he continued observing her, he would have caught a 'look of ineffable contempt'. A few nights later she saw him again at the Green Room. He had learnt the lesson of her scorn and did not attempt speaking. After suffering from his indifference, it was some comfort to snub him in such fashionable places and in such aristocratic company.

From Lady Kingsborough's point of view, the concerts were more successful and she must momentarily have congratulated herself on impressing her governess when, after she had given her tickets for both days of the Handel commemoration – the *Messiah* had first been performed in Dublin – Wollstonecraft admitted herself 'obliged'. She had already heard Handel's music in Bath or London and been raised by it 'from the very depths of sorrow'. Now again Handel impressed with his 'sublime compositions' and the Hallelujah chorus haunted her.[8] 'Lady K. and I are on much better terms than ever we were,' she wrote, adding that her employer 'really labors to be civil'.

Yet she was not won over. In private she continued to judge 'this female' harshly, as foolish, unamusing and intruding, and she deeply resented the time with her: 'The defect is in her nature,' she wrote. 'She is devoid of sensibility – of course, *vanity only* inspires her immoderate love of praise –

and *selfishness* her *traffick* of civility – and the fulsome untruths, with all their train of strong expressions without any ideas annexed to them.' Wollstonecraft herself occasionally tried to be amiable, talking 'of getting husbands for the *Ladies* – and the *dogs*' and being 'wonderfully entertaining', but she did not often strain candour by good manners and she was not much impressed with their exercise in others. Lady Kingsborough was jealous, she thought, especially of her being noticed in polite company. 'Why she wishes to keep me I cannot guess.' She had the comfort of believing she had reduced her employer to fear – much like Mrs Dawson in Bath.

The tension in the relationship between the two women is well caught in an awkward social moment with the Earl of Kingston, Lady Kingsborough's father-in-law, in which Wollstonecraft took the kind of pride she had felt in her performance at the masquerade. Lady Kingsborough had been dining with the Earl, together with Miss Moore and her sister Mrs Ogle, and the formidable governess had seemingly been a topic of conversation. The Earl was curious to see the lady. Upstairs, wrapped in her habitual melancholy, Wollstonecraft had seated herself to write to her sister when Miss Moore and Mrs Ogle disturbed her, closely followed by Lady Kingsborough. All requested her to come down to the drawing-room to meet the Earl. At first she refused, they pressed her, and still she held out. Lady Kingsborough bit her tongue at this rude behaviour, but Miss Moore grew more persuasive until at last Wollstonecraft consented. It is a remarkable social scene where Mrs Ogle, her sister and Lady Kingsborough all try to persuade the governess to descend and be civil to the elderly Earl of Kingston, whose house they were inhabiting.

When she did comply, with bad grace, she was surprised that Lady Kingsborough tried to get rid of her before the other gentlemen arrived, although this withdrawal was usual social behaviour for a governess. 'Nay would you believe it,' she told Everina, 'she used several arts to get me out of the room before the gentlemen came up – one of them I really wanted to see Mr Ogle.' Of course she refused to budge, whatever 'arts' her ladyship used, and she was still in the drawing-room when the men arrived – including Ogle. She enjoyed the rivalry with Lady Kingsborough: the latter had chosen him for her (chaste) '*flirt*'. Wollstonecraft could not think why she bothered, except to outwit her governess, since she neither understood nor relished good conversation. She supposed she wished 'to be taken particular notice of by a man of *acknowledged* cleverness'.

With herself, of course, it was different. Ogle had the sensitivity she wanted in a man and the taste to appreciate her pathos and intellect, without any grossness in his admiration – indeed 'his sensibility has ever lead him to pay attention to a poor forlorn stranger', she told Everina. Such an unhappy 'genius ... you may suppose would catch your sister's eye'. He had not seen her for some time, so when he now entered the room he immediately sat down beside her. Then he began a series of '*fanciful* compliments' and gave her some poems, 'melancholy one[s], you may suppose as he thought they would accord with my feelings'. Lady Kingsborough must have been thoroughly put out at this display by the pair of them. She was further irritated when she observed her husband's surprise to find the governess still lingering in the room and noted the latter's blush when he bowed respectfully to her. All in all it was a memorable evening.

Assuming Mary's very real depression a fashionable affectation, over the next weeks the interesting Mr Ogle continued to pay court. When she described him to Everina she found she was describing her interesting self, displayed for an appreciative male gaze. In *Émile* the heroine Sophie views herself as the object of desire and expresses her own desire through such narcissism:

> deprived of the only comforts I can relish, I give way to whim – and yet when the most sprightly sallies burst from me the tear frequently trembles in my eye and the long drawn sigh eases my full heart – so my eyes roll in the wild way you have *seen* them. A deadly paleness overspreads my countenance – and yet so weak am I a sudden thought or any *recollected* emotion of tenderness will occasion the most painful suffusion. You know not my dear Girl of what materials, this strange inconsisten[t] heart of mine, is formed and how alive it is to tenderness and misery. Since I have been here I have turned over sever[al] pages in the vast volume of human nature, and what is the amount? Vanity and vexation of spirit – and yet I am *tied* to my fellow-creatures by partaking of their weaknesses – I rail at a fault – sicken at the sight – and find it stirring within me – new sympathies and feelings *start* up – I know not myself – ''Tis these whims,' Mr Ogle tells me, 'render me interesting' and Mrs Ogle with a placid smile quotes some of my own sentiments – while I cry the physici[an] *cannot* heal himself – This man has *great* faults and his wife *little* ones – They vex me – yet he say a witty thing and genius and sensibility lights his eyes – tenderness illumines her's, and her face is dressed in smiles of benignity – I forget reason – the present pleasing *impulse* rules the moment and it *flies*–

In much the same way in her fiction she would portray the heroine observed in her sympathetic postures by the admiring hero and describe her appearance when a man looks at her.

Other details suggest a growing fascination with the erotic milieu of the Kingsboroughs, the 'dissipated lives the women of quality lead'. Images of sensuality flitted into her mind, sex, drink and gluttony. Men and women in high life were married solely for procreation and money, not companionship; seldom alone except in bed, they were emotionally separate even then, the husband drunk and the wife's head 'full of the *pretty* compliment that some creature, that Nature designed for a Man – paid her at the card table'. Perhaps the flirtations Wollstonecraft noticed were not as harmless as she had supposed.

The first shock came from 'poor half-mad Mr Ogle'. She had been so sure that his attentions to her and Lady Kingsborough were pure, but then she doubted, either from experience or household gossip. She was bitterly disappointed: 'I am sorry to hear a man of sensibility and cleverness talking of sentiment sink into sensuality – such will ever I fear be the case with the inconsistent human heart when there are no principles to restrain and direct the wayward impulses of it.' Interestingly, she had described *herself* as 'half-mad' when she noted her own heightened vivacity.

Much of her misery fell on Everina, but she also used men she hardly knew for comfort: the publisher Joseph Johnson and the clergyman-tutor Henry Gabell. To these she conveyed her dejection but giving some rational cause. Providence and mental suffering seemed more appropriate than 'nervous fever' and love-sickness for male correspondents. Earlier she had stressed the horror of dependence to Johnson; she tried this again while also indicating a vague psychological predicament: 'I am still an invalid – and begin to believe that I ought never to expect to enjoy health. My mind preys on my body – and, when I endeavour to be useful, I grow too much interested for my own peace.' She was lonely, excluded from 'rational conversation, and domestic affections ... a poor solitary individual in a strange land, tied to one spot, and subject to the caprice of another'. How could she be contented? 'I am desirous to convince you that I have *some* cause for sorrow – and am not without reason detached from life.' One posture she knew from literature appealed to sensitive men: that of mother, and she assumed it for Johnson: 'I feel all a mother's fears for the swarm of little ones which surround me...'

To Henry Gabell she had sent a copy of *Thoughts on the Education of Daughters*, together with a short, rather intimate note moaning of existence; she feared he might accuse her of 'always running on in the same strain', especially since she had also been gloomy when they met. It mattered since she wanted to impress Gabell. Later she used his name for the sickly hero of her first novel, which she admitted was 'drawn from Nature', although Godwin insisted that only the female friendship portrayed in the novel was autobiographical. Gabell had little in common with the fictional Henry except in his tendency to fend off the sensitive lady and the sad childhood as a second, unloved son might rather have called on the experience of her own missing brother. When she wrote again, Wollstonecraft knew of Gabell's engagement and was more detached but still eager to impress. With other correspondents she rambled confusedly about the causes of her state – poor nerves, a broken heart, or excess sensibility – with Gabell she insisted simply that her miseries were divinely inflicted.[9] He doubted that God created misery, but she argued that the sensitivity of temperament that allowed deep suffering *had* to be ordained, not accidental: surely 'an All-wise and good Being created nothing in vain. He cannot be mistaken, or cause *needless* pain.' If only this world mattered, there would be no purpose to self-improvement:

> A *good* understanding prevents a person's enjoying the common pleasures of this life – if it does not prepare him for a better it is a *curse*. Why have we implanted in us an irresistible desire to think – if thinking is not in some measure necessary to make us wise unto salvation ... the more I reflect, the less apt am I to concur with you – if I did, I should envy *comfortable* folly ... The main hinge on which my argument turns is this, refinement genius – and those charming talents which my soul instinctively loves, produce misery in this world – abundantly more pain than pleasure. Why then do they at all unfold themselves *here*? ... Surely *peculiar* wretchedness has something to balance it!

It was a valiant attempt to integrate her religious, social and psychological experience.

Despite this display of intellect, the correspondence lapsed, leaving Wollstonecraft to fear once more that attractive men were repelled by intelligent women. She had, however, become convinced of one thing in her dealings with men over the last years: that even measured against them rather than her own trivial sex she herself was extraordinary and that, with the intellectuals of Newington Green, the aristocrats of Dublin, and university-educated clerics, she could hold her own.

# 11

*'The kind of company I find most pleasure in'*

However low in spirits she felt in Dublin, Wollstonecraft dreaded returning to rural Mitchelstown. So she was heartened to learn that she was to accompany the Kingsboroughs on a planned Continental tour. They would cross the Irish Sea at the beginning of June. She (almost) looked forward to the trip, eager to see France and improve her inadequate French. Before reaching the Continent they would visit Bristol Hot Wells to sample the medicinal waters. Wollstonecraft would not have chosen this place for, like Bath, it was primarily a resort for the rich, leisured and ill, but she was glad to be returning to England. After the Hot Wells, she would take a short holiday with her sisters.

Once established in Bristol Hot Wells, Mary found life the usual strenuous struggle. Perhaps Gabell's reasoning had touched her a little, tipped the balance in her vacillation between providence and physique. In her letters to her sisters she wrote far more of her 'nerves' and delicate body than of her soul: 'My nerves daily grow worse and worse – yet I strive to occupy my mind even when duty does not force me to do it – in a trifling way I net purses, and intend having two smart ones to present to [Eliza] and Everina . . . I shake my head but it remains heavy – I *ruminate* without digesting. I have several neighbors; but none of them please me.'

Now in England she was taking increasing comfort in regarding herself as an author. The identity made her feel a superior being to her sisters: 'When I have more strength I read Philosophy – and write – I hope you have not forgot that I am an Author . . . I have lately been reading a book which I wish Everina to peruse. It is called Paley's philosophy. The definition of virtue I particularly admire – it is short. "Virtue is the doing good to mankind in obedience to the will of God, and for the sake of everlasting happiness." ' She was still filling her mind with edifying quotations, useful to pass on to her less resourceful sisters – and perhaps to embroider future writings. William Paley, a kind of theological utilitarian, put morality within life and supported women's education and independence. She did not let him unsettle her belief in the value of painful sensibility.

The proposed vacation with Eliza and Everina set her scheming again.

Although unmentioned in the letters, possibly Everina alone had received some Roebuck money, so gaining a modest annuity, insufficient to keep her but something to brighten servitude now that she took the plunge and left Ned for a teaching job in Henley. But, to make a real difference, both sisters needed substantial capital; this Mary was trying to raise. Someone promised it, but she was not permitted to name the benefactor. He or she remains a mystery. Possibly it was George Ogle, but, since he had tumbled from favour, she would not wish to be beholden to him. Mrs FitzGerald was openly the source of small advances; she too was an unlikely donor. After all the difficulty over the initial loan, Mrs Burgh could not have been approached again; besides, Mary had declared that she wished to avoid depending on someone holding improper views. A possibility is Joseph Johnson, offering an advance for a new work, but, in that case, the secrecy seems odd. Another possibility is Lord Kingsborough, though she did write cryptically at this time, 'Lords are not the sort of beings who afford me amusement – nor in the nature of things can they . . .' But, if he promised money rather than amusement, the secrecy would be explained.

According to Godwin, at Bristol Hot Wells Wollstonecraft composed her second work and first novel: *Mary, A Fiction*; the unexpected form probably derived from her French reading, both of Rousseau's novelettish *Émile* and of the Baroness de Montolieu's sentimentally serious *Caroline de Lichtfield*. She may well have begun her own novel in the fraught months in Dublin when noting Rousseau's idea that a genius will educate itself. This was used as a summary of her book, which presented a female Émile educating herself through sensations, nature and solitary thinking.

*Mary, A Fiction* continued her habit of writing primarily from personal experience. Hence the paradoxical name, which also drew attention to the public's scepticism about a 'thinking' heroine. As she declared, 'Those compositions only have power to delight, and carry us willing captives, where the soul of the author is exhibited, and animates the hidden springs.' The tale was 'artless' – Wollstonecraft still prized her adolescent spontaneity. The emotional configuration of her own family was mapped on the castle: 'Mary' became the daughter of an aristocrat who petted her dogs not her children, but died languidly like Elizabeth Wollstonecraft. The identification fell foul of her later strictures against novels being invariably set in high society.

The fictional Mary's father has a disturbing sensuality, possibly drawing on Edward Wollstonecraft – as well as George Ogle and Lord Kingsborough. He is given to immoderate dinners, whose 'cumbrous load' he somnolently digests through the afternoon. The sexual encounter he then requires is a kind of dessert, and, since he is a gourmand in women, he leaves his genteel wife for more appealing fare. The heroine Mary cries for her vicious father, comparing him with her worthy self.

Wollstonecraft was as harsh on his feeble wife, Mary's mother, who lives through fantasy. Agreeing with male moralists in opposing trivial women's fiction – despite her momentary yearning for light reading for the King girls – she made her heroine's mother read trashy novels. The preface even repudiated the most culturally respectable fiction, Richardson's *Clarissa*, which presented a strong woman implacably defending her chastity and integrity through submission and self-destruction; it left out intellect, Wollstonecraft thought. Also repudiated was Rousseau's depiction of Sophie in *Émile*. Instead of novels Mary read poetry: Thomson's *Seasons*, the 10,000 gloomy lines of Young's *Night Thoughts*, and Milton's *Paradise Lost* and *Il Penseroso*, with its dark pines and dim religious light. It was the correct taste, touchstone of female value – ironically within the very women's novels Wollstonecraft so much despised. To reject these authors revealed deep flaws in fictional heroines; to approve them augured well for their ethical future.[1]

Mary, whose virtue, like her author's own, sprang from neglect and unhappiness, was of course a woman of 'sensibility'. This was the classless quality which separated Wollstonecraft from Lady Kingsborough and attracted Ogle. It made a woman tremblingly alive to afflictions: of others sometimes, but also of her own. The heroine's 'rhapsodies' on sensibility, close to some of Wollstonecraft's letters, were the novel's main appeal and were excerpted in sentimental collections. In them Mary extolled sensibility and, accepting that she might be 'under the influence of a delusion', still believed it proved her '*of subtiler essence than the trodden clod*', to quote the poet Young: 'These flights of the imagination point to futurity; I cannot banish them.' In the ardent benevolence born of sensibility she became heaven-directed and 'almost forgot she had a body'. Yet, for all the approval of Mary and disapproval of her mother, parent and daughter combine in yearning and self-pity and there seems no absolute distinction between the heroine's unsensual and virtuous sort of sensibility and her mother's sensual irrational type – as the novel is fitfully aware: 'Not curbed by reason, [sensibility] is on the brink of vice talking, and even thinking of virtue,' muses the heroine towards the end of her emotional career.

The centre of the novel is the friendship of the sensitive Mary and Ann, following fairly closely the outward events in the relationship with Fanny Blood. In the story this tie replaces Mary's unsatisfactory arranged and unconsummated marriage. Given her affectionate references to Fanny in the personal letters, it is shocking to find how inadequate in the end the fictional Ann appears to the benevolent and loving heroine, how much she is not what Mary wished.

Mary is at first attracted to Ann through her air of sadness, but this proves circumstantial not temperamental. An 'ill-fated love has given a bewitching softness to her manner, a delicacy so truly feminine, that a man of any feeling could not behold her without wishing to chase her sorrows away'. Mary feels ambivalent towards this 'femininity', so desirable to a man. Indeed it seems that, as an object of desire, the feminine Ann fascinates her friend when the latter takes the man's role; as an equal companion she repels. Ann's intellect is weak: she likes the pretty over the great, harmony over genius. Still, Mary makes the best of her and forms her into the object of benevolence. Indeed, at times she seems infatuated less with her friend than with her own image of herself loving her friend. Benevolence is most provoked when Ann is diagnosed with consumption. As she hastens to death, she becomes a purer object of devotion, for Mary can pour out her benevolent love unstintingly – all sexual possibilities are stanched and she reveals affection in the convulsive hug and tearful glance. In an early letter Wollstonecraft had hinted that she had 'leaned' on Fanny Blood; here Ann is the 'bruised reed' who leans on Mary, 'her only support'. As Ann dies, Mary tends her. The scene is so affecting that it attracts a sensitive spectator, Henry, the next object of love.

The story of Ann and Mary was an extraordinary betrayal of a woman who had for so long meant 'all the world' to Wollstonecraft. Perhaps the need for demolition sprang from the hurt at Fanny's defection in marrying and dying; perhaps it responded to a need in herself to move on and see her absorption in her friend as an encumbrance in her life, a stage she had to outgrow. Although Godwin conjectured that the book 'renewed her sorrows [for Fanny] in their original force', in some ways in its disloyalty it formed a farewell to the dream of female community and surrogate families. Wollstonecraft would continue to have a warm spot for the Bloods, but they would never figure in her plans for her own life.[2] And she would not again try to satisfy emotional needs with a woman. Indeed, she would never again have a very close woman friend. The book enacts the replacement of a female loved object by a male. That both die was a reflection of its author's mood rather than her rational expectations.

The man who takes the failed friend's place as she is dying is a curious object, invalid and slightly duplicitous. Although she pursues fancy over reason at times and is more intuitional than rational, Mary is a woman of intellect, the Advertisement declares, 'accustomed to think'. In the gendered society she cannot escape, this intellect threatens men and she appeals to those who do not see her as a sexualised and sexy being but rather as a clever child: men of a philosophical turn or 'past the meridian of life' or sick. Henry is such a man. And, since Mary is married, he cannot act as the usual storybook hero and rescue her romantically from danger or folly. He could promise a more equal relationship and the heroine need not become the conventional domestic wife.

Yet the pull of conventional romance is strong, 'I cannot argue against instincts,' declares the narrator and the hero's admiration for the heroine in her benevolent and sentimental postures comes close to romantic indulgence. To her effusions he responds, 'Dear enthusiastic creature . . . how you steal into my heart'.[3] Mary tries to make Henry into a quasi-paternal figure – she wished she had such a father, she exclaims – but the father has already appeared an ambiguous, unresolved presence. Henry is deeply attractive and Mary, in a sexless marriage, soon loves him as much as she loved Ann, displaying in the process the inconsequential speech and disordered emotions that marked her creator's Irish letters. Henry responds with caution and retreat until it is clear he too is fatally ill; then the pair embrace in a storm. As with Ann, physical closeness, burgeoning with debility, leads to death, for in the storm Henry catches a cold from which he dies; he declares, 'I could have wished, for thy sake, that we could have died together.' Mary is left longing but pure. She returns to her husband, feeling only nausea when he approaches her sexually.

Wollstonecraft was troubled by the sensuality of relationships, whether of pity or love, witness her response to the sensual Ogle. Yet she also feared retreat into solipsism. Severely intellectual and yet ecstatic in religious thoughts, the heroine of *Mary, A Fiction* finds her feelings 'do not accord with the notion of solitary happiness'. She searches for an object of love but none quite suits. She finds momentary completion in the sublime, but concludes that nothing earthly can fulfil her desire: 'Every thing material must change; happiness and this fluctuating principle is not compatible. Eternity, immateriality, and happiness, – where are ye? How shall I grasp the mighty and fleeting conceptions ye create?' The book ends in psychic tumult and religious yearning for an uncoupled Biblical heaven, while more mundanely it expresses yet again Wollstonecraft's overt rejection of marriage, together with the body and the sexual subordination it implies: '[Mary] was hastening to a world *where there is neither marrying* nor giving in marriage'. In the context of the novel, the other 'world' seems ultimate solitude.

The only two conventional fiction plots were the comic one of courtship and marriage and the tragic one of seduction and death. Neither was right, as previous writers on sensibility like Sterne had realised when they settled for fully formed, static heroes of sensibility and very little plot. Despite the conventional placing of her story in the upper ranks, Wollstonecraft had tried to create an untraditional work in which her heroine grew to need love and respect from a single sensitive person, while desiring learning and significance in the world. No marriage or love affair could answer these needs; no plot could show the development of mind *and* heart.

She did not expose the external world that thwarted desire but stayed inside the single tortured feminine sensibility, too often collapsed into her own and declared beyond 'discussion'. The depiction of this sensibility portrayed in an unconsummated marriage and a relationship with the ailing Henry revealed her growing obsession with her own sexuality: the passionate love, easily controlled in *Thoughts*, became unruly in fiction. If Wollstonecraft had loved someone in the Kingsborough months, he had stirred her profoundly.

The fictional Mary was presented as sentimentally taciturn. In this she differed from her creator. By now there were open hostilities between her and the woman she had caricatured as an inadequate dog-petting aristocratic. Mrs FitzGerald had not accompanied the family to Bristol Hot Wells and they missed the tempering influence. Wollstonecraft always thought she restrained the hauteur of her stepdaughter, while no doubt she calmed the overwrought governess. Lady Kingsborough was still introducing her into company but with an arch tone. Wollstonecraft blushed with irritation at slights she could not combat. Lady Kingsborough, who must earlier have noticed the reddening of her cheeks when her Lord approached, probably also noted this genteel reflex, rather above a governess's station. She was sick of being despised by a social inferior. The affair with Ogle still rankled.

She was further irritated by the pull exerted over her daughters, especially her eldest, Margaret, whose affection had been entirely alienated. She knew the girls feared her; this was common in the aristocracy where mothers did not see much of their children, and she accepted that they would run to a hired woman for protection. It was fitting for a governess to become fond of her charges and they of her. But things had become indecorous. Wollstonecraft was convinced that young people should frankly if respectfully judge their parents: Margaret had seen 'her m[o]ther's faults – and sometimes ridicule[d] them'. This was intolerable: rupture was inevitable.

The Kingsboroughs and their entourage had moved to London, intending the Continental tour. Before this, Wollstonecraft would have her vacation. Feeling the approaching loss, Margaret grew distressed; her mother disapproved the unseemly display and violent quarrels between employer and governess ensued. Later, Margaret defended Wollstonecraft, declaring that, without her, she would have become 'a most ferocious animal'. Her mother considered her one already. As for the governess, she had restrained herself too long, and, without Mrs FitzGerald's calming presence, no doubt told some home truths. She was dismissed.

Curiously, she was surprised. She had been fending off Lady Kingsborough so long she must have expected her patience to be elastic despite her adverse judgements. She was amazed she had not been let go months before and amazed she was now dismissed: 'It disconcerted me at first; but I will not describe *what* I suffered – though I long expected something of the kind would happen.'

Although the catalyst was Margaret's behaviour, dismissal also resulted from general exasperation in her beautiful, spoilt but often well-meaning patron, who had once made Wollstonecraft think she was a 'GREAT favourite'. As Charlotte Brontë would indelibly show in *Jane Eyre*, the role of the governess was ill-suited to a woman who regarded herself as morally superior to her employer. Wollstonecraft left with her wages but without the mysterious loan. She had been in the Kingsborough household for only a year but, some time later, when both the first and third daughters fell from respectability, there were mutterings about the influence of the extraordinary governess on impressionable girls. Indeed, the adult and republican Margaret flaunted the brief association and 'glorie[d] in having had so clever an Instructress, who had freed her mind from all superstitions.'4

Twenty-eight, without home, money or employment, tactless, self-absorbed, depressive and energetic, Wollstonecraft had to find a way of earning a living outside governessing and teaching. She would need to stop being the disempowered sentimental lady who, she was starting to realise now she had completed her novel, had almost no purpose except to be chosen by a man. Since this was eluding her, she would aim to value independence; she would try no longer to see it as the horror described in *Thoughts*.

In pursuit of independence she went straight to St Paul's Churchyard, centre of the London book trade. There booksellers lived in stately houses next to packed warehouses or camped above their shops. Literary life had centred here since the seventeenth century, attracting leisured consuming gentlemen, politicians, authors and would-be authors. Here she sought out Joseph Johnson.

The son of a Baptist landowner and tradesman from Everton near Liverpool, Johnson was a convert to Unitarianism, a confirmed bachelor, possibly latently homosexual, possibly not – it is difficult to judge in an age so appalled at sodomy: he was not sexually interested in women, but was certainly a good friend to many. At forty-nine, he was a 'squat little' asthmatic man with large dark eyes and an unpretentious manner.[5] He had built up a flourishing business, printing, publishing and selling serious, usually liberally tending books, on religion, medicine, law and politics, as well as some fiction and poetry. Now he ran his business with the help of an adopted nephew, Roland Hunter.

He was reputed to be cautious and mean, but this reputation was not borne out by his dealings with Wollstonecraft and his occasional publication of unknown women – the year before, he issued the poems of two 'lisping Sapphos' of seventeen and fourteen. When she first met him, Wollstonecraft found him formal and stiff, but soon saw that outward reserve hid a tender concern for those he valued. He was immeasurably helpful: 'I informed Mr Johnson of my situation: he insisted on my coming to his house, and contrived to detain me there a long time – you can scarcely conceive how warmly, and delicately he has interested himself in my fate.' She could even talk to him about her feelings of responsibility for her sisters. In short he saved her 'from despair, and vexations I shrink back from – and feared to encounter'. There *were* alternatives to governessing, companioning and teaching for a woman who could write and talk, he agreed; they were unconventional and risky, and most successful female writers remained amateur or had powerful patrons, like the popular novelist Frances Burney. Wollstonecraft had no problem with risks and determined to try for a literary living in London: of all that Johnson said she remembered most his assurance that, if she exerted her 'talents in writing', she could support herself 'in a comfortable way'. They resolved to work together; she could stay with him for a few weeks, then Johnson would find her a house.

Before embarking on her new life, she visited her sisters. First she went to Henley, where Everina was at Miss Rowden's school, as miserable as with Ned and despised as a mere teacher by inferiors.[6] She was twenty-two, tall, sturdier and not quite as pretty as Eliza; sometimes she showed her older sister's vivacity. Mary pitied her, especially as Everina envied her life in Ireland. She tried to persuade her that being despised in Henley was no worse than being lonely in a glittering masquerade.

Although she found Everina easier to deal with than Eliza, Mary kept from her the secret of her dismissal and London plans: she was too leaky a vessel. So she felt awkward when she heard Everina considering a renewed proposal from George Blood: that they all join with him in founding a school in Dublin. George must have urged this plan during his stay in London and, as

Everina grew more lonely and sad in Henley, it grew in attraction. Although it had had its difficulties, she now remembered the time together with her sisters as remarkably pleasant; almost anything would be better than life with Ned or with the 'vulgar' in Henley. Mary had clearer memories of the Green with its jealousies and petty aggravations. *She* would never return to Ireland, and Eliza and Everina lacked the qualities to run a school alone. Besides, Everina did not want to encourage George's romantic hopes, on which much of his enthusiasm was founded.

So, after discussion, Mary convinced her sister of the foolishness of the Dublin plan. She herself wrote the deflating letter to George, honestly declaring that her sisters were unsuited to business without her management: 'Eliza wants activity; and Everina's vivacity would by the injudicious, be termed giddiness; – her youth too would furnish another pretext for doubting her abilities; and besides they could not pretend to teach French, and without a knowledge of that language it is vain to attempt any thing in the school line.' Forgetting how much she had once boasted of them, she downgraded her Irish connections: 'I am not so inexperienced as to imagine [they] would be of much use ... vague professions of friendship are not to be relied on, especially when made to an inferior, in point of rank[;] self-interest, or vanity, is the cement of worldly friendship; two Girls without fortune, or a consequential name, could not expect to be supported much because related to one who is, perhaps, forgotten.' She may have remembered the gossip she had aroused: 'Dublin too has not the advantages which result from residing in London; every one's conduct is canvassed, and the least deviation from a ridiculous rule of propriety (which might arise from conscious rectitude) would endanger their precarious subsistence.' Everina had fallen foul of their brother's standards in London if rumour were credited.

George was disappointed to have his 'fabric' knocked down, especially as Mary and Everina could not 'raise a better'. Everina did not even trouble to write. Mary had said that her sister would tell him about her life and 'describe the companion, the only companion, she has to converse with after the labors of the school have rendered a little relaxation necessary'. But, when he came to the bottom of the paper, he found only a short postscript from Everina apologising for silence and moaning at being 'disagreeably situated'; she had not smiled in Henley until Mary came, she said. George was unimpressed by the excuse and did not reply at once.

Seeing Everina's misery and feeling her own guilty secret, Mary applied to Gabell, presenting her sister rather like a daughter: 'she has fine spirits, I grieve to see them broken so soon; nor do I desire to pour premature knowledge into her mind – if it was *possible* for me to persuade her that the pleasures she sighs for would prove fallacious when attained.' She hoped Gabell could find her something genteel: 'She has a small annuity, and I wish to place her in a Gentlemans family 'till fortune smiles on me – or she gains experience.' Gabell answered speedily but, no more than Mary, could he think quite what to do with the genteel and spirited Everina.

However much they provoked her anxiety, her sisters were becoming Mary's past. She would work for them – 'I would fain be their mother and protector,' she wrote – but not keep them. She remained fond of George too, but would not again share her inner thoughts with him. She had left him so far behind intellectually that she could now warn him not to read above his ability. The poor man had been trying to impress the sisters; Mary was unmoved: 'I had rather you would not read Dr Price's sermons,' she informed him, 'as they would lead you into controversial disputes, and your limited range of books would not afford you a clue.' George might look into Price's other works, more suited to his capacities since 'less entangled with controversial points'. George was capable in matters of feeling, less so of intellect: he could understand what came 'warm from the heart', but 'the sermons require more profound thinking, [they] are not calculated to improve the generality.' George must have sighed to see himself included in the 'generality'. To ensure that he did not again read beyond his capacities, she sent him suitable books.

Wollstonecraft's own future lay with intelligent men. To them she continued creating herself as melancholy lady, but her long depression was lifting with anticipation, and she was eager also to be seen as an independent bluestocking. To Johnson she wrote:

Since I saw you, I have, literally speaking, enjoyed solitude. My sister could not accompany me in my rambles; I therefore wandered alone, by the side of the Thames, and in the neighbouring beautiful fields and pleasure grounds: the prospects were of such a placid kind, I caught tranquillity while I surveyed them – my mind was still, though active. Were I to give you an account how I have spent my time, you would smile. – I found an old French bible here, and amused myself with comparing it with our English translation; then I would listen to the falling leaves, or observe the various tints the autumn gave to them – At other times, the singing of a robin, or the noise of a water-mill, engaged my attention – partial attention – for I was, at the same time perhaps discussing some knotty point, or straying from this tiny world to new systems. After these excursions, I returned to the family meals, told the children stories (they think me vastly agreeable), and my sister was amused – Well, will you allow me to call this way of passing my days pleasant?

Such self-conscious style must have amused Johnson. He knew she could write sentimental effusions as well as tart paragraphs of common sense. Now she was seeking a personal style that had the potential to be less self-indulgent. She had some way to go, but her earnestness was heartening.

More plainly she wrote of her exciting future outside the normal feminine sphere:

> Have you yet heard of an habitation for me? I often think of my new plan of life ... Your sex generally laugh at female determinations; but let me tell you, I never yet resolved to do, any thing of consequence, that I did not adhere resolutely to it, till I had accomplished my purpose, improbable as it might have appeared to a more timid mind. In the course of near nine-and-twenty years, I have gathered some experience; and felt many *severe* disappointments – and what is the amount? I long for a little peace and *independence*! Every obligation we receive from our fellow-creatures is a new shackle, takes from our native freedom, and debases the mind, makes us mere earthworms – I am not fond of grovelling!

A week later she returned to London, then set off on the public coach for Market Harborough. She wrote up her journey for Johnson, again eager to suggest her writerly sensibility: her fellow passengers were repulsive tradesmen and 'the sable curtain concealed the beauties of nature' – happily since she was not yet adept at nature descriptions. The response of one of the scorned tradesmen must have been encouraging to Johnson: he judged her 'a useful partner in a good *firm*'.

Eliza had left her school and was now companion to a Mrs Tew. Mary, who vividly remembered her own time in Bath, imagined this could not be an improvement. She had dreaded seeing her sister; Eliza grumbled as much as herself and, being so dependent, could be trusted even less than Everina with her plans. She would desperately want Mary to take her to London; it was the last thing her sister intended. She could, she hoped, give Eliza a holiday, although at the moment she did not see how to pay for it.

Desiring to hide her future also from Mrs Burgh, she avoided calling, instead sending £20, probably the half-wages from her dismissal. Her creditors would rightly expect her to get another governessing position. If she saw them and admitted she was now poor and facing a hazardous future, she would both feel guilty and receive a barrage of unwanted advice. She was determined on her course, and did not want to argue her case.

# Part II

# 12

*'I am ... going to be the first of a new genus'*

Johnson found Wollstonecraft a pokey little house south of the river in a fairly new three-storeyed terrace, 49 George Street. He acquired a relative from the country as her servant and initially dealt with tradesmen, a duty she hated. She moved in at the end of September with just enough furniture to manage. She had no bed for guests and did not immediately want one. For the first time in her life she was living without immediate constraint and relished it: she could be robustly severe without the pressures for adornment exerted by the frivolous Kingsboroughs.

Not far from Blackfriars Bridge, her new home was within walking distance of Johnson's St Paul's shop across the Thames. After Ireland, even Dublin, she was glad to be back in a big city. She liked the mixture of anonymity and good company, the choice of isolation or sociability London allowed. The surrounding streets were muddy and thronged; she did not have her own carriage and often had to walk rather than take a hackney coach, but she did not grumble about being cramped or jostled or getting her petticoats dirty. London was home: if she belonged anywhere emotionally and physically, it was here. She cast no longing glances back at her fashionable parlour in the Kingston townhouse or the Palladian grandeur of Mitchelstown. When she wanted society she could go to Johnson's and meet 'the kind of company I find most pleasure in': his variety of 'standing dishes'. But she was not yet on the level of these authors and feared being patronised – she had had her fill of unequal relationships. Besides, she had work to do and felt her age: 'the seed-time' was passing. 'I see the necessity of labouring now – and of that necessity I do not complain,' she wrote. Godwin believed that the first three years with Joseph Johnson were 'the most active period of her life'.

For many weeks after moving, Mary delayed writing to her family, worrying that they would try to persuade her against her attempt or mock her presumption. At last, in early November, she told Everina that, in Johnson's words, she was trying 'to live by literary exertions and be independent': 'I *have* left Lord K's.'¹ The Kingsboroughs were still in England, having abandoned the Continental trip, and were planning to return the following week to Mitchelstown. When they left without her, the secret of her dismissal would be out. Mrs Burgh would hear of it through the Priors. Still she hoped to keep the secret of her new life from her old friend and from her father and Ned. So, as prelude to telling Everina more, she cautioned, 'Before I go on will you pause – and if after deliberating you will promise not to mention to any one what you know of my designs (*though you may think my requesting you to conceal them unreasonable*) I will trust to your honor – and proceed.' As usual she gave her sister few options.

She would be an author and a special one: 'I am then going to be the first of a new genus,' she boasted. 'Providence has been very kind to me – and when I *reflect* on past mercies with respect to the future I am not without hope – And freedom *even* uncertain freedom – is dear ... This project has long floated in my mind. You know I am not born to tread in the beaten track – the peculiar bent of my nature pushes me on.' Her crowing to Everina, playing precisely the role she herself had found wanting, was a touch tactless, but Mary needed hyperbole, being either at the apex or the nadir of existence much of the time.

Her move to London was extraordinary for her and Johnson. Her secrecy about her living arrangements argues her awareness of the strangeness of a respectable unmarried woman being protected by an unmarried man, as well as the novelty of her role. She was not actually 'the first of a new genus', but she would be one of a small band of independent literary women making a living in the market. Once the overflow of her unsatisfactory life, writing would become a source of income and significance.

Usually dilatory, Everina wrote back at once, desperate for details. So, before addressing Eliza, Mary again wrote to Everina admitting, 'All this will appear to you like a dream'. She still wanted secrecy: 'If you pay any visits you will comply with my whim, and not mention my place of abode or mode of life.' Realising how far she had mentally moved from her sisters, she protested her continuing care – and gloom: 'I only live to be useful – benevolence must fill every void in my heart.' If her literary plan succeeded, her 'dear Girls' could turn to her in sickness and have a refuge for a few months each year. (Subsequently this became 'two months' as Everina must have noted.) Mary would try hard to get 'poor uncomfortable' Eliza a situation near London, so that the three sisters would be close: 'you and Eliza are the only part of the family I am interested about – I wish to be a mother to you both.' But she still had no spare bed.

Keeping her sisters at a distance, she also fended off her favourite brother, Charles, who was no doubt disliking life at Ned's as much as Everina had done. Only 'if he behaves properly' would she meet him – and then not at her house but on the neutral ground of Johnson's shop. Charles was talkative and she did not want her affairs discussed by her brother's family.

She had given Johnson the manuscript of *Mary, A Fiction* and begun another novel 'The Cave of Fancy', partly again in yearning autobiographical mode, with a fantasised rescue of a young girl by a fatherly sage who teaches her the recognition and value of true sensibility. Drawing on Dr Johnson's melancholy philosophical tale *Rasselas*, it provided through this sage a cautionary tale of sensibility in passionate women, thereby explicitly discussing an erotic longing while allowing its rhapsodical imaginary nature. The tale suggested a movement in Wollstonecraft's conception of sensibility: less compensatory and quasi-divine than in *Mary, A Fiction*, more a matter of 'finely fashioned nerves' and vibrations causing violent mood swings – 'exquisite pain and pleasure'. The heroine of the inset tale seems to her husband to be superior in sensibility while actually being distressed by a lost, improper love. Like Mary she is predominantly approved but is more clearly chastised for her over-indulgence in sensibility.

Perhaps Wollstonecraft stopped writing 'The Cave of Fancy' because she was sick of worrying over this cultural problem which seemed so personal: what was sensibility and how could it be channelled away from pain and illicit desire? More and more she was concluding that in women it was not often combined with reason but developed as its expense and that it was worryingly close to a death-wish. Or perhaps Johnson persuaded her to turn to a genre more suited to her talents.

There was a growing market for children's fiction; indeed a distinct literature was coming into being, especially in Dissenting circles, and his neighbour John Newbery had made a good living from it. Formerly children learnt to read through simplified Bible stories, chapbooks and fairy tales, but now serious parents wanted books delivering their values of probity, benevolence and thrift in more realistic settings. The Dissenting poet and educationist Anna Laetitia Barbauld could be a model; possibly for this reason Johnson introduced them. Wollstonecraft had no need of models however. Though deeply serious and rather shy in society, Barbauld was mocked for perpetually grinning; perhaps this repelled the gloomy Wollstonecraft. Besides, although they shared a liberal politics and admired the Dissenting traditions of education, Barbauld, a clergyman's wife, did not disapprove trivial femininity as Wollstonecraft did, and she saw no reason to make common cause with other would-be literary females. 'There is no bond of union among literary women, any more than among literary men,' she later wrote.[2] She had refused an offer from the bluestocking patron, Elizabeth Montagu, to become the principal of a female academy, declaring that she disapproved of intellectual women; it was enough for them to be 'good wives or agreeable companions', she said. By the age of fifteen, girls were so influenced by their feelings that they could learn little.

Wollstonecraft preferred Sarah Trimmer, who, inspired by Barbauld, had just published a popular book of animal tales. In *Fabulous Stories*, robins conversed pleasantly and improved and amused the child; a female authority-figure Mrs Benson interpreted the world for her charges, teaching them to respond critically. Weighed down with her own large brood, Trimmer did not move in London literary circles or threaten Wollstonecraft's uniqueness. The women enjoyed a day together.

Johnson pointed at Trimmer's success as well as Madame de Genlis's with her *Adelaide and Theodore*, which Wollstonecraft had read in Mitchelstown. Rousseau had had a male instructor for Émile but in Genlis and Trimmer a powerful mother or governess guided children to maturity through incidents and anecdotes.[3] She could do something similar Johnson urged and she knew she could. As with *Thoughts*, she made the new genre her own by referring to her experience.

*Original Stories* – its full reforming title added *from Real Life; with Conversations, Calculated to Regulate the Affections, and Form the Mind to Truth and Goodness* – is a sort of governess fantasy, in which children are rescued from sophisticated aristocrats by a discerning surrogate, Mrs Mason, as the Kingsborough daughters were rescued by Mary Wollstonecraft.[4] Parenthood (and to some extent auto-didacticism without guidance) had failed the heroine of *Mary, A Fiction* as they failed the girls in *Thoughts*: surrogate motherhood is a medicine for the disease of biological parents, the only route to moral regeneration.[5] The financial and emotional independence forced on unfortunate women in *Thoughts* is embraced, the change happily reflecting Wollstonecraft's changed circumstances; austerity fits girls for the real world of struggle and possible loneliness, for rational and moral autonomy. Their comfort is religion; as their creator had in the letter to Gabell, they must accept that suffering is sent by God to teach fortitude.

The book was more overtly and intellectually pious than any other of Wollstonecraft's published works, and less rhapsodically religious than *Mary, A Fiction*, in this respect reflecting her attitudes in Newington Green rather than her months in Ireland. Although it favoured Locke's notion of the newborn mind as a blank sheet over the idea of original sin, it gave a powerful impression of juvenile corruption similar to the old Christian one, but owing to society not God. The religion that emerges so strongly is a human-centred one, in which ants and bees exemplify thrift and forethought, tulips superficial beauty, and breakfasting pigs human gluttony. Storms dissipate noxious vapors, and suffering prepares people for the next world.

The fantasy of the book mainly inheres in Mrs Mason, illustrated for a later edition by the poet and engraver William Blake as a willowy version of Mary Wollstonecraft – although the independent fictional character has more in common with Mrs Burgh than her younger friend.[6] Rousseau's Émile had a ubiquitous tutor, somewhat like Mrs Mason in that he gave his charge the illusion of freedom, the sense that he was learning from experience when he in fact faced a simulacrum, but Émile was not to know how much he was watched and controlled; Mrs Mason is open in her manoeuvring and her morals.

Unlike an ordinary governess, she does not act for money but out of high-minded compassion, so avoiding the ambiguous status of the governess against which Wollstonecraft so repined. She is a landowner, with income allowing extensive benevolence. In her recent *Oeconomy of Charity*, Sarah Trimmer had stressed that middle- and upper-class women had to educate and benefit the lower class wherever they could, from contributing for schools to buying from struggling shopkeepers. Mrs Mason knows that charity is a virtue and virtue delivers the only true pleasure and self-esteem. The objects of her compassion are gratifyingly thankful, like honest one-eyed Jack, the heroic sailor who praises God for leaving him one eye.

Wollstonecraft had no truck with the coming idea that children had separate wisdom of their own, and the gap between her benevolent knowing adult and ignorant children remains until the latter mature into good adult ways and become 'candidates' for friendship. Mrs Mason's goal is to make her pupils 'fit for the society of angels' and herself – poor women call her their 'angel'. The girls wilt at any sign of displeasure and 'all their consequence seemed to rise from her approbation', hence the only punishment is withdrawal of affection. It appears a pedagogic dream of a woman who has abandoned teaching for ever, although Godwin insisted that Wollstonecraft believed she had had this effect on children.[7] As for the powerful mentor, the melancholy Mrs Mason herself, she was strengthened by patience and a dignified acceptance of her lot in life, virtues quite beyond any of the Wollstonecraft sisters.

Although heavy with morality, some of the stories in the book are so grim they require an afterlife to become palatable. Crazy Robin, for example, was an industrious young man who had too large a family, lost children and money, and was imprisoned for debt. His wife dies after working too soon after labour and his other children follow, until only two remain. They and the dog come to him in prison, which they leave to beg by day. They fall prey to jail fever and die; Robin goes mad, escapes and lives with his dog in a cave, eating berries and receiving scraps from Mrs Mason. Then the dog barks at a rich rider and is shot; Robin dies of grief.

The implied message is a social one, that the rich should cease tyrannising over the poor, but this is not what Mrs Mason is preaching; when the children reasonably exclaim that nothing could be so cruel, she declares it could and starts on a worse story of a Bastille prisoner who befriends a spider, only to see it crushed by spiteful authority. The closest Mrs Mason comes to blaming society is when the girls learn that the poor are impoverished and degraded by the rich delaying to pay their debts, and that foreign imports destroy local manufacturing. Here she argues beyond her usual charitable message, insisting that justice is superior to compassion as a foundation of virtue, but she does not elaborate. Throughout *Original Stories*, the tie between higher and lower remains charity, and story after story which cries out for resolution in social reform is answered by personal benevolence.

Wollstonecraft provided a belligerent preface, drawing attention to her 'simplicity of style', her hatred of ornament and artifice in life and literature. She would not flatter parents with 'unmeaning compliments' since she had written her stories because of their corruption:

> These conversations and tales are accommodated to the present state of society; which obliges the author to attempt to cure those faults by reason, which ought never to have taken root in the infant mind. Good habits, imperceptibly fixed, are preferable to the precepts of reason; but, as this task requires more judgment than generally falls to the lot of parents, substitutes must be sought for, and medicines given, when regimen would have answered the purpose much better ... to wish that parents would, themselves, mould the ductile passions, is a chimerical wish, for the present generation have their own passions to combat with, and fastidious pleasures to pursue, neglecting those pointed out by nature: we must therefore pour premature knowledge into the succeeding one; and, teaching virtue, explain the nature of vice.
>
> Cruel necessity.

She hoped Lady Kingsborough would read her words.

Johnson wanted this irritable address muted, but Wollstonecraft refused, tartly remarking, 'If parents attended to their children, I would not have written the stories.' Most families were dysfunctional and education was remedial. The few sensible parents would not be hurt and the foolish were 'too vain to mind what is said in a book intended for children'. In any case she was averse to revising on other people's advice. She always had a sense of the value of her writings and, now that she was a professional author, this sense was burgeoning. She liked her robust preface: 'I hate the usual smooth way of exhibiting proud humility.' In the eighteenth century the discourse about individual ownership of property which Locke had encouraged had been fused with the notion of value in original composition to make authors claim property in their writings and sentiments. Wollstonecraft was very much aware that, though she might sell her copyright to Johnson, she was the ultimate owner of her words. Her stubbornness did no harm. The book proved popular; Johnson brought out three more editions during the 1790s, and French, German and Danish translations appeared in the same decade. Wollstonecraft had shown she could do a professional job to order.

At Christmas Johnson encouraged her to bring her sisters to London, and, though she feared the interruption in her busy schedule, she invited them. They came with alacrity. Indeed Everina burnt her boats by giving in notice at Henley. In London they met some of their sister's friends and saw Anne Cristall, whom Everina especially liked. Since she lived out at Blackheath, possibly they had met her originally through the Bloods when both families were south of the river. Like Everina she was having to teach, which she disliked. Both must have envied Mary's independent living.

Neither Eliza nor Everina was happy. Mary could do nothing for Eliza immediately, though no doubt being urged. Perhaps she even kept her house minimal to avoid any suggestion of her sister's moving in. But something had to be found for Everina or she would be on Mary's hands. What she needed was proficiency in French. Then – and only then – she might be fitted for a decent governess position such as Jane Arden had obtained at her age. The best place to learn French quickly was France and Mary set about finding a way to get Everina there. Since she had sent her Kingsborough wages to Mrs Burgh, she had to borrow from Johnson; she would pay him back when her books were published, she reasoned.

Towards the end of January Eliza trailed miserably back to Market Harborough, while the luckier Everina remained at George Street before being dispatched to Paris to lodge with 'Mademoiselle Henry, Rue de Tournon, Faubourg St Germaine' to learn French. She was to stay for about six months at the cost to her sister of around fifteen guineas.[8] She left in mid-February and soon Mary received long letters 'full of accounts, of disasters and difficulties'. She was relieved: a contented Everina would be unnatural; besides, happiness was not good for people, it made them lazy.

The Christmas vacation together with her sisters had shown Mary once more the unsuitability of their presence in her new life. As her first year progressed, she grew surer: 'I have determined on one thing, *never* to have my Sisters to live with me, my solitary manner of living would not suit them, nor *could* I pursue my studies if forced to conform.' Holidays would be enough.

She was not quite family-less. Despite determining to keep him at arm's length, she had met Charles, found him charming, with youthful high spirits and dancing eyes, and had entered into rivalry with Ned over his control. She regaled Charles with lectures on firm principles; presumably he thought a preachy sister better than an irritated brother for he came more and more to rely on Mary.

There was, too, another problematic Blood at hand, sunk even below the usual family standard. Mrs Burgh had written to say that the Islington parish officers had been enquiring for Mr Blood. They wanted to pass on his daughter Caroline, picked up off the streets 'in a dreadful situation'. She was now in the Islington workhouse, where she could remain only if someone paid half a crown a week. Mrs Burgh was not volunteering. Wollstonecraft could not bear to think of the poor girl's being thrown back on the streets but she also refused the charge; nor would she visit Caroline or let her know where she lived, since the wretched girl would stick on to her limpet-like. It was Mr Blood's responsibility but she was not hopeful. She had heard that the good effects of Fanny's death had diminished and he was again displaying his 'selfish sensuality'. Her indignation rose. After all she had done, he cared only for himself and his ease. She had a mind to dispatch Caroline to him forthwith; yet, she could not augment Mrs Blood's vexation – she suffered enough with such a husband. 'What is to be done my dear boy?' she wailed to George, who held his father in equal contempt.

She answered her own question. There would be no steady flow of money from Mr Blood but he could send a lump sum of £10 now. This was below the sum she had given for him to go to Ireland when she could ill afford it. He should deposit it with Mrs Burgh, whose shortcomings were forgotten in the need for help. Mrs Burgh would organise Caroline's keep. But first she herself would buy the poor girl clothes and set up the boarding arrangement in the workhouse; this she was generously intending before anything came from Ireland. If the £10 were unforthcoming, she would send Caroline to Dublin, however dismal home life would become. The threat roused Mr Blood and he sent £10.

Charles and Caroline were not the burdens Eliza, Everina and George had been. Later in the year Mrs Burgh died; the event was unmarked in Mary's letters. Her death may have wiped out the unpaid portion of her debt; if so, for a brief time Mary was freed from financial anxiety to think about other aspects of existence.

She still trusted in the afterlife and was thus much comforted in her continued mourning for Fanny by a sermon she went to hear from her old friend from the Green, John Hewlett. It concerned 'the recognition of our friends in a future state' and was delivered especially for her. Hewlett looked sickly, she thought; she ascribed it to 'domestic vexations'. She knew he had made the wrong choice of marriage partner.

She read David Hume, but more as an historian than as a philosopher, so was untroubled by his anxiety over subjectivity, whether the self was the same from one day to the next and whether personality really existed. She had a sense of an immutable self, the possession of ultimately authentic identity, whatever the means by which this identity might be influenced. Yet she still needed to explain her endemic misery: she had vacillated between a notion of her sufferings as special and God-given and of her 'nerves' as peculiarly sensitive. Now the latter notion was shifting.

There had always been a moralistic component in nerve theory. In *The English Malady* (1733) George Cheyne confined nervous disorders to 'the Wealthy, the Voluptuous and the Lazy', seeing them as a by-product of the nation's increasing luxuries and leisure. Dr Johnson reinforced this when, responding to the death of Lady Tavistock from grief at her husband's death, he remarked, 'She was rich and wanted employment . . . so she cried till she lost all power of restraining her tears: other women are forced to outlive their husbands.' Had they put Lady Tavistock 'into a small chandler's shop, and given her a nurse-child to tend, her life would have been saved,' he continued. 'The poor and busy have no leisure for sentimental sorrow.'[9] The anecdote impressed Wollstonecraft, who began to think that misery might be part habit, part physically produced.

In 1788 Joseph Johnson published *Elements of Medicine*, an English translation from the controversial and eccentric John Brown. It was made because of the 'decaying state of the knowledge of the Latin language'; so its theories were open to women.[10] Wollstonecraft, always fascinated with medical theories, could not have avoided a work which was the talk of the town; in *Thoughts* she recommends medicine to girls and the heroine of *Mary, A Fiction* studies physic.[11] Brown, an English but Scottish-educated doctor, was a pupil, then enemy, of William Cullen, famous for his theory that all disease was a modification of nerves. The aim of Brown's 'science of life', which its author immodestly insisted would supersede volumes of diagnostics, was to give people an holistic sense of the body and mind, not to allow the mind *or* the body to define health.[12]

A lapsed theologian who left religion to its 'proper guardians', Brown, unlike the now old-fashioned John Armstrong, declared that everything could be reduced to the interaction of exciting powers with the body's excitability; there was no need to posit a soul. The powers could be external agents like heat, diet and air or internal like thinking and emoting, but, whichever they were, their effect remained the same in kind, and the 'sedative affections' were simply a lesser degree of the exciting ones. Passion could be discussed in the same way as diet. Moderate stimulus produced health; too much exhausted excitability. Whatever part was over- or under-excited would affect the whole body in indirect debility.

For her own predicament Wollstonecraft could have read the passages on 'hypochondriasis', a disease of debility – more associated with women than men, but either sex could suffer.[13] Its symptoms were aching belly, anxiety, a sense of being iller than one was, obsession of mind, and a fixation on one pursuit. Such symptoms were not a sign of ladylike superiority; to recover the sufferer needed stimulation and agreeable company rather than rest.

Like many in Johnson's coterie, Wollstonecraft was probably impressed with Brown's work. While holding to pain as divinely ordained, she was increasingly attracted to rationalist rather than sentimental explanations of human ills and often let her subjectivity include the whole of her body. She could now ascribe her ailments to the unnatural sedentary life of middle-class ladies, not simply to sensitive 'nerves'. In some circles it was not acceptable to describe bodily parts. In 1782 the maid dressing Mrs Thrale's hair 'burst out o' laughing at the Idea of a Lady saying her stomach ach'd', but Wollstonecraft was uninhibited in her investigation of mind and body, and unself-consciously named veins and blood. In the new formulation, the reason for aches and pains lay in the head *and* the body.[14] She was intrigued by the interaction:

I have lately been a little too studious, and the consequence is the return of some of my old nervous complaints. I will try to shake them off as the spring advances – I do not take sufficient exercise I know, I am eager to catch at any excuse for staying at home, and I blame myself, without correcting the fault. Even now I am suffering; a nervous head-ache torments me, and I am ready to throw down my pen – almost unable to direct it – my thoughts are frozen – I cannot thaw them – or force them to flow glibly from my pen – I shall write nothing but tautology – well – well – Nature will sometimes prevail, 'spite of reason, and the thick blood lagging in the veins, give melancholy power to harass the mind; or produce a listlessness which destroys every active purpose of the soul. – I am not however going to complain; for I have abundant reason to be thankful to Providence for the many comforts I at present enjoy, and the evils I have escaped.

It was a rare moment of religious and medical acceptance. Fearing complacency, however, Wollstonecraft declared in her old pious language that the world was a 'good one, when considered as a road – but no abiding place for those that feel'.

# 13

*'I succeed beyond my most sanguine hopes'*

Johnson needed a regular supply of translated books and Wollstonecraft was soon at work, translating from languages she knew even less than French. It suited her plan of self-improvement.

She had setbacks. Sometimes the task proved too hard. Italian handwriting was a 'stumbling-block' and she returned the commission, declaring, 'I cannot bear to do anything I cannot do well.' Occasionally she embarked on a project begun by another translator, as with the pastor, Johann Kaspar Lavater's *Essays on Physiognomy*. Too slow, she was overtaken by Johnson's friend, Thomas Holcroft. She bore no grudge and, when an unofficial abridgement appeared, she attacked it as 'surrepticious' and defrauding.[1] Although she gained nothing financially, she profited from a study of Lavater's physiognomy, a rudimentary theory of phrenology systematically relating character to the bone formations of the face. It accelerated her sense of the mind and body's interdependence and helped further destabilise her notion of sensibility as simply superior emotional fineness.

With less competition she abridged and 'almost rewrote' an English version by John Hall of the Dutch Maria de Cambon's *Young Grandison*, didactic letters using some of the characters in Richardson's last novel, *Sir Charles Grandison*. Like *Original Stories*, this fictional conduct-book sought to exercise children's minds and teach the value of moral achievement over rank and riches; virtue was enjoined on boys and girls, although the latter had to pursue it in a domestic setting. As in her original writings, Wollstonecraft could not resist inserting herself and family: a nasty boy is called Edward, a nice one, Charles.

She was not fluent in French but at least she now had the rudiments and so could tackle a more ambitious translating project: *Of the Importance of Religious Opinions* by the French politician, Jacques Necker, who, out of office, was eager to promote piety as consolation for reversals. She would undertake the work if she found its author's life accorded with his sentiments, she said primly.

For this project Everina in Paris was useful: she could learn 'the character of the man in domestic life and public estimation &c and the Opinion the

French have of his literary abilities'. Everina satisfied her queries and she was soon hard at work on Necker's French, pleased with her progress, and making 'free with the author' when he seemed obscure or bombastic. She liked his emphasis on constant self-improvement and his praise of reason as a divine gift in agreement with religion. Later, when she disapproved Necker's political activities before the Revolution, she came to despise his book, describing it as 'various metaphysical shreds of arguments' in a style as 'inflated and confused as the thoughts were far-fetched and unconnected', but for now she was impressed with it and herself.[2] So much so that she later favourably reviewed her own translation.

Her last 'translation' came out serially – possibly it took a long time or bored her. It returned her to the juvenile market: Christian Salzmann's *Elements of Morality, for the Use of Children; with an Introductory Address to Parents*. It was an adaptation more than a translation for she knew little German and had begun it as an exercise to help her learn the language – she told Johnson to send her a grammar. She was glad to find it 'a very rational book'; it agreed with her view, wavering but still held on balance, that pain, whatever its physical cause, was in God's plan and led to good character. She approved, too, its opinion that happiness was not the measure of virtue and its aim to 'insinuate a taste for domestic pleasures into the hearts of both parents and children'. She kept the moral stories Salzmann had written and added one herself to persuade children to consider Indians their brothers, a more relevant tale for British than German youth. She toned down the sentimental effusions and the ingratiating remarks about the upper orders.

Again she let her own concerns emerge – and her family: the nice boy is Charles and the sensitive girl, Mary. As an adult, Wollstonecraft hated the fuss and bondage of female dress; it was worse for a child and she graphically described little Mary struggling within a pair of stiff stays constructed of bones so tight she could hardly breathe. Over it she had a severely laced silk slip and over that a long gauze dress 'so stuck out with trimmings and artificial flowers that she could scarcely move'.[3] For more than an hour the child was tormented by her hair being pulled and frizzed: her naturally flowing locks were twisted hard into papers and then pinched with hot irons. Naturally she could not sleep and woke with a headache. Irritation at the treatment of the castle misses of Mitchelstown illuminated this depiction.

As with *Original Stories*, Wollstonecraft insisted on a controversial address to parents. Impurity, it declared, would be eradicated if adults spoke to children about 'the organs of generation as freely as we speak of the other parts of the body, and explain to them the noble use which they were designed for'. The sentiment was worthy but unwise; it was much ridiculed when she became notorious.[4] In the mean time the address, like its predecessor, did the work no damage, and *Elements of Morality* went through several editions in England, America and Ireland.

With her several books and translations Wollstonecraft was now an authority on teaching morality to the young, part of the collective effort of Johnson's authors to improve society through education. The Dissenters in Newington Green believed in reading English aloud as part of this education – Mrs Burgh's husband had written a treatise on the subject, *The Art of Speaking*. Practice in elocution and talking in what was becoming standard English improved one's style and, since the passages chosen were uplifting, helped enforce morality. With this in mind Dr William Enfield, the rector of the Warrington Dissenting Academy, had published with Johnson *The Speaker*, to prepare boys for careers of useful public speaking. Wollstonecraft adapted his form for girls, though not intending them to 'become public speakers or players'. It was not her aim to attack the proper 'diffidence and reserve' of female youth or encourage women to obtrude their persons and talents on the public, but simply to enable them 'to read with propriety', to communicate with society as well as entertain. Unlike Enfield, she included devotional pieces aimed at helping girls sustain their lot in life and 'still the murmurs of discontent'.[5]

Her *Female Reader* was a series of improving extracts in verse and prose to be read aloud and sometimes memorised. Items came from the Bible; the seventeenth-century conduct book by the Marquis of Halifax, which recommended a domestic role for women to accord with nature and divine will; from Trimmer, Barbauld, Genlis and the much respected Dr Gregory; from Shakespeare, Milton and, of course, William Cowper, the most excerpted among living writers, whose poetic persona of almost feminine Christian domesticity appealed to an aspect of her own personality. No early women appeared; many such as Aphra Behn or Eliza Haywood might seem unsuitable and most had fallen into oblivion during the eighteenth century, but other contemporary women writers did refer to some respectable predecessors such as Mary Astell or Elizabeth Rowe; Wollstonecraft is unusual in her ignoring or ignorance.[6]

She published the book anonymously but fed her self-regard by including three excerpts from her own *Thoughts*, as well as probably supplying four original prayers signed 'O'.[7] More ethical than devotional, these thanked God for making her 'an intelligent being', confessed to much impatience in daily life, and urged acceptance of death as the prologue to 'a new and glorious day'. A preface informed the young reader that she would be edified by the contents but should not parrot them in company: 'a blush is far more eloquent than the best turned period.' Yet the stress on reasoned talking and self-reliance qualified this traditional one on the eloquence of the female body: 'As we are created accountable creatures we must run the race ourselves,' she concluded.[8]

Letters to Everina in Paris went through a business associate of Johnson, M. Laurent.[9] Mary forwarded some from Eliza and Charles, as well as from their common friend Anne Cristall. She also sent her own and, predictably, received insufficient in return. Everina had complained about her eyes and Mary suggested applying bark and bathing them with cold water. She had, she wrote, once worried that Everina might pick up 'vulgar French', but she was glad to hear that this was not the case. She herself was, of course, studying French for translating and she wished she had Everina's chance of conversing with French people: 'if I have ever any money to spare to gratify myself, I will certainly visit France, it has long been a desire floating in my brain'. Paid for by her sister, Everina must sensibly have felt her generosity. For once, both were properly educating themselves. They noted the circumstance, though Mary could not resist ascribing her own activity to her aching heart, 'the worm that will gnaw the core – and make that being an isole, whom nature made too susceptible of affections.' Everina would not have been Everina if she had not grumbled about 'trifling vexations'. They were both conscious that, at the moment, Eliza's was the hardest lot.

She knew she had much to congratulate herself on. Johnson's gamble had paid off. She was working hard and her austere inclinations meant that she was making herself not only independent but also free of dependants. She conveyed her pride in her achievements to George Blood:

> I succeed beyond my most sanguine hopes, and really believe I shall clear above two hundred pounds this year, which will supply amply all my wants and enable me [to] defray the Expences of Everina's journey, and let her remain at Paris longer than I at first intended. I am thankful to Heaven for enabling me to be useful, and this consideration, sweetens my toil, for I have been very diligent ... I have had some difficulties at the onset which imperc[ep]tibly melt away as I encounter them – and I daily earn more money with less trouble. You would love Mr Johnson, if you knew how very friendly he has been to the princess.

Yet she needed her old friends and wanted them to write often, however derelict she might be through overwork. She had sent George a copy of *Mary, A Fiction* – rather a surprising gift considering its fictional depiction of his sister – and he should pass it on to Betty Delane, who was planning a visit to London. Betty valued Fanny's memory almost as much as she did and

Mary looked forward to her coming; she knew Betty would not mind her Spartan domesticity.

Then Betty had to cancel. She had suffered a disappointment, possibly in her hopes of marriage. Wollstonecraft's better spirits evaporated and she felt again her 'deep rooted sorrows'. The misery of yet another young woman distressed her and sensitised her to inappropriate happiness elsewhere. This was how she viewed what she now learnt about Fanny's widower, Hugh Skeys, always a troubling presence. He had remarried, and perhaps the good luck had to do with his wife, though apparently she had been as poor as Fanny when he married her. Whatever it was, Wollstonecraft could not be glad at it and the news invoked bitter memories of his treatment of Fanny. She brooded 'over past tumultuous scenes of woe – thinking of that dear friend – whom I shall love while memory holds its [s]eat'. Why had fortune not come to Fanny?

Now that she was writing steadily for a living, Wollstonecraft's output of letters slowed. Her arrival at St Paul's Churchyard had coincided with a new venture of Johnson's. Thomas Christie, a clever and vivacious young Scot, was an avid reader of foreign journals and he proposed a magazine review to be called the *Analytical Review* that would bring the material to a general educated British public, the intelligent man of leisure and the busy professional. This serious, radical periodical would set a new standard of taste and refashion the national canon on liberal lines – not a very popular enterprise in a mostly conservative country, and no one expected huge sales; indeed the print run was only to be a third of the popular, middle-of-the-road *Gentleman's Magazine*. It would primarily consist of book reviews, the lead ones long like essays except for their copious quotations; these would allow readers to judge a book critically for themselves, as well as considering the views of the reviewer. Since reviewers were paid by the space they filled – a guinea for a sheet of sixteen pages – the practice had advantages for them as well. There would also be short reviews, especially of the increasing number of novels and advice books aimed at women and children. All the reviews would be unsigned except for initials, some indicating the reviewer, others simply arbitrary; several initials could be used by the same person to suggest a larger reviewing staff than existed.[10] Famous authors like Cowper were pressed into writing – the anonymity made this more attractive since contributing to magazines was not much esteemed – but there was also work for someone unknown such as Wollstonecraft who could be used as a composer of short notices. It was an exciting project.

In early summer, the *Analytical Review* began publication and Wollstonecraft entered the first volume as reviewer of women's fiction, the genre so condemned in her own novel. Her first statement was typical: '*The Happy Recovery* [a novel 'By a Lady'] is an heterogeneous mass of folly, affectation, and improbability.' She reprimanded the abusers of that sensibility that still gave her so much trouble, as well as the Ogle-like varnishers of sensuality with sentiment:

> Young women may be termed romantic, when they are under the direction of artificial feelings; when they boast of being tremblingly alive all o'er, and faint and sigh as the novelist informs them they should. Hunting after shadows, the moderate enjoyments of life are despised, and its duties neglected; the imagination, suffered to stray beyond the utmost verge of probability, where no vestige of nature appears, soon shuts out reason, and the dormant faculties languish with want of cultivation ... the heart is depraved when it is supposed to be refined, and it is a great chance but false sentiment leads to sensuality, and vague fabricated feelings supply the place of principles.[11]

Even when involved with 'folly' and 'trash', as she was soon calling the books, reviewing gave Wollstonecraft a sense of herself as an arbiter of public opinion. For this she had the radical's contempt: 'The voice of the people is only the voice of truth when some man of abilities has had time to get fast hold of the GREAT NOSE of the monster,' she told Johnson. Already she was aligning herself with those who did not run with the herd or hold commonplace opinions. As a new literary partisan she vigorously attacked the rival, more established journals: the *Critical Review* was 'timid, mean', she declared, and the *Monthly Review* tame and sycophantic. No one could accuse her of these faults.[12]

Inevitably the excitement of her new activity and position wore off, but slowly. As a former governess, teacher and companion, roles with little social and intellectual status, she knew well what it was to be subject to other people's wills. The new life working on her own felt liberating for a longer time than it might for a man. Except for deadlines, she was free to think her own thoughts and try them out on paper or in talk. Godwin, who had made a more usual transition from minister to hack writer, described the effect of such work too negatively when he summed up this period of Wollstonecraft's life in the *Memoirs*:

> It perhaps deserves to be remarked that this sort of miscellaneous literary employment, seems, for the time at least, rather to damp and contract, than to enlarge and invigorate, the genius. The writer is accustomed to see his performances answer the mere mercantile purpose of the day, and confounded with those of

persons to whom he is secretly conscious of superiority. No neighbour mind serves as a mirror to reflect the generous confidence he felt within himself; and perhaps the man never existed, who could maintain his enthusiasm to its full vigour, in the midst of this kind of solitariness. He is touched with the torpedo of mediocrity. I believe that nothing which Mary produced during this period, is marked with those daring flights, which exhibit themselves in the little fiction she composed just before its commencement. Among effusions of a nobler cast, I find occasionally interspersed some of the homily-language, which, to speak from my own feelings, is calculated to damp the moral courage it was intended to awaken.[13]

Himself without private income, Godwin knew what he described. Yet he did not comprehend how much Wollstonecraft was struggling to break the mould in which he liked to see her best: a lady of self-pitying sensibility and author of the effusions of *Mary, A Fiction*. It was the homiletic language which he disliked that she would later use in her distinctive moral writing. As for the reviewing, it was not noticeably dampening her mind; instead it was influencing her beliefs – away from trust in sensibility in literature and life, for example – she was no longer so sure that an education largely in accomplishments and an attitude of piety and achieved resigna-tion were enough for anyone. Reviewing also gave her an intellectual security for which an educated man would not need to struggle so hard. It was teaching her different voices behind the '*phalanx*' of the editorial 'WE' and allowing some playfulness with the authorial persona: the quotation comes from a review of Rousseau's *Confessions* in which the writer declares herself male and so contemplates without impropriety the 'naked' heart of Rousseau.[14]

It was also teaching her some much needed humour, absent from her letters. Her dismissals of trivial feminine poetry and fiction, as well as her mockery of male pomposity, were the funniest things she had written. 'Much ado about nothing,' she wrote airily of one work. 'We place this novel without any reservations, at the bottom of the second class.' Again, 'This insignificant knot of adventures ... has not a shadow of interest to make the reader for a moment forget the absence of common sense.' Writing misses were told to 'throw aside [their] pen' and do something useful. Plots were so predictable that only a few readers were awake till the end of a novel. Worse, most were trivially immoral: 'why is virtue to be always rewarded with a coach and six?' 'Alas poor Yorick!' she exclaimed, contemplating the effect on women writers of Sterne's sentimental hero, 'If an earthly wight could punish thee ... thou woudst be condemned to review all the sentimental wiredrawn imitations.'

Such tart reflections stood her in good stead when she chose to ridicule as well as refute the great male philosophers of her time.

Since she saw Johnson frequently, Wollstonecraft had little occasion to write to him, but she did send some formal notes about her work. She also had to address him about money.

At the outset of her period in London she had been amazed at her earning power and had for a time jettisoned financial anxieties. But she had grossly overestimated what she could realise and had overcommitted herself as a result. It was sensible to keep Everina in Paris although her stay was costing more than anticipated and there were countless other calls on her purse – from Caroline Blood and young Charles for a start. She had therefore often to rely on Johnson's resources to make up the shortfall.

As a result, Johnson was coming to fill the place vacated by Mrs Burgh as her chief creditor, but, since she coincided with him in opinion, presumably she did not worry unduly. She was working hard, but reviews were not immensely lucrative, even when packed with quotations. Sometimes she felt agitated at her indebtedness, but mostly she was careless of the burden. 'Remember you are to settle my account, as I want to know how much I am in your debt,' she wrote, but added, 'do not suppose that I feel any uneasiness on that score. The generality of people in trade would not be much obliged to me for a like civility, but you were a man before you were a bookseller.' Johnson must have wondered what he had let himself in for; he had not entirely decided to be a benefactor not a businessman. It was, however, a role in which she frequently placed him:

> I am, of course, over head and ears in debt; but I have not that kind of pride, which makes some dislike to be obliged to those they respect. – On the contrary, when I involuntarily lament that I have not a father or brother, I thankfully recollect that I have received unexpected kindness from you and a few others. – So reason allows, what nature impels me to – for I cannot live without loving my fellow creatures – nor can I love them, without discovering some virtue.

The relationship with Johnson went beyond money. When not indulging gloom Wollstonecraft could openly express affection: 'I feel at this moment particularly grateful to you – without your humane and delicate assistance, how many obstacles should I not have had to encounter – too often should I have been out of patience with my fellow-creatures, whom I wish to love!' Johnson knew his function as semi-counsellor. He saw how hard she found reticence and tact, how often she had to speak volubly to relieve her feelings. He was glad to be a receptive ear. Later he summed up his role:

During her stay in George Street she spent many of her afternoons & most of her evenings with me, she was incapable of disguise, whatever was the state of her mind it appeared when she entered, & the tone of conversation might easily be guessed; when harassed, which was very often the case, she was relieved by unbosoming herself & generally returned home calm, frequently in spirits.[15]

Occasionally, when Wollstonecraft was especially needy, the relationship became strained. Then she would blame Johnson for indifference and declare how much her mental stability depended on careful handling, how much he had replaced the men who should have sustained her, Ned and her father: 'You are my only friend – the only person I am intimate with. – I never had a father, or a brother – you have been both to me, ever since I knew you.' Sometimes she regretted her petulance, the bouts of ill humour to which she subjected him. In the light of his affection and patience they appeared 'crimes'.

Once when she felt ashamed that she had indiscreetly revealed a secret, she turned to Johnson as confessor, giving full hyperbolic vent to her erratic symptoms:

I am sick with vexation – and wish I could knock my foolish head against the wall, that bodily pain might make me feel less anguish from self-reproach! To say the truth, I was never more displeased with myself … Perhaps you can scarcely conceive the misery I at this moment endure … Surely it is hell to despise one's self! … I shall not call on you this month – nor stir out. – My stomach has been so suddenly and violently affected, I am unable to lean over the desk.

Johnson himself was not expressive and tended to think that emotions might better be controlled than displayed. So at times he met Wollstonecraft's depressive panics with a touch more detachment than she wished. One night in particular he seemed more stoical than was proper, and she accused him of being 'very unkind, nay, very unfeeling'. Her 'cares and vexations' arose from her 'disinterestedness and unbending principles' and from concern for others, she insisted: 'that mode of conduct [cannot] be a reflection on my understanding, which enables me to bear misery, rather than selfishly live for myself alone.' Should Johnson be unconvinced, she appealed to the experience of Dr Samuel Johnson: her new free-thinking acquaintances regarded him as religiously gloomy, too prone to 'dwell upon the dark & unamiable part of our nature',[16] but she retained a reverence: 'I am not the only character deserving of respect, that has had to struggle with various sorrows – while inferior minds have enjoyed local fame and present comfort. – Dr Johnson's cares almost drove him mad – but, I suppose, you would quietly have told him, he was a fool for not being calm, and that wise men striving against the stream, can yet be in good humour.' She would now moan to God, the only being who properly appreciated her worth, one 'who perhaps never disregarded an almost broken heart'. Her practical response was to stay in bed till eleven o'clock.

# 14

Wollstonecraft was striking and firm-minded, and she attracted a man she met fleetingly at Johnson's. With sufficient money for a wife and knowing her poverty, he yet lacked the temerity to approach such a formidable lady. Tentatively he mentioned to friends that he would like to propose marriage; the idea was put to Johnson.

She was past the usual marrying age and Johnson sensed her curious ambivalence towards the state; perhaps he caught her confused yearning for a male protector from her habit of making men, including himself, into paternal substitutes. A similar message emerged from her loud complaints, her constant need for money, and her hatred of dealing with tradespeople. Might she not welcome a husband? He did not quash the proposal but would not act as broker. So the idea was broached through another mediator. No doubt the man was awkward in expressing himself, stressing too much the financial advantages for her. He cannot have expected his reception.

Wollstonecraft reacted to the idea of being sought in marriage with fury and horror. She showed the envoy the door, then worked herself up into a lather. How could anyone have dared think that she was for sale or that her independence was a plea for insulting protection? She dashed off an outraged note to Johnson berating him for his part in the affair: 'My poverty makes me proud – I will not be insulted by a superficial puppy.'

Of her suitor she was contemptuous. He might assume intimacy with 'Miss—', she sneered, and make such a proposal 'to his cousin, a milliner's girl', but not to *her*. If she ever met him again at Johnson's, she would leave since she could not 'pull him by the nose'. The mere thought of how he viewed her made her ill: 'God of heaven,' she exclaimed, 'save thy child from this living death! – I scarcely know what I write. My hand trembles I am very sick – sick at heart.'

Time did not diminish the 'tumult of indignant emotions'. She never for a moment considered the man's motives or took his offer of himself as a compliment. The proposed marriage implied nothing less than the 'prostituting [of] my person for a maintenance'. The hurt she expressed to Johnson was transformed into fiery anger at the go-between. She would have been appalled if her *friend* Johnson had relayed the proposal, but he was only a 'civil acquaintance': 'The privilege of intimacy you had no claim to'. She wished never to see him again, not even to receive his apology. Asserting her proud independence, she armoured herself in ringing periods worthy of the theatre:

> I am, sir, poor and destitute. – Yet I have a spirit that will never bend, or take indirect methods, to obtain the consequence I despise; nay, if to support life it was necessary to act contrary to my principles, the struggle would soon be over. I can bear any thing but my own contempt.

In her dramatic response she assuredly did not have that. She can have feared no second attempt.[1]

Such a huge reaction to what might have been indelicate but had been kindly meant argues how much marriage troubled her, how much she needed to believe herself superior to its blandishments. She was horrified to appear so universally needy, to seem a mere ordinary woman who would prostitute herself to be kept.

The few letters of the remainder of 1788 and all of 1789 reveal her exasperation with the Bloods, about whom she became increasingly frank. George was in financial difficulties again, having lived beyond his means. Mary berated him: 'I thought you had paid for your experience – how could you be so inconsiderate!' He was still at home, allowing his lazy father to live off him. No longer idealising Ireland, she saw George's affability as an Irish desire to impress people: he must be more principled if he wished to flourish. The delinquent sister Caroline had reformed and become 'so industrious she is mentioned as a pattern by the mistress of the house'; yet, after the initial £10, nothing came from the Bloods and, with Mrs Burgh dead, she herself paid the next instalment. George must reimburse her and pay the money directly to Mrs FitzGerald, from whom she had borrowed to help Betty Delane. The money had been 'swallowed in the quicksand; but I do not forget it – and wish to get it out of my mind'. George should not mention this repayment to his father since 'his notion[s] of justice are so lax, he would call honesty romance.' George was feckless and his father dishonourable while she exulted of herself, 'Blessed be that Power who gave me an active mind! if it does not smooth it enables me to jump over the rough places in life. I had had a number of draw-backs on my spirits and purse; but I still I cry avaunt despair – and I push forward.' George had put up with a good number of reproaches but this letter was excessive.

For the moment she was more patient with her own family. It was the first time she could really help them, using her (and Johnson's) money and contacts to advance them. Once Edward Wollstonecraft had disintegrated into a beggar, Ned should have assumed the role of parent to his younger siblings. Yet now she, with none of his advantages in money, education and love, was a 'mother' to them all. She was not always sensitive in her efforts, but together they represent a remarkable record of generosity.

The most satisfactory were her two sisters. Although complaining, Everina was doing well in Paris; she should be equipped for a good governess post. With Eliza too, Mary had some success. Probably again with borrowed money, she moved her from Market Harborough into Mrs Bregantz's school in Putney, where she would be a parlour boarder. When she returned from Paris at the end of the year Everina was also dispatched to Putney, where she did some French translating for Johnson. Putney was close enough for Mary to reach by boat up the river. The pleasant trip could include a visit to Johnson, who had a country house at Purser's Cross, Fulham.

After the exceptional intimacy of Eliza's escape, the elder sisters had not been consistently close, but there must have been moments of companionship in Newington Green which made the move to Putney attractive. Without feeling as resentful of her parents as Mary, Eliza as wife and no wife was questioning cultural values: the family, law and English 'liberty'. She was aided by Mary and her radical friends, for occasionally she and Everina visited George Street and St Paul's Churchyard and conversed with authors daring to criticise the status quo.

The men of the family were also managed. Shipped off to sea when only a boy, James had evaded formal training. When he returned to London, Mary took him home, then paid for him to be taught at the Military Academy, Woolwich, by John Bonnycastle. The gaunt, long-headed Bonnycastle 'goggled over his plate like a horse' so that 'a bag of corn would have hung well on him', but he was a celebrated mathematician and she was lucky to arrange such education. No doubt Johnson was crucial in the matter since the two were close friends.[2]

Then there was their father in Laugharne, living on remittances from his property through Ned, convinced his son was cheating him. She persuaded Johnson to help her rescue him from Ned's clutches. Reluctantly Johnson agreed and soon he and Mary had to handle the rents from the Primrose Street houses, with all the problems of collection and repairs: 'she had the care of her father's estate, which was attended with no little trouble to both of us,' Johnson recorded. Edward Wollstonecraft did not regard himself as any better served.

Ned cannot have appreciated his sister's interference, which intensified his irritation with young Charles, his articled clerk. The Roebuck lawsuit had soured relations between Ned and the younger siblings, who also took their father's side in disputes over the Primrose Street houses. Old Edward Wollstonecraft was therefore eager to get Charles away from Ned, and Mary concurred. When the brothers quarrelled, she had to find Charles a new attorney for his articles. She had high hopes for the young man with his pleasing manners and enthusiasm.

But her delight vanished when Charles was ignominiously discharged from his new post. Since Ned had probably expressed his dissatisfaction, she must have known of Charles's liking for drink and high living, his untrustworthiness with money. Yet in the rivalry with her brother she had ignored these failings. Now she understood that Charles's charm coexisted with extravagance. Frugal in her habits, she found it disturbing.

Charles's ingratitude and imprudence plunged her into depression. She scolded him and punished her body; her nerves were harried and she was actually sick: '[H]e has wound[ed] a heart that was full of anxiety on his account – and disappointed hopes, which my benevolence makes me regret, more than reason can justify ... I would fain have made him a virtuous character and have improved his understanding at the same time,' she sighed; 'had I succeed[ed] I should have been amply reward[ed] – but he has disappointed me – disappointed me, when various cares pressed sorely on me – when I was searching for a little remnant of comfort.'

He could be bundled back to Laugharne, but she feared their father's influence, as well as his anger at a son who threw away chances – as he himself had done. Ned's door was, of course, closed. The only solution was to dispatch him to Ireland, at her expense again; perhaps he could make something of himself there. He left in April without her forgiveness. He was supposed to contact George Blood when he arrived.

Forgetting the severe criticism she had so recently levelled at him, she wrote plaintively to George: 'Let me now request you to have an eye on [Charles's] conduct, and if you can get him into any employment you will relieve me from a heavy weight of care.' The thought of what he had thrown away flooded her and her hand trembled – a fact she relayed to George, who was used to hearing of the physical results of her vexations: 'I beg you if you have any love for me – try to make him exert himself – try to fix him in a situation or heaven knows into what vices he may sink!' She felt less angry now Charles had actually gone: 'you may tell him that I feel more sorrow than resentment – say that I forgive him – yet think he must be devoid of all feeling if he can forgive him self – ... I know he will plunge into pleasure while he has a farthing left – for God [sake] endeavour to save him from ruin – by employing him.'

George did not respond to her lament and remained stubbornly silent. She was puzzled. Five months elapsed and she heard nothing. She grew irritated. George was unkind not to bestir himself when he knew her anxiety about Charles and his own situation. 'Pray write immediately and borrow one half hour from sleep to tell me where you are, and what you intend to do,' she ordered. Then she began again on the general ineptitude of the Bloods: old Matthew must work and George must make him or he would loll in 'sensual idleness'. George had not moved out – this was weak of him: he was being imposed on by an 'artful selfish man'.

This rebuke brought George to heel no more than the earlier ones. So she complained to Betty Delane. Betty asked her to be patient and suspend judgement, but she was in no mood for patience. Two more months passed before George finally wrote and then, instead of sending Mrs FitzGerald the bill of exchange for £10, he dispatched it to her. He had been silent not only because of financial troubles but because he was hurt.

She was furious about the mistake with the money and incensed by the 'strange unfriendly conduct'. She refused to accept that George might have grown weary of her nagging or have struggled to raise the £10. Once she admitted that her temper was volatile, but now she insisted she was implacable and, as with the suitor, she reacted to suspicion of disrespect with savage rejection. George had neglected a friend who had cared for him: 'I am not unreasonable – you might have written to me a few lines to account for your conduct – you were not shut up in the Bastile . . . in short, you have obliged me to alter my opinion of you'. As usual, she stoked resentment with writing: 'If I were to write to a volume, I should only repeat the same things [–] I cannot use my India rubber to obliterate the traces of sorrow and disappointed affection your behaviour has left on my memory . . . I do not think it probable that I shall ever be able to respect and trust you as I habitually did.' She loved him no longer; all that was left was the 'reflected affection' he could command as Fanny's brother.

After such an outburst, correspondence between Mary and George trailed off. Mr Blood did not support Caroline and the duty fell to George, always in arrears. She was disgusted at the weakness of both. She did not visit the young woman often, since, had she done so, she would have been dunned for the debt.

Charles did not flourish in Ireland and soon became a drain on the Cork relatives. By March of the following year, his sister had made him a cautionary tale for Anne Cristall's brother Joshua, a friend of Charles's and an apprentice in Thomas Turner's china factory in Shropshire. He had asked her for advice on becoming a London artist. 'Charles is now at Cork eating the bread of idleness – and living on the kindness of relations who do not respect him,' she wrote. 'His example ought to impress you – it is a great disadvantage to a young man to be thought unsettled ... a false step in the beginning of life frequently throws a gloomy cloud over the fairest hopes.' Her exasperation at both Charles and the Bloods fuelled her: 'I know that you earnestly wish to be the friend and protector of your amiable sister and hope no inconsiderate act or thoughtless mode of conduct will add to her cares – for her comfort very much depends on you.' She called on her own experience when she snapped, 'You scarcely know what industry is required to arrive at a degree of perfection ... in the fine arts how dreadful it is to plunge into the world without friends or acknow[l]adged abilities.'

Some months later, as the young man wavered, she grew more censorious. If he continued, he would 'instead of being useful to your sisters, become a burden to yourself'. He must decide 'like a man' whether art was to be 'the business or the amusement of your future life.'³ There were too many indecisive young men around for her to be patient. Even young women were irritating when not firm and forthright – like herself. So she preached to Joshua about his poor sister Anne: she had a difficult, jealous but fortunately sea-going father and cultivated mother, and had to teach for a living – the usual sort of thing, Wollstonecraft must have thought. She was another Fanny Blood, all sensitivity and insufficient grit: 'I have seldom seen your sister since you left town. I fear her situation is very uncomfortable. I wish she could obtain a little more strength of mind. If I were to give a short definition of virtue, I should call it fortitude.'

The ineptitude irritated Wollstonecraft, who solaced herself with writing. By July 1788 she had impressed Johnson and Christie as a reviewer, and was sometimes moving from 'trash' to substantial literature, such as Dr Johnson's *Sermon ... for the Funeral of his Wife* written in 1752 but published only after his death. She found its melancholy therapeutic.⁴

So she used the short review to express her emotions. Depressed and missing the dose of piety to which she had become used in Newington Green, she found her 'soul' again with Johnson: 'it has been for some time I cannot tell where'. Though she now insisted that religion and reason were together, when miserable she found her old ardent religion more comforting; for 'untoward spirits' reason was 'not a good bracer'. Johnson's subject, loss, brought back the 'vacuity' of grief for Fanny Blood. This death, his wife's, and Dr Johnson's merged into one sadness: 'We read this sermon deliberately, and paused at some passages to reflect, with a kind of gloomy satisfaction, that the heart which dictated those pathetic effusions of real anguish now ceased to throb, and that the mind we had often received instruction from, was no longer disquieted by vain fears.' So moved was she that she abrogated the judgmental reviewer role in which she usually delighted: 'After the emotions these reflections raised we *cannot* criticise; trifling remarks appear impertinent, when we tread as it were, on a grave recently closed, before the clods have formed one common mass.'

Joseph Johnson found the review too personal and protested. But Wollstonecraft was attached to her writing and her emotions. She would improve her grammar if necessary but stood by the contents: 'If you do not like the manner in which I reviewed Dr J's s— on his wife, be it known unto you – I will not do it any other way – I felt some pleasure in paying a just tribute of respect to the memory of a man – who, spite of his faults, I have an affection for – I say have, for I believe he is somewhere – where my soul has been gadding perhaps; – but you do not live on conjectures.'

The comment suggests how threatened she sometimes felt in her piety by the many agnostics and free-thinkers that surrounded her at Johnson's. She had had a legacy of religion, modified in the Green, and she had called on it while in Ireland. As much as her austere intellectuality, it separated her from the flippant and unserious. She was, she could acknowledge, less miserable in London than in Mitchelstown despite her unsatisfactory siblings, but this did not cancel her need for otherworldly comfort, especially in periods of lowness when reason was insufficient. The afterlife had perhaps become less compensatory as this one appeared less appalling, but she did not waver in her belief in its existence and purpose.

In *Mary, A Fiction* she had bade farewell to one meaning of Fanny Blood in her life – as an erotic object displacing romance and men – but the dead woman was still a potent force, perhaps even an increased one in the early London months. Now she was more alone than ever; she imagined herself talking to Fanny of her life and thoughts. Her dead friend was still the person who had come closest to filling her intellectual and emotional needs.

Missing this companionship and dissatisfied with her acquaintances and siblings, she began to yearn for a close tie that would not disappoint her, that she could control. She remembered the relationship with the teenaged Margaret King, for whom she had felt 'all a mother's fondness'. For a while she had surreptitiously corresponded through George Blood, and been pleased to note the continuing regard of 'poor, dear Margaret' for her: 'She says, every day her affection to me, and dependence on heaven increase, &c. – I miss her innocent caresses – and sometimes indulge a pleasing hope that she may be allowed to cheer my childless age – if I am to live to be old.' Despite the social gap, it was not an entirely absurd notion, since Margaret had been profoundly moved by her governess. Still, the correspondence had lapsed and Wollstonecraft was hurt.[5] Could she try surrogate parenting once more on her own behalf?

So she took into her house the seven-year-old niece of the second Mrs Hugh Skeys, a motherless girl who needed a home. Ominously for readers of *Mary, A Fiction* the child was called Ann, the name of the inadequate fictional friend. Possibly Wollstonecraft tried too hard to educate her as 'a child of nature' within the corruptions of London, or, given her own self-absorption, devoted too little time to her charge.[6]

As Ann grew older, Wollstonecraft became alarmed at her high spirits but continued to regard her as 'affectionate, artless'. Visitors congratulated her on her upbringing but Wollstonecraft was not sure. Ann was a fine girl and had 'great animal spirits and quick feelings', but not much sensibility. In *Original Stories* the governess Mrs Mason improves and helps her girls but, when she has done her work, they are only candidates for her friendship not real friends. She did not approve of giving unconditional love. Ann, Wollstonecraft surmised, was not earning her friendship; she would never be 'the kind of child I should love with all my heart'. Then one day she caught her pilfering and learnt that she had habitually been stealing sugar: 'the artful way she managed it, not to mention the lies, really vexes me.' Ann had become another of Wollstonecraft's disappointments. In time she was shunted on to Everina and then into the charge of a friend; after a few enquiries made about her, she faded from her adopting mother's story.

*'Falling a sacrifice to a passion'*

Although diffident himself, Johnson kept a sociable table, probably in the garret of the house leased behind his shop. His weekly dinners in the 'little quaintly shaped upstairs room, with walls not at right angles', were attended by 'a sort of Menagerie of live Authors', unpolished frank people all convinced they were right. His invitations were brief: '[a] good humoured face ... cordial shake of the hand, and "How d'ye do, sir? I dine at three" brought in the company. There was wine and plain food: boiled cod, roasted veal, vegetables and rice pudding. The guests, a touch 'straitened for space', came for the talk and often stayed arguing until well into the night.[1]

The company was mainly male although Anna Laetitia Barbauld was occasionally present. At some time it included Dr Price and Hewlett from the Green, as well as the equine Bonnycastle; the poet William Blake, introduced into the circle at about the same time as Wollstonecraft; the old radical and philologist Horne Tooke; the tall, ugly and hook-nosed veteran of the American revolution, Thomas Paine; the American poet and pamphleteer, Joel Barlow, friend of Price and author of an interminable Miltonic epic on America; the Scottish lecturer-physician George Fordyce, renowned for his careless dress, manners and habit of eating one huge meal a day – presumably on these occasions at Johnson's expense; the forthright novelist and playwright Thomas Holcroft, whose rise from peddler's son and stableboy to dramatist and man of letters was as steep as any round the table; and his friend, the ex-minister and present philosopher, William Godwin. Wordsworth came briefly in the early 1790s. Most were freethinkers, English versions of the French *philosophes*, some deist, some atheist, some simply sceptical. They thought human nature could progress both intellectually and morally and that truth, happiness and virtue should fall together through reason and education.

One of 'the standing dishes' when Wollstonecraft joined was an old and close friend of Johnson's, Henry Fuseli from Zurich; when Johnson reminisced about Wollstonecraft's long visits, he added, 'F. was frequently with us ... they were so intimate and spent so many happy hours in my house that I think I may say he was the first of her friends.'[2] Fuseli fancied himself a wicked lady's man and, in the past, had flirted with the artists Angelica Kauffman and Mary Moser, as well as Magdalena Hess of Zurich. When Wollstonecraft met him, he had recently married a young model, the uneducated and pretty Sophia, not included in Johnson's intellectual dinners. His earlier bisexuality emerged from passionate letters to Lavater when both were young Protestant pastors; later he expressed similar passion for Lavater's niece.

As self-obsessed as Wollstonecraft, the 'straddle-legged' Fuseli believed himself a 'genius'.[3] He was the most 'conceited man' Godwin had ever met. He was also irascible and his past was littered with lost friends, including the medical poet John Armstrong, with whom he had travelled to Italy. In 1788 he was basking in fame after years of struggle, having succeeded with his exhibition of Shakespeare illustrations. His short, slight stature, white hair and trembling hand – the last two attributes from an earlier fever – belied his vehemence. He was known for his malevolent wit, and friends used the word 'formidable' of him: Blake called him a mixture of 'Turk and Jew', savage and crafty. Speaking forcefully, often caustically, with a heavy German accent, he must have been a dominating presence at the dinner table. He had to be the centre of attention and Johnson warned Bonnycastle: 'if you wish to enjoy [Fuseli's] conversation, you will not attempt to stop the torrent of his words by contradicting him.'[4]

When she had first met Ogle, Wollstonecraft declared him the sort of man that most attracted her: 'between forty and fifty – a *genius*'. This could describe Fuseli. He was a revelation, an exotic combining the idealised attributes of father and lover, a man who had actually met Rousseau. She 'always thought, with some degree of horror, of falling a sacrifice to a passion which may have a mixture of dross in it', but she feared nothing with Fuseli, despite the lurid voluptuousness of his art – most notoriously he had painted the weird erotic *Nightmare*, which imaged desire through a male demon riding a recumbent female body.

Fuseli was the 'soul mate' she craved, a person of learning and creativity. He knew the horrors of dependence as a tutor and concluded that, like her, he 'was not framed to live with courtiers'; both she and he were 'designed to rise superior' to their 'earthly habitation'.[5] Before Fuseli she had seen no man 'possessed of those noble qualities, that grandeur of soul, that quickness of comprehension, and lovely sympathy' she required. In the *Memoirs* Godwin described the revolutionary events of 1789 as a profound shock to Wollstonecraft, who suffered a 'vehement concussion' of her prejudices. Her emotion for Fuseli was equally concussive.

*

Initially she had reason to be engaged: Fuseli had put himself out to be kind where she most appreciated it, for her family. He had helped organise Everina's trip to Paris through his relations there. Without such help, Everina could not so expeditiously have been placed and she would have remained in Mary's cramped house.[6] When Everina returned and joined Eliza out in Putney, both she and Eliza met Fuseli and his wife. He raised equivocal feelings in Eliza.

About art Wollstonecraft knew little, but was eager to learn. Visits to Fuseli's house and studio and trips to the theatre – she reviewed plays for the *Analytical* – augmented formal dinners and evenings with Johnson. 'I have conversed as man to man [about] the proportions of the human body with artists,' she later wrote, 'yet such modesty did I meet with, that I was never reminded by word or look of my sex'. Since later visitors described a studio hung round with 'galvanised devils', it is difficult to see how she avoided thinking of her 'sex', but she was determined to have pure thoughts.[7] For some months Fuseli was rarely out of her sight or mind. He entered her reviewing in a new aesthetic appreciation of imagination and genius – not every work absolutely had to teach, she now thought – and in her beginning doubts about evil as inherent in the divine plan. He was also present in her satiric swipes against the conventional, added to her usual scoffing at fools.[8]

As Henry Crawford remarks in Austen's *Mansfield Park*, 'We all talk Shake-speare, use his similes, and describe with his descriptions.' Wollstonecraft was no exception. She had moodily used *Hamlet* in her letters to Everina and George Blood, echoed *King Lear* in *Thoughts* and *Macbeth* in *Mary, A Fiction* and excerpted the plays for *The Female Reader*. Yet, before meeting Fuseli, she quoted Shakespeare less than one would have expected. Although she had received George Blood's present of the text in Dublin, it was Fuseli who made the tragedies felt presences in her mind. She responded to their alienated heroes.

At the outset Fuseli encouraged her feelings for him – her enthusiasm puffed his vanity – although Wollstonecraft was always the more involved. Years later the poet Browning portrayed a nervous lady with 'power / To pounce on [her] prey,' but the contemporary art historian Allan Cun-ningham implied mutual interest in his ridicule: the lady, he claimed, was infatuated at once while Fuseli, 'instead of repelling, as they deserved, those ridiculous advances, forthwith, it seems, imagined himself possest with the pure spirit of Platonic love – assumed the languid air of a sentimental Corydon – exhibited artificial raptures, and revived in imagination the fading fires of his youth.' Although he believed that Sophia Fuseli had no reason for alarm, he mentioned the 'uneasy mind' with which she regarded 'the philandering of these originals'. For his own part, he considered 'The coquet-ting of a married man of fifty with a tender female philosopher of thirty-one can never be an agreeable subject of contemplation'.[9]

The comedy lay in the bluestocking image Wollstonecraft constructed for herself and which cannot have charmed the sensual Fuseli. His friend and first biographer John Knowles recorded the anecdote about her Spartan entertaining of a sophisticated French politician: 'when Prince Talleyrand was in this country, in a low condition with regard to his pecuniary affairs, and visited her, they drank their tea, and the little wine they took, indis-criminately from tea-cups.'[10] Her appearance was even more austere. Fashion had somewhat calmed down by the late 1780s: plumes and powdered hair still surmounted silk gowns and satin brocade shoes, but the hoops mocked in Salzmann's stories had diminished. Remaining appalled at any frivolity, Wollstonecraft had become a 'philosophical sloven' and Knowles described her 'usual dress' as 'a habit of coarse cloth, such as is now worn by milk-women, black worsted stockings, and a beaver hat with her hair hanging lank about her shoulders'.[11] He probably exaggerated but there was nothing coquettish about her attire.

After July 1789, her plainness of costume and lifestyle seemed radical – lank hair differentiated French revolutionaries from powdered royalists and aristocrats, and in England some sympathisers adopted the style. Whatever its symbolism, austerity did not entirely suit her. When in 1791, she had her portrait painted, albeit with unrevolutionary powdered hair, she disliked her stern image. Perhaps in part it prompted a change which Knowles ascribed wholly to Fuseli. Knowles also believed she moved to more spacious lodgings in Store Street, north-east of Bedford Square and close to the present British Museum, to be nearer to him and appeal to his taste:

> [she] moulded herself upon what she thought would be most agreeable to him. Change of manners of dress, and of habitation were the consequences; for she now paid more than ordinary attention to her person, dressed fashionably, and introduced furniture somewhat elegant into commodious apartments, which she took for that purpose.
>
> But these advances were not met with the affection which she had hoped to inspire in Fuseli, – for he admired her chiefly for her talents; and in the warmth of her disappointed feelings she constantly vented complaints of being neglected. These availed so little that sometimes when Fuseli received letters from her, thinking they teemed only with the usual effusions of regard, and the same complaints of neglect, he would allow them to be some days unopened in his pocket.[12]

This last behaviour is confirmed by other sources: after her death, Godwin, wanting to use Wollstonecraft's letters to Fuseli for his *Memoirs*, was given a sight of them, but refused access; he noticed that many remained unopened.[13] No more than Jane Arden or George Blood did Fuseli care to be bludgeoned into behaving as Wollstonecraft wished.

Yet, in other respects, Knowles overstressed the one-sidedness of the affair – he never met Wollstonecraft and took his facts from man-to-man conversations with the elderly Fuseli who deplored 'viragoes' and the castrating effect of strong women on men; he was also famous for betraying friends.[14] Fuseli prated much of his appetites, and was at the time he associated with Wollstonecraft painting his wife Sophia as domestic wife and dominatrix – perhaps he needed to believe that no single woman could be enough for him.

No one actually asserted that the relationship was consummated, but the overt sexuality of Fuseli's art ensured it was erotically charged – at his death he left a large collection of obscene drawings. In the *Memoirs*, Godwin treated the affair delicately, for he was referring to a passion of his dead wife's when its object was still living and well-known to him. It was, he implied, a marriage of minds, not a sexual affair. Yet Godwin was startlingly honest. Wollstonecraft had been celibate all her adult life, inevitably so since 'the rules of polished society condemn an unmarried woman' to this. Fuseli aroused her physically but, since she would not acknowledge her own desire, she took no steps to combat it. For her, passion posed no problem: neither Fuseli's marriage nor her friendship with Sophia need be a deterrent when all she wanted was a share of a mind.

In *Mary, A Fiction* she had almost described sexual longing, but the hero died just as the heroine was forced into appreciating her feelings. In *Thoughts*, she had shown that she understood sexual self-deception: 'Nothing can more tend to destroy peace of mind, than platonic attachments ... if a woman's heart is disengaged, she should not give way to a pleasing delusion, and imagine she will be satisfied with the friendship of a man she admires ... The heart is very treacherous.' Now, under the onslaught of unexpected feelings, she did not heed her past words or pursue her analysis of sexual relations. Rather, she insisted that her feeling for Fuseli avoided the self-deceptions of other women. It was simply a stronger version of what she felt for Johnson. She was no libertine, she did not believe in free love or condemn loving marriage, and she had no wish to defy society's rules.

Godwin saw the source of Wollstonecraft's passion in a mutual intellectual esteem and admiration.[15] Yet they were not entirely congenial. Although after their meeting he occasionally portrayed young women corruptly controlled by duennas and procuresses, in the main he did not share Wollstonecraft's developing views on the cultural construction of feminine women or the collusion of literature. She repudiated Richardson's novel *Clarissa*, while he called it 'exquisite' and declared he 'never read it without crying like a child'.[15] When she saw his illustrations to Milton, whose depiction of the unfallen Eve disturbed her as much as his depiction of love inspired her, she told a common acquaintance:

> Our friend Fuseli is going on with more than usual spirit – like Milton he seems quite at home in hell – his Devil will be the hero of the poetic series; for, entre nous, I rather doubt whether he will produce an Eve to please me in any of the situations, which he has selected, unless it be after the fall.[16]

She distrusted voluptuous innocence and the childishness men found so appealing in pretty women. Eve was the creation of Milton and Fuseli, not God.

With such an overwhelming need growing in her, Wollstonecraft had difficulty keeping up with work. Debts mounted. Although she had graduated from parlour-boarder to teacher, Eliza needed money in Putney and Mary found it hard to raise enough, especially as she was dunned elsewhere. One painter was so insistent that she finally had to apply to Johnson. Having paid off the painter along with a few other determined creditors, she was broke again.

The Primrose Street houses were troublesome: she had to collect and send money to her father, but the agent was irregular, and she feared appearing importunate. She hated haggling. It was an aspect of independent life she rebelled against as a genteelly raised lady; possibly she had been sensitised by her parents' constant battle with tradesmen. She knew her father relied on the money, however, and probably she sent some of her own to Laugharne to tide him over. Again she had no alternative but to apply to Johnson, although aware how little she was doing for him. Her reviewing was trailing off and she had started no new book.

Part of her inactivity she ascribed to renewed ill health, a consuming fever, and, in the vicious circle she had entered, her anxiety over rising debts. She tried medicinal bathing, but it was costly and did not bring immediate relief, so she left it off. Her malaise made her idle and idleness rendered her unhappy. She was still upset over Charles, about whom she heard nothing: both he and George Blood remained silent. She began dreaming of her brother 'being in distress – and losing his watch &c'.

The huge significance of Fuseli for Wollstonecraft cannot be gauged from extant letters, though from early 1790 he starts discreetly appearing. When young Joshua Cristall wanted to become an artist she used Fuseli as warning: 'Mr F. with his original genius and uncommon diligence had a very precarious support until the Shakespearian plan commenced.' To William Roscoe, a Liverpool attorney whom she met through Johnson, she stressed Fuseli as artist and professional. He was having trouble attracting subscribers for his Milton project (as in the Shakespeare one, he intended to exhibit the literary pictures for a fee, then sell engraved reproductions). He would have done better had Johnson been more of a publicist for this was a 'puffing age'. What he needed was a rich sponsor who could advertise his name throughout London. She wrote in strict confidence, she told Roscoe, for she valued Johnson and did not want Fuseli to know her misgivings.[17] When she met the latter she simply encouraged him, 'for on this work the comfort of his life, in every sense of the word, seems to depend'. The solicitude for Fuseli was punctuated with some familiarity: she 'love[d] the man and admire[d] the artist'. An enquiring and sensitive person who knew both parties, Roscoe probably saw how things stood.[18]

In her more fraught correspondence with her sisters, Mary continued the secrecy habitual since Bath. Yet, without mentioning Fuseli, she revealed to Eliza the emotional strain now telling on her work, health and income: 'Heaven grant me patience! I hope it is my body which thus weighs me down, but I know not what to do with myself ... I never was in the state, I am at present, for such a length of time – I really do every thing which reason suggests and still have this dreadful complicated, lingering illness ... My head is now very bad – and I scarcely know what I write.' Her first mention of a 'lingering' sickness had been in response to the powerful effect of her dominating father when she was a girl.

Knowles was plainer:

> She falsely reasoned with herself, and expressed to some of her intimate friends, that although Mrs Fuseli had a right to the person of her husband, she, Mrs Wollstonecraft, might claim, and, for congeniality of sentiments and talents, hold a place in his heart; for 'she hoped,' she said, 'to unite herself to his mind.' It was not to be supposed that this delusion could last long.[19]

Seeing her growing intensity, Johnson suggested a break. So, in August 1790, she visited Gabell and his new wife Ann; he was now headmaster of the Warminster School near Salisbury. Domestic felicity was perhaps not entirely appropriate to her case, but a change of scene was desirable. She might have gone to her sisters in Putney, but Johnson by now knew their harassing effect; Mary could never enjoy their company for any length of time. With Eliza in particular she fell into arguments. On political matters they should have agreed, on social ones not necessarily so.

Wollstonecraft made the Yorkshire countryside near Beverley her standard and was disappointed by the slice of southern England she saw as she rode into Wiltshire. Without considering how her mood contributed, she lamented that the landscape afforded her no pleasing prospects. Still, she made do with 'green fields' and planned long walks, especially in the morning. When she was low, she always woke early.

Ann Gabell was as bound to disappoint as the undistinguished scenery, and Wollstonecraft wrote a measured account of her hostess:

> I did not find Ann the kind of woman that my imagination had sketched – She has it is true light full eyes with scarcely any eye-brows, a fair complexion and soft brown hair, yet she is rather a fine than a pretty woman – and has an expression of bluntness instead of the gentleness which I expected to see in her countenance. Her person is large and well proportioned – She made me think of a Doric pillar, for proportion without beauty – symmetry without grace, appears in her person, and activity and ease in her gestures. Indeed her activity is quite exemplary and she manages her large family [her school] with a degree of cleverness that surprises me, considering how little experience she has had; but her hearts and thoughts are at home.

In her writings Wollstonecraft valued harmonious families, influenced by Milton's powerful picture of the first couple in Paradise, rewritten as virtuous domesticity by Cowper. Disliking the erotic innocence of Fuseli's portrayal, she remained fascinated by the notion of felicitous companionship: 'Domestic happiness, thou only bliss / Of Paradise that has survived the Fall...'[20] Yet in life she was ambivalent about the home life of others:

> [the Gabells] find most pleasure in each others society – of which Milton has given a description, when he speaks of the first pair – Mrs B. [Eliza] may smile, but still I must tell her, that in this House she would find domestic felicity... you can scarcely imagine *how much* happiness and innocent fondness constantly illumines the eyes of this good couple – so that I am never disgusted by the frequent *bodily* display of it – they seem in short just to have sufficient refinement to make them happy without ever straying so far from common life as to wish for what life never affords – for only for a moment. The quietness of the scene and a view of their innocent pleasures have calmed my mind and gratified my heart more than you can conceive.

The result of all this domestic togetherness was her longing for the sight of her own room, a chance to walk through London Streets to St Paul's Churchyard.

Once the longing had been expressed, she became more honest. The Gabells were hospitable without invading her privacy. She was 'mistress' of her 'room and time'. When she appeared, each partner was eager to please. She *should* have been happy, especially as each was excellent in a different way: 'His conversation is superior to what one can generally meet with, and she has great rectitude of mind and common sense.' But she could not sustain the tact: 'the circle of [Ann's] thoughts seldom extends beyond her family and never enters into the labyrinths of sentiment and taste ... her voice is harsh and a blunt laugh often disconcerts me – in [other] words, she has tenderness without sensibility – clearness of judgment without comprehension of thought.' It was a damning indictment of a person whose 'unaffected good nature' she had just praised, the more convincing for appearing to fall inadvertently from her pen.

She ended her letter to Everina with a curious question: 'Can you understand my account of myself and the worthy family I am with?' Possibly Everina read jealousy, but, without some further clue, she could not have taken her sister's meaning. If Eliza saw the letter, she probably had a clearer idea of Mary's mind and emotions.

A few days later, Mary wrote again to Everina in Putney about a possible position in an aristocratic French family: a country one looking after teenaged girls and requiring good needlework and an understanding of French. Mary had reason to doubt her sister's competence in the former.

She had cooled even more towards the Gabells, oppressed by their married bliss. For all their kindness, their open affection for each other made her feel an intruder. The weather, so hot in London that she had assumed it contributed to her ailments, was now dreary and she could not take walks. She had struggled out one picturesque morning just after dawn, but had got wet feet and a headache lasting all day. She did not repeat the excursion and mostly the wet weather confined her indoors.

There she was thrown on her hosts' society. Now their happiness seemed not only excluding but trivial. Happiness, she concluded, was appropriate only for lesser sorts of people. She was not suited to the life of the Gabells: 'my die is cast. – I could not now resign intellectual pursuits for domestic comforts – and yet I think I could form an idea of more elegant felicity – where mind chastens sensation, and rational converse gave a little dignity to fondness.' As so often, her mocking repudiation of feminine domesticity jostled her affectionate yearning for domestic culture.

So far the holiday was doing what Johnson hoped: making her appreciate what she had. Beside the ordinary Ann Gabell, even Everina and Eliza seemed 't[w]o very clever, and most agreeable women', as she gracelessly informed them. She was honest enough to admit that her enthusiasm depended on their absence, for she well remembered that she and Eliza had parted on bad terms, each judging the other haughty.

When she wrote to Everina a week later, her thoughts were fixed on London. She was even worrying about her chimney. Everina had not welcomed the French post and Mary had independently decided against it. The family was offering only twenty-five guineas a year 'and some presents'; it was 'meanness' with 'promises to veil it'. Their offer to treat the governess as a 'child of the house' was, at the least, ambiguous, while their country location was isolating. She remembered life in Mitchelstown and advised Everina to try for a family spending at least winters in town. She did not seem unduly worried that neither sister was bringing in sufficient money for her keep.

As in the past, she had intended approaching Gabell for advice over the now French-speaking Everina. A well-connected schoolteacher, he might have been asked to recommend a governess to a genteel family. But the Gabells were too complacent to be useful to others: '*happiness* is not a softener of the heart – and from them I should always expect little acts of kindness and grateful civilities – but never any great exertion, which might disturb, for a moment, the even tenor of their loves and lives.' '[G]ood folks' like the Gabells were inferior to miserable driven people like herself. Indeed now she even took a lofty attitude towards the original couple:

Whenever [I] read Milton's description of paradise – the happiness, which he so poetically describes fills me with benevolent satisfaction – yet, I cannot help viewing them, I mean the first pair – as if they were my inferiors – inferiors because they could find happiness in a world like this – A feeling of the same kind frequently intrudes on me here – Tell me, does it arise from mistaken pride or conscious dignity which whispering me that my soul is immortal & should have a nobler ambition leads me to cherish it?

Her sisters were not especially pious and probably did not answer this rhetorical question. Eliza noticed the self-esteem her sister was stoking in herself.

She was ready to be persuaded back to London. She would return in a few days but, if Everina needed her, she could come now: 'to say the truth the sacrifice would not be very great – for I am grown a little weary too, and my heart and thoughts turn towards home.' In Warminster her jealousy at exclusion had mingled with her pride in independence, but she returned to London more single-minded. The common wifely woman was distinct from her extraordinary self. Unfortunately, she also felt the disparity between the ordinary domestic man and the genius Fuseli.

Without more of the missing letters to Fuseli, it is impossible to know when Wollstonecraft realised the significance of the Bastille's fall in July 1789, although the guests at Johnson's dinnertable were all devotees of revolution. Christie actually abandoned the *Analytical Review* and set off to Paris to see events for himself. The Dissenters of Newington Green were equally welcoming; they hoped the Revolution would progress to England and free them from their political and religious oppressions. Later, Wollstonecraft assessed the revolutionary moment in Dissenting terms, 'Evils are passing away; a new spirit has gone forth, to organise the body-politic ... Reason has, at last, shown her captivating face beaming with benevolence; and it will be impossible for the dark hand of despotism again to obscure it's radiance.'[21]

In December 1789 she reviewed a sermon given by her old friend Dr Price to the annual gathering of a society commemorating England's Glorious Revolution of 1688 – the beginning of religious and political tolerance within monarchical government. Price hailed French events and reiterated English radical principles: that the king was a servant not sovereign, that people had 'the right to liberty of conscience in religious matters ... the right to resist power when abused ... the right to chuse our governors; to cashier them for misconduct; and to frame a government for ourselves.'[22] Truth, liberty and virtue were blessings of human nature, and the first concern of a patriot should be to enlighten it.

In Dissenting and liberal circles these aims were commonplace, but they became ominous through Price's vision of 'THIRTY MILLION of [French] people, indignant and resolute, spurning slavery, and demanding liberty with an irresistible voice; their king led in triumph, and an arbitrary monarch surrendering himself to his subjects'. Wollstonecraft quoted the passage in full at the end of her review.[23]

The following year, the English voice of tradition asserted itself against such fervour. The ageing Edmund Burke, once 'friend of the people', supporter of American independence, and enemy of excessive monarchical power, wrote *Reflections on the Revolution in France* to render such enthusiasm absurd and un-English. The book put the conservative case for the aristocratic status quo, for old hierarchies and values, and warned the propertied classes that abrupt change weakened aged and valued fabrics. Burke had been boring parliament for years with his speeches but now his powerful and emotional arguments galvanised the government and realigned public opinion, giving him a 'glorious revivification' as Wollstonecraft mocked. Tom Paine, once a friend of Burke's, knew the book should be countered, for it drew on so many cherished British beliefs. Also, it sold 30,000 copies.

Wollstonecraft was confirmed in her values. The being that had once justified itself only to God had duties to itself as a rational being made in his image. It was a free moral agent endowed with political individualism and rights. These Dissenting liberal certainties were being questioned by Burke and she too saw the need of opposition. She was especially outraged by the attack on Price as a traitor, an alien to the traditions of England, and a vulgarian for mingling politics and religion – although she accepted that Price was more 'Utopian' than she. To her Burke was a venal opportunist who had once gathered statistics from asylums to prove George III indelibly mad so that his unsavoury son could seize power and make Burke paymaster-general. Though no lover of monarchs, she felt appalled at Burke's thundering that the Almighty had hurled the poor mad king from his throne by afflicting him.

Fresh from her country vacation and itching to make her mark in London, to be somebody in the literary world rather than the domestic, Wollstonecraft was ready for Burke. She may at first have meant to savage him in a long review but, realising how much she had to say, she let her writing swell into a pamphlet. Johnson was encouraging: at last she was turning her emotional energy into powerful print.

Price's 'careless dignity' was the style she aimed at, contrasting with Burke's inflated images, some of which she cleverly incorporated – and helped make notorious.[24] It was a practice learnt from reviewing. In the past she had tried to rescue good from bad sensibility. In Burke she saw the latter used for propaganda; his prose style was artificial though masquerading as impulsive. She wanted to make Burke both a shrewd manipulator *and* a crude victim of passion. As for herself she would assume a new role for which her pedagogic work and austerity had prepared her: of severe reasoner. The conventional gender roles were reversed: Burke lost his 'manly' subtlety, she gained 'masculine' logic. Comically, she still employed extreme sentimental techniques: contemplating his 'infantine sensibility', his mourning 'for the idle tapestry' decorating the gothic pile while 'man preys on man', she exclaimed: 'Such misery demands more than tears – I pause to recollect myself' – signifying her interruption by the lines of dashes that stood for feelings in so many rebuked novels.[25]

Although speedily begun, her work was not easily concluded. As usual with topical pamphlets, the sheets were printed as she wrote; there was no chance of afterthoughts. Mostly the habit suited her voluble style: she was not a careful writer given to much erasing. However, half way through this piece she lost her nerve. Fuseli filled her mind and she may have feared his censure. On first returning from Warminster she had been self-confident, warmed by a reactive flow of self-esteem, but the mood wore off and she sank into lassitude and torpor. She regretted she had begun so large and presumptuous a project, one so out of her usual way.

Determined to stop writing whatever the embarrassment, but expecting Johnson to protest at the waste in labour of herself and the printers, she broached the subject on an evening call. As always she was frank about her feelings, neither exaggerating nor dignifying them with cogent causes. As she spoke, she probably realised the irrationality of what she was doing.

By now Johnson knew how to handle his impetuous employee. Instead of urging her forward, thus provoking reaffirmation, he treated her with friendliness and agreed that she should not struggle against her feelings. As for what he had already printed, he would 'cheerfully' destroy it if this would make her happy. The response threw her. She immediately saw that what she had written meant much to her and was piqued that anyone should agree to destroy it. Her mind was concentrated and she returned home eager to finish the work. She had been composing with such naked emotion, calling so heavily on her own experience that Johnson's proposal to destroy her pages felt like an offer of mutilation.[26] Admitting that some pages were 'the effusions of the moment', she rushed onwards making A Vindication of the Rights of Men the first of forty-five answers to Burke written in the year following publication. Appearing on 29 November 1790, twenty-eight days after Reflections, it anticipated Tom Paine's inflammatory The Rights of Man by several months.

The vision of society revealed in A Vindication of the Rights of Men was one of talents, where entrepreneurial, unprivileged children could compete on equal terms with the now wrongly privileged. It was absurd to believe that noble descent made the upper orders virtuous; quite the contrary, it gave 'factitious pride that disembowelled the man'. Against Burke's reverence for the accumulated wisdom of generations she asserted her Enlightenment version of progressive history. The past did not contain knowledge and culture, instead recording benighted, gross and prejudiced acts and attitudes. Using the architectural imagery he so loved, she asked Burke 'why was it a duty to repair an ancient castle, built in barbarous ages, of Gothic materials'. She mocked his reactionary view of the Revolution as a usurpation from genteel natural leaders by mercenary business men and corrupt lawyers. Her cast of villains was otherwise – and would have been familiar to her usual correspondents: feckless parents, aristocratic females, and spoilt eldest sons. Class and gender privileges and hereditary property made civilisation 'partial', causing selfishness and injustice in men, while needy women were forced into marriage as 'legal prostitution'. Fury fuelled her prose as she contemplated the mess of her own and her sisters' lives, from their lack of inheritance to their pride in suffering delicacy. Such inequities could not withstand the rational rights of humanity based on God and reason rather than fallible history. The truths of religion were still secure but the Church of England as an institution was venal and feudal, corruptly enthralled to temporal power. In one of her few references to Christ she co-opts him for change and nastily imagined the anti-Semitic Burke as a Jew crucifying him to prevent such change. Misery and poverty remained God-given – she had not entirely renounced her argument against Gabell – but they worked to improve an individual not a society and must be combated by all together with equally God-given human reason.

With her disdain, so recently confirmed, for clever men choosing the trivially feminine over the androgynously intellectual, she attacked both Burke's *Reflections* and his earlier book, *A Philosophic Enquiry into the ... Sublime and Beautiful*, in which he had made gentle beauty feminine – 'beauty in distress is much the most affecting beauty' – and the sublime masculine. The categories had nothing to do with sex, she sniffed, but were based on simplicity and truth. The work's influence confirmed her fear of representations. It is unknown where Wollstonecraft resumed her work after her crisis of confidence but her argument takes fire in this late section on gendered aesthetics.

The gendering in *Reflections* irritated her as well. Burke was a 'chivalrous knight', owing proud submission to helpless ladies born to inspire 'pleasing sensations' in men. She was incensed at his melodramatic account of the October march to bring the king from Versailles to Paris, the event which Price honoured as a popular victory. The 7000 or so market women who had helped secure the Revolution by tramping through twelve miles of mud were for Burke 'the vilest of women'. Wollstonecraft responded briskly, 'probably you mean women who gained a livelihood by selling vegetables or fish, who never had any advantages of education'.[27] She had not often praised women's work outside the home, but it was no disgrace. She was even crosser at Burke's gallant vignette of the humbled queen Marie Antoinette: 'I thought ten thousand swords must have leaped from their scabbards to avenge even a look that threatened her with insult.' The treatment of women displayed a society's values; Burke's attitude was corruption by glamour, an affectation of sensibility: 'This laxity of morals in the female world is certainly more captivating to a libertine imagination than the cold arguments of reason, that give no sex to virtue.'[28] To the serious Wollstonecraft, Marie Antoinette was an aristocratic doll, a vacuous Lady Kingsborough, a kind of half-being created by a dissipated male imagination. Impatiently, she reduced her: 'The Queen of France – the great and small vulgar – claim our pity; they have almost insupportable obstacles to surmount in the progress toward dignity and character.'

One aspect of *The Rights of Men* clearly suggested her intellectual move-ment since Newington Green. Although her Dissenting friends advocated equality, some continued to stress individual benevolence, very much part of Wollstonecraft's doctrine as late as *Original Stories*. Now, however, under the influence of Johnson's radicals, she thought poverty should not be per-sonally alleviated but politically eradicated; benevolence did not exist to gratify the sensitive rich: 'Sensibility is the manie of the day, and compassion the virtue which is to cover a multitude of vices, justice is left to mourn in sullen silence and balance truth in vain.' In *Original Stories*, where the children had to learn the value of the poor, the latter had been movingly grateful to benefactors, but in *Mary, A Fiction* where the emphasis had been on the heroine's inner life, Mary had been shocked by the ingratitude of those she aided; now, although the distinction of deserving and undeserving poor remained, all should be helped and the 'aversion which men feel to accept a right as a favour, should rather be extolled as a vestige of native dignity, than stigmatised as the odious offspring of ingratitude'.[29] Social reform not individual benevolence was needed.

*The Rights of Men* was moderately successful, selling for 1s 6d, half the price of Burke's book. It appeared anonymously and early reviewers assumed male authorship. There was some speculation, as she learnt from Dr Price, to whom she sent a copy. Although sick and near to death, he had replied at once, declaring his 'pleasure . . . from the perusal':

> He has not been surprised to find that a composition which he has heard ascribed to some of our ablest writers, appears to come from Miss Wollstonecraft. He is particularly happy in having such an advocate; and he requests her acceptance of his gratitude for the kind and handsome manner in which she has mentioned him.[30]

She was glad to receive the testimony and kept his letter. A few months later he was dead.

Three weeks after the first, a second edition appeared carrying Wollstone-craft's name. She dispatched a copy to the most eminent woman polemicist of the day, the liberal historian Catherine Macaulay, accompanied with a letter:

> Now I venture to send you [*A Vindication of the Rights of Men*] with a name utterly unknown to you in the title page, it is necessary to apologise for thus intruding on you – but instead of an apology shall I tell you the truth? You are the only female writer who I coincide in opinion with respecting the rank our sex ought to endeavour to attain in the world. I respect Mrs Macaulay Graham because she contends for laurels whilst most of her sex only seek for flowers.

Busy writing her own more historical and specific response to Burke, Macaulay welcomed the new female political voice, the sort little heard since Aphra Behn and Delarivier Manley weighed in for the Tory party in the late seventeenth and early eighteenth centuries. She replied warmly:

> The receipt of your letter with one of the copies of the second edition of your excellent pamphlet in vindication of the rights of men gave me a pleasure derived from a variety of causes. I was pleased at the attention of the public to your animated observations, pleased with the flattering compliment you paid me in a second remembrance, and still more highly pleased that this publication which I have so greatly admired from its pathos & sentiment should have been written by a woman and thus to see my opinion of the powers and talents of the sex in your pen so early verified.
>
> Believe me Dear Madam I shall ever be happy in your valuable correspondence, and when opportunity offers shall with great pleasure avail myself of it for changing the lesser satisfaction of a correspondence by letters to that of a personal acquaintance.[31]

Another enthusiastic reader was the Liverpool lawyer Roscoe, whom Wollstonecraft met as the book was being published. He was so enchanted by it and the author that he commissioned a portrait of her and included her in his satirical verses on Burke's 'mad career':

> And lo! an amazon stept out,
>  One WOLLSTONECRAFT her name,
> Resolv'd to stop his mad career,
>  Whatever chance became . . .

There were two more similar stanzas allotted to her. She had moved on in her taste for doggerel since Beverley days but was mildly polite: 'I like . . . some stanzas in your ballad.'[32]

Fuseli was not much impressed, nor was the waspish man of letters, Horace Walpole, who memorably called Wollstonecraft a 'hyena in petticoats' for her attack on Marie Antoinette. Fuseli's friend William Godwin, at work on his own system of politics and justice, was not keen either. He looked into the book, then threw it aside noting its bad grammar and carelessness. He regretted that this non-too-reasoned tirade should be the first to counter the powerful prose of Edmund Burke.

The work did not encourage him to seek the author, but in mid-November, just after publication, when Wollstonecraft was mitigating her usual gloom with self-satisfaction, he met her at one of Johnson's dinners. Paine was to be of the party and, since he knew Paine was composing a substantial reply to Burke, Godwin was eager to hear him. She turned out worse than her prose, hogging the conversation and speaking over others. In mixed company Paine was more reticent than in the all-male society of taverns, but he managed to make a few shrewd comments. (She later wrote that 'we know nothing of Thomas Paine's private life'; perhaps she gave him little chance to describe it.) Despite his hope of avoiding her, the bulk of the conversation lay between Godwin and Wollstonecraft. She annoyed him with her injudicious criticism of people he admired, her tendency to dismiss the equivocal and make the subtle crudely clear. She had followed this mode with Burke and he disliked it. In conversation it was more galling. At the end of the afternoon he left Johnson's dissatisfied with himself for having argued with so shallow a thinker.

Whatever 'literary men' thought of her and her work, *A Vindication of the Rights of Men* firmly associated Wollstonecraft with radicals, especially Paine, whose *Rights of Man* appeared with éclat the following year. According to the *Gentleman's Magazine*, both were designed to 'poison and inflame the minds of the lower class of his Majesty's subjects to violate their subordination'. Eliza, who by now held strongly liberal views herself, was proud of her forceful sister, and repeated the compliments that her headmistress Mrs Bregantz relayed to her from a Swiss admirer: 'he had read the pamphlet and was delighted with it; and he wished with all the warmth of a Swiss for half an hours conversation with *Miss W* and the great *Pain!*'[33]

The *Analytical Review* was favourable but less proud than might have been expected. It placed Wollstonecraft with Catherine Macaulay rather than Tom Paine when it reviewed both women's replies to Burke, remarking:

How deeply must it wound the feelings of a *chivalrous knight*, who owes the fealty of 'proud submission and dignified obedience' to the fair sex, to perceive that two of the boldest of his adversaries are women![34]

# 16

*'I shall shut up all my private sorrows in my own breast.'*

The younger Wollstonecrafts were not flourishing – apart from James in Woolwich. Charles had slunk back to Laugharne. The Putney school was foundering and Mrs Bregantz was in 'constant ill humor', especially with the indolent Everina. Both sisters needed to find places. The idea gave Eliza 'a universal languor that I can not shake of[f]', while Everina displayed her usual array of symptoms, including sore eyes. Mary suggested three doses of salts each day. This would also cure the ugly spots that erupted on Eliza's pale face; her sister cannot have appreciated being reminded of this blemish. Miserable over Fuseli, Mary tried once more to anticipate an early grave. Yet she knew the notion 'fanciful' and sometimes suspected that her main problem was 'a painful sensation of *loneliness*'.

By the end of 1790, the strain of supporting her sisters was telling. Their misery exacerbated their dependence: they felt like millstones round her neck. When they had been apart they imagined being together bliss; now together, they remained dissatisfied, working on each other's resentment of Mary and her more glamorous life, which she would not share. Mary was equally resentful. Neither sister was treating her with 'greatness of mind' or appreciating the stress of her life. Once, on a visit to Putney before Christmas, she rounded on them venomously.

She had been working at home one evening when she received upsetting letters, probably demanding payment. She hurried round to consult Johnson. On her way she realised how little private conversation they had recently had. When she arrived, Johnson provided supper, then gave some unwelcome news; he was not a grumbler and so any complaint was serious. He had had sensations in his head and arms which, with his medical knowledge, suggested an oncoming stroke. Apprehending death, he was settling his affairs.

Wollstonecraft was deeply shocked and could not sleep. In the morning she felt emotionally drained and stayed in bed but felt no better. Writing was out of the question. That afternoon she dined with Johnson, intending to tell him to consult Dr Fordyce rather than relying on his own conclusions, but he left promptly on business. So she planned to speak to him at supper next day. But, before that, she was summoned by Everina in Putney and assumed 'something dreadful had happened'.

Yet, *en route* she grew exasperated with her sister. Everina often hinted at sorrow which turned out trivial and selfish, unlike Johnson. It was so this time. Mary was vexed. She told her sisters how troublesome they were, how little peace she had had with them and how, when her health seemed improved, they pulled her down. Had she not bothered about them, her last two years in London would have been easy: she would have had no money troubles. To this diatribe, Eliza and Everina responded sourly. They doubted that Mary gave them much thought: she was far too big-headed and self-centred. Both parties had some reason. Mary did trample on her sisters' self-esteem; yet she assessed her finances correctly. Johnson reported, 'She could not during this time I think expend less than £200 upon her brothers & sisters.'[1]

The sisters' togetherness allowed them to act badly, she supposed. She was especially hurt that Everina stopped Eliza from explaining before she left. Hurrying home she wrote an impetuous letter. Then she received one from Eliza declaring how upset she had been. A little mollified, she took up her pen again to apologise for her outburst. But, as she relived the event, as usual she rekindled anger. She had 'behaved in a manner ... I blush to recollect'; in future she would 'shut up all my private sorrows in my own breast'. She concentrated on herself: 'I have hitherto struggled through great [difficul]ties ... I shall live independent or not live at all.' Her solace came not from her sisters but from two men: Johnson and the unnamed Fuseli. Were Johnson to die, she would lose 'a father and brother ... who bore with my faults – who was ever anxious to – serve me – and solitary would my life be'. '[T]he only friend who would exert himself to comfort me is so peculiarly circumstanced he cannot – and he too is sick – yet I know while he lives I shall never want an indulgent warm friend – but his society I cannot enjoy.' Mary had persuaded herself that Fuseli, temporarily ailing, would be with her if he could.

The flurry of truculent but apologetic letters patched things up. The sisters and an 'improved' James managed to spend Christmas in Mary's lodgings. It was the last time they would be together, and they sensed the coming diaspora.

In spring 1791 Eliza accepted the demise of the Putney school and took a job as governess at Upton Castle, Pembrokeshire. Upton had been a large estate owned by the ancient family of Malefants, but the line had died out and part of the estate had been bought by a miserly nabob called Tasker. He was a bachelor and his heirs were his three nieces, who shared the castle. It was for them he was hiring a governess. Upton was close to Cresselly where the Allens lived, but this was now no use to Eliza.

Probably friends did not find her the job, which may have come through an agency, the sort dismissed as a slave market for the 'governess-trade' by the refined Jane Fairfax in Austen's *Emma* or perhaps through the news-papers, which advertised for companions and teachers. The fact that Eliza did not have the desirable French marked the post as not of the highest, although it paid £40 per annum, Mary's wage in Ireland. Eliza would care for almost grown girls on whom she feared she could have little influence. The Upton post was uncannily close to that described by her sister in *Thoughts* when she imagined a refined lady having to work for vulgar employers and train insensitive, mocking girls. Despite their enlightenment and refinement, Mary had complained of the aristocratic Kingsboroughs; this upstart Welsh family had no such advantages.

Given the years of petty resentments, Eliza felt little pain at parting from Mary. With the others it was different. She and Everina were close in their reliance on Mary and their helplessness in the marketplace, and, though constantly grumbling, they comforted each other. Later letters suggest that James promised to rescue his sisters when he succeeded in the navy, by giving them portions from prize money. Such promises and his manly affection revived in Eliza some memory of male attention, from which as a separated woman she was for ever barred: 'I felt more at parting with poor James, than I could well *analyse* on *recollection*, without *blushing*. Well what will not bear to be analyzed is as well not talked of.'

Pembrokeshire was almost as far west as possible, at least four or five days' stagecoach ride and a Severn boat trip. The journey, retracing the one taken long before to Laugharne, was eventful: near Bath Eliza met their old friend from the Green, the musician Hinxman, now unwelcoming, poor and selfish. One stage was solitary, while the Severn crossing involved a boatload of indecent, drunken men. The nadir was Laugharne. The letter to Everina describing their father reveals the melancholic temperament she shared with Mary as well as the reality of old Edward, whose spectre Wollstonecraft was combating in her vigorous polemics against patriarchy. Eliza and Everina had not cut themselves off so definitively as Mary: for them their father remained a discomfiting presence.

Eliza had lived briefly in Laugharne and been moved by its beauty. She hoped she would be remembered by childhood friends, but 'not one eye have I met, that glistened with pleasure at meeting me unexpectedly; and I revisit our old walks with a degree of sadness I never felt before. The Cliff-side the church-yard, &c &c are all truely romantic and beautiful – a thousand times more so than I imagined; yet all creates a sadness I cannot banish.' Worst of all was her father, an example of life misspent:

> The sight of my father's ghastly visage haunts me night, and day, for he is really worn to a mere skeleton, has a dreadful cough that makes my blood run cold whenever I listen to it; and that is the greater part of the night, or else he groans most dreadfully; yet he declaires he has good nights. There cannot be a more melancholy sight than to see him not able to walk ten yards without pantting for breath; and continually falling.

But there was pugnacious life in him: he ate and drank heartily and rode ten miles each day. Eliza agreed that, without this exercise, he might die quickly, but in general she deplored his extravagance. He was 'mad to be in London', believing he could force money from Ned. Eliza told him Mary had gone short to help him, but he fell into a 'passion': 'I represented matters as they are that he might abridge himself of some unnecessary expenses; but now he is too weak – in mind and body for to act with prudence.' In the context of this selfish man, the much maligned Lydia seemed 'truely a well meaning woman ... willing to do the little she can do to lessen the debts.'

As for Charles, he was almost as distressing as his father. The pair tormented each other: Edward nagged his son while doing nothing to help. Why had he not sought to get him into the lucrative Excise? Charles could gauge casks and sniff out smuggling, but entry needed influence, which his father failed to seek; so Charles remained jobless, running around 'half naked'. Yet, for all his wild appearance, he was improved, sobered literally and figuratively by the disastrous last years: Eliza noted he drank 'never any thing but water'. He was all submission to her but she remained cool: '[I] have said all I can say to rouse him but where can he go in his present plight?' He thought to list 'for a soldier [–] if he does, there is an end of him'.[2]

Lowered in spirits Eliza continued the few miles to Pembrokeshire, called 'Little England beyond Wales' for its racial mix of Flemings, English and Welsh. Although dreading her work, she wistfully wondered if Upton might be a 'Haven'. When she arrived she saw advantages. The elderly steward, Mr Rees, was amiable, the scenery splendid and the place, almost surrounded by water, picturesque. Little of the old castle remained except the entrance, romantically overgrown with ivy between two turrets, in which she had her room; she was given sole use of a good library. Like Mary in Ireland she determined on self-improvement and tried the writers her sister recommended: Blair and Paley. She also dutifully read Welsh history. The place brought it alive: a disused chapel once part of the castle complex, with tombs of old Malefant warriors and robed ladies, and a curious sculptured clenched hand attached to the wall as candelabrum. Like other ladies, the Wollstonecraft sisters appreciated scenery, but Eliza had more sense of visual qualities than Mary.

She had arranged for her portmanteau to be delivered but had mentioned some anxiety to her father. It gave him excuse. Three days after her arrival, when she was strolling with the girls, Mr Rees rushed to warn her: '[W]ho do you think is come to Upton?' he asked. 'Your father! in his [old] clothes too! poor man! he thought you had lost your box.' Tactfully he supposed her father *chose* to look shabby.

What Edward really wanted was a square meal at another's expense. She had to invite him to stay the night and since her castle employers would not provide a room for such a tramp, he slept with her. As in Laugharne, his wracking cough kept her awake all night. Next morning he was put on the road home, cross not to be asked to spend longer at the castle.

Left alone, Eliza soon realised that no natural or cultural sights could redeem her situation: the employee of a vulgar, mean master still attached to his rural Welsh roots: 'I deem it quite as *mad* to expect a *home* in a state of *dependance*, as the thought of finding a *Friend* when friendless!'

Her consolation was a 'noble Newfoundland dog' which, glancing at Mary's early amour, she named Neptune, and a greyhound, whom she took on long walks. The big girls in her charge were bad-tempered or vacant; both were indolent and moved only out of bed or away from the fire. No one, not even Mr Rees, was interested in her famous sister, which, despite her envy, disconcerted her. So she was pleased when, at a local dance, a visitor learning her name exclaimed warmly, 'you are dancing with the *cleverest* Woman in the World.' She 'made him *understand I was but her sister*'. But he persisted, and 'I can hardly tell you with how much pleasure I took his hand.' It seems that she danced *as* Mary. The sisters were interchangeable.

As they were in another incident. Back in London, Everina received a marriage proposal from George Blood. He was working with Skeys in Dublin and felt able to keep a wife. Despite her precarious state, Everina did not hesitate. The Wollstonecrafts felt superior to the Bloods but it remains remarkable that all three sisters avoided, escaped or evaded marriage. There was a surplus of genteel ladies in the late eighteenth century which made marriage difficult without money or beauty, so they were not unusual; yet most spinsters had no choice. Despite their earlier coolness over Caroline and Charles, Mary wrote delicately to George refusing the proposal. This allowed Everina to correspond as if nothing had happened. Nonetheless, it suggests strange vicariousness. George replaced one sister with another: Everina received a proposal, Mary replied.

Now my dear George let me more particularly allude to your own affairs – I ought to have done so sooner, but there was an awkwardness in the business which made me shrink back. We have all my good friend a sisterly affection for you – and this very morning Everina declared to me that she had more affection for you than for either of her brothers – Edward is, of course out of the question; but accustomed to consider you in that light she cannot view you in any other – let us then be on the old footing – love us as we love you – but give your heart to some worthy girl, and do not cherish an affection which may interfer with your prospects when there is no reason to suppose that it will ever be returned. Everina does not seem to think of marriage, she has no particular attachment.

Instead of marrying, Everina went to look after the children of the Samuel Boyses in Bishopshall near Waterford, South Ireland, not a very prestigious post despite her Parisian French. Perhaps the lack of 'fancy-work' told. Though she would be close to the Cork relatives, she would be separated from Eliza by sea. As she watched her sisters leave, Mary felt ambivalent: relieved that there would be no frequent holidays in London, that she would be freer of them than she had been since their mother's death, yet anxious knowing what they faced. The journey to Ireland allowed Everina to visit Upton. Though Eliza tried to be bright, they ruined their time together by moaning, each remembering Mary's miserable letters from Mitchelstown. When they parted they resolved to write often; Mary would be a frequent subject.

In the autumn James suddenly quit Woolwich and his training and returned to sea. He had 'condescended to take the command of a trading vessel' on 'a voyage of speculation' of which Mary had few hopes. Yet, Eliza surmised that she was glad to be rid of him: Mary was 'in good spirits, and ... brimful of her friend, Fuseli, a visible pleasure at her brother's departure is expressed,' she told Everina. The ringing words from the Putney quarrel stuck in her mind and she remembered Mary's desire to shuffle them all off. Bitterly Eliza mused on the money squandered on James that might better have been spent on *her*.

As one brother left, another entered. Charles now quitted Laugharne and threw himself on Ned's protection. Given Mary's supposed relief at James's departure and her continuing resentment of Ned, Eliza advised him to keep out of their sister's way. Then she rescinded her advice, realising that only Mary could do anything for him. But weeks had elapsed and Mary was annoyed; Eliza blamed herself – and Mary more: 'our sister rather wonders she has not seen [Charles]. At the same time [she] condemns him for being with his brother, she is a strange inconsistent being.' Later she wrote huffily: 'Her resentment appears to me very childish; but I will make no comments on the motives that influence her conduct.'

In fact Charles had long been Mary's 'blister'. Before he arrived from Laugharne she unsuccessfully tried to insert him into the East India Service, then approached her friend Roscoe in Liverpool: 'My present care ... is a younger brother (he is just of age) and loitering away his time in Wales. He was bound to my eldest brother; but my father took him away, when the dispute about the property commenced – since which he has been unsettled.' This was a fine understatement. Unconvincingly, she recommended the young man: 'He was with me some time. He is a thoughtless youth with common abilities, a tolerable person, some warmth of heart, and a turn for humour. If he remains much longer idle, he will, of course, grow vicious. His boiling blood could only be cooled by employment and I cannot procure him a situation.' She assured Roscoe that any place would do, 'were it but a temporary one, to employ him till something better occurred'. She wished him not to be left too much to himself. Despite her lukewarm testimonial, Roscoe found something, possibly in the law, but Mary hung back, doubting Charles's 'professional knowledge'. Perhaps, after writing, she thought better of recommending her rascally brother to a man she valued. Still, she was grateful to Roscoe for trying.

Once Charles arrived in London he became 'a constant weight'; yet he had his old knack of charming and disarming. The time in Laugharne had taught him to appreciate Mary and to determine to regain her affection. So, after the initial unwise absence, he called on her and soon she felt all her old fondness. Again she found him delightful, while he was overjoyed by her 'kindness and affection'.

## 17

*'A book . . . in which I myself . . . shall certainly appear, head
and heart'*

While her siblings took their different roads, Wollstonecraft was battling her infatuation for Fuseli by some ground-breaking work. Instead of pursuing a secular investigation of sexual feeling and sensibility, tentatively begun in some letters, she swerved towards a simpler rationalist explanation for the sufferings of women, including herself. She would write herself again as reasoner.

Although she had once yoked sensibility and ardent piety, and although reason sometimes seemed less comforting than religion, philosophically God and reason easily co-existed, partly because both were so immaterial. In *The Rights of Men*, she had not denied that God had put evil into the world but she had not stressed this. Now she saw that immortality did not necessarily demand earthly suffering and that God's creation was good, his gift of reason to both sexes his kindest act. In the new formulation Wollstonecraft was not unhappy because of special misfortune or refined nerves but because of the cultural corruption of her sex. She had been a victim of the erroneous association of femininity and delicacy made by Burke and male conduct-book writers. Femininity embodied the corrupted power relations of civilisation.[1]

The rationalist critique explained much, from resentment at her brother's privileges to obsession with ill health and her misfortune with insufficiently enlightened men. Fuseli was not responding because he had learnt to believe he wanted artificial feminine women or 'play-things'; the critique was less successful in explaining her obsession with him.

Johnson's dramatic pains, so upsetting to Wollstonecraft, had subsided, and he decided he was not dying. He was ready to encourage her again both because her arguments fired her and because they promised lucrative controversy – perhaps to prepare for death he had taken stock of his outstanding debts. *The Rights of Men* had delivered esteem and made Wollstonecraft equal with any of his authors in her own mind; she could prove herself again.

In October 1791, she wrote to George Blood, a little reinstated in her good opinion after his disappointment with Everina: 'I do not complain, I have some reason to hope that I shall overcome all these difficulties and whilst I struggle I catch some gleam of sunshine – tranquillity does not fly from my quiet study, and the pictures, which fancy traces on the walls, have often the most glowing colours.' Mary did not often speak of tranquillity and a less perceptive man than George could guess that something was happening. Late in November Eliza also felt something stirring: 'I shall be happy to hear from you what she is now absorbed in,' she wrote to Everina. 'Is [it] *A Love?* or Study, pray let me know.' For the moment 'Study' was predominating.

When reporting on the portrait he had commissioned, Wollstonecraft divulged her new project to Roscoe:

> Be it known unto you, my dear Sir, that I am actually sitting for the picture and that it will be shortly *forthcoming.* I do not imagine that it will be a very striking likeness; but, if you do not find me in it, I will send you a more faithful sketch – a book that I am now writing, in which I myself, for I cannot yet attain to Homer's dignity, shall certainly appear, head and heart – but this between ourselves pray respect a woman's secret!

This 'woman's secret' was an angry companion to *The Rights of Men: A Vindication of the Rights of Woman.* Godwin said it took her six weeks; it was more like three months although her arguments had been much rehearsed.

When reviewing her *Rights of Men,* the *Gentleman's Magazine* remarked sarcastically, 'we were always taught to suppose that the *rights of woman* were the proper theme of the female sex'. The 'rights' they envisaged were not the Enlightenment rights to education and self-determination that Defoe or Lady Chudleigh proposed, but the sexual and coquettish ones of contemporary femininity. Lacking knowledge of the earlier feminist tradition, Wollstonecraft would reinterpret the phrase from within her culture. Her 'rights of woman' were neither feminine nor primarily masculine ones extended to the second sex, but freedom from the degradations which she now believed had played such havoc with women's lives, including her own. The book would swerve from the primarily political matter of *The Rights of Men* into something more basic: the psychological and philosophical construction of sexual difference, competitive and cultural femininity analysed from a rationalist point of view. She was revising *Original Stories* for a new edition: the work reminded her of the power of formal education but also of the greater power of 'opinions and manners' in society. Women might make a difference politically, but first they must reform. She would use the cultural critique of the Dissenters and Paine to become a Mrs Mason teaching the nation from a new angle. Burke had lamented the 'revolution in sentiments, manners'; she ran with his phrase, demanding a 'revolution in female manners'.

Paine's answer to Burke, his phenomenally successful *Rights of Man* had linked the political and the social in arguing that despotic states fostered men's power over women and children or, to reverse the point, that despotic states presupposed despotic households. The argument was useful for Wollstonecraft, as was Paine's title, which he may have encouraged her to echo. 'Man' was a resounding abstraction and recalled the recent French revolutionary *Declaration of the Rights of Man*, as well as her own earlier book. The phrase 'the Rights of Woman' shocked those liberals who insisted on leaving women out of the political equation.

In emphasising women's freedom as well as education, Wollstonecraft travelled beyond Paine and overtook their friends more concerned with tyrannies of class than sex. Christie, for example, had just published another answer to Burke, in which he provided an English translation of the French constitution. This divided people into active enfranchised citizens and unenfranchised passive paupers, beggars, vagabonds, servants, debtors and bankrupts. Women entered this second category since '[the French] do not give the Sex the privilege of Active Citizens, or any share in the government.' The little control they were to have over family property should be removed, Christie thought, because it might lead to a 'reversal of the laws of Nature, by appointing women to rule over men'.

Although he acknowledged her intervention in the Revolution debate and referred to his friend Mary Wollstonecraft as an 'animated writer', he believed that the French had 'manifested superior wisdom, in showing that they knew where to draw the line, and so to honour the sex as not to injure their *real* happiness, or endanger the welfare of society. They have rightly judged, in not raising them out of their natural sphere; in not involving them in the cares and anxieties of State affairs, to which neither their frame nor their minds are adapted.'[2] Wollstonecraft's book denied this view, while accepting that women as they were fell short of what they might be. It argued for education for girls on a par with boys, so that they could in time take a proper place in society.

Perhaps even more than *The Rights of Men* which he had inspired, Dr Price influenced the new book. Compared with *Original Stories*, it was less insistently pious, but, for all her association with freethinkers, she lacked the intellectual security or the temperament fully to embrace scepticism, any more than the atheism of Godwin or the mythical humanism of William Blake. Too little had been given her in this life to allow a full dependence on it, although she was now eager to meliorate it where she could. Although she had stopped regularly attending church, she had hopes beyond the grave and the rigorous reasonable education she wanted for women still primarily prepared for the next world, though it would help them in this. When she had lived in Newington Green, Price had been revising his 1758 work on morality, which argued that 'practical virtue supposes LIBERTY' and that, where liberty was wanting, 'there can be no moral capacities.'[3] Freedom implied guidance by one's own will and 'licentiousness and despotism are more nearly allied than is commonly imagined.'[4] Women could not be moral without independence, Wollstonecraft realised, while refusing with Price to problematise the relationship of virtue and freedom. Independence for women demanded autonomy, an escape from male expectations.

Here she was helped by Catherine Macaulay's recently published *Letters on Education*. This too was severely moral and religious, arguing against the present system of trivial female upbringing and for serious-minded co-education. There was no innate intellectual difference between the sexes: both could be taught to reason abstractly. Although not much acknow-ledging Macaulay's arguments – she needed to feel original, the 'first of a new genus' – Wollstonecraft paid her predecessor a handsome tribute: 'the woman of the greatest abilities, undoubtedly, that this country has ever produced'. Macaulay appeared like a mother-figure in the book, one whose daughter wanted simultaneously to stress her newness and to receive parental 'approbation'. Sadly, the two mutually admiring women never met. Twenty-eight years her senior, Macaulay died shortly before the publication of *The Rights of Woman*. The unexpected death left Wollstonecraft feeling a 'sickly qualm of disappointed hope, the odd excessive expression distinguishing her style from both her mentors.'[5]

With its religious and moral emphasis, the book was little concerned with political 'rights'. Yet, that Wollstonecraft meant her work as a political inter-vention appears in the dedication to the French politician Talleyrand, who was helping to extend the principles of the *Declaration of the Rights of Man* by writing women out of the new constitutional order. He had submitted a report to the National Assembly on education, arguing for difference based on different political identities: 'It seems incontestable to us that the common happiness, especially that of women, requires that they do not aspire to exercise rights and political functions. One must seek their best interest in the will of nature.' This nature implied 'delicate constitutions' and 'peaceful tendencies', so they should pursue 'gentle occupations' and the cares of the interior.'[6] Wollstonecraft did not harshly attack Talleyrand whom she met between the first and second editions of her book, hoping she could still influence him. She knew she had common sense on her side, for what sort of universal rights excluded 'one-half of the human race' from citizenship and education? She addressed both Christie and Talleyrand, 'the *rights* of humanity have been ... confined to the male line from Adam downwards ... Who made man the exclusive judge, if woman partake with him the gift of reason?'

Controversially, Wollstonecraft insisted that the sexes were psychologically identical, basing this on her continuing religious sense of an immortal soul: virtues were not sex-specific. It is not enough, as the moral philosopher Adam Smith had recently argued, to imagine an 'impartial spectator', so viewing ourselves as we suppose we are viewed, since any 'spectator' has his or her own and the culture's prejudices. The view must be God's, internalised in the individual. Since the culture had associated sensibility with women, she now had frontally to attack this false authority, though prizing it for so long. To do this she degraded it from the moral, mental and magical to the material and medical, helped here by the physician's manuals she had been reading: 'over exercised sensibility' makes women unstable and 'trouble-some'.[7] Constructed and controlled by men as objects of desire, women colluded by exaggerating sexual attractiveness and gaining corrupt power in a society that repressed them in any other character. In them 'the mind shapes itself to the body'. Middle-class women must stop aping aristocratic ladies, a synonym for arrested development. Dr Johnson had been right when considering that Lady Tavistock would not have sensitively grieved to death had she coped with a shop and baby. She too imagined transplanting fine ladies from their carriages into 'a little shop with half a dozen children looking up to their languid countenances for support. I am much mistaken, if some latent vigour would not soon give health and spirit to their eyes, and some lines drawn by the exercise of reason on the blank cheeks.'[8] Women should be more like the Dissenting image of mercantile men, robustly pros-pering through their unrestricted, unalienated labour. And yet she could not quite dismiss as false consciousness her own 'lingering' sicknesses, noting that the 'weakness of women' may also come from their being 'kept down by their parents'. Indeed parenting was much to the fore: she remembered being prematurely forced into adulthood, and, reaching adulthood, being forced back into childish dependence.

Through Burke she had learnt to fear men's talk of women, the revered literature which conditioned men's (and women's) minds from Moses and the Bible onwards; even Milton, whose work she had so thoroughly imbibed, was corrupting in his placing of man between woman and reason. She attacked writers once valued and excerpted: the enlightened educational writer Dr Gregory, for example, was blamed for 'speciously' supporting 'opinions which ... have had the most baneful effect on the morals and manners of the female world'. Gregory wanted his daughters happy, so advised them to conform. Be cautious in displaying good sense, he warned them – to Wollstonecraft's disgust; if you have learning conceal it. His was a system of 'dissimulation': why should not women improve themselves until they 'rose above the fumes of vanity; and then let the public opinion come round,' she exclaimed. 'This desire of being always women, is the very consciousness that degrades the sex.'[9] Above all, he praised what she once valued in herself, 'extreme sensibility', an 'encumbrance' to men but 'engaging' in women. Female writers were no better. Madame de Genlis inculcated '*blind submission to parents*'; her works were full of 'obstinate prejudices, and absurd rules of conduct'.

Her main fire was reserved for Fuseli's hero, Jean-Jacques Rousseau, and his educational novel *Émile*. As with Milton, she admired hugely – even now she was writing in the *Analytical Review*, 'surely [Rousseau] speaks to the heart' – and was all the harsher because she had been slow to gauge his implications, so much had his conflicted sensibility seemed to mirror her own. Her mind had been contaminated by reading the extraordinary education in narcissistic passivity and cultural sexualisation given to Sophie.

Rousseau argued that sexual difference was part biological, part cultural, so distinguishing his views from Locke's environmentalism. Difference needed reinforcing through a political programme. The argument tangled on 'modesty': a *natural* female attribute that could stimulate and control male passion, while needing construction by women – themselves *naturally* sexualised. Modesty became a female wile, an artificial, artful and provocative veneer. Women, Rousseau thought, were physically weaker than men, so must be subject and agreeable to their masters. Yet, with their facility to excite desire, they controlled pleasure. Men had to please to obtain women's consent that they be the strongest. Women should glory in a weakness that allowed them mastery and sexual submission. They should not straightforwardly seek power: visibility of public women was always a sign of political degeneracy.

Being different, men and women required distinct educations: the woman's should 'be always relative to the men. To please, to be useful to us, to make us love and esteem them, to console us, to render our lives easy and agreeable: these are the duties of women at all times, and what they should be taught in their infancy.' Given this aim, girls, though not intrinsically stupider than boys, must be early accustomed to confinement and self-suppression – the physical debility that might follow could also be cultivated as pleasing 'languor'. They should learn to enhance beauty through dress, and practise agreeable gestures, modulation of voice and easy carriage; they should study to adapt looks and attitudes to time, place and occasion. If they talked, they should think not of content but reception.[10]

Wollstonecraft was appalled at the stress on appearance at the expense of morality and principle, on the education in restraint needed to make women servile to the free man. She was uninterested in men's corrupt expectations: 'I do not wish [women] to have power over men, but over themselves.' People must not play the game of her parents or the inhabitants of Mitchelstown Castle. Women should not be slaves to 'love or lust'; Rousseau should not make them in this debased image. Through reviewing for the *Analytical Review*, she had learnt the mocking effect of quoting chunks of a book out of context and running separate passages together. She used the method powerfully against Rousseau, made to appear ignorant of his subject: women. The reduction of so large a cultural icon was the most telling part of her work.

Female novelists colluded with male desire and gave their women characters a sense of self through reflection in a man. They had not the power over the culture that Rousseau was assuming, but their analysis was still shaming. In a review of Elizabeth Inchbald's *A Simple Story*, she noted that 'all female writers, even when they display their abilities, always give a sanction to the libertine reveries of men'. Women's fiction genuflected to male fantasy with pictures of weak women swooning and in tears, who yet had amazing power over libertine-rakes. Women internalised this fantasy as romance and took their identity from it.[11] The identity was eroticised; eroticisation was produced by culture.

In *Mary, A Fiction* and 'The Cave of Fancy' she had allowed the expression of passion to be romanticised. In *The Rights of Men*, she had still written, 'Sacred be the feelings of the heart! concentred in a glowing flame, they become the sun of life; and, without his invigorating impregnation, reason would probably lie in helpless inactivity, and never bring forth her only legitimate offspring – virtue': in this curious sexy reversal of Burke's gendering of feeling as female, there was perhaps some mockery of her own youthful and Burke's mature style.[12] But then she went on to insist that the rights of the heart become rights of the mind and asked, 'In what respect are we superior to brute creation, if intellect is not allowed to be the guide of passion?' Now in this new book she went even further towards reason. Sensibility was demoted to the 'polished instinct' of a Burke and, though it might sometimes be prompted by feeling, reason *must* be the foundation of action, thought and worship. Only through identifying with the rationalist God and forgetting irrelevant gender could women gain a proper sense of self. Reason was God-made and part of God's plan, the image of God within mankind. Its dignity became a moral source.[13]

For day-to-day living, too, reason should be cultivated, and all the gendered virtues of sensibility, delicacy, modesty and chastity be rationally redefined away from sexual allure. Women should become open and frank; truth and equality should exist between the sexes inside a companionate relationship which replaced coquetting femininity; the manipulating dissimulations of conventional marriage equalled adultery.[14] Women needed the chance to become reasonable and intelligent: love of men should be part of life, not its purpose and ground. Here, however, Wollstonecraft faced a difficulty. The sole other mundane identity outside wifehood she offered at length was motherhood, a civic as much as a domestic role in her view, but necessarily implying some difference from men's status.[15] Beyond this lay ill-defined 'independence', a share in 'the art of healing', 'benevolence' and 'business of various kinds'. Governessing was a 'humiliating situation ... a degradation ... a fall in life' for the 'educated' gentlewoman. When they read the work, Eliza and Everina must have noted the lack of any detailed plan of rescue.

Wollstonecraft could be stern on emotion because she insisted on disdaining the passionate sexual love that stayed fixed on earth. Her rational love was capitalist, an equitable transaction. Sex should be demystified and human reproduction openly discussed: she had anticipated the point in the Salzmann preface.[16] Yet, though women's 'common appetites' should be acknowledged along with men's, passion emerged in awkward intense disclaimers – 'excepting with a lover ... unless where love animates the behaviour'. Called 'voluptuousness' it entered metaphors, and even chaste love became curiously erotic when accompanied with the 'sublime gloom of tender melancholy'. Instead of being liberated as twentieth-century feminists wished, female sexual passion *had* to be curbed by reason; otherwise it undermined women in society. In the sexual game as then played by aristocrats and libertines and those who followed them, women would always come off worst. Nothing she learnt later contradicted this view, although she came to understand the difficulty of the curbs, and the price to pay for them.

Given her views on physical control, it is a surprise to find her straightforwardly declaring Rousseau's personal problem to be sexual repression. He was naturally warm, she wrote, and became lascivious when thinking of women, his apparently virtuous restraint inflamed his feelings. 'Had he given way to these desires, the fire would have extinguished itself in a natural manner; but virtue, and a romantic kind of delicacy, made him practice self-denial.' As a result he 'debauched his imagination'.[17] Did she apply such reasoning to herself? She seems not to have urged it on Fuseli.

As with *The Rights of Men*, the printing of *The Rights of Woman* was not smooth. Publishing had begun at the end of 1791 and continued into the new year. In the final stages she felt hurried; the habit of printing pages at once forbade correction and she was dismayed at a mounting list of errata. Roscoe as 'a gentleman author' could understand her annoyance, although those who had 'never dabbled in ink' might mock. Usually she accepted the custom, but her subject was original and important, and now she regretted not insisting on more time. She felt vexed but could not blame Johnson, who would probably have humoured her. She was victim to her vain desire to have her book out quickly. It was not false modesty to wish now she had 'written a better book, in every sense of the word'. But it was done and, on 3 January 1792, she handed in her last sheet. Her only hope was to do better in volume two: 'I intend to finish the next volume before I begin to print, for it is not pleasant to have the [printer's] Devil coming for the conclusion of a sheet before it is written.'

However difficult its birth, *The Rights of Woman* stirred many readers and reached a wide audience from Glasgow to Blackburn and Lichfield. Anne MacVicar Grant from Scotland reported that it was so in demand that one had no time to read it before having it snatched away, while Rachel Prescott in Blackburn said the book 'first induced me to think'. Believing it carried its ideas of equality too far, the poet Anna Seward in Lichfield yet termed it 'that wonderful book' which applied 'the spear of Ithuriel' to the systems of Rousseau and Gregory.[18] It had its moment in the sun and was widely reviewed, often favourably as a sensible work on education. Johnson republished it within the year and it appeared in America and in French and German translations, the latter by Salzmann, much concerned with female education but eager to blunt any subversive message. Like Wollstonecraft, with whom he had been corresponding, he made free with his foreign text and added 'edifying improvements'.[19]

Inevitably many readers were irritated. Although the *Analytical Review* had praised the book as 'strong and impressive', the critical Godwin called it rawly written, 'a very unequal performance ... deficient in method and arrangement'. Probably Fuseli was unimpressed too: he could not have relished her attack on the 'sensual homage' of men for beautiful women. The playwright Hannah Cowley thought the book horribly '*unfeminine*', while the *Critical Review* ungallantly advised the young author to assume some of the feminine graces she despised, so she would become more pleasing and 'infinitely happier'.[20] A 'mother' wrote to the *Ladies Monthly Museum* to lament that her four daughters had been corrupted by the book: one lost her 'softness' and indulged in horse-racing, fox-hunting and betting; a second had taken up Latin and Greek; a third was scientifically dissecting her pets; and a fourth was challenging men to duels.

Despite his earlier advocacy of contemplative calm, Thomas Taylor the Platonist had grown cantankerous, wanting to burn everyone who disagreed with him, among whom was his old fellow-lodger in Walworth, Mary Wollstonecraft. Failing this, he sought to ridicule her (and Paine) by extending their 'amazing rage of liberty' to animals – vegetables and minerals would follow. His *Vindication of the Rights of Brutes* discussed female rights by implication, through unsavoury anecdotes of animal-woman copulation. Wollstonecraft is 'a virgin' and as such connected to the elephant's tale: 'From his prodigious size [the elephant is] very well calculated to become the darling of our modern virgins', who 'are seldom intimidated at any thing uncommonly large'. In the next anecdote, a dragon, prevented from enjoying his nightly visits to a naked lady, found her out and 'with the folds of his body, having first bound her hands and arms, he lashed the calves of her legs, with the end of his tail; expressing by this means a gentle and loving anger'. The rights of woman must lead to sexual chaos, while, in an unhierarchical world, women would always be violated.[21]

Although it deeply affected many individual women, compared with the huge body of establishment conduct literature on education by such writers as Hannah More, *The Rights of Woman* had little immediate effect on English culture. More's *Strictures on the Modern System of Education*, with its advice to women not to indulge in 'impious discontent with the post to which God has assigned them', sold 11,000 copies in the three years between 1799 and 1801, and her grimly didactic novel, *Coelebs in Search of a Wife*, sold 14,500 in the first quarter of the nineteenth century. Even more spectacularly, her *Cheap Repository Tracts*, written as 'antidote' to the 'fatal poison' of Paine allegedly reached over two million, a quarter of the population. By contrast *The Rights of Woman* sold only about 1500 to 3000 copies in its first five years in print and very little throughout the next fifty. It continued to be stocked in libraries and came out in inexpensive paperback editions during the 1840s Chartist agitation, but it never joined such works as Paine's *The Rights of Man* or Shelley's poem *Queen Mab* in the radical canon and it never had a clear radical constituency to disseminate its ideas. As for the influential Mrs More herself, she was 'invincibly resolved' not to read the work; its very title was 'fantastic and absurd'. Yet Mary Berry, a reader of them both rightly noted that the rivals agreed 'on all the great points of female education'.[22]

Few of its readers were prepared to meet Wollstonecraft's arguments head-on. (Indeed she had some problem envisioning her female readers, at one moment including them with herself – 'Let us, my dear contemporaries' – at another separating herself and similar strong-minded women from the 'hapless woman' she addresses.) Even now the book is difficult to assimilate, although in its contentions, digressions, contradictions and asides it antici-pates most positions of modern feminism. The logic of eighteenth-century Enlightenment equality was to attack the ultimate hierarchy of the sexes. This is now a commonplace and the difficulties Wollstonecraft ignored have emerged more strongly.

First, she wanted to destroy traditional complementarity – where women were emotional, intuitive and tender, and men rational, ambitious and strong. Without erroneous cultural training, the sexes would revert to equal-ity. But she was never quite sure that the natural order denied *all* subjection and she never saw the complementary abstract terms as themselves culturally constructed. Meanwhile the autonomous regenerated male political subject remained the norm, though so much of what she wrote suggested its fic-tionality. Second, she wanted to transcend the body. In earlier times, women's social subjection was extrapolated from scripture with its implication of the cursed, dirty female body and its contaminating blood. In the late eighteenth century inequality was grounded on women's nervous physique. To make her protest Wollstonecraft had to shy away from her own occasional sense that the unsatisfactory body controlled the brain and disturbed reason. If the female body were emphasised, woman would be omitted from the Enlightenment experiment and perhaps suffer another millennium of oppression.

Two centuries on, it is easier to see how Wollstonecraft underestimated the power of polarisation and physical difference. As later feminists realised when they contemplated the 1970s feminism of equal rights, it was an over-simplification. Yet it is important not to belittle the achievement. If women were to make any educational and social advance, Wollstonecraft had to argue for intellectual and psychological equality, even identity; so, whatever her private experience, she must ignore sexual difference, on which the edifice of subjection was founded. She could not be straightforwardly revo-lutionary like Paine, who wanted society transformed through a change of institutions; instead she sought a basic psychological and personal reform that must come from change in individual attitudes. Her strength was to say clearly and ringingly what was not said again for another two hundred years and which constantly needs resaying: 'This desire of being always women, is the very consciousness which degrades the sex.' Or in modern terms, 'Can anyone fully inhabit a gender without a degree of horror? How could someone "be a woman" through and through without suffering claustrophobia?'[23]

# 18

*'We must each of us wear a fool's cap'*

*The Rights of Woman* made Wollstonecraft a minor celebrity. Public acclaim excited her; she had preached to a nation and part of it had listened. In recognition she took the title, 'Mrs'. Unmarried women often did this at about forty, signifying removal from the marriage market – though the governess Agnes Porter who adopted it joked she might yet 'be mistaken for a little jolly widow and pop off'.[1] A younger woman could suggest some status, as Wollstonecraft was doing. She did not disguise her feelings; she swelled with elation.

Although Eliza sometimes admired her sister's success, the new notoriety bred resentment. She, the prettiest of the three, was ignored, while Mary was applauded. Correspondence between London and the sisters dwindled, and neither bothered to increase it. In their separate spaces Eliza was consumed with envy, Everina with misery, and Mary with contradictory feelings. Each hugged her own emotions making no imaginative leap into another life. Eliza came to believe that Mary's 'fame' and consequent pride threatened the family. Was it worth sacrificing their tranquillity to temporary achievement?

So alienated was Eliza that she soon found it hard to name Mary or regard her as a relative, leaving her to appear in letters as 'his' or 'your sister', the words scrawled in the ugly characters into which her writing degenerated in crises. As she lay sleepless in the Welsh night, she even imagined Mary dead: 'I never think of *our sister* but in the light of a *friend* who had been dead some years . . . and when all here is fast asleep and naught is to be heard but the screech-owl I sigh to think we shall never meet, as such, again – though perhaps in a better world the *Love of Fame cannot corrupt the soul.*' Displaying Mary's judgmental tendency, she added, 'Ought not this sudden change in such a character make one feel less indignation and surprise when one meets weak minds, wholly lost in foolish pride.' When she read *The Rights of Woman*, she registered its powerful arguments but marked it only by the question, 'Have you nought to say about your sister's Rights of Woman?'[2]

During the next months Eliza heard nothing from Mary but she did sometimes receive tantalising snippets from Charles: '[He] informs me too that *Mrs Wollstonecraft* is grown quite handsome[;] he adds likewise that being conscious she is on the wrong sid[e] of thirty she now endeavors to set of[f] those charms (*she once* despised) to the best advantage.' The glimpses further embittered the self-obsessed Eliza. She had suspected her sister's fascination with Fuseli and, unlike young Charles, probably ascribed her change to this, but, in her pit of envy, could not imagine a rejected or unhappy Mary.

Then Everina fell ill. Eliza feared she would be left with no sisters, so completely had she literalised Mary's metaphoric death:

> I have not heard from [Charles's] sister for above three months – thus was I mad enough to *forget* the *past* – and give way to a feverish anxiety that bid me anticipate from to-*morrow's Post what thirty long years experience* tells me *is not* to be *found* – oh that I could banish from my heart the dread I now feel of losing you my only comfort! Yet this idea often haunts my imagination – I want but this blow to compleat all – Mary *already* dead! And you half gone—

Back in London, Mary knew nothing of this alienation. Her sisters were not well placed but she believed them 'tolerably settled for the present'. She had long since stopped expecting consideration from Eliza and was not puzzled by her silence, and, though surprised at Everina, reflected: 'she is very apt to forget the absent when amused by the present.' She did not really believe Everina 'amused' – she remembered too well being a governess herself – but she could not always be burdened with her sisters' dissatisfaction. Her father remained her running sore: 'I live in continual fear of having him thrown upon me for his whole support.' The Primrose Street houses had been mismanaged and were not generating enough income. When nothing went to her father he had nothing to live on unless she contributed.

She also worried about Charles. What if their father died? Who would get his share of the property? The Primrose Street houses represented the only hope of capital for the younger children now the Roebuck legacy had largely gone. She must watch out for their interests. So she wrote again to Roscoe as lawyer seeking advice about obtaining power of attorney: 'you will readily perceive that my dear-bought experience makes me anxious to guard against conti[n]gencies lest by some quirk of the law my eldest brother, the Attorney, should snap at the last morsel.' If Charles went abroad, she wanted to manage his interests in England, and, were both he and her ailing father to die, see that Everina and Eliza got their brother's share. She was always concerned with family money: it had value in itself and gave status as no amount of earned capital could do.

Her specific reason for asking was that she had managed to press a new acquaintance into serving Charles, who would soon be leaving for America. Joel and Ruth Barlow, American friends of Paine, had been in France peddling American land. They were now in London where Barlow had published with Johnson *Advice to the Privileged Orders*, another reply to Burke. The Barlows, the very type of frank and energetic Americans, had made a most acceptable offer: they were shortly returning to America and would take young Charles. He could board at a farm until he gained experience; then he would obtain land and set up on his own. Everyone approved the plan – the anxious Mary had probably been lobbying them all. 'Mr Paine assures me that he could not be recommended to a more worthy man, and that there is not a doubt of his earning a respectable livelihood if he will exert himself.' Fuseli 'insisted on making Charles a present of ten pounds, because he liked the scheme.' The Barlows grew expansive: 'Mr B. has some thoughts of keeping him in his own family; but he waits till he sees more of him before he avows his intention.' This would be 'desirable', since the older man could keep an eye on the happy-go-lucky Charles. 'The other day he clapped C., in his dry way, on the knee and said – that as his wife and he could never contrive to make any boys they must try what they could do with one ready brought up to their hands.' Mary was overjoyed though not without a nagging fear of her brother's relapse, 'I am particularly anxious that C. should behave properly for unless he forgets himself I have not the least doubt of his doing very well. He is in great spirits and I think very much improved.'

Mary resumed correspondence to communicate her excitement to Everina. She was also asking for a contribution since, while he waited for the Barlows, she was expensively preparing Charles for his new life. She placed him in a farm in Leatherhead to study agriculture and equipped him with suitable new clothes. Everina, who also had a soft spot for Charles, responded to the call and helped out.

Wollstonecraft did not really *like* Joel Barlow. He was cold, even calculating, had 'a sound understanding with great mildness of temper' but no 'natural good humour'. As a follower of the pacifist Newington Green Dissenters, she distrusted his stand on violence, which he believed necessary in a revolution. She appreciated Ruth, however. She was her first American friend, a breath of fresh air in the artifice of London.

Then, instead of going to America, Joel returned to Paris, ostensibly for a few weeks. Ruth was left alone and Wollstonecraft developed the friendship. As with the Gabells, she winced at signs of marital bliss, but they were a small price for the company of a frank, open-hearted woman. As she wrote to Everina:

The Barlows are, indeed, very worthy people, and she has been gratified by my attention to her during her husbands absence. I do hope that he will soon return and then I shall be able to form some judgment respecting their future plans. Mrs B. has a very benevolent, affectionate heart, and a tolerable understanding, a little warped it is true by romance; but she is not the less friendly on that account. Delighted with some of her husband's letters, she has exultingly shewn them to me; and, though I took care not to let her see it, I was almost disgusted with the tender passages which afforded her so much satisfaction, because they were turned so prettily that they looked more like the cold ingenuity of the head than the warm overflowings of the heart – However, she did not perceive that the head and heart were gadding far away, when he calls 'her arms his heaven', in search of fame on this same dirty earth – so all was well.

Having placed one sibling, Mary turned with renewed enthusiasm to the others. She had described to her new friend the unpleasant situations of Everina with 'brawling brats' in Waterford and Eliza with vulgar girls in Upton; Ruth began scheming at once: 'she is continually saying how well you might be settled in America. European women, very absurdly, are particularly respected in America, and she confidently asserts that you and Eliza might live, by tak[ing] a few young people under your care, and be respected by the first families; nay, marry well, but this entre nous.' With gusto the childless Ruth imagined including the sisters in plans for Charles: 'She has even said that you might come and live with her, and Eliza keep Charles's house, till you could look about you – I almost wish that you would begin a correspondence with her, it might be of use to Charles.'

Mary had little memory of being a governess in rural exile or else she might not have babbled to Everina about such improbable schemes, all depending on her new friend's liking for their famous sister. More reticent, Eliza and Everina wanted Mary to plan for them but may have recoiled at their needs and failures being displayed at London dinner tables.

The excitement over Charles's prospects was matched by excitement about her own quickened social life. Mary bragged to Everina about new friends: the Cornish artist John Opie was a constant caller, she wrote. Rather a curiosity in London, the self-educated son of a carpenter, he had been patronised by Dr John Wolcot (real name of the political satirist Peter Pindar), who had urged him on public notice as a crude, rude genius – beside his talent for portrait-painting he had a strong Cornish accent and appalling table manners. Opie introduced her to his pretty, frivolous wife, whom Mary predictably disapproved. Another intelligent worthy man was yoked to a trivial woman: Mrs Opie was 'too much of a flirt to be a proper companion for him'. However, both Opies treated her with 'uncommon civility' and she enjoyed their attention. John may even have painted her portrait, again with the powdered hair and serious expression of the previous year but in more attractive pose.[3]

Marriage too was on her mind and she boasted with mock formality: 'be it known unto you that my book &c &c has afforded me an opportunity of settling *very* advantageous in the matrimonial line, with a new acquaintance; but entre nous – a handsome house and a proper man did not tempt me; yet I may as well appear before you with the feather stuck in my cap.' She wanted to impress Everina as fancy-free, yet the object of men's attentions. The arch, stilted language suggests insecurity: Mary was especially insensitive when insecure.

In late summer, a fellow-writer Mary Hays introduced herself, praising *The Rights of Woman* as 'a work full of truth and Genius'. Wollstonecraft now accepted such commendation as her right. The conservative author Hannah More might believe sincerity and humility the predominant virtues, but Wollstonecraft honoured only the former. In contrast to Catherine Macaulay's response to her letter of compliment, she answered Mary Hays's overture haughtily,

> Madam,
> Intending to call upon you I put off answering your letter from time to time till, as is usually the case, it became a task and I could not recollect what I thought of saying when I first read it. I will then simply acknowledge the receipt of your testimony of esteem merely to have an opportunity of telling you that when I return to Town I shall be glad to see you. I should, indeed, have invited you ... but some family cares, among the rest the settling a brother in life, drove secondary objects out of my mind.

A little frostiness could not deter. Hays held radical views on women's place in society and had been writing a work on their oppression which analysed the resulting emotional and psychological damage. Pipped to the post by Wollstonecraft, she laid her work aside and prepared to admire her rival. Persistence triumphed; she persuaded Joseph Johnson to arrange a breakfast meeting. Soon Hays called at Store Street, and the visit went well: 'I was extremely gratified by this interview. This lady appears to me to possess the sort of genius which Lavater calls the one to ten million. Her conversation, like her writings, is brilliant, forcible, instructive and entertaining. She is the true disciple of her own system, and commands at once fear and reverence, admiration and esteem.'[4] Hays was never wonderfully perceptive about others.

Later in the year, she experienced more hauteur. Johnson had agreed to publish *Letters and Essays* by Mary Hays with two tales by her sister Elizabeth; Hays sent in the preface and title page for an opinion, along with a covering letter declaring her 'honour' at acceptance. Wollstonecraft disposed of the title page: 'trifles of this kind I have always left to [Johnson] to settle'. And the letter: 'you must be aware, Madam, that the *honour* of publishing, the phrase on which you have laid a stress, is the cant of both trade and sex; for if really equality should ever take place in society the man who is employed and gives a just equivalent for the money he receives will not behave with the obsequiousness of a servant.' Then she turned to the preface, which thanked well-placed admirers, expressed authorial modesty, and regretted inadequate education, the usual sentiments of a woman before the public.[5] With Christie in France, Wollstonecraft's role on the *Analytical* had increased; so it was as seasoned editor as well as celebrated writer that she took her pencil to what she judged authorial vanity and weak-kneed writing. Years before, when composing her irritable preface to *Original Stories*, she condemned a 'smooth' exhibition of 'proud humility' – she discerned it in Hays. She had little sense that the other woman was a fellow professional:[6]

I do not approve of your preface – and I will tell you why. If your work should deserve attention it is a blur on the very face of it. – Disadvantages of education &c ought, in my opinion, never to be pleaded (with the public) in excuse for defects of any importance, because if the writer has not sufficient strength of mind to overcome the common difficulties which lie in his way, nature seems to command him, with a very audible voice, to leave the task of instructing others to those who can. This kind of vain humility has ever disgusted me – and I should say to an author, who humbly sued for forbearance, 'if you have not a tolerably good opinion of your own production, why intrude it on the public? we have plenty of bad books already, that have just gasped for breath and died.'

The last paragraph I particularly object to, it is so full of vanity ... An author, especially a woman, should be cautious lest she too hastily swallows the crude praises which partial friend and polite acquaintance bestow thoughtlessly when the supplicating eye looks for them. In short, it requires great resolution to try rather to be useful than to please ... Rest, on yourself – if your essays have merit they will stand alone, if not the *shouldering up* of Dr this or that will not long keep them from falling to the ground ... the preface, and even your pamphlet, is too full of yourself. – Inquiries ought to be made before they are answered; and till a work strongly interests the public true modesty should keep the author in the back ground – for it is only about the character and life of a good author that anxiety is active.

Since Wollstonecraft strode into her own works, presumably she regarded herself as 'a good author', quite devoid of 'vanity'.

Hays took some of the genuinely good advice, dropped mention of her high-placed friends and converted the preface into a eulogy of Wollstonecraft as the 'admirable advocate for the rights of woman' whose words concerning the desultory nature of female education she now used to make her less fulsome apology to the reader. Mollified, Wollstonecraft agreed to read the proofs of *Letters and Essays* quickly – as long as she had nothing more important to do. Hays should have the printer's boy deliver them and wait while she corrected grammar and expression: 'I shall use a pencil so you may adopt or erase my corrections without much trouble.' She had now read Hays's earlier piece on public worship, a 'sensible little pamphlet' with 'fewer of the superlatives, exquisite, fascinating, &c, all of the feminine gender, than I expected.' Hays sometimes remained obscure, but she could improve with Wollstonecraft's advice: 'if you continue to write you will imperceptibly correct this fault and learn to think with more clearness, and consequently avoid the errors naturally produced by confusion of thought.' Had they seen this letter, Fuseli and Godwin would have been much amused.

While quick to find fault in others, Wollstonecraft was not bestirring herself. With fame she should have been writing the second volume of *The Rights of Woman*, as she told Roscoe she would. Her friends were publishing away: in February Paine brought out the second, more radical part of his *Rights of Man*, aware that, when one had 'got the ear of the country' one should go on filling it with revolutionary calls, while Joel Barlow followed with *A Letter to the National Convention* urging the French to 'improve the morals of mankind' at the expense of tradition. But Wollstonecraft frittered time away as she had rarely done in the early months at George Street: 'her exertions seem to have been palsied, you know the cause,' Johnson later remarked.[7] Never a fan of her moodiness, he must have lamented that, when jettisoning the ladylike virtues, she included the ideal of stoical self-command.

Despite the impression given to Everina and Mary Hays, Wollstonecraft was growing ever more obsessed with Fuseli. Yet she refused to see herself as Brown's 'hypochondriac', debilitated by obsession. The security of opinion about emotions expressed in *The Rights of Woman* hid any realisation that her profoundest feelings were conflicted. She insisted that, with Fuseli, she was aiming for the nurturing friendship experienced with Johnson. Rousseau's views that sex and sexual difference marked and marred all relations between men and women were mythical. The commonsensical diagnosis of Rousseau's sexual repression provided in *The Rights of Woman* could not apply to her: repeatedly she pleaded to Fuseli the 'strength of feeling unalloyed by passion'.

For twelve months after completing *The Rights of Woman* she composed nothing but reviews. These lacked the fire and zest of her earlier notices, but were enough to prevent indigence. Probably prodded by Johnson, Fuseli became concerned. Although he had quarrelled with her old friend, the medical poet John Armstrong, he followed his system for health, which precluded cherishing the 'poison' of passion unnerving body and soul. So, according to his biographer Knowles, he 'reasoned with her, but without any effect, upon the impropriety of indulging in a passion that took her out of common life. Her answer was, "If I thought my passion criminal, I would conquer it, or die in the attempt. For immodesty, in my eyes, is ugliness; my soul turns with disgust from pleasure tricked out in charms which shun the light of heaven." ' Feeling the absurdity of what she said but powerless to refute it except by the grossest argument, Fuseli gave up.

She was exhilarated by a plan for Johnson, the Fuselis and herself to visit France together in early August. To Everina she described it as 'a summer excursion to Paris' of about six weeks. She had just taken money from her sister for Charles, so needed to assure Everina that her journey would not be expensive 'or I should put if off till a more convenient season, for I am not, as you may suppose, very flush of money.' Charles was wearing out his new farming clothes in Leatherhead, but 'his indolence' had 'received a shove' and he had transacted some business for Joseph Johnson. He still awaited the date of the Barlows' departure for America.

The Revolution was at an interesting stage and, like Christie and Barlow, Johnson, Fuseli and Wollstonecraft wanted to see it at first hand. In revolutionary France divorce and unconventional family arrangements were discussed; perhaps she hoped that, in the freer atmosphere, a clearer role might be found for her with the Fuselis.[8] For the moment she was simply excited by the prospect of travelling as a famous author in the company of a famous artist: 'I shall be introduced to many people, my book has been translated and praised in some popular prints; and Fuseli, of course, is well known.'

Given such contacts, she could now help Eliza, she told Everina, unaware of the huge resentment her sister was fermenting. Eliza envied Everina's time in France and a similar stay would make her eligible for superior posts and rescue her from the wet Welsh winter which exacerbated her rheumatism. The French excursion was communicated through Everina, together with the plans for Eliza; they caused a paroxysm of bitterness. Why did not Mary take her with her now? Why did she not make her part of her life, as she had once done? She scorned the notion that her sister might do something in future. All she saw was proud Mary's desire to shed her relatives. Although the relationship with Fuseli remained unexpressed, Eliza, barred from romance herself, read the symptoms – unlike Everina:

> So the author of the rights of Woman is going to France I dare say, her chief motive is to promote her poor Bess's Comfort! or thine my girl or at least I think she will thus reason – Well, in spite of *Reason* when Mrs W reaches the Continent she will be but a woman! I Cannot help painting her in the height of all her wishes, at the very summit of happiness, for will not ambition fill every Chink of her Great Soul? (for such I really think her's) that is not occupied by *Love*? After having drawn this sketch, you can hardly suppose me so sanguine as to expect my pretty face will be thought of when matters of State are in agitation[,] yet I know you think such a miracle not impossible[.] I wish I could think it at all probable, but alas! it has so much the appearance of Castle building that I think it will soon disappear like the 'Baseless fabrick of a vision and leave not a wrack behind' –
>
> And you actually have the vanity to imagine that in the National Assembly Personages like M. and F[useli] will bestow a thought on two females whom nature meant to 'suckel fools and chronicle small beer' . . . I blush to own that my temper is now so *soured*; and continually ruffled that I almost despies myself . . .

Eliza might have been less sour had she known Mary's underlying mental state during this summer, as well as the outcome of the Paris plan. The party set out, but in Dover received troubled news from France. The Revolution had turned threatening: the king's palace was assaulted and his guard massacred. It was the end of monarchy and, in some people's opinion, the start of anarchy. Fuseli, Johnson and Wollstonecraft were well-wishers but retreated before disorder and violence. They turned back towards London. Perhaps there were rifts among them, which made politics a useful excuse.

Deeply disappointed, Wollstonecraft solaced herself by going to the country, taking the ailing Johnson along – she had a good friend called Mrs Cotton in Berkshire, who seems sometimes to have provided a refuge. It is unlikely she tried the Gabells again – she had had her fill of amorous domesticity. The departure of Johnson and Wollstonecraft led to gossip. As she reported to Roscoe in Liverpool, 'I am told the world, to talk big, married m[e] to [Johnson] whilst we were away.' Given the truth of things, she could only smile wryly at the rumour.

On her return in mid-September she saw Charles who had been working hard for Johnson: 'the habit of order which he is acquiring, by attending to business will, to use Mr Paine's phrase, "do him no harm in America"; besides, the company he mixes with at this social table opens his mind.' She was less satisfied with Barlow, who, though 'a worthy man', was 'devoured by ambition'. He ignored the fact that Charles was costing her money and still gave no definite date for returning to England. France enthralled him, she suspected, either because of its politics or, more likely, because of its business possibilities. There was always some excuse why he lingered 'amidst alarms instead of returning to the peaceable shades of America.'[9] Rest, she believed, was 'the rack of active minds, and life loses its zest when we find that there is nothing worth wishing for, nothing to detain the thoughts in the present scene, but what quickly grows stale, rendering the soul torpid or uneasy.' The adjectives described the unquiet Barlow.

She was right to be suspicious. The noble pioneer had become the speculator, another American type she would soon know well. Charles must make his own way to the New World alone. The voyage need be postponed no longer.

Now it was close, she felt sad, so much so that she could not even write to tell Roscoe until he was actually going. Lazy and extravagant Charles might be but he had charm and, though a dependent, never threw himself on her as others sometimes did. She told him nothing of Fuseli and he suspected nothing, but his uncomplicated presence comforted her. He was a favourite too with Eliza and Everina; even more than brother James he sustained with dreams of money and of living happily ever after together. So far he had burdened them, but he would repay them all a hundredfold. He was to leave through Liverpool, where he would call on Roscoe.

The failure of the French trip combined with the loss of Charles, which left her unusually family-less, clarified matters: Fuseli was absolutely necessary to her. She must be open about this. Had she not promoted frankness between men and women in *The Rights of Woman*? Would she not be following her principles? She was not asking for sexual sharing – she had just written resoundingly against polygamy – but for constant emotional closeness. Surely he would pity her. Pity was her prevailing passion and led to firm love. Perhaps it did so in a man. In this she later believed herself mistaken: men were more sex-obsessed than women and women loved with more steadiness and warmth. But now she was influenced by her theories and could not allow sexual difference to disturb them.

Fuseli's biographer Knowles described events:

At length Mrs Wollstonecraft appears to have grown desperate, for she had the temerity to go to Mrs Fuseli, and to tell her, that she wished to become an inmate in her family; and she added, as I am above deceit, it is right to say that this proposal 'arises from the sincere affection which I have for your husband, for I find that I cannot live without the satisfaction of seeing and conversing with him daily'. This frank avowal immediately opened the eyes of Mrs Fuseli, who being alarmed by the declaration, not only refused her solicitation, but she instantly forbade her the house.

Wollstonecraft left without further remonstrance. She was humiliated, bested by a woman with half her significance. And this after she had conquered her lifelong demand for primacy. Presumably Fuseli made no effort to contradict the banishment; Wollstonecraft was left with neither hope nor dignity.

There was nothing to be done but retire. Her high-minded aims were reduced to sexual jealousy between women: for all the self-esteem revealed to Mary Hays and Everina and the vanity of fame so resented by Eliza, she had been displayed as simply a rejected lover. Summoning up what remained of her self-respect, she apologised to Fuseli 'for having disturbed the quiet tenour of his life'.[10]

Hers was not the only scandal of the season. In Paris Christie had acted unsuccessfully for a London mercantile house, leaving immense debts and financial victims. He returned to London with a married Frenchwoman, who bore his child. They were awaiting the change in French divorce laws so they could marry. But, when the baby was some weeks old and divorce about to be loosened, Christie married an English heiress, Rebecca Thomson, and became a partner in her grandfather's carpet business in Finsbury Square. The couple left for Paris on a wedding trip, taking with them Christie's sister Jane.

There they joined the large Anglo-American community, including Paine, who had fled from London as the book police closed in on him. According to one story, Blake, hearing of a warrant for his arrest, warned him, 'You must not go home, or you are a dead man!' He left England to the howls of a Dover crowd, threatening to duck, tar and feather the 'great Satan'; he arrived in Calais to a hero's welcome: soldiers at attention, a gun salute, officers embracing him and women giving him the national cockade.[11] The English government tried him *in absentia* for seditious libel; he was found guilty and exiled forever. In Paris he became part of a 'British Club' of revolutionary sympathisers who met at White's Hotel to applaud French successes and foster revolution in Britain. Its members included many of those who had sat at Johnson's dinner table.

Christie's precipitate journey and the existence of so many friends in Paris persuaded Wollstonecraft to cross the Channel and do by herself what she had yearned to do in company. There she would not risk encountering Fuseli or suspect the sniggering of common friends. Despite the news of atrocities, the rush of émigrés into England and the intellectual retreat of some of the radicals, she would go to Paris, without men to accompany her. Anywhere was better than a mocking London.

Godwin summed up the plan: 'the cordial intercourse of Mr Fuseli, which had at first been one of her greatest pleasures', had become 'a source of perpetual torment to her. She conceived it necessary to snap the chain of this association in her mind; and, for that purpose, determined to seek a new climate, and mingle in different scenes.' As before, she intended to go for about six weeks.

She arranged to stay with Aline Fillietaz, daughter of Eliza's old head-mistress, Mrs Bregantz at Putney, and now married to a well-to-do French-man. Reversing the usual pattern, she asked to borrow £30 from her sisters, justified by her intention of finding them better positions. They should send it to Johnson on whom she could then draw. Everina was willing since Mary had paid her expenses in France, but Eliza was suspicious. She doubted Mary would be any use to them anywhere. Her reaction was unfair: considering that £15 was expected to keep Everina for six months, the larger sum for six weeks suggests that she did intend to find her sisters posts and support them in France when they arrived. She had little sense of how discomposing a revolution could be.

Before she left, Wollstonecraft wrote her miseries to those who could understand, chiefly Roscoe, to whom she had already hinted much, and of course Johnson. As news of atrocities filtered out of France, magnified in British newspapers, Roscoe found his radicalism making him unpopular in bourgeois Liverpool, where those who had once approved the French desire for civic liberty now saw France as the enemy of property, a bad influence on restive English artisans. Since the projected trip with Fuseli and Johnson, the September Massacres had consumed 1400 priests, prisoners and aris-tocrats, while individual attacks had reached new depths: rumour had Marie Antoinette's alleged lesbian lover, the princesse de Lamballe, dragged through the streets by the mob, her breasts and vulva cut off – the latter worn as a moustache – her head dressed and carried on a pike, swayed to and fro outside the queen's window. News of this sort revolted the English, whipped up into anti-French patriotism by their anxious government.[12]

Wollstonecraft was not wavering, and she urged Roscoe to stand firm. He was writing a cultural biography of the Renaissance Lorenzo de' Medici, depicting him as a republican spirit, epitome of the true patriot and patron. Distrusting the project, however embued with revolutionary sympathies, she hoped he was not exhibiting 'the glossy tide of aristocracy' and allowing his studies to make him too critical of modern politics. He must not 'forget the order of the day, or I shall think your praises of Liberty mere headwork'. She also feared that Roscoe might be influenced by public opinion: 'let me beg you not to mix with the shallow herd who throw an odium on immutable principles, because some of the mere instrument[s] of the revolution were too sharp,' she counselled. 'Children of any growth will do mischief when they meddle with edged tools.' Yet she must have known that by now the 'shallow herd' she urged Roscoe to avoid included most people in London and the provinces.

The bread-and-butter note she wrote on Charles's behalf revealed more than concern for the purity of Roscoe's politics. She wanted his under-standing for what, underneath her flippancy, he must realise she was suffer-ing. Probably he knew of the Fuseli débâcle and she was eager to insist that, however it looked, she had acted rationally. Roscoe had admired her as author and she did not want pity as a rejected woman:

> When do you think of again visiting the metropolis? Not very soon, I hope, for I intend no longer to struggle with a rational desire, so have determined to set out for Paris in the course of a fortnight or three weeks; and I shall not now halt at Dover, I promise you; for as I go alone neck or nothing is the word. During my stay I shall not forget my friends; but I will tell you so when I am really there ... I am still a Spinster on the wing. At Paris, indeed, I might take a husband for the time being, and get divorced when my truant heart longed again to nestle with its old friends; but this speculation has not yet entered into my plan.

To another radical she could mock marriage as an unstable institution that any government could change and any person choose and unchoose. Back in September the French legislators had declared it simply a civil contract and established divorce as a right of any free individual. In reality, nothing in Wollstonecraft's private or public writings suggested she believed in any-thing less than monogamy and lifelong commitment. She had been prepared to devote herself to Fuseli in a platonic manner and had not suggested her commitment should be passing or that she and Fuseli should rid themselves of passion with a sexual affair. She was deceiving herself if she thought she had a 'truant heart'.

Although she had assured Roscoe that nothing would make her stop at Dover this time, when departure neared she began to falter. '[I]n going I seem to strive against fate, for had I not taken my place I should have put off the journey again,' she wrote to Everina a week before. This was a reasonable response to a political situation which even she found 'rather alarming'. England and France seemed about to go to war; if so, she would be travelling to an enemy nation.

At the same time her reluctance was emotional: it was hard to escape habitual pain. The only respectable face of anxiety was worry over Johnson's ill health; of Fuseli she could say nothing to her sisters: 'My spirits even sink; but I go – yet should any accident happen to my dear and worthy friend Johnson during my absence I should never forgive myself for leaving him – These are vapourish fears – still they fasten on me and press home most feelingly a long comment on the vanity of human wishes.' Her worry was no doubt genuine: Johnson was ill again with asthma and she sensed that she added to his suffering by selfishly complaining.

When she wrote her publisher a final letter, she was open about Fuseli and the insecurity caused in all her relationships. She could no longer believe her unconquerable misery God-given: it was not proof of superiority but a subtle mixture of physical and mental failing. The emotions which the *Vindications* had ringingly asserted should be ruled by reason were rebellious: 'I am a mere animal, and instinctive emotions too often silence the suggestions of reason.' She had made herself sick with uncontrolled feelings: 'I have been very ill – Heaven knows it was more than fancy – After some sleepless, wearisome nights, towards the morning I have grown delirious.'

Her dreams merged wish-fulfilment and anxiety. One time she imagined Fuseli 'thrown into great distress by his folly; and I, unable to assist him, was in an agony.' She woke to find her nerves in 'a painful state of irritation'. Only society could calm her and she desperately sought Johnson. Suddenly she felt uneasy: rejected in one place, why not in another? She remembered how much she had plagued and hassled her publisher 'with childish complaints, and the reverses of a disordered imagination'; anxiously she wondered if she were simply tolerated, not liked. Johnson never called on her; it was always she on him whether or not she were unwell. Perhaps he did not really want her. She had been so sure of herself, so secure in her new significance. Now fame seemed hollow, deceptive. But she did not quite eat humble-pie: mortification always included some resentment.

She was in such a raw state Johnson could do nothing right. She was hurt by a note; she gave it 'a kind of winterly smile, which diffuses a beam of despondent tranquillity over the features', but had no clear reason for her edgy detachment. She knew she was making her own misery or colluding in its generation and she tried to be as honest as possible:

I have nourished a sickly kind of delicacy, which gives me many unnecessary pangs. – I acknowledge that life is but a jest – and often a frightful dream – yet catch myself every day searching for something serious – and feel real misery from the disappointment. I am a strange compound of weakness and resolution! However, if I must suffer, I will endeavour to suffer in silence. There is certainly a great defect in my mind – my wayward heart creates its own misery – Why I am made thus I cannot tell; and, till I can form some idea of the whole of my existence, I must be content to weep and dance like a child – long for a toy, and be tired of it as soon as I get it.

We must each of us wear a fool's cap; but mine, alas! has lost its bells, and is grown so heavy, I find it intolerably troublesome. – Good-night! I have been pursuing a number of strange thoughts since I began to write, and have actually both wept and laughed immoderately – Surely I am a fool...

She could not bring herself to use the rational language of *The Rights of Woman* on herself; her own life was always delivered in the language of sensibility.

# Part III

# 19

*'How silent is now Versailles!'*

Paris was a shock when she arrived in mid-December. Having sailed to Ireland and been tossed in storms in the Bay of Biscay, Wollstonecraft is unlikely to have found the Channel crossing disconcerting, but, like many English people, she may have expected France to be warmer than it was and she arrived with a heavy cold. It soured her mood. She had set out to discover whether the French Revolution was 'a noble glow of patriotism' or a 'phosphoric burst produced by levity'.[1] She was quick to suspect the latter: 'when I first entered Paris, the striking contrast of riches and poverty, elegance and slovenliness, urbanity and deceit, every where caught my eye, and saddened my soul . . . The whole mode of life here tends to render the people frivolous.'[2]

Nursing her cold, she went straight to 22 rue Melée (Meslay) off the Boulevard Saint-Martin, to find her hostess, Aline Fillietaz, away and the house grander than expected. Servants met her: 'you will easily imagine how awkwardly I behaved unable to utter a word,' she told Everina. Her cold became a chesty cough and she felt too poorly to attack the town. She had walked briskly around London for health and business, but here going out was difficult: she was ignorant of Paris and the streets were dirtier. Not understanding people, she was quick to see a mob and felt surges of hatred whenever she failed to catch an individual within the mass.

So she stayed in the large six-storey house alone struggling with French: 'I apply so closely to the language, and labour so continually to understand what I hear that I never go to bed without a head ache – and my spirits are fatigued with endeavouring to form a just opinion of public affairs.' During the mistress's absence the servants tried to make her comfortable, but merely suggested how little spoken French she knew. She felt irritated by one, a pert young maid who insisted she knew English because she had taught in an English boarding-school. She seemed eager to help but, when Wollstonecraft asked her to do something, nothing happened. She described the predicament to Everina: 'dust is thrown up with a self-sufficient air, and I am obliged to appear to see her meaning clearly, though she puzzles herself, that I may not make her feel her ignorance; but you must have experienced the same thing.' It was easy to address Everina on whose memories she could draw.

Unaware of the extent of Eliza's resentment, a week or so after arriving, Mary wrote to her also. So far her experience was comically at odds with Eliza's visions and her tone was subdued. She had tried to find a place for her sister in supposedly cheap Geneva, but as France grew unstable, so Swiss currency strengthened. She then wrote to Fuseli, giving her views on French affairs and begging him to write occasionally. He did not reply.

This December the city was especially tense. France had provoked war with Austria and Prussia, then experienced military defeat. Internal subversives were blamed, including the king, whose presence must encourage enemies abroad and provoke conspiracies at home. Louis XVI was therefore to be tried for his life. Paine opposed the death penalty, wanting the king humiliated, not martyred. English history with Charles I had taught him the foolishness of letting a king star in a fatal drama. At the moment Louis was held in the King's Prison at the Temple close to Wollstonecraft's lodgings.

From the Fillietaz house she now witnessed the king passing through the streets to his trial. She described it to Johnson in a new kind of personal prose, neither strident nor sentimental, the hallmark of her best later writing. Like her mentor Richard Price, she was never a full republican though using a republican analysis to attack the injustice of all inherited privilege. She had little time for actual kings, yet the insanity of George III, perhaps echoing her own brother Henry's, incited pity in the face of Burke's ridicule and she was always moved by lonely suffering, royal or otherwise. The Fillietaz servants had gone out to swell the standing crowds and she was alone watching from the attic.[3] It was an unaccustomed place, which exaggerated her sense of isolation:

> About nine o'clock this morning, the king passed by my window, moving silently along (excepting now and then a few strokes on the drum, which rendered the stillness more awful) through empty streets, surrounded by the national guards, who, clustering round the carriage, seemed to deserve their name. The inhabitants flocked to their windows, but the casements were all shut, not a voice was heard, nor did I see any thing like an insulting gesture. – For the first time since I entered France, I bowed to the majesty of the people, and respected the propriety of behaviour so perfectly in unison with my own feelings. I can scarcely tell you why, but an association of ideas made the tears flow insensibly from my eyes, when I saw Louis sitting, with more dignity than I expected from his character, in a hackney coach going to meet death, where so many of his race have triumphed.

My fancy instantly brought Louis XIV before me, entering the capital with all his pomp, after one of the victories most flattering to his pride, only to see the sunshine of prosperity overshadowed by the sublime gloom of misery. I have been alone ever since; and, though my mind is calm, I cannot dismiss the lively images that have filled my imagination all the day. – Nay, do not smile, but pity me; for, once or twice, lifting my eyes from the paper, I have seen eyes glare through a glass-door opposite my chair, and bloody hands shook at me. Not the distant sound of a footstep can I hear. My apartments are remote from those of the servants, the only persons who sleep with me in an immense hotel, one folding door opening after another. – I wish I had even kept the cat with me! – I want to see something alive; death in so many frightful shapes has taken hold of my fancy. – I am going to bed – and, for the first time in my life, I cannot put out the candle.

The French people were not always so majestic and she was shocked by the habitual disorder and violence, which, unlike Burke, she had not expected to accompany a revolution. She was appalled by the greed and selfishness of those who fed on disorder. 'Liberty is the mother of virtue,' she had written in *The Rights of Woman*. She was no longer sure and, as her abstract enthusiasm for French radicalism dissipated, she experienced her own mental revolution. Dismayed, she forgot her previous warning against judging people and events prematurely.

In London at Johnson's table she had learnt mainly of political and social tyranny. Paine's *Rights of Man* argued that, for freedom, egalitarian principles must be extended to economic as well as political life. In France she understood this point: as power moved from one group, it could settle on another equally unjustly. In *The Rights of Men* she had attacked the system of hereditary property favouring men; now she saw how much the definition of the citizen and the privileging of the male depended on possession of *any* property, inherited or earned, from which most women were barred. The new order was not one of upstanding Dissenting merchants, but of greedy entrepreneurs; it might be no better for women, or indeed humanity, than the old order of hereditary privilege. She was aghast to think that a sullied nation like France might never become pure and that disorder led inevitably to vice. Her horror emerged from her 'Letter on the Present Character of the French Nation', intended as the first of a series for Johnson, dated 15 February 1793, only two months after her arrival:

I would I could first inform you that, out of the chaos of vices and follies, prejudices and virtues, rudely jumbled together, I saw the fair form of Liberty slowly rising, and Virtue expanding her wings, to shelter all her children! I should then hear the account of the barbarities that have rent the bosom of France patiently, and bless the firm hand that lopt off the rotten limbs. But, if the aristocracy of birth is levelled with the ground, only to make room for that of riches, I am afraid that the morals of the people will not be much improved by the change, or the government rendered less venal . . .

Before I came to France, I cherished, you know, an opinion, that strong virtues might exist with the polished manner produced by the progress of civilization; and I even anticipated the epoch, when, in the course of improvement, men would labour to become virtuous, without being goaded on by misery. But now, the perspective of the golden age, fading before the attentive eye of observation, almost eludes my sight; and losing thus in part my theory of a more perfect state, start not, my friend, if I bring forward an opinion, which at first glance seems to be levelled against the existence of God! I am not become an Atheist, I asure you, by residing in Paris: yet I begin to fear that vice, or, if you will, evil, is the grand mobile of action, and that, when the passions are justly poized, we become harmless, and in the same proportion useless . . .

She had suspected that pain was the pre-condition of wisdom; could vice be the pre-condition of action? It was not atheism but a negative version of her old psycho-religious beliefs subverting her new rationalism.

The horror was that human nature could not progress: 'names, not principles, are changed' and 'the turn of the tide has left the dregs of the old system to corrupt the new.' Pride in office and power remained, exacerbated since the possessors were new: each 'endeavours to make hay while the sun shines' and each 'stalks like a cock on a dunghil'.[4] It would have been better, she implied, if the French Revolution had been carried out by the virtuous citizens of Newington Green and Johnson's dinner guests.[5]

The return of the Fillietazes improved her life. Aline's husband was not 'what is termed a polite man' but he had 'great softness of manners'. The bourgeois French were what she expected, easy and superficial, urbane and fashionable like their furniture. Paris was just the place for someone wishing to live cheerfully without deep emotions. It was a good recipe for her present state.

Yet her hacking cough kept her depressed. The weather was bad and she still could not easily walk out, so she had to spend a fortune on hiring coaches. She hated confinement: 'The streets of Paris are certainly very disagreeable, so that it is impossible to walk for air, and I always want air,' she confessed to Ruth Barlow, left behind in London. She remained bashful about her bookish French. She wanted to distinguish herself from unskilled

English people who 'talk away with an unblushing face'; at the same time she knew herself too inhibited.

It was not only bashfulness that silenced her, it was also homesickness. As in Ireland, she longed for England once out of it. As she told Ruth, 'when my heart sinks or flies to England to hover round those I most love all the fine French phrases, ready cut and dry for use, fly away the Lord know where.' Sometimes she was so preoccupied she simply replied 'Oui, oui,' to whatever was said. A gentleman warned her she might say it at quite the wrong time.

Her homesickness was sometimes so great she was even tempted to leave before she had given Paris a chance. People were quitting the city and passage out was hard to obtain. A man had offered her 'a place in his carriage to return to England' and she had wavered. 'I knew not how to say no.' But she resisted; it would be foolish to go back after taking such trouble to come. Ruth probably knew the state of things between her and Fuseli and understood that her friend was still grieving when Wollstonecraft confessed, 'I am afraid that I have a strange spirit of contradiction in me physically and morally, for though the air is pure I am not well, and the vivacity that should amuse me fatigue[s] me more than you can conceive.' The French could not yet compete with her friends in London: 'All the affection I have for the French is for the whole nation, and it seems to be a little honey spread over all the bread I eat in their land.'

Over the next weeks she cheered up and socialised. Soon neither her own situation nor France's seemed so dire. At 10.22 on 21 January 1793 Louis Capet, as the king was now called, was guillotined before a crowd of 80,000 spectators. His head and body were deeply buried and covered with quicklime. Paris did not fall into turmoil, as many hostile British expected.

The expatriate community was large and varied: enthusiastic British, speculating or liberating Americans, and idealistic Germans. With these she relished again the sort of intellectual dinners attended so garrulously at Johnson's. Even though the political climate had worsened, many foreigners were enjoying themselves: the lawyer Thomas Cooper, who had come to Paris with the steam-engine inventor James Watt to deliver a declaration of support from the Manchester Constitutional Society, claimed that the four months he spent there were the happiest of his life. He admired Wollstonecraft and she probably read his work – he wrote on materialist and medical issues and was fascinated by Cullen and Brown – as was Christie, who was making a schematic outline of Brown's system for the 1795 edition of The Elements of Medicine. Cooper also had the distinction, with her friend Dr Price, of being attacked by Burke for revolutionary enthusiasm.[6]

The group of British and American friends passed their 'Evenings together very frequently either in conversation or any amusement [which] might tend to dissipate those gloomy impressions, the state of affairs naturally produced. Miss Wollstonecraft was always particularly anxious for the success of the Revolution & the hideous aspect of the then political horizon hurt her exceedingly. She always thought, however, it would finally succeed. Sometimes we met at Mr Paines or formed dining parties,' recorded a young man called I. B. Johnson.[7]

Paine and Joel Barlow were often at White's Hotel, made infamous in England by a political dinner in the previous November held by the 'Friends of the Rights of Man' or the British Club, fifty revolutionary sympathisers, with Paine at their head. On this occasion Barlow had presented his Letter to the National Convention, from whom he and Christie received the title of *Citoyen*. Then they drank to the abolition of hereditary rank, the success of the French, and 'the coming Convention of England and Ireland'.[8] The event was much reported in English newspapers, which reacted with amusement or outrage. Some found the last toast treasonable.

Paine was in the thick of politics despite his lack of fluent French. He and Condorcet, a seemingly cold and reticent man but the most concerned of the major revolutionaries for women's rights, were sketching out a new constitution and involved in several committees considering such topics as education and land reform. Wollstonecraft told Ruth Barlow that she was working on a 'plan of education' and it is most likely that the invitation came through Paine or Condorcet, a member of the committee on public education. He might well have wanted to hear the opinions of someone who supported coeducation and community schools as well as female rights.[9]

Through Christie, Wollstonecraft had arranged to receive drafts of money from Johnson. Despite difficulties between the countries, trade continued: commercial men always knew how to move money. Having failed in his last entrepreneurial project in France, Christie was now Paris agent for the London firm of Turnbull, Forbes & Co. trading in flour. He too was deep in politics. His home life was complicated by his French mistress's return with their child to Paris, not best pleased with her treatment: she was trying to keep her baby while gaining compensation for Christie's many broken promises.

Wollstonecraft spent much time with Thomas and Rebecca Christie, who were great entertainers of expatriates. Through them she met the rich Silesian count, Gustav von Schlabrendorf, an enthusiastic revolutionary who was living 'on almost nothing' to avoid adverse comment on his wealth.[10] He was struck by Wollstonecraft's manner and appearance; later he recalled her 'charming grace' and face 'full of expression ... There was enchantment in her glance, her voice, and her movement' and she was 'the noblest, purest and most intelligent woman I have ever met'.[11] He declared he had been in love with her during their time together, but the count was a susceptible man and was in fact (temporarily) engaged to Jane Christie, Thomas's lively sister. Still, the testimony underscored a truth about Wollstonecraft: that passion took her to the depth but she sprang up with congenial society and the possibility of other relationships. 'New-born affections', she once said, were the only method to rub off the 'rust of the mind'. She was most attractive to men with her assertiveness a little moderated by grief. Just like her heroine in *Mary, a Fiction*.

Wollstonecraft did not seek out the women's clubs, so much a feature of the early Revolution. Neither did she try to meet individual radical women, not the most extreme, Pauline Léon or Claire Lacombe, who wrote 'free woman' after her signature. Not even the more moderate Dutch woman, Etta Palm, who campaigned for universal suffrage without property qualifications; or the prolific author Olympe de Gouges, who had just anticipated Wollstonecraft in asking men, 'Who has given you the sovereign authority to oppress my sex?' Palm and Gouges made clearer political claims for all women than Wollstonecraft, who had aimed her *Vindication* mainly at the middle class. Even they had to change before being fit to enter political life. Indeed, she had only half suggested that women might be represented in legislatures.[12] By contrast, Gouges called ringingly for a female national assembly and the adoption of a 'Declaration of the Rights of Woman and Citizen'. Paraphrasing the 'Declaration of the Rights of Man', she demanded equal legal treatment for the sexes, equal admission to public office and equal property rights.[13] Gouges' power base was the women's clubs and street demonstrations. Believing change should come through individual rationality, Wollstonecraft could not support mass protest, which tended to rely on prejudice and simplified emotional appeals; the individual must act alone through reason.

Other women carried pikes and marched in the streets in red and white trousers. The most flamboyant was Théroigne de Méricourt, who believed the Revolution as much women's as men's. Back in 1789, dressed in scarlet riding-dress and black-plumed hat, she had embraced and harangued the women marchers to Versailles, so vilified by Burke. It had rained heavily and they were bedraggled; she had tried to warm them with some of her fire. Short, pretty, loud and promiscuous, she insisted that, as in early times, women could fight and rule with men; believing that courage and intrepidity should compensate for want of strength, she had formed a battalion of women warriors. Later she organised civic banquets and fêtes at which women danced the patriotic dance of war and liberty.[14] Wollstonecraft liked this martial parade even less than street demonstrations – perhaps it reminded her of the Amazon Hannah Snell: in *The Rights of Woman* she declared women should not 'turn their distaff into a musket'. She had, too, a general fear of force, the legacy of her family and of the Newington Green Dissenters, who profoundly distrusted popular violence. No discussion between Théroigne and Wollstonecraft is recorded, although they were in each other's company and Théroigne knew well many members of the British Club, including Christie.[15]

Wollstonecraft was more inclined to react favourably to moderate republican bourgeois women than to street revolutionaries. She mixed with *salonnières* rather than activists, and became a firm friend of an English lady, Helen Maria Williams, rather than of the streetwoman Théroigne. Williams, once the giver of literary tea-parties in London, which Wollstonecraft did not attend, now held a glamorous political salon on the rue Helvétius, paid for in part, it was suspected, by some reporting on her friends alternately to the British and French authorities. It was no great disgrace: few British people in France avoided being caught up in this informal and ubiquitous espionage.

Williams's enthusiastic dispatches from the early Revolution had done much to warm English opinion to the French political adventure. Where Wollstonecraft's *Rights of Men* had mocked Burke's vision of *ancien régime* chivalry, Williams's *Letters from France* had replaced it with a new one of revolutionary chivalry. Her words inappropriately prepared Wollstonecraft for a romantic Paris marked by 'its noble contempt of sordid cares, its spirit of unsullied generosity, and its heroic zeal for the happiness of others'.[16] During her impeccable youth in England, Williams had been patronised as a sentimental poet by bluestocking ladies like Anna Seward, and Dissenting clergymen and famous authors, including Dr Johnson and the physician Dr John Moore. He perhaps had given her the form in which she would have most success, the familiar reminiscence mingling personal anecdote with history and critical observation.

Now Helen Maria Williams was in her radical maturity: at the White's Hotel dinner, a song of hers had been sung and toasts drunk to the 'Women of Great Britain ... who have distinguished themselves by their writing in favour of the French revolution'. Among these were Williams and Charlotte Smith – whose partisan revolutionary novel *Desmond* had just appeared in England – but not Wollstonecraft. It was two years since she had opposed

Burke and supported the Revolution, but it is strange that Barlow, who had been complimented by Smith just before he left England and was probably the reason for her inclusion in the toast, did not also bring Wollstonecraft to the attention of the guests. Perhaps he did not like her any more than she him.[17]

Surrounded by her family of mother and sisters, Williams was now allegedly the mistress of John Hurford Stone, president of the British Club, a married man whose revolutionary sympathies antagonised the London government but who was as much concerned with business as politics – more in the line of Christie and Barlow than Paine. Wollstonecraft may have met Stone earlier when he was a member of Price's Newington Green chapel but now he showed little admiration for her. Her frank opinionated manner contrasted with Helen's artful social style and he could not approve her friendship with Christie, once his business partner, now his debtor. Stone thought Christie a thorough crook.

Helen Maria Williams did not escape British public censure for her opinions. It was one thing to support the fall of the Bastille, another to praise revolutionary principles after they had shown their ugliness. For her continuing allegiance to 'savage anarchy', Boswell erased the word 'amiable' from his description of her in his Life of Johnson and Anna Seward, who always thought she showed only the 'sunny-side' of the Revolution, urged her to 'return, while yet you may, to your native country', to fly 'the land of carnage' and the 'influence of the equalizing system'.[18] Wollstonecraft, however, was predisposed to approve of Williams. In a review of her novel Julia in 1790 she remarked, 'Without any acquaintance with Miss W. only from the perusal of this production, we should venture to affirm that sound principles animate her conduct, and that the sentiments they dictate are the pillars instead of being the fanciful ornaments of her character.' When she reviewed her French chronicles just before leaving England, she found them 'unaffected', displaying 'the goodness of the writer's heart'.[19]

Now she met Williams in the flesh, her views were modified. 'Unaffected' was not the adjective most people applied to her. Like so many of her acquaintances, Wollstonecraft noted her new friend's gushing social manner – though failing to appreciate the shrewdness that would help her survive the Revolution and its aftermath:

> Miss Williams has behaved very civilly to me and I shall visit her frequently, because I rather like her, and I meet french company at her house. Her manners are affected, yet the simple goodness of her heart continually breaks through the varnish, so that one would be more inclined, at least I should, to love than admire

her. – Authorship is a heavy weight for female shoulders especially in the sunshine of prosperity.

Wollstonecraft must have confided in Williams about Fuseli, for a common acquaintance remarked on Williams's solacing her in her grief. She may have provided more comfort by her example: through her – as indeed through Christie – Wollstonecraft could see that in France there was life after failed marriages and liaisons, and that there were mutually fulfilling heterosexual relationships without the bonds of matrimony. At the beginning of her address to Talleyrand in *The Rights of Woman*, she had admired French salons but feared them as adulterous and corrupt. In Ireland she had been appalled at the hypocritical sensuality of refined social life. Now she found Williams's salon less corrupting than exhilarating.

Through Williams or Paine, Wollstonecraft may have met another celebrated but more Spartan *salonnière*, Manon Roland, now at modest apartments on the rue de la Harpe. She could not have accompanied Paine to the twice-weekly dinners since Madame Roland received no women on these serious occasions, believing that they should not show their disputatious talents in public, but Wollstonecraft would have heard much of them.[20] Madame Roland too had a passion outside marriage, for a deputy called Buzot, but, like Wollstonecraft, had refused to surrender to '*impulsions brutales des sens*'. In Wollstonecraft, Madame Roland could have seen a woman who, like her admired Catherine Macaulay, had achieved significance on her own not, as she had done, through service to a man. It must have seemed an attractive route as she contemplated her own literary and political abilities, superior to those of her older husband. Though idealistic, neither Helen Maria Williams nor Manon Roland was radical in her views on women and Wollstonecraft's knowledge, actual or by report, of these charming and thinking ladies may have helped her see the attractions of some of the conventions of femininity denigrated in *The Rights of Woman*, as well as confirming her in the notion that public and private spheres were indistinct.

A further fruitful introduction was to Madeleine Schweitzer, formerly Magdalena Hess of Zurich, Fuseli's one-time beloved, whom Wollstonecraft mistakenly assumed was Lavater's niece, another former object of his passion. Madame Schweitzer was wife to a Swiss banker of revolutionary leanings, Johann Carl. After some wariness, the two women became friends and met frequently at the luxurious Schweitzer home. Wollstonecraft was not secretive about her past among these sophisticated gossiping people and their shared experiences may have made a bond between her and Madeleine, although the latter sometimes resented her new friend's overbearing and opinionated manner.[21] Her husband, who did not care for his wife's past, came to like Wollstonecraft rather more and later rebuked Fuseli for his hard-heartedness towards her.

The expatriate community was embedded in French political life. Godwin exaggerated when he said that Wollstonecraft 'was personally acquainted with the majority of the leaders of the French Revolution', but at the various salons and dinners she met many of the political movers and thinkers, as well as some eccentrics. She was struck by the communitarian François-Noel Babeuf, who she thought had huge abilities and strength of character. Her enthusiasm is curious since he advocated common ownership of land and the means of production, views far more radical than her own reformist desire to see large estates broken into small farms.[22]

Most of the English were attached to the faction in power in the Convention, the Girondins. These were often accused by the more radical Jacobins – Robespierre, Marat and Danton among others – of being in league with monarchists, although most were openly republican. They were also blamed for appearing overly anglophile and being dominated by a mere woman, Madame Roland. The Jacobin Danton in particular mercilessly mocked his antagonist, and she returned his contempt.

The leading Girondin was the pale, thin and learned Jean-Pierre Brissot, a pastry-cook's son who had become prominent in the Revolution through writing radical articles. He had status as a former prisoner in the Bastille under the old regime. Wollstonecraft had reviewed his work on America, praising it for expressing the old Commonwealth and Dissenting ideal supported in *The Rights of Woman*: private virtue nurturing public spirit. His faction included the aristocratic feminist philosopher, Condorcet, and François Lanthénas, who translated Paine's speeches into French for him, as well as Madame Roland's husband, Jean-Marie, for a short period minister of the interior in the revolutionary government.

By the time Wollstonecraft joined the expatriate group, it was waning in importance. The more moderate Girondins were struggling to hold power against the Jacobins and Helen Maria Williams, a staunch Girondin supporter, had moderated her earlier optimism. A revolution did not require perpetual insurrection as the Jacobins seemed to think, and a tyrant was a tyrant whatever his provenance and principles. Williams disliked the foreign wars, the French notion of *imposing* liberty on others (in her chronicles she downplayed the Girondin support for these adventures). Soon factions were brawling in the Paris streets. Soaring inflation was accompanied by shortages of essentials – soap, candles and fuel – and there were bread riots in the market. In February, war had been declared with England, and France was now fighting an array of European powers. Foreigners were no longer welcome and had to identify themselves on their doors; surveillance increased. Citizeness Marie Wollstonecraft thought of removing to Switzerland for ease and economy but found it difficult to get a passport. Places in coaches out of Paris were at a premium.

In April the Committee of Public Safety was set up to bring order and control the city; quickly it became the supreme power. Rumours of English plots abounded. In the Place de la Révolution beside the Tuileries Gardens the guillotine was increasingly used; many regarded it as a new humane way of killing: it was quick and, although it caused a tremor to seize the corpse, the head always looked placid and pale, its eyes decently shut. Beside the grotesqueries of hanging it was an enlightened mode of execution.

At the end of May the Girondins fell. Helen Maria Williams criticised their leader, Brissot, for underestimating malice and being 'the dupe of the wicked'. In June Madame Roland, blamed by many for accelerating the crisis through her implacable hatred of Danton, was arrested and imprisoned. She was visited by Williams, to whom she gave some of her manuscripts for safe-keeping – later reluctantly burnt when Williams was also imperilled. The educational author Madame de Genlis left Paris, as did many foreigners, including young Johnson, who went to Switzerland, and Cooper, who returned to England, having learnt he was about to be denounced by Robespierre (he arrived home to be denounced in Parliament for marching in a revolutionary parade carrying national colours). The White's Hotel group disbanded and even the supportive Scot Christie was attacked and he and his family temporarily arrested before he too left France. The British were speeded on their way by Robespierre, who proposed that all should be expelled. Paine fell into depression and drank heavily, his usual response to defeat or failure.

The English who had associated with the disgraced faction might compromise their friends: Wollstonecraft could not 'think of staying any longer at Madame F's.' So with the Fillietazes' help she moved out of Paris to a nearby village, Neuilly-sur-Seine, not far from the Longchamp tollgate of the city, north of the Bois de Boulogne. The solitary house and garden were tended by the old Fillietaz gardener. He was sometimes fearful for his intrepid guest who thought nothing of walking in the gloomy tangled woods despite his 'recounting divers horrible robberies and murders that had been committed there'.[23] She even trekked over to the deserted palace of Versailles, sight-seeing in a revolution.

*

In England, Prime Minister Pitt had been reluctant to declare war: the country was unprepared and, underestimating the ideological changes in France, he thought that economic chaos would bring the revolutionary government to its knees. When this did not happen, he moved into hostile mode, prosecuting war with vigour and controlling activities at home. He was following national opinion, sharply swinging against France. Radicals who still supported it were distrusted.

Back in January Joel Barlow had praised the execution of Louis XVI and even suggested that 'George's poll' should be next; in consequence he was vilified in England. Ruth felt ostracised by former friends and concluded that London was no place for the wife of a notorious francophile. So she joined Joel in Paris. Now, as Americans, they were not in immediate danger and so, occasionally, Wollstonecraft came out of hiding to breakfast with Ruth in Meudon. She also sometimes visited Madame Schweitzer and saw in terrorised Paris scenes she could never have supposed would result from ideals of liberty and equality:

> She happened one day to enter Paris on foot ... when an execution, attended with some peculiar aggravations, had just taken place, and the blood of the guillotine appeared fresh upon the pavement. The emotions of her soul burst forth in indignant exclamations, while a prudent bystander warned her of her danger, and intreated her to hasten and hide her discontents.[24]

Most of the time she remained in Neuilly. She composed a few letters to her sisters but, with all correspondence surveilled, she could not be frank and she doubted that much would get through. She had heard from James in a letter written back in April (predictably asking for money) and she had news of her sisters through Ireland, possibly from George Blood or Hugh Skeys rather than directly. But she was entirely cut off from people in England: nothing came from Johnson, and there seemed little point in writing more. After so much corresponding, it was strange to be without this prop: 'I feel quite lonely here now the communication is shut,' she admitted.[25]

But she had other projects. Ashamed of her long months of lassitude in London, she determined not to 'return to England without proofs that I have not been idle'. Probably with Johnson's earlier prompting and inspired by Helen Maria Williams' successful chronicles, she had begun work on a multi-volumed history of the French Revolution – 'a great book' she called it.[26] Her female sympathisers in England might have hoped for a second *Rights of Woman* from Wollstonecraft's Paris sojourn, a volume addressing the French feminist arguments for women's complete citizenship. But perhaps personal events had eroded her once sustaining belief in a rationalist solution to the problem of women's lives or perhaps political events pressed her to make general sense of the country she was now inhabiting and so to write a sequel to *The Rights of Men* rather than *The Rights of Woman.*

Williams had more first-hand knowledge than her friend of the past and present and had once called on Christie and Stone for help with battles and campaigns. But Wollstonecraft had thought long about revolutionary principles, their impact on individuals and nations, and she intended to discuss the relationship of ideas to actions without presenting them within a personal record in Williams's manner. She was interested in the workings of ideas over time rather than the totality of the present or in personal biographies, mocked in *The Rights of Woman* as no better than romance. She would not write a mixture of annals, lives and memoirs, but history in the way the great Catherine Macaulay had composed it in her Whig accounts of England and Blair had defined it in *Letters on Rhetoric*: instruction in virtue as well as a recording of truth, the sort of history that shows 'the spirit and genius of nations'. The King girls in Ireland had been ignorant despite reading '*cart*-loads of history'; her sort of history would show causes more than facts.[27]

When she had written *The Rights of Men*, her main attack had been on aristocracy and hereditary prerogative; this book would critique the system by telling the 'progress of the human mind'.[28] She would rewrite events as moral and judge characters and eras according to unprejudiced reason, much as she had judged women in her *Rights of Woman*. France, like women, had been voluptuously ensnared, cozened into false sensibility and arrested in development by old institutions and culture, but it would soon feel the value of 'intellectual improvement' and move towards 'perfection'. The blood-letting was a detour. She had progressed from her initial fear that evil alone motivated people. The arrested French had spoiled their revolution, but not its principles. It remained a 'monstrous tyranny' to exclude the majority of citizens from 'a chance of improvement'.

Yet trivial Paris and recent disorder had dented her optimism. She had become confused about violence, at one moment condemning it, at another seeming to justify it if there appeared no alternative way to combat despotism. To cover her confusion, she argued that years of tyranny and not revolutionary ideals had created present disorder and that some violence was probably inevitable from false consciousness. Once, she had been appalled at Burke's notion that particular people could be sacrificed for general good; now she accepted the necessary destruction of aristocrats, with no sense that these were individuals. The 'sympathizing bosom' might be chilled by terror but one had to support reason over gut feeling; otherwise one could not believe in the 'uncontaminated mass of the french nation'.[29] Her earlier Christian belief in the providential value of pain helped with this secular interpretation of painful events: in the frequently made analogy of individual and state, violence was childhood misery toughening the adult. Belief in compensatory heaven could be recycled as belief in a better future.

In her interpretation of historical events Wollstonecraft shared Helen Maria Williams's difficulty. Both needed to modify their earlier enthusiasm to account for later horror; both struggled to reconcile theory and aghast observation. Both sought revolutionary scapegoats: in Marat or the turncoat Duke of Orléans. Wollstonecraft's distaste for the latter may have been connected with her revised views of the once-admired author Madame de Genlis, governess to Orléans's children, now discovered as his mistress and procuress. The 'despicable duke of Orléans' was found behind the persecution of the royal family, especially Marie Antoinette, described as fleeing with the dauphin from marauders through the palace – a picture not far removed from Burke's melodrama – though in Wollstonecraft the queen's misery is brought on by her vulgar disregard for revolutionary hopes and symbols. Indeed, Burke's hysterical version of events, seemingly so idiosyncratic in 1790, now appeared less absurd and, despite her earlier taunting, she did not attack Burke directly in this fuller history, though her defence of revolutionary principles was still in partisan dialogue with his book.[30]

With his gold, Orléans was even made instigator of the market women's march to Versailles, an event supported in the more egalitarianly feminist *Rights of Men*. Burke's general reasoning was still wrong, she thought, but he was right to see the event as preface to greater atrocities. Since Théroigne had urged on this march, perhaps the image of the 'Amazonian' woman was influencing her change of opinion. Now she sneered, 'That a body of women should put themselves in motion to demand relief ... is scarcely probable.' From being independent market-traders, the female marchers sank into 'rabble', 'the lowest refuse of the streets, women who had thrown off the virtues of one sex without having the power to assume more than the vices of the other'; their band even included men in drag.[31] The event, which paled in destruction beside the September massacres, was described by Wollstonecraft as sullying the annals of humanity. Partly this must be due to her horrified reaction to the later exploits of the mob inspired by Robespierre and the Terror, but the change also fitted with her reluctance in her book – and in her letters – to treat women's early involvement in the Revolution and her lack of comment on the stifling of the female clubs by the Jacobins. Ironically, the suppression had been justified by the Rousseauian rhetoric of female physical weakness she had so much opposed in *The Rights of Woman*.[32]

For by now many of women's rudimentary freedoms were endangered. Condorcet had been denounced, his proscription ending any formal effort to include women in the institutions of the new republic. A few days later, fired with heroic notions of aiding the fallen Girondins, Charlotte Corday stabbed the Jacobin Marat in his bath. A furious reaction followed against moderation and female meddling. Conspicuous political women were silenced. Corday was swiftly guillotined. Théroigne was stripped by a mob in the Tuileries Garden and her head violently beaten with stones; later she became deranged and spent the rest of her life in an asylum. Olympe de Gouges was imprisoned, then executed, partly as a feminist – she had wanted to be 'a man of state' – but more as a federalist in a republic wedded to the concept of centralised power. Wollstonecraft was learning the truth of Rousseau's perception, that degenerate courts favoured politically active, powerful women where republics were rigidly masculine.

She did not address the point but instead swerved into praise of French bourgeois life before the revolutionary Terror, perhaps sensing that this at least had the virtuous female element despised in aristocratic courts and entirely lacking in the representative bodies of the new republic. Or perhaps she simply listened to Helen Maria Williams nostalgically remembering the old days when

> many french families ... exhibited an affectionate urbanity of behaviour to each other ... The husband and wife, if not lovers, were the civilest friends and tenderest parents in the world – the only parents, perhaps, who really treated their children like friends; and the most affable masters and mistresses ... Their hospitable boards were constantly open to relations and acquaintance, who, without the formality of an invitation, enjoyed there cheerfulness free from restraint; whilst more select circles closed the evening, by discussing literary subjects. In the summer, when they retired to their mansion houses, they spread gladness around, and partook of the amusements of the peasantry, whom they visited with paternal solicitude.[33]

It sounds more like an ideal bourgeois version of the Kingsborough house than the revolutionary society coming into being. In Ireland Wollstonecraft as governess had been as close to the 'peasantry' in dependence as to mansion-owners in education; perhaps it was her sense of being treated as an equal by people of modest birth but high social status that made her now feel she would like to settle in France, however disconcerting its politics.

The bourgeois domestic ideal shadows the most eloquent section of her new book, a set-piece description of Versailles recently visited in its pillaged state. She was no longer as fearful of eloquence as when writing *The Rights of Men*; now more open to all sorts of sensuousness, she admitted that the 'advantage of eloquence' was that it might give 'wings to the slow foot of reason'. Burke had ensured that any great edifice empty or in ruins would have imaginative Gothic power and, for liberals, it had symbolic significance as the triumph of liberty over despotic authority. Empty grandeur and crumbling castles evoked in most sensitive people of the 1790s a mixed response of melancholy and complacency – as Versailles did in Wollstonecraft; 'old palaces' were 'historical documents':

> How silent is now Versailles! – The solitary foot, that mounts the sumptuous stair-case, rests on each landing-place, whilst the eye traverses the void, almost expecting to see the strong images of fancy burst into life. – The train of the Louises, like the posterity of the Banquoes, pass in solemn sadness, pointing at the nothingness of grandeur, fading away on the cold canvass, which covers the nakedness of the spacious walls – whilst the gloominess of the atmosphere gives a deeper shade to the gigantic figures, that seem to be sinking into the embraces of death.
>
> Warily entering the endless apartments, half shut up, the fleeting shadow of the pensive wanderer, reflected in long glasses, that vainly gleam in every direction, slacken the nerves, without appalling the heart ... The very air is chill, seeming to clog the breath; and the wasting dampness of destruction appears to be stealing into the vast pile, on every side...[34]

Aristocratic grandeur was decaying: she, an example of the new coming order, was contemplating its decline. Eighteenth-century commentators on culture had insisted that civilisation developed through the invention of the sciences and industry, connected to the bourgeois order with its stress on fact, practicality and comfort, rather than through the arts beloved by aristocracy. She agreed. But, as the old luxurious civilisation faded and the scientific bourgeois one developed, so people should become 'domestic, and attached to ... home'. She did not entirely gender the spaces she considered, but the aristocratic did signify an heroic male order for her, where the domestic space was associated with the female. Concord could now replace male conflict; domesticity supersede chivalry. Liberty would no longer be a fierce warrior but a motherly bird who, having revealed her 'sober matron graces' in America, was flapping her 'maternal wing' and 'promising to shelter all mankind'.[35]

Two years before, she had shied away from the domestic insularity of the Gabells, but, in the tumult of events in France, the extremes of empty grandeur and sordid commerce, she was increasingly drawn to an ideal of domestic life. Even with the Gabells when she had contrasted her intellectual existence with their cloying domestic one, she had imagined a higher form of their bliss, something more elegant and rational. Then she had been a devotee of chastity, imagining sensations chastened by the mind. Now she could envisage domesticity allied to sexual love and intellectual dignity. Fuseli had offered her none of these, but they might be found in another man. In France everything was changing, anything was possible.

# 20

*'I fear not their* knives'

During Mary's last painful months in London, Eliza had been shut away in Wales, consumed with resentment. Now, however, she experienced a reversal. In Mary's initial letters from France she noted the tonal change. Gone was the infuriating smugness born of fame. 'I am *convinced* M. has met with some great disappointment lately,' she told Everina, 'her letters are not in the same strain as when she was in London; she complains of lowness of Spirits ... Mary seems rather *disgusted* with the French in general[,] yet I am sure there [is] a Cause.'

She had suspected Mary's preoccupation with Fuseli, but he had not accompanied her and Eliza began to think she could again engross her sister: Mary might fulfil the implied promise made when she rescued her from Bishop's house, that she would look after Eliza for life. Though their relationship had deteriorated, Mary remained the only route to France out of Wales and vulgar servitude.

More than her sisters, Eliza craved gentility and culture. She doubted she would ever achieve them in her own right, but, if she could acquire a proper command of French, she could work in a more elevated family and mix with the sort of people who would not affront her intelligence. Mary was rash but resolute: '[She] is not one that ponders, when she ought to act.' Now in her muted letters she was giving reality to the idea of escape by promising to find Eliza a place in France by the spring.

So Mary became '*my* sister', a living not a 'dead' being. Again Eliza reposed on her the full weight of her neediness and desire, becoming as eager now to remit money as she had been reluctant before. The large amount demanded seemed in retrospect proof that Mary was thinking of her sister: to send it was but investing in her own future. Over the next months as she whined and moaned to Everina, her attitude to this money marked the true state of her hopes, whatever surface despair she expressed.

Mary wanted the money sent swiftly: 'the exchange is greatly in favor of the English, & the thirty pound will now go as far as forty or fifty at any other time'. Prepared to ask for a loan from the steward against her quarterly payment, Eliza worried about her earlier caution. How stupid she was not to have realised the money was for her all along! 'If [Mary] should ever be too generous while at Paris I shall not feel I am distressing her, when she sends me only what we lent,' she mused. The selfishness might appear remarkable but so, in relation to their wages, was the amount the sisters were being asked to remit.

Everina found her employers disordered, disorderly and finical – Eliza described her sister's life as 'imbittered by sideboards, folly and super-stition!' – and was considering a move to the Irwins of Fortich's Grove, possibly met through the Skeyses, who lived nearby. Mary and Eliza urged her on, but she remained indecisive. Still, Eliza managed to enjoy a Christmas with her in Ireland and felt 'risen from the dead'. True, she and Everina spent too much and had a 'foolish week' in Dublin with George Blood, who somehow disgraced himself, but Mary advised her to forget this and remember only the 'pleasure'. In better spirits, Eliza returned to Upton where she found the family trying to avoid 'disgusting' her with their 'vulgarity'.

By late January she was her old self. The Upton ménage was again 'intoler-able'; she had a heavy cold and her usual rheumatic trouble. Though she retained her belief in the Paris escape, she was disheartened by Mary's silence: 'I am weary of expecting a letter from France.' Yet she no longer blamed Mary alone: she had heard 'the cry of *War* and the horrid *Butcheries that are hourly committed in Paris*'.

'Butcheries' were no deterrent to hope: 'I have so long dwelt on visiting the Continent, that I should now find it very difficult to prevent my heart's wandering that way.' No public horrors could exceed the dreary private ennui of Pembrokeshire; atrocities impinged mainly as they decreased her chance of leaving: 'I fear not their *knives* and would "rather dwell in the midst of alarms than reign in this horrible place" – still when I hear every creature reecho the same opinion – I can hardly anticipate the day when I shall behold that Land of *Equality*!! Recollect it is not cowardice that makes me despair; but the dread of disappointment.' Eliza would prefer to be Mary in the midst of massacres than herself at peaceful, boring Upton. The sisters were so temperamentally alike that the same was true of Mary.

Eliza's enthusiasm was not simply hatred of Wales and service. She per-sisted in holding genuinely liberal views, unlike many erstwhile radicals now succumbing to the government line and equating patriotism and con-servative ardour. In Lichfield, Anna Seward, a supporter of liberal causes like American independence and abolition, paralleled her growing alarm at the revolutionary Helen Maria Williams with complacency about the national system: 'Never do I remember such an universal glow of loyalty, such a grateful and fervent sense of the blessings of our balanced government, as seem now to pervade all the orders of British society,' she enthused.[1] Eliza disagreed. She remained as convinced as Mary of the soundness of revolutionary principles and, in a sea of reaction, stood faster than Everina – and even Mary – in her belief in revolutionary France. She hated dependence and, like Mary, extended the personal to the political. What would not a people be justified in doing to become free? What would she not do?

Her political views were so at odds with those of the castle inhabitants that, whenever she expressed them, they left the room or abruptly turned the conversation to 'Murphy or Irish Potatoes, or Tommy Paine, whose effigy they burnt at Pembroke the other day'. They knew of her notorious sister; so it was with a gleeful cruelty that they told her people were thinking 'of immortalizing Miss Wollstonecraft in the like manner'.

Their talk consisted merely of slogans and clichés:

all end[s] in Damning all Politics[:] what good will they do men? ... I heard a clergyman say that he was sure there was no more harm in shooting a frenchman, than in lifting his piece at a Bird – and a gentleman, I cannot find out [who], sent me this receipt [recipe]: –

'An effectual cure for the bite of a Mad Frenchman. Mix a Grain of common sense in the milk of human nature, with two grains of honor, and half a dram – of Loyalty[;] let the Patient take this night and morning; and he will be in his senses all day.'[2]

A fire was in her room: she suspected it was provided so that the family could get rid of her.

Then she heard from Mary. She wrote cheerfully while admitting 'disappointments'. Again she promised she would not leave Paris before settling her sister; it was as well she had not come earlier since Paris was confused and cold.

Such efforts at comfort did not impress; Eliza wanted a date. 'I yesterday received the long wished for letter from Paris,' she told Everina; it 'suppressed all the childish expectations that suspense had left me prey to.' Mary meant 'to be friendly by indulging hope; but did not succeed as I felt every pang that disappointment could bring'. News of brother James aggravated misery. He had written to Mary to tell her he was in London wanting to try for naval promotion. If he could only become a lieutenant he would have an annuity for life. But he had no money to equip himself. Used to her siblings' failures, Mary was philosophical: 'I would willingly most willingly, forward any plan that would lead him to sea again,' she told Eliza, but she could not apply again to Johnson: 'you will readily grasp my vexation & reluctance.'

Eliza, in whose mind had lingered a vague promise of rescue from James, was appalled. The pair had become close last winter and James had assumed the manly role of protector to her dependent female, a part for which, despite occasional revulsion, she often craved. She was sickened by his fecklessness, his absurd posturing at their expense. To Everina she reviewed the many hollow schemes:

> ...Brother's Cottage in the New World, or the still more stately Edifice, that Jamey *once* more crossed the Pacific ocean to erect for his *helpless sisters*!! This Philosopher, I own has dreadfully disappointed me – you *know*, I *looked* forward with hope, to the time when he would return; and be happy to pay M., what his extravagance has extorted from her ... how finely are my hopes crushed, on hearing he is returned to London; and again applied for *Money* to Equip him to appear in the Navy, like an accomplished youth, just arrived from making the *Tour* of France ... while I deny myself the *few* comforts I might here enjoy – and have even *hardly* left you a sixpense for the half year; but why do I dwell on James? who I own I feel a great contempt for.

The day after this letter was written, Louis XVI was executed; on 1 February, France declared war on England; official postal services were disrupted. In distant Pembrokeshire Eliza heard the news, heavily overladen with anti-French propaganda; she disliked French violence but more the vulgar use made of it in Britain:

> War my dear Everina, is now *inevitable*[.] *Never oh! never*, did I lament the *horrors* of war! in the way I do at *present* ... I own I now tremble for the Cap of Liberty! and its attendant *Egalite! sounds* so pleasing to a poor *dependant's Ear* – I should like my dear girl, to know what you felt on first hearing Louis Death. I own I was shocked; but not deluged in tears. In short, I could bear to hear it read, and hoped they had some motive for such an act of cruelty that our newspapers did not explain – but to hear him cryed up as the *best* of men; and that no man's sufferings or *fortitude* equaled the King of France's is to me quite novel.

She summarised the crude attitudes around her: 'that the French are *all* Atheists; and the most bloody Butchers the world ever produced ... the world is going to be at an end! That these *Assassins*, are *Instruments* in the *hand* of Providence'.[3]

War could not destroy her obsession, 'I should not dread going to France in the midst of war.' Yet she could see it meant longer exile and she plunged into hyperbolic despair. She had tasted so little of what Mary had had, never been the famous bluestocking or argued politics at Johnson's dinners or indeed with Dr Price on the Green. Yet through Mary she had known a little of what it was to 'mingle with beings I could love – that I could admire, or to speak more rationally, beings that I could reap some improvement from; while the sad hours of life were *rolling* away.' Paris was her sustaining dream. Melodramatically she described receiving 'a *blow* that struck me to the very heart – and will for ever prevent its beating to that something like hope'. Mary's renewed silence, obviously explicable by events, became suspicious: '[W]ould it not be kind to take me from the rack?' she moaned. Then it hit her that Mary might use money intended for her on the undeserving James. Had Everina secretly heard from Mary? Was she actually in England? Suspicion lurched into paranoia: 'put me out of doubt for the worst thing wld be more acceptable than the *cruel suspense* that now devours my peace.' A 'feverish kind of anxiety ... almost deprives me of my reason ... Picture to yourself how I wait every night, for a boy that I contrive to send to the postoffice, in spite of storms, he *returns* and I in vain endeavour to study, or amuse myself...'

Then, in the midst of her jumbled panic and suspicion, she received a 'cordial', an encouraging letter, and her mood flipped over again. Mary asked her to be 'quietly resigned' for a time, but her spirits soared when she noted a *precise* date for rescue: May.

> I yesterday received *the much wished* for letter: which has again bid me hope – as, Mary still says she will not leave Paris till I am settled there, or in the country, I own I should prefer the city, for I dread lest childish fears (if I was far from the Capital) would prevent all improvement; but these are matters, I will *not quarrel* about, so I but *once* get into the Land of *Liberty*!! and *Equality*! Yet M. says, I must remain here two months longer ... no plan has yet occurred to her, that has proved successful and I believe [she] wishes to see how the war will go on in France – before she fixes me.

The hope was too extreme. Could she trust it? Mary had so often had crazy plans: 'We know Mary sometimes to be very sanguine; and even shortsighted; but I do pray that she has, on this occasion used Spectacles,' she told Everina. Yet – and again the money was the test – Mary had actually called the money 'her money' by saying that the exchange rate was "greatly in *my favor*" (meaning me)'. It convinced Eliza. Now at last funds were sent.

It was some time since Mary had begun requesting the £30 and she must have wondered at the reluctance of sisters she had supported so long.

For over a month Eliza and Everina heard nothing. In Britain the war increasingly resembled a holy crusade in support of religion, morality and property against French atheism and anarchy. The government moved against revolutionary sympathisers, especially targeting English 'Jacobins', who might politically exploit the lower orders, now growing restive in response to steeply rising prices. Subversive publications were suppressed or prosecuted; Habeas Corpus was sometimes suspended; public meetings discouraged, and writers who had no weapons except their prose proscribed and sent to Botany Bay. The republican and reforming longings of such men as Godwin, Holcroft and Horne Tooke suddenly sounded treasonable.

Other measures constrained the movement and thought of ordinary people. Anyone who travelled to France was to be punished unless armed with 'his *Majesty's* licence, under the privy-seal'. Swimming in a sea of propaganda and ignorance, Eliza grasped her liberal principles: 'Call you this Liberte? – ? – I feel it to be *bondage* – to be *Slavery* Personified – and e'er long expect to read that the Bastile is rebuilt to ornament the banks of the Thames.' Her letters were remarkably antagonistic: 'as to the fate of poor France I own I am *sanguine*! – though all cry out she will soon be *Crushed*!!' – this about a country with which her own was at war.

Of course she restated her despair, 'Know then, that every hope is now *Crushed* – nay torn up by main force from the bottom of my heart … it is even criminal, thus to lament a visionary plan, as if it was a real misfortunate; but to my *shame* I own I have *allowed* myself to *dwell* with too much eagerness on this journey.' Yet, of course it was not quite despair and each evening she sat in fear that she would receive the letter from Mary that would truly end hope. She anticipated Everina's response to this paradoxical behaviour: 'I think I hear you exclaim Eliza are you Mad? Is this your resignation! Well have patience for I will strive hard … Ah Everina if I had gone with [Mary] I should not now regret the horrors of war on my own account.'

Spring now held no joys, for it would not bring the promised escape and, like Mary before her, Eliza felt her body wasting away with decaying hope. Even her hair was falling out in 'handfuls'. Silent weeks passed and she remained 'on the rack'. Mail packet boats had been stopped between Dover and Calais; now they ceased between France and Ostend, another port from which they had customarily sailed to England. The two countries were closing themselves up and Eliza was in the wrong one.

For once she was actually glad for *Mary's* sake that she and Everina had sent money and the thought led to a rare appreciation of her extraordinary sister – though she could not keep off herself for long: '[The money] must be very acceptable at this juncture, for heaven only knows when she will return, not that [I] imagine her in real danger; yet, in this land of *superstition*, it is natural to feel momentary fears for her safety – yet we know M. will rather rejoice at encountering what others shudder at (even in idea) and I still regret I had not gone with her.'4 She made, too, a rare approving reference to her ideas and life: 'Mary was certainly right in saying, she never saw a handsome woman who had not a look of *weakness*[.] I now perfectly agree with her,' and 'Mary will be hurt at not being allowed to correspond with friends in London ... I envy her the language she is now Mistress of; and from my very soul would rejoice to hear some tidings of all her new friends.' Her loyalty was partly reactive: as she wrote to Everina, 'did I tell you? How much the gentry of Pembroke are shocked at M's book[;] every one declares it the most indecent Rhapsody that ever was penned by men or women. Mr B[ois] is continually dwelling on the parts that *wound* his Modesty most.'

Anticipating her escape from Bishopshall to the Irwins, Everina was cheering up. It disconcerted Eliza, who warned her not to become too happy – she would be disillusioned. Besides, she loved Everina's 'melancholy letters best'. May came and went and nothing arrived from France. Eliza's desperate hopes of a Parisian life should have diminished; yet she was not blaming Mary for her silence. She had managed to see a newspaper and learn that in France no one was allowed to correspond with people in a hostile country; Mary *could* not be sending letters. Indeed, as French news became more violent, Eliza's hopes re-expanded, for it clarified that her sister's silence was due to public not personal events. If it were simply a matter of massacres, the Paris dream need only be postponed: she would go in the autumn. She began studying French again and saving up for her trip.

Then at last Mary's letters, written in June in Neuilly, were delivered to Wales, probably through Barlow's American business associates in London. Mary had, she wrote, been uneasy over the ending of relations between Britain and France, especially as it seemed to destroy her hopes of getting a passport for Eliza. She had in the end obtained it, but only after she had moved to Neuilly and could do nothing.

What was quite uncharacteristic was the buoyancy combined with solicitude. Mary was 'in better health and spirits' while declaring herself saddened by her despondent sisters, her disappointing of Eliza. It would 'be madness' now to try to get her to 'this distracted Land', though something might be done if peace broke out. But she had something quite different to offer. She had to write 'with reserve' because all letters were opened:

> [I] have actually a plan in my head which promises to render the evening of your life more comfortable. I cannot explain myself in a clearer manner, and knowing how sanguine you are I am almost afraid to set your Imagination to work and

lead you to rekindle hope with all your might and main, whilst you are talking in heroics of despair – ... as absence renders my friends more dear to me my heart bounds, when I think of you with the emotions of youthful fondness.

Not best pleased at the description of herself in her early thirties as approaching 'the evening' of life, Eliza could not see the need for such circumspection about a private matter. She was agitated by the unusual elation, used to a gloomy Mary; also, she had admitted preferring melancholy letters. The new impression aroused old suspicions; morosely she wished that 'Mary would not write from the feelings of the moment – for it awakens feelings I wish not to rouse'. When she had copied out the letters for her sister, she exclaimed: 'What say you Everina now to the *Continental air.* – Or is it A *Love?* Ambition or Pity? that has wrought the Miracle?'[5]

Eliza was right in her first conjecture, but, as radical as she was in her politics, she could not in her wildest dreams have imagined the radical change in personal life that Mary had experienced. After years of preaching deferred gratification and rational living, sexless marriage and pure affection, Mary had complemented the French Revolution with her own revolution: she had entered a sexual relationship outside marriage.

*'Mary's sweetheart affair goes well.'*

The plan of rescue so tantalisingly produced for Eliza concerned a farm in America in which, once sufficient capital had been raised, all three sisters would share. The centre of it would be the new man in Mary's life, he who had chased away her melancholy over Fuseli and put her in 'better health and spirits', an American 'Captain': Gilbert Imlay.

She had met Imlay, a tall, thin, rather handsome and self-assured man in his late thirties at the Christies' house in April shortly after his arrival in Paris from London. She was nursing her sadness from the Fuseli affair but was galvanised by good talk. Like von Schlabrendorf, Imlay was attracted to this forceful, famous but now slightly muted woman, but, unlike the count, his attraction made him pay 'her more than common attention'.[1]

Wollstonecraft was not immediately impressed, perhaps seeing one of the rather shady adventurers preying on revolutionary France. She knew the type through Barlow, who, expressing impeccable liberal principles, had yet seen the chaos as a business opportunity. Her initial unfavourable impression was soon overlaid: for all her emphasis on rational affection, her earlier flirtation with the dashing Joshua Waterhouse suggested her attraction to handsome men when revealing some attraction to her and one account of her stresses her response to male gallantry: 'She was ... very pretty and feminine in manners and person; much attached to those very observances she decries in her work; so that if any gentleman did not fly to open the door as she approached it, or take up the handkerchief she dropped, she showered on him the full weight of reproach and displeasure.'[2] In a matter of weeks any hesitation at Imlay's pointed attentions gave way to affection, then passion. Her careful version of equitable, profitable love described in *The Rights of Woman* was jettisoned for traditional romance, the cancerous growth whose origins lay deep in the battered psyche.

For the first time in her life, she was dealing with a man who saw no occasion to hold back. He was not married or bent on marriage, not inhibited by social class or rebuking social mores. He had had relationships before, enjoyed them, and extricated himself. He had no reason to retreat from the welcoming response of a famously revolutionary woman who had already scandalised society with her frank, unanswerable books and her honest enthusiasm for a married man. On her side she was excited by Imlay's attention; any resemblance to her father was at first concealed, for he differed where it mattered most: in temper. Her father and Fuseli had both been irascible men, alternating cloying fondness with tantrums; the manly, affectionate Imlay avoided scenes. After the misery with Fuseli she was ready to abandon her search for difficult men of 'genius'. Here was a simple man of action and feeling, a tall, handsome one as well. She loved him and he her: it was easier than she had supposed as she agonised in her parlour in Ireland or her house in Store Street.

Never able to conceal her emotions, Wollstonecraft revealed herself to the watchful Joel Barlow, who wrote home to Ruth, 'Between you and me – you must not hint it to her or to J[ohnson] or to anyone else – I believe [Mary] has got a sweetheart, and that she will finish by going with him to A[meric]a a wife. He is of Kentucky and a very sensible man.'[3] Hence the dream of an American farm, conveyed to her amazed sisters.

Imlay was neither from Kentucky nor sensible. He came from a middle-class family of businessmen and judges from Monmouth County, New Jersey, a more prosaic provenance than 'the back parts of America'.[4] A professional 'American' in self-confidence, he promoted himself as a New World Émile, simpler, wiser and more 'natural' than corrupt Europeans. He had served briefly in the War of Independence and assumed the rank of captain: it gave him glamour among British sympathisers.

Now, like Barlow, he was primarily a speculator. As a veteran he had claimed rights to land taken from the Native Americans in Kentucky; he was appointed a deputy land surveyor and helped erect an iron works, but, though he tried to line his pockets, he was soon in debt and pursued by lawsuits. He became more unsavoury by associating with the notorious General James Wilkinson who, while working to acquire the Spanish colony of Louisiana for the US, was in Spanish pay and simultaneously campaigning for an independent state west of the Alleghenies. Imlay left America in 1786 to avoid prosecution for his activities; now he was working with Barlow to sell American land to those tired of revolutionary Europe.

Imlay's image as a frontiersman was supported by his recent publication of *A Topographical Description of the Western Territory of North America* (1792), the preface of which quoted a patriotic petition by the people of Kentucky to the US government, probably written by General Wilkinson.[5] The work was popular and well received by the *Analytical Review* and most other liberal journals. Cleverly, it described simple, unfettered rustic life in the New World while making the land appear ripe for capitalist development: 'In contemplating the vast field of the American empire, what a stupendous subject does it afford for speculation.' It was just the message in the early 1790s when many disaffected British were thinking of emigrating – it was estimated that by 1796 about 2000 had been lured to America by such lyrical works. Many were disillusioned and crept back and *The British Critic* of January 1795 had some justification in criticising those who persuaded people to part with hard-earned money through false promises. In a review of two rival schemes, the Manchester lawyer Thomas Cooper's in the Susquehanna valley and Imlay's in Kentucky, it mocked the pair as 'rival auctioneers', 'show-men, stationed for the allurement of incautious passengers'; Imlay was a con-artist feeding on the gullible.[6]

In 1792 and 1793 the author's aims still seemed benevolent. In addition, his sentiments were impeccably revolutionary, supporting everywhere 'the spirit of liberty'. Much of the book opposed African slavery, a popular cause among liberal British and French; it declared for gradual emancipation and even contemplated inter-marriage between races.[7] But Imlay was less generous towards Native Americans, who should be civilised or confined to particular districts.

Imlay's anti-slavery opinions, as well as his knowledge of American terrain and his earlier connection with Louisiana schemes, persuaded Thomas Cooper to introduce him to Brissot, the Girondin leader. Brissot was immediately keen to bring him into his own Louisiana scheme, this time to benefit revolutionary France with the tacit approval of the new US government which feared an English takeover.[8] Imlay wrote two proposals for the Committee of Public Safety, his plan being to carry out the enterprise with American citizens, himself in some leadership role. The rumoured imminent departure of both Imlay and Wollstonecraft had to do with this Louisiana scheme, although Wollstonecraft seems to have known little of it; her dreams of America were domestic.

Imlay was known to have had other sexual affairs; he mocked marriage and told Wollstonecraft of his recent enthralment to a 'cunning woman' – did she recollect that this was how Rousseau described his ideal female? – but she had little experience of this male type and felt no fear.[9] The men she had been attracted to had hung back; Imlay pursued her, letting her feel some dominance. Also, unlike other men who had interested her, he did not grow bored with the recitation of her miseries. Surely he must have a good heart. Soon Barlow recorded that Wollstonecraft's 'sweetheart affair goes well. Don't say a word of it to any creature.'

Probably she was influenced in her view of Imlay by the novel he had recently written or may still have been writing when they met, another brochure for western America called *The Emigrants*. Ostensibly composed in Kentucky, it hailed from Europe, which was much castigated for its corruption beside American purity. The book was gallant rather than feminist, stressing man's superiority of activity deriving from his superiority of strength, but insisting this superiority should not be translated into tyranny over soft, tender women. Both sexes needed rational education – though women had little to do with theirs.

The plot of *The Emigrants* is simple and sentimental. An English family, ruined by fashionable, improvident parents, is forced to flee to America and live in the backwoods. After misunderstandings and adventures, the beautiful and sensitive heroine, Caroline, is rescued from Indians and united with the handsome and sensitive Captain Arl—ton. Together with Caroline's sister Eliza, who, like Eliza Bishop, has been persuaded to leave her brutal husband, they form an ideal community of order and moderate equality on the banks of the Ohio river. The book attacked English marriage customs, which caused so much misery to beautiful young ladies. Caroline mentions the dangers for women of flouting these, but they seem lessened near the Ohio, and Caroline's uncle declares that he would 'never be the cause of procrastinating, by a regard to idle ceremony, the completion of our joys'; happily, no offensive flouting is required since Eliza is conventionally freed for another more satisfactory union by her husband's suicide – the parallel with Eliza Bishop breaking down here. Ignoring the book's florid style which, as the austere *Analytical* reviewer, she would have mocked, Wollstonecraft might have fantasised herself and Imlay in the gallant captain and Caroline, and imagined that, in spite of her determination never to be near her sisters again, fiction could become fact and they all live happily together in the western states of America. If she did, she was not the only one to be imposed on; the young poet Samuel Taylor Coleridge was so impressed that he first planned to set up his pantisocracy in Kentucky before opting temporarily for Thomas Cooper's Susquehanna vision.

In late summer, about the time she moved to Neuilly, a sexual affair began between Wollstonecraft and Imlay. In *The Emigrants* the hero urged consummation while the heroine accused him of sophistry, then felt persuaded by his arguments. In the context of Wollstonecraft's earlier writing, the first sexual act was momentous. Sensuality had troubled and appalled her in Ireland and in *Mary, A Fiction* the lovers died or hoped for death rather than contaminate themselves with sexual love. Such love, though natural, when it became passionate was the enemy of female independence and self-respect in *The Rights of Woman*. But the months of obsession with Fuseli had taught Wollstonecraft something about herself: she was not content with platonic affection, nor with sharing a man in however high-minded a way. Again she had to have 'first place or none'; she wanted a body *and* a mind, Brown's holistic 'living body'.

In the heady atmosphere of revolution and new society, her views on sex had shifted. *The Rights of Woman* had revealed a puritanical attitude towards pleasure, consonant with her experience and upbringing. Although pro-creative sex was proper, recreative sex was in the main distasteful and unwise, despite her indulgence of the repressed Rousseau. In Paris, she began accept-ing with Brown that sex was a need like hunger or thirst and that erotic love should not simply be heaven-directed. She did not mention her first close reading of Rousseau's explosive novel *La Nouvelle Héloïse* but it might have been now. In London her reading had been dominated by review work; in this she had mentioned *Héloïse* but without involvement. Her own writing had been primarily educational and political, and she had most noted Rous-seau's books that dealt with these issues. Now perhaps she took the measure of the extraordinary depiction of a young girl's ecstastic love for her seductive tutor, Saint-Preux. To the shock of a Europe raised on Richardson's chaste *Pamela* and *Clarissa* the unmarried love is consummated, then thwarted by parents and duty.[10]

With its portrayal of open desire, boudoir fetishes, and the titillating signs of sexuality, it was certainly the first book in which Wollstonecraft could have grasped not the sex act but the emotional, almost religious intensity of sex. Later she wrote of an autobiographical heroine's initiation: 'She had read this work long since; but now it seemed to open a new world to her – the only world worth inhabiting.'[11] Something similar may have happened to her within the society that had generated the book. If she wanted a more philosophical justification of sexual openness she could have turned to Diderot's fable, 'Supplément au voyage de Bougainville', much discussed in Paris where it was circulating in manuscript: it confronted a bewildered Christian missionary with the frank sexual enjoyment of the South Sea Islanders.

Beyond books she met people who separated sex and guilt, finding good in sexuality itself. As Saint-Just remarked, 'happiness is a new idea in Europe'. She was no longer thinking of this life *primarily* as a preparation for the next. Sexual abstinence became only a social rather than a moral virtue, and, now that social constraints were removed, it had no rationale. '[W]hat is often called virtue, is only want of courage to throw off prejudices, and follow the inclinations which fear not the eye of heaven prevented,' she wrote in her

*French Revolution.*[12] Her friend von Schlabrendorf reported a conversation between her and a Frenchwoman occurring at some point during her stay in France. The Frenchwoman 'had boastingly said to her: *"Pour moi, je n'ai pas de tempérament."* She replied, *"Tant pis pour vous, madame. C'est un défaut de la nature."* ' Wollstonecraft now saw sexual desire as natural and right for women; indeed she went on to affirm that 'chastity consisted in fidelity and that unchastity was an association with two people at the same time'.[13] It was a striking change of view and one that would change everything in her life.

Yet, although she might joke with Roscoe about a temporary lover in Paris and believe that sexual pleasure was innocent, she remained essentially her old self and did not enter the affair with Imlay flippantly. She was still caught by sentimental romance with its exaggerated expectations of intimacy, and she remained true to conventional ideas of love as permanent. She might declare to von Schlabrendorf that chastity need not imply sexlessness but it did demand fidelity to one person.

As she saw herself, so Godwin portrayed her at this moment of liberation:

> her whole character seemed to change with a change of fortune. Her sorrows, the depression of her spirits, were forgotten, and she assumed all the simplicity and the vivacity of a youthful mind. She was like a serpent upon a rock, that casts its slough, and appears again with the brilliancy, the sleekness, and the elastic activity of its happiest age. She was playful, full of confidence, kindness and sympathy. Her eyes assumed new lustre, and her cheeks new colour and smoothness. Her voice became chearful; her temper overflowing with universal kindness; and that smile of bewitching tenderness from day to day illuminated her countenance, which all who knew her will so well recollect, and which won both heart and soul, the affection of almost every one that beheld it.

For a few weeks the passion seemed complete. At thirty-four Wollstonecraft had found the love she craved and it did not endanger the independence on which she set such store. There was no financial need, for on 2 May she cashed a bill through Christie, using money advanced by Johnson, possibly for her history; on 13 July, after her sisters' money had been remitted, she cashed another bill for £20 again through Christie.[14] Of the social horrors of sexual indulgence described in *The Rights of Woman* she seemed to have no fear: 'the creature of sensibility was surprised by her sensibility into folly – into vice; and the dreadful reckoning falls heavily on her own weak head, when reason wakes.'

The first extant letter to Imlay from Neuilly shows how far Wollstonecraft had travelled from the platonic posturing of the Fuseli period, how easy she was with her sexuality. She was no longer scornful of endearments or familiar embraces. She yearned for ordinary domesticity and companionable communication between a man and a woman.

> My dear love, after making my arrangements for our snug dinner to-day, I have been taken by storm, and obliged to promise to dine, at an early hour, with the Miss [Williamse?]s, the only day they intend to pass here. I shall however leave the key in the door, and hope to find you at my fire-side when I return, about eight o'clock. Will you not wait for poor Joan? – whom you will find better, and till then think very affectionately of her.

The fantasised future on an American farm confirmed the present, 'You can scarcely imagine with what pleasure I anticipate the day, when we are to begin almost to live together; and you would smile to hear how many plans of employment I have in my head, now that I am confident my heart has found peace in your bosom ... I like the word affection, because it signifies something habitual; and we are soon to meet, to try whether we have mind enough to keep our hearts warm.'

Like her ideal of female friendship, Wollstonecraft's dream of modest rural domesticity was culturally conditioned. Using the pastoral tradition and poets like Cowper and Thomson, the late eighteenth century idealised a virtuous cottage life of frugal plenty. The vision drew on liberal belief in a primarily agrarian, more egalitarian society; moral writers, political economists and reformers all used cottage domesticity as a standard of future schemes. Yet the ideal was in many ways anachronistic, a middle-class emotional and aesthetic vision antagonistic to the dynamic commerce shaping town and country alike – and certainly at odds with the overcrowded apartments of the urban poor and the dirty hovels of rural labourers. Paine might anticipate the future by imagining great states giving out pensions, and marriage and death benefits, but Wollstonecraft remained wedded to the ideal of small estates and farms of 'cheerful poultry' owned by autonomous families, the sort of ideal held by the worthy pre-revolutionaries whom she pictured having literary evenings and spreading contentment around.[15] It required a certain kind of man to act out the ideal amidst a revolution and unprecedented commercial possibilities.

Since Imlay as an American could stay in Paris while Wollstonecraft was exiled to Neuilly, the pair met at the barrier, one of the fifty-four tollgates or customs posts in the city wall. Self-consciously she displayed herself in pastoral mode for Imlay, coming towards him over the fields with her basket of grapes on her arm. Together they talked, made love, and planned their future. Yet, with all her heady pleasure, her old fears and melancholy remained and, after each surge of depressive feeling, each display of vulnerability, she apologised to the man who was giving her such unwonted happiness: 'I will be *good*, that I may deserve to be happy; and whilst you love me, I cannot again fall into the miserable state, which rendered life a burden almost too heavy to be borne.' It was a pact: if Imlay loved enough, she would curb her depressive tendencies: 'Cherish me with that dignified tenderness, which I have only found in you; and your own dear girl will try to keep under a quickness of feeling, that has sometimes given you pain.' Her sisters and Jane Arden had been 'dear girls' to her; now Imlay was using this vulnerable term for her.

Occasionally she was unsure. 'I shall not . . . be content with only a kiss of DUTY,' she told him, 'you *must* be glad to see me – because you are glad – or I will make love to the *shade* of Mirabeau.' She was deep in her Revolution book and the politically moderate but fiery orator Mirabeau was its first hero, the kind of awkward genius admired in the past. But Imlay need have no fear: he was dead and she had moved on from the type. With an oblique glance at Fuseli, she considered she could have made something of the confused and overbearing Mirabeau, but also knew it 'the vanity of my heart'.

When she spent evenings alone, her feelings surged towards Imlay. 'I obey an emotion of my heart, which made me think of wishing thee, my love, good-night! before I go to rest . . . good-night! – God bless you! Sterne says, that is equal to a kiss – yet I would rather give you the kiss into the bargain, glowing with gratitude to Heaven, and affection to you.'

At last Wollstonecraft had a male correspondent with whom she could be open and loving. It made for attractive, unwily letters. She had no truck with the old conduct-book line for women, that they should hide their love and respond only when the man pursued.

With the Gabells she had learnt to distrust Milton and his vision of domestic bliss in Eden. Now it seemed more beguiling. When Eve spoke to Adam, 'Milton insinuates, that, during such recitals, there are interruptions, not ungrateful to the heart, when the honey that drops from the lips is not merely words.' She wanted Imlay to respond to her like this, to praise with his eyes. Yet, remembering how cloying the Gabells' fondness had been and how irritated she felt reading Joel Barlow's endearments, she put her love letters aside when anyone entered. An interruption made her poetic: 'Hush! here they come – and love flies away in the twinkling of an eye, leaving a little brush of his wing on my pale cheeks.'

It was an idyllic time; Wollstonecraft demanded that Imlay act his loving part and make the idyll last.

# 22

*'The elm by which I wish to be supported'*

On 28 August the British fleet overcame the French garrison at Toulon. News reached Paris on 2 September. Outrage followed and, in xenophobic reaction, the government threatened all British expatriates with imprisonment until war ended. To keep her safe, Imlay registered Wollstonecraft at the American Embassy as his wife, so implying her American citizenship. They did not marry but she took his name. She had never attacked marriage, although accepting Dissenting opinion that it was useful rather than sacred.[1] Probably she wanted it now, especially as she suspected she might be pregnant, but to friends she made the decision appear a mutual, revolutionary choice. Also she had debts and by marrying would encumber Imlay with them.

The registration left her free to quit Neuilly. She went with a pang, for love and work had happily coexisted there and she had experienced the 'elegant felicity – where mind chastens sensation'. Perhaps it had been so good because Imlay was a visitor. Now she would live openly with him in Paris, possibly at his lodgings in Saint-Germain, where the affair had begun.

Imlay had acted appropriately: between 10 and 14 October, about 250 British subjects were imprisoned in the Luxembourg, including Stone and Helen Maria Williams. Later Williams described feeling 'the knife of the guillotine suspended over [her] head by a frail thread' – though her apprehension did not prevent her composing sonnets and translating St Pierre's *Paul and Virginia* while inside.[2] Back in England Anna Seward trembled for her friend's 'life in that murderous city' seeing her 'encircled with a nation of blood-hounds'. Smugly she concluded that Williams 'dearly pays for that misleading enthusiasm which led her to follow the wandering fire of imaginary freedom'.[3] Wollstonecraft's admirer von Schlabrendorf was also arrested: still careful not to declare his wealth, he frugally 'lived on bread and boiled plums' instead of acquiring more luxurious supplies.[4] His precautions were unavailing, and on two consecutive mornings he was due to be guillotined: on the first he mislaid his boots and on the second the authorities forgot to call his name. He greeted each subsequent morning with anxiety. Others of Wollstonecraft's revolutionary friends fell foul of Saint-Just's dictum that 'those who make revolutions by halves dig their own graves'.

The longed-for time of living with Imlay was brief and much interrupted. Soon he left for Le Havre. With the Girondin fall, his connection with Brissot and the Louisiana affair ended and he had to find other ways of earning money. He also had to prove loyalty to the new regime. So, with Barlow and a merchant with French connections, Elias Backman, he hatched a plan to evade the British blockade of France and import grain, soap and iron from neutral countries; payment would be in Bourbon silver, which they had permission to export to Sweden.[5] Backman would set up in Gothenburg and provide money and material; Imlay would handle shipping from Le Havre. It was a daring plan which, if successful, would endear them to the French government and make them rich. He and Wollstonecraft could then settle comfortably in domestic America with their child.

It was a cold, dreary September. She had few friends in Paris except the Barlows – though she visited both von Schlabrendorf and Williams in prison. The blockade destroyed regular correspondence with her sisters and London friends, and she solaced herself with writing letters to Imlay. When Godwin later read them, he was deeply moved, calling them 'the offspring of a glowing imagination, and a heart penetrated with the passion it essays to describe'. 'Glowing' certainly, but anxious too, for Wollstonecraft was quick to display the victimised woman and, when hurt, blame Imlay in the generic terms used for men in *The Rights of Woman*. The bliss of the Neuilly summer had not transformed her temperament or eradicated memories of Neptune and Fuseli. Her letters are moving, but, *en masse*, perhaps better to read as third party than recipient.

The first was written as Imlay travelled to Le Havre: 'I have been following you all along the road this comfortless weather; for, when I am absent from those I love, my imagination is as lively, as if my senses had never been gratified by their presence – I was going to say caresses – and why should I not?' Already the letter revealed all was not quite well, for Wollstonecraft was turning her critical gaze on her lover as she had on her sisters:

> I have found out that I have more mind than you, in one respect; because I can, without any violent effort of reason, find food for love in the same object, much longer than you can. – The way to my senses is through my heart; but, forgive me! I think there is sometimes a shorter cut to yours.
>
> With ninety-nine men out of a hundred, a very sufficient dash of folly is necessary to render a woman *piquante*, a soft word for desirable; and, beyond these casual ebullitions of sympathy, few look for enjoyment by fostering a passion in their hearts. One reason, in short, why I wish my whole sex to become wiser,

is, that the foolish ones may not, by their pretty folly, rob those whose sensibility keeps down their vanity, of the few roses that afford them some solace in the thorny road of life.

I do not know how I fell into these reflections, excepting one thought produced it – that these continual separations were necessary to warm your affections. – Of late, we are always separating. – Crack! – crack! – and away you go.

It was lightly done, but her imagining of her deserted self touched her.

In these letters Wollstonecraft was no longer primarily the rational analyst. The sad lady of sensibility, subdued when writing *The Rights of Woman*, had re-emerged; sensibility was being remythologised. She stressed her changing moods which Imlay must bear, her 'melancholy tears', her 'glow of tenderness' and 'the vagaries of a mind, that has been almost "crazed by care", as well as "crossed in hapless love"' – Ophelia and Sterne's mad Maria were haunting her again. She knew her mind fed on itself and countered melancholy with visions of an active future: 'When we are settled in the country together, more duties will open before me, and my heart, which now, trembling into peace, is agitated by every emotion that awakens the remembrance of old griefs, will learn to rest on yours, with that dignity your character, not to talk of my own, demands.' That she was worthy of love she remained sure, 'I think that you must love me, for, in the sincerity of my heart let me say it, I believe I deserve your tenderness, because I am true, and have a degree of sensibility that you can see and relish.' She would not leave the observation to her lover.

At the end of October Imlay briefly visited Paris. It was a momentous political time. The guillotine was working at full capacity. The slaughter of the great began with Marine Antoinette; facing death with 'indignant sorrow' in the words of Helen Maria Williams, she was beheaded on 16 October. Then on the 31st, as Wollstonecraft sat in her lodgings, Imlay entered and remarked, 'I suppose you have not heard the sad news of to-day?' She asked, 'Is Brissot guillotined?' Imlay's reply was shattering, 'Not only Brissot, but the *one-and-twenty* are.' These, the Girondin deputies, had approached the guillotine 'with all the calm of innocence,' breathing 'their last vows for the safety and liberty of the republic'. Serious before the immensity of death, Brissot had 'mourned over the fate of his country and not his own.'[6] At the news Wollstonecraft felt 'a sort of indefinite terror'; she visualised the faces of the dead she had known and, overwhelmed with emotion, sank lifeless on the floor.[7]

A week later Madame Roland went dramatically to the guillotine, her death lengthily portrayed by Williams. Just before her execution she bowed before the statue of liberty in the Place de la Révolution, uttering the famous words, 'O liberté, que de crimes on commet en ton nom!' When he heard the news, her husband committed suicide by falling on his sword in Roman fashion. Wollstonecraft later told Godwin that her anguish at these appalling events was 'one of the most intolerable sensations she had ever experienced'.[8] It was the end of an era. Nearly 35,000 people were killed in the Great Terror, but for Wollstonecraft it was the dead she knew who made the strongest impression.

In November, Imlay was back in Le Havre. This time he wrote her the affectionate letters her heart craved. Her fainting at news of executions might mark her horror at Robespierre's blood-letting, but also, along with 'some gentle twitches', confirmed she was 'nourishing a creature who will soon be sensible of my care'. It was a dark time to be bearing a child; yet, if France was politically topsy-turvy, it was less personally disturbing than conservative England. There, a woman, fearing the label of whore, would hide her shame until she might emerge childless. The *York Courant* ran a typical advertisement for 'Pregnant Ladies whose Situation requires a temporary Retirement'. On offer was an apartment for lying-in and promise of treatment with 'Honour, Attention, and Secrecy'. When delivered, infants were 'humanely taken Care of'. Even more ominously the advertisers offered an 'effectual Remedy to remove all Obstructions and Irregularities'.

Wollstonecraft stifled any alarm and declared her trust in Imlay and desire for the child. A common belief, strengthened by Lavater's work, was that the foetus felt what the mother felt, that the maternal body transmitted harmful emotions. Wollstonecraft determined to be tranquil. She must nurture herself physically and avoid abrupt movements. When she hurt herself lifting a large log of wood, she 'sat down in an agony, till I felt [the] ... twitches again.' She had 'an overflowing of tenderness' for this object of 'mutual interest'. Pregnancy made her more than ever want words of endearment, never enough or too passionate, and she pestered Imlay:

> write to me, my best love, and bid me be patient – kindly – and the expressions of kindness will again beguile the time, as sweetly as they have done to-night. – Tell me also over and over again, that your happiness (and you deserve to be happy!) is closely connected with mine, and I will try to dissipate, as they rise, the fumes of former discontent, that have too often clouded the sunshine, which you have endeavoured to diffuse through my mind.

Towards the end of the year, Wollstonecraft warmed herself by remembering sexual pleasure and, as in her Irish letters, describing her own sentimental reactions:

I have thy honest countenance before me – Pop – relaxed by tenderness; a little – little wounded by my whims; and thy eyes glistening with sympathy. – Thy lips then feel softer than soft – and I rest my cheek on thine, forgetting all the world. – I have not left the hue of love out of the picture – the rosy glow; and fancy has spread it over my own cheeks, I believe, for I feel them burning, whilst a delicious tear trembles in my eye, that would be all your own, if a grateful emotion directed to the Father of nature, who has made me thus alive to happiness, did not give more warmth to the sentiment it divides – I must pause a moment.

However much she loved, she wounded Imlay with her 'whims' and 'querulous humours', partially blamed on his depressing her spirits. She was no devotee of 'a milk-and-water affection ... when the temper is governed by a square and compass ... [T]he passions always give grace to the actions'; she trusted his affection despite ups and downs. Yet, since they had come to Paris, 'I do not know why, but I have more confidence in your affection, when absent, than present.'

Also there was his mercenary side which, ominously, he shared with the shallow 'calculator', Burke. She did not like his 'money-getting face' although admiring his energy and purpose, seemingly so different from the indolence of her younger brothers and George Blood. Her father had lost money in farming but had taken his biggest tumble through business and she instinctively feared it. Commerce might be associated with great republics as Paine thought, with industriousness and abstemiousness as James Burgh and the Newington Green Dissenters believed; it might be the motor of civilisation and progress – indeed, when she herself had looked to the future in *The Rights of Men*, she had supported the entrepreneur against the privileged aristocrat. Yet she had deplored money-mindedness in the French on first arrival. Commerce could dry up the bourgeois virtues that should be replacing aristocratic selfishness – cultural critics had been saying this since the time of Defoe and Addison; it could also endanger family life and chase out affection. Exchange value was not real value. She hoped her lover would not lose himself and her in schemes, forgetting their domestic purpose.

With Imlay away in Le Havre, Wollstonecraft probably had Christmas dinner with Helen Maria Williams, newly released from prison with the help of her sister's French fiancé. Her freed companion, John Hurford Stone, was absent suffering from gout, but he recorded that, during the season, he enjoyed a 'pleasant and agreeable society ... the Barlows, Payne, Williams, Wolstencroft' reading the English newspapers together. The 'trickster' Christie had decamped to Switzerland after a brief imprisonment in August; apparently he owed Stone the huge sum of £40,000 and his French mistress another £1200, awarded by the French authorities for seduction.[9] Wollstonecraft was still working on her book and Stone rudely reported, 'Rights of Women is writing, a huge work; but it will be as dull as Dr Moore's Chronicle, and probably as inaccurate.' John Moore had published several volumes describing and reflecting on his periods in France. Stone, who helped Williams write her campaign sections, preferred annals to historical chatter and pontificating; also he probably resented Moore's admiration of Williams, to whom the doctor had earlier written admiring verses. Had Wollstonecraft heard the comparison rather than the criticism, she could not have objected; she had read Moore's work back in London, found his travel writing 'ingenious', and his sadistic novel *Zeluco* full of 'sound principles'.[10]

Williams, who knew the political dangers of criticism in France more than Wollstonecraft, although perhaps exaggerating them for a person far from people in power, later advised her to 'burn' the manuscript. Wollstonecraft ignored the advice, but it might have influenced her for the moment to stop her story in the early Revolution. As might the sudden fate of Paine, who, long fearing the call of the guillotine, was dragged off to the Luxembourg prison from White's Hotel just after Christmas.

With such happenings the season renewed depression. If Imlay *knew* he was going to be away so long, why had she not gone with him? She tried comforting herself with writing a stream of short, almost daily notes, growing increasingly critical as his image receded. At the end of December she could be jocular: 'You seem to have taken up your abode at H[avre]. Pray sir! when do you think of coming home? ... I shall expect (as the country people say in England) that you will make a *power* of money to indemnify me for your absence ...' Yet she still scolded: 'I will cork up some of the kind things that were ready to drop from my pen, which has never been dipt in gall when addressing you; or, will only suffer an exclamation – "The creature!" or a kind look, to escape me, when I pass the slippers – which I could not remove from my *salle* door, though they are not the handsomest of their kind.' Slippers were the metonym of domesticity. Their owner might stray but had left this sign of his true familiar identity.

The next day arrived a batch of letters and books. One 'melancholy letter' was from Eliza, which 'harrassed' her mind.[11] Knowing nothing of the marriage manoeuvre, the London papers had reported that Mary had been arrested with other British residents, and the event had crushed Eliza both through her sister's danger and her own failed hopes. Trying to retain some dignity by mentioning alternative plans – working near Everina in Ireland –

she yet screamed her miseries. Mary could do little to help and did not immediately reply. She had a very different letter from Charles in America: she was cheered, apparently forgetting his sanguine temperament. Even without the immediate help of the Barlows he had made good.

Another 'very long and very affectionate' letter probably came from Johnson. Like Eliza's it troubled her since it suggested all was not well. The books probably also came from him. 'I shall not look into them till you return,' she told Imlay, 'when you shall read, whilst I mend my stockings.' The books were presumably for her history and she did not often mention sewing or communal reading, but lovers' sharing books was a motif in sentimental fiction expressing tasteful courtship and happy marriage, while the husband's reading to the sewing wife was a frequent scene in conduct books and didactic novels – indeed she herself had made one for a virtuous wife in *Original Stories*.

Imlay had not been in Johnson's circle in London; now she wanted him to know this man whom she regarded as a more presentable father than fate had provided. 'Love him a little!' she urged. 'It would be a kind of separation, if you did not love those I love.' She dreamed of welding together friends and relatives in cosy domesticity: of Charles she wrote, 'There is a spirit of independence in his letter, that will please you ... I think that you would hail him as a brother, with one of your tender looks, when your heart not only gives a lustre to your eye, but a dance of playfulness, that he would meet with a glow half made up of bashfulness, and a desire to please the – where shall I find a word to express the relationship which subsists between us? – Shall I ask the little twitcher? – But I have dropt half the sentence that was to tell you how much he would be inclined to love the man loved by his sister. I have been fancying myself sitting between you, ever since I began to write, and my heart has leaped at the thought!'

All her visions turned to her lover and, despite her concern for others, it was Imlay's letter that meant most and nullified the pain of Eliza's moanings and her friend's troubles. She found it a 'cordial' of 'so much considerate tenderness' that 'if it has not made you dearer to me, it has made me forcibly feel how very dear you are to me, by charming away half my cares.'

With such a reward, she quickly resumed her pen, and a few hours after one letter she was ready with another. She hoped Imlay needed to hear often. She knew she had returned to her old role of sensitive lady – only in affairs of the heart, for she insisted her *mind* remained untouched – and she suspected Imlay had emotional needs as well, despite his struggling to appear 'manly'. He should acknowledge them, for she loved to see sensibility 'striving to master' his face. '[T]hese kind of sympathies are the life of affection: and why, in cultivating our understandings, should we try to dry up these springs of pleasure, which gush out to give a freshness to days browned by care!'

However she fantasised a sentimental Imlay in a loving huddle of publisher and brother beside a domestic fire, New Year became a lonely moment of stock-taking which renewed melancholy. Outside, the guillotine continued to slash off heads: personal and public worlds seemed equally in disarray.

Her response was gloomy introspection. In her *Vindications* she had criticised western Europe's major literary icons and the way they helped construct sexual difference. In proportion as she grew sad she recalled their images, internalised when she was a hungry adolescent in Beverley or a solitary governess in Ireland. They wrote of men of course, but gender seemed less important when contemplating her own internal life. Shakespeare's and Milton's heroes answered deeper needs than the resilient matrons of Catherine Macaulay and Sarah Trimmer:

> The face of things, public and private, vexes me. The 'peace' and clemency which seemed to be dawning a few days ago, disappear again. 'I am fallen,' as Milton said, 'on evil days;' for I really believe that Europe will be in a state of convulsion, during half a century at least ... The world appears an 'unweeded garden' where 'things rank and vile' flourish best.[12]

As New Year's Day closed, she was at her desk, loneliness preying on her. Now for the first time she understood the physical and social burden of pregnancy. Women were glancing censoriously from her face to her belly, making pointed remarks. She announced 'simply that I was with child: and let them stare! and —, and —, nay, all the world, may know it for aught I care!' Yet she added plaintively, 'I wish to avoid —'s coarse jokes.'

Some anxiety at being an unmarried mother must have touched her. Catherine Macaulay lost her reputation by making, in Horace Walpole's words, 'an uncouth match', marrying in middle age a man twenty-six years her junior; Macaulay had remarked the bizarre morality imposed on woman: 'Let her only take care that she is not caught in a love intrigue, and she may defame, she may ruin her family with gaming, and the peace of twenty others with her coquetry, and yet preserve her reputation and her peace.' Wollstonecraft echoed this when she noted that woman's reputation was confined to 'a single virtue – chastity'. In the social world she needed Imlay more than he needed her, or as Rousseau asserted: 'he could do without her better than she can do without him.'[13]

At the same time she reflected on the unit of mother and child. When she had rescued Eliza from marriage, she had largely accepted that the baby belonged to the father. She felt differently now: 'Considering the care and anxiety a woman must have about a child before it comes into the world, it seems to me, by a *natural* right, to belong to her.' Yet she felt the vulnerability of this maternal unit in a world ruled by men and male values; men's lack of care for it jolted her into the kind of thinking she had avoided since publishing *The Rights of Woman*: 'When men get immersed in the world, they seem to lose all sensations, excepting those necessary to continue or produce life! – Are these the privileges of reason? Amongst the feathered race, whilst the hen keeps the young warm, her mate stays by to cheer her; but it is sufficient for man to condescend to get a child, in order to claim it. – A man is a tyrant!'

The thought brought herself and Imlay into focus as gendered types: she concerned with feelings and sensibility, he with pleasure and money. She had believed such gendering limiting when composing *The Rights of Men*, for it justified female subordination and separate education. But she and Imlay were embodying its most intractable aspect – she giving all to love, he straying: 'You may now tell me, that, if it were not for me, you would be laughing away with some honest fellows in L[ondo]n. The casual exercise of social sympathy would not be sufficient for me – I should not think such an heartless life worth preserving.' In response to these serious reflections, she asserted an independence hard to achieve at any time and no longer much wanted: 'If you do not return soon – or, which is no such mighty matter, talk of it – I will throw your slippers out at window, and be off – nobody knows where.'

Perhaps had she not been pregnant and alone she would have freed herself from someone she sometimes feared was retreating, but it is unlikely. For so long she had desired such a relationship and Imlay's resemblance in character if not temperament to her father and Fuseli suggested how fast she was caught. Where Imlay displeased, she insisted, as with Fuseli, that he was not what he seemed, that they were really alike. Desperately she wanted him to be lover and parent, constant suitor and nurturing protector. His slippers denoted his presence; they promised his return and, in their domestic comfort, declared his wished-for vulnerability.

Then she panicked. One of Imlay's business partners, possibly the American land speculator Colonel Blackden, whom she disliked, confirmed her suspicion: that Imlay knew he would be in Le Havre for a further three months and had hidden the news. She dashed off a furious note. According to Godwin, 'further letters' following in this week were so ferocious that Imlay destroyed them. She accepted their destruction while retaining her belief that *whatever* she wrote, even peevish or uncontrolled, had value.

The extant letters resumed a few days later when Wollstonecraft had pulled herself together. She had received a reply from Imlay but, fearing a rebuke, even withdrawal, sat racked by trembling before opening it. When she did, she found reassuring words and felt mortified, realising that, however she softened, Imlay held proof of her defection and would receive more resentment through the slow post. Desperate to neutralise it, she wrote a 'penitential letter', blaming her moods on her physical state. She was pathetic not aggressive, an appealing lover not a harridan. She would be feminine, gentle, a devoted mother-to-be, never more letting 'folly' threaten 'fatal consequence' in her womb:

> I have just received your kind and rational letter, and would fain hide my face, glowing with shame for my folly. – I would hide it in your bosom, if you would again open it to me, and nestle closely till you bade my fluttering heart be still, by saying that you forgave me. With eyes overflowing with tears, and in the humblest attitude, I entreat you. – Do not turn from me, for indeed I love you fondly, and have been very wretched, since the night I was so cruelly hurt by thinking that you had no confidence in me.

Her erratic emotions had made her ill: stomach and bowels were disordered and nothing she ate or drank stayed down. She was ashamed of hurting the baby: 'the notion that I was tormenting, or perhaps killing, a poor little animal, about whom I am grown anxious and tender, now I feel it alive, made me worse.' She tried to be cheerful, 'Do you think that the creature goes regularly to sleep? ... You perceive that I am already smiling through my tears – You have lightened my heart, and my frozen spirits are melting into playfulness.' She ended by imploring Imlay to write at once. He could scold her when he saw her but must not be angry by post – she could not bear it: 'God bless you, my love; do not shut your heart against a return of tenderness; and, as I now in fancy cling to you, be more than ever my support. – Feel but as affectionate when you read this letter, as I did writing it ...' It was intended to be emollient, but the effect, though loving, remained demanding and self-conscious.

Perhaps it was some dissatisfaction with her style, as well as anxiety to form her lover's opinion that made her write another letter a few days later. Pain made her defensive and angry, she knew; it was a lifelong response for which she had often chided herself: 'One thing you mistake in my character, and imagine that to be coldness which is just the contrary.' Again she promised, 'I will never, if I am not entirely cured of quarrelling, begin to encourage "quick-coming fancies" when we are separated.' Forgetting the advice of *The*

*Rights of Woman*, that self-respect was more important than respect of others and that the source of happiness should reside in the self, in her next letters she stressed how physically and mentally weak she was: 'Sorrow has almost made a child of me, and ... I want to be soothed to peace.' Her 'own happiness' depended wholly on Imlay: she was 'MARY IMLAY', his 'poor sick girl'.

To calm her, Imlay invited her to visit Le Havre. Although desperate to see him, she hesitated, fearing that, since she was so weak, the journey in such a cold time might further harm the tormented foetus. Possibly in a few days she could manage it; she was now taking care of herself, getting into a warmed bed at night, and keeping out of draughts. She knew she had stayed indoors too much; women often remained as inactive as possible through pregnancy but the latest medical opinion, even in France, urged exercise, and walking was the best on offer.[14] She would start at once. Then she would come to Le Havre.

Next morning she began her healthy regime. It was a fine January day and the clear bracing air could invigorate the baby. It was just the weather for a walk *together*. Since supplies of wood and food were erratic, she probably used her excursions to help her maid get what they needed to keep well and warm. With each succeeding day she felt stronger; playfulness was returning and she asked pardon of the unborn child. She could not see how to hug it but the idea suggested she meant well.

Like other pregnant women she probably prepared her belly for labour with some sort of oil or fat. She was fastidious and clean in her habits but would not have taken baths, even had she had enough wood to heat so much water: baths relaxed muscles, provoking suspicion that the woman wanted a miscarriage.[15] With all her care she expected an easy delivery: 'I cannot boast of being quite recovered, yet I am (I must use my Yorkshire phrase; for, when my heart is warm, pop come the expressions of childhood into my head) so *lightsome*, that I think it will not *go badly with me*. – And nothing shall be wanting on my part, I assure you; for I am urged on, not only by an enlivened affection for you, but by a new-born tenderness that plays cheerly round my dilating heart.'

The child would be the first of many and she made a consoling hint from her lover into a full vision of fecund bliss: 'What a picture you have sketched of our fire-side! Yes, my love, my fancy was instantly at work, and I found my head on your shoulder, whilst my eyes were fixed on the little creatures that were clinging about your knees. I did not absolutely determine that there should be six – if you have not set your heart on this round number.' Instead of allowing Imlay's business to underpin their domesticity, she was ready to complement her picture of six clinging children with a sentimental idealisation of poverty: 'I do not think a *little* money inconvenient; but, should [the projects] fail, we will struggle cheerfully together – drawn closer by the pinching blasts of poverty.'

Her good resolutions paid off: her health improved and her mind was calmed by trying to sympathise with Imlay's business alarms: 'I cannot but respect your motives and conduct. I always respected them; and was only hurt, by what seemed to me a want of confidence, and consequently affection. – I thought also, that if you were obliged to stay three months at H[avre], I might as well have been with you.' She would not nag him about returning, sure he would come when he had 'attained (or lost sight of) the object of your journey'. She could never resist a dig.

Though his letters are lost, Wollstonecraft's replies reveal that, whatever his actions, Imlay's words were frequently reassuring. At other times, either he was unclear or he expressed his feelings ambivalently. Prevarication followed reaffirmation of love. In the latter he was temporarily sincere; the hold of Wollstonecraft over Imlay was not as great as his over her but it surely existed.

When she could stand Paris alone no longer, she determined to go to Le Havre, to be with him even if she were not quite well and it proved dangerous for the child. Since she had not completed her 'great book', she could not expect more money from Johnson and apparently she had taken nothing from Imlay for herself. So she borrowed from Ruth Barlow, intending to repay her once the history was published. A couple of letters informed Imlay that his importunate lover had a passport and was *en route*. She would set out on Thursday, arriving on Friday evening in Le Havre, in time, she hoped, to say good-night to him in her new apartment. She, he and love would be together and 'in spite of care' he would 'smile' her to sleep, for, as she wryly reminded him, 'I have not caught much rest since we parted.' Now that she was about to see him, she could express all the longing and clinging she had been trying to suppress. The conventional vocabulary of 'lofty pine' and 'graceful vine' once abjured seemed wonderfully apt:

> You have, by your tenderness and worth, twisted yourself more artfully round my heart, than I supposed possible. – Let me indulge the thought, that I have thrown out some tendrils to cling to the elm by which I wish to be supported. – This is talking a new language for me! – But, knowing that I am not a parasite-plant, I am willing to receive the proofs of affection, that every pulse replies to, when I think of being once more in the same house with you. – God bless you!

Indeed it was not the language of *The Rights of Woman*, where the feminine desire totally to depend on a man and be supported by heterosexual love had been mocked as the culturally conditioned disease of femininity: 'To see a mortal adorn an object with imaginary charms, then fall down and worship the idol which he had himself set up – how ridiculous!' she had written. Now she forgot her belief that she should look round man to God and that God alone could lift the burden of existence. She was aware of inconsistency but rationalised rather than investigated it. In her predicament she would not dare to let a perceived cultural problem turn into a psychological one.

Her last note from Paris was meant to arrive just before herself, an '*avant-coureur*, without jack boots'. She was 'on the wing' like the heart-whole spinster she had imagined as herself when first setting out for France over a turbulent year ago. Proximity was exciting but unsettling. She had written fiercer letters than he; yet, now she had surmounted her fear of losing him, she recollected it was he who started the quarrel by his deception. Penitence, so lavishly expressed, must be paid for by resentment. Was she so much less emotionally controlled than he or had they colluded in thinking so? New security allowed her to consider that perhaps she was no more at the mercy of her moods than he. Well, she was near now, and resolved not to ruffle his temper for a 'long, long time – I am afraid to say never.' In her pleasure she forgot the tremblings, headaches, panics, stomach and bowel pains: 'I am well, and have no apprehension that I shall find the journey too fatiguing, when I follow the lead of my heart. – With my face turned to H[avre] my spirits will not sink – and my mind has always hitherto enabled my body to do whatever I wished.'

They met in Le Havre and ironed out creases made during too long an absence. Given the anxious epistolary prelude, their life together went better than one might have expected. Wollstonecraft was not always sympathetic, not always polite to the business associates who had replaced the dashing revolutionaries of the Paris days, and there must have been tension. Imlay's friend Colonel Blackden visited and drank too much and she hated drunkenness. But she was now concerned with her own affairs and had less time minutely to criticise his friends, appraise her feelings, or scrutinise Imlay's. She looked forward to the approaching birth and the completion of her book, now long overdue.

# 23

*'Nothing could be more natural'*

Imlay and Wollstonecraft rented a spacious house near the harbour on the rue de Corderie in the Section des Sans-Culottes owned by John Wheatcroft, an English soap merchant. They kept several servants including a cook and scullery-maid and dined and entertained formally – happily not much with Blackden, who was shipped off drunk to Lisbon. It was as conventional a life as she had ever led.

Having stifled her panics, she set about finishing the last part of *The French Revolution*. However painful the previous months, she was glad she had come to France when she had; otherwise she could never have formed a 'just opinion of the most extraordinary event that has ever been recorded'. She was treating only the early Revolution, but, by gloomily suggesting a glorious dawn followed by a shoddier day, she would be giving offence and she was right in thinking 'my life would not have been worth much, had [the manuscript] been *found*' in France. Yet it was worthwhile taking risks. Over the last months she had mostly been concerned with Imlay, but she had felt the uproar outside and the 'sad scenes' she had witnessed in Paris left a lasting impression.

She had known extremes unheard of in England: though 'death and misery, in every shape of terrour' still haunted the country, she had 'met with some uncommon instances of friendship, which my heart will ever grate[ful]ly store up, and call to mind when the remembrance is keen of the anguish it has endured for its fellow creatures, at large – for the unfortunate beings cut off around me – and the still more unfortunate survivors.' It was the inevitable mode. Helen Maria Williams was filling her chronicles with the killings of the Jacobin regime, individual acts of capricious sadism, state executions and vicious mass drownings in fake-bottomed boats in icy rivers. Horror bred the sensational courage no peace could demand, and her account was punctuated with heart-warming anecdotes of friends dying for each other, nuns begging their faces be covered modestly in death, mothers taking their daughters' places for the guillotine. But before these chronicles were printed Williams and Stone had prudently decamped to Switzerland.

If it was worth taking risks for history, it was less so for correspondence.

Brother James had sent her so indiscreet a letter that, had it been opened, she might have found herself in trouble. Despite his experience of war, James had little sense of the dangers faced in an enemy land. She hoped he would receive her letter of warning before writing again.

More than with James she wanted to re-establish contact with her sisters, but, when she sat down to write, she felt horribly out-of-touch. From Eliza's last depressing letter, she assumed the sisters were together in Ireland, quite underestimating Eliza's Paris obsession. She wanted to assure her she still cared for her and planned a future, but, even as she wrote, she felt how far she had travelled from the imagined community on an American farm.

Over the months she had written many letters to her sisters with no evidence any had been received. She assumed they had done likewise. So it was no pleasure to write stale news, but she would attempt it for, with Imlay's international associates, including their landlord Wheatcroft, who often journeyed abroad, as well as the easier boat travel from Le Havre, she could more likely get news through to Ireland. So, about three months after arriving in the rue de Corderie, she wrote again to Everina and this time her letter arrived. She reiterated her generalisations about the French and their climate. Forgetting her miseries in cold Paris, she declared the weather uncommonly fine and the country pleasant. The French were superficially cheery and friendly; when depressed she found them trivial and frivolous but, more contented now, she saw 'ease, and even simplicity, in . . . manners'.

Politically things were, of course, dreadful, but she skirted round this dangerous topic. She even feared to provoke opinions in reply. Imlay was in delicate negotiations, which depended on keeping the goodwill of French authorities; he had impressed on her the need to be circumspect. She hinted at this when she told Everina she was afraid to request an answer 'lest I should involve others in my difficulties, and make them suffer for protecting me.' Her sisters were more sensitive than James but they must have been bombarded with English propaganda and might write something indiscreet in her volatile context.

She had hidden so much it was difficult to know where to begin and end. There was as yet no child, so no need to stress cohabitation outside marriage. It was one thing in revolutionary France, another in provincial Ireland. She knew her sisters, especially Eliza, were sympathetic to revolutionary ideas, but both might have quailed before her private reality. How could they understand the slow growth of affection, her new sense of sex as part of love, and her unexpected trust in a man, especially after her vigorous stance against foolish romance? Like her when panicking, they might have seen a fallen woman unsure of her lover and about to bear his illegitimate child.

So she mentioned neither her new name of Imlay nor the impending birth, but admitted she had the 'protection' of an American:

> A most worthy man, who joins to uncommon tenderness of heart and quickness of feeling, a soundness of understanding, and reasonableness of temper, rarely to be met with – Having also been brought up in the interiour parts of America, he is a most natural, unaffected creature. I am with him now at Havre, and shall remain there, till circumstances point out what it is necessary for me to do.

Occasionally Imlay returned to Paris. Wollstonecraft, of course, pursued him with letters, displaying herself as a woman contentedly affectionate and cured of melancholy moods but still vulnerable, still affected by any diminution of love or lengthening of absence:

> I could not sleep. – I turned to your side of the bed, and tried to make the most of the comfort of the pillow, which you used to tell me I was churlish about; but all would not do. – I took nevertheless my walk before breakfast, though the weather was not very inviting – and here I am, wishing you a finer day, and seeing you peep over my shoulder, as I write, with one of your kindest looks – when your eyes glisten, and a suffusion creeps over your relaxing features.

When she forgot something she meant to enclose she jocularly put the error down to love 'at the fag-end of a letter of business': 'You know, you say, they will not chime together. – I had got you by the fire-side, with the *gigot* smoking on the board, to lard your poor bare ribs – and behold, I closed my letter without taking the paper up, that was directly under my eyes!'

She also wrote to Ruth Barlow, happy that her friend knew her circumstances and understood life with a preoccupied man of business. As winter became spring, Imlay worried about delays and the restrictions the French authorities placed on his trade. She conveyed the anxiety to Ruth, writing as part of the firm: 'Let but the first ground be secured – and in the course of the summer we may, perhaps celebrate our good luck, not forgetting good management together. – There has been some plague about the shipping of the goods, which Mr Imlay will doubtless explain.'

To Ruth she could also reveal pride in coupledom – she underlined 'us' and joked, 'you perceive that I am acquiring the matrimonial phraseology without having clogged my soul by promising obedience &c &c.' Ruth had probably witnessed her panic in Paris and she wanted to overlay the impression with more carefree love. She took pleasure in telling her friend about her domestic life, that she had found linen shirts for Imlay and needed none sent.

Other things she did need: calico or dimity for a morning gown. Happily, as she noted in her history, revolutionary fashion had veered toward the simple – light draped shawls and bright or white dresses – rather easier for pregnancy. Stays were still worn although they were not obligatory in France or quite so tortuous as before to the fuller figure. Men from Locke to Rousseau and Sir Joshua Reynolds had inveighed against tight-lacing, rather as they attacked wet-nursing, but few women thought to give up stays altogether – Wollstonecraft did not, though she moaned of the cramping of female limbs and minds. Yet, though she now followed fashion to some extent, she was never greatly interested in dress or worried over the quality of cloth. Where other ladies might swathe their rounded bellies in spotted muslins and expensive silks and lace, she ordered only cheap cottons from Ruth, either plain white or light coloured with ribbing for ornament.

From Joel Barlow she wanted copies of the journals printing National Assembly decrees and debates so that she could complete her book. He must have sent them speedily for she wrote the last words in late spring. She ended the final volume with very tarnished hopes. Atrocious government had sunk the French below savages and obliterated their morality; consequently the Parisian mob were 'barbarous beyond the tiger's cruelty'. She had often favoured baroque physical images and the notion of painfully opened bowels was apt in her ripely pregnant state: the Terror became 'excrementitious humours exuding from the contaminated body' of France. The only mitigation was that the cause of barbarity lay in the tyrannical past.[1] When finished, she sent the pages at once to Johnson who had been receiving the work in instalments. She was eager to be rid of it before bodily events intervened. Now she could assure Ruth, 'I am still very well; but imagine it cannot be long before this lively animal pops on us – and now the history is finished and every thing arranged I do not care how soon.'

Grandly entitled *An Historical and Moral View of the Origin and Progress of the French Revolution* (as Stone had surmised, it *was* rather like Dr Moore's latest work, *View of the Causes and Progress of the French Revolution*), the book discussed a past she had not witnessed, thereby avoiding direct presentation of the king's trial which had so moved her and the horrifying Reign of Terror she was living through.[2] She based her work on secondary sources, extensively the English *Annual Register*, and made few historical (though many moral) observations of her own. Her sexual passion for Imlay and her desire to absorb him completely perhaps made her uneasy at past self-images: in the new book, the narrative voice was rarely gendered. She would not be stridently unfeminine as in *The Rights of Men*, or allude with proud frequency to her rational femaleness as in *The Rights of Woman*.

Rousseau had emphasised sexual difference; she was starting to feel it as her body swelled while Imlay's remained lithe and spare. Yet, that she had written so weighty a book in pregnancy countered Rousseau's limiting gender theories. In *Émile*, he declared that biology was personality. The performance of female functions, especially pregnancy, birth, and nursing, required 'a special constitution'; so female bodies and minds were governed by 'the general laws of nature' that made it a 'woman's business to be a mother' even when not breeding. With such a body, a woman could not reach to 'abstract knowledge'; she was 'limited in her range of observation'.[3] Yet Wollstonecraft's *French Revolution*, concluded during a first pregnancy, ranged widely, was heavily abstract, and induced John Adams, later president of the new United States, to call her 'a Lady of a masculine masterly Understanding'.[4]

At two in the afternoon on 14 May 1794, her baby was born. It was 25 Floréal in the revolutionary calendar (called Flowery by English wags, who translated other months as Sneezy, Freezy and Nippy), the month when Robespierre established his Cult of the Supreme Being in place both of Christianity and scepticism, a new era by any standards. Wollstonecraft was thirty-five, old for a first delivery, but she had little fear of labour and childbirth. Despite the dismal, depressive letters about her pains and shattered nerves over the years, she had a good constitution and the happiness of the months in Le Havre as well as her regime of exercise kept her healthy. She knew of the quarrels between female midwives and male obstetricians for the control of childbirth and, though favouring the former, was not hostile in theory to the medical knowledge male 'professionals' had amassed. For the *Analytical Review* she had summarised without much comment a general work on biology by the foremost expert on midwifery from the mid-eighteenth century, William Smellie, who combined his progressive belief that the uterus rather than the child did the expelling in childbirth with a disturbing sense of the maternal body as a kind of obstructive machine that had to be worked on by male mechanics.[5] In her own case she saw no need for arcane or specialised knowledge and, in *The Rights of Woman*, had argued that women should help themselves and not unnecessarily turn to men.

She had employed only a midwife, possibly on ideological grounds, possibly because she feared French hospitals and physicians. In hospitals the newly discovered disease of puerperal fever had become rampant and no one seemed quite clear what to do about it – except give ipecacuanha. Physicians had high status in France, but they tended, like Smellie, to regard the female body as obstructive and women patients as too unenlightened to be listened to. They were opposed by a thriving medical counter culture, which, by attending to women, preyed on them. The most famous charlatan of the 1770s and '80s was Franz Anton Mesmer with his flamboyant 'animal magnetism' cures based on the notion of a universal fluid permeating all sentient things. To the medical establishment his cures appeared disturbingly erotic since they included touching within a context of soft furnishings and music. Mesmer specialised in nervous and ambiguous cases which other doctors could not heal and claimed that with his methods women, cursed in Genesis, could bear children without pain. As a former student of John Arden, who had taught her scientifically about magnetism, Wollstonecraft was scornful of women's credulity; she called magnetic cures 'hocus pocus tricks'.[6]

Happily the birth was easy although the baby had a large head, and she was proud of not succumbing to the usual fears and follies of women in her condition. '[N]othing could be more natural or easy than my labour,' she wrote gleefully to Ruth six days after the birth, 'still it is not smooth work – I dwell on these circumstances not only as I know it will give you pleasure; but to prove that this struggle of nature is rendered much more cruel by the ignorance and affectation of women.'

Although much medical opinion demanded a month's lying in bed or on a couch for the new mother, she was up next day, shocking the midwife, who was convinced that she would kill herself and the child. But, 'since we are alive and so astonishingly well, she begins to think that the *Bon Dieu* takes care of those who take no care of themselves'. Later she wrote, 'I managed myself so well that my lying-in scarcely deserved the name; I only rested, through persuasion, in bed one day and was out a walking the eight.' With the common superstitions of birth she had nothing to do: the French rural custom of tying the umbilical cord of a boy a couple of inches from his stomach, while tying the girl's as close as possible or tipping the first bathing water of the girl on the ashes of the hearth to keep her at home, while the boy's was thrown outside since he had to deal with the world. If she knew of such customs, she had denied their principles in her own wandering life.

Of course she suckled the baby, following good revolutionary and liberal principles. Rousseau had lyrically advocated breast-feeding for all mothers and, back in London, she had favourably reviewed Ben Lara's *Essay on the Injurious Custom of Mothers not suckling their own Children*, which argued that not to breast-feed was bad for the *mother's* health.[7] Yet, for all this propaganda, she did not find breast-feeding quite the idyll men portrayed, and she was 'incommoded' by a too lavish supply of milk. But she persevered since she had always resented her own mother for suckling only her eldest son and, unlike the majority of mothers in her class, she believed that such feeding bonded mother and child and made the child more tender – though Ned failed to fit the theory. She impressed her attendant with her vigorous dealings: 'My nurse has been twenty years in this employment, and she tells me, she never knew a woman so well – adding, Frenchwoman like, that I ought to make children for the Republic, since I treat it so slightly.'

The baby girl was named Frances or Fanny after her dead friend. Perhaps it compensated a little for the fictional betrayal. Inevitably there was some echo of Eliza's dead baby, the one who had united them all as Mary Elizabeth Frances. That child had begun healthily too, yet died, but this one would retain her mother, her mother's milk, and her father.

Under the name Françoise Imlay the baby was registered as legitimate in the Maison Commune of Havre-Marat (as Le Havre was now called). Their English landlord, John Wheatcroft, and his wife were witnesses. Ruth Barlow had briefly visited Le Havre in April with Joel and had been busy making caps for the expected baby. Wollstonecraft was proud to say they were all too small: 'let me tell you that I have got a vigorous little Girl, and you were so out in your calculation respecting the quantity of brains she was to have, and the skull it would require to contain them, that you made almost all the caps so small I cannot use them; but it is of little consequence for she will soon have hair enough to do without any.'

To Ruth, her 'Dear Friend', Wollstonecraft could convey her excitement. Imlay seemed pleased to be a father and she called him her 'affectionate companion', but she suspected that only a woman could truly understand her feelings. She had not felt them at once; motherly emotions were not automatic – hence her stress on breast-feeding – but they could be cultivated. This she had done: 'I feel great pleasure at being a mother,' she confided to the childless Ruth, conscious that she was rattling on about babies and childbirth in a way she would earlier have mocked. But she could not restrain herself and three days later she added a proud maternal postscript: 'My little Girl begins to suck so *manfully* that her father reckons saucily on her writing the second part of the R[igh]ts of Woman.'

Fatherhood could not engross Imlay as much as motherhood could her. Sometimes women avoided intercourse after childbirth, as the affair with Eliza and the importunate Bishop hinted. Perhaps Wollstonecraft was eager to follow this custom; perhaps Imlay did not much care for milky, breast-feeding women who had not regained their figure. Whatever the reason, there seems to have been some abstinence and Imlay found it unappealing. He must have thought of alternatives, if not in Le Havre then elsewhere.

Also, business affairs were importunate. To further the trading scheme, he had associated with a young Norwegian shipmaster, Peder Ellefsen, in whose name he purchased a French cargo ship called *La Liberté*, renamed it *Maria and Margaretha*, and certified it as Norwegian. Ellefsen would sail it from Le Havre to Norway under a Danish flag, thus avoiding the English blockade. It would carry the cargo of Bourbon silver with the huge value of £3500 to exchange for grain. There were delays however and Imlay grew tense during these delicate and dangerous manoeuvres.

Sadly, from May through the momentous political summer of 1794, any letters Wollstonecraft wrote to her sisters have vanished. A shorter hiatus occurs in the correspondence between Wollstonecraft and Ruth Barlow; only in July did she receive a letter from Ruth written in May. Another letter from Joel was lost. She was dismayed since it had enclosed one from Charles, presumably sent through a business friend of Barlow's in America.

So Wollstonecraft's ebbs and flows of emotion, the matter of most of her letters, are hidden during this pivotal personal and political time, when she tasted and lost the domestic life she craved and heard of the final slaughters of the Terror as the Jacobins turned on each other until, at the end of July, Robespierre fell. The one letter to Ruth showed that she was registering the times: 'The French will carry all before them – but, my God, how many victims fall beneath the sword and the Guillotine! My blood runs cold, and I sicken at thoughts of a Revolution which costs so much blood and bitter tears.'

Inevitably the child filled much of her life. After so many months of irritable bowels and upset stomachs, she felt well. She had the usual maternal pride in the baby's natural development, always seeming greater than that of other children. But, as usual, she herself was centre stage, ascribing the baby's precocity to her method of nursing: 'my little Girl [is] not only uncommonly healthy, but already, as sagacious as a child of five or six months old, which I rather attribute to my good, that is natural, manner of nursing her, than to any extraordinary strength of faculties. She has not tasted any thing, but my milk, of which I have abundance, since her birth.' However natural and desirable breast-feeding might be, she intended an early weaning and in a month or two would begin Fanny on starchy solid food. The bread in Le Havre was poor and she asked Ruth to send her some of the 'fine biscuits' presumably brought as a present when she visited Le Havre. Weaning was considered a difficult transition for mother and baby; it was important to get it right.

As befitted an authority on education Wollstonecraft took child-rearing seriously. Later when she compiled a series of infant lessons, she based them on little Fanny within a nuclear family:

When you were hungry, you began to cry, because you could not speak. You were seven months without teeth, always sucking. But after you got one, you began to gnaw a crust of bread. It was not long before another came pop. At ten months you had four pretty white teeth, and you used to bite me. Poor mamma! Still I did not cry, because I am not a child, but you hurt me very much. So I said to papa, it is time the little girl should eat. She is not naughty, yet she hurts me. I have given her a crust of bread, and I must look for some other milk.

The cow has got plenty, and her jumping calf eats grass very well. He has got more teeth than my little girl. Yes, says papa, and he tapped you on the cheek, you are old enough to learn to eat? Come to me, and I will teach you, my little dear, for you must not hurt poor mamma.

In 'Lessons', 'Papa' is always there.[8]

Despite stressing Imlay's fatherhood, Wollstonecraft expected passionate love to continue; any diminution alarmed her. She herself was being careful not to let the lover be subsumed in the mother, although this was not her counsel in *The Rights of Woman*: there lovers did not make good mothers, and children had a better chance of attention when parents were distant. She quoted instances of Imlay's affection for her as mother but was unsure how much interest he really had in her in this role. She herself cared little for *his* other roles: businessman and male companion. How often in these relatively happy months did she tell him that commerce was not all there was in life or lament the replacement of their radical Paris set by coarse money-grabbing businessmen? About his inner life and hopes she seemed strangely incurious.

Then Imlay fell ill. Wollstonecraft ascribed it to a mind harassed by business disappointments for the government put constant restrictions in his way. She tried to enter into his anxiety by translating desire for money into concern for honouring his word. He had contracted to send so much to Backman and must ensure it was received: 'I cannot help sharing his disquietude,' she told Ruth, 'because the fulfilling of engagements appears to me of more importance than the making a fortune.' This was probably not Imlay's view.

In August Ellefsen finally sailed from Le Havre on the *Maria and Margaretha* and Imlay's work was done. His fever left him and he was impatient to go to Paris to find how matters stood after Robespierre's fall. The independent woman he had cherished had turned into a needy mother and he was relieved to escape from reproaches and demands.

# 24

*'Come back quickly to play with your girls.'*

Wollstonecraft determined not to panic while Imlay was away; she would be active and maternal. Seeing a sad analogy between her love for baby and father, she hugged and kissed her 'little darling':

> Poor thing! when I am sad, I lament that all my affections grow on me, till they become too strong for my peace, though they all afford me snatches of exquisite enjoyment – This for our little girl who was at first very reasonable – more the effect of reason, a sense of duty, than feeling – now, she has got into my heart and imagination, and when I walk out without her, her little figure is ever dancing before me.

She made enchanting images for Imlay to control her moods and lure him back: 'the little damsel ... has been almost springing out of my arm – she certainly looks very like you – but I do not love her the less for that, whether I am angry or pleased with you,' she closed a letter. Fanny was 'a little sprite' at one moment, a 'little Hercules' at another.

She continued her social life, but her accounts were sour. She called on an ill-assorted French couple who lacked the fineness of herself and Imlay: the woman had the 'manners of a gentlewoman, with a dash of the easy French coquetry, which renders her *piquante*', but her husband, neither gentleman nor lover, cut an awkward figure. Another couple were ugly and had a house smelling of 'commerce from top to toe'. The abortive attempts at taste only showed it could not be bought. She especially noticed a *'pendule* – A nymph was offering up her vows before a smoking altar, to a fat-bottomed Cupid ... kicking his heels in the air.' '[K]ick on,' she mused, 'the demon of traffic will ever fright away the loves and graces.' Imlay would tell her to leave 'the square-headed money-getters alone' and be less severe.

Soon she was openly rebuking her own 'money-getter': 'I merely thought of business; and, as this is the idea that most naturally associates with your image, I wonder I stumbled on any other.' Imlay must rise above commercial obsession, she urged, be more imaginative, less materialistic – more like her: 'as common life, in my opinion, is scarcely worth having, even with a *gigot* every day, and a pudding added thereunto, I will allow you to cultivate my judgment, if you will permit me to keep alive the sentiments in your heart, which may be termed romantic, because, the offspring of the senses and the imagination, they resemble the mother more than the father, when they produce the suffusion I admire. – In spite of icy age, I hope still to see it, if you have not determined only to eat and drink, and be stupidly useful to the stupid.' 'Suffusion' was a word associated with sexual fulfilment: she insisted that sex was imaginative for her, for Imlay it seemed mere lust.

When asking about Tallien, the renegade terrorist who helped topple Robespierre, she declared she admired his 'dignity of conduct'; he was a man of rhetorical ability, unusually combined with an 'openness of heart, which is the true basis of both public and private friendship'. She feared, she said, that Imlay would see this remark as an oblique rebuke; presumably she meant one. Their life together in Le Havre must have been larded with criticism for her to continue this niggling by post:

> Do not suppose that I mean to allude to a little reserve of temper in you, of which I have sometimes complained! You have been used to a cunning woman, and you almost look for cunning – Nay, in *managing* my happiness, you now and then wounded my sensibility, concealing yourself, till honest sympathy, giving you to me without disguise, lets me look into a heart, which my half-broken one wishes to creep into, to be revived and cherished. – You have frankness of heart, but not often exactly that overflowing (*épanchement de coeur*), which becoming almost childish, appears a weakness only to the weak.

She was remaking Imlay in the image she wanted and blaming him for not conforming.

As in the last absence she was piqued by Imlay's failure to write often enough. For two days she waited impatiently and then, having learnt nothing from earlier remorse, sent off an irritable complaint. She was precipitate and two letters from Imlay arrived together. Again her lover would receive disgruntled words while she read kindly ones. She apologised but apology reprised the original provocation, and she fell into that condescending preacherly mode that so often alienated those she loved:

> I do not think it false delicacy, or foolish pride, to wish that your attention to my happiness should arise *as much* from love, which is always rather a selfish passion, as reason – that is, I want you to promote my felicity, by seeking your own. – For, whatever pleasure it may give me to discover your generosity of soul, I would not be dependent for your affection on the very quality I most admire. No; there are qualities in your heart, which demand my affection; but, unless the attachment

appears to me clearly mutual, I shall labour only to esteem your character, instead of cherishing a tenderness for your person.

Alone in the Le Havre house, she grew increasingly uneasy. The place reeked of Imlay. Once it had been only his slippers she cherished as sign of intimacy, but now she was surrounded by spurs to memory. It was painful to sit alone in the dining-room. When the maid brought in the meat she picked up the carving-knife to act the husband but was overwhelmed by loneliness. Tears sprang to her eyes and she could not eat. She described the moment to Imlay: such open displays of emotion cannot have hastened his return. She was aware of the vulnerable impression and tried to forestall it: 'Do not ... suppose that I am melancholy – for, when you are from me, I not only wonder how I can find fault with you – but how I can doubt your affection.' However hard she tried she could not stop herself from doing either.

Wanting her own money – and the self-esteem of authorship – she needed to write. Since the new political climate allowed her to address the violent part of the Revolution while still remaining in France, she was planning the next volume of her history; for this reason she asked Imlay about Tallien. She also wanted gossip about the dead Robespierre, famously cold and austere. She heard he had kept mistresses. Was it true? She could not believe such a man was voluptuous; he must have kept them from vanity. Her own sexual fulfilment had much influenced her attitude towards sensuality.

Although she later claimed she had written a 'considerable part' of two or three further volumes, these, like the promised sequel to *The Rights of Woman*, do not exist. If she had written so much, Johnson might have judged it unpublishable. England had changed since she was last there and any support for the French experiment, however muted, appeared unpatriotic. To the British, Burke's rather than Paine's prophesies had been fulfilled. In 1792 radicals had already been falling out of favour, but, in the month in which she finished the first volume of her *French Revolution* and bore Fanny, Pitt's Tory ministry translated them from misguided fools into traitors. The political agitator, Horne Tooke, link between the mid-century reformism of Wilkes and Price and that of the 1790s, was arrested, along with the radical shoemaker Thomas Hardy; to make common cause with them, Holcroft surrendered himself voluntarily to the chief justice. As a publisher involved in the printing and selling of Part II of Paine's *Rights of Man*, Johnson was implicated.[1] Then, amidst much publicity and pamphleteering – the most famous pamphlet was authored by Godwin – Horne Tooke was tried for high treason but acquitted by a jury, after which the prosecution dropped its case against all the defendants. It was all rather foolish but frightening. Had Wollstonecraft been in London, she might have heard that her once favourite pupil, Margaret King, now Countess of Mount Cashell, had revealed her libertarian passion by ordering a pair of shoes from Hardy. They were badly made and, returning them for altering, she remarked, 'Mr Hardy, I am very sorry for it but my feet are democratical and your shoes are aristocratical, and they don't agree at all.' Hardy made a new pair and refused payment, delighted that a countess would receive his gift.[2]

Neither Hardy nor Lady Mount Cashell was typical. Wollstonecraft's first volume of *The French Revolution* was well received as a philosophical work by liberal magazines, but, like the later chronicles of Helen Maria Williams, it was not attuned to the national mood.[3] Her continuing antagonism towards Marie Antoinette jarred: analysing now rather than simply condemning, she still saw the dead queen as a frivolous harlot who had foolishly neglected the 'frippery' which concealed her and France's 'deformity' – this while the nation was sighing over her death, the beautiful hair bleached through suffering. Her remarks were moderate beside those in *The Rights of Men*, but seemed tasteless now. The proper feminine response came from the poet and novelist, Mary Robinson, who exclaimed: 'Shunn'd be the Fiend, who, in these dreadful times, / Would brand Her mem'ry with Infernal Crimes! / Shunn'd be the Monster, who, with recreant art, / Beyond the Grave, would hurl Detraction's dart!'[4]

By now Imlay doubted the wisdom of trusting Ellefsen with his rich cargo. Correctly he suspected foul play: the young captain had no intention of taking his ship to Backman. Instead, on arrival in Norway, he transferred ownership to his family, then moved the ship from one small harbour to another, hiding out at Arendal for a month. What he did with the cargo remains a mystery. Knowing nothing for certain, Imlay grew frantic. Wollstonecraft commiserated on some 'knavery' but was probably ignorant of the potential loss.

In late August Imlay visited Le Havre. He was on his way to London where he might be able to contact people about his missing investment or perhaps, as Wollstonecraft suspected, he had entered other schemes. By now he had tired of domesticity and fancied the life which she had once playfully accused him of wanting: the bachelor existence of men, with occasional sexual adventures. He would see that she was right financially: she could call on him for money through his friends.

Wollstonecraft had accepted sex outside legal marriage but had emphasised fidelity: anything else was 'unchaste'. Imlay did not hold this high-minded view and initially may have seen her willingness to live outside matrimony as a sign that she would accept open or multiple relationships. If he ever thought this, he must by now have been undeceived. He did not quite know what he intended for the future. He could have hoped that Wollstonecraft would make a move to free him or possibly he half intended returning to try monogamy again. He was fond of the child, and indeed of her mother. In his playing with possibilities, he could have had little notion of the few options open to a woman with a baby. Wollstonecraft was especially aware of them at this time for little Fanny caught smallpox and took all her mother's attention.

It was a serious illness, especially for the young. Earlier in the century Lady Mary Wortley Montagu had popularised the eastern idea of giving children weak doses to guard against the strong, but the practice had dangers: about one in a hundred died and it required incisions and long preparation and recovery time. Still, had she been in England, she would probably have had Fanny inoculated since Johnson had recently printed a work advocating the method.[5] But, cut off from her British friends, she had to deal with the devastating disease alone. The child had a severe case and was covered in spots. Again distrusting French doctoring and remembering the damaging treatment of Margaret King for her fever, she decided to nurse the baby herself; it sounds as though she was following Brown's medical advice, adapting the cure to the cause, avoiding bleeding and sweating and 'putting her twice a-day into a warm bath'. Fanny recovered and her mother was convinced it was due to her treatment.

The effort, anxiety and constant care took their toll and, when the child was better, the mother fell ill. It was hard at such a juncture to face a new separation from her lover.

Carrying letters from Mary to Eliza and Everina, Imlay went on the boat from Le Havre in September. He left a sick 'wife' who watched him sail with the deepest misgivings. He would return in two months, he promised. Meanwhile, he urged her back to Paris though they would keep on the Le Havre house.

Wollstonecraft was fearful. She had already revealed her nervousness when Imlay was still in the same country; now he was across the Channel in enemy land. Going to Paris was travelling farther from him, but Le Havre felt so desolate that she was soon eager to leave. Some of her surviving friends had been freed since Robespierre's fall, and might be a comfort, although Williams and Stone were in Switzerland, Joel and Ruth Barlow in Hamburg; Paine was still in prison (he was not to be released until November). So, despite her poor health and the baby's recent sickness, she set off for Paris. Probably she took a maid and a nurse for Fanny, but otherwise travelled alone in a public coach. The English were not in danger as formerly, but the two countries remained at war and foreigners were not entirely welcome. As she anticipated, the trip was fatiguing and the coach overturned four times, but the baby liked its motion.

Paris improved on provincial Le Havre. Her lodgings were not as comfortable and spacious, but she had hated being alone, and, in the greater anonymity and bustle of the city, she recovered some spirits. A fête was on and she joined in. Jacobins still controlled parts of Paris and were reburying the corpse of their revolutionary hero, Marat, in the Panthéon – so volatile was the situation that it would be removed four months later. The baby was bubbly, excited by the scarlet military waistcoats and loud music. Rousseau was honoured as well, since he too was in the Panthéon. She bought the baby a sash in commemoration, admitting, 'I have always been half in love with him'.[6] In the political and emotional turmoil of the last months Rousseau had become less the creator of charming, contingent Sophie, so mocked in *The Rights of Woman*, and more the investigator of selfish inequality, the mocker of greedy commercial enterprise which was ruining society and her own life.

With the fall of Robespierre the press resumed some freedom. It remained unwise for a foreigner to say too much and she continued circumspect in letters, but she could mention recent events without fear of upsetting the secret agents who prowled Paris. She had no pity for persecuted Jacobins now suffering the ultimate penalty, but she did 'fear the last flap of the tail of the beast'. It was a common fear as a weak government assumed power, in time eased the repression, and yet had to face the problems for which the Terror had been instituted: counterrevolution, foreign invaders and domestic discontent in a collapsing economy.

She contacted her old friends, including a German lady who had just lost her first child but who now had one about Fanny's age. She and her husband were poor but affectionate, and the sight of their modest contentment pleased and pained her. She remet the susceptible Count von Schlabrendorf, who retained his revolutionary faith despite imprisonment. He had appreciated her visits and still found her 'enthralling'. She liked his company and admiration. After the crude businessmen of Le Havre, she enjoyed intimate friendships with men, a chance to talk poetry and principles in intellectual, sensitive company.

With a freeing of political tension she received news of her family. Charles had written with more good tidings. She knew he was sanguine but remained

The earliest known portrait of Mary Wollstonecraft, by an unknown artist,
commissioned by William Roscoe, 1791

Dr Richard Price by
Thomas Holloway after
Benjamin West

Robert and Caroline King, Lord and Lady Kingsborough, artist unknown

Joseph Johnson by
William Sharpe after
Moses Haughton

Illustrations by William Blake to Wollstonecraft's *Original Stories,*
second edition, 1791

Henry Fuseli by
John Opie,
exhibited 1794

Self-portrait by John Opie, 1785

A portrait of Mary Wollstonecraft by John
Opie, painted *c.* 1792

Helen Maria Williams by J. Singleton, stipple engraving, published August 1792

Mary Wollstonecraft by an unknown artist, published 1798

Elizabeth Inchbald by George
Dance, 1794

William Godwin (right) and
Thomas Holcroft at the
Treason Trials, by Sir Thomas
Lawrence, 1794

Amelia Alderson, later
Opie, from Religious
Tract Society, 1855

William Godwin by J. W. Chandler, 1798

Mary Wollstonecraft by John Opie, *c.* 1797

heartened by his optimism. James too had returned to sea and was in line for bounty, but, not sharing Charles's temperament, he wrote 'in a querulous strain'. Still nothing came from her sisters and once again she told them her news, taking Everina's knowledge of the child for granted and assuming it would imply marriage. She helped the impression by now signing herself 'Mary Imlay'. As with Ruth Barlow, she expressed affection for the baby in her pride, 'I want you to see my little girl who is more like a boy – She is ready to fly away with spirits – and has eloquent health in her cheeks and eyes – she does not promise to be a beauty, but appears wonderfully intelligent; and, though I am sure she has her father's quick temper and feelings, her good humour runs away with all the credit of my good nursing.' She would have no worry that Fanny might not grow up beautiful – beauty had been little help to Eliza – but her need to equate intelligence, spirits and easy humour with maleness is strange. Perhaps her own temperament was making her wonder quite what was cultural, what biological.[7]

The correspondence had lapsed for too long for her to explain her emotional state had she wanted to. Besides, she had long acted more as mother than sibling and, while she could moan of depression and nerves, she never divulged social slights or neediness. So, ironically, just when she dreaded the meaning of his absence, she had to show Everina her security in Imlay and revert to the kind of visions of sisterly togetherness described at Neuilly – though the sisters must have noted these were now presumed temporary: 'I hope the time is not very distant when we shall all meet ... Should peace take place this winter what say you to a voyage in the Spring, if not to see your old acquaintance to see Paris, which I think you did not do justice to.'

She was of course writing copiously to Imlay, her letters going through his business associates. She disliked being beholden to such men, especially one American on whom she had also to depend for money.

She would, she said, write as often as possible. There was criticism in her thoughtfulness: 'I know I should be disappointed at seeing any one who had left you, if you did not send a letter, were it ever so short, to tell me why you did not write a longer.' Indeed, she criticised at every turn, making less effort than before to soften her words. Imlay was corrupted and mercenary: 'There is nothing picturesque in your present pursuits ... you are embruted by trade and the vulgar enjoyments of life.' Her antidote was nostalgia for the Neuilly idyll and its pastoral images: she carrying her basket of grapes or gazing at the waving corn, he with his happy smiling face uncorrupted by thoughts of 'alum or soap', as she contemptuously termed his trade.

It was only four years since she had rounded on Burke for attacking those who thought of nothing but 'pepper and coffee, callico or tobacco, or some such low concern'.[8] Did she remember her criticism of his snobbery when he exclaimed that such men could have no sense of higher morality and culture? She had read Burke carefully; now in her misery, his arguments and techniques seeped into her writing. Moving with the times, she dignified the elevated form of sensibility Imlay lacked as 'imagination', a less gendered word than 'sensibility'. In the medical discourse that had permeated her writing in the *Vindications*, imagination, once a privileged Lockean quality that made sense impressions complex and vivid, had often been associated with disease and excess. Now she cut it loose from this medical context and placed it firmly with aesthetic and moral taste:

> Believe me, sage sir, you have not sufficient respect for the imagination – I could prove to you in a trice that it is the mother of sentiment, the great distinction of our nature, the only purifier of the passions animals have a portion of reason, and equal, if not more exquisite, senses; but no trace of imagination, or her offspring taste, appears in any of their actions. The impulse of the senses, passions, if you will, and the conclusions of reason, draw men together; but the imagination is the true fire, stolen from heaven, to animate this cold creature of clay, producing all those fine sympathies that lead to rapture, rendering men social by expanding their hearts, instead of leaving them leisure to calculate how many comforts society affords.

Influenced by motherhood and oppressive sexual love, she was sounding more like the author of *Mary, A Fiction* who praised passionate imagination as prophetic of futurity than the reasoned vindicator of the rights of woman. The rational revolution, even if successful, would not have been enough, she now saw; it would have given too little to the personal, feeling side of humanity. In some ways, her attitude retreated from the feminism of a few years before; in others, it was an effort to make that revolutionary feminism into a transformation based on individual inner development in men and women. Yet she still demanded this personal imaginative transformation in the language of rational rights.

If Imlay regarded her paean to emotion and imagination as 'romantic', even 'nonsensical', if he refused to reform, turn back the clock, and accept her value system, she would see him as spoilt. He must resume his 'barrier-face': without it, he should have nothing to say to his 'barrier-girl' or her mother: 'I shall fly from you, to cherish the remembrances that will ever be dear to me,' she promised.

Of course she would not. Perhaps she did not know her emotional need or used such threats to defend herself against the rejection she was afraid to contemplate. The limited independence available to her had never actually been very attractive, except as alternative to family tyranny and sub-ordination. Now, as a mother and dependent lover, it was impossible to achieve – as Imlay must wryly have noted. To try the other tactic of provoking jealousy she could only summon up dead literary men like Mirabeau or Rousseau, whose emotional fineness was meant to rebuke the coarsening Imlay. Of the admiring von Schlabrendorf she said nothing.

She found herself sinking into reveries. Her mind was overactive, she composed letters in her head, endlessly entering conversations in which she convinced and controlled. Her restlessness and busy brain kept her awake at nights; in the mornings she was exhausted.

As in Le Havre she used the child to attach the father. '[A] sweet little creature' with 'little intelligent smiles', the baby was entwining herself round her heart. She loved her quickness and sensitivity: 'she has an astonishing degree of sensibility and observation,' she wrote. 'She is all life and motion, and her eyes are not the eyes of a fool – I will swear.' It pleased her to make maternal tableaux: 'I have been playing and laughing with the little girl so long, that I cannot take up my pen to address you without emotion. Pressing her to my bosom, she looked so like you ... every nerve seemed to vibrate to the touch, and I began to think that there was something in the assertion of man and wife being one – for you seemed to pervade my whole frame, quickening the beat of my heart, and lending me the sympathetic tears you excited ... I know that you will love her more and more.' Again she could not restrain criticism: the baby looked like her father only in his 'best looks', not his 'commercial face'.

In fact, while motherhood had pleasures, it also had pains. She had brought a nurse from Le Havre, but the girl was useless in Paris. Now she was pregnant; so her mistress had to assume more of the child-nursing. She enjoyed breast-feeding, but hated disturbed sleep and was irked at being woken up early in the mornings when Fanny was at her liveliest: 'I still continue to be almost a slave to the child,' she lamented. In truth, life had become so difficult domestically that she sometimes wished she had never left Le Havre.

All the time she wrote and wrote, while her desire to hear from Imlay grew. When she could not send letters, she still wrote, as if needing to address him to believe in his reality: 'Take care of yourself,' she ended one letter, 'if you wish to be the protector of your child, and the comfort of her mother.' She wished it herself so much it hurt.

*

Given the difficulty of corresponding, Wollstonecraft cannot have known whether Imlay's silence came from indifference or the post's carelessness. To inspirit herself she kissed the baby and imagined it Imlay's kiss; she reread the soothing letters written during the earlier absence when she had panicked. She had no access to her own or they might have given her pause.

Imlay was not writing as much as before; yet, when he did, he frequently gave her what she wanted: an explicit date of return. She would then convince herself of his honesty and veer between hope and disappointment as ships arrived and left. Each time he did not come, what could she do but pick herself up and trust once more?

The irregular correspondence disturbed her. Several men heading for England promised to take letters but delayed. Since she wrote continually, she always had a stack ready, some in 'a low-spirited strain, a little querulous or so' but she wanted to send them none the less and was cross when prevented. 'Tant mieux!' she could imagine Imlay saying as she complained of the intermittent service; perhaps he was right, for she too, when so far away, would hate to receive petulant words: 'The letter which you chance to receive, when the absence is so long, ought to bring only tears of tenderness, without any bitter alloy, into your eyes.' She judged from her own feelings, for Imlay did not write querulously, he simply did not write or write enough.

Perhaps at this point he sent a particularly generous bill of exchange or perhaps she received payment from Johnson for her *French Revolution*. She dispatched the 'helpless' nurse to Le Havre and in her place hired a new Parisian girl with more 'vivacity'; she was called Marguerite, and, although this vivacity would sometimes irritate, she served her mistress well. Wollstonecraft also hired another nurse and the burdens were lifted. However attractive motherhood occasionally seemed as she hugged little Fanny, her spirits always rose in proportion as she avoided its drudgery. It was more fun to meet her smiling child in the street than to deal with perpetual demands:

> this said little girl, our darling, is become a most intelligent little creature, and as gay as a lark, and that in the morning too, which I do not find quite so convenient. I once told you, that the sensations before she was born, and when she is sucking, were pleasant; but they do not deserve to be compared to the emotions I feel, when she stops to smile upon me, or laughs outright on meeting me unexpectedly in the street, or after a short absence. She has now the advantage of having two good nurses, and I am at present able to discharge my duty to her, without being the slave of it.

So, no longer the 'slave' to Fanny, she cheered up considerably. She was making progress with her French again and had met some interesting friends, including one of the tribunal judges who she found had 'humanity, if not *beaucoup d'esprit*'. Echoing the threats of disloyalty and independence made to Imlay in her misery, she could play again on the notion of another love, 'let me tell you, if you do not make haste back, I shall be half in love with the author of the *Marseillaise* [Claude Joseph Rouget de l'Isle], who is a handsome man, a little too broad-faced or so, and plays sweetly on the violin.' But now there was no shred of seriousness – as, of course, she self-consciously explained: '*entre nous*, I like to give way to a sprightly vein when writing to you, that is, when I am pleased with you.' Imlay should 'be a good boy, and come back quickly to play with your girls?' She could even pretend to be jealous of the baby: 'I shall not allow you to love the new-comer best.'

The numerous letters to Imlay declare that Wollstonecraft did nothing in Paris but yearn for him. Yet, momentarily at least, she could be absorbed by other men. In company she was often vibrant and engaging, and, keeping her darkest fears to herself, could talk intimately to men and women about her longings, her child and her worries about returning to England.

When she visited Madeleine Schweitzer, she was pleased to find her reading a German translation of Imlay's topographical description of America. Madame Schweitzer was puzzled about Wollstonecraft: seemingly sensitive and feminine, she preached rationalism, and, while declaring herself within a *grand amour*, responded intently to other men. She had 'excessive sensibility', no doubt, but also appeared an ordinary woman obsessed with male attention. To make her point Madame Schweitzer described a country evening they shared with the Baron de Wolzogen. It included a ravishing sunset: 'Come, Mary – come, nature lover, – and enjoy this wonderful spectacle – this constant transition from colour to colour!' Madame Schweitzer cried. But 'to my great surprise, Mary was so indifferent that she never turned her eyes from him by whom she was at the moment captivated. I must confess that this erotic absorption made such a disagreeable impression on me, that all my pleasure vanished.'[9]

Another absorbing acquaintance was Archibald Hamilton Rowan, a rich, cheerful, rather self-regarding Irish patriot lawyer, whom she met at the Marat fête. He had been secretary of the Dublin United Irishmen – an organisation working with the French for Irish separation from England; he had been caught and imprisoned, then escaped to France, where he was first taken for an English spy, then fêted and lodged by the Committee of Public Safety at its own expense. Now Rowan had to remain in Paris feeling increasingly less revolutionary as events unfolded. Like that of Madeleine Schweitzer, the picture he painted for his wife in Ireland, suggests that Wollstonecraft was not always dismal, but that she had lost some of the brashness that so upset Godwin when she silenced Paine two years before. At the same time, his shocked response to a woman who, he admitted, charmed him reveals what she might expect in England, were she to return with a child and no husband:

> Mr B[ingham] . . . joined a lady who spoke English, and who was followed by her maid with an infant in her arms, which I found belonged to the lady. Her manners were interesting, and her conversation spirited, yet not out of the sex. B. whispered to me that she was the author of 'The Rights of Woman'. I started! 'What!' said I within myself, 'this is Miss Mary Wollstonecraft, parading about with a child at her heels, with as little ceremony as if it were a watch she had just bought at the jeweller's. So much for the rights of women,' thought I. But upon further inquiry, I found that she had, very fortunately for her, married an American gentleman a short time before the passing of that decree which indiscriminately incarcerated all the British subjects who were at that moment in this country. My society, which before this time was entirely male, was now most agreeably increased, and I got a dish of tea and an hour's rational conversation, whenever I called on her.

Rowan learnt that his new friend had a 'republican marriage' only, and they argued over it. Perhaps there was some desperation in her defence: she needed to convince herself as well as Rowan of its value. Yet, despite her curious opinions, and her belief (troubling to him as an absent husband), that a man's neglect justified a wife's, she behaved like a conventional spouse: 'she took care of [Imlay's] house and commercial concerns during his absence on different speculations, and was treated as his wife by all who knew her'.[10] Though mocking business she had learnt something through her father's and Imlay's affairs it seems. He also noted that her informal tie 'had with her all the sanctity and devotedness of a matrimonial engagement'. She agreed: when she spent a night at Imlay's old lodgings, she described the emotional effect: 'I slept at St. Germain's, in the very room (if you have not forgot) in which you pressed me very tenderly to your heart. – I did not forget to fold my darling to mine, with sensations that are almost too sacred to be alluded to.'[11] In the absence of the Christian rite, the little ceremony at Saint-Germain suggests how much she had sanctified her sexual relationship with Imlay, how much she wanted it to have for him the binding force of marriage.

# 25

*'Why have you so soon dissolved the charm?'*

However she might flirt with Rowan and others, in her heart Imlay alone had place. Her passion for Fuseli was not so far in the past but she rarely alluded to it except as part of earlier unhappiness. The difference now was sexual love and a child, emotional equivalence to societal marriage in their binding. She had supported freedom in love when arguing against the traditional Rowan; did she stand in Rowan's place when she spoke to her lover? Imlay's actions she sometimes regarded as at odds with his principles, but the principles she never dared investigate.

Early winter 1794 continued politically volatile. There was organised violence in the streets; many released Girondins and returned émigrés shouted for revenge. The Jacobin Club was finally abolished. Wollstonecraft continued to imagine a better future for herself predicated on Imlay's certain return: 'I hope indeed, that you will not be so immersed in business, as during the last three or four months past – for even money, taking into account all the future comforts it is to procure, may be gained at too dear a rate, if painful impressions are left on the mind.' But now, with a happier social life and less burdensome parenting, she was less critical; she remembered happy moments of their life and did not need so insistently to delineate her lover's failings: 'Separated, it would be almost impious to dwell on real or imaginary imperfections of character. – I feel that I love you; and, if I cannot be happy with you, I will seek it no where else.'

Anticipating rebuke, she had feared to open letters during the last absence. Now she delayed to heighten pleasure. In her new relaxed mood she accepted Imlay's business life: he had to make his way in the world and she would not 'childishly' demand his return before he was done; she only hoped he could arrange things so that they need not part again.

Towards the end of the year, Imlay informed her more convincingly that he would leave England imminently. Her spirits soared. According to Godwin, he really did set out. He got as far as Ramsgate when 'he was recalled, as it should seem, to London, by the further pressure of business now accumulated upon him.'[1]

Possibly this was true, for Imlay knew for certain now that Ellefsen had stolen his silver ship and perhaps his recall had to do with the affair. On his behalf a Stromstad merchant, Christoffer Nordberg, and the district judge, A. J. Ungar, had begun making enquiries; when they failed to find the ship they had lodged a complaint before the Arendal court. Ellefsen declared he knew nothing of ship or silver and intended to plead innocent.[2] Backman, Imlay's partner, in Gothenburg, took the matter up at a higher level, and, at the time Imlay set out for Paris, the Swedish minister in Copenhagen brought it before the Danish government; a royal commission was set up to investigate and might well have wanted something urgently from Imlay.

For Wollstonecraft, on tenterhooks in Paris, none of this had the least importance. She simply saw that Imlay had not arrived, because either his boat had miscarried or he had reneged on his promise: 'I have been … for some days tormented by fears, that I would not allow to assume a form – I had been expecting you daily – and I heard that many vessels had been driven on shore during the late gale.' Then she learnt he had never left England. She tried to be glad he was safe.

She had become used to the cold spells in France but this one was exceptional. Burke's fear of the reign of merchants and hagglers was fulfilled and, as commerce was liberalised and controls in imports removed, prices soared. The new government continued the Jacobin rationing of bread and meat but cut the amount of bread while allowing meat to become almost unobtainable. Prices of other commodities spiralled beyond all except the rich. There was a severe shortage of firewood. Everything required lengthy queuing and bargaining. So in discontent and discomfort the second lonely Christmas season passed, and the summer months of happiness between seemed little more than a dream.

At first, influenced by a sympathetic letter from Imlay, Wollstonecraft stayed calm. She hated separation but continued to understand how business crowded in. She must try not to welcome poverty and see togetherness as all-important, for this sort of thinking dejected her: 'I do, my love, indeed sincerely sympathize with you in all your disappointments.' She rallied him as her 'dearest friend, husband, father of my child!' all ties that glowed in her heart and brought tears to her eyes; desperately she hoped they did the same for her lover.

But she knew she was skirting melancholy for she awoke remembering sad dreams: 'feeling that I am happier than I ever was, do you wonder at my sometimes dreading that fate has not done persecuting me?' The child remained a comfort but sadly was growing up fatherless. Imlay was not watching her mind unfold, seeing her first tooth or helping her crawl. Often

Wollstonecraft imagined them both together taking pride in the baby – as well as sharing the burden. She had written that the bonding of parent and baby was neither natural nor inevitable but forged through habit.[3] How could Imlay care for someone he hardly knew? She tried to convey her maternal feelings by comparing them to the sexual ones he understood:

> You talk of 'dalliance', but certainly no lover was ever more attached to his mistresses, than she is to me. Her eyes follow me every where, and by affection I have the most despotic power over her. She is all vivacity or softness – yes; I love her more than I thought I should. When I have been hurt at your stay, I have embraced her as my only comfort – when pleased with you, for looking and laughing like you; nay, I cannot, I find, long be angry with you, whilst I am kissing her for resembling you ... Fold us both to your heart.

Despite her understanding of Imlay's sexual needs, her rival for his attention remained business. It was too painful to suspect a human one or think he might not want to return to her strenuous monogamy. His commercial friends did not care for her values, seeing unprecedented opportunities in a war with embargoes. Those with few principles and sufficient contacts and cunning could reap large rewards. Wollstonecraft had no sympathy with the view and extended her ill humour at her lover to his friends. In London Imlay was engrossed by new schemes, speculating again in land for would-be emigrants. It irritated him that Wollstonecraft shared none of his enthusiasm. So in his letters he could convey only disappointments to explain his absence; his plans and projects were discussed with male friends and perhaps with more understanding women.

As days passed she sensed she was fighting for Imlay's soul with the hostile American friend in Paris. Anxiously she saw their letters travelling together. Imlay must be influenced only by her, she insisted. This man might be consumed by the 'idle desire' of commerce but 'we who are governed by other motives, ought not to be led on by him. When we meet, we will discuss this subject. – You will listen to reason, and it has probably occurred to you, that it will be better, in future, to pursue some sober plan, which may demand more time, and still enable you to arrive at the same end. It appears to me absurd to waste life in preparing to live.' There was nothing glamorous in dreams of wealth: they were other people's dreams. Why, she asked repeatedly, did he have to hurt her and himself? Latterly he was talking of other projects, other journeys. She could not have it. He *must* come the moment he had settled the present business. Otherwise – and she knew she was making an empty threat – 'the little woman and I will be off, the Lord knows where'. Quickly she defanged it, 'I will not importune you. – I will only tell you, that I long to see you, and, being at peace with you, I shall be hurt, rather than made angry, by delays.'

As the year declined, she wrote daily long, repetitive letters, scolding Imlay for indifference and attacking commerce. Complaints grew sterner, 'How I hate this crooked business! This intercourse with the world, which obliges one to see the worst side of human nature! Why cannot you be content with the object you had first in view, when you entered into this wearisome labyrinth?' As did irritation: 'I know very well that you have imperceptibly been drawn on; yet why does one project, successful or abortive, only give place to two others? Is it not sufficient to avoid poverty?' How could he let her rival succeed with his poisonous letters? '[W]hy do I talk to you? – If he can persuade you – let him! – for, if you are not happier with me, and your own wishes do not make you throw aside these eternal projects, I am above using any arguments, though reason as well as affection seems to offer them.' Threats took on more flesh: 'let me tell you, I have my project also – and, if you do not soon return, the little girl and I will take care of ourselves; we will not accept any of your cold kindness – your distant civilities – no; not we.' This time her threat was but 'half jesting': 'if you chuse to run about the world to get a fortune, it is for yourself – for the little girl and I will live without your assistance, unless you are with us.'

Up to now she had blamed Imlay for delaying, but, as she wrote, new suspicions struck her. He could not be deserting her exactly, but might he have no intention of returning to France? '*If you do* – stay, for God's sake; but tell me the truth – if not, tell me when I may expect to see you, and let me not be always vainly looking for you, till I grow sick at heart.' In *The Rights of Woman* sensual fascination peeped through rationalist principles; now in her letters, though business was her surface worry, she revealed a covert fear: 'The common run of men have such an ignoble way of thinking, that, if they debauch their hearts, and prostitute their persons, following perhaps a gust of inebriation, they suppose the wife, slave rather, whom they maintain, has no right to complain, and ought to receive the sultan, whenever he deigns to return, with open arms, though his have been polluted by half an hundred promiscuous amours during his absence.' She had not suggested before that Imlay was involved with other women, so it was a strange out-burst. She gave it point by adding, 'if a wandering of the heart, or even a caprice of the imagination detains you – there is an end of all my hopes of happiness – I could not forgive it, if I would.'

Her half-formed suspicion was fed by Imlay's friend. As she continued her morose visits to send letters and receive money, he became less tactful, indicating that Imlay chose to stay away. She remembered the hints of his need for 'dalliance', his enjoyment of variety, his restless looking for diversions. She must not dwell on the idea. It was better to generalise male cruelty:

> You know my opinion of men in general; you know that I think them systematic tyrants, and that it is the rarest thing in the world, to meet with a man with sufficient delicacy of feeling to govern desire. When I am thus sad, I lament that my little darling, fondly as I doat on her, is a girl. – I am sorry to have a tie to a world that for me is ever sown with thorns.

She failed in her resolve not to send 'ill-humoured' letters, but they resulted from her fears, 'the strongest proof of affection'. She tried hard to sustain her spirits, not write the dread and bile she felt or, if she wrote, not send the letter, but his friend's innuendoes touched her to the quick. If the restless search for wealth was more important than their life together, Imlay should go now: 'Say but one word, and you shall never hear of me more'. They could 'struggle with poverty – with any evil, but these continual inquietudes of business.'

In the early days of 1795 Wollstonecraft caught a cold. She had expected that Imlay would arrive this week or next, so had not prepared for a long winter alone. Paris shortages were difficult to cope with at any time, but with a baby they felt worse. Wood was dear; black-market traders charged the shivering inhabitants dearly; so she had insufficient to keep a fire going. She and Fanny huddled in the cold damp house and thus she fell ill. She did not look after herself and the cold settled on her chest; soon she was wracked by coughing.

Her debility harmed the baby and she determined, once the weather improved, to wean her. She had been breast-feeding for eight months or so, the usual period being eighteen to twenty-four months, but, noticing how pale and drawn she looked, friends advised weaning now.[4] She believed misery not breast-feeding was the problem. Although she had intended to wean the baby early, she did not relish it now for the intimacy was precious. Also such weaning contradicted her fantasy of a father's case: when she had imagined it, she had seen a father gently murmuring, 'Come to me, and I will teach you, my little dear, for you must not hurt poor mamma.'

Depression usually threatened in winter months and added to her discomfort. She still believed that mind and body were interconnected but she found it increasingly difficult to control the mind with external stimuli. Imlay increased her gloom by doubting he would return to Paris even in February. She was no better than Eliza at hoping; without certainty both sisters collapsed into self-pity. Now she responded by assessing a life that seemed a series of miseries, interrupted by one mistaken vision of joy:

Fatigued during my youth by the most arduous struggles, not only to obtain independence, but to render myself useful, not merely pleasure, for which I had the most lively taste, I mean the simple pleasures that flow from passion and affection, escaped me, but the most melancholy views of life were impressed by a disappointed heart on my mind. Since I knew you, I have been endeavouring to go back to my former nature, and have allowed some time to glide away, winged with the delight which only spontaneous enjoyment can give. – Why have you so soon dissolved the charm?

She respected letter-writing, the expense of paper and the power of words to make absence presence. She had berated her sisters for failing to fill their pages where she habitually wrote to the bottom. Now, where she had once hoarded his letters, she was dismayed at Imlay's untidy scrawls, his 'dozen hasty lines'. Such carelessness argued her a 'secondary object'. She never believed his claim that his longer letters had gone astray.

She was giving a weak impression she knew, perhaps remembering that it was to the independent assertive woman that Imlay had been attracted. She had boasted of her firmness to Johnson, assuring him that she did everything she set out to do. Yet, as she threatened an emotionally improbable independence, Imlay read her continued dream of the rural American life he had unwisely promised: 'I should have been content, and still wish, to retire with you to a farm.' This had been based on the Louisiana schemes; these had collapsed. He knew she knew the money it took to stock a farm – her own father had been a casualty of the dream; she also probably knew by now that he had debts in America.

Mid-January was an emotional oasis. At her gloomiest, Wollstonecraft received two proper letters from Imlay written just after Christmas; 'anger died away'. She replied briskly with a pretty picture of the unweaned Fanny:

My animal is well; I have not yet taught her to eat, but nature is doing the business. I gave her a crust to assist the cutting of her teeth; and now she has two, she makes good use of them to gnaw a crust, biscuit, &c. You would laugh to see her; she is just like a little squirrel; she will guard a crust for two hours; and, after fixing her eye on an object for some time, dart on it with an aim as sure as a bird of prey – nothing can equal her life and spirits. I suffer from a cold; but it does not affect her. Adieu! do not forget to love us – and come soon to tell us that you do.

It could not last. No further inspiriting letters arrived; instead Imlay replied coldly to the dismal ones he was receiving by every post. Exasperated, he told her some home truths about himself and her.

*He* demanded more than the bare subsistence to live on, did not welcome poverty, and liked pleasure, good cheer and jovial company. *She* was histrionic and refused to make the best of things. If she pulled herself together she could live contentedly while they were apart. They would come together one day, but she must not hold unrealistic expectations of their union. Meanwhile she was too concerned with 'the secondary pleasures of life' and was grumbling too much about Paris. Life was difficult for everyone; it could not be quite as uncomfortable as she made out for she was only facing the 'common evils of life'. She must have wondered grimly how much Imlay knew of bringing up a baby in post-revolutionary Paris.

Had he read *The Rights of Woman*? If so, he was feeding back her own thoughts, that people should find their strength and comfort within themselves. He wished she could be happier with less, that she could rest on what they had, rather than constantly striving to make him conform to an ideal.

After her surge of optimism, the disappointment was cruel. She had hoped for too long to muster resilience and by the end of January was sinking again. Imlay's friend sneered at her; she retaliated by blaming him for wrecking her life. Hostilities increased: she denouncing the vulgarising effect of commerce, he exulting 'very unmanlily . . . over me, on account of your determination to stay.' It was no matter: she had 'drunk too deep of the bitter cup to care about trifles.' But she did care, and sometimes she stopped at his doorstep too fearful to proceed: 'In the bitterness of my heart, I could complain with reason, that I am left here dependent on a man, whose avidity to acquire a fortune has rendered him callous to every sentiment connected with social or affectionate emotions. – With a brutal insensibility, he cannot help displaying the pleasure your determination to stay gives him, in spite of the effect it is visible it has had on me.' Rather than face him, she would borrow money elsewhere.

Then she added a fresh cold to her persistent cough and her visits had to stop – but not her writing. She wrote furiously, sarcastically noting that Imlay's *financial* interests in Paris were suffering by his absence. As for his rebukes, she saw no reason to endure what could be helped: 'If . . . you accuse me of wanting the resolution necessary to bear the *common* evils of life; I should answer, that I have not fashioned my mind to sustain them, because I would avoid them, cost what it would.'

Ten days later, she was confirmed in misery. For all her reproachings, she had not understood that Imlay could actually desert her and their child, imagining it simply to shock him back to her arms. But the new realistic tone hinted that their life together might be over, that she had 'leaned on a spear'. She took no comfort from the stern words in *The Rights of Woman* about the stupidity of women who put their trust in romantic hopes or in her mockery of Hester Piozzi for arguing that all women's attainments and arts 'are employed to gain and keep the heart of man; and what mortification can exceed the disappointment, if the end be not obtained?'[5] She now knew the power of romantic love if not its rules, and no longer much cared whether its hold on women was cultural or natural.

So she began the slide into the deep depression suffered earlier in Ireland, but now it was not divinely ordained. Instead, as in the first London months, she began by declaring it primarily physical, partly to fit it to her new philosophy, partly to have hope of an ending in death. Sometimes she thought to anticipate this, but, looking at the child, knew she should not. She stirred herself to plan for the future. She could face poverty, she had been there before, and nothing could be worse than the recent heartbreak. She never cared for money; she cared less now she saw what it was doing to the man she most admired. 'I can still exert myself to obtain the necessaries of life for my child, and she does not want more at present. – I have two or three plans in my head to earn our subsistence; for do not suppose that, neglected by you, I will lie under obligations of a pecuniary kind to you! – No; I would sooner submit to menial service. – I wanted the support of your affection – that gone, all is over!'

Such proud determinations were not sustaining. Soon she abandoned all appearance of self-control: 'So many feelings are struggling for utterance, and agitating a heart almost bursting with anguish, that I find it very difficult to write with any degree of coherence.' Why not nag? She had been ailing when he had left her before Christmas, yet he had not cared. Now she was weaker than ever through a neglected cold and misery. How could Imlay treat her so? How could she have fallen so low?

> my head turns giddy, when I think that all the confidence I have had in the affection of others is come to this. – I did not expect this blow from you. I have done my duty to you and my child; and if I am not to have any return of affection to reward me, I have the sad consolation of knowing that I deserved a better fate. My soul is weary – I am sick at heart; and, but for this little darling, I would cease to care about a life, which is now stripped of every charm.
>
> ... Do not insult me by saying that 'our being together is paramount to every other consideration!' Were it, you would not be running after a bubble, at the expence of my peace of mind.
>
> Perhaps this is the last letter you will ever receive from me.

Over the next grim months, Wollstonecraft would often declare she was writing for the last time.

To her own friends she kept up a façade. She was not writing to her sisters and, when brother James unexpectedly called, she appeared contented. She had moaned to Helen Maria Williams and Madeleine Schweitzer about Fuseli, but this betrayal was another thing. The affair had been so public and Fanny was proof of its seriousness and sexuality. There was really no one to cry to except Imlay; despite the ending of her last letter, she wrote again next day. 'You will think me mad,' she told him, 'I would I were so, that I could forget my misery – so that my head or heart would be still.'

She wished to die and, as when depressed before, convinced herself death was near: 'The inquietudes of the last winter have finished the business, and my heart is not only broken, but my constitution destroyed. I conceive myself in a galloping consumption, and the continual anxiety I feel at the thought of leaving my child, feeds the fever that nightly devours me.' She had consulted the usually despised French doctors, who diagnosed a lung infection, especially dangerous for breast-feeding mothers. 'They lay a stress ... on the necessity of keeping the mind tranquil – and, my God! how has mine been harrassed! But whilst the caprices of other women are gratified, "the wind of heaven not suffered to visit them too rudely," I have not found a guardian angel, in heaven or on earth, to ward off sorrow or care from my bosom.'

Anticipating death, she made arrangements for Fanny – it gave her a pretext for writing to Imlay. Having recently received 3000 livres, she would visit the hated American businessman only once more, obtain a final lump sum to pay her servant's wages, presumably Marguerite's since the extra nurse had gone; then earn her own living until she died. Imlay would have no leisure to write to her sisters, so she would do that when calmer. Last year she had told him she envied a poor but contented German lady with a child Fanny's age. She would abandon her own lodgings and move in with her: it would be cheap and prepare Fanny for her mother's death when she would live with the German lady. Then, as if sending a suicide note, she cursed and blessed Imlay, while affirming her own worth and esteem:

When you first entered into these plans, you bounded your views to the gaining of a thousand pounds. It was sufficient to have procured a farm in America, which would have been an independence. You find now that you did not know yourself, and that a certain situation in life is more necessary to you than you imagined – more necessary than an uncorrupted heart – For a year or two, you may procure yourself what you call pleasure; eating, drinking, and women; but, in the solitude of declining life, I shall be remembered with regret – I was going to say with remorse, but checked my pen.

As I have never concealed the nature of my connection with you, your reputation will not suffer. I shall never have a confident: I am content with the approbation of my own mind; and, if there be a searcher of hearts, mine will not be despised. Reading what you have written relative to the desertion of women, I have often wondered how theory and practice could be so different, till I recollected that the sentiments of passion, and the resolves of reason, are very distinct ... God bless you! Adieu!

For Wollstonecraft the horrors of the French Revolution now paralleled personal horrors and made them more heroic; public and private coalesced in individual suffering: 'This has been such a period of barbarity and misery, I ought not to complain of having my share. I wish one moment that I had never heard of the cruelties that have been practised here, and the next envy the mothers who have been killed with their children.' After being in such a crucible of misery, she must have wondered how she had ever been able to write of politics and human misery in that abstract Enlightenment way of *The Rights of Woman* and *The French Revolution*. The books were not wrong but they did not go far enough.

As for Imlay he must have received the solemn farewells with a touch of irony. No one, he supposed, died of a broken heart, certainly not so assertive a woman as Mary Wollstonecraft.

She had reached the nadir. Even as she melodramatically prepared for death and wrote of her decease to Imlay, she felt depression lifting. Ten days after her death-obsessed letter, she was no longer planning to die. Her cough continued but it was not now a galloping consumption; she had not given up her lodgings or Marguerite, and had not written to her sisters of her impending death. She would begin a new life in Paris with Fanny by finding work; she had failed so far only through low spirits. She sensed her shift, but found each mood justifiable in its own terms; she was rarely disposed to apologise for her temperament.

Then she changed again. However suitable for rearing a child and however unjudgmental Paris seemed, by spring she could stand it no longer. The depression of these weeks belies the extraordinary fact that, responding to the reams of miserable prose, Imlay had actually invited Wollstonecraft to come to London and she was reluctant. He was asking only out of duty, she snapped; since he had not completely abandoned Paris, there was no point in her going abroad. Yet it seems an inadequate reason to play the martyr alone. Partly she hesitated because, with her irregular marriage, she feared life in censorious England. Londoners had starched notions, '[A]m I only to return to a country, that has not merely lost all charms for me, but for which

I feel a repugnance that almost amounts to horror, only to be left there a prey to it!'

Now, given the gap in letters, Imlay may have responded to her reluctance by visiting Paris and persuading her to join him. He realised he could not support her for ever and knew she had a better chance of earning money in London – and perhaps of attaining some calmness among old friends. Perhaps he was charmed again. Although she had once claimed she trusted in his love more in absence than presence, he was always harsher when they were apart. When he saw her, he softened. Now he wrote more lovingly than for some time, 'Business alone has kept me from you. – Come to any port, and I will fly down to my two dear girls with a heart all their own.' It was irresistible.

Yet horribly unwise. She had earlier felt the futility of joining Imlay after so long an absence; with the passing of time her going was less appropriate. Imlay had been in London for months alone, publicly living a bachelor life. Given his often expressed desires, he must at least have had other women, even if she did not truly expect a single rival. But, with the kind words ringing in her ears, she could not act rationally any more than she could abide by her repeated intentions of silence. She would overcome reason and her 'repugnance' for England. Later she told Godwin that she had reacted to Imlay's expressed wishes. He had, she said, sent a servant to Paris to accompany her on her journey. Perhaps her memory was faulty.

She would go to Le Havre by public coach, look in on their old house, still leased from Wheatcroft, then take the longer Channel crossing. Since she was not necessarily returning to France in the near future, she would take her possessions. She had not accumulated many clothes but she had books which needed watertight boxes, and Fanny and Marguerite had their own baggage. In Le Havre she would add the household linen. The journey would not be easy. Boats were irregular and could not be planned in advance and it was early spring, when crossings were often rough. Fanny was under a year old, and Wollstonecraft was delivering another young child to England; she disliked the commission, which delayed her, but she undertook it for Imlay's sake. She grumbled a bit, but knew he would have no sympathy.

For the past months the Le Havre house had drained their finances, but it was useful now; she moved in gratefully. She had had some of her happiest times there and memories provoked tears. She and Imlay would have no further need of the place and she must look out for a tenant until the end of the lease. She tidied it up in preparation.

In the mean time, it could serve her friend Rowan, *en route* from Paris to

America.[6] She put a little store of provisions in a closet to cheer his arrival. Their old scullery-maid who tended the house had been well paid and would look after him, and Wheatcroft would hold any luggage sent on ahead. After Rowan the house had been promised to his friend, possibly Thomas Russell, a member of the Ulster United Irishmen. He was coming with his family and she regretted there was not a lot for them to use since her kitchen furniture had been sold and she was about to remove her linen. Still, it was better than staying at an inn. When she had been in Le Havre for a little time, she heard of a possible tenant, however; so she was no longer sure this arrangement could be honoured. She would leave the matter with Wheatcroft, who could tell Rowan what to say to his friend.

She completed her weaning of Fanny. Remembering how their sex life had dwindled after the birth, she believed this would free her to concentrate on her lover; the child would be querulous and she did not want anything to disturb their meeting. She had come to realise that women's sentimental fiction overplayed the attractions of motherhood to men – or rather she sometimes feared that Imlay was not the heroic husband imagined in *The Rights of Woman* but rather that other man whose heart had been 'rendered unnatural by early debauchery' and who was thus unmoved 'at seeing his child suckled by its mother'. But, however necessary, weaning was painful for it separated her from the baby who had kept her living these terrible months. For three or four nights she tried putting Fanny in another room, but felt so sad she fetched her back. It was one of the many burdens she had to carry, she told Imlay.

When not bustling around about the house or coping with Fanny, she wrote. The days in Le Havre were busy; yet the picture she drew was of static and lone misery, the mood that came over her whenever she began a letter: 'I sit, lost in thought, looking at the sea – and tears rush into my eyes when I find that I am cherishing any fond expectations. – I have indeed been so unhappy this winter, I find it as difficult to acquire fresh hopes, as to regain tranquillity. – Enough of this – lie still, foolish heart! – But for the little girl, I could almost wish that it should cease to beat, to be no more alive to the anguish of disappointment.' Imlay hoped she would travel in a more sanguine mood, but could have had no illusions about what faced him when he read 'I shall not attempt to give vent to the different emotions which agitate my heart – You may term a feeling, which appears to me to be a degree of delicacy that naturally arises from sensibility, pride – Still I cannot indulge the very affectionate tenderness which glows in my bosom, without trembling, till I see, by your eyes, that it is mutual.'

On 9 April, she found a boat and hastily wrote a couple of notes to Rowan telling him of arrangements. She was sorry she had not seen more of him. Rowan knew the marriage was not legal and this, as well perhaps as her fears, made her refer to Imlay as her 'friend'. The dream of America was still alive for she imagined visiting Rowan there one day. Now she wished him to give her love to brother Charles.[7]

After waiting so many days she was told she had an hour to get her party on the boat. She hurried herself 'out of breath', but, once on board, they were at the mercy of an unskilled pilot who ran them all aground within a few hours. She and her little entourage disembarked, no doubt getting very wet in the process.

They arrived back to empty rooms, made more desolate by the final packing. She wished she had a friend to visit but there was nothing to do but count the seconds, or listen to the ticking of an absent clock. In due course the boat was righted and they set out again.

Calling herself Mary Imlay and using the same phrase, 'on the wing', as when she had left England nearly two years before – repeated when she had left Le Havre and her happiest period of domestic life – she stepped off the boat in Brighton. Marguerite had a tendency to seasickness, so Wollstonecraft would have cared for Fanny and the other child. Still, she arrived in a cheerier mood than she had been in for some time. She preferred even uncomfortable travelling to passive waiting.

Imlay was not there to meet her, but she had told him not to come and she was not immediately downcast. She dashed off a note: 'Here we are, my love, and mean to set out early in the morning; and, if I can find you, I hope to dine with you to-morrow. – I shall drive to —'s hotel, where — tells me you have been – and, if you have left it, I hope you will care to be there to receive us.' It must have been some comfort to Imlay that the woman approaching him was not his legal wife in England, but he was still nervous about the encounter and put it off as long as he could.

Since her own furniture was in store, he had taken a furnished house for her and Fanny at 26 Charlotte Street, Rathbone Place, in Soho. It was in a newly built development named after Queen Charlotte and it included artists and architects. Imlay had done what he could to make her comfortable and respectable. But all Wollstonecraft wanted was his love and her heart sank when she met him and found him cold. Her own 'very affectionate tenderness' was not 'mutual'. He was embarrassed and she did not know why. Yet he was intending to live with her.

Together they tried to settle in the house, and over the next few weeks talked and talked over their predicament. Imlay explained his need for variety and a zestful life, while she argued the value of what they had made together. In *The Rights of Woman* she had imagined a relationship where passion subsided and parenting took its place: 'In the exercise of their maternal feelings providence has furnished women with a natural substitute for love, when the lover becomes only a friend, and mutual confidence takes place of overstrained admiration – a child then gently twists the relaxing cord, and a mutual care produces a new mutual sympathy.'[8] In reality parents did not feel 'a mutual care', for fatherhood differed from motherhood and did not define masculinity as she had once hoped, while the loss of love and admiration was, now she experienced it, harder to bear than she had supposed. Seeing Imlay every day, she was dissatisfied with remote friendship and tried to renew the sexual intimacy which had meant so much to her. He drew back and she was stung. He decided to move out until they could resolve their relationship.

Wollstonecraft still did not admit that she could be rivalled by more than business and Imlay's own mental frivolity. She accused him of wanting many and various women as he wanted a variety of food, drink and pleasures, and she knew what she thought of this, 'how grossly is nature insulted by the voluptuary'.[9] In the *Memoirs*, Godwin reported that Imlay was having an affair with 'a young actress from a strolling company of players', but Wollstonecraft did not know this. She only sensed that he did not want her either emotionally or physically. She was deeply hurt.

She had nowhere to turn for support. In Paris she could retain a belief in Imlay and the possibility of reunion. Now, when he left their house for no reason except distaste for her, the loss was overwhelming. She was largely avoiding her old London friends. Johnson perhaps she confided in a little, but, ailing and phlegmatic, he had little experience of her predicament, disapproved of indulging in melancholy, and had only recently ceased comforting her over Fuseli.[10] The Christies had returned to England, much preoccupied with money problems; also they seemed more Imlay's friends than hers. At this sorry moment, she visited Fuseli for solace but he refused it. Some months later, she wrote bitterly, 'I have long ceased to expect kindness or affection from any human creature, and would fain tear from my heart its treacherous sympathies.'

At the end of May, near little Fanny's first birthday, she could cope no longer and decided to end her life. Despite the utopian rationalism of *The Rights of Woman*, she accepted, as before, that exclusive, mutual love was a want of her heart and that she could not concentrate her emotions and intellect on any goal without it. She had often envisaged death releasing her from pain and recently had mused on suicide as resolution, staying her hand only with thoughts of the unprotected child. Now nothing could stop her. So she took or meant to take an overdose of common poison, perhaps laudanum, the usual method for women. Before she swallowed, she remade her plans for Fanny and wrote a public letter of explanation. She laid no blame on Imlay for the catastrophe, she averred, but how could she explain without giving some? Godwin received only a vague report, unsure whether she was caught by Imlay before or after the attempt: 'It was perhaps owing to his activity and representations, that her life was, at this time, saved. She determined to continue to exist.'

*'You will, perhaps accuse me of insensibility'*

One of the griefs of Wollstonecraft's life is that, when she most needed them, she alienated the sisters for whom she had taken such strenuous if sometimes insensitive care. The resemblance in temperament, especially between Mary and Eliza, both self-pitying, self-regarding, clever and petulant, both apt to see their sufferings as unique, and both extreme when provoked, made communication treacherous. When most hurt, they hurt each other.

Mary imagined no subjectivity outside her own. While experiencing to the full her particular neediness, she feared others' neediness. For the first fortnight in London she wrote nothing to her sisters. She had been ill, but knew this was no excuse. Finally she addressed Everina – in a letter sent through Skeys, so out of touch had she become.

She had dispatched £10 to her father. She offered a similar 'trifle' to Eliza, though £10 had never been a trifle to any of them. Her urge to hide her pain translated into fantastic promises: when she could rely on Imlay for nothing and felt shamed at taking his money, she spoke of vast sums to her impoverished sisters: 'I know [Imlay] will give me for you and Eliza five or six hundred pounds, or more if he can – In what way could this be of the most use to you?' What reaction can she have expected?

More than the exaggerated sums of money, the letter to Everina shocked by its expression of exclusive coupledom, as much outside her grasp as £600. It was as if, understanding her own emotional dependence, Mary at last appreciated Eliza's and was aghast: 'I do not wish to have a third person in the house with me – my domestic happiness would perhaps be interrupted without my being of much use to Eliza,' she told Everina. 'This is not a hastily formed opinion, nor is it in consequence of my present attachment, yet I am obliged now to express it, because it appears to me that you have formed some such expectation for Eliza – you may wound me by remarking on my determination still I know on what principle I act and therefore you can only judge for yourself.'

For the last year and a half, during which Eliza had hardly heard from her eldest sister, she had lived her French dream, sending money she could ill afford in the hope that Mary would establish her there. The fact in part explains the catastrophic effect when she received her own version of this seemingly complacent and patronising letter.

It succeeded a long correspondence with Everina, alternating bitterness at and confidence in the sister who had rescued her from marriage, repeatedly let her down but also inspired her with glamorous schemes. The letters reveal how dependent all the family were on each other, how much of a burden the moody James, the charming Charles and their feckless father were to Everina and Eliza, not just Mary, how much the sisters lived projected lives, how much all of them fantasised 'rescue'. Like Mary's depression, Eliza's pain was conveyed in the language of nerves and nervous sensibility, as well as in an irritating habit of self-reference as if that way her morbid introspection and fragmentation were justified.[1]

Now in her early thirties Eliza felt herself marooned in Wales. Delighting in its scenery, she loathed its ignorant inhabitants. She had not grown more religious and her political views remained liberal; so she continued to hate the pervasive propaganda. With all that had happened in France, she still wailed: 'how much more kind it would have been, to have taken poor Bess! to the Continent with her.' Her obsession even made her fear a kindly offer through Everina's employers of a well-paying post in Sligo in western Ireland. She was kept awake 'one whole night' fearing it 'a *final* bar to a jaunt that is for ever lurking near my heart – (and of course will never be put onto execution) . . .'[2]

Charles had been in America for a year and James's whereabouts were unknown; some time before he had walked from Dover to London, which argued him broke again. Their father was 'perfectly restored to health, though his leg is still tender, never was man so near the brink of the grave', wrote Eliza after a visit to Laugharne; the illness had used money that should have gone to pay debts. Meanwhile, Mary had disappeared into revolutionary France: 'I am half afraid poor Mary is not perfectly secure, for you have undoubt[e]dly read in the papers of her having been arrested; I hope in God she is safe, yet the contrary idea haunts and makes me forget her few faults. She is certainly in greater danger than a more insignificant character.'

Anxiety bred affection: 'I would to God Mary had quitted that unhappy country . . . [she] haunts me continually; and her virtues appear more daz- zling than ever, while the failings of human nature are no longer remembered, for my heart reproached me for having been *too severe* on a heart capable of all that commands respect and Love.' Yet, while realising the blindness of her '*Confidence* in the french', she did not really believe the newspapers and, though she wished from her 'very soul that M was returned to England', she admitted she would '*gladly at this moment* be in Paris'.

*

By new year 1794 Eliza was 'croaking' again – as she called her moaning. James seemed to be doing well out of the French war and to have prize money; he was rumoured to have been made a captain.[3] The news could not offset other worries. When she did not hear from Everina she concluded her sick again, while Mary's silence continued to disturb. Her own temper, she thought, had been ruined not by great misfortune but by petty cares: 'reason tells me that nothing can occur for Eliza, I feel it now more forcibly than ever[.] I have been at Upton near three years yet are not the goodly prospects more distant than ever? ... I long to know something more of Mary, she must be still in poor France, or we should hear from her. I flatter myself that she is safe, but not that it will be practicable to quit it in a hurry so we must have patience.' The Upton girls remained unmanageable but she now had an unexpected solace in little John, sent to Upton Castle from India, a responsive ear and heart for her teaching.[4] Over the weeks the 'sweet babe' became 'still more dear': 'I never had so much power over any child, or loved a child with such affection.' He was a lively sensitive boy and his 'look ... of tenderness' reminded her of Fuseli.

By the end of the month she reported that her vulgar girls were being courted by boorish men and her dear little John had croup because the miserly family deprived him of proper shoes. Every day was a 'dreary blank' and she had received no word from 'our unfortunate Emigrant', despite a rumour that she had gone to Switzerland. Eliza doubted this but, since Johnson was cheerful, she concluded Mary safe. Holding fast to her liberal, pro-French views, like Mary with Roscoe, she was concerned that Everina remain true too: her sister must not 'go with the *stream*'.[5]

By the time she replied, Everina had had to leave the pleasant Irwins and was now with the family of David Mounsell in Dublin, not a change for the better. Still, she wrote reassuringly: she imagined Mary back with them, 'the celebrated authoress' but no longer distinguished by pride. Eliza appreciated the vision and 'fondly imagine[d], it would restore me a friend – I have long thought dead – At any rate, the horrid scenes M. has been an *Eye* witness of, will awaken her tenderness for those she once loved. I would to God she was safe landed in England.'

Like Mary in Paris, she had received an enthusiastic letter from Charles, the last of several, he declared. He had done wonderfully, become a 'Speculator' in Pennsylvania, bought land and, as if following Imlay's novel, contemplated a company to buy 300,000 acres to form a settlement of English emigrants. Within a year he expected all to be flourishing and 'Then Eliza will give up romantic plans; and resolve to leave England – she will find not only a home but a brother in America'. Eliza doubted the undelivered letters and hoped Charles was not being 'too sanguine'.

Conservatives had tried to stir up anti-French feelings by publicising revolutionary attacks on the church and its property, a difficult task since anti-Catholic feeling equalled anti-French. Ever since August 1792, when the revolutionary government had expelled refractory priests, exiles had been landing on British shores – at least 6000 in the first months. *The Times* suspected some to be spies, while others regarded them as persecuted but still fundamentally *French*. Burke began a charity campaign and both Frances Burney and Hannah More, though recoiling from Wollstonecraft's meddling with politics, were persuaded to write pamphlets in this '*moral*' cause: the priests were martyrs to militant French atheism. Eliza saw all this as cynical manipulation of public opinion: 'I have been attacked by every body because I would not give towards the general Collection that has been made for the french Clergy.'

So there was some irony in her reaction to two brother priests washed up on a nearby coast. The elder was a fifty-year-old bishop called Graux, looking, Eliza thought, remarkably like Joseph Johnson – her references outwards were mostly to Mary's London friends. Graux confirmed her views of the Welsh: his sufferings in revolutionary France paled beside his treatment in 'free' Pembroke:

> they landed near Haverfordwest and were used *worse* they *declare* than if they had been *in Paris* – the P[rimate] (though he fainted among the savages) had a stone flung at his head – and [was] guarded all night (though he expected every moment to be his last) – for ... they were treated as republicans – and this good creature compelled to walk three miles, fainting at every step he took, surrounded by men women and children gazing, not at his pale face, but at a handkerchief that supplied the place of a wig, that the waves had stole from him. The moment he was housed at Pembroke all the children were admitted into the room where he sat for many hours, his head sunk on the table, – at last [he] was allowed to go to bed.[6]

Similar events were happening in other parts of the country. Bodies of émigré French wrecked on British shores had fingers and hands hacked off for the rings and bracelets they wore.

With her views Eliza was not a natural ally but in Graux she saw less a priest than an emissary from France. Whatever his politics, he spoke French and she needed training. So, when he recovered, she planned to take three French lessons a week with him. Her xenophobic employers refused entry to a foreigner, nor would they help her travel the muddy roads from Upton to Pembroke; she therefore proposed to stay with the priests from Saturday to early Monday, learning French for a guinea a month. If this were rejected, she threatened to quit Upton. The castle gave in, but she had to pay for a horse each way, as well as another 4s for lodgings.

Further drain on her resources came from Laugharne. Back in November her father and Lydia had seemed reasonably comfortable, but for the last six months they had been 'almost starving'. Her father wanted desperately to go to London to wring more money from Ned, who had resumed control of the Primrose Street houses in Mary's absence. In the mean time, 'They were so distressed ... that I was obliged to send a couple of guineas for the wants of the day.'

Eliza's spirits rose when she began her new regime. Pembroke was a small, handsome walled town, really only one street and a large castle but an improvement on isolated Upton. Learning French fed her dreams of Paris and allowed her to avoid the '*wretched Sundays*' with the lumpen family. She liked her ailing teacher though judging him 'a *Royalist from principle* and *warmly attached to his country*.'[7] James actually sent money to their father, and there was further good news of Charles. So contented was Eliza for the moment that she took in her stride (though doubting its truth) the extraordinary rumour that Mary was not in prison but married: 'I could not even (for a moment) suppose Mary Married!' she exclaimed.

Then she received an even more glowing letter from Charles in Philadelphia. He was rich, with $10,000. Having travelled 700 miles mostly on foot, visiting 'the original natives', he had returned to Philadelphia to purchase uncharted tracts – like Imlay largely untroubled by any connection of 'natives' and land. He was euphoric, expecting to be worth the huge sum of £13,000 by next year. He was even hinting at a wife. True, he had no cash but in the autumn he would send £100 for Eliza's passage, then give her a room in his house and a horse. She would have 'that elegant ease you have often longed for'. Everina could have £500 as a dowry and receive interest before marriage. He would send something for immediate relief. He also fleshed out the Mary rumour. He had met one of Imlay's American friends returned from France and, knowing nothing of her sorrows, the latter had painted a pleasant picture of her, Captain Imlay – and a baby.

The letter excited and puzzled Eliza. 'Can all this be more than a dream?' she demanded of Charles's projected bounty. But, 'it is *ungrateful* to harp on the horrors of *our* comfortless fate *at* the moment, when my very soul rejoices; and eagerly sighs to share this momentary happiness with thee.'[8] She remained sceptical about Mary:

Mary cannot be *Married*!! It is mere *report*. It is natural to conclude her protector is her *Husband* – Nay, on reading Charles's letter, *I* for an *instant*, believed it true – I would, my Everina we were out of suspense for all at present is uncertainty; and the most cruel suspense[.] Still Johnson does not repeat things at random and that the very same tale should have crossed the Atlantic makes me almost believe that the *once* M. is now Mrs Imlay, and a mother – Are we ever to see this *Mother and Her Babe*[?]

To Everina, Eliza wrote that she would remain at Upton 'till all the many Wonders are made *Clear*'; to Charles she wrote that she would come as soon as she received money for travel. She wrote him three times to ensure he had her reply.

In October Everina heard from Mary that she was married and contented. Now Eliza's envy burgeoned and the trust she had tried to nurture faded. Life at Upton was intolerable, while her weekly meetings in Pembroke were spoilt by her difficult journeys. Her money was seeping away and she would never be proficient at this rate. She had to quit either Upton or French. It was no contest; she would leave the castle and live with Graux, beard the scandal, and perfect her skill. Three to six months of constant instruction were all she needed. Fooling herself that she had put the dream of Paris behind her, she declared she was preparing for Ireland and life near Everina: '*Bread* is not *even* to be procured without french – in Dublin it is as much wanted as in London.'

Despite her resolution she was again agitated by a letter from Mary sent through Imlay, now in London. It promised France next spring:

Mary's letter gave me a dreadful complaint in my b—s, and all I felt was a degree of ill humor with the whole world I never before experienced[.] I read her letter a dozen times – yet my heart not once beat with joy ... If possible in spring, my Everina, why not have gone with Mr *Imlay*[?] Could he not have written to us? If Mary was afraid to be more explicit I wonder *had* M. Eliza, or poor Bess, in her mind's Eye when she gave her – heart to this Genereux – I feel now as if mine could never more be tranquillized –

For her Pembroke plan, Eliza needed money; she deeply regretted having sent anything to Mary. She had received help from George Blood and could touch him no further and she had been 'mortified by Johnson' who, already her creditor, had perhaps balked at more. In this predicament she turned to Everina and wrote directly to Imlay in London, care of Johnson; after all his 'wife' was in her debt.

Imlay took time to reply. When he did, he wrote formally, with none of the charm that was dangling Wollstonecraft on a string in France. He presented himself as a loving husband sadly deprived of his family. Such conventional expressions of coupledom would have cheered Wollstonecraft had she seen them, but, with the admission that they had no money and could do nothing for Eliza, cannot have pleased their recipient:

> Mr Johnson gave me your acceptable favor inclosing one to Mrs. Imlay saying it was for her; which leaving me ignorant of being included I could not return an immediate answer since which time I have been out of Town. I hope this circumstance will appear to you a sufficient apology for my silence; and that you will be pleased to consider it a good reason for preventing a forfeight of that claim to humanity, or at least respect & esteem for a person so affectionately loved by my dear Mary as yourself which you say had already been impressed on your mind –
>
> As to your sister's visiting England, I do not think she will previous to a peace, and perhaps not immediately after such an Event – However be that as it may, we shall both of us continue to cherish feelings of tenderness for you – and a recollection of your unpleasant situation, and we shall also endeavour to alleviate its distress by all the means in our power – The present state of our fortune is rather [words omitted]. However you must know your sister too well and I am sure you judge of that knowledge too favourably to suppose that – whenever she has it in her power that she will not apply some specific aid to promote your happiness[.] I shall always be happy to receive your letters, [but as] I shall most likely leave England the beginning [of next] week I will thank you to let me hear from you as soon as convenient, & tell me ingenuously in what way I can serve you in any manner or respect[.] I am in but indifferent spirits occasioned by my long absence from Mrs. Imlay and our little Girl while I am deprived of a chance of hearing from them.[9]

The stuffy kindness, coupled with the smug 'we', was chilling to Eliza, hoping desperately for money or an invitation. She tried to regain dignity by declaring she intended to go to America next spring. She later believed Imlay had not received her letter, ignorant of the disparity between his written intentions and acts.

Probably a little after this Everina received an undated letter from Mary coupling Imlay and the sum of £100,000 – very much like the exuberant Charles. *Two* prospects entailing such vast sums were more than Eliza could credit:

> A *Hundred Thousand*!! – and you are *really* – mad enough to suppose it possible!

To have made *such* a fortune, in a few months – It is truly in the Novel style my Everina – and so similar to Castles we have built on in days of yore that I am actually afraid to *Hope*! I was sure my eyes had deceived me when I first read the letter – Alas! the cruel past still deprives me of the power of anticipating impossibilities. –

I wish to God it may prove *true*. I know no one more deserving of *even so large* a fortune than Mary or more worthy of such a companion as Imlay – A propos I am a little surprised that he should not recollect, at this juncture, poor I – for he is in my debt – But I am sick of conjecturing...

By mid-November Eliza was ready to leave the 'dungeon' of Upton, though the separation from her 'poor dear Boy, who I shall for ever love', pained her: 'I would much sooner see him in the agonies of death than leave him among such *a set*,' she wrote melodramatically. 'I never had before *nor* shall again! the like affection for a child – he had become so a part of myself that it was like loosing a limb to leave him *behind* ... he was the only child I ever found a pleasure to teach ... This is the *Last* child I ever *Love*! While I have the power of loving!'

Instead of receiving largesse from Mary or Charles, Eliza had to give again. Their father was in the 'greatest distress' and threatening to attack Ned in London. Eliza feared Mary might be there by then, furious at finding him begging after all her efforts. So to prevent his journey she sent off 'a five guinea bill', the money she had stinted herself to save for Graux, though he and she were not quite so close now she knew enough French to discuss politics. The gift pushed her into penury: 'Alas! my Everina *should* Mary return we shall both be penniless – which I cannot help lamenting on every account – in particular as Madam Bishop is in want of almost every thing – But I hear thee exclaim Thy *wants shall all be replenished* in Spring ...' She was ageing and, while others lured her into spirits with mythical fortunes and schemes, she feared she was really of little account; nobody quite wanted her enough to send for her in earnest: 'At moments I feel that M. is lost forever to her *sisters* – and again I sigh to behold her babe[,] herself – her husband! Are you still dreaming of seeing france *again*? – I fear a little rouge will be necessary for us both when that period arrives.'

Then everything collapsed. First the grandiose American dream. She had never quite credited it but it had sustained her in moments of intense misery. At the least she had hoped for the promised travel money; if sent, she supposed Mary had it:

[The] '*one Hundred Pounds* which were to have *arrived* in autumn' has without doubt been carried into France ... I declare my dear Everina that Charles' *unpar-*

*donable* Ingratitude gives me a thousand times more pain than all the other disappointments his folly has produced … not even a trifling present for either of us – How gladly would I have pinched myself for a twelvemonth (at the time he left England) to have sent an other Ten – I own I never expected from *this brother* – not even after all that happened in days of yore.

Then James's promises to help his sisters faded. Eliza had forgotten his handwriting and, for a moment, assumed his letter Imlay's. She was doubly disappointed. His prize money would just fill his own needs:

I came home in consequence of ill health and therefore have an excuse which you may be sure I shall profit from as it accords so well with my inclination – I must tell you nothing of my past transactions nor my motives for coming home, for you will I know, disapprove of them all[;] however that you may not be at a loss to account for my present conduct, know that I cannot yet conquer my aversion to the sea, and now only wish for permission to live quietly on my halfpay and the prize money I have made; so thus I wait in hopes of soon seeing an end to the war, and when that happens I shall go immediately to *France* where I can live handsomely, and, from the past I think contently. You speak with rapture of going also, when the war is over let us gang together, believe me E. I should be very happy if we could; I shall run no more wild-goose chaces, my future movements are to be for improvement & must be regulated with economy &c &c. –

Coming on top of disappointments from Charles, it was a cruel blow. Eliza had never received 'a more *unacceptable* Epistle'. She replied furiously, mocking James's offers and relating how she had impoverished herself to help their father, something *he* ought to have done. Having sent her letter she repented, as so often, and suggested that Everina make things up. Still, she was right: '[James's] conduct appears to me actual *madness* and equally mean[.] I should not be surprised if he quits the sea, critical as *the* moment is, was there really peace his folly would be more excusible [–] he has surely forgot the *Portion so long promised* to *dear* Everina and poor Eliza – But [it] is in vain to argue the Case and childish to anticipate aught from this brother.'

Finally there was Mary. James had visited her in Paris, then Imlay in London: 'Mr Imlay … is a fine handsome fellow, and he tells me Mary is to be in England in *April* and that she will spend a few months in England.' Here was discrepancy indeed and Eliza suspected deceit. 'I am certain Imlay has *Concealed* Mary's intention of remaining in this country – You find she is not *expected* till next month.' Her reaction was extreme (horribly echoing Mary's at the same moment): 'Ah! Everina, what are we to hope! – I never anticipated, or longed for *the Morrow* so little, as at this juncture – a kind of despair has taken stronger root than ever in *Bess* heart and all I now dwell on, is the thought of seeing you soon.'

Her period in Pembroke expired on 20 May; after that she was broke and must rely on Everina, 'that is, *if* my fortune does not arrive from America before that period is elapsed.' Then she added, 'Not that I have any objection to share in the Hundred Thousand Pounds – or to behold Imlay his friend and brat.'[10] The last scrawled words show how close to the edge she had come, unemployed and watching her meagre savings and loans evaporate. She had grown so poor she no longer had clothes with which to approach a respectable employer. A noose tightened round her as her money seeped away and all routes closed except passage to Ireland and servitude. Although she promised, 'you will see your Bess as Lambish as in days of yore and only sensible to the many good qualities of her Everina', she delayed, so hard was it to abandon hope.

Again the parallel with Mary was uncanny, for as one sister sat unhappily in Paris, so the other waited in Pembroke, both in poor health, their minds preying on their bodies. Eliza had violent headaches, Mary violent colds; both imagined their own deaths. As Eliza dreamt of rescue by Mary, so Mary dreamt the same from Imlay. It was a grim circle of desire.

It was at the end of this roller-coaster of hopes and disappointments, as Eliza faced destitution, that she at last received a letter from Mary in Charlotte Street, declaring that she wanted no threesome in her house. Perhaps Mary enclosed the 'trifle' of £10:

I arrived in Town near a fortnight ago, my dear girl, but having previously weaned my child on account of a cough, I found myself extremely weak. I have intended writing to you every day, but have been prevented by the impossibility of deter- mining in what way I can be of essential service to you. When Mr Imlay and I united our fate together he was without fortune; since that [time], there is a prospect of his obtaining a considerable one; but though the hope appears to be well founded I cannot yet act as if it were a certainty[.] He is the most generous creature in the world and if he succeed, as I have the greatest reason to think he will, he will, in proportion to his acquirement of property, enable me to be useful to you and Everina – I wish you and her could adopt any plan in which five or six hundred pounds could be of use. As to myself I cannot yet say where I shall live for a continuance it would give me the sincerest pleasure to be situated near you – I know you will think me unkind – and it was this reflection that has prevented my writing to you sooner, not to invite you to come and live with me – But Eliza it is my opinion, not a readily formed one, the presence of a third person interrupts or destroys domestic happiness – [Excep]ting this sacrifice there is nothing I would not to do to promote your comfort[11] – I am hurt at being obliged to be thus explicit and do indeed severely feel for the disappointments which you have met with in Life – I have not heard from Charles nor can I guess what he is about – What was done with the fifty pounds he speaks of having sent to England? – Do pray write to me immediately and do justice to my heart[.] I do not wish to endanger my own peace without a certainty of securing yours – Yet I am still your most sincere and affectionate friend Mary.

In her stark misery, of which she gave Eliza no hint, Mary had forgotten the other sort of gnawing misery to which she had succumbed in Ireland, when she too had been a lonely governess, lowered by nerves and headaches. She intended to be comforting with her promise of money, more than had ever before been mentioned among the sisters. Who knows whether for a moment she believed the retreating Imlay would advance this sort of sum, whether she was deceiving herself or only Eliza or Everina?

Eliza's response was extreme: 'Alas! at the end of four long years could despair itself [have] dreampt of such studied *Cruelty*[?] No – inquiries after my *present wants*, &c &c no wish [to] *see us*.' Her reply to Mary was her shortest extant letter. She did not dare touch on the excluding vision of domestic bliss and answered only the wrong assumption that she had had help from Charles. 'Mrs B. has never received any money from America.' Then, since brevity felt unnatural, she angrily copied out Mary's words, dispatching them to Everina with an hysterical letter of injury and jealousy:

This I have just received my Everina[.] What I felt, and shall for ever feel it is childish to talk of after lingering above a fortnight in such a cruel suspense[.] Good God what a letter! how have I merited such pointed cruelty? I may say *insolence*[.] When did I ask to live with her at what time wish for a moment, to interrupt *their Domestic* happiness? Was ever a present offered in so humiliating a style – ought the poorest domestick to be thus insulted – Are your Eyes opened, at last, Everina? – What do you now say to our goodly prospects – I have such a mist before my lovely eyes that I cannot see what I write[.] But this clearly [I] make out that M is *now* positively determined to quit [...] latter end of next month and [I] as positive in intention of going to Dublin[.] So instantly get me a situation in Ireland I care not where – Dear Everina – delay not to tell me you can procure me bread – with what Hogs I eat it nay if exactly the Uptonian breed – Remember I am serious[.] If you disappoint me my misery will be compleat[.] I have enclosed this famous letter to the author of the Rights of Woman – without any reflection. So she shall never hear from *poor Bess again*. Remember, I am as fixed as my misery – and nothing can change my present plan. This letter has so strangely agitated me that I know not what I say but this I feel, and know that if you value my existence you will comply with my request for I am positive I will never torment our amiable friend in *Charlotte* Street[.] Is not this a goodly Spring my dear Girl[?] At least poor Bess can say it is a fruitful one. Alas, poor Bess!

Desperately needing a saviour, Eliza even reconsidered the disappointing Charles: 'To receive aught now from your Mary appears to me the height of meanness – Would to God we were both in America with Charles – Do you think it would be possible for us to go from Dublin in an American ship to Philadelphia ... I am sure our sister would be delighted with this plan, and our *New brother* of course display all his Energy of character to render it practical.' In fact her only realistic hope was Ireland and a little kindness from George Blood – as perhaps she knew: 'If it is impossible to procure me *Bread* immediately,' she wrote to Everina, 'perhaps George would permit me to remain with him till you could succeed – Recollect I *value* not what situation you get me agreeable or disagreeable will be equally acceptable to the Sister of the Author of the Rights of Woman.'

All thoughts and roads led to Mary and, calling herself the famous author's sister, she clarified how contingent a being she had always felt, how much she had resented her subordination while taking her little significance from Mary. Frantically she analysed Mary's letter. Had she done right in returning it? Was it an impulse she would regret? There was a hole where Mary had been which no one, not even Everina, could fill. 'I now have not the smallest wish to quit Wales – nor are my prospects in the least cheered by the idea of seeing you so soon – For I am sick to death of arguing and accounting for the unaccountable Events of this Wretched Life, and as thoroughly tired of the lingering existence I have dragged on year after year, *Spring* after spring.' It was a horrid irony that, just as her sister was planning to take her dose of poison 250 miles away, Eliza was bitterly repeating, 'I am so dull and weary of my miserable – life – Is not this – a Goodly Spring – and is not Bess a Lucky *Girl*[?] The amiable Mary pined in poverty, while Mrs I. enjoys all her heart can sigh [for]'. She wrote an uncontrolled hand and her frequent habit of self-referral became infantile.

Back in London Mary mournfully described the exchange to James, who repeated it to Eliza. His letter revealed how tense were the epistolary relations between all the Wollstonecraft siblings:

This is the fourth time I have attempted to write to you[;] I never could get through a letter fearing to give pain[.] I thought silence best. Mary says you returned her letter. – She appears less composed and happy than formerly ... It was not in my power to send my father more money; for though I make a good deal of prize money yet it is all in Spain and I may not receive it these six months, and then owing to the continuance of the War shall lose considerably in remitting it home. I sent my father five pounds and M. sent ten in my name which I am sorry for, because he has been thanking me for what I do not merit – God Bless you. When writing to you or Everina there are always such contending passions struggling about my heart, that I am almost deprived of reason [–] I am very unhappy.

'What say you to James' "struggling passions?" ' Eliza wrote caustically to Everina.

Like Mary, Eliza liked making grand gestures of silence and endings, but was not good at following them up. So, though Mary was supposedly 'dead' to her and she had made a 'positive' resolution never to communicate again, she itched to write. She even contemplated travelling to London and throwing herself on Mary. Graux, to whom she had boasted of her famous sister, supported the idea; perhaps in his troubles he had come to depend on Eliza and thought the risk worth taking for them both. Wisely she hesitated: 'Would it be meanness even to think of going to London – after such a letter – and at present my only *Hope* is Bread!' Mary's offer swam into her mind but she had no energy left: 'Even with the money offered what could we do[?] I sicken at a school and how very uncertain our success *friendless* as we are.'

Despite low spirits, with only one more week in Pembroke, Eliza had to exert herself. As a poor, genteel and lone woman with no servant, she must arrange her own transport. She 'bid [little John] farewel for ever', then wrote to Everina for instructions on arrival in Ireland. She had to remove herself, a desk, three boxes and two large picture cases; she also had to get her greatcoat from London so that this could travel with her. She must pay porters, giving them just enough not to be abused. Then she would cross the sea to Ireland and rely on the inevitable sickness to raise her spirits. Like Mary she knew that uncomfortable travelling relieved mental pain.

Yet an aftershine of the Paris dream lingered and Eliza found it difficult *absolutely* to commit herself to going west. So despite all her resolutions she *did* write again to Mary. Then she went to Laugharne to say good-bye – and await an answer. She could surely delay a little.

In Laugharne she received a short, hasty letter, presumably written in the aftermath of Mary's suicide attempt. With no key to her sister's state, Eliza could not interpret. It gave her a violent headache and she did not reply at once. She also heard from George Blood, who invited her to spend time with his mother until Everina found her a job. It was kind and friendly; yet she vividly remembered being disappointed by George and his promises. Could she take his offer seriously?

She had to, as she was honest enough to admit to Everina: 'If ... you cannot get me a tolerable employment immediately it is the only step I can take.' George suggested he meet her at Waterford in the south east of Ireland, a much cheaper and nearer route for her to take from Pembroke than going north to Dublin. He was keen to have Everina in his house ready to meet Eliza. All these arrangements would, she feared, be expensive – or perhaps she feared that, with George's improvidence, she would end up paying; she dreaded 'being lead imperceptibly into *extravagance* ... let *us* be governed by prudence'.

Still she paused, still wrote again to Mary, still waited in Laugharne for something to nourish hope.

Then it shrivelled from report of Mary's cheerfulness. James had correctly seen her melancholy; yet she obviously *looked* good following childbirth, plumper and less strained, and it was to this aspect that the less perceptive Johnson responded when he declared that 'he *never* saw Mary so well or so happy'. The remark was relayed to Eliza; it plunged her into despair. But she did not stop waiting for Mary to write.

The suspense was maddening: each day she expected the letter, each day was disappointed. It was absurd that, for the sake of this forlorn hope, she disturbed plans and delayed: 'Eliza's Peace [is] strangely disturbed.' She blamed herself for not answering Mary at once; perhaps she had offended. If she did not get an encouraging reply now, she really would write to George.

For the next four days she was tense and anxious, yet not daring to move in case she missed the letter by an hour. She met with resounding silence and could do little but scrawl painful words to Everina:

> [I have been] *lingering* here a week longer than I intended – *after writing to Mary* –
> No answer –
> Not a *line* – ...
> Her letter was written a month ago[;] I know not what to think on the subject[.]
> I am weary to death – So *expect* me *to-morrow* week – so for if I have promise[d]
> myself aught on earth I *will positively* be in Waterford on Sunday – I have just
> written to George.

Finally Eliza crossed to Ireland, taking the boat from Pembroke past Milford Haven and the South Welsh islands and out into the Irish Sea to Rosslare. Probably she was seasick since the crossing could be choppy and the journey often took three days and nights if there were storms.

The two younger sisters were reunited. They had both looked forward to this time and occasionally in their month together Eliza enjoyed the Irish scenery of mountains and glens. More often she was gloomy, letting a 'horrid langueur of mind and body' embitter everything. While Everina sketched, she urged her to contemplate the 'black abyss' of their future. When separated again she regretted she had destroyed 'the little gleam of sunshine ... by my incessantly Croaking over irremediable ills'.

Yet, with all her 'croaking', Eliza had come through her worst period. She was at last relying a little more on herself and, with better health from walking in Ireland, could admit at moments to being 'very snug'. She gave up hopes of rescue from Charles who had proposed that he settle his sisters in Wales or a country town in England, thus clarifying that he did not really want them in America and making Eliza '*doubt every* offer he has yet made'. In due course she managed to run her own school in Dublin for a dozen day boys near Everina. It is not known at what point she learnt how desperate Mary's position had been when she wrote her terrible letter and understood why she had had no reply to her appeals from Laugharne. Mary was no longer in England.

# 27

*'My soul has been shook'*

Wollstonecraft had 'determined to continue to exist', but what should she do? Her feelings were unchanged and she disturbed Imlay: as a public person she was noticed and she lacked reticence. Imaginatively they found a solution to both their problems, personal and commercial: the suicidal 'wife' who had nagged about commerce would go to Scandinavia as his business envoy and speak with the Commissioners appointed to investigate the lost silver ship. She would be gone for a few months, perhaps do him some good, and save him notoriety.

Wollstonecraft did not relish sea-crossings, but, like Eliza, knew their emotional value. Brown had suggested long journeys with new scenes, projects, wine, light and pure air to stimulate neurotics: Scandinavia with its long, clear days was custom-made for cure. The bizarre plan was sweetened by Imlay's promise to join her in Basel after she left Hamburg on her return. They could take a short holiday together.

The idea of activity cheered her. She contacted Joseph Johnson, who gave her a commission to execute, possibly correcting a translation of Manon Roland's prison memoirs, an improved second edition of which he wanted to publish.[1] She also resolved to take notes to work into a travel book; so she read the most recent account of the area, William Coxe's *Voyages and Travels* (1784). She may have carried it with her for occasionally she set her observations against Coxe's. She also probably took George Blood's gift of Shakespeare: the Jacobean heroes were useful companions in dramatic wanderings.

In Scandinavia she should try to hasten legal proceedings or settle with Ellefsen, arrested at the beginning of the year but released on bail since his family was rich and influential. She should go first to Backman, then with him to Stromstad to see the commissioners Nordberg and Ungar. On 19 May Imlay scrawled a fulsomely complimentary document, as much for the bearer's eyes as for those of businessmen. She was 'Mary Imlay my best friend and wife', a phrase Wollstonecraft must often have contemplated in the coming grim weeks. It authorised her 'to take the sole management and direction of all my affairs and business which I had placed in the hands of Mr Elias Backman negotiant Gottenburg or in those of Messrs Myburg &

Co. Copenhagen', and to collect the sum awarded in a suit against Ellefson for violation of trust. As his 'dear beloved friend and companion' she was given his complete confidence.²

With this commercial solution to their romantic predicament Imlay felt emotionally freer. He cared about his self-image and wanted to be seen parting on good terms with his old lover; so he wrote an affectionate letter, blaming his apparent withdrawal on business cares and suggesting dinner. Penitent, Wollstonecraft replied with a mixture of shame, hope, humble gratitude, and continued misery: 'I have laboured to calm my mind since you left me – Still I find that tranquillity is not to be obtained by exertion; it is a feeling so different from the resignation of despair! – I am however no longer angry with you – nor will I ever utter another complaint – there are arguments which convince the reason, whilst they carry death to the heart.'

Recently she had tried to overcome 'irritable nerves' by visiting old friends, attending the theatre and dining out. With annoyance she noticed that her health was mending, but she remained bitterly unhappy: 'Every emotion is now sharpened by anguish. – My soul has been shook, and my tone of feelings destroyed.' She could not let Imlay be: 'My friend – my dear friend – examine yourself well – I am out of the question; for, alas! I am nothing – and discover what you wish to do – what will render you most comfortable – or, to be more explicit – whether you desire to live with me, or part for ever?' It was not the letter Imlay wanted, still demanding impossible emotional commitments and introspection.

Wollstonecraft had promised that, when he came for a last dinner, she would assume a cheerful face. She could not and the afternoon failed. Perhaps Imlay clarified how much he wanted to safeguard his reputation and asked her for her suicide letter to him. The request agitated her and, when she forwarded it, she added a hurt note: 'I am tempted very laconically to wish you a good morning.' But she could not be laconic: 'a strong conviction seems to whirl round in the very centre of my brain, which, like the fiat of fate, emphatically assures me, that grief has a firm hold of my heart.' She ended, 'God bless you!' a phrase she almost used as a curse when she contemplated Imlay in the context of her death.

In June, without replying to the frantic Eliza waiting in Laugharne, Wollstonecraft set off to Hull accompanied by Fanny and the maid Marguerite to take ship for Sweden. Since she was on the mail coach, there were changes of horses but few stops, and it was a long tiring journey. It was high summer and they could at least have the windows open – when shut the inside quickly became stagnant – but summer or winter coaches were cramped and passengers thrown together: a single chatterbox could prevent all from sleeping. Great friendships were commenced on mail coaches, but some people grew murderous towards their irritating fellows.

The other passengers cannot have welcomed a baby. Fanny, who had been so good on the road between Le Havre and Paris, was restless and demanding and through the night would stay only with her mother. She remained in high spirits, loving the noise of the coach's horn as it neared towns and trying to imitate it. Wollstonecraft arrived in Hull exhausted.

They took a room in a damp, tomb-like house, resolving to move as soon as possible. But first she must write to Imlay, rushing to catch the post which went early from Hull. Privy to recent events in London, Marguerite must have felt reluctant to hurry with a letter that could do little but uselessly tell her mistress's woes:

> I will not distress you by talking of the depression of my spirits, or the struggle I had to keep alive my dying heart. – It is even now too full to allow me to write with composure. – [Imlay], dear [Imlay], – am I always to be tossed about thus? – shall I never find an asylum to rest *contented* in? How can you love to fly about continually – dropping down, as it were, in a new world – cold and strange! – every other day? Why do you not attach those tender emotions round the idea of home, which even now dim my eyes? – This alone is affection – every thing else is only humanity, electrified by sympathy.

The end of the letter, which promised that Wollstonecraft would write daily and demanded he do the same, must have sunk Imlay's heart.

Hull was a busy port but the most advertised routes were to London and across the Atlantic; finding a boat for Sweden would take time. Feeling unsociable and biased against provincials, she had only reluctantly brought a letter of introduction to a doctor in the town. In fact she found him interesting, but, when his pretty wife came to offer her an outing, she exclaimed to Imlay over the vague arrangements: 'why talk of inconveniences, which are in fact trifling, when compared with the sinking of the heart I have felt! I did not intend to touch this painful string'. Yet she was grateful to the couple. Fanny, who had long been alone with her mother or Marguerite, 'was never so happy in her life, as amongst their young brood'.

When they had discussed their relationship in London Imlay had hinted he was no longer sexually attracted to her, that, like other men, as he aged he needed 'variety'. In Hull she had time to brood and fantasise conversations. He was careful not to be too provoking when he wrote now, fearing perhaps she might return directly; yet he reiterated that he *did* like a zesty life. She had no hesitation in facing the admission.

The needs he described existed only in the 'common run of men', she explained, not in those with 'imagination' which converted 'appetite into love' cemented by 'according reason'. It was 'one of the most serious misfortunes' of her life that she had not met Imlay 'before satiety had rendered your senses so fastidious, as almost to close up every tender avenue of sentiment and affection that leads to your sympathetic heart. You have a heart, my friend, yet, hurried away by the impetuosity of inferior feelings, you have sought in vulgar excesses, for that gratification which only the heart can bestow.' The analysis was not calculated to rein in an erring lover.

In the early phase of their relationship, Wollstonecraft had accepted that she was hypersensitive and had tried to change. Now however she reverted to seeing her miseries as due to misfortune, while believing again that emotional quickness was a virtue, her unhappiness the price of her special combination of feeling and intellect, her 'true, unsophisticated heart'. It was a secular version of her earlier belief in divine affliction. Her identity was not simply made by a Brunonian balance of inner and outer forces but a superior disjunction between desire and fulfilment, the ordinary world and her imagination. Given her own experience, she was no longer inclined to think with Dr Johnson, that occupation and a baby could prevent female despair. So, just when she most needed to present an appealing image of herself, she was fixated only on changing Imlay or rather changing him back to an original virtue she insisted in seeing, a virtue overlaid by a brutish mercantile morality that had sought and consumed money and women. That she was inevitably alienating her lover with criticism meant less to her than self-justification.

Firmly she contrasted her good self with his errancy. Rousseau opposed sex as pre-reflective, pre-cultural instinct with 'moral love', which could not be satiated. *Her* sexuality was, like Rousseau's ideal, more refined than Imlay's; he should become, with her, less 'common'. Despite her description of love being saturated with religious imagery, she had rather forgotten her earlier notion that proper love looked ultimately towards God:

Ah! my friend, you know not the ineffable delight, the exquisite pleasure, which arises from a unison of affection and desire, when the whole soul and senses are abandoned to a lively imagination, that renders every emotion delicate and rapturous. Yes; these are emotions, over which satiety has no power, and the recollection of which, even disappointment cannot disenchant; but they do not exist without self-denial. These emotions, more or less strong, appear to me to be the distinctive characteristic of genius, the foundation of taste, and of that exquisite relish for the beauties of nature, of which the common herd of eaters and drinkers and child-begeters, certainly have no idea. You will smile at an observation that has just occurred to me: – I consider those minds as the most strong and original, whose imagination acts as the stimulus to their senses.

Well! you will ask, what is the result of all this reasoning? Why I cannot help thinking that it is possible for you, having great strength of mind, to return to nature, and regain a sanity of constitution, and purity of feeling – which would open your heart to me. – I would fain rest there!

Significantly, 'child-begeters' – fathers, were now associated with 'money-getters' – improper capitalists; motherhood, a more imaginative business of production and consumption, was unfortunately tainted by the notion. She had long associated reason with self-restraint and self-denial, so dignifying it in her puritanical mind. Now sensibility, troublesome when it tended to excess and indulgence, was converted into Rousseauian imagination through self-denial. 'Imagination' had been used for an undisciplined and tyrannising fancy when she had been lambasting the uncurbed Burke and the licentious aspect of Rousseau; now as she moved from perception of Rousseau as writer of *Émile*, then critic of capitalism, to Rousseau as introspective author of the *Confessions* and especially of *The Reveries of the Solitary Walker*, she embraced his notion of a faculty that distinguished the élite from 'the common herd'.[3] It might create sympathy, but could also promise a general alienation.

Rousseau and she were heroic misfits who attempted to live out their values and beliefs. As she thought on Imlay's unworthiness and her own worth and puzzled over her infatuation, she began sinking again. Occasionally she yearned for a death that would include Fanny and obliterate motherhood: 'I have looked at the sea, and at my child, hardly daring to own to myself the secret wish, that it might become our tomb; and that the heart, still so alive to anguish, might there be quieted by death.' Renewed fear of hopelessness brought tears and she addressed Imlay in a series of emotional, unanswerable questions, trying to force him into her mode of thinking:

Are we ever to meet again? and will you endeavour to render that meeting happier than the last? Will you endeavour to restrain your caprices, in order to give vigour to affection, and to give play to the checked sentiments that nature intended should expand your heart? ... Examine now yourself, and ascertain whether you can live in something like a settled stile. Let our confidence in future be unbounded; consider whether you find it necessary to sacrifice me to what you term 'the zest of life;' and, when you have once a clear view of your own motives, of your own incentive to action, do not deceive me!

Imlay had often declared he wished to promote her happiness, but had not been specific about means. She knew what they were: he must give more of himself.

She could not sustain her assertiveness. Soon she was overwhelmed by her own pathos, the contrast between Imlay in the London fleshpots and herself and baby on their lonely, arduous journey: 'I cannot indeed, without agony, think of your bosom's being continually contaminated; and bitter are the tears which exhaust my eyes, when I recollect why my child and I are forced to stray from the asylum, in which, after so many storms, I had hoped to rest, smiling at angry fate.'

Imlay was still cross about her lax notions of reticence. After all he had not abandoned her and was keeping mum about many aspects of their relationship. But she did not see things his way. What was reputation beside a broken heart? Everyone knew how much she adored him, how could she hide it? 'You were certainly wrong, in supposing that I did not mention you with respect; though, without my being conscious of it, some sparks of resentment may have animated the gloom of despair – Yes; with less affection, I should have been more respectful. However the regard which I have for you, is so unequivocal to myself, I image that it must be sufficiently obvious to every body else.' It sounds as though she had destroyed a letter intended for public consumption justifying her suicide; in any case it had been 'written (of course warmly in your praise) to prevent any odium being thrown on you'. Imlay must have been glad she had not been able to make public her long-suffering praise.

By now she had spoken to a boat-captain planning to sail for Scandinavia in a few days but doubted his commitment; perhaps her Hull friends warned her of the North Sea's contrary tides. Imlay must go on writing. She needed his letters to convince herself that they were not parting, that he was still a father: 'my little darling is calling papa, and adding her parrot word – Come, Come! And will you not come, and let us exert ourselves? – I shall recover all my energy, when I am convinced that my exertions will draw us more closely together.'

To help her pass the wearisome time, the doctor and his wife took her in their carriage to Beverley a few miles away. She had not seen it since a girl and found it changed and unchanged. Walking on Westwood Common, she happily recalled her former chattering rambles, but, after London and Paris, the town itself, once so elegant and cultured, seemed little more than a village. She recollected how excited she had been by the talk of books and ideas, but then her contrast was with the hamlet of Walkington. Industry and farming had developed, she saw, but there were unwelcome social changes. The French Wars had provoked nationalism everywhere, as Eliza's letters testified; here the results were more fervent Protestant sects and greater stress on social stability and class, a new respect for aristocracy. Whatever the Revolution might in the end do for France, it had not improved England.

Her main response to Beverley was the usual one of a person who had lived too intensely and moved too often: that it was wonderful to see people exactly where they had been so many years before: 'when I found that many of the inhabitants had lived in the same houses ever since I left it, I could not help wondering how they could thus have vegetated, whilst I was running over a world of sorrow, snatching at pleasure, and throwing off prejudices'.

Probably one of these static people was her childhood friend Jane Arden. She was still there, still unmarried, still running her school.[4] While Mary was increasingly questioning the doctrines that had formerly sustained her, Jane was growing conventionally pious: she would soon warn her pupils never to open a volume of the wicked new poet, Lord Byron.[5]

The trip could do little against her prevailing mood. Back in Hull the wind remained in the wrong direction, seeming stuck in its ways, and there was no chance of sailing. Each morning, whether rested or not, she trembled uncontrollably as in Paris and feared she was falling ill again. Everything seemed too much trouble, even little Fanny got on her nerves. Her mind was filled with Imlay and his next letter; she begged him to write to sustain her.

The commercial tie where 'confidence' could be 'unbounded' renewed hope of an emotional one: openness in a public sphere must be duplicated in private. He had deceived her about business when he left Le Havre; now he was dealing honestly and she felt her self-esteem rising. If his plans failed – and she felt she had a right to advise – he could fall back on her, 'convinced that a true friend is a treasure'. Putting the suicidal thoughts behind her as well as memories of Imlay's complaints of her faint-heartedness, she declared herself proud of her strength: she would not mind struggling with the world again. Her feelings swelled with the thought: 'Accuse me not of pride – yet sometimes, when nature has opened my heart to its author, I have wondered that you did not set a higher value on my heart.' The scheme of *Mary, A Fiction* is reversed: divine love should here have implied earthly.

Business talk dissolved into desire to obliterate business with her loving image: 'Often do I sigh, when I think of your entanglements ... and your extreme restlessness of mind. – Even now I am almost afraid to ask you whether the pleasure of being free, does not overbalance the pain you felt at parting with me? Sometimes I indulge the hope that you will feel me necessary to you – or why should we meet again?' She asked a lot of questions, but rarely those that he could or she could not answer.

Then the wind changed suddenly to a south-westerly one and she had to rush herself and her party on board in a few hours. Although she could not warm to Hull, she was sad to leave its kind people; she would not meet them again. Mostly she sighed for Imlay's next letter; she was assured it would be forwarded but was reluctant to leave without it.

Expecting seasickness, poor Marguerite must have looked glumly at the grim, choppy, grey water. The North Sea could be stormy and newspapers regularly listed ships and people lost, even strong swimmers defeated by sudden swirls and surging water, their dead bodies flung on to the mud and sand. In Hull just before they arrived, there was a particularly ferocious storm that killed many fishermen.[6] Wollstonecraft was too concerned with her broken heart to care much for her body; as on her trips to Portugal, Ireland and France, she insisted that mental storms exceeded nature's.

In Paris she had feared England, now she feared leaving it:

My spirits are agitated, I scarcely know why – The quitting England seems to be a fresh parting. – Surely you will not forget me. – A thousand weak forebodings assault my soul, and the state of my health renders me sensible to every thing. It is surprising that in London, in a continual conflict of mind, I was still growing better – whilst here, bowed down by the despotic hand of fate, forced into resignation by despair, I seem to be fading away – perishing beneath a cruel blight, that withers up all my faculties.

The baby was fine, but no one and nothing else was. She had no special presentiment of evil but felt an 'inexpressible sadness'. During Eliza's abduction, she had prided herself on being especially chosen for divine suffering; some of this religious thinking remained in the secular context when she called her heart 'a mark for misery'. She wrote her letter to Imlay and prepared to leave.

Fanny, Marguerite and Wollstonecraft embarked in mid-afternoon. They were the only passengers and, on first sight, the vessel seemed comfortable. Wollstonecraft was glad to have a cabin to herself. The captain appeared polite and open-hearted and the cabin-boy played with Fanny, who became 'as gay as a lark'.

By evening the wind had veered round to the wrong direction and they could make no real headway. All nerved to go, they were becalmed. It was misty and Wollstonecraft felt adrift in a nothingness of flat sea and thick air.

It felt eerie. She had brought books to help while away the time but in this dead period could not read, only write 'effusions'.

She was echoing Mary of *Mary, A Fiction* who rhapsodised on her miserable voyages, needing to write to contain her emotions. Yet, unlike her heroine, Wollstonecraft was an author and knew the value of her writing. Some of it she probably thought to use in the future; some went into the letters she continued at every spare moment to address to Imlay, full of the questioning that had become her mode:

> My dear friend, my heart sinks within me! – Why am I forced thus to struggle continually with my affections and feelings? – Ah! why are those affections and feelings the source of so much misery, when they seem to have been given to vivify my heart, and extend my usefulness! But I must not dwell on this subject. – Will you not endeavour to cherish all the affection you can for me? What am I saying? – Rather forget me, if you can – if other gratifications are dearer to you. – How is every remembrance of mine embittered by disappointment? What a world is this! – They only seem happy, who never look beyond sensual or artificial enjoyments.

The comfort of her 'effusions' strengthened her intention to write of herself and her travels.

Twenty-four hours later, she was still stuck on the cold, choppy sea with a violent headache, a little comforted by a letter from Imlay delivered to the boat by a pilot. She answered at once, while the pilot waited. Marguerite was in a terrible state, the motion of the anchored ship rendering her so seasick she was quite helpless. So Wollstonecraft had to look after Fanny herself and found it irksome, especially since the child had teething troubles. Once appearing commodious, the boat now felt dirty and smelly. Sailors were famous for caring for rigging, shrouds and braces but being careless in their persons and habits. She felt disgust rising.

It was near midsummer but the north-east wind chilled, and she looked bleakly at the monotonous flat land merging into the sea. She was imprisoned in a landscape of sky, sea and mudflats. But – as usual: 'These are ... trifling inconveniences, compared with anguish of mind – compared with the sinking of a broken heart. – To tell you the truth, I never suffered in my life so much from depression of spirit – from despair.' She had begun dreaming of Imlay again and her dreams made frightening pictures of alienation: 'I do not sleep – or, if I close my eyes, it is to have the most terrifying dreams, in which I often meet you with different casts of countenance.' She wanted to calm not deaden her painfully active mind, but could not: 'One thing let me tell you – when we meet again – surely we are to meet! – it must be to part

no more. I mean not to have seas between us – it is more than I can support.'
Still she was sleepless: 'I lie awake, till thinking almost drives me to the brink
of madness – only to the brink, for I never forget, even in the feverish
slumbers I sometimes fall into, the misery I am labouring to blunt the sense
of, by every exertion in my power.'

Friday came and went and Wollstonecraft managed *not* to write to Imlay.
Instead she brooded on herself and the different being she was when, ten
years earlier, she set out for Portugal. She had had enough 'elasticity' of mind
to ward off weariness and had held smiling visions of a rainbow future.[7] Her
memory was playing her false – she had been depressed then, though young
and ignorant of what she now knew. Her insomnia was bad and it was hard
to keep a grip on the present, let alone the past.

To break the monotony, on Saturday she and Fanny planned to accompany
the captain on a rowing boat to a spot on the coast. Although the weather
remained poor, the wind cold, they could avoid the stench of the boat, take
a walk and buy milk and fresh food in a village. The exercise might help her
sleep and take Fanny's mind off her teething. Before she set out, Wollstonecraft began a serial letter, determined not to miss a chance of sending
to Imlay from ashore:

> This is the fifth dreary day I have been imprisoned by the wind, with every
> outward object to disgust the sense, and unable to banish the remembrances that
> sadden my heart . . .
>
> I am going towards the North in search of sunbeams! – Will any ever warm
> this desolated heart? All nature seems to frown – or rather mourn with me. –
> Every thing is cold – cold as my expectations! Before I left the shore, tormented,
> as I now am, by these Northeast *chillers*, I could not help exclaiming – Give me,
> gracious Heaven! at least, genial weather, if I am never to meet the genial affection
> that still warms this agitated bosom compelling life to linger there . . .
>
> I hope this will be the last letter I shall write from England to you – are you not
> tired of this lingering adieu?

The next day, the captain offered to return to Hull instead; Wollstonecraft
was indifferent so long as she escaped the boat. The sea looked rough and
the trip to land on choppy water was bound to be dangerous, but she was
determined to go.

So they set off and, though disagreeably buffeted, arrived in Hull without
mishap. She went straightaway to the post office to enquire for a letter,
though she had told Imlay they were about to sail. None was there and she
scolded: he should have second-guessed the wind. 'Had you written one
haphazard, it would have been kind and considerate – you might have

known, had you thought, that the wind would not permit me to depart. These are attentions, more grateful to the heart than offers of service – But why do I foolishly continue to look for them?'

Then, the wind turned westerly again and they had to hurry back on board. She finished the truly last letter from England: 'Adieu! adieu! My friend – your friendship is very cold – you see I am hurt. – God bless you! I may perhaps be, some time or other, independent in every sense of the word. – Ah! there is but one sense of it of consequence. I will break or bend this weak heart – yet even now it is full'. This time the sails swelled and they went out with the tide.

So Wollstonecraft left on a characteristic note of reproach. She knew Imlay to be retreating; yet she could not resist constantly telling him how to behave. Despite her experiences, she continued to misunderstand romantic passion and insist it be rational, argued into being. She would not accept that Imlay might not love as much as she did. At least in *The Rights of Woman* she had separated sexual love from reason and accepted the irrationality and danger of the former. Passionate love was there 'an arbitrary passion' reigning 'by its own authority, without deigning to reason.' Now she was trying to bring them together, unaware that romance and Enlightenment notions are strange bedfellows.

Since she did not appreciate Imlay's otherness, Wollstonecraft's ideology remained what it had been: that of equality between the sexes, an equality that, thoroughly acted out, would preclude the passion she was feeling. Her sense of sexual identity meant that the male other must be equivalent to herself and her desire be rational. Had she not scorned the literature of passionate women and the conduct-book manuals with their pragmatic sexual politics, she would have learnt that, in the culture as it existed, frankness and judicious evaluation of a lover's character do not attract the straying male and that intensity of affection, especially an initiatory or pursuing one, will not catch a man.

She also showed little knowledge of masochism: 'Who can caress a man, with true feminine softness at the very moment when he treats her tyrannically. Nature never dictates such insincerity,' she wrote in *The Rights of Woman*. Her past and present experience should have told her that tyranny and softness were not incompatible, often indeed went closely together. Imlay wrote letters that were sometimes warm, but now she knew he could be cruel. The tyranny and warmth kept her caressing.

Yet, if the Hull letters were similar to earlier ones in their strain of irritated misery, they also flash with insight and suggest what is to come. There is no doubting the reality of her suicidal depression, continuing from the awful months in Paris and London, but in some letters there is a self-dramatising quality slightly different from the dreary introspection of Ireland and New-ington Green. Wollstonecraft was aware of her pathos, a lonely and aban-doned woman with a child travelling into the wild regions of the north. As mention of her 'effusions' suggests, she had decided that, whatever she wrote to Imlay – and she knew she could not stop writing – she would also write her feelings in the melancholy landscape, as Sterne had written his sentimental traveller, Rousseau his solitary wanderer, and Imlay in *The Emi-grants* his sensitive English lady. She felt the comfort of self-dramatisation, but in earlier years she had been partly ashamed at the dismal self-image she was creating. Now, as she accepted that it was Imlay who was wanting, not her unhappy self, she considered her self-image more favourably. With insufficient replies, she was eschewing the dialogue of letters, filling her own frame while progressing from the sentimental presentation of *Mary, A Fiction* and the Kingsborough era into something more imaginative. It was, of course, insufficient consolation for a broken heart.

# 28

*'Emotions that trembled on the brink of extacy and agony'*

The English literary traveller went south, took some portion of the Grand Tour of France, Italy and the Rhine parts of Germany and Switzerland. The Baltic states were largely unvisited except for business or diplomacy.

It was rare for a woman to journey on business and few business people of either sex went in so melancholy a mood or mingled economic observations with such elegiac reflection. Although she often declared herself languid and fancied herself suicidal, Wollstonecraft needed immense energy for her strenuous voyage.

It began with eleven days on a rough sea. The cargo boat got progressively dirtier. Marguerite continued seasick and the teething Fanny remained exacting; once more her mother had the burden of care. Yet the child was her reason for living; later she told Imlay how she had gazed at the sea and thought to plunge in, but been stopped by Fanny's little smiling face. Inevitably the first sight of coast gladdened them all.

She had planned to land in Arendal in Norway or Gothenburg in Sweden, near where Imlay's partner Backman lived, but contrary wind blew them past both towns in the night. They backtracked towards a lighthouse, perhaps the double beacon of Nidingen seen from their ship. The captain hoped to lure a pilot's boat from shore; otherwise his passengers would have to accompany him to Elsinor, his next port of call. No boat came and Wollstonecraft was forced to conclude, against her anti-capitalist bias, that some things were better in mercenary England:

> Despotism, as is usually the case, I found had here cramped the industry of man. The pilots being paid by the king, and scantily, they will not run into any danger, or even quit their hovels, if they can possibly avoid it, only to fulfil what is termed their duty. How different is it on the English coast, where, in the most stormy weather, boats immediately hail you, brought out by the expectation of extraordinary profit.[1]

Desperate to disembark, she persuaded the captain to lend her a boat and sailors to row the three of them to land; it was unusual to allow the ship's boat out except in emergency and she was elated by her success.

The weather had improved and little clouds scudded across a fine blue sky.

When they reached the shore they found it silent and uninhabited but for two old men in a wretched hut. Since the captain had stipulated that his sailors should row them only to the nearest land, she had to bribe them with two guineas to go the eight or ten miles on to where the old men claimed that pilots were living. It was risky for her crew: the captain might harness the slight westerly breeze and abandon them.

The sailors knew no more than she where they were, and the little boat wandered about under the hot sun close to huge dark rocks. Weakened by two weeks of seasickness, Marguerite was terrified, but her mistress remained calm. Finally they came close to land near the pilots' hut. No one appeared and, still in moralising mood, Wollstonecraft inferred that the sluggish men were so 'near the brute creation', so 'rooted in the clods they so indolently cultivate', that they were largely destitute of civilising curiosity. Like the greed of the English, the inquisitive triviality of Parisians, lambasted on her first arrival in France, now seemed attractive, 'a proof of the progress they had made in refinement'.[2]

The sailors found the pilots, but even bribery would not persuade them to take the passengers to their lieutenant, and she was forced to retain her sailors. Happily a boat carrying the lieutenant was seen heading towards them. He spoke English. Wollstonecraft immediately trusted herself, her party and baggage to him – much to Marguerite's consternation. At last the weary sailors were dismissed.

The lieutenant's house on the Onsala peninsula had a splendid view of the coast and bay; more importantly after the squalid days at sea, it was clean, fresh and smelled of juniper. Wollstonecraft's mood improved. Though not well off, his family offered lodging in a bed laid with white muslin and pressed food on her, fish, butter and cheese on white linen. They also brought coffee, a forbidden substance here, and too much brandy, which she strongly disapproved. It was, she said, 'the bane of this country'. Some years before, the English middle classes had drunk deeply but, perhaps in part with the growth of Dissent – James Burgh had written a firm pamphlet, *A Warning to Dram-Drinkers* – there had been a marked fallingoff, though the lower and upper orders were as drunken as ever. Puritanical about alcohol and associating it with male violence, Wollstonecraft assumed that increased sobriety followed increased enlightenment.

Despite this present blot on the country, she appreciated the general kindness and much enjoyed the admiration she received: the lieutenant and his wife, with whom she could only exchange smiles, judged her a 'lady' by her hands and a neighbour called her 'a woman of observation, for I asked him *men's* questions'.

After so long at sea she was relieved to have rational conversation and to talk of what so much interested her, the connection between government and the psychologies of the governed. Now the rural Swedes seemed less cloddish than at first, simple in a golden age sort of way. The landscape was sterile – she was not Romantic enough to find barren land entirely satisfactory – but she began to see its 'rude beauties', grateful for the moment-ary distraction. Soon she was clambering on the rocks, feeling better than she had since her excursion to Beverley. She borrowed a telescope and saw her old ship departing; no speck appeared in the calm bay: her sailors were safe on board.

Perhaps aware that, unlike Helen Maria Williams, she had not sufficiently exploited her stay in France for a personal record, Wollstonecraft was careful to record details of her unusual journey. There was comfort in interweaving among the political and social comments a dramatising of herself as forsaken, restless lady and sentimental mother, on the lines of Charlotte Smith in *Elegiac Sonnets*. A reader would want facts and figures about so strange a region as Scandinavia but would value even more the intrusions of her imaginative self. *The Rights of Woman* with its outbursts of her assertive and impatient personality had been more popular than the more studied *French Revolution*.

So, in one of the first long evenings she made a self-image for herself, not Imlay:

> I contemplated all nature at rest; the rocks, even grown darker in their appearance, looked as if they partook of the general repose, and reclined more heavily on their foundation. – What, I exclaimed, is this active principle which keeps me still? – Why fly my thoughts abroad when every thing around me appears at home? My child was sleeping with equal calmness – innocent and sweet as the closing flowers. – Some recollections, attached to the idea of home, mingled with reflec-tions respecting the state of society I had been contemplating that evening, made a tear drop on the rosy cheek I had just kissed; and emotions that trembled on the brink of extacy and agony gave a poignancy to my sensations, which made me feel more alive than usual.[3]

A flower, heartsease, became an omen: she pressed it in one of Imlay's inadequate letters – only the 'cruel remembrance suffused my eyes'. Then the moment 'passed away like an April shower', while Fanny contentedly played, 'regardless of omens or sentiments'. This puncturing of melodramatic self-consciousness was used to good effect in the published account of her journey but did not enter the unrelentingly melancholy letters to Imlay. To him she wrote at dusk and dawn, her tears staining her pages as she acted out roles of friend, child, lover, and mother, business agent and social observer.[4]

However interesting she found herself in nature, her business lay in Gothenburg with Backman. It was time to go the twenty miles north to the town. The kindly lieutenant hired an open carriage with post-horses – they had had enough of boat travel. He asked for 11 or 12s, which seemed so cheap after England that she pressed a guinea and a half on him, as well as something for her board and lodging. He demurred over this last, eventually accepting a guinea on condition he accompany her. They would leave the following day.

The night was so fine it was hard to go indoors but, since she had to rise early, she reluctantly retired. Sleep eluded her and she listened to the waking birds before experiencing any night. She rose before six and, with Marguerite, had morning coffee and milk. Then, because the carriage could not approach the house, they walked with Fanny over the rocks to the road. The lieutenant took their baggage by boat.

Although she had moments of energy, Wollstonecraft's weeks of stress, misery, suspense, and untended colds had taken their toll and the slackening of tension delivered a convulsion or fainting fit. She had no warning and, as she fell lifeless to the ground, she banged her head hard on the rocks, remaining unconscious for fifteen minutes. Marguerite was terrified. Slowly she came round, bruised and slightly concussed.

She had to continue. Probably she remembered Brown's discussion of convulsion from debility or diminished excitement; stimulation was the remedy.[5] So, after resting, she, Marguerite, Fanny and the lieutenant climbed into the carriage to go along the rocky road to Gothenburg. The driver was careful, but Marguerite was apprehensive of the steep drops; so again Wollstonecraft had the care of Fanny. Sometimes she wondered quite why she had brought Marguerite.

It was late by the time they reached Gothenburg and found a comfortless inn, more like a stable. No one would provide a fire or hot food since dinner was officially over. Still confused from her fall and desperate to go to bed, Wollstonecraft yet discovered when the post would be collected; hearing it was soon, she wrote her first Scandinavian letter to Imlay. As usual she did not downplay her suffering: 'how I escaped with life I can scarcely guess ... I am not well, and yet you see I cannot die.' Then she wrote to Backman, hoping he would invite them to his house in the country – as he did.

They moved in. She was relieved to be comfortable again but too miserable for gratitude: 'I am overwhelmed with civilities on all sides, and fatigued with the endeavours to amuse me, from which I cannot escape.' With Marguerite's incapacity, the teething baby had been more of a burden than a pleasure these last weeks. Soon Wollstonecraft felt herself slipping into suicidal thoughts, even as she tried to keep up appearances before the hospitable Backmans. Her head still hurt and she often longed for the quietness unobtainable in a strange home. She wrote again and again to Imlay:

> My friend – my friend, I am not well – a deadly weight of sorrow lies heavily on my heart. I am again tossed on the troubled billows of life; and obliged to cope with difficulties without being buoyed up by the hopes that alone render them bearable. 'How flat, dull, and unprofitable' appears to me all the bustle into which I see people here so eagerly enter! I long every night to go to bed, to hide my melancholy face in my pillow; but there is a canker-worm in my bosom that never sleeps.

*Hamlet* was an inevitable presence for any forlorn literary traveller in Scandinavia and the prince's bleak soliloquies often swam into her mind as she tramped around the alien rocks. Imlay must choose dependence or independence for her, knowing the first as impossible as the second. If his 'inclination' leant 'capriciously' towards the latter – as she loadedly put it – he must say so. To prove his commitment, he should promise to meet her. They had decided on Basel, but why not Hamburg? She could be there in two months; by then he could have settled his Parisian affairs. She ended her letter in a mode he must have felt ominous, 'God bless you!'

Then her mood lightened a little, partly because she received a letter from Imlay in which she detected some 'gloominess' – unlike her he would quickly return to his irritating cheerfulness – and partly because she was recovering her youthful 'elasticity'. She slept better and had healing dreams which affected her waking mind. She started to look about and grew poetic, sounding at times more like Burke's man of taste than her old rationalist self. She found 'eternity' in the liminal moment, the days that 'scarcely softened into twilight' and evenings where 'the moon ... burst forth in all her glory to glide with solemn elegance through the azure expanse.' 'Who fears the falling dew?' she asked with self-conscious lyricism, 'It only makes the mown grass smell more fragrant.' She was surprised at her better health, ascribing it to the pure air and country nights – though she did not let them demolish her melancholy. Fanny was delighting her again, 'I grow more and more attached to my little girl – and I cherish this affection without fear, because it must be a long time before it can become bitterness of soul. – She is an interesting creature.'

Her better health and the slightly depressed letter allowed her to write to Imlay more tranquilly. For the first time she hinted that she too might be sensually tempted if she lacked self-control and, in a curious aside, lamented it was her 'peculiar misery' to follow her strict 'principles':

My friend, I have dearly paid for one conviction. – Love, in some minds, is an affair of sentiment, arising from the same delicacy of perception (or taste) as renders them alive to the beauties of nature, poetry, &c, alive to the charms of those evanescent graces that are, as it were, impalpable – they must be felt, they cannot be described.

Love is a want of my heart. I have examined myself lately with more care than formerly, and find, that to deaden is not to calm the mind – Aiming at tranquillity, I have almost destroyed all the energy of my soul – almost rooted out what renders it estimable – Yes, I have damped that enthusiasm of character, which converts the grossest materials into a fuel, that imperceptibly feeds hopes, which aspire above common enjoyment. Despair, since the birth of my child, has rendered me stupid – soul and body seemed to be fading away before the withering touch of disappointment.

She no longer sought a deadening of emotion as in Ireland. The feelings she now had were worthy, explicable and right.

Despite asserting her virtue, she knew she had lost Imlay's esteem with her clinging love. Repeatedly she assured him she would withstand anything rather than disturb his peace: if he wished, she would hide her sorrow and be simply a faithful friend. She twisted the faint offer of release into an urge for self-respect:

I have the sincerest esteem and affection for you – but the desire of regaining peace, (do you understand me?) has made me forget the respect due to my own emotions – sacred emotions, that are the sure harbingers of the delights I was formed to enjoy – and shall enjoy, for nothing can extinguish the heavenly spark.

Still, when we meet again, I will not torment you, I promise you. I blush when I recollect my former conduct – and will not in future confound myself with the beings whom I feel to be my inferiors. – I will listen to delicacy, or pride.[6]

However dignified she intended to be, Wollstonecraft could not stop 'tormenting' Imlay. Always she expected more letters than she received; she counted every missed delivery in Gothenburg, every opportunity not taken to gratify her. Always she reproached, always asked her impossible questions: 'why do not you love us with more sentiment? – why are you a creature of such sympathy, that the warmth of your feelings, or rather quickness of your senses, hardens your heart?' Always she justified and promoted herself: she was worthy of love, why did he not love? 'It is my misfortune, that my imagination is perpetually shading your defects, and lending you charms, whilst the grossness of your senses makes you (call me not vain) overlook graces in me, that only dignity of mind, and the sensibility of an expanded heart can give.'

After her days cooped up in the boat, Fanny happily played in the garden with the friendly Backman children. Despite her misery, Wollstonecraft's health continued to mend. She enjoyed country walking and energetically tackled the rocks, feeling better for the struggle. During the same month Eliza noticed the same phenomenon as she tramped the Irish hills, feeling healthier even as she determined to depress Everina.

'I am more alive, than you have seen me for a long, long time,' Wollstonecraft admitted. 'I have a degree of vivacity, even in my grief, which is preferable to the benumbing stupour that, for the last year, has frozen up all my faculties. – Perhaps this change is more owing to returning health, than to the vigour of my reason – for, in spite of sadness (and surely I have had my share), the purity of this air, and the being continually out in it, for I sleep in the country every night, has made an alteration in my appearance that really surprises me. – The rosy fingers of health already streak my cheek – and I have seen a *physical life* in my eyes, after I have been climbing the rocks, that resembled the fond, credulous hopes of youth.' She had a greater sense of her body than before her sexual involvement with Imlay, feeling herself from within and through the gaze of others – perhaps she was looking more in the mirror than formerly. The 'rosy' suffusions she had seen in Imlay were sexual; she was suggesting there were other sensual enjoyments beyond promiscuous sex. Unused to the more tranquil mood, she soon returned to familiar gloom – it was an old garment without which she felt naked; yet she admitted improvement and, though her letters continued self-absorbed, Imlay must have believed the trip might fulfil his hopes.

Now she had energy for sightseeing. She liked Gothenburg, a clean, airy, Dutch-built town of canals and neat rows of trees, though she despised its wealthy merchants – rather in the style of the Le Havre burgers. They too relished their money and believed they could buy culture. They were cosmopolitan, some Swedish of course, but others German and many Scottish. In irritation at the business she had come to facilitate along a coast inevitably involved more in trade than agriculture, she lamented the economic effect of war on neutral countries. The influx of unearned wealth from advantaged commerce 'embrutes' its owners, she declared. Private and public judgements had fallen together.

Outside the town she visited notable houses and gardens, displayed as if to invite comparison. She liked nature improved not regulated, and one of the estates close to a lake had a tasteful, Gothic garden, a rhapsody of grand cliffs and flowery streams, much in the Burkean manner of Sublime and Beautiful, which, when it did not draw on prejudices of gender, she tended to accept as standard. Another, the country house of a Scots merchant, was vulgar and grandiose, its only redemption being that its vanity employed many labourers in a poor region.

The main pleasure of these coarse rich people was the table. In England this was becoming more orderly, with the meal segmented, but here it was spread with an overspiced and sugared 'caricature' of French food, accompanied by 'the constant use of spirits'. With disapproving Englishness she watched course follow course in the homes to which she had been kindly invited: bread and cheese, raw salmon or anchovies prefaced salt fish or meat, followed by fish, flesh, and fowl for two hours at least, till finished by strawberries and cream, now reeking with the smell of meat since the food had been set out together. The whole was rounded off with coffee, punch, ale, tea, cakes, and raw salmon – so the day went on, and the next, 'a never-ending, still beginning feast'. Hospitality was an overrated virtue: people were hospitable in proportion as they were bored and mentally vacant. As with sex, so with eating and drinking, imagination was necessary to refine sensual grossness. She was on her hobby-horse.

She also disapproved the treatment of babies and female servants. Babies were bundled up even in summer with flannels and rugs, never properly washed, and fed crude food like brandy and salt fish, even when still at the breast with no chance of exercising it off; consequently they were squalid, stinking and puny. Female servants were at the bottom of all hierarchies. Men struck lowlier men, who struck women, left with the most laborious and menial tasks. Pityingly she realised that these drudging bundled-up beings had in winter to wash the linen of indolent masters, their hands cracked and bleeding from the cold water, their feet bare, earning for their pain only £1 or so a year. She thought of the treatment in England, concluding that in the 'boasted land of freedom, it is often extremely tyrannical'. In *Thoughts* she had lamented any contact between children and menials; now she thought it agreeable to see 'servants part of the family'.[7] The revolutionary stirrings throughout Europe had made men less subservient to their masters, but women remained untouched. Yet her sympathy towards these wretches did not blind her to their faults. In general, Swedish lower-class women were not admirable. Like those in Ireland, Wales and America they were lewd and promiscuous. The fact that English girls were more refined and restrained proved that, with all its faults, her native country was in a more advanced state than these ruder, cruder regions.

Had she been travelling for pleasure, Wollstonecraft would have gone to Stockholm, for, though aware a country should be judged by its regions, she felt more at home in capital cities. Two of the judges on the Board of Inquiry lived in Strömstad close to the Norwegian border, however, and Backman suggested this as her next port of call. He would accompany her and they would take post-horses. His German servant could drive.

So they headed north through 'the most uncultivated part of the country' where a few log huts shivered on naked rocks. She had no fear of highwaymen or footpads; the country was too sparsely inhabited to produce such men, the spawn of city life. Again she responded with mingled rapture and disquiet to the wild beauty. The Burkean contrasts of high and low, light and shade moved her, but she did not easily give in to the influence: any increased sensation should be surrendered to pain or she was betraying love. To Imlay she wrote little of what she saw, registering her sense of the sublime only in the occasional quickening of her prose. Mainly she gave him her misery, her disappointment that he was no longer the lover he had been.

Whatever her better health portended, her momentary tranquillity was over and her letters, written at every stop on the way north, resumed their suicidal eloquence. Imlay had almost ceased writing and she was deeply hurt. Time and again she sent Marguerite to the post offices of towns they passed, knowing that Imlay had her itinerary, but nothing was there. A year ago, he would have written on the off chance she would stop; her memory was playing her tricks, for it was longer than a year since Imlay had been vol-untarily attentive, but the past and her imagined past were all she could hold on to.

Some misfortunes were so great they silenced words, she told Imlay. Yet she could not be quiet. Instead she sent him pictures of her sorrowing self: 'there is such a thing as a broken heart! There are characters whose very energy preys upon them; and who, ever inclined to cherish by reflection some passion, cannot rest satisfied with the common comforts of life. I have endeavoured to fly from myself, and launched into all the dissipation possible here, only to feel keener anguish, when alone with my child.' She would die soon, she was sure. The post had arrived. She sent to ask for letters. None was there. Her fiery brain burnt. She rushed from the room for air.

Yet outwardly she was an intrepid woman travelling with a business col-league, a maid and baby. Each night they dispatched a scout ahead to hire horses at the next post. Sometimes these were poor specimens, but mostly they were little spirited animals that trotted briskly along the surprisingly good roads. Travelling cost about 1s for six miles, cheaper than in England. The inns were satisfactory but she hated the soft down beds boxed in and spread with another down cover – like sleeping in a grave. She always disapproved too much material or soft furnishings, preferring cleanliness and airiness to luxury. She carried her own wheat bread, disliking the ubiquitous rye of the peasants, hard because baked only once a year.

On the second evening at sunset they arrived at Kvistram. As they descended a rocky mountain Wollstonecraft had a view of fir-clad slopes, wild flowers and meandering stream; her mood swelled into uneasy rapture, quickly punctured when she registered the ubiquitous stench of rotting herrings used for manure. She felt comfortable with spoilt pleasure. They found an inn under the rocky ridge; while Marguerite tended Fanny, she strolled before supper, sitting a while on the flowery bank of the stream thinking philosophical thoughts but smelling putrefaction. She returned to the inn and was lulled to sleep by the sound of water.

The next day they set off again under dreary skies. As they approached the Norwegian border and the sea, the farms, always small in these northern lands, grew poorer, with fewer gardens or vegetable patches. The flowery scene gave way to bareness, the beautiful to the sublimely dismal. It was easy to understand sun-worshipping. Who would not worship a thing so rarely seen? Probably humanity started here, then men ran to all parts of the earth in search of warmth. She had heard there were still wild bears; she watched out but saw none.

The sun reappeared but the border town of Strömstad still looked dreary. It was built on and from the rocks, only three or four weather-beaten trees interrupting its bleakness. Out she went to see the sights: a church with a steeple, a few houses, barrenness and an immense sea. Then the sun shone and the bare rocks grew intolerably hot, while the wind blustered and cut and the herring smell assailed her. Happily, as at Gothenburg, she was hospitably received, this time by the merchant Nordberg, who had made enquiries on Imlay's behalf. He was a rich man, with a fine family of girls, whose fresh sparkling complexions she approved. They could speak only a few French words and no English, so, as with the lieutenant's wife, there was much smiling. Nordberg urged Wollstonecraft and her party to stay with him and they had a good night. She rose early.

# 29

The next call was Tønsberg in Norway, where Wollstonecraft would interview Backman's former agent, Jacob Wulfsberg, who had accompanied Nordberg and Ungar on the original inquiry. He was one of the commissioners appointed to the Ellefsen case. She would proceed to the lawyers in Larvik and then on to East Risør.

Tønsberg was north of Strömstad. The roads were rocky and slow and it was difficult to obtain suitable transport. So she determined to go by sea, although this part of the Swedish coast was notoriously dangerous; rocks lurked just below the water close to the shore. The visit would be brief and, in view of the danger it seemed best to send Marguerite and Fanny back to Gothenburg, presumably with Backman. The weather was humid and the child, still teething, would be fractious on a sea journey. Wollstonecraft hired a boat – expensive at fifteen dollars but strangers were fair game – and ordered a carriage to be ready in Larvik to take her to Tønsberg.

Marguerite was terrified at parting from her volatile and vulnerable mistress. The fainting fit had alarmed her and she feared being abandoned in a strange land with a baby whose melancholy mother might never return: she must have heard much of her mistress's musings on death. Wollstonecraft was adamant. She cared little for her personal safety.

The weather was boisterous; so she could not sail at once and she had a day to spare. She could not converse with her hosts and had seen the town. Some gentlemen, possibly including Backman, proposed a day-excursion by carriage to Halden just inside Norway, about eighteen miles away. She agreed, preferring it to being alone in her room. She would leave Fanny and Marguerite but take along the eldest and prettiest of the Nordberg daughters: she liked pretty women when Imlay was absent.

They intended to take the ferry to Norway, but to reach it had to climb some of the sheerest cliffs in Sweden. The scenery was spectacular, full of precipices, chasms, lakes and sudden lush meadows, but the road was sometimes so bad they had to walk. This, together with their failure to order post-horses ahead of time, meant that their outing took longer than intended. Soon they were thankful to stop at a farm to eat a simple dinner of ham, butter, cheese and milk. The cost was small and Wollstonecraft 'scattered a little money' among the farm children.

The slow ferry finally reached Halden, where, since the journey had lengthened, they had only a short time. None the less she was eager to compare the national character of the Swedes and Norwegians, who each accused the other of knavery and hypocrisy. Declaring that 'dogmatical assertions' were absurd, she proclaimed the Swedes more sluggish, the Norwegians more industrious.

They left Halden at nine in a warm fine evening and were delayed at the ferry because their Swedish passports were unsigned. It was near midnight though still light from a sky resplendent with bright moon and loitering sun. She felt enchanted, especially as her companions did not snore – in sentimental literature snoring precluded sensibility. She was glad they slept, for it left her alone with sublimity. She felt most alive when she appeared the sole consciousness within a scene. She watched as the balmy night became a silvery-streaked grey dawn. Then she 'saw the sun – and sighed'.[1] The party returned to Strömstad at five in the morning.

The contrary wind had died down and her boat was ready. She hugged Fanny, said farewell to Marguerite, then, without sleep but with a change of linen and a dish of coffee, set out by water for Tønsberg. She had recently found Fanny troublesome but was sad at leaving her – though, with her grand sorrow, this seemed merely 'weak melancholy'. On the journey she was soothed into welcome sleep by the open boat's placid rocking. When she awoke, she felt solitary.

The voyage was uneventful though they had to tack about to enter Larvik, arriving at about three. It was a clean, pleasant town with an iron-works; after so much Swedish poverty, she rejoiced at signs of industry. Here she had no cause to lament the Scandinavian lack of curiosity for people rushed forward to study her and her strange clothes, offer assistance and find a carriage. She was touched; it was sympathy dropping from the clouds. She knew she was especially sensitive because of her troubled mind and was moved more than she need have been.

Her thoughts dwelt often on Fanny. At night in a tolerable inn she imagined her babbling. For almost the first time she saw the child's independent life in an alien world, noting that the development of inwardness she so prized made social conformity more difficult. She wanted Fanny to be a superior being like herself and dreaded the suffering implied. Moved by her own predicament as much as her daughter's, she wrote her thoughts on the problem so long harassing her. What was the value of sensibility, of emotional fineness?

> You know that as a female I am particularly attached to her – I feel more than a mother's fondness and anxiety, when I reflect on the dependent and oppressed state of her sex. I dread lest she should be forced to sacrifice her heart to her principles, or principles to her heart. With trembling hand I shall cultivate sensibility, and cherish delicacy of sentiment, lest, whilst I lend fresh blushes to the rose, I sharpen the thorns that will wound the breast I would fain guard – I dread to unfold her mind, lest it should render her unfit for the world she is to inhabit – Hapless woman! what a fate is thine![2]

To Imlay she did not send this cultural lament but, still harping on Fanny, concentrated on herself, using the literary allusions now so frequently in her mind: 'Poor lamb! It may run very well in a tale, that "God will temper the winds to the shorn lamb!" but how can I expect that she will be shielded, when my naked bosom has had to brave continually the pitiless storm? Yes; I could add, with poor Lear – What is the war of elements to the pangs of disappointed affection, and the horror arising from a discovery of a breach of confidence, that snaps every social tie!' Sterne, who sentimentally believed that God would temper his winds, gave way to Lear's dramatic haranguing of the elements.

She had wanted an inn room to herself but her hosts were so attentive she could not hurt their feelings by withdrawing. Yet she found opportunity to write to Imlay. There was always business to convey to him, so she had an excuse, but it was also a drug she could not do without. She felt supremely lonely and it struck her how much her passion for this one man had closed off other comforts. He used to write that he wanted her happiness; strange way of making it! Now he had stopped writing and she was hurt, 'Very well! Act as you please – there is nothing I fear or care for! When I see whether I can, or cannot obtain the money I am come here about, I will not trouble you with letters to which you do not reply.' Complaining loudly, she declared, 'I will not complain.'

Despite her continual misery and sadness at leaving Fanny, she felt enlivened by escape from the baby for the first time since her birth. Released from childcare she tended to cheer up; when burdened she grew more miserable. Now she even managed a laugh when she finally got on to the road. The ordered carriage had not materialised and she hired a crude cabriolet with a half-drunk driver. She was to share her seat on this vehicle with a Danish ship's mate, while his captain, unused to horses, rode behind. They made a grotesque sight and she wanted to indicate to a genteel passer-by that she knew it by greeting his smile with a broad laugh. Yet, the horses proved swift and soon she was rolling over the more beautiful, fertile but less romantic scenery of Norway. The roads were better here for farmers were obliged to keep them in repair near their homes.

At evening she arrived at the ancient, bustling, mercantile town of Tønsberg, the oldest settlement in Norway, full of painted wooden houses. The first lodgings available were unsuitable; she was then offered a place in a quiet private house, beautifully situated in an amphitheatre of woods by the sea. She took it and went straight to bed, for once silent about the soft mattress.

The next day she met Wulfsberg, now mayor of Tønsberg, and realised with a pang that she would need several weeks to conduct her business, which included a trip to Oslo (Christiania). It saddened her to think she had left Fanny behind for so long. Then she roused herself to record more observations; she was passing through scenes she would not see again and must notice everything. Possibly she also did some of her work for Johnson; if so, it gave her confidence and she declared in a brisk note to Imlay: 'I have begun —, which will, I hope, discharge all my obligations of a pecuniary kind. – I am lowered in my own eyes, on account of my not having done it sooner.'

No one at her lodgings could communicate with her, so Wulfsberg found a young woman with a little English to translate when necessary. Wulfsberg spoke tolerable English and was a sensible, cheerful man, but he was busy and could not spend much time with her. So she was more alone than usual, could dine by herself as she had so often wished. Inevitably, she grew introspective again, sometimes sounding like the self-conscious heroine of *Mary, A Fiction* lamenting her acute sensitivity; at others, more like the tasteful gentleman of Burke's *Sublime and Beautiful*, or something between Cowper's gentle, divinely-inspired enthusiast and the male Romantic poet finding his emotions mirrored in external nature.

> Nature is the nurse of sentiment, – the true source of taste; – yet what misery, as well as rapture, is produced by a quick perception of the beautiful and sublime, when it is exercised in observing animated nature, when every beauteous feeling and emotion excites responsive sympathy, and the harmonized soul sinks into melancholy, or rises to extasy, just as the chords are touched, like the eolian harp agitated by the changing wind. But how dangerous it is to foster these sentiments in such an imperfect state of existence; and how difficult to eradicate them when

an affection for mankind, a passion for an individual, is but the unfolding of that love which embraces all that is great and beautiful.[3]

Although feeling the power of her subjectivity and physical plenitude in nature, Wollstonecraft continued to wrap herself in melancholy. She now decided to avoid writing directly to the unresponsive Imlay, though she thought always of him and the sexy, rosy hue of which the morning's tint reminded her. Occasionally the two Fannys floated into her mind: her dear friend, whose 'soft voice' she could hear on the heath, and the baby, too young to question her mother's pain.

She also thought a good deal about mortality – in a more general way than when she had contemplated suicide. This was provoked by the sight of embalmed bodies in the Tønsberg church. They were worse than natural decay, she thought, a kind of 'treason against humanity'. It was an Enlightenment view, which, rejecting the dead, wanted little relationship with them. Corpses were sources of contagion; if not used as tools of research, they should be hidden in impenetrable tombs. Looking at them improperly exposed, she wondered at the principle of life and reflected on self-consciousness – 'Where goes this breath? This *I*, so much alive? In what element will it mix, giving and receiving fresh energy?'[4]

Writing seven or so years after *Mary, A Fiction*, she avoided following her question as then with worried concern for an individual immortality. Intellectually she had travelled some distance since she had sought eternity solely outside the world and been sure that the '*I*' would find a *compensatory* afterlife for all its sufferings. Subjectivity remained her concern, once aided by her individualistic religion, then by the political theories of rights which accepted the value of a personal self. Now she joined the eighteenth-century secularising effort to comprehend spiritual longing without a firm belief in a particular biblical God, an effort that would be accelerated by the Romantic poets with their notion of a cosmic spirit moving through nature and expressing itself in human minds. Although she too yearned at moments like this to make the self, the identity, transcend brain and body as the poets would do – 'my very soul diffused itself in the scene – and, seeming to become all senses, glided in the scarcely-agitated waves, melted in the freshening breeze' – she would not usually take their route, instead finding selfhood primarily in time and imaginative narrative. Even in this passage she continued, 'or ... fancy tript over new lawns, more beautiful even than the lovely slopes on the winding shore before me,' and ended thinking of her neuter 'Creator' whose 'footstool' was the earth.[5]

Such usage suggests that she might have been convinced by Paine's deist arguments. While waiting for the Terror to reach him in Paris in 1793, he had written *The Age of Reason* denigrating Christianity as revelation and system but arguing that 'The creation we behold is the real and ever-existing Word of God, in which we cannot be deceived.' Wollstonecraft believed something like this during these months in sublime nature. She seems to have felt deserted by God in her miseries in France and England; now when he was present to her in Scandinavia he came less as the idealised father figure or the severe rationalist of *The Rights of Woman* than as a being partaking of the human, sensual imagination. This imagination was a distillation of the sensibility on which she had earlier prided herself; it felt less self-indulgent, less common a property.

Tønsberg proved a refuge. She believed she was making headway with the lawsuit and she had ample leisure too. She had no guilt over leaving Fanny since she heard regularly that the child was well. She looked about her, her mind more at ease than for some time.

Denmark ruled Norway but not heavily, except in its regulation of shipping. The existence of small farms – the social unit she so approved – tended towards some social equality. When rich merchants died, they left their wealth *among* their children. She liked the custom, though noting that boys received twice the girls' portion. In general the Norwegians seemed a pretty free people, if a touch litigious.

It was a fine summer and the long days had wonderfully luminous evenings. She was out of doors much of the day, walking heartily and riding on horseback, exercise which, like her father, she enjoyed. She bathed in the cool water and watched the white sails passing the cliffs. The nights were so mild she could sleep in the fields. She visited saltworks, churches, a deserted fort by the bay, and one of only two large estates in Norway. The house was empty and chill but the fine gardens freshened her. There were pines, oaks and musical aspens; the pines dull by day, magical in the evening. She did not approve of aristocrats, but admitted that they alone had the money and breadth of knowledge to bring back improvements and stimulate inferiors to think.

At the end of July, she received two letters from Imlay written a month before. Since June she had written many times and it was strange to hear a voice so out of touch with her. The letters cheered her a little: her greatest horror was Imlay's indifference and his silence had seemed to betoken this. Any communication except the coldest and most rejecting improved on nothing. She wrote at once: she was beyond pausing for strategy.

She had been rehearsing her points incessantly; now she could take up the argument: Imlay must return to her. She deserved it because she was worthy and had suffered. So she urged her misery and value, avoiding the humour recorded in her notebooks as well as the self-conscious irony of her sublime scenes. She buried the news of her good health in customary moaning: 'Write to me then, my friend, and write explicitly. I have suffered, God knows, since I left you. Ah! you have never felt this kind of sickness of heart! – My mind however is at present painfully active, and the sympathy I feel almost rises to agony. But this is not a subject of complaint, it has afforded me pleasure, – and reflected pleasure is all I have to hope for – if a spark of hope be yet alive in my forlorn bosom.'

The correspondence reawakened dreams of domestic life and again she pleaded motherhood to justify them. Given their recent past, it was more feasible to demand a father than a lover. Parental affection could only come from 'habitual tenderness'. Were she to die, Fanny would be protected only by Imlay's sense of duty unless he worked now at fathering. As for her, had she not been a mother, she would simply have licked her festering wound in silence 'without wincing'. Imlay had heard before that this demanding woman had no wish to disturb his peace. Still she went on: 'If I am destined always to be disappointed and unhappy, I will conceal the anguish I cannot dissipate; and the tightened cord of life or reason will at last snap, and set me free.' Again she asserted her significance, one that Imlay had never denied, 'This heart is worthy of the bliss its feelings anticipate – and I cannot even persuade myself, wretched as they have made me, that my principles and sentiments are not founded in nature and truth.' She ended by demanding: 'Write to me immediately – were I only to think of myself, I could wish you to return to me, poor, with the simplicity of character, part of which you seem lately to have lost, that first attached [me] to you.'

It was not a seductive letter, but Wollstonecraft despised seduction. Rational frankness and honest self-esteem formed her mode and she could not change. Not even though she accused Imlay of enjoying the games of cunning women.

Whatever her mind felt, her body grew stronger, plumper and more vigorous. The fever nursed since her cold the previous winter and her weaning of Fanny had left her. She continued to walk and ride, bathe in the sea and row on the lakes. The last was a new, enjoyable sensation. Her oar caught jelly fish floating just below the surface: looking like 'thickened water' they intrigued with their intangibility. Like the Swedish bears, the Norwegian seals kept out of her sight; she was rather glad. (Later she enquired after the Kraken, a leviathan supposedly living in northern seas. Weighing evidence she decided it was mythical and should not be left in geography books to fool young persons.) Outside Tønsberg there were mineral springs and she took the waters. Her body pleased her: it was 'exquisite delight' to feel it in the dramatic scenery, the wildernesses and untamed confusion of sea, sky and land.

Being more confident physically, she returned to her sense of the body's power over the mind, ascribing her greater mental tranquillity to the air, exercise and variety: 'I have seldom been in better health; and my mind, though trembling to the touch of anguish, is calmer,' she admitted to Imlay. But she added the rider, 'yet still the same', for, despite excitement in health and nature, she knew she could not be happy alone. '[O]n examining my heart, I find that it is so constituted, I cannot live without some particular affection – I am afraid not without a passion – and I feel the want of it more in society, than in solitude.' She continued to arouse herself with her thoughts and writing. When she described herself forlornly, she felt the more forlorn; as she wrote to Imlay, the tears that had dried when riding and rowing filled her eyes; as she determined to confine her 'anguish' to her own bosom she yearned to express it to its cause.

Wulfsberg introduced her to people who entertained her, a rich liberal-minded merchant, for example, whose indolent female relatives exclaimed over a woman's travelling alone on business; they found her solitariness 'terrible'. Once again she singled out the 'prettiest' woman, delighting in her kiss and glance. The next day she heard the women had liked looking at her as well and was pleased. But always the meals felt too long; there was too much food, too few interesting people. So she continued most to enjoy her solitary walking along the shore and her sleeping beneath the stars on mossy downs.

Hearing nothing further from Imlay, she wrote again. She was missing her baby and, in her absence, felt keenly the romance of motherhood. So she tried again to coerce him into fulfilling the fatherly role in which he showed no interest. She wanted love for Fanny; if he failed to supply it, she would support her alone and the reward would be undivided affection: 'She must be a comfort to me – if I am to have no other.' If Imlay were not to live with them, she would stop writing and be 'dead' to him. The articulation of these impossible promises cut into the wound: 'I cannot express to you what pain it gives me to write about an eternal separation.'

Constantly she brooded on the past. What had gone wrong? Could she have acted differently when they tried to live together in London? Imlay had accused her of wanting too much. Maybe she had. But it had been difficult to act sensibly when feeling so wretched. Now she could see that she had ruined what they had by demanding more: 'I let the pleasure I might have caught, slip from me.' She could not bring herself to admit it directly but she was coming to suspect that Imlay had another specific relationship. She should not *want* to live with him in the circumstances, but she knew she did.

Often she began letters by admitting some tranquillity, but, as she worked up her rhetoric and emotion, arrived at a state of misery that must be expressed: 'Little reason have I to expect a shadow of happiness, after the cruel disappointments that have rent my heart ... for God's sake! spare me the anxiety of uncertainty! – I may sink under the trial ... I scarcely know what new form of misery I have to dread.' So many times in her letters of complaint she included the promise, 'I will not complain'.

By now Wollstonecraft might have learnt the lesson of the slow post. 'Peevish' and too frank writing had got her into trouble before. But she saw her error only when she received a batch of five letters from Imlay, probably sent on from Gothenburg by Backman. One was clearer about his feelings than she was used to. Ironically it was written on the day when she was accusing him of secrecy.

Her immediate response was pain. Perhaps she had merited some rebuke after her behaviour in London but, in view of her suffering, she had not expected it. Imlay accused her of tormenting him with her constant reproaches – he had not Fuseli's cold self-command which allowed him to leave letters unopened. Her heart must have sunk as she realised how many scolding words were sailing towards him. There was nothing to do but try to respond with dignity: 'you shall not be tormented with any more complaints. I am disgusted with myself for having so long importuned you with my affection.'

As she read over Imlay's letters again and again, however, she found that she could not sustain this response. She was numbed by fear, so disoriented that she tried to convince herself that she had now crossed a threshold of misery, an absolute point of development. Surely these letters had changed her; she would never again yearn for so much: 'What a long time it requires to know ourselves; and yet almost every one has more of this knowledge than he is willing to own, even to himself. I cannot immediately determine whether I ought to rejoice at having turned over in this solitude a new page in the history of my own heart.'

# 30

*'Self-applause is a cold solitary feeling'*

A few days after receiving Imlay's letters she concluded her business at Tønsberg, having achieved less than she once hoped. She paid her largish bill – Norway was dearer than Sweden. Then, with a heavy heart, she said goodbye to the Wulfsbergs and the town: she had been more contented there than for many months, feeling kindness and enjoying solitude.

She was returning to Larvik to meet Imlay's lawyers. No public transport offered and she hired horses and probably a servant to help her. As she journeyed she had ample opportunity to muse. The cocooned life she observed in other women was not hers and, while at times lamenting her unprotected state, she exulted in her self-reliance, the intrepidity of her lone travels in alien lands. She could never be a Mrs Gabell or an overstuffed Tønsberg wife.

Outside herself she remarked the effect of a grove of towering beeches in an otherwise monotonous landscape. She noted the neat log houses and thought on the tolerant social system of the Norwegians, caused largely by the absence of a corrosive aristocracy. The farmers with whom she stopped to drink coffee were decently unmercenary. Again, however, she deplored the endemic drunkenness, looking forward to a time when refinement would modify it. Whatever she had seen in France she remained sure that the world would continue to improve in morals and politics, and that austere revolutionary principles would help it along.

Continuing to enjoy the rural simplicity, she thought of the city-country divide. She would not herself choose to live in a backward place, preferring the 'polished circles of the world' to sublime wildernesses. Paris and London remained her norms: for all her Yorkshire phrases and memories, she was a Londoner through and through. But, having admitted this unfashionable sentiment, she recollected city vices and follies and tried to imagine burying herself in deserted woods. There she could know 'the wisdom and virtue which exalts my nature'.[1] Rather like sex, the country needed imagination to ennoble it.

When she reached the little town of Larvik, her thoughts contracted. She found a better inn than last time, paying a good deal for it. Again she judged the townspeople civil though not as pleasing as in Tønsberg. She kept her contempt for the shrewd and selfish lawyers acting in Imlay's case, her reaction suggesting that they did not like her either; perhaps they resented working with a woman. Sounding like Burke in his *Reflections*, she deplored legal pedantry and mercenariness, the selfishness that confounded right and wrong. Heartily she supported a new system of mediation being set in place to precede legal action. Lawyers or 'locusts' would diminish as people became more enlightened, she (mistakenly) concluded.

Then she hired a cabriolet, sent on her baggage by water, and braced herself for the most difficult part of her business, in East Risør where Ellefsen lived. She did not know whether he was there, but the meeting either with him or his agents would be tricky. She had found Larvik inferior to Tønsberg and was warned that things deteriorated as one went west.

Happily she found another travelling companion, going in another cabriolet apparently to a place beyond Risør. He spoke English and had reasonably enlightened views; she was glad of his company and his help with negotiating prices. Indeed she quite took to him, declaring him a person of 'warm heart'. He did not possess passion and imagination like herself, to be sure, but sympathy and tenderness were something.

Part of the way they used cabriolets, then had no choice but to ride horses on a wretched path or take a boat, the coast being so rugged. They chose the boat and in the dusk travelled down the rocky side of steep fjords, past several barren islands. The coast was almost deserted and, for all her appreciation of her companion's warmth, she felt solitary. It began to rain and grow dark, and the pilot decided not to press on but put in at Portor, a little haven of half a dozen houses under the curve of a rock. He brought in the boat dextrously, having to navigate a narrow pass through crags, and landed his passengers at about ten o'clock. They found comfortable clean lodgings kept by an old widow and Wollstonecraft slept in the too soft bed, dreaming of Fanny.

The next day rain delayed them, and she spent time studying the widow, whom she admired but suspected of a little smuggling to augment her income. Then the rain stopped and she dashed out to enjoy the sensation of her 'nerves [keeping] time with the melody of nature'. Momentarily she was happy, while always aware of underlying misery. In the *Vindications* she had criticised those who could not face reality but took refuge in physical sensations and fictional bliss. She herself had been guilty of the latter while an alienated young companion in Bath; now she echoed her earlier self, praying to the phantoms to enclose her in their 'magic circle' and wipe out memory.

Soon it was time to leave. The sea was rough and their pilot nervous of going further. He offered to return them one of their dollars and let them travel by a local boat with a new pilot who better knew the dangerous coast. They agreed and were relieved that they had when they saw how rocky the sea was and how fierce the waves.

By now she was tired of barren grandeur and viewed the coast wearily. Its unproductiveness set her imagining an opposite: the earth perfectly cultivated. Then the population would rise, maternity in excess – the nightmare again revealing the ambivalence of Wollstonecraft's feelings about motherhood. Soon there would be no further places to cultivate. The earth would fail to support humanity, becoming a vast prison. It was an endemic fear of the time as agriculture improved in England and population increased. The apocalyptic moment was some way off but Wollstonecraft was used to millennial thoughts.

A smaller prison was Risør, entirely surrounded by ocean and high steep cliffs: 'Talk not of bastilles!' she exclaimed. 'To be born here, was to be bastilled by nature.' About two hundred houses were huddled together close to the sea in such a jumble that only a quarter saw the water. They were joined by planks instead of paths, or occasionally ladders since some were so steeply ranged they could only be reached that way. There was no escaping this dismal place: even walking out was impossible. The cliffs were so slippery it was easy to fall. Anyway, why bother? What was there to see? She was no longer in a mood for sublimity and did not care to struggle only to view 'a boundless waste of water'. She longed for green fields.

Her horror may partly have arisen from difficulties encountered in Risør, but, if she met Ellefsen's representatives, her account has not survived. In her extant writing she blamed her sinking mood on the boulder-filled landscape and its dreary inhabitants. They matched their town, shut out as they were from anything that opened understanding or enlarged the heart: 'I felt the confinement, and wished for wings to reach still loftier cliffs ... I felt my breath oppressed.'[2] The primitive here implied robbers and brigands, not golden age peasants; in any case she was beginning to wonder if the state of nature had much to teach civilisation. Did she ever investigate her own vision of a farm in backwoods America? How would she have coped?

Still stung by his words and trying to sustain her notion of self-transformation, she had stopped sending letters to Imlay. None the less she wrote copiously, probably intending to dispatch some of her thoughts when she received encouragement. Writing was her only amusement, for available company was boorish, consisting of men drinking and making deals in air thickened by pipe smoke. She shuddered to think of making love to one of them. These were the most brutish people she had met on her travels and she judged that the grim scenery had helped to coarsen them – as had their main business: contraband trade. She could not resist the dig at Imlay.

She was less appalled by the ménage of a nearby English vice-consul, possibly John Mitchell, whom she visited at the end of her stay. Presumably he was a last resort in pursuit of her case. The vice-consul again offered too much brandy and his women were too 'loaded . . . with finery', but his house was open to the sea and fragrant. Also there was some talk of politics and plays. She spent a pleasant evening with the family and finished by listening from a boat to the sounds of a French horn on the water.

A few days later she left Risør, again by sea. It was not easy, for the wind had dropped and it took nearly fourteen hours to go about twenty-six miles. Landing in the village of Helgeroa, she felt emancipated from a rocky prison. Never had she been so keen on placid green fields; sometimes nature was simply too grand. She hurried on with her journey back to Tønsberg, gladdened by 'elysian scenes' of rivers, lakes, groves, and peasants in their picturesque farms. When at noon she saw the town, it felt like home.

Her pleasure dimmed at the thought that no one waited there: 'I dreaded the solitariness of my apartment, and wished for night to hide the starting tear, or to shed them on my pillow, and close my eyes on a world where I was destined to wander alone.' She moved into her old groove, lamenting that virtue and sensibility did not deliver happiness, forgetting perhaps that she had known this before she fell in love. In her earliest writings she had accepted that virtue did not produce earthly happiness – the world was a staging-post and God rewarded in another life the sufferings of this. Then in her more rationalist phase she had been sure that it could also produce earthly content if one judged rightly. Now she was unsure: 'The satisfaction arising from conscious rectitude, will not calm an injured heart, when tenderness is ever finding excuses; and self-applause is a cold solitary feeling, that cannot supply the place of disappointed affection.' She was reworking the problems that had troubled her when she had written to Gabell in Ireland. Why had she been given such refined feelings if they only opened her to misery? She had no answer. She could not consider that perhaps it was not the foundation on 'conscious rectitude' that was weak, but rather her melancholic temperament, romantic love and a philandering man. Wrapping herself in this 'rectitude', she never bared herself to the kind of analysis that might have found both herself and Imlay unsuitable to the idyllic domestic life she thought she craved.

With nothing except pain to show for her musings she interrupted them by exercise, walking herself into tiredness and sleep.[3]

*

In Tønsberg Wollstonecraft probably saw the hospitable Wulfsbergs again. Then, towards the end of August she set off north to Oslo. It was a capital city at last, clean and neat but graceless, with large, square undecorated wooden houses. She had a good reception, being invited to dine with 'some of the most fashionable people of the place'; indeed, she almost imagined herself 'in a circle of English ladies'. The company included Bernard Anker, a leading Norwegian merchant, Fellow of the English Royal Society and brother of the Norwegian financier and politician who had earlier interested himself in Imlay's case at Backman's instigation. His son, Peder, owned a large country estate and English garden outside Oslo, which she was taken to see. She found the garden contrived. Since she added 'Mary Wollstonecraft' to the names carved on an old rustic house, she was clearly travelling as the famous radical author rather than a 'wife'.

She enjoyed hob-nobbing with the great when treated as an equal, but the lavish hospitality could not stop her observing 'the cloven foot of despotism'. In thrall to the Danes, the Oslo Norwegians acted like conquered people, in turn oppressing underlings. She was appalled to see men working in chain-gangs in the streets. She blamed the social ills partly on the colonial hier-archies and partly – yet again – on an exaggerated concern for commerce which stamped everything from houses to inhabitants with meanness.

Quickly she did her business, then thought of returning to Tønsberg, then Fanny. Yet she admitted she enjoyed travelling and, displaying the wanderlust born of a peripatetic childhood, as well as the emotional need always to imagine better places and people, she wished she could go further north. Unlike the coastal inhabitants, natives there were allegedly uncontaminated with cunning and commerce: she wished to see them. But winter was approaching. June and July were the months in which to see Norway; in August clouds began gathering. Besides, she was on a journey of business, not pleasure. So she headed back.

Now on the home journey she felt a lowering of spirits. Again the image of Imlay rather than Fanny flooded her. As she grew melancholy she became careless of the body that had recently given her such pleasure. On one occasion she was indifferent to being wet until a kindly hostess at an inn alerted her. While waiting for the boat at Hull, she had remembered her trip to Lisbon when she had felt 'elasticity' of mind. She recalled this imagined state again: the contrast made her think of decline and death.

She made a detour to visit the cataract at Fredrikstad. Finding it amidst dark cavities, she used it opportunistically to correlate with her morbid mood. Why should she be 'chained to life and its misery'? The question excited her and she grasped at 'immortality ... I stretched out my hand to eternity, bounding over the dark speck of life to come'. Like her suicide attempt, from which she had emerged with new resilience, the contemplation of death was exalting.

About three in the afternoon she set out from Fredrikstad in a rowing boat, expecting to reach Strömstad by nightfall. Her guide did not know the way and the boat glided under dark rocks without any sense of purpose. Eager to order horses in advance for Gothenburg, she insisted they return to an inhabited place and obtain information of their whereabouts. When they saw a light they pulled in. She remained in the boat while her guide scrambled ashore. He was gone so long that she grew cold, wondering if he were merely slow or smoking a pipe with a new friend. Finally they reached Strömstad. It was after midnight, too late to go on. She arranged to leave for Gothenburg early next morning.

Further delays darkened her mood and she prepared to spend an extra night at Kvistram, but the inns were full, for the fair was in town. Balefully she stared at the alien merriment, which she knew would end in 'gross debauch'. After a plate of fish meal for which she paid the exorbitant charge of a dollar and a half, she set out in an open carriage through the night, noticing on her way, the drunken revellers by the roadside, polluting noble groves of trees.

After the first stage her driver refused to budge, even with bribes. The post-house was foul, eight or ten smelly people in a room with dogs, cats, pots, pans and washing-tubs, but she had to stay the night. Half suffocated by the stench, she went through to an upstairs bedchamber. Fastidiously she opened the window and took clean towels from her overnight bag to spread on the dirty bed. Only then did she conquer disgust and sleep.

Rising with the grey dawn and singing birds, she picked her way through the human pigsty and got on the road again. The weather was fine and she enjoyed moments by rocks, rivers, lakes and farms. Once she was struck by the sight of a harvest-cart with a little girl clinging to her father; her domestic dreams burgeoned. She envied the mother, who, she assumed, was preparing their meal – though with rare honesty admitting she herself disliked cooking. 'I was returning to my babe, who may never experience a father's care or tenderness. The bosom that nurtured her, heaved with a pang at the thought which only an unhappy mother could feel.'

At the end of August, after a gap of six weeks, the reunion with Fanny in Gothenburg delighted her. Once again she held the child and watched her as a miraculous separate being running about and playing alone or with the

Backman children. She was growing intelligent and sensitive, and her mother rejoiced to see a developing mind.

Delight was destroyed by three chilling letters from Imlay, the last sent only three weeks before and accusing her of torturing him with reproaches. He accepted his paternal responsibility he said; for the child's sake he would try to be tender to the mother but surely by now she could see their minds were uncongenial. She was becoming a burden to him. He could pity her suffering but her continued complaints did not arouse love.

She was appalled. The letters seemed to destroy hope of the Swiss or Hamburg meeting; she understood that, although she had considered herself changed after the last letters, she had, in fact, held to this promise of reunion. The blow was so great that from now on she found she could not easily escape her misery in sublime nature, brisk company, self-dramatising or tiring uphill walks. Even the child, so yearned for, reminded her too forcibly of the father – though once more her mother determined never to abandon her through suicide.

In a state of renewed misery, the following morning Wollstonecraft wrote again to Imlay, inviting yet more anguish by asserting what she could not make true: that she would trouble him no more. Bitterly she repeated his point about the uncongenial nature of their minds. Indeed so, she agreed, for she had 'lived in an ideal world, and fostered sentiments that you do not comprehend – or you would not treat me thus'. Stung by his honesty, she snapped that she would not be 'merely an object of compassion – a clog, however light, to teize you'. She did not need his 'protection without affection'. London was distasteful but she would return and earn her own living. Imlay should forget she existed and she would cease tormenting where she could not please.

The effort to imagine a future alone was too much for her and, as so often in writing, she worked herself into hysteria. As she finished, her whole body was convulsed, her veins circulated fire and her lips trembled. She told him so, of course.

Despite her dramatically conveyed suffering, Wollstonecraft knew she had to continue being a mother and a business envoy. She also had to be an author, for only through writing could she keep herself and Fanny. When she returned she would have to make a success of her Scandinavian travelogue. So she continued noting customs, weighing up civilisations, and forming moral and political opinions suitable for her future book. This sort of thing, she remarked, was the purpose of travel – especially if, like her, one were not enjoying it. So, without much enthusiasm she went on trips, to the Trolhätte

Canal for example, being dug to connect a lake near Gothenburg to the North Sea. It was a grand proof of human industry and ingenuity but the nearby waterfall was more to her taste; she wished it had been left to its 'solitary sublimity'.

Her *French Revolution* had been written in an impersonal style. In Scandinavia she claimed to find it difficult to note down observations in this way. She often managed it, however, and perhaps there was some irony in doing so during this last miserable lap of her journey. As she despaired of Imlay, blamed him for his calculation and commerce, so she herself became more insistently numerical, more keen to note interest rates in Norway and precise amounts of taxation. Perhaps, though, it was what she could most manage; one needed some ebullience to describe rocks and fields, to mock funny customs and condemn lumpen men.[4]

The day after the Trolhatte expedition she set out with Fanny, Marguerite and probably a manservant or two for Copenhagen, where she would seek people of real power. She was the head of her small party, making arrangements for inns and stops, horses and boats. She journeyed with a leaden heart and, hardly commenting on what she saw, passed down through Sweden, staying at cheap, moderately comfortable inns. She was not in the mood to appreciate little towns, although some compared favourably with those in Wales or northern France.

They crossed the water into Denmark. Considering the pervasive influence of the moody introspective character of Hamlet on her sense of herself in the Scandinavian wilderness, she must have been miserable indeed to dismiss the sight of Elsinor castle as 'pleasant', mentioning only that she paid 'three rixdollars for my boat'.

Arriving in the town of Elsinor they entered an inn to await horses. There she sat down to write impressions, focusing her mind on the depressing Scandinavian society, its poverty and drunkenness. Then they were on the road again, a good one, and they easily covered the twenty-two miles to Copenhagen. The flat plain had nothing to recommend it except its agriculture. All she could say was that the houses did not disgust her.

She had anticipated some pleasure at Oslo, but her darker mood prevented any surge of feeling for Copenhagen, a more important capital. It was prefaced by a dismal encampment of people made homeless from a recent fire. The sight deepened her melancholy, as did the signs of fire in the city. With what was left standing she was unimpressed; nothing roused 'the idea of elegance or grandeur'. She was disgusted to see a crowd of well-dressed people returning from a public execution; horrified, she learnt that two men had drunk the criminal's blood, an alleged remedy for apoplexy. This sort of thing had happened in terrorised Paris but the times had been exceptional.

In Copenhagen as in Oslo she was hospitably received but remained censorious. Danes were greedy and selfish, more so than their subject nation, the Norwegians. Children were spoilt; yet again Wollstonecraft had reason to lament that parents were allowed to rear their young. She was equally appalled at sexual relationships, all power on one side, cunning on the other. Men were 'domestic tyrants', women ignorant. In later life husbands became sots, wives scolds. She was on a hobby-horse: 'How can I avoid [the subject], when most of the struggles of an eventful life have been occasioned by the oppressed state of my sex: we reason deeply, when we forcibly feel.'

She went to the theatre but dismissed the actors as poor. She visited the public library, the museum and the royal Rosenborg Castle, the last reminding her of Versailles, though now she had no heart for fine writing. She admitted she might be looking at everything 'with the jaundiced eye of melancholy – for I am sad – and have cause.'

The immediate cause was that in Copenhagen she had received another careless and hasty letter from Imlay. His image was everywhere: in one place signs of his triviality and sensuality, in another of his commercial mania. Although asking tenderly after Fanny, he had continued to reject her mother. He wanted her happy, he insisted, but she gave him too much pain with her endless complaints. Could she not pause and take a rest? She replied immediately but for once did not send her letter. Even she knew it expressed too much bitterness of soul.

Then she reread Imlay's letter and felt that, though intentionally wounding, it was still not *absolutely* explicit, not quite as repudiating as the Gothenburg letters. Why had he not cast her off properly with a complete negative? She found herself yearning for this final blow, to be hurt once more and harder. Brutal rejection suggested passion and passion was preferable to indifference. She wrote at once to taunt Imlay into action. She supposed his emotionally muddled letter had been written after dining well with her enemies. Her own head was also disturbed, not by wine but by poring over his meaning. Why could he not be clear? He must write once more.

The next day she wrote again, taking further sustenance from his ambiguity: 'We live together, or eternally part! – I shall not write to you again, till I receive an answer to this.' She was dubious about the pain he complained she caused him; she had insufficient vanity to imagine it could be much. Hers was great however: 'Gracious God! It is impossible for me to stifle something like resentment, when I receive fresh proofs of your indifference. What I have suffered this last year, is not to be forgotten! I have not that happy substitute for wisdom, insensibility – and the lively sympathies which bind me to my fellow creatures, are all of a painful kind. – They are the agonies of a broken heart – pleasure and I have shaken hands.' She was sick of travelling. The journey had some purpose when she expected Imlay at its end. Now she was tired of seeing dull, ugly towns and conversing with commercial, sensual people. When she found contented families joined by affection or at least principles, they strengthened her depression. Why had she met only with unkindness? Why had she been abandoned when she had done her duty? She had a soft heart, why had she reposed it on a stone?

Despite the written anguish, Wollstonecraft energetically carried on her legal business. In pursuit of the case, she now had an audience with the liberal statesman, Count Bernstorf, the 'real sovereign' of Denmark and Norway. Since she described him as rather vain and cautious but worthy, he probably did not give entire satisfaction, but he might have helped her tackle the Danish Courts where Backman had started the legal process. She needed all the help she could get since she had received little from Imlay's lawyers in Larvik. Perhaps considering that Bernsdorf had been behind the system of mediation she had praised, he advised her to come to an out-of-court settlement with Ellefsen. She could not go higher up and he of all people knew the relationship of the law to vested interests of important commercial families – especially since there was no trial by jury. She would have been foolish not to take his advice.

Having done what she could to settle the case or head it towards con-clusion, she decided to move on to Hamburg, where she had once thought to meet Imlay. The recent letter allowed a sliver of hope or she might have found a way to return directly to England. She knew she must leave Copenhagen before the colder autumn winds began blowing.

She had met a gentleman whose company she enjoyed. They had planned to travel together from Copenhagen to Hamburg, but he had had to go on ahead before she concluded her business. She wrote to ask him to arrange accommodation for her arrival: she had heard Hamburg was difficult for visitors.

Without waiting for a reply she hired a manservant to accompany her party and they set off across the dull, flat, rich Danish land of Zealand. At Korsor they took a barge across the Great Belt to the island of Fyn. There was no direct wind but the crossing took only three and a half hours. She beguiled the time by talking politics with a German baron. The French revolutionary armies, which had started out defending their Revolution, were on the crusading offensive. They had conquered or liberated – the two were becoming interchangeable for the French – Holland and the Palatinate and by now only Austria and Britain remained in the war, which was spreading up through the Rhineland provinces. The area was restless enough already and the baron was alarmed when he heard that French armies were approaching his estates.

She and Fanny had no trouble with seasickness. Marguerite did, but in her desolation Wollstonecraft was careless of her maid's comfort. Indeed, she sometimes felt her presence oppressive, 'as our train of thoughts had nothing in common'. In the uncouth north she had come to appreciate the trivial briskness of the Parisians, but, at close quarters in Marguerite, she still found it irritating. It was as well that Marguerite and Fanny were often asleep for neither provided adult company. While awake, the city-bred maid tried to cheer her mistress by recounting funny stories of their travels, describing outlandish costumes and uncouth languages. Wollstonecraft sourly imagined her telling these tales to her French family, boasting of the extraordinary journeys she had made, stammering out a few foreign phrases and displaying pieces of strange money. 'Happy thoughtlessness,' exclaimed her mistress, 'aye, and enviable harmless vanity, which thus produced a *gaité du coeur* worth all my philosophy.'

This kind of condescension was a touch unfair. On such a trip with no other permanent domestics, Marguerite would have been acting not only as nanny, but also as lady's maid and general factotum. She had made endless trips to strange post offices. She would have helped with packing and moving bundles, with arranging carriers and coachmen. It was summer but they would still need considerable clothing, Wollstonecraft especially, since she was dealing with businessmen, and an incontinent child would want many changes of linen. Yet, if Wollstonecraft sounds unfairly censorious, she probably confined her opinions to writing. When Madeleine Schweitzer, her friend in Paris, lamented her dominating manner with equals, she remarked, 'to her servants, inferiors, and the wretched in general she was gentle as an angel'. Godwin made the same point, 'To her servants there never was a mistress more considerate or more kind.'

For the rest of the day Wollstonecraft and the Germans travelled across Fyn, meeting together in the post-houses to change horses. After the Scandinavian tongues which she had not learnt, it was agreeable to hear people talk in a language she partly knew.

The man hired in Copenhagen, who knew the terrain and heard that the wind was contrary, advised her to go an extra twenty miles on land to a narrowing of the channel so as to avoid passing the Little Belt into mainland Germany, the Danish duchies of Schleswig and Holstein. He was overruled by the Germans. Fooled by the name, Wollstonecraft expected a brief crossing. For the Great Belt she had unnecessarily brought refreshments in case they were detained; this time she had nothing and was dismayed to find that for ten hours they tacked about without gaining on the opposite shore. Fanny was crying with hunger. Wollstonecraft felt a dreadful mother.

The crying ceased when they landed and Fanny had bread and a basin of milk at a comfortable inn. Her mother supped with the Germans, with whom she now had to part. Her emotions were so fragile that every separation seemed a kind of death. She had merely picked up friends on the highway but the baron in particular moved her and she wished he could stay and travel with her. But he was desperate to get home before the French armies arrived and he galloped off leaving her more mournful than before.

The rest of the journey was difficult on sandy roads though the weather continued fine. The towns were mainly on bays of the Baltic, picturesque with their neat tree-lined streets. In them she saw a cheerfulness and cleanliness absent in the impoverished Danish peasants sitting silently in their tomblike houses. She was surprised: the Germans were vassals and *ought* to have been unhappy. If she looked further, she could probably uncover some 'lurking misery', she concluded. At Schleswig she saw soldiers and was confirmed in her prejudice about German despotism. Such men were bred solely to destroy life, she mused, but, then, was not life destroyed everywhere? It seemed to be nature's plan.

She set about sightseeing as a duty, visiting the heavy, gloomy castle of the Hesse-Cassels, empty since there was no separate reigning duke. She took a pleasant walk in the grounds, surprised to find them tastefully laid out to make winding paths under shady trees in the manner that Cowper and William Gilpin, theorist of the picturesque, had popularised. There was something democratic in a walk; any person of taste could appreciate it. The castle, entered over a drawbridge, was a mere shell, ponderous and magnificent, too big and too military. Like empty Versailles, it spoke of decaying royalty and toppled greatness. She was in philosophic mood and the absurdity of the aping grandeur of this little court made her smile disdainfully. *She* was not taken in by all this, *she* was not playing her part by rote. Earlier in life she had believed herself chosen by God for special suffering; now her significance was social, less personally rewarding but more useful and emotionally gratifying. In Hull she had called her heart 'a mark for misery'; the dignified image was painfully apt and she repeated it. It was just such original and distressed spirits as she who were 'marks set up to be pelted at by fortune; or rather as signposts, whilst forced to stand still themselves amidst the mud and dust'.

The next lap of the journey was a little better than the last, with more trees and less monotonous landscape. Also there was more bustle and, when they put in at farmhouses, they found clean and commodious stables, joined to family quarters. She liked the cosy arrangement. On one refreshment stop she saw a remarkably pretty woman with celestial blue eyes, dressed in a simple cotton jacket with blue ribbon knots. She liked the style. Thinking her the maid for she would not sit when invited, Wollstonecraft gave her money. The woman handed it to the girl who had brought in a slice of bread for Fanny, so indicating she was the mistress. Customs were strange when unusual: seeing the lightness of Fanny's clothes in a land that bundled up babies, her hostess exclaimed over her in pity.

Though the beds were still too soft, the inns were reasonably comfortable and inexpensive, the people civil and not obsequious. Her sorrow over Imlay continued to gnaw her, of course, but she arrived in the free town of Hamburg in a tolerably relaxed state.

It had a suitable revolutionary past since it had greeted the events of 1789 with civic banquets, but it was predominantly a commercial town and now in the war had prudently removed to the counter-revolutionary English side. From a distance along a tree-lined road, it had appeared fine, but, like Oslo and Copenhagen, she found it disappointing – especially as it indeed proved difficult to find lodgings. Although she determined to go to nearby Altona the next night, they had to stay in Hamburg for this one: the town gates shut at dusk and, if they sought outside, might be unable to return. After going from house to house, they bedded down in a disgusting room. The sad and lonely arrival in yet another alien place reminded her of her painful return to England the previous spring: 'I play the child, and weep at the recollection – for the grief is still fresh that stunned as well as wounded me.'

The reason for renewed anguish was that, having begged Imlay for a final letter, she had sent expectantly to the post office and found nothing. Why did she have to suffer like this? Was she not innocent like a child? Why not have its happy thoughtlessness? She wrote the words to comfort herself; they made her a sad deserted female and, perhaps she realised, a literary lady, for she was using the rhetoric of novels.

Soon she was obsessively numbering empty posts, as her sister Eliza had been doing in Upton when she awaited news from Mary in France. Three mails brought nothing. She had declared herself dead to any hope of meeting, yet there she was in Germany hoping that a letter would come and make all right. None did. Although she had declared she would never write again unless she heard from Imlay, she wrote to complain. She gave her note to a friendly captain met in the town. He was returning to England and offered her a passage, but she did not take it. Was there not still that faint hope? She waited again.

Another delivery arrived, with no letter. Once more she wrote: 'this silence is a refinement on cruelty'. She began to regret that she had not taken the offered passage. What was she doing there? Kneading her misery.

Misery had not entirely obliterated the need for physical comfort. It was only a short walk to Altona from Hamburg and, had she gone there the first night, she would have found that accommodation had been arranged for 'herself and brat' by the gentleman to whom she had written for help. They moved at once. The new lodgings were expensive and tolerably comfortable, but not completely convenient since Marguerite and Fanny had to cross several rough streets before reaching any level place for play and the Elbe had no path for walking by its edge; meanwhile the smell of glue manu-factured nearby polluted the air. The circumstance allowed her to make her usual reflection on commerce, how it deflected taste and destroyed beauty. Yet she could see the aesthetics of the riverscapes and the bustling shipping, the meandering tranquil river that bent across the flat land.

Altona was crowded with French exiles fleeing the revolutionary armies. The educational writer Madame de Genlis, once admired, then denigrated, had been living there under a false name; a former president of a French parliament kept an inn with his cheerful wife; there was a French theatre which Wollstonecraft attended. Humbled aristocrats and their emulators were preferable to a vulgar, grasping bourgeoisie.

She found good society to dine with: a civil gentleman who attached himself to her, and John Dickinson, an elderly friend of Imlay who had written articles opposing British colonialism in America. Perhaps her plumper appearance and more vital health made her attractive, for at every stage of her journey she had met charming gentlemen who wanted her company. With Dickinson she enjoyed mocking commercial Hamburgers and their narrowed minds. Commerce also distorted bodies, he remarked, 'you will not meet with a man who has any calf to his leg; body and soul, muscles and heart, are equally shriveled up by a thirst for gain.' Why had Imlay moved so far in his thinking from this admirable friend?

The country houses of the merchants sat on the banks of the Elbe – so their masters could watch the packet-boats come in, she sneered; it was easily done since, without England's window-tax, Hamburg dwellings were half-fronted with glass. Again she grumbled while being kindly entertained. Had she been intending to stay or been happier, she would have sought out interesting inhabitants – Hamburg was full of anglophiles who had read English books supplied through a contact of Joseph Johnson – but she had no time or inclination and she simply ate the food of the boorish and affluent, then mocked them and their fare.[5]

Hamburg personified Imlay in the mercenary guise she hated. Commerce was a 'whirlpool of gain', a dishonourable 'gambling' with people's lives and content. Everywhere she was disturbed by the 'din of trade'. She longed for the tranquillity of Norway, where rocks shut out sorrow and peace stole along the lakes. Here there were only the tricks of trade, the carelessness of other people's feelings. Bitterly she contemplated men's sacrifice to money of all the domestic virtues and happiness she craved. She was a Cassandra crying out against this debased modern world:

> Ah! shall I whisper to you – that you – yourself, are strangely altered, since you have entered deeply into commerce – more than you are aware of – never allowing yourself to reflect, and keeping your mind, or rather passions in a continual state of agitation – Nature has given you talents, which lie dormant, or are wasted in ignoble pursuits – You will rouse yourself, and shake off the vile dust that obscures you, or my understanding, as well as my heart, deceives me, egregiously – only tell me when?

She did not send this warning directly to its object. Nor did she send her final apocalyptic generalisation of her betraying lover: 'The sword has been merciful, compared with the depredations made on human life by contractors, and by the swarm of locusts who have battened on the pestilence they spread abroad ... Why should I weep for myself? – "Take, O world! thy much indebted tear!" '[6]

She had been living with her sliver of hope. Now a further, colder letter disillusioned her. It was the worst ever received from Imlay, harsh, without trace even of friendship. She had become simply a burden he wanted to offload. Why did she go on asking questions the answers to which she perfectly well knew? How unnecessary was her frothing herself up into anger. He had made himself absolutely clear; it was now for her to decide her future. He accepted responsibility for her and the child and would try to promote their happiness by giving financial and emotional support. She could take the offer or leave it.

It was not a surprising letter but she was stunned. She accepted there would be no meeting and that their relationship was over. Or she said she did. She would go home to England at once; with the advancing French armies, she would have found it hard to travel through Germany to Switzerland as they had planned, and the best of the summer was over, but these were not real reasons for, like Eliza, she did not much care for physical danger when unhappy. She was abandoned and weary of travelling; the continual partings from new friends simply reminded her of her greatest loss.

Before she left she poured out her grief to Imlay, recapitulating the sorry disjunction of their minds. Imlay had to say the word, not she: he knew how loving she still was. Her letters had well, too well, displayed 'the agonies of a distracted mind'. What more could she say? He had fooled her repeatedly into thinking they would meet when her business was over. Why had he deceived her?

> The tremendous power who formed this heart, must have foreseen that, in a world in which self-interest, in various shapes, is the principal mobile, I had little chance of escaping misery. – To the fiat of fate I submit. – I am content to be wretched; but I will not be contemptible. – Of me you have no cause to complain, but for having had too much regard for you – for having expected a degree of permanent happiness, when you only sought for a momentary gratification.
>
> I am strangely deficient in sagacity. – Uniting myself to you, your tenderness seemed to make me amends for all my former misfortunes. – On this tenderness and affection with what confidence did I rest! – but I leaned on a spear, that has pierced me to the heart. – You have thrown off a faithful friend, to pursue the caprices of the moment. – We certainly are differently organized; for even now, when conviction has been stamped on my soul by sorrow, I can scarcely believe it possible. It depends at present on you, whether you will see me or not. – I shall take no step, till I see or hear from you.[7]

Once more she tried to recover self-esteem through reverting to professional plans, but she found it painful to imagine herself in London alone. She would write to a friend there, probably Johnson, to arrange obscure lodgings for a few months, then in secrecy earn enough to go with Fanny to Paris. When peace came, ready English money would find a good rate of exchange and she could educate the girl, buy her a small estate and introduce her into good society. Then she herself would die in longed-for peace, knowing she had done her duty.

It was an emotional rather than practical plan. Peace was not imminent while French armies roamed Europe; more than a few years were needed to earn money for an estate and a fancy education; and exchange rates were unstable. In any case, this was promised only *if* the next letter echoed the last. So, after all Imlay's harshness, there she was, like Eliza in Laugharne, still expecting another letter, clinging to failed promises. The postscript said it all, 'I am not in a state of mind to bear suspense – and ... I wish to see you, though it be for the last time.' It was not the first time she had declared that she wished to see Imlay for one last time.

She left as planned. Her little party went down one of the steep narrow harbour stairs, then sailed down the Elbe between the banks of Holstein and Hanover. It was a difficult and dangerous route; although the river was large, the navigable channel was small and boats travelled only by day so that pilots could see buoys and markers. If the ship rolled violently as it hit the open sea, if doors flew open and boxes and bottles tumbled out and clattered, she did not record it. Her spirit of observation had fled. She was going home.

Did her journey to Scandinavia have any legal and commercial value? There is no secure evidence either way. Commission documents from Copenhagen and Oslo for this period have disappeared.

Later in autumn after she left, John Wheatcroft, their Le Havre landlord, arrived in Norway, possibly to help pursue the case. Ellefsen's defence lawyers then challenged the right of Judge Wulfsberg to be on the commission because of his earlier association with Backman. This objection was upheld at the beginning of the next year. In November 1797 the court at Arendal announced that witnesses would be called in the case, but the development was foiled by Ellefsen's defence, which argued that no new statements had been made since Wulfsberg's dismissal; the hearing was closed.

Perhaps the *Maria and Margaretha* foundered on the sharp Norwegian rocks, but, if so, no one discovered its wreck. Perhaps, though, with Wollstonecraft's help, it was reunited with Backman to whom it had originally been heading. Two days after she arrived in Dover the captain of a ship called the *Maria and Margaretha* signed on a crew in Gothenburg; its owner was listed as Elias Backman.[8] There was no mention of the missing Bourbon silver.

In all this mystery what seems relatively clear is that Wollstonecraft herself received no money from her voyage of three and a half months – except what she might make from exploiting it in writing.

# 31

*'Let my wrongs sleep with me!'*

In *Thoughts on the Education of Daughters*, written at the outset of her literary career, Wollstonecraft described the horror of loving a man whom one could not respect. After much painful experience, she was still unprepared to consider that sexual love had little to do with esteem and could coexist with contempt. When everything pointed to her need to go, she could not pull free or accept that such a destructive relationship was better placed in a sentimental novel. She deserved to be loved, she believed, had a *right* to be loved, forgetting that in her vindicating she had never rationally claimed this for anyone except children. It was not far from the demands of the girl who wrote to Jane Arden in Beverley that she *had* to be first.

In *The Rights of Woman* she argued for a transparent rational tie, believing that sexual difference should be abolished. Now she refused to apply to herself the book's harsh prescription: that sexual desire must be combated or it would undermine women. Yet even in *The Rights of Woman* she had exempted the grand romantic passion. Hers was now a grand passion but she would not allow it to swing free from rationality and she would not channel her emotions in the gendered way the culture proposed, through dissimulation and manipulation. She often assumed that she was not keeping Imlay because she was too equal and frank, and because Imlay was corrupted into needing the seductive game of Rousseau's 'cunning woman' which, though she knew such a female had entranced Imlay, she could not play. As a result she made her lover act the culturally feminine role of duper and deceiver in their correspondence. That Imlay sometimes fed Wollstonecraft's romantic errors appears from what she quoted of his missing letters.

She had been thrown too much on herself and her resources as a girl and young woman, and had followed a depressive and excessive independence with a dependence of such mammoth proportions that she herself believed it could only be broken in death. The tie with a man, an option, a dream in her austere youth, had become a basic need, the ground of her being. With Fuseli she had barely controlled her psychological neediness but refused to acknowledge sexual hunger, a social disease brought about in women by constraint and subordination she thought. She had thoroughly bonded with

Imlay, her first sexual partner, accepting the romantic belief that a sexual encounter had especial, almost transcendental meaning. She was not helped by Rousseau's insight, that adult sexuality, which seemed to require an imaginative transformation into an equal relationship of different beings, constantly became a tussle of domination and subordination. She never asked Godwin's question: 'Why did she thus obstinately cling to an ill-starred unhappy passion?' He answered: 'Because it is of the essence of affection, to seek to perpetuate itself.'¹ She was sure she was unhappy owing to improper treatment and Imlay unkind owing to bad company and ideas. She could connect her feminist resentment to family grudges but rarely her adult desire to the craving of an unloved child.

Despite the hopes of sexual identity expressed in *The Rights of Woman* and her insistence on an ideal Imlay beneath the corrupted surface, Wollstonecraft glimpsed a part of her lover's make-up: that, while a woman might respond to male neediness, he, a man, found female neediness unattractive. In being drawn to her, both Fuseli and Imlay had seen an independent woman whom they had then sought to destroy. If women had a belief in a maternal father figure representing nurturing parents, some men, it seems, had an image of the independent, articulate, maternal woman, whom they alone could silence, whom they could abuse and violate but who would always be ready for more. Both sexes colluded in blaming this masculine need on feminine behaviour.

After a long, tiring journey the three arrived in Dover. Wollstonecraft was ill-disposed to appreciate the celebrated white cliffs, seeming 'insignificant' beside the grandeur of Scandinavia. It was early October; always attuned to seasons, she felt the colder, shortening days lowering her spirits. Imlay was not there of course. Once, he had told her he would fly to any port to meet her and Fanny, and she had believed him. Now she had less reason for credulity: recent letters had been frigid; no one but a lover could doubt their meaning. As depressed and obsessed as when she left Hull, she again let desolation call up other lonely arrivals when she had retained some hope. Yet, she waited at Dover in an uncomfortable inn, just as she had at Hamburg, in case Imlay should change his mind and come.

Fanny was at her liveliest. In her anguished state, her mother could not respond to the untimely flow of spirits. She walked out alone to get away but found the town dirty.

Her excuse for writing was that Imlay might not have received her last letter in which she had mocked his insistence that *she* should decide their future. She had already decided, had told him so repeatedly: they should live together for the sake of Fanny and for her 'own comfort'. Imlay might not want this yet, but, some years hence when 'the tumult of business was over', he would desire 'to repose in the society of an affectionate friend, and mark the progress of our interesting child, whilst endeavouring to be of use in the circle you at last resolved to rest in; for you cannot run about for ever.' She painted a pathetic picture of their plight in Dover, hoping to make her old lover rush to her side: 'the extreme anguish I feel, at landing without having any friend to receive me, and even to be conscious that the friend whom I most wish to see, will feel a disagreeable sensation at being informed of my arrival, does not come under the description of common misery. Every emotion yields to an overwhelming flood of sorrow.' Meanwhile, she could not easily explain her waiting: it was for Fanny's sake, she said, and because she did not want to surprise Imlay by arriving unexpectedly.

She told him her lodgings, offering, if he preferred, to meet him on the London road. He must write with instructions by return of post to the local post-office; already she was haunting it. 'Do not keep me in suspense,' she begged, 'I expect nothing from you, or any human being: my die is cast! – I have fortitude enough to determine to do my duty ... I am unable to tear up by the roots the propensity to affection which has been the torment of my life – but life will have an end!'

She waited a while, then took the public coach to London. There she found Imlay. As when she arrived from Le Havre, he settled her and Fanny in lodgings and did what he could to make them comfortable, hiring servants and seeing to their immediate needs. But, also like last time, he seemed withdrawn and she felt humiliated. She had been scolding him; perhaps he had taken offence. Yet she had also displayed her inordinate affection, her seemingly unquenchable passion. She had painted pictures of herself as pathetic victim, assertive woman, and passionate lover. She had no more roles.

That he was trivially promiscuous she accepted, but in response to Imlay's hints she had in a recent letter alluded to a possible rival. She made little of it, always assuming her main opponent his cupidity, but now she was alerted and at last she suspected a more formidable opponent than 'alum or soap'. She did what she despised herself for doing, questioned the cook Imlay had hired for her.

So she discovered what would most hurt her, that all her analysis of love and relationships had been wide of the mark: Imlay simply had a new mistress and had set up an alternative household. She could neither hope for the domestic life of her dreams nor for a dignified separation in which she could remain Mrs Imlay while he stayed Fanny's father. Reduced from the radical experimenter of sexual relationships, she was an abandoned woman whose lover had tired of her.

As energetic in despair as hope, she dashed round to the couple to convince herself of the truth. An anguished night followed and, after months of intermittently contemplating suicide, she determined to commit it through drowning. A more convincing route than poison, it was still regarded as female by eighteenth-century cataloguers of suicide; as cynics noted, it was less disfiguring than stabbing or shooting.

Wollstonecraft always felt herself the product of defective mothering and, though she wished to be a good mother, had no experience to call on, only theory. In the event, any cultural belief in motherhood or biological fondness for Fanny was too weak to withstand the overwhelming dependency she felt on a man and her definition of herself in terms of this one person. In spite of her resolve in London and Scandinavia to be mother as well as lover, to exist for her child, in the face of Imlay's great rejection she felt she could abrogate her own responsibilities – as if his defectiveness excused her own. In all her rationalisation of suicide later, she did not mention her huge failure in mothering, that, for the sake of a passion for a man whom she declared imaginatively beneath her, she was prepared to leave her daughter motherless.

As rationalism eased Wollstonecraft to unrequited passion, so it helped her to suicide. Although Enlightenment had made inroads into conventional Christian thinking, most English people thought 'self-slaughter' a sin – indeed, it could still technically be punished with staking at the crossroads. Wollstonecraft, however, had thrown off such superstitious beliefs. She agreed with Godwin and the philosopher David Hume, who considered that suicide could be entirely rational, justifiable if it hurt no one and concluded irremediable misery. She had, too, imbibed the French republican notions of the revolutionary years when suicide became a valorous public act to circumvent the guillotine. M. Roland had been an heroic example.[2]

The individualistic view had crept into sentimental literature as well; most famously Goethe's hero, young Werther, had taken his own life after much talk of superior sensitivity, very much in Wollstonecraft's manner. He had luxuriated in imagining his dead body viewed by his beloved – 'when you read this ... the cool grave will already cover the stiff remains of the restless, unhappy man'. He died, he declared, for his Charlotte, sparing her no pain, hinting at haunting, and gaining exquisite comfort from her projected tears and tremblings. The literary event was rumoured to have inspired some susceptible readers to follow suit.

Wollstonecraft would seek to take her life as a rational not a sentimental act. Yet, when she came to write a suicide note, the sentimental models bore in on her, including that of the melodramatic Werther with his desire for posthumous power.[3] She had often prepared for this note: in Paris when she anticipated a natural death; in London before leaving for Sweden; in Scandinavia when dramatising herself in the elegiac, monitory mode of the suicide. This time it was no rehearsal:

> I write to you now on my knees; imploring you to send my child and the maid with —, to Paris, to be consigned to the care of Madame —, 2 rue —, section de —. Should they be removed, — can give their direction.
>
> Let the maid have all my clothes, without distinction.
>
> Pray pay the cook her wages, and do not mention the confession which I forced from her – a little sooner or later is of no consequence. Nothing but my extreme stupidity could have rendered me blind so long. Yet, whilst you assured me that you had no attachment, I thought we might still have lived together.
>
> I shall make no comments on your conduct; or any appeal to the world. Let my wrongs sleep with me! Soon, very soon, shall I be at peace. When you receive this, my burning head will be cold.
>
> I would encounter a thousand deaths, rather than a night like the last. Your treatment has thrown my mind into a state of chaos; yet I am serene. I go to find comfort, and my only fear is, that my poor body will be insulted by an endeavour to recal my hated existence. But I shall plunge into the Thames where there is the least chance of my being snatched from the death I seek.
>
> God bless you! May you never know by experience what you have made me endure. Should your sensibility ever awake, remorse will find its way to your heart; and, in the midst of business and sensual pleasure, I shall appear before you, the victim of your deviation from rectitude.

Like its rehearsals, the note must have mitigated her shame. As an appeal for love, however, it was surely as little effective as the letters from Scandinavia which repeatedly declared Imlay's flaws. In keeping with these, it presented the writer as betrayed, stern, moral and rational: the living man was sensual, effeminate and threatened with ghosts.

She planned to go to Battersea Bridge but considered it too public. So she rented a rowing-boat to Putney. It was night and raining violently. To make her clothes heavy with water, she walked up and down about half an hour. She paid the halfpenny toll to get on to the wooden bridge, climbed to the top, and jumped. She did not sink at once and she pressed her clothes round her closely to weigh her body down.

Did Wollstonecraft mean to be rescued? Perhaps in part. She had been seen by the boatman and noticed by fishermen as she jumped. Before leaving she had sent her suicide note, indicating the manner and vaguely the place of death. But, if she faintly hoped for rescue, she also yearned for annihilation – as indeed she had at intervals during all her adult years. In reality in the cold river it took a long time coming and the pain of drowning proved greater than anticipated – quite different from the ease of Werther, who simply slid into the 'broad embrace of death'. Wollstonecraft struggled for some time, then when she managed to force herself into sinking suffered intensely as she gasped into unconsciousness and her lungs filled with the filthy waters of the Thames.

Unconscious, she floated downstream, until pulled out of the river by fishermen, doubtless used to suicides – especially in autumn, the preferred season. The Royal Humane Society had been set up to pursue the enlightened policy of thwarting self-murders by receiving and, if possible, resuscitating bodies found floating in the Thames.

She was taken to an inn where she was revived. *The Times* probably described this incident, without knowing the infamous name of the 'elegantly dressed' victim. Its reporter found the attempt rather trivial, influenced perhaps by the Humane Society, which saved a good number of 'desponding ladies':

> On Saturday fortnight a Lady elegantly dressed, took a boat from one of the stairs in the Strand, and ordered the waterman to row to Putney where landing, she paid him 6s. and immediately going upon Putney Bridge, threw herself from the frame of the central arch into the Thames: fortunately she was picked up by a fishing-boat, and being carried to an inn at Fulham, was soon restored by the skill of one of the medical persons belonging to the Humane Society. She told her place of abode, and added, that the cause of this, which was the second act of desperation she had attempted on her life, was the brutal behaviour of her husband. In about two hours afterwards, her coach came, with her maid, and a proper change of apparel, when she was conveyed home, perfectly recovered.[4]

If this is Wollstonecraft, her brush with death made her conventional. As with female depression, so with suicide, the general opinion was that the physiology of women rendered them vulnerable to emotional upheavals and denied moral judgement. It was against this kind of assumption that she had written *The Rights of Woman*, but her suicide attempt seemed to fulfil it, as the *Gentleman's Magazine* asserted when it contemplated her act: 'From a mind of such *boasted* strength we naturally expect fortitude; but, in this instance, she was weak as the weakest girl.'[5]

Presumably the coach in *The Times* was hired and sent by Imlay, alerted by the suicide note.[6] He could hardly assume his resurrected lover into his new ménage and she could not just go 'home' as the newspaper supposed. So it was to the Christies' house in Finsbury Square, not far from her first home in Primrose Street, that she was taken to recuperate. There Rebecca nursed her back to health; given his own complicated past and his belief in the power of mind over matter, Thomas may have responded ambiguously. As for Wollstonecraft, she moaned a lot but was physically strong and her months in the mountains of Scandinavia had left her robust. She made a good recovery.

Despite her rational posturing, she was haunted by shame and disappointment. Since Imlay did not visit her, she was aware that, if there had been manoeuvring in the attempt, it had failed. Imlay would not have been haunted; her death would have had no meaning for him.

Then she received a note. It roused her to welcome anger. Imlay made his usual claim that he would do what he could to make her comfortable. She supposed he meant money but she would not take it from someone so unfeeling. She had withstood poverty before and could do so again. Besides, he was only acting to bolster his reputation. She was even more furious at his claim that he knew not 'how to extricate' them from the 'wretchedness into which we have been plunged' and that he had not visited her out of 'delicacy'. Disdainfully she replied, 'You are extricated long since.' How would he have been indelicate in seeing a wretched friend? '[Y]our new attachment is the only thing sacred in your eyes,' she concluded.

She deeply resented the untimely rescue into 'living death':

I have only to lament, that, when the bitterness of death was past, I was inhumanly brought back to life and misery. But a fixed determination is not to be baffled by disappointment; nor will I allow that to be a frantic attempt, which was one of the calmest acts of reason. In this respect, I am only accountable to myself. Did I care for what is termed reputation, it is by other circumstances that I should be dishonoured.

... When I am dead, respect for yourself will make you take care of the child.
I write with difficulty – probably I shall never write to you again. –
Adieu! God bless you!

As in the suicide note itself, here too she allowed no external authority, from religion, the state, or humanity. The 'comfort' she sought held oblivion more than heaven. When she spoke of the suicide to Godwin much later, she did not imply it was wrong or that she would never take the route again if misery demanded. Drowning had been agony, however, and she determined to avoid this method in future.

She had learnt little from her sufferings. Even now, after every proof of Imlay's indifference, she could not resist the notion that he was not what he seemed, that she had a right to him because of her love, whoever now held his body. So, when he finally called to comfort her, her obsession conquered her need to be first in regard. Imlay may have declared his new affair trivial; if so, she clutched at his remark, and soon imagined further domestic scenarios including herself and Fanny. She would accept the new mistress, and, as suggested to Fuseli and his wife, form a *ménage à trois*. With all her passionate lack of self-control, she did not abuse the woman for whom she was deserted, rightly judging the blame Imlay's. She would take her rival under her wing and 'improve' her.

Amazingly, Imlay went along with the plan, so forceful did he find Wollstonecraft's personality when they met. They even looked at a possible house. Then common sense reasserted itself. The new mistress may have demurred when she heard the agenda. Once again Wollstonecraft declared she would now leave Imlay alone: 'I am compelled at last to say that you treat me ungenerously ... My child may have to blush for her mother's want of prudence – and may lament that the rectitude of my heart made me above vulgar precautions; but she shall not despise me for meanness. – You are now perfectly free. – God bless you!' Imlay took her at her word and moved into the new house without her.

Acutely aware of the figure he was cutting, he tried to visit once more, while asking after her among common friends, who reported that she was 'tranquil'. If they had, they must be heartless, she responded. He also let it be known he was offering her money. How could he? She would rather die than take it. Yet she wondered where money *could* come from.

She was still thinking of ultimate escape to France: 'Have but a little patience, and I will remove myself where it will not be necessary for you to talk – of course, not to think of me,' she told Imlay. But she could not let go. After all that had happened to them both, all the painful rejecting letters that had repeatedly obliterated hope, the suicide attempts that had brought no reconciliation, she still demanded that Imlay give that final mythical blow that would kill or cure: 'let me see, written by yourself – for I will not receive it through any other medium – that the affair is finished.'

Then her mood altered. She continued to demand Imlay's last rejection but her anger was energising her. She needed no further care from the Christies and determined to get her own lodgings – probably learning that it was not so easy with a baby. Since her own furniture was in store, she rented rooms and contents. The move allowed her to remain close to Rebecca, but enabled the Christies to socialise again with Imlay. She wrote to inform him: 'I shall go this evening to the lodging; so you need not be restrained from coming here to transact your business . . . you need not fear that I shall publicly complain. – No! If I have any criterion to judge of right and wrong, I have been most ungenerously treated: but, wishing now only to hide myself, I shall be silent as the grave in which I long to forget myself. I shall protect and provide for my child. – I only mean by this to say, that you have nothing to fear from my desperation.'

Imlay may well have believed she would not soon reattempt suicide despite her immediate reaction, but he must have doubted she would become 'as silent as the grave'.

16 Finsbury Place was in a pleasant area close to but not in the City, with James Lackington's famous Temple of the Muses nearby, a capacious purpose-built shop selling thousands of remaindered books round a circular counter. She could walk to St Paul's Churchyard, though the area between was not the most attractive: overcrowded Cripplegate, which included Grub Street itself (near where the Barbican now stands), a narrow road of printers, taverns and lodging-houses, homes of many poor hangers-on of literature, ghost writers, copyists and indexers. The streets would remind her of what she might sink to if she did not exert herself.

She was not friendless, and, in her grief and mature handsomeness, soon became an object of interest to several men. One unidentified admirer who knew of Imlay's desertion pleaded for 'a cold second place in her heart'.[7] But she was not easily deflected. Her old lover haunted her still.

Determined to take nothing from him, she had to earn a living for herself and Fanny. She abandoned The French Revolution and decided she might utilise her misery in an extraordinary new project: writing her life seriously but within a comedy. Apparently she composed a draft, which was presented to two publishers, who turned it down. Godwin later destroyed the manuscript as too 'crude'. Grimly she found her failure pleasing: 'an accumulation of disappointments and misfortunes seems to suit the habit of my mind.'

Perhaps in pursuit of the bizarre project, Wollstonecraft asked Fuseli to return her letters and, despite his lack of response on her earlier arrival in London, took the opportunity to ask for sympathy. Fuseli gave none, did not visit and, although having no sentimental attachment to her letters, many unopened, did not return them. She did not respond to his unresponsiveness but wrote as if therapeutically communing with herself. The cynical, sophisticated Fuseli can hardly have wanted to read the following: 'I am alone. The injustice, without alluding to hopes blasted in the bud, which I have endured, wounding my bosom, have set my thoughts adrift into an ocean of painful conjectures. I ask impatiently what – and where is truth? I have been treated brutally; but I daily labour to remember that I still have the duty of a mother to fulfil.'

Imlay was also asked for letters; he was more obliging and enclosed a note with the package. She did not see it at once; viewing the bulk of her own recorded misery agitated her. She glanced at the letters and pushed them aside.

He and his new lover had set off for Paris, possibly pursuing the business of which Wollstonecraft had often reminded him or perhaps he was sick of gossip. Thinking he was going without contacting her, she furiously followed him with letters, intercepting him as he reached Dover. Then she found the farewell note. In it Imlay declared that his actions had been unambivalent and that in time she would understand. He had had to be cruel to be kind. He had acted by the liberated 'exalted' principles he had always professed and which she knew well. When she had become calmer, she would judge him more coolly. He was offering 'friendship' as he had always done.

Her first response was angry but rational, meeting argument with argument. Could not passion be clouding his reason as much as hers? Such principles as he professed led to self-gratification. Friendship was cold comfort to a lover and, in any case, it had dwindled into the vulgar offer of money. Then a knife twisted in the wound and self-pity welled out. Making the self-indulgent, self-lacerating image she had avoided in the past angry weeks, she grew half-mad again, unaware who and where she was, a passionate distraught woman buried alive in the tomb of her emotions. Again she became the ghostly presence haunting an unregenerate lover – the self-portrait of the suicide note:

My affection for you is rooted in my heart. – I know you are not what you now seem – nor will you always act, or feel, as you now do, though I may never be comforted by the change. – Even at Paris, my image will haunt you. – You will see my pale face – and sometimes the tears of anguish will drop on your heart, which you have forced from mine.

I cannot write. I thought I could quickly have refuted all your *ingenious* arguments; but my head is confused. – Right or wrong, I am miserable!

Then she pulled herself together, renewed anger and returned to refutation:

It seems to me, that my conduct has always been governed by the strictest principles of justice and truth. – Yet, how wretched have my social feelings, and delicacy of sentiment rendered me! – I have loved with my whole soul, only to discover that I had no chance of a return – and that existence is a burthen without it . . .

I have been treated ungenerously – if I understand what is generosity. – You seem to me only to have been anxious to shake me off – regardless whether you dashed me to atoms by the fall. – In truth I have been rudely handled. *Do you judge coolly*, and I trust you will not continue to call those capricious feelings 'the most refined,' which would undermine not only the most sacred principles, but the affections which unite mankind. – You would render mothers unnatural – and there would be no such things as a father! – If your theory of morals is the most 'exalted,' it is certainly the most easy. – It does not require much magnanimity, to determine to please ourselves for the moment, let others suffer what they will. . . .

Beware of the deceptions of passion! It will not always banish from your mind, that you have acted ignobly – and condescended to subterfuge to gloss over the conduct you could not excuse. – Do truth and principle require such sacrifices?

A week later, she was still writing bitterly but with less garrulous determination to control her fleeting lover. Her excuse was, as so often, that he might not have caught her earlier letter. She remained 'stunned', still within 'a frightful dream', still threatening to haunt Imlay, still haranguing: 'You will feel something like remorse, for having lived only for yourself – and sacrificed my peace to inferior gratifications. In a comfortless old age, you will remember that you had one disinterested friend, whose heart you wounded to the quick. The hour of recollection will come – and you will not be satisfied to act the part of a boy, till you fall into that of a dotard.'

At the same time she was clearly regaining composure with her arguments: 'That I have not been used *well* I must ever feel; perhaps, not always with the keen anguish I do at present . . . You may render me unhappy; but cannot make me contemptible in my own eyes.' She was blaming him for lesser faults than destroying her. He had used 'cunning', that Rousseauian feminine quality she so despised, and been mean with her family. When they had lived together she had not sent money to her father and sisters, being unclear about Imlay's needs. When going to Scandinavia, she had asked him to remember them, especially Eliza, whose appeals had been so ill-timed. But Imlay did nothing, although, on both arrivals in London, she had found him living in high style. He had not even paid one or two debts of hers as promised. If friendship were delivered as money, he was not a friend, 'Will you not grant you have forgotten yourself?' There was change here and Imlay might momentarily have believed this a final letter.

It was not and the drug of writing still controlled her. Giving in to its

power, she could begin in one mood, end in another. She stimulated passion
with her words, then, still writing, helped it subside. She felt compelled to
use the dramatic phrases 'for ever' and 'for the last time' again and again. She
could not resist juxtaposing her threats of eternal separation with plaintive
appeals for renewed closeness. As time went by Imlay must reasonably have
thought himself caught in the web of her writing for life, bound eternally to
play the villainous role in her drama of abandonment.

It was even more confusing since she gave him a prelapsarian image
as well, one entirely under her control: 'I know the soundness of your
understanding – and know that it is impossible for you always to confound
the caprices of every wayward inclination with manly dictates of principle.'
He had spoken words of love and these existed in her present as thoroughly
as in his past, '[Imlay], believe me, it is not romance, you have acknowledged
to me feelings of this kind. – You could restore me to life and hope, and the
satisfaction you would feel, would amply repay you.'

In making such an image she exonerated herself from foolish obsession.
He had led her to believe he was struggling 'with old propensities' and so
she had licence to conclude that she 'and virtue should at last prevail', that
he had 'a magnanimity of character' with which to conquer himself. So with
such manoeuvring she ended back where she had been before two suicide
attempts, tomes of passionate writing, lonely wanderings and reams of analysis:

> In tearing myself from you, it is my own heart I pierce – and the time will come,
> when you will lament that you have thrown away a heart, that, even in the moment
> of passion, you cannot despise. – I would owe every thing to your generosity –
> but, for God's sake, keep me no longer in suspense! – Let me see you once more!

Apparently, Imlay did not reply.

In *Persuasion* Anne Elliot remarks that 'no private correspondence could
bear the eye of others'. Wollstonecraft kept her letters and must have assumed
another eye. Why?

Perhaps it was simply her attachment to anything she wrote. She was a
significant being and could imagine all her works important to others after
her death. Her letters were sometimes dashed off, sometimes more carefully
composed, and, though they often ignored the peculiar needs of the recipient, they had a literary ring. Their craftedness put them as a collection in
the tradition of female laments going back to Ovid's fictional Heroides –
Sappho and Dido – or the medieval nun Héloïse's letters to her lost Abelard.
Something of the literary line pressed on Wollstonecraft and gave her courage

to send as well as write what she must have suspected would do her no good. However she was repulsed and however they were rejected, her letters had value and consequence.[8] The very concentration on herself and her virtues, the berating of Imlay as lover and failed reader – for he was misunderstanding the message – rendered them valuable documents of her inner life, as much as parts of an exchange.

The absence of Imlay's letters makes for one-sidedness – did she not keep them as he, for a time, kept hers? did she send them back to be destroyed? – but she gives enough in her answers to suggest his tenor and words. Indeed, she uses on Imlay the techniques of her reviews and the *Vindications*, the telling quotation of individual phrases out of context. But his letters were never equal to hers in quantity or quality and much of her complaining centred on his failure as correspondent. His hasty notes were far from her great symphonies of pain.

When Godwin decided to publish the letters to Imlay, he did so as part of his honest presentation of a beloved partner. Also because he admired them as literary constructions, the proper self-expression of a sensitive woman. He was extreme in their praise. Possibly they contained 'the finest examples of the language of sentiment and passion ever presented to the world'. He used the most celebrated modern collection of love letters to place them: 'in the judgement of those best qualified to decide upon the comparison, these Letters will be admitted to have the superiority over the fiction of Goethe. They are the offspring of a glowing imagination, and a heart penetrated with the passion it essays to describe.'[9]

Well, yes. But Godwin would not have written such self-indulgent letters himself and Goethe grew ashamed of Werther's sentimental, narcissistic 'effeminacy'. Godwin's sense, not at all accepted by Wollstonecraft even in her letters, that women were all intuition and feeling beside men's reason and composure helped make her a female Werther. So, although their publication would have a devastating effect on their author's reputation, it is easy to see why Godwin could not destroy them or even keep them to himself. It is just as easy to see why another person would have destroyed them – as the Shelley family presumably cremated the Fuseli correspondence.

Yet the letters to Imlay *are* extraordinary: such an open exposure of raw need is not often kept. Not until Charlotte Brontë wrote to the unresponsive M. Heger in the nineteenth century is there such another extant series from a major writer. They are also wilfully blind, partly hiding what she must have known and partly struggling to convey something that could never quite be grasped in language. What she wrote often seemed untrue the moment it was displayed in words, and Wollstonecraft frequently broke off – in passion she said, but also in frustration. Only so much can be conveyed in the language of any time; she seems to want to express what the culture was refusing her, an easy articulation of a desire both adult and infantile that was now beyond repressed sex. Would the language of psychoanalysis have helped her? Probably not, for it brings its own limitations and hides truths she allowed.

Inevitably there is irony in the correspondence. The exhortations of the letters are so frequently inappropriate as to seem grimly comic. The communications are often misjudged and mistimed. They ebb and flow in intensity, replying to moods long since dissipated in their recipient, fostering relationships that would collapse on first physical sight. Yet they are important for Wollstonecraft's intellectual development. They allowed her to consider the value of imagination, now replacing sensibility as a favoured term. No substitute for the reason on which she had so long prided herself, imagination could yet be a valued component of personality. She had not thought it all out, but was grasping again a psychological point that made *Mary, A Fiction* stimulating despite its fictional flaws: that reason could coexist with passion, and intelligence with extreme sensitivity.

# Part IV

# 32

*'There is "sophistry" on one side or other'*

By the winter of 1795 Wollstonecraft was acutely aware of her indebtedness, especially to Johnson. She began preparing *Letters from Sweden* for publication, knowing that in her observations and self-portraits she had a potentially popular work. In her first months with the *Analytical Review* she had added travelogues to her novels and juvenile-book reviewing: she had considered Alexander Jardine's letters from Barbary to Portugal, Hester Piozzi's journey through France, Italy and Germany, and J. Hassell's tour of the Isle of Wight, each assessing culture and noting picturesque sights; she had also reviewed more pastiches of Sterne's sentimental travels than she cared to remember. She knew well the hybrid form of observation and effusions and could adapt it with *éclat*. It was a stroke of genius to ignore the failure of the personal letters to seduce Imlay and use her relationship to seduce the public. In the published book her suffering would become appealing.[1]

It was a fertile time for women's personal writing, although moralists like Hannah More warned against 'egotism'. In her earlier books, whatever their tenor, Wollstonecraft had stressed intellectual merit; in this new one, she would openly declare herself the heroine and insist on the value of the personal – she would allow 'feeling to be my criteria' and her remarks and reflections would flow 'unrestrained'. Other contemporary writers were doing the same. Perhaps it was her location close to Lackington's vast bookshop that brought to mind his recent self-promoting *Memoirs* (1791), in which he had declared his peculiar individuality – 'I, great I, the hero of each tale', a phrase she quoted in her 'Advertisement'. Among women there was even more autobiographical activity. Charlotte Smith was referring to her unhappy life in her novels to mixed acclaim and censure, while Mary Hays was about to scandalise the public by using actual love letters in fiction. Wollstonecraft did not go so far, and it was the secrecy of her work – the affair with Imlay is nowhere described, any more than the legal business – that formed much of its attraction. In the personal letters Wollstonecraft had insisted on her openness; the published book, declaring itself open, gained much power through secrecy. Unlike Hays, she would not be part of a real-life epistolary couple in the mode of Richardson and Rousseau – only *her* side of the story would be given.

Possibly her rereading of her letters suggested the limitations of her frank self-image, as well as the display of neediness that screamed from their pages. So, when she prepared the work, she allowed the absence of Imlay to recall powerful stereotypes: he became the villain from the most popular genre, Gothic romance. Unlike the fictional villains, however, he was retreating rather than pursuing his lady. She, of course, became the maiden with all the ethical power of the victim.

The goal of her journey, the defeat of Ellefsen, does not appear in the book, but perhaps something of Ellefsen's image seeps through the portrait of the unscrupulous Imlay. For herself she also exploited the more conventional image of the desolate woman and mother, something closer to Smith in *Elegiac Sonnets*. In confessions by women who had fallen beyond the pale, motherhood screened notoriety; in the sentimental late eighteenth century, a maternal body might obliterate a sinful, sexual one. Very occasionally in her personal letters Wollstonecraft had feared boring her readers with her misery; the remedy here was to add melodrama. She could translate suffering into care for a child and lament for a lost domestic paradise while just hinting at sexual abandonment. Through motherhood too she could compensate for her unpopular treatment of Marie Antoinette by sympathising with another royal mother – whom Imlay had also venerated: Caroline Matilda, sister of the English king, George III.[2] Matilda had married the debauched, mentally defective Danish king Christian VII and had tried to be an enlightened mother in his backward court. Together with her lover, the German physician Struensee, she had helped introduce liberal reforms to Denmark until both were overthrown by a reactionary establishment. She was imprisoned and Struensee executed. For Wollstonecraft, her fate mirrored the suffering of all well-meaning women and mothers who inspired hatred in the illiberal: 'Poor Matilda! Thou hast haunted me ever since my arrival; and the view I have had of the manners of the country, exciting my sympathy, has increased my respect for thy memory!'[3] Finally, in her self-image she exploited the theme of solitude so powerfully conveyed by Rousseau in his *Solitary Walker*. The withdrawing and loneliness that caused her such pain in Ireland, and indeed often in Scandinavia according to her letters to Imlay, here became a Rousseauian quest for a higher state of consciousness and self-knowledge.

Responding to such attractions the public *was* seduced by *Letters from Sweden* and favourably compared its sensitive author with the strident rationalist of *The Rights of Woman*. The young would-be writer, Amelia

Alderson, wrote enthusiastically to Wollstonecraft, 'I remember the time when my desire of seeing you was repress'd by fear – but as soon as I read your letters from Norway, the cold awe which the philosopher had excited, was lost in the tender sympathy call'd forth by the *woman* – I saw nothing but the interesting creature of feeling, & imagination'.[4] Rather ambiguous praise, Wollstonecraft must have thought. Other women were more censoriously aware of disparity: Anna Seward was surprised that the author of *The Rights of Woman* should, 'beneath the sense of inflicted cruelty, perfidy, and ingratitude, give way to those expressions of passionate and desponding tenderness, which we find so frequent in her tour. If her system could not steel her own heart, as it seeks to fortify that of her sex in general, we should at least have expected her to conceal the weakness, whose disclosure evinced the incompetence of all her maxims.'[5]

Within her old male circle in London the book made a stir – as it should for, whatever its genesis in personal sadness, it was marking Wollstonecraft's movement with the times, adding to her Enlightenment radicalism that inner concern, that brooding self-consciousness that was becoming the fashion in high English culture.[6] Godwin, who had been so repulsed by the garrulous vindicator at Johnson's, was rapturous: 'If ever there was a book calculated to make a man in love with its author, this appears to me to be the book.' 'Calculated' was an ironic word: it was part of the feminine myth that, when women were most seductive, they were the least calculating.

Despite the sentimental appeal of the work, the bulk was in fact about commerce and politics. With a political reputation to sustain, Wollstonecraft cleverly combined her maternal image with a masculine subject matter. The work ended with appendices on military numbers, interest rates, and Norwegian taxation. Caught between feudalism and Enlightenment, the Scandinavian countries allowed her to observe their economic systems and contrast them with those of England and France. When she saw the old tyranny of aristocracy in Norway, she noted the need for economic fuel, although, echoing her observations in *The French Revolution*, she remarked: 'England and America owe their liberty to commerce, which created a new species of power to undermine the feudal system. But let them beware of the consequence; the tyranny of wealth is still more galling and debasing than that of rank.' When she commented on idealistic revolutionaries failing through lack of maturity, she thought no doubt of France and Imlay, rarely it seems of her own would-be revolutionary private life.

Given her financial predicament, Wollstonecraft was especially pleased with her book's success when Johnson published it early in 1796. He added to it a new edition of *The Rights of Woman*, perhaps hoping it would be carried by this gentler, more appealing work. With literary acclaim, her self-esteem, dented by rejection, began to mend: she was a unique professional writer again, earning her 'independence'. Reviews were heartening and the book achieved continental currency, being swiftly translated into Swedish, German, and Dutch.[7] The future poet laureate, Southey, said it made him fall in love with 'a cold climate, and frost and snow, with a northern moonlight'.[8] An imaginative triumph since there was no snow in the book.

*Letters from Sweden* was not entirely cathartic; Wollstonecraft's emotions still betrayed her when she thought of her retreating lover. At the beginning of the new year she remained determined to take Fanny to France whatever the cost, and leave her there when she suffered her expected early death. Paris cannot have been inviting though: prices were still rocketing out of control and the new rich under the Directory were flaunting their wealth. In this time of inegalitarian misery, her old acquaintance Babeuf tried, with the help of a Jacobin remnant, to act out his communistic ideal of an equal society. He was betrayed to the government, now moving in quite another direction, and executed.

Yet in England her position was uncomfortable: she knew she would be almost friendless if her real state were known and that it was only through Imlay's silence that she could pass as a married woman. She wanted desperately to confide, but in whom could she trust? From her sisters she remained estranged. So she turned to new people like Archibald Hamilton Rowan, her Paris acquaintance, now in America. It was a measure of her continuing need that she wrote so openly to a comparative stranger who had not written to her. Rowan had seen her as a 'wife' in Paris and been so impressed with her description of Imlay that he wished to meet him. She had to destroy this image.

In America Rowan had met Charles; together they became involved in a calico mill. Writing to him might elicit news of her brother, but her most salient need was comfort. She was frank about her misery – 'I am unhappy – I have been treated with unkindness ... even cruelty' – but a little guarded about exactly what had happened: 'I have been very ill – Have taken some desperate steps'. She left her 'agitated hand', an 'incoherence' of style, and a self-weariness to communicate her state: 'I live, but for my child ... there is nothing good in store, my heart is broken'. Rowan had his own troubles with money and an uncomprehending wife who did not see why he sacrificed so much for feebly-held ideals and he found it difficult to answer this *cri de coeur* although it touched his heart. He did not reply.

Wollstonecraft sent similar moanings and pleas for comfort to her Swedish admirer in France, the Graf von Schlabrendorf, who had realised his romantic feelings for her too late. Again she got nothing back.

Without the solace she sought she was none the less moving onwards and, at last, she managed a real break with Imlay.

He had returned from Paris at the end of February and one evening, despite her friend Rebecca's best endeavours to head off an encounter, she met him at the Christies' house. Since she had Fanny with her, she may have planned the meeting, unable to resist a chance of tormenting herself. With other company present, Imlay suggested a private talk, and, as ever when faced with Wollstonecraft, he wavered and trimmed; he even hinted that reconciliation might be possible. Her hopes soared at his 'gentleness' and the pair agreed to dine next day.

Disappointment inevitably followed. The night apart firmed Imlay's resolve; Wollstonecraft was persuaded to leave London for a time.

She went to her old friend Mrs Cotton in rural Berkshire near Maidenhead. Mrs Cotton was an enthusiastic, sensitive lady, an acquaintance of all the sisters, possibly made during their time in Newington Green. Wollstonecraft had much in common with her and she in turn valued her famous friend. She offered appropriate, soothing companionship. In Berkshire Wollstonecraft had no chance of an arranged or haphazard meeting with Imlay and was distant from those who knew more than they should about her personal life. In the gentle landscape of green fields and slow-moving river, she learnt more moderation of response than she had been mistress of in the sublime and lonely wilderness of Scandinavia.

Mrs Cotton introduced her to a neighbouring couple, Sir William and Lady East living at the grand modern house, Hall Place, in Burchetts Green, Hurley. Happily, they did not display the damp connubiality so irritating in the Gabells or the frivolity of the Kingsboroughs. Lady East was even more fascinated with her bodily symptoms than the younger Wollstonecraft had been, and the pair might have exchanged views on the value of bathing, rhubarb grains and camphor julip for headaches and stomach pains. Both Sir William and Lady East had read Paine and Helen Maria Williams, but not the *Vindications* when they were first published; probably they knew little of metropolitan scandals or of scandalous authors.[9]

Given her interest in education, perhaps Sir William mentioned the success of his own recalcitrant son Gilbert, who had preferred dancing to Virgil as a child but who, through the prudent management of George and Cassandra Austen, had managed the gentlemanly route through Oxford. It is just conceivable that the neighbouring gentry, the Leigh-Perrots of Scarlets, aunt and uncle of Jane Austen, visited the Easts during these weeks and met the melancholy guest. If so, it might have been through them or the Easts that Jane Austen came to be acquainted with Wollstonecraft's life and be confirmed her sense of the danger (and compelling power) of indulged feeling.[10]

The visit to Berkshire was the right medicine. Long walks improved her mood while a discouraging and self-satisfied letter from Imlay, forwarded by Rebecca Christie, may have strengthened her resolve to sustain her new calm. Imlay found her indelicate and himself forbearing; she knew whom she thought 'indelicate'. When, after a month away, she returned to Finsbury Place in March, she accepted the hopelessness of any relationship. Now she had the courage to respond appropriately – though even at this last gasp she maintained intact her sense of superior virtue:

> You must do as you please with respect to the child. – I could wish that it might be done soon, that my name may be no more mentioned to you. It is now finished. – Convinced that you have neither regard nor friendship, I disdain to utter a reproach, though I have had reason to think, that the 'forbearance' talked of, has not been very delicate. – It is however of no consequence. – I am glad you are satisfied with your own conduct.
>
> I now solemnly assure you, that this is an eternal farewell. – Yet I flinch not from the duties which tie me to life.
>
> That there is 'sophistry' on one side or other, is certain; but now it matters not on which. On my part it has not been a question of words. Yet your understanding or mine must be strangely warped – for what you term 'delicacy' appears to me to be exactly the contrary. I have no criterion for morality, and have thought in vain, if the sensations which lead you to follow an ancle or step, be the sacred foundation of principle and affection. Mine has been of a very different nature, or it would not have stood the brunt of your sarcasms.
>
> The sentiment in me is still sacred. If there be any part of me that will survive the sense of my misfortunes, it is the purity of my affections. The impetuosity of your senses, may have led you to term mere animal desire, the source of principle; and it may give zest to some years to come. – Whether you will always think so, I shall never know.
>
> It is strange that, in spite of all you do, something like conviction forces me to believe, that you are not what you appear to be.
>
> I part with you in peace.

She had been declaring stoutly that she would die rather than take money from a man who withheld love, but the reality of her own and Fanny's situation did not allow heroics. She had published nothing for many months. Recently she had had success with *Letters from Sweden*, but she would have to write much more to pay her debts. So, weighing sense against sensibility, she accepted a bond from Imlay, strictly for Fanny.

Perhaps in her heart of hearts she wanted a link. In those first weeks after she formally ended her relationship she must have felt naked without her old pain. Such prolonged misery had put her on a different level from ordinary keepers of houses and raisers of children. Then she saw Imlay by chance on the New Road (Euston Road near King's Cross). He was on horseback, she on foot; he dismounted and walked beside her. To a spectator ignorant of the past they were ordinary acquaintants chatting amiably. All passed calmly and she was surprised she felt so little after such turbulent passion.

Yet her letters refused this neat closure. In May, long after the final break, she wrote again to von Schlabrendorf, open about her misery and Imlay's failure. She had more reason than with Rowan[11] to suppose he might not have received her earlier appeal, for continental Europe continued in chaos: 'I think you would have answered my letter had you received it – for I wrote you in quest of your comfort and I am sure you would not have neglected a wounded spirit.' She always found von Schlabrendorf congenial and his own gentle disasters in personal relationships united them. Both were lonely: 'the attention of friendship is a moral want that torments us both. I was led to expect that I had found it, only to be cruelly deceived ... The man on whom I relied with the utmost confidence has betrayed me, used me ill,[12] dishonourably – and ceasing to esteem him I have almost learned to hate mankind.'

While Wollstonecraft was fighting to accept romantic rejection, an old acquaintance and admirer, Mary Hays, was struggling less successfully close by in Hatton Garden. At the end of 1795 Joseph Johnson asked Wollstonecraft to invite Mary Hays to dine. She had just moved from her mother's home south of the river to live alone in lodgings, and needed new society. She was about to be one of his authors and would be useful as a jobbing reviewer – though, having an annuity of £70 per annum, she was less needy than Wollstonecraft. The encounter of the two women led to a sense of mutual misery and no doubt much discussion of sexual relationships in a corrupt world.

Hays's misfortune was to have fallen in love with an admirer of her pamphlet on public worship, the leading radical Unitarian, William Frend. He had just lost his Cambridge fellowship (and been tried for blasphemy) for refusing to retract his opinion that civil and religious policies needed reforming and that the French Revolution was a fine stimulus. He had admired Hays before he met her, impressed that a woman could think so soundly, but he never shared her intense passion – though there is evidence he avoided commitment partly for money reasons. In a series of awkward self-revelatory letters to him she poured out her sorrow at his obtuseness and her predicament as a genteel lady caught in a 'magic circle' of convention, repression and desire. Like Wollstonecraft with Imlay, she aimed to persuade Frend into rational love. He was unmarried, where was the impediment?

She also wrote copiously to Godwin, to whom she had recently introduced herself as one '[d]isgusted with the present constitutions of civil society'. She had, she declared, been raised from 'a depression of spirits' by a 'few puissant and heavenly endowed spirits', who included Godwin. Initially she had written to borrow his book, too expensive to buy (*Political Justice* cost three guineas). Godwin lent it, was helpful and called, alone or with his close friend Holcroft. Yet he did not quite relish his role as respondent to the 'free disclosure of . . . opinions in the epistolary mode.'[13] Soon he had to apologise for inattentiveness to Hays's romantic confessions: 'I always admire your letters, &, when I read them, am sorry that invincible circumstances preclude me from having often the pleasure of seeing you. I am sorry too, that the nature of my avocations restrain me from entering into regular discussions in the epistolary mode.'[14]

To help Hays, Godwin tried to convince her of the culturally conditioned nature of her hysterical responses, the self-destructiveness of romantic passion, and the danger of self-indulgent female sensibility, the kind of thing Wollstonecraft preached in *The Rights of Woman*. In turn, Hays argued that Godwin had not sufficiently considered the economic and psychological dependence of women when he composed his rational social systems and that male philosophy needed reforming to take into account the 'feminine' aspects of life. Abstract principles could not always govern people and it was foolish to underestimate individual feeling.

Some of Hays's letters, written to Godwin early in 1796 and mentioning Wollstonecraft, form comments on the correspondence with Imlay: in an extreme way they underline the predicament of a thinking woman of the 1790s, intellectually emancipated yet socially and emotionally constrained. They also suggest how useful to a rejected lover was the notion of commerce and greed, and how melodramatic was the only style in which women could express personal feeling. Beside them Wollstonecraft's overwrought responses seem almost restrained:

You think me incapable of heroism, I fear so do I, yet, I am call'd to great exertions – I do not repine at trifles – believe me, I do not, but a blow that has been suspended over my head, for days & weeks, months, years, has at length descended, *& still I live*, & tho' my tears will flow, in spite of my struggles to suppress them, they are not tears of blood – & my heart, tho' pierced thro' & through is not broken! – *My friend*! Come & teach me how to be happy – I am wearied with misery – all nature is to me a blank – I shall, I doubt, never be a philosopher – a barbed & invenomed arrow, rankles in my bosom – philosophy will not heal the festering wound – But you, tho' a philosopher yourself, will not despise me, you have ever shown a humane & tender consideration for my feelings, it is a proof of the sensitivity & of the goodness of your heart, & that a dear friend, the other evening, affected to [?] upon it, she has told me that it has raised you greatly in her esteem – I was pleased to see her so lively tho' I know the gaiety to be very superficial. She had been a great sufferer & with all her strength of mind, her suffering had well nigh proved fatal – happy for her, & happy for me she is, yet, preserved! I shall ever love her, for her affectionate sympathies, she has a warm & generous heart! Yes, I have many excellent friends, & I am sensible of their value – &, yet, ungrateful that I am – *I am exquisitely miserable!* ...

Torn by conflicting passions, & wasted in anguish – my life is wasting away, a burthen to myself, a trouble to those who love me, & worthless, I doubt, to everyone! ...[15]

A month later, in February, when Wollstonecraft was rehearsing her grief to Rowan, Hays was becoming philosophical about her misery, needing to calm her mind by abstracting principles from her woe. Like her friend she looked bitterly at the independence so painfully achieved. Her predicament was Wollstonecraft's with Fuseli – but with awareness of her sexual needs: 'I am a woman, I mean by this, that education has given me a sexual character.' With Wollstonecraft, Hays hated the idea of superior but sensual men being captivated by trivial and pretty women rather than those 'of sensibility & virtue'. Again like Wollstonecraft with Imlay, her comfort was that the retreating Frend was not what he seemed.

Mine, I believe, is almost a solitary madness in the 18th century – It is not on the altars of love, but of gold, that men now come to pay their offrings. The man who has sacrificed me, if I am not much mistaken, is a votary at the shrine of Plutus, & has had some struggles to ice his heart & stifle his humanity. Why call woman, miserable, oppres'd, & impotent, woman, crushed & then insulted – why call her to an 'independence' which not nature, but the accursed & barbarous laws of society have denied her? ... It is from chastity having been render'd a sexual virtue, that all these calamities have flow'd ... My conduct was not altogether so insane as I have been willing to allow. *It is certain, that, cou'd I have gain'd the end proposed my happiness wou'd have been increased* – I will say, with my friend Mrs

W, 'It is necessary for me to love & admire or I sink into sadness'.

Still she nursed her pain. Frend was, she knew, not all excellence but, if she had 'won him to her arms', she could have elevated and purified him. Now she must become a 'comfortless, solitary, shivering, wanderer' like her friend in Scandinavia, but her wandering was the more painful for being in London and in the 'wilderness of human society'. She had not quite the self-esteem of Wollstonecraft, but could still dramatise herself as a person of extraordinary emotional consequence, whose thwarting was dangerous. Like Imlay, who was to be haunted by his dead lover, Frend would know he had been stabbed or criminalised by the passionate lady he had rejected:

I cou'd have encreas'd the felicity & improvement of a small circle of indi-viduals – & this circle, spreading wider & wider, wou'd have operated towards the grand end, general utility … I am put out, & now perhaps shall do mischief – The placid stream, turn'd out of its channel, lays waste the meadows. The man I too tenderly loved, appears to me at this moment a great criminal, on my principles of morality – He wou'd not receive & confer happiness – such an opportunity may never present itself to him again – He is degrading himself – he will sink yet lower, he has laid waste my mind, & he has, or I much mistake, given a mortal stab to his own.

Godwin found this more than he could bear, as apparently did Mary Woll-stonecraft when she returned from her convalescence with Mrs Cotton and received similar complaint. The time that was just beginning to heal her was not yet working on Mary Hays, who had no child to divert her and no memory of sexual fulfilment. Wollstonecraft firmly addressed her friend:

Pray do not make any more allusion to painful feelings, past and gone – I have been most hurt at your not *labouring* to acquire more contentment; for true it is wisdom, I believe, to extract as much happiness, as we can, out of the various ills of life – for who has not cause to be miserable, if they will al[l]ow themselves to think so?

This was rich coming from Mary Wollstonecraft.[16]

For recovery she had one material advantage over Hays: she had grown more handsome over the last months. Hays described her as tall, well-proportioned, full of form, with pleasing, expressive features and soft voice; when she and Hays were caricatured, Hays was mocked as repellent, Woll-stonecraft as sexually alluring.[17] Motherhood became her: the severe angular woman of the Roscoe portrait had softened and rounded. In romantic terms her passionate past did her more service than authorship of *The Rights of Woman*; probably a good number of men dreamt of the amorous lady philosopher. Amelia Alderson reported a man's describing her as a 'very *voluptuous* looking woman', where poor Mary Hays remained 'old, ugly, & ill-dressed'.[18] Also, Hays had bad luck with men. One cold morning Godwin called unexpectedly, since both had declared they despised formal etiquette. He found her inelegantly dressing in front of her sitting-room fire.

Proof of Mary Wollstonecraft's attractions comes in a bizarre love-letter addressed about this time to 'Mrs Imlay'. The neat handwriting resembles that of the thrice widowed Holcroft, possibly the earlier suitor mentioned in her letters, a man in his early fifties. A close friend of Godwin and enemy of indissoluble unions – in his novel *Anna St Ives* he proclaimed the absurdity of binding 'body to body' and 'soul to soul' – he was on the lookout for a new relationship and perhaps responded to the desire for domestic affections expressed in *Letters from Sweden*. Although he had recently told his elderly father he had had 'marriage enough for one man', his reason was that 'the woman whom I could truly esteem is not easily found; and, if the discovery were made, it would be strange if she were wholly disengaged.'[19] Now he was sending the presumably married Mrs Imlay a love-song, beginning 'Eliza, when, with female art, / You seem to shun and yet pursue . . .' which she had requested. These lines had been written by the portly Peter Pindar (John Wolcot) to celebrate the virtue of the writer and former actress Elizabeth Inchbald, whom Holcroft himself – along with many other men – had courted. The letter accompanying it veers wildly between sentiment and pastiche, as occasionally do Holcroft's novels and plays – in earlier reviews Wollstonecraft herself mentioned his 'highly wrought' style, 'over-wrought' characters and 'fustian'.

The letter began solemnly enough, declaring that the writer and she ought to act rationally to secure happiness. She had been on his mind for some time, although he was haunted by the notion that her heart was 'prepossessed . . . irrevocably given to another'. But he could repress his feelings no longer:

I think I discover the very being for whom my soul has for years been languishing: one who, the woman of reason all day, the philosopher that traces compares and combined facts for the benefit of present and future times, in the evening becomes the playful and passionate child of love: one who would realise all the fond raptures of my fanciful and ardent youth and by the very remembrance of whom I perceive myself restored as it were to all my boyish simplicity: One in whose arms I should encounter all that playful luxuriance, those warm balmy kisses, and that soft yet eager and extatic assaulting and yielding known only to beings that seem purely etherial: beings that breath and imbibe nothing but soul.

Yes: you are this being … Well, well: I never touched your lips; yet I have felt them, sleeping and waking, present and absent. I feel them now: and now, starting in disappointment from the beatific trance, ask why I am forbidden to fly and fall on your bosom and there dissolve in bliss such as I have never known, except in reveries like this … consider the subject well: answer me, and tell me why I should not; or bid me once more come and try if this Lover's Millenium may not yet be ours.[20]

Still grieving – the letter was sent in January – Wollstonecraft was unprepared for such an amorous millennium, but, if she knew the anonymous writer to be Holcroft, she handled the situation with unusual tact. Two days later, the miserable Mary Hays tried to cheer up her equally gloomy friend with a small party at her lodgings which included Holcroft – perhaps it was even his idea. The party went smoothly and had the advantage of reintroducing Wollstonecraft to Holcroft's friend, William Godwin.

# 33

*'One sex did not take the priority'*

Godwin had not been overjoyed by the invitation, but, perhaps for Holcroft's benefit, he replied politely. He would be 'happy to meet Mrs Wollstonecraft' despite the fact that she had 'amused herself with depreciating me'.[1] He went to tea and the two got on well. Probably to Hays's disappointment, her friend did not descant gloomily on female wrongs as at Johnson's disastrous dinner.

Wollstonecraft was better disposed to Godwin than he to her. With the publication of *Political Justice* and his novel *Caleb Williams*, combining horror of class oppression with distaste for a superficial radicalism in the lower orders, he had become one of the capital's leading intellectuals, with a wide circle of male and female friends. Like Paine he never really considered the situation of women in the utopias he imagined or confronted the disruptive power of sexuality – as Hays argued. Yet he appealed to Wollstonecraft with his pacifism, for he combined revolutionary principles with refusal to condone *any* violence, legal or revolutionary; after some wavering in France, she was again sympathetic to this attitude. Also Hays found him considerate to her broken heart; it endeared him to her similarly wounded friend.

At forty, shortish, large-headed, long-nosed and pedantic, with the unpowdered and parted revolutionary hairstyle he had recently adopted, Godwin had not the immediate attractions of the tall, handsome and easy Imlay, though he occasionally arrayed himself in green coat, crimson under-waistcoat and sharp-toed, red morocco slippers.[2] He was both proud and diffident, with the loud, unmodulated peal of laughter of the constrained. He had been born in Wisbech in the Cambridgeshire Fens to a poor Dissenting minister's family, seventh of thirteen children, only five of whom reached middle age. There were resemblances with Wollstonecraft: he too resented being put out to a wet-nurse; he too survived an awful, violent childhood with a sense of his own extraordinary significance and now felt responsible for most of the rest of his family; he too had progressed from hack writer to respected author; he too was sometimes reluctant to compromise independence with good manners. The differences were as salient. While Wollstonecraft was reading Beverley doggerel, Godwin was suffering James Janeway's accounts of children's joyful deaths. Where Wollstonecraft had tumbled up with some schooling, Godwin had been much educated in a day-school, a private house, and finally, for five years, at the Dissenting Academy at Hoxton, which taught the rigorous analysis of language and the world. Now he lived in Chalton Street, Somers Town, just north of St Pancras and Camden Town; sometimes he shared his mean, disorderly lodgings with an admiring hack writer, James Marshall, occasional amanuensis and friend since student days.

Godwin remained unmarried – more violently opposed to marriage than Holcroft, he called it 'the worst of all laws ... an affair of property' – but he seemed recently to have discovered women and was now pursued by several lively ladies. Truthful and sincere to a fault, he found it difficult to flirt. He had met the twenty-two year old Sarah on a trip to her father, the philosophical clergyman Dr Parr; when she visited London she began writing saucily to him. Perplexed, he was unable to respond and she ended a note, 'I am so angry that I could marry thee in downright spite, if I did not hold sacred the oath I swore six years ago never to marry – a wise man'.[3] This comic resolve followed her mother's advice not to unite herself with a clever man, since Mrs Parr had not enjoyed marriage to an argumentative philosopher. Godwin's very seriousness continued to provoke coquetry and, just before he met Wollstonecraft, he had learnt sometimes to respond with awkward gallantry.[4] On her side, she had had her fill of charming, worldly men and was perhaps ready to appreciate the sort of complicated 'genius' with whom she had once been infatuated.

In mid-January, Wollstonecraft and Godwin were at a dinner party together, along with Rebecca Christie, alone now Thomas had gone on business to Surinam.[5] In his diary Godwin recorded that he then spent three days reading *Letters from Sweden*, realising in the process how much the strident vindicator had softened: 'She speaks of her sorrows, in a way that fills us with melancholy, and dissolves us in tenderness, at the same time that she displays a genius which commands our admiration.' He was glad: he did not care for 'a man in a female form, though that form was the form of Venus'. Yet, although he found Wollstonecraft more womanly, the effect was not powerful enough to make him call on her immediately and she remained preoccupied with grief.

Perhaps he held back knowing Holcroft's hopes or perhaps he was too busy to add another lady to his schedule. His diary was filled with intelligent women. Mary Hays, of course, and Sarah Parr, but, more important to him, the widowed Elizabeth Inchbald, 'a piquante mixture between a lady and a milkmaid',[6] former actress, now playwright and novelist in her forties. He saw her frequently and loved looking at her; she was a lively talker and put him at ease. Then there was the pretty young Amelia Alderson of Norwich, staying with friends out in Southgate and being chaperoned about London by Inchbald. She had achieved some notoriety by kissing Horne Tooke after his acquittal from treason, and she had badgered the philosophers Godwin and Holcroft into intimacy with her sprightly talk, happy that such famous men respected her writing talents and paid her attentions. She displayed the pair amusingly for a friend in Norwich: 'You have no idea how gallant [Godwin] is become; but indeed, he is much more amiable than ever he was. Mrs Inchbald says, the report of the world is that Mr Holcroft is in love with her, *she* with Mr Godwin, Mr Godwin with *me*, and I am in love with Mr Holcroft!'[7] This merry-go-round including the two close friends gives some support to the notion that Holcroft was the writer of the recent love-letter to Wollstonecraft: seemingly the pair entered love-games in tandem. Finally and most significantly, there was the married Maria Reveley. As his daughter later admitted, for her Godwin experienced more 'tenderness and preference' than for any other.[8]

In mid-February he made time to call at the Christies' house expecting to find Wollstonecraft, but she was nursing her wounded heart in Berkshire. When she returned, she moved again. Rebecca Christie had been her main-stay, but once Thomas had quit London she often stayed away, and Woll-stonecraft had little reason to remain in Finsbury Place. Her new lodgings were at 1 Cumming Street, just off the Pentonville Road approaching Isling-ton; her furniture remained in store, for Paris was still her goal – Italy or Switzerland, anywhere except where she was. She met Hays again and the pair encouraged each other's morbid moods. 'Mrs Imlay is returned,' Hays told Godwin. 'I am sorry to add, her health appears in a still more declining state. It does not signify what is the cause, but her heart, I think, is broken.'[9]

Although she continued to moan promiscuously, Wollstonecraft's 'heart' was in fact on the mend and in mid-April she called at Godwin's lodgings, conveniently within walking distance of Cumming Street, to repay the February visit. It was an unconventional but characteristic step. Godwin wrote unconventionally but it was left to Wollstonecraft to live so.

On the same day Godwin visited Amelia Alderson, but on the next he had tea with Wollstonecraft; a week later he saw her again. From this point the name Wollstonecraft or Imlay appears often in his diary, sometimes with Hays, sometimes with Rebecca Christie. At much the same time he made another new friend – Mary Robinson, former actress, mistress of the young Prince of Wales and then of the dashing soldier, gambler and MP, Banastre Tarleton. She had been carrying Tarleton's child when, rushing after him to

Dover, she suffered a bungled miscarriage which left her crippled. She was now a writer supporting a daughter and mother with her work and an erratic royal annuity of £500. Vilified by the press as 'this once all-conquering impure', she appeared to Godwin the most beautiful woman he had ever seen.[10]

Godwin introduced Wollstonecraft to his society of ladies: the visiting Sarah Parr and Amelia Alderson, Mary Robinson and Elizabeth Inchbald. Though admiring his intellect, Alderson had declared Godwin's person disappointing; it was otherwise with Wollstonecraft, who shared with 'the lakes of Cumberland' the rare distinction of living up to her expectations. She was eager to become better acquainted; her new friend inspired affection because she obviously felt it. Soon Alderson was sending presents of game from Norwich and referring to her as Cleopatra.[11] Mary Robinson was equally delighted with Wollstonecraft. Sharing experiences of chequered pasts and illegitimate pregnancies, of France, miserable Channel crossings, desertion, social opprobrium, and a propensity to put life into works, the two women got on well and often took tea together. If Wollstonecraft read her new friend's 'Stanzas Written between Dover and Calais, in July, 1792' to her fickle lover Tarleton, she would have seen her own more recent past emotions poetically expressed:

> Proud has been my fatal passion!
> Proud my injured heart shall be!
> While each thought and inclination
> Proves that heart was formed for thee!

Wollstonecraft and Inchbald found each other less congenial. They agreed on much: both were impressed with Rousseau's natural pedagogy and believed conventional female education corrupting. Yet, although Inchbald had cautiously welcomed *The Rights of Woman*, she probably remembered the mocking reviews of her earlier work as insipid and pandering to male prejudice, which, since they were signed 'M', she may reasonably have supposed to be by Godwin's new lady friend.[12] And she could not have relished the recent review of her new work, *Nature and Art*, which damned her with faint praise: 'philosophical' but without enough 'lively interest to keep the attention awake'; morally correct but 'improbable': 'were we to characterize Mrs I.'s peculiar talent, we should unhesitatingly say *naïveté*.'[13]

If Mary Hays did not quite receive the emotional comfort she desired from either Godwin or Wollstonecraft, she must have been pleased to hear that the latter had taken up her feminist pen to write a sort of sequel to her *Rights of Woman*, the second volume of which had never materialised. This work would concern the *wrongs* of woman and accept that women could not simply be inserted into the male Enlightenment enterprise, as the earlier book implied. Feminine feeling was destructive in the world as it was, but might also be beneficial, and the choice between reason and sensibility once presented to women was simply too stark, as the letters to Imlay indicated. In *The Rights of Woman* Wollstonecraft had blamed women for preying on themselves and others; concentrating more on material oppression, she now portrayed them less as weak tyrants than as slaves and victims. Their misery would be displayed in political as well as psychological terms, using the emotive words that the Revolution had popularised, 'tyranny', 'despotism', 'oppression' and 'justice'.

No doubt Hays encouraged this line, as would their common friend Eliza Fenwick, wife of another of Godwin's friends, the radical editor John Fenwick. Eliza had recently published a dark feminist novel, *Secresy*, featuring a romantic, idealistic young woman who, believing the marriage ceremony unnecessary, was betrayed by a conventional mercenary man; her isolate education was criticised for not developing her rational faculties, but in her benevolent, artless state she was superior to the corrupt and trivial world that destroyed her. Fenwick's present poverty appeared in her austere grey gowns worn with no linen visible; soon she would separate from her clever drunken, famously sponging husband, and experience the difficulty of women outside marriage as she tried to keep herself and her children in the strenuous way of teaching, governessing, and hack-writing.[14]

Fenwick, Hays, Alderson, and certainly Inchbald, were all more skilled novelists than Wollstonecraft – in terms of plotting, dialogue and control of material – and they may have persuaded her from her natural bent for straight polemical prose, especially since all except Inchbald admired her abilities. Wollstonecraft knew the pitfalls of the didactic novel and had begun a predominantly favourable review of Holcroft's *Anna St Ives* by blaming it for too obviously conveying the author's (correct) sentiments. Yet she agreed with Imlay that fiction was 'the most effectual way of communicating moral instruction', as well as with Godwin, who had written *Caleb Williams* to trace the 'modes of domestic and unrecorded despotism by which man becomes the destroyer of man'. Of woman, too, she would show.[15]

The expectations of friends who regarded Wollstonecraft as their natural leader must have been daunting. She herself was severe: writing to Godwin, Amelia Alderson noted, 'Mrs Imlay is a more rigid critic than you – but I acquiesce in the justice of most of her remarks – happy, most happy shall I be if the efforts, and application to which I am hastening, may entitle me to

the praises of you both.'[16] Wollstonecraft was never nervous about criticising – she rebuked Paine for offending 'against the subjunctive', Mary Hays
for effusiveness, the successful novelist Charlotte Smith for grammar, and
Mary Robinson for writing careless and confused books. Told to compose a
quick review of Jane West's new didactic novel, *The Gossip's Story*, Hays was
instructed what to think and how to express herself: to give 'a short summary
of the contents, or an account of the incident on which the interest turns'.
Hays obliged and, significantly, urged 'superiour writers' to use the novel for
moral and political reform.[17]

Yet there was also a new restraint. Wollstonecraft had resumed reviewing
for the *Analytical* in April, her first contribution appearing in May; by August
she was reading fast, for in the October issue, compiled during the previous
months, she contributed all the short novel notices. In these she reiterated
her desire for psychological realism and moral responsibility to readers but
toned down her earlier contempt for poor writers: where once she had been
amusingly scathing, she was now prepared to take earnest authors seriously.
She herself had a far more innovative conception of her subject than other
reforming women novelists but she would have more trouble than any with
the need to dramatise what she so urgently felt. In theory she knew what to
do, not in practice: 'the writing of a good book is no easy task' were the last
words she would publish in the *Analytical*.

With new friends, a final break with Imlay, and revived literary activity, by
the summer Wollstonecraft had stopped yearning for Paris and death.
London was still a small town; one could walk across it comfortably in an
hour or so and it felt familiar. The bond with Imlay should help with Fanny's
keep and she could support herself as before. Marguerite was still with her.

Slowly she resumed her old life. She went to the theatre, one of the earliest
plays she saw in the new season being a dramatic version of Godwin's *Caleb
Williams* with the politics omitted. *The Iron Chest*, a stage adaptation by
George Colman the Younger, had premièred in March to general disapproval,
in part because the famous actor John Philip Kemble, who played the lead,
had a heavy cold, which he tried to cover with opium; later, revised and cut,
the play achieved great success. On this night Hays was of the party as well
as Wollstonecraft. Godwin did not record his opinion of this travesty of his
work or the reactions of his women companions. At other times Wollstonecraft was entertained by Kemble and his sister, Sarah Siddons, who
setting up for maternity herself, admired the maternal *Letters from Sweden*
as Wollstonecraft admired Siddons's 'dignified delicacy' in her heroic acting.
On one occasion at Kemble's house, Wollstonecraft talked of 'Love' with her

host, Godwin and Inchbald: she had much to contribute.[18] She had met the famous actor and actress through their scholar brother-in-law, Francis Twiss; on every third Sunday she dined with the gaunt Twiss and his fat wife, Fanny.

Fuseli's tutelage had given her an appreciation of art and the vocabulary to discuss it. So she felt at ease with painters such as Godwin's old friend James Barry, an eccentric and belligerent historical artist. Opie, now famous for his portrait-painting and expensively divorced from his flirtatious wife, called often, as did young Basil Montagu, illegitimate son of the Earl of Sandwich. Once a law student, he became Godwin's admiring pupil, even moving to Chalton Street to be close. Wollstonecraft, of course, continued to visit St Paul's Churchyard, where Johnson was again prepared sometimes to play father to his difficult daughter. She also had regular dinners or evenings with the Fuselis.

Unhappily, in this mellower time Wollstonecraft was not reconciled with Eliza, from whom the estrangement had been too great, but she wrote again to Everina. James turned up suddenly, tired once more of sea-faring life and declaring himself, belatedly, a convinced revolutionary. She dispatched him to Paris with a written recommendation for citizenship to Lanthénas, who had betrayed the Rolands and thus survived the Terror. As a result of Lanthénas's endeavours, James was allowed to remain as a student, but a couple of years later, apprehended as a spy, was ordered to quit France. He then turned to Helen Maria Williams and John Hurford Stone. Stone tried Talleyrand but with no success and James had to leave. Mary did not see him again.[19]

Of Charles she heard nothing and it was in part to obtain news that she wrote in mid-September to the silent Rowan, enclosing a copy of *Letters from Sweden*. Since her earlier letters had been so mournful, she also wanted to indicate her changed life: 'I feel an inclination to avail myself of the present opportunity to inform you of the state of my mind. – It is calmer.' She rehearsed her past sorrows and rectitude, then coyly ascribed her new contentment to growing 'self respect ... on which alone true happiness is built'. Lamenting that she had never met Rowan's large brood of ten children, she confided that her own child grew and prattled apace, 'She is a motive, as well as *a reward*, for existi[ng].'

Despite her openness about Imlay, what Wollstonecraft did not say to Rowan was that she had found a replacement in 'an intimate friend', William Godwin.

The relationship with Godwin was not a grand passion, although, when it suddenly terminated, it assumed this quality for the abandoned lover. The humourless, tactless Godwin seems an unlikely successor to the seductive and charming Imlay: the word 'love' did not occur in *Political Justice*, where the choice of partner was a rational act. However, this had to some extent been Wollstonecraft's view too a few years before. Where Hays was perturbed by Godwin's uncompromising advice in her emotional troubles, Wollstonecraft was in a mood sometimes now to appreciate truth over tact. On his side, Godwin was ready to modify his view in *Political Justice*, that universal benevolence would only come about when individuals were freed from relationships of a filial or marital kind.

By the summer, each had expressed interest, though there would be many feints and withdrawals. Well aware of Wollstonecraft's previous hungry love and of Hays's repeated lament that women could not decently initiate affection, Godwin later insisted that neither made the first move. He was the last of at least three men in her life, since a 'fusty old pedant of a painter' and an 'imprudent and unprincipled debauchee' had anticipated him very publicly, and he feared appearing the dupe of a famously fallen woman. Theirs was 'the purest and most refined of love':

> It grew with equal advances in the mind of each. It would have been impossible for the most minute observer to have said who was before, and who was after. One sex did not take the priority which long-established custom has awarded it, nor the other overstep that delicacy which is so severely imposed. I am not conscious that either party can assume to have been the agent or the patient, the toil-spreader or the prey, in the affair.[20]

Wollstonecraft was equally concerned with her self-image. In the novel she was writing she described a woman loving for the second time: this woman did not show 'a decided affection' for 'fear of outrunning' her new lover's; so she often seemed cold or indifferent 'even when giving way to the playful emotions of a heart just loosened from the frozen bond of grief'.[21]

Not a natural romantic Godwin tried to woo Wollstonecraft in poetry. The attempt amused her and allowed her to write with an archness not assumed since the early Imlay days, 'I want ... to remind you, when you write to me in verse, not to choose the easiest task, my perfections'. But she had not learnt to stifle her pedagogic urge and she needed to show Godwin how to write a love-letter much as she had had to teach Imlay how to feel: 'give me a bird's-eye view of your heart. Do not make me a desk "to write upon", I humbly pray – unless you honestly acknowledge yourself *bewitched*.'

In July, Godwin travelled to Norfolk to visit his mother. While there he called on Amelia Alderson's father, a Dissenting doctor living in Colegate,

Norwich. Then he set about writing a pastiche of the love-letter Wollstonecraft ordered:

> Now, I take all my Gods to witness ... that your company infinitely delights me, that I love your imagination, your delicate epicurism, the malicious leer of your eye, in short every thing that constitutes the bewitching tout ensemble of the celebrated Mary ... Shall I write a love letter? May Lucifer fly away with me, if I do! No, when I make love, it shall be with the eloquent tones of my voice, with dying accents, with speaking glances (through the glass of my spectacles), with all the witching of that irresistible, universal passion. Curse on the mechanical, icy medium of pen & paper. When I make love, it shall be in a storm, as Jupiter made love to Semele, & turned her at once to a cinder. Do not these menaces terrify you?[22]

He ended by asking Wollstonecraft to let Marguerite tell his janitor he was returning in a week, 'to depart no more'. It was a domestic detail that suggested the intimacy she craved. She was not keen on most of the letter – she disliked facetiousness – but she was warmed by the final sentence, which seemed to make friendship permanent.

While he was away, she finally took her furniture out of storage, then moved from Cumming Street to 16 Judd Place West on the edge of Somers Town, close to Godwin. By now she had augmented Marguerite with a maid called Mary, a general servant who cooked and ran errands.

On the 20th she expected Godwin and waited in for him. When he did not come she was cross and, next day, wrote a tart note: 'I mean to bottle up my kindness, unless something in your countenance, when I do see you, should make the cork fly out – whether I will or not.' In fact, Godwin had not returned from Norfolk when intended, reaching London on the 24th. He called promptly on Wollstonecraft but it was too late. She was not quickly pacified and continued to complain of his inadequate attentions: 'I suppose you mean to drink tea with me, *one* of these day[s] – How can you find in your heart to let me pass so many evenings alone.'

Aware that she had been wilfully blind to Imlay's betrayal, she began revealing a flirtatious jealousy of Godwin's other women, especially Inchbald and Alderson. Given his honesty, Godwin probably told her how much he admired Inchbald's beauty and that she had obtained the nickname 'Mrs Perfection' through her superlative praise of *Caleb Williams*. So Wollstonecraft quipped: 'I did not wish to see you this evening, because you have been dining, I suppose, with Mrs Perfection, and comparisons are odious.' A couple of days later she wrote that she had heard the middle-aged Godwin had been ready to devour Amelia Alderson when she called at his cramped lodgings. Could so old a man be transformed by love into the polished courtier Amelia wanted? She tried to diffuse the threat by discussing Godwin with Amelia, who wondered whether the philosopher had ever actually kissed a lady. Well she might, for he had once tried to 'salute' her but withdrawn when courage failed. 'As you do not like to solve problems, *on paper*,' Wollstonecraft told him, 'TELL her *before* you part – She will tell *me* next-year.' So she mocked both him and her; she was learning some guile in matters of the heart.

A week later at Wollstonecraft's lodgings, Godwin declared the love long brewing. They became intimate but not complete lovers. She was perplexed, he agitated. It was probably his first sexual experience and the old puritan minister peeped through the cosmopolitan philosopher. Some years before, Maria Reveley, who greatly attracted him, had apparently made a sexual advance and been rebuffed.[23] Now, faced with a similar more serious assault, he imagined himself feverish and ill. The next day, he failed to call as Wollstonecraft expected, instead going to dine with Holcroft in Newman Street as he usually did on Sunday. The following day she visited his lodgings but he remained awkward and self-absorbed. The next morning she tried to rally him with a playful note sent by Mary and little Fanny, asking 'did you feel very lonely last night?' But Godwin had taken fright and, after a sleepless night, wrote gracelessly: 'I have been very unwell all night. You did not consider me enough in that way yesterday, & therefore unintentionally impressed upon me a mortifying sensation. When you see me next; will you condescend to take me for better for worse, that is, be prepared to find me, as it shall happen, full of gaiety & life, or a puny valetudinarian?' He followed the letter with defiant absence.

There was nothing to do but advance; Wollstonecraft hurried round. She tried embracing him only to be spurned with a lecture on how things should be between people of the opposite sex.

Now seriously alarmed she too lay awake during a painful night. In the morning she could not eat her breakfast, worried that she had been too forward and that Godwin despised her. She wished she and Fanny were in France, Italy, anywhere; yet she knew it was not the place but she that was wrong. 'My imagination is for ever betraying me into fresh misery, and I perceive that I shall be a child to the end of the chapter,' she wrote, echoing her despair when, three years before, she contemplated her inelegant behaviour with Fuseli. Godwin's seeming retreat recalled other rejections and she was afraid to trace emotions backwards only to resurrect past agonies. No man would ever understand her.

The following morning she wrote a letter of protest and constrained affection, hoping that her own expressed intention to retreat would bring Godwin to heel, as it had never brought Imlay. As with her former lover, she defined herself in Rousseauian imaginative terms – a 'Solitary Walker', now in opposition, not to a materialist speculator but to a cold rationalist.

> Is it not sufficient to tell you that I am thoroughly out of humour with myself? Mortified and humbled, I scarcely know why – still, despising false delicacy I almost fear that I have lost sight of the true...
>
> I would not be unjust for the world – I can only say that you appear to me to have acted injudiciously; and that full of your own feelings, little as I comprehend them, you forgot mine – or do not understand my character. It is my turn to have a fever to day – I am not well – I am hurt – But I mean not to hurt you. Consider what has passed as a fever of your imagination; one of the slight mortal shakes to which you are liable – and I – will become again a *Solitary Walker*. Adieu! I was going to add God bless you!

Hays was due to call in the afternoon, but Wollstonecraft's mind was not on casual visitors.

By midday the letter had done its work. At last Godwin realised Wollstonecraft's vulnerability, her separate not entirely knowable consciousness, and felt his abstract theories shift. He wrote back a better letter than he had yet addressed to her, still didactic but a real love-letter:

> You do not know how honest I am. I swear to you that I told you nothing but the strict & literal truth, when I described to you the manner in which you set my imagination on fire on Saturday. For six & thirty hours I could think of nothing else. I longed inexpressibly to have you in my arms. Why did not I come to you? I am a fool. I feared still that I might be deceiving myself as to your feelings, & that I was feeding my mind with groundless presumptions. I determined to suffer the point to arrive at its own denouement. I was not aware that the fervour of my imagination was exhausting itself. Yet this, I believe, is no uncommon case.
>
> Like any other man, I can speak only of what I know. But this I can boldly affirm, that nothing that I have seen in you would in the slightest degree authorise the opinion, that, *in despising the false delicacy, you have lost sight of the true.* I see nothing in you but what I respect & adore.
>
> I know the acuteness of your feelings, & there is perhaps nothing upon earth that would give me so pungent a remorse, as to add to your unhappiness.
>
> Do not hate me. Indeed I do not deserve it. Do not cast me off. Do not become again a *solitary walker.* Be just to me, & then, though you will discover in me much that is foolish and censurable, yet a woman of your understanding will still regard me with some partiality...

Be happy. Resolve to be happy. You deserve to be so. Every thing that interferes with it, is weakness & wandering; & a woman, like you, can, must, shall, shake it off. Afford, for instance, no food for the morbid madness & no triumph to the misanthropical gloom, of your afternoon visitor. Call up, with firmness, the energies, which, I am sure, you so eminently possess.[24]

Two hours after his letter, in mid-afternoon, Godwin saw how blind he was still being to Wollstonecraft's offers of sexual love. He wrote again even more penitently:

Intent upon an idea I had formed in my own mind of furtive pleasure, I was altogether stupid & without intelligence as to your plan of staying, which it was morally impossible should not have given life to the dead . . .

I have now only left to apologize for my absurdity, which I do even with self-abhorrence. The mistake being detected, it is for you to decide whether it is too late to repair it. For my own part, I have not the presumption to offer even a word to implore your forgiveness.[25]

Before he had delivered this, Wollstonecraft arrived with her own letter at Chalton Street, written at two o'clock in response to Godwin's earlier one, which she had recognised for the defensive love-letter it was. Relieved after all the repulses from Imlay, she was able to give free rein to her bossy and emotional modes at once: 'I like your last – may I call it *love* letter? better than the first – and can I give you a higher proof of my esteem than to tell you, the style of my letter will whether I will or no, that it has calmed my mind . . . it is almost gone – I mean all my unreasonable fears and a whole train of tormenters, which you have routed – I can scarcely describe to you their ugly shapes so quickly do they vanish – and let them go, we will not bring them back by talking of them.'

She asked him to come to dine with her and Fanny at 4.30: he had ruined her breakfast and it was only fair he should season her dinner. Also, the little girl had been exiled during the emotional altercation and needed attention. If he could not make that engagement, he could come in the evening. Hays was due to arrive but she seldom stayed late. If not in the evening, then he could come next day. As long as he came soon. Poor Hays cannot have had much of her friend's attention during this tense time – she was still there when Godwin called. Did she suspect the intimacy her social efforts had allowed?

Wollstonecraft wanted to avoid some of the mistakes made with Imlay and yet she could not shake off the habits that had been so much part of her most intense and very recent relationship. So again she analysed herself and her new lover, keen to bifurcate their psychologies and justify her sensitivity, even touchiness:

> our imaginations have been rather differently employed – I am more of a painter than you – I like to tell the truth, my taste for the picturesque has been more cultivated – I delight to view the grand scenes of nature and the various changes of the human countenance – Beautiful as they are animated by intelligence or sympathy – My affections have been more exercised than yours, I believe, and my senses are quick, without the aid of fancy – yet tenderness always prevails, which inclines me to be angry with myself, when I do not animate and please those I [?love].

Although she had calmed Godwin, she had not had a chance to talk things over. He called at her house but Marguerite was in the next room and they could neither converse intimately nor embrace. Meanwhile, she had the common reaction of the comforter to the comforted: slight resentment that she had had to take such trouble. By Friday it was she who most feared the future. She worried she was repeating her mistake with Fuseli and Imlay. She wanted to be made much of, to be repeatedly reassured by loving words. Awkwardly, she tried to elicit comfort from Godwin, yet convey her fears about love and sex. She did it by composing a fable of a sycamore.

> This poor deciduous (female) tree was growing among evergreens and all through the winter snows, as the wind whistled through her thin branches, she shivered and envied the foliage of her more fortunate neighbours. Her only comfort was that it would soon be spring and she too would have warming leaves. But she did not know the proper signs of spring and so, whenever the sun shone on the snow, she asked the other trees if it had really come and she should put out her leaves.

She did so prematurely and 'the next day came a frost that shrivelled up her unfolding leaves and changed all her green to brown'. A neighbouring tree told her she should 'learn to distinguish February from April.' Wollstonecraft ended plaintively, 'Whether the buds recovered, and expanded, when the spring actually arrived – The Fable sayeth not.'

Her story was appealing and genuinely anxious, but it failed to elicit the hoped-for response. Unused to lovers' fears, Godwin was blind to its desire. Insecure and anxious himself, he saw only withdrawal on Wollstonecraft's side, misery on his. He wrote back at once, his alarm making him pompous and literal: 'I have no answer to make to your fable, which I acknowledge to be uncommonly ingenious & well composed.' He felt her criticism and responded with justification and an effort at particular interpretation far from its meaning: he could not apply the fable to the time when Hays called or when Marguerite's presence constrained them. Then he proceeded severely:

> Your fable of to day puts an end to all my hopes. I needed soothing, & you threaten me. Oppressed with a diffidence and uncertainty which I hate, you join the oppressors, & annihilate me. Use your pleasure. For every pain I have undesignedly given you, I am most sincerely grieved; for the good qualities I discern in you, you shall live for ever embalmed in my memory.[26]

When she received this Wollstonecraft understood her error. She dashed round at once to Godwin's place; they spent the following evening 'chez elle' as Godwin recorded in his diary. On the next day, Sunday, it was 'chez moi, toute' and one may assume that at last they made love without any catastrophic results – though it needed another month and half before he could write 'chez moi, bonne'.

# 34

*'It is not rapture. It is a sublime tranquillity.'*

The morning after 'toute', Wollstonecraft wrote to reassure and provoke reassurance. She was sometimes 'painfully humble', she said, and needed a line or two of comfort. Could he oblige? Still thrown by his experience, Godwin yet responded to this clearly stated desire with the kind of flattery he was at last learning to give women, 'Humble! for heaven's sake, be proud, be arrogant! You are – but I cannot tell what you are. I cannot yet find the circumstance about you that allies you to the frailty of our nature. I will hunt it out.'[1]

Over the next weeks, there was much advancing and withdrawing, much coldness followed by extra warmth, much warmth followed by frigidity. Both talked too much, providing endless possibilities for offence. Wollstonecraft tried to control her lover's responses, as she had Imlay's, but less desperately: Godwin must learn to avoid stray wounding remarks and become 'fastidious' in feeling. Her depressive, volatile nature confused him and he often retreated from her moods and demands into the society of men and easier women. Or he stood dogmatically on principle, as he had before Hays's emotional outbursts. According to his diary there was a good deal of sex.[2]

Despite their praise of openness they revelled in the secrecy of the affair. Wollstonecraft used it to set off public appearance against private truth, playing the flirtatious game of rivalry – especially with Elizabeth Inchbald, with whom Godwin sometimes dined alone. On one occasion in late August she prefaced his setting out with a short note reminding him of his 'fealty' to her whatever the other woman's charms. To which Godwin replied, 'I will report my fealty this evening'. On another, Inchbald praised Godwin so highly that Wollstonecraft almost fancied her in love with him. It pleased her: by now she knew her own firm hold and was styling herself privately 'your Mary'.

Eager for the domestic life enjoyed fleetingly in Paris and Le Havre, she tried to include Godwin in the family – 'Give Fanny a biscuit – I want you to love each other' – and she stressed the homeliness of her invitations. Godwin should come to her 'fireside' or, instead of taking a walk, bring his work to her house, where they would sit cosily together. They would be 'snug' and, like old married couples, feel happier contenting the other than themselves. Godwin was easier to turn into a father than Imlay, and he and Wollstonecraft sometimes jocularly addressed each other as 'mama' and 'papa'. Little Fanny grew attached to him and stayed often in his lodgings, where he gave her cakes and pudding. Wollstonecraft encouraged the treats but told Godwin not to give her butter.

Just occasionally she wrote Godwin the kind of frank, loving and sexy letters she had sent Imlay from Neuilly. When they had spent a late evening together making love, they had to part, with a too intense memory of sexual arousal. She woke in her own lodgings full of the sense and smell of him:

> Now by these presents let me assure you that you are not only in my heart, but my veins, this morning. I turn from you half abashed – yet you haunt me, and some look, word or touch thrills through my whole frame – yes, at the very moment when I am labouring to think of something, if not somebody, else. Get ye gone Intruder! though I am forced to add dear – which is a call back –
>
> When the heart and reason accord there is no flying from voluptuous sensations, I find, do what a woman can – Can a philosopher do more?

Or she sent a coy note in which the ominous 'God bless you' to Imlay became a Sternean kiss: 'I only write now to bid you Good Night! – I shall be asleep before you – and I would leave you a God bless you – did you care for it; but, alas! you do not, though Sterne says that it is equivalent to a – kiss – .'

Mainly they wrote quick notes, making secret arrangements, asking for books and commenting on moments in company, for by day they led separate lives, seeing friends, reading and working. Some notes were sent to sweeten or season dinner, or regret a meal eaten alone. When they expressed intimacy, it was often in embarrassed French, 'Mon Bien-aimé' or 'Adorable maitresse'.

Wollstonecraft wanted Godwin to respect her intellect, not just love her for some sexual and fugitive charm available in another woman. She must stir his heart and imagination so that he loved involuntarily *and* reasonably: 'I want to have such a firm throne in your heart, that even your imagination shall not be able to hurl me from it, be it ever so active.' Yet she was conventionally proud to believe her man her superior: 'I am glad to discover great powers of mind in you, even at my own expence,' she told him.

She grew sensitive about her writing. She had played with reticence in her *Letters from Sweden*, but it was circumstantial, a matter of hiding shame and shady commercial dealings. Now she returned to her ideal of writerly frankness, her need to feel she was expressing all a valued self, forcing a published work to share the intimacy of a private letter. Like Fuseli before him, Godwin recoiled from this emotional style when the subject was not personal life and he urged Wollstonecraft to reveal ideas more systematically. But they were two rival writers as well as lovers: 'I do not intend to let you extend your scepticism to me – or you will fright away a poor weary bird who, taking refuge in your bosom, hoped to nestle there – to the end of the chapter,' she wrote. For her new difficult writing she wanted only a *little* criticism; Godwin's scrupulous comments disheartened her. He had had the same effect on Amelia Alderson, who reported a friend's saying, 'you must mind your *p*'s & *q*'s when you write to Citizen Godwin,' and wondered if her hesitation in writing was due to fear of his criticism.[3] In fact they were all liable to severe strictures on each other. Even the serviceable Marshall could upset Godwin by telling him he had an uncouth style and wrote 'on stilts'.[4]

*The Wrongs of Woman* was being composed with greater care than the *Vindications* but she was not a natural novelist and found it difficult separating herself from her central character and judging with detachment. One Saturday in early September, some time after he had read her manuscript, Godwin assessed her work in general; he was unusually frank. There was a disparity between aims and style, she was not conveying what she wanted. The defect was 'a worm in the bud'. Deflated, she brooded all Sunday morning; with such disapproval she could write nothing, out of patience with Godwin *and* herself. Then she decided to counter the argument.

First, she wrote from necessity: 'I must either disregard your opinion, think it unjust, or throw down my pen in despair; and that would be tantamount to resigning existence; for at fifteen I resolved never to marry for interested motives, or to endure a life of dependence.' However, she was not writing *only* for subsistence: she wanted to be a *successful* author, and her sales suggested she was. 'I shall not be content merely to keep body and soul together – By what I have already written Johnson, I am sure, has been a gainer.' Most important, she wrote distinctively:

> I would wish you to see my heart and mind just as it appears to myself, without drawing any veil of affected humility over it, though this whole letter is a proof of painful diffidence, I am compelled to think that there is some thing in my writings more valuable, than in the productions of some people on whom you bestow warm elogiums – I mean more mind – denominate it as you will – more of the observations of my own senses, more of the combining of my own imagination – the effusions of my own feelings and passions than the cold workings of the brain on the materials procured by the senses and imagination of other writers.

More controlled and effective than her usual justifications of her imaginative temperament and spontaneous writing, the letter impressed Godwin. He rescued her Sunday by rushing round with soothing words – tactful ones too, since by the end of their talk he managed to persuade her to let him teach her grammar. No one since Fanny Blood had dared do that.

In *Paradise Lost* in those scenes which so fascinated and disturbed Wollstonecraft, wise Adam and lovely Eve punctuated their conversation with 'kisses pure'. In recent years such mingling of talk and embraces had appealed to Wollstonecraft and she used the image to attract Imlay in the first heady days of their romance in Neuilly. Now with Godwin she invoked it again, hoping that the first grammar lesson would follow this agenda: '[A] word in your ear, I shall not be very angry if you sweeten grammatical disquisitions after the Miltonic mode.' So pleasant was the sensation that she could refer lightly to his criticism: 'now you have led me to discover that I write worse, than I thought I did, there is no stopping short – I must improve, or be dissatisfied with myself'.

Their happiness continued, snugly fitted into individual lives. Fanny had so taken to Godwin that, when she neared Chalton Street, she piped, '[G]o this way Mama, me wants to see Man.' But her mother respected her lover's privacy and, when she glimpsed a caller in a blue coat at his door, probably belonging to one of his lady friends, she turned away. She had so internalised him that she could speak to him lovingly in her head without seeing him. In return he should simply love her with no testing or experimenting, no 'wild-goose chace after a-wise man'. She needed little signs, all the same. 'Send me one line – if it be but – Bo! to a goose,' she wrote. Godwin obediently replied 'Bo'.

Occasionally Wollstonecraft worried over the effect of their love on Mary Hays. She remembered her own distaste for the amorous Gabells and even for the Barlows in their soppy letters. More honest than her friend, Hays admitted she found other people's love intolerable. Probably for this reason she was acting strangely. Feeling generous in her new contentment, Wollstonecraft determined to write a kind note: 'when I am happy myself, I am made up of milk and honey, I would fain make every body else so.' She saw no need to confide however: when Hays entered, she hastily put her love-letter aside.

Sometimes the secrecy was inconvenient, with different demands made on their public and private selves. On one occasion when she had a cold, she hoped to go to the theatre where Godwin would be; then she wanted to see him at his house afterwards for their private time. But she would be accompanied by someone else, perhaps Opie or Montagu, and, to keep up appearances, would have to appear to go home and tuck herself up for the evening. To visit Godwin after that would be odd.

If the secrecy appeared silly before close friends such as Hays and Alderson, who already coupled the pair in their minds, with the maid Marguerite it was even more absurd. Godwin was never sure whether or not she was in the know or whether he should be constrained. She had been with Wollstonecraft so long, been a second mother to Fanny, and seen her mistress through the depressions of Scandinavia, suicide attempts and the long parting from Imlay. Marguerite had irritated Wollstonecraft with her frivolity when she was at her gloomiest in Denmark and she may not have wanted to make her a confidante. Or perhaps it was embarrassment rather than any sense of her maid's unworthiness that kept her quiet about so speedy a successor to her 'husband'.

With Imlay, Wollstonecraft had venerated places of passion, especially in Paris where their affair had begun and at the barrier gate where Fanny was conceived. She wanted to recapture this sense of significant geography with Godwin by going somewhere together where none of their friends would interrupt. The place would have special association in memory and become a landmark in the growth of affection. Courting or clandestine couples often took small excursions from the fishbowl of central London, a favourite place being Greenwich, to which only a year before Godwin had secretly gone – together with the married Maria Reveley – only to draw back when Mrs Reveley interpreted the outing in the usual way.[5] Now there were no longer such hesitations. It was mid-September and the weather was fine, not yet autumnal, and Wollstonecraft wanted to do her 'vagabondizing' before summer was quite over. Godwin readily agreed. They would have complete nights together for the first time, alone. They had had delicious excursions to the countryside as a threesome, but this would be different.

Then plans were interrupted. Fanny had been out of sorts for some time; now the cause became clear: chicken-pox. It was some relief to know what had been ailing her, but the disease prevented the outing. The child was fretful and clinging, and her mother felt she should stay at home. Next day the spots were beginning to abate though Fanny remained poorly. Godwin was ready to travel, but Wollstonecraft felt reluctant. Besides, the weather was no longer as inviting. 'We must then woo philosophy *chez vous* ce soir, nest-ce pas; for I do not like to lose my Philosopher even in the lover.'

As so often in recent years, motherhood did not easily outweigh sexual love. Before little Fanny had recovered, they decided to have their loving excursion but stay for only one night. Leaving the child with Marguerite, they set out north for the village of Ilford near Barking, about seven miles from Somers Town. There they spent their first complete night together. Being close by, they visited Wollstonecraft's childhood home near Epping, the old house she had inhabited before her father's decline. It was ruined now and set in a neglected garden, but it still spoke of a grander beginning than Godwin's in rural East Anglia.

When they returned to Somers Town, she was glad she had not stayed a second night. Fanny had grown worse and, on the morning of her mother's absence, fretted herself into renewed fever. She had missed her mother and, when Wollstonecraft was sick and breakfasted out of the way in bed one morning, Fanny became especially affectionate, fearful of losing her again. Wollstonecraft carried her in her arms, trying to stop her scratching the scabs on her face, but was not entirely successful: as the child recovered, her mother noted wryly that spirits and health were returning faster than beauty. In less high-minded households, this would have been a tragedy.

The itchy nature of Fanny's chicken-pox made her restless through the nights, inevitably disturbing Wollstonecraft, who felt woken up every half-hour. The caring took its toll and, in spite of the Ilford break, she soon felt tired and low. She too became querulous, blaming Godwin for making only flying visits. The different duties of men and women were borne in on her again. While she had to minister to another as well as keeping up her writing, Godwin as a man had only himself to serve. She wanted to force him to consider the female caring role, even to take it on, so that he might under-stand what it felt like to suffer constant demands: 'It is I who want nursing first, you perceive – are you above the feminine office?'

Godwin did not rise to the appeal and she grew more demanding, until she tipped over into behaviour even she disapproved. Then she apologised for acting childishly and promised in future to be sensible and 'demure'. Anxiously, she demanded, 'Say only that we are friends.' This time Godwin knew what to do: he replied gallantly: 'Friends? Why not? If I thought otherwise I should be miserable.'[6]

Her being 'demure' suggested a chaste evening, for in the same breath she exhorted Godwin not to 'leave the philosopher behind'. Both were phil-osophers and lovers, and, with these identifications, evolved a code to signify when they wished temporarily to avoid sex, either because she had a period or because he felt out of sorts or practised 'self-government'. In his diary Godwin was plotting Wollstonecraft's menstrual cycle, possibly believing they could avoid pregnancy by negatively following the ever-popular but much discredited manual, *Aristotle's Master-piece*, which taught how to ensure conception. It declared that frequent sex reduced its likelihood – it being widely noted that whores were seldom pregnant – and that it occurred most easily during the few days after menstruation. The dashes and dots suggest that Godwin followed this unfortunate system, although, since he was attending lectures given by Dr Anthony Carlisle, surgeon at the charitable Westminster Hospital, he may have had more sophisticated advice. Whatever his method, he did not always adhere to it since his lover sometimes noted his 'failure of resolution', the fading of the 'philosopher'. She too was not always as 'demure' as she intended.

With her domestic desires rekindled, Wollstonecraft yearned for something regular and public, even hinting to Godwin she might like marriage. Sex had been a revelation; so had the sexual rejection after Fanny's birth in Le Havre and again after her return from France. Although Godwin was a different man from Imlay, she was anxious about keeping a lover when she was not pleasing him sexually. When she had a period she accepted abstinence but wanted reassurance that she was desirable. She hungered for marks of bonding and shared domestic rituals.

For Sunday dinners they went their separate ways, she often to the Twisses, he invariably to Holcroft, as mutually agreed. Yet she missed him and suggested that they always dine together on a Saturday to prepare themselves for Sunday's deprivation. Other evenings she might walk over at about eight o'clock to talk or make love. Sometimes she arrived and he was not there, often because she was late through her many duties. He had once spoken of giving her a key. Could he not do so? Then she would let herself in whenever she came, not worrying about the time 'which I cannot always punctually observe in the character of a woman, unless I tacked that of a wife to it'. It was an odd concession and must have made Godwin, the thunderer against marriage, uneasy.

All in all, it was the best time of their love. She did not indulge the romantic dream of elms and clinging vines as with Imlay, but she enjoyed entwining a man in her life and relished increasing security. Despite her worry that she would be wounded by anyone on whom she placed her 'mighty stock of affection', he forced her to love him 'more and more'. She was reading his new essays, especially those on education and social justice; they raised him in her esteem still further – though she urged him to temper his severe rationalism by rereading Rousseau, who wrote about the irrational desires that had played such havoc with her life.[7] '[E]steem' was a 'cold word' – was it not really love? Admiration and love were fused: mind, eyes, lips and voice all cohered, in the way she had so passionately desired with Imlay:

I shall cork up all my kindness – yet the fine volatile essence may fly off in my walk – you know not how much tenderness for you may escape in a voluptuous sigh, should the air, as is often the case, give a pleasurable movement to the

sensations, that have been clustering round my heart, as I read this morning –
reminding myself, every now and then, that the writer *loved me.* Voluptuous is
often expressive of a meaning I do not now intend to give. I would describe one
of those moments, when the senses are exactly tuned by the rising tenderness of
the heart, and according reason entices you to live in the present moment, regardless of the past or future – It is not rapture. – It is a sublime tranquillity. I have
felt it in your arms Hush! Let not the light see, I was going to say hear it – These
confessions should only be uttered – you know where, when the curtains are up –
and all the world shut out.

As with misery, so with joy, she excited herself through writing. So after this
love-letter, she had to repress her overflowing feelings to get on with the day.
She invented loving anxieties. What if the rain were wetting her lover?

But it was never plain sailing. After much expressed anticipation, the
encounter could not be as rapturous as expected. Godwin did not give
himself with the required abandon. She reacted immediately, complaining
he dampened her spirits. If reason ruled conduct, why could it not command
one's mood? It was a mystery. Sometimes 'we are so happy . . . when we least
know why'; at others he seemed afraid of letting himself go and she felt
rejected: 'Can you solve this problem? I was endeavouring to discover last
night, in bed, what it is in me, of which you are afraid. I was hurt at perceiving
that you were – but no more of this – mine is a sick heart; and in a life, like
this, the fortitude of patience is the most difficult to acquire.' She used her
mother's dismal word 'patience', still often in her mind.

In the second week of October, Godwin fell ill with fever. The tell-tale dashes
in his diary indicating sexual intercourse ceased. His doctor friend Carlisle
visited, while Wollstonecraft saw to his household linen. With her yearning
for domesticity, she relished the task; indeed, it allowed her to hint again at
marriage: when she sent the linen she confessed she felt 'a sensation of
pleasure at thus acting the part of a wife, though you have so little respect
for the character'. She wanted to convince him of the magic of habitual
affection, of accepted and trusted love: 'I have been more gratified by your
clasping your hands round my arm, in company, than I could have been by
all the admiration in the world, tho' I am a woman – and to mount a step
higher in the scale of vanity, an author.'

Absorbed in Godwin, she had been neglecting old friends who had sustained her in the dreary past. Mary Hays, whom she had earlier tried to
soothe, now felt particularly upset at being pushed to the margins. She
conveyed her hurt by returning a book without any covering note. Woll-

stonecraft understood her dismay. Friendship did not wither without a cause, she assured her, and with Hays she had none. She ascribed the hurtful neglect to the weather, business and engagements. Rebecca Christie had come to London for only a few days and Wollstonecraft needed to talk to her: possibly Imlay had used Christie to organise the bond for Fanny; possibly she wanted to comfort Rebecca, who might already have heard that Thomas had died in Surinam some weeks before. In addition, Godwin had been ill and Woll- stonecraft had to care for him: 'I have frequently been with him, as well to amuse as to see that the things proper for him were got. He is much better, but I believe had rather not see any company for a few days.' However benevolent Wollstonecraft's intentions, this letter must surely have alerted Mary Hays to her friends' growing affection and her exclusion.

Just as Godwin was recovering and she anticipated resumption of clan- destine sexual intimacy, she learnt that Mrs Cotton from Berkshire planned a visit of 'a *few* days'. Mrs Cotton was a dear close friend who had given much needed solace only eight months before, but now Wollstonecraft exclaimed, 'Heaven and Earth!'[8] There was nothing to be done, however.

By the end of October Mrs Cotton was installed in Judd Place and Godwin came to supper to meet her. Two days later he was there again, as he was on the next day. He then entertained the guest at his own house in Chalton Place. By this time Mrs Cotton must have suspected a good deal, although she saw that her friend entertained other men callers such as Opie and Montagu alone. Happily, Godwin made a good impression and 'almost captivated Mrs C'.

Back on their own, the couple celebrated by going to the theatre in a large party including Hays, her sister, and Horne Tooke. Wollstonecraft enjoyed even more the resumption of her sexual life in the evening. In their great books, *Political Justice* and *The Rights of Woman*, both had firmly associated sex and procreation. 'Reasonable men', Godwin thought, would 'propagate the species, not because a certain pleasure is annexed to this action, but because it is right the species should be propagated,' while she had scorned women who frustrated the 'purpose' of sexual appetite by practising birth control. The intervening years had modified their views.[9] Looking back on her infatuation with Fuseli, she now knew what had been wrong – as she knew what had been right with Imlay despite the sad outcome. So she was gladdened by the renewal of sexual relations and wrote happily to Godwin on the morning after their first evening alone:

If the felicity of last night has had the same effect on your health as on my countenance, you have no cause to lament your failure of resolution: for I have seldom seen so much live fire running about my features as this morning when recollections – very dear, called forth the blush of pleasure, as I adjusted my hair . . .

Winter brought problems. Despite all their mutual loving, each still had to teach the other about relationships. Each could seem too wary and each took immediate cover from hurt in pomposity and principle. Wollstonecraft had to learn that she could reject out of neediness and be forgiven; Godwin had to recognise codes of courtship and understood seductive play. From time to time both feared, but neither fled like Imlay or despaired as the old Wollstonecraft had done.

Occasionally she tried to play the mistress, a role she believed she despised, but, for which, like that of wife, she often yearned: 'How do you do this morning – are you alive? It is not *wise* to be cold during such a domesticating season, I mean then to dismiss all my frigid airs before I draw near your door, this evening . . . entre nous, *little* marks of attention are incumbent on you at present . . .' To which Godwin replied obtusely, 'Yes, I am alive. Perhaps I am better. I am glad to hear how enchanting & divine you will appear this evening. You spoil little attentions by anticipating them.'[10]

Instead of simply taking offence as she would so recently have done, Wollstonecraft tried to explain to her exasperating lover the need for playfulness. She wished he could distinguish between jest and seriousness and, to reassure him, she promised she never played 'with edged-tools'. Indeed she did not play at all when hurt or angry. In the main she was right, but Godwin probably remembered the fable of the sycamore, which he felt too playful for the circumstances and which had nearly destroyed them.

Wollstonecraft held her ground. She needed lightness to express her new-found happiness. 'Still allow me a little more tether than is necessary for the purpose of feeding, to keep soul and body together – Let me, I pray thee! have a sort of *comparative* freedom, as you are a profound Grammarian, to run round, as good, better, best; – cheerful, gay, playful; nay even frolicksome, once a year – or so, when the whim seizes me of skipping out of bounds. Send me *a bill of rights* – to this purport, under your hand and seal, with a *Bulletin* of health.' It was an attractive scenario, but Godwin replied plaintively, 'I can send you a bill of rights & a bill of health: the former *carte blanche*; the latter, much better (as I think). But to fulfil the terms of your note, you must send me a bill of understanding. How can I distinguish always between your jest & earnest, & know when your satire means too much & when it means nothing? But I will try.'[11]

Although she had reacted moderately to the altercation, Godwin's grace-lessness rankled. As so often, she felt irritated at having to calm or explain when she regarded herself as in the right, and the irritation grew when the other made no allusion to the event or acted as though it had never been. So some days later Wollstonecraft reverted to the tiff: 'You tell me that "I spoil little attentions, by anticipation." Yet to have attention, I find, that it is necessary to demand it.'

It was November and the weather was frostier than usual; thick clouds promised snow. She caught a heavy cold which lasted in full force for ten days, greatly trying her temper. She knew from experience how lingering her infections could be and coddled herself. Inevitably she had conflicting wishes. She thought it wise for Godwin to stay away, but berated him for keeping only himself warm with his love. She would not risk going to a play and getting fresh cold, wanted him to go alone, and hoped he would not: 'I was a little displeased with you for mentioning, when I was seriously indis-posed, your inclination to go – and was angry with myself for not permitting you to follow your inclination.' Why did he not try to tempt her to go, however unwise?

She hated to be left out. She could not bear to think of Godwin's socialising without her or of his passing her lodgings without entering. No doubt she imagined blue coats waiting at his doorstep. She longed to be in the 'kennel', as she termed his cramped quarters. Sometimes he did the right thing and made cosy, sexless visits: 'Our *sober* evening was very delicious – I do believe you love me better than you imagined you should – as for me – judge for yourself.' At other times she wanted to come to Chalton Place but realised she would only cough at him. Notes of assignation flowed between them or Godwin was instructed to look up at her window when passing for a sign whether he should enter or not. Always there was slight anxiety that, in her present state, she was 'disappointing' him. Men were odd creatures and she had learnt how little she knew them.

By late November, she felt well enough to amuse herself, she said, and would trouble him no further. She did not mean it and Godwin's diary showed she visited Chalton Place that very evening. They had sex, as they had not done for some days during the worst of her illness. They were intimate again at the end of the month. Since Wollstonecraft menstruated in mid-November when she complained of being 'feverish', Godwin may have thought this a particularly safe time. It was an unfortunate assumption.

The cough persisted into early December. Ill health delivered low spirits which crept over her during the evening and night, then lay like a load on her next morning. Yet, unlike on so many earlier occasions – in Ireland and with Imlay – she declared she would try to act against melancholy rather than feed it by grumbling and writing.

To pursue her resolution, she determined to cheer herself by struggling to the theatre one evening, to see Holcroft's *The Force of Ridicule*. She had been to another play a few days before with Godwin, but the effort had taxed her so much she decided not to try the experiment again. So Godwin had asked Inchbald to go with him to the next play instead. When Wollstonecraft changed her mind, he had to find another ticket for her, as well as procuring a companion. It was at the last minute and he could only get poor seats – he knew they would not please but he could not put off a lady already invited and squire Wollstonecraft instead.

As expected, she hated the exclusion. She was irritated by her companion, not the person she wanted to be seen with at the play – perhaps Godwin's sister Hannah – and by the hopeless seats. She was thrust into a corner in the third row where she could neither see nor hear. It was as bad as being in the cheap gallery with servants. When she got home, she wrote at once to scold, 'I am determined to return to my former habits, and go by [my]self and shift for myself – an amusement loses its name when thus conducted.' Her real annoyance was seeing Godwin and Inchbald comfortably situated in better seats. She was always envious of this beautiful, successful woman, and the vision irked her, 'You and Mrs I— were at your ease enjoying yourselves while, poor I! – I was a fool not to ask Opie to go with me – had I been alone I should not have minded it.' The rebuke brought Godwin round to Judd Street with soothing words.

Wollstonecraft's low spirits continued, as did her cough, and she found it hard to write with her aching head. She resented the different working patterns of herself and Godwin. She could not concentrate with visits and callers, instead needing to hole up alone for several hours. At the same time she knew isolation made her dull, 'I want winding up,' she admitted. Godwin, however, integrated the various facets of his life. He could write and gad about town: 'I do not know how you make authorship and dissipation agree, my thoughts are sometimes turned adrift.'

A subtext was their different gendered duties. When he was ill she had fussed about his household linen, and no doubt other women came to minister to him despite her efforts to warn off Hays. None had done the same for her. Also she had a child to care for where he had only himself to please. In her dissatisfaction she felt vulnerable and it was often then that she became most feminist. Women's lot was exacerbated by clothes. Although fashions now emphasised vertical lines rather than outlandish curves, were less constraining than they had been or would be fifty years on, long dresses remained inconvenient. Godwin's friend, Alexander Jardine, had proposed short skirts, so women could move more easily – they should wear drawers or knickers underneath. Wollstonecraft had called the author a 'manly Englishman' in her review but had not discussed his remarks on female underwear.[12] In Scandinavia, she noted the way women were bundled up in layers of clothing which impeded free movement and aggravated their chores; in England she deplored women's gowns trailing in the mud. As she wrote to Godwin, 'The dress of women seems to be invented to render them *dependent*, in more senses than one.'

Imlay had been largely indifferent to her complaints about the general predicament of women. Godwin was often similarly unmoved. He had not loved her for *The Rights of Woman* but for her Scandinavian letters. Now he did not respond to her generic or particular lament. Indeed he was beginning to find her efforts to control his life a touch annoying and her appeals to her oppressed state as a woman left him cold. She was turning into a nagging wife, making him a hen-pecked husband.

So, at Mary Robinson's one evening, he responded with coolness. She was piqued: 'there is a manner of leaving a person free to follow their own will, that looks so like indifference, I do not like it.' She knew the effect she was having, did not 'intend to *peck*', and proposed calling at three next day. Godwin was softened and replied honestly: 'I own I had the premeditated malice of making you part with me last night unwillingly. I feared Cupid had taken his final farewel. Call on me at three as your propose, unless you see me first in Judd Place.'[13] She called and, according to his diary code, they made successful love.

The pre-Christmas period found Wollstonecraft more contented than for many past seasons. Their snug times together were affectionate and secure and she revelled in them. 'Was not yesterday a very pleasant evening? There was a tenderness in your manner, as you seem to be opening your heart, to a new born affection, that rendered you very dear to me.' A few years ago in *Political Justice*, Godwin had argued relentlessly that emotions muddied clear perception, that reason should always overrule passion, and that no special hearing should be allowed to personal love; notoriously he had insisted that, if one had a choice between rescuing a close relative or an important philosopher and benefactor of humanity like Fénélon, one should choose the philosopher. Now this man was surrendering to his affections, 'There are other pleasures in the world, you perceive, beside those know[n] to your philosophy.'

Feeling better now, she began again to 'gad' about. She saw more of other women than when she had been a raw London author, dependent for most of her society on Johnson's intellectual circle. She especially appreciated Mary Robinson, who, having brought up her child to become an affectionate daughter, remembered Wollstonecraft was a mother. For one dinner she sent round her carriage to pick up 'little *Fannikin*' (Robinson was unusual in running a carriage, costing around £200 a year, but, since she was paralysed, it was a necessity). Wollstonecraft liked having Fanny included because she wanted to educate her through company; at the same time she was a little embarrassed to be urging her forward: 'You will smile at having so much of the womanish mother in me,' she admitted.

With her men friends she continued dining alone. She saw Johnson of course, and spent whole days with Opie. He was preparing to put his pictures on show at Robert Bowyer's Historic Gallery in Pall Mall: his admiration of strong women, including no doubt herself, led to inclusion of 'two Amazonian *heroines*', Boadicea and Joan of Arc.[14] Wollstonecraft and Opie seemed so publicly comfortable together that, writing from Norwich, Amelia Alderson reported a rumour they were to marry 'Law willing'. For her part she believed Opie would gladly marry Wollstonecraft, but not she him.[15] This was as well, for it was not many months afterwards that she herself accepted the proposal of John Opie.

# 35

*'The inelegant complaint'*

During her last coughing weeks Wollstonecraft had been conscious of another ailment. Signs of trouble were indigestion, nausea, irritability and bruised eyes, but the clearest was a late period. Hers should have arrived in early or mid-December; it had not. She was 'at a loss what to say', the event rested 'in the womb of time'.

Her maladies and distractions ate into her writing. She was doing reviews, but her book languished. She had been unable to repay her loans to Johnson since returning and her debts increased. Her father kept bothering her: she and Johnson had written to Charles after he declared his good fortune, hoping he might assume some of the burden, but no reply came. Although she had accepted a bond from Imlay for Fanny, nothing was paid; indeed Imlay had even reneged on joint debts. Poverty and pregnancy were good reasons for anxiety.

Along with Mary Hays, a few days after Christmas she and Godwin planned to attend one of Horne Tooke's regular dinners in Wimbledon. This famous old radical was conservative about women, but Wollstonecraft did not give this as a reason for her reluctance to visit him now. She was simply in no mood for political talk of any sort. New worry mingled with bitter memories of past Christmases. She was indulging herself but could not help it: 'I dare say you are out of patience with me,' she exclaimed to Godwin, who bore the brunt of her low spirits.

Indeed he *was* rather 'out of patience' and by the end of the year her moodiness was taking its toll. Because she felt superior in suffering, she assumed the right to say whatever she liked; as depression enveloped her, she attacked him from its depths. Godwin was prepared to soothe her when anxious, but not to be mocked or scourged for his pains. In one particular quarrel at the end of December she went too far, wishing she had never met him, wanting to take back all she had written and cancel everything between them. Having got this bile off her chest, next day she felt better, but her words stuck on Godwin and he could not slough them off. Like Johnson, he was dismayed at the notion that selfish behaviour could simply be ascribed to temperament and forgiven by the more self-controlled as Wollstonecraft expected. He wrote her a stern rebuking note, complaining of her 'extreme unkindness'. Especially hurtful was her apparent calm. Did she want to convey indifference?

Fretful and anxious, Wollstonecraft could not console. She was aware her affection wavered with her spirits. Godwin failed to understand what she faced in being once more pregnant and unmarried. The plight of women, from their womb to their stupid clothes, was borne in on her and she had little comfort to give any man, however distraught. She stood on her hurt pride and the mythical independence so often invoked with Imlay:

> This does not appear to me just the moment to have written me such a note as I have been perusing.
>
> I am, however, prepared for any thing. I can abide by the consequence of my own conduct, and do not wish to envolve any one in my difficulties.

Having displayed such raw emotions, the couple spent New Year's Eve together at Wollstonecraft's and did not make love.

Next morning her spirits were unrelieved and she felt unwell. There must have been moments of sheer terror: she had found one child difficult to cope with; two would be more than twice the trouble. Although conceived by a woman of high moral principles, two illegitimate children with different fathers could not be explained to the conventional. She would be mocked for her moral books about companionate marriage and decorous child-rearing. Without spelling out her predicament she demanded sympathy. 'You do not, I think make sufficient allowance for the peculiarity of my situation. But women are born to suffer.' Godwin was nearly out of wine but she wanted a bottle sent round. Though a stern critic of alcohol, what was she to do but have a drink?

She also remained alive to her poverty, no longer the contented state imagined in the Imlay days.[1] Much to her and Godwin's dismay, her predicament was known. Inchbald, who lived so parsimoniously that she managed to get a good income from savings and leave at her death the substantial sum of £5000, obliquely referred to her new acquaintance's profligacy, while a curious incident with Amelia Alderson in Norwich suggested that the news had travelled afar.

In mid-November Alderson had written to Godwin:

> A rich-ish old-ish bachelor who is never so well pleased as when he spares from his superfluities to the wants of persecuted patriots, & distressed authors, has written to me in consequence of his having heard that Mrs Imlay is in very

distressed circumstances, such circumstances as to make 5 guineas an acceptable present to her – Is this true? – If it be, I have his order to find some means of conveying that sum to her, the *giver unknown* – If she wants it, *surely* she thinks too justly to scruple accepting it – but I wish to have *your opinion* on the subject, & then I shall think further about it.

Godwin relayed the quaint proposal to Wollstonecraft, although Alderson had wanted only his confirmation or denial. Then the pair scorned the offer: 'Mrs Imlay has laugh'd with me over the story of y[ou]r rich-ish, generous gentleman – for my part, I have no patience with such fellows.' Wollstonecraft added further 'illiberal reflections' on the would-be donor, as well as some censure of Alderson.

The young woman was dismayed by criticism from Wollstonecraft, a person whom her 'too enthusiastic feelings' led her 'almost to *adore*', but furious with Godwin.[2] He had been her 'pope' in matters of principle; now she was appalled at his 'expressions of the most *contemptuous* kind'. The donor was not a rich man but a university fellow eager to honour 'suffering merit'; his offer provoked 'perhaps a degree of ridicule which he is far from deserving'. The 'merriment' at the expense of a 'well-meaning man' was unworthy. Her friend had wished to give a distressed woman genius 'his mite'; 'for this he is laughed at – & by whom?' Godwin: a man who prided himself on benevolence and patience. She was shocked.[3]

Despite the scorn with which she greeted the Norfolk bachelor, it is possible that Wollstonecraft herself had appealed to public charity: a curious item from Waugh's MS Account Book, possibly of St Pancras, for June 1796 records the acceptance of a 'Mary Wolsoncroft' as pensioner with 6s per month; she has 'a bastard child aged 5'. Fanny was only two; Wollstone-craft seems more elevated than this; and there exists a contemporary Mary Wolsoncroft from Clerkenwell. Still, it is a remarkable coinci-dence of name, parish and circumstance, and it remains possible that her needs were so great that she sometimes had to swallow her pride and admit her status.[4]

Godwin had a more respectable resource and offered it. For the past couple of years he had had a rich young admirer, Thomas Wedgwood, son of the pottery manufacturer Josiah Wedgwood of Etruria, who had changed the eating manners of the middle classes by providing good-quality, mass-pro-duced crockery, so converting an initial £10 into a legacy of half a million. Under the influence of Godwin's political theories and a fearful digestive system, young Tom determined not to marry but use his inherited money to help perfect human behaviour through education and habits of self-scrutiny. At nineteen he wrote, 'I mean to exert myself for the good of my fellow creatures.' An ally was Godwin.

Some years before, they had discussed patronage. Godwin saw gifts as 'a pampering of superfluous luxuries', an ignoble 'species of commerce'; nothing should be exchanged except 'the suggestions of the mind'.[5] Wedgwood considered this over-scrupulous; *he* gave without strings. Godwin tacked, 'If the loan or the gift of £100 would . . . be of eminent service to me in my pursuits, I think it probable that I ought to ask you for it without scruple, & that you ought to advance it', but he added 'I am not sure that I should think it my duty, when the case occurres.'[6] Both knew there *was* 'selfishness' in giving. For all his good intentions young Tom was demanding – he ended a long letter, 'Tell me, are you at all pleased, or edified, by these my lucubrations? I have a book full of similar matter' – and, for all his pride, Godwin took when necessary.[7] One principle of *Political Justice* was that money should roll down to the deserving, without need for gratitude.

Wollstonecraft distrusted rich young men, ailing or well, with or without benevolent ideas, knowing their propensity to think too well of themselves. Tom Wedgwood was clever in his own right – he would become famous as the precursor of photography with his experiments on light-affected nitrate and chloride of silver – but she saw a narcissistic and favoured son bolstered by hereditary wealth and family prestige; perhaps she also perceived with distaste a latent homosexuality in his avoidance of marriage. She had no objection to receiving loans and gifts, resembling Godwin in regarding her indebtedness as a privilege for her creditors, but she liked to approve her creditor. Also, she knew that, while Godwin encouraged the young man, he did not much like him. It was easy to dissuade him from writing.

Having mocked the Norwich bachelor and refused Godwin's Wedgwood offer, Wollstonecraft was desperate to make her own money from writing. Yet nothing was turning out as it should.

At this moment Mary Hays's raw autobiographical novel of unrequited female passion, *Memoirs of Emma Courtney*, appeared. Based on her miserable courtship of William Frend and seen by many as a straight transcription of her life, it was quite different from other more decorous attacks on female ills – like Inchbald's or Fenwick's for example – and it was another rebuke to Wollstonecraft's slowness with *The Wrongs of Woman*. Mary Robinson admired it, especially the main story, but was displeased with the melodramatic ending, which, not content with indulgently revealing the hero as loving beneath his rejection and killing him off, also violently disposed of the heroine's husband.[8] The book should have stopped with the hero's death.

Wollstonecraft agreed: she too lost interest then. She ascribed this to knowing Hays and the originating event: she had 'had a peep behind the curtain' so to speak. Not usually a fan of the intense Hays, Amelia Alderson was even more enthusiastic; though deeply flawed, the book was a *tour de force*: 'I am delighted with Miss Hays's novel! I would give a great deal to have written it,' she told Wollstonecraft.

Alderson knew that, however admirable, the work would be generally condemned and prided herself on her daring in appreciating it publicly.[9] Although a weak preface tried to transform a manifesto into a warning and Hays admitted the book a 'memento of [her] own folly and madness', there was no escaping the heroine's declaration, 'My friend – I would give myself to you', or her assertion that 'the individuality of an affection constitutes its chastity'. Hays's friends had to defend the book throughout London against the conservative and conventional. Anna Laetitia Barbauld's unstable clerical husband, with whom Wollstonecraft now dined, sneered at the author as 'a Philosophess – a [G]odwinian'. With her tongue firmly in her cheek, Wollstonecraft reassured him that, unlike Godwin's works, this novel would not undermine religion, private morality and the state. Hays must have appreciated her bold friend's support, but neither did the other much good. More than once, Hays was dismissed as 'the baldest disciple of Mrs Wollstonecraft'.[10]

It snowed incessantly. Cold weather always reinforced Wollstonecraft's gloom and she sometimes felt too depressed and lethargic even to visit Godwin. At others, she was hindered by her state, afraid to walk out in case she slipped. Everything worked against females. '[Y]ou have no petticoats to dangle in the snow,' she groaned. 'Poor Women how they are beset with plague – within – and without.' No man could understand her suffering. As January closed she wrote disconsolately: 'I am still an invalid – Still have the inelegant complaint, which no novelist has yet ventured to mention as one of the consequences of sentimental distress.'

Although not laid low by pregnancy, she had more chronic ill health than earlier. She felt neither sick nor well, simply out of sorts, irritated at being suspected of malingering. Biology was unjust: 'Women are certainly great fools; but nature made them so. I have not time, or paper, else, I could draw an inference, not very illustrative of your chance-medley system.' It was probably Godwin's 'chance-medley system' that had caused her predicament. Now Godwin was visiting the theatre and she was staying alone. When they did finally attend together at the beginning of February, along with Holcroft and John Fenwick, they appropriately saw Dryden's satire on marriage and sexual relationships, *Marriage à la Mode*. Presumably she had changed her earlier opinion that comedy of the past age was 'censurable', shocking a 'chaste ear' with 'indecencies'.[11]

Given the new situation, Godwin felt he needed medical information. According to his diary he was visited by Lady Lanesborough, whom he asked about the St Marylebone Dispensary. This was a London hospital founded in 1785 in Cavendish Square, its aim being to help 'poor and distressed sick persons' and provide advice to pregnant women.[12] Its catchment area included their lodgings. Lady Lanesborough was probably a patron, very much the kind of person with whom Godwin might easily converse about his and Wollstonecraft's predicament. She was no stranger to gossip: before the death of her husband, the Viscount, she had been linked to a friend of Godwin, the rich, shady Jewish money-lender, John King, who was accused of blackmail and swindling as well as radicalism; she later married him after he had divorced (or, as scandal declared, not divorced) his wife. Perhaps her connection with the Dispensary was a charitable way of aiding a needed social rehabilitation.[13]

Godwin also talked to his medical friend Carlisle, not an authority on pregnancy but a man he respected. Through such means he learnt about the theories of obstetrics, when intervention was advisable and who best served the interests of mother and child: the experienced midwife or the male obstetrician able to use his forceps to deliver a recalcitrant baby. He also knew something of the peculiar bodily rhythms and troubles of the pregnant female.

Wollstonecraft too was eager to talk to a doctor and she visited an old acquaintance from the Johnson-dinner days, Fordyce of St Thomas' Hospital, another close friend of Godwin's. She might have consulted Carlisle but never caught him alone and did not accompany Godwin to his lectures. She intended to ask his help when she wrote a new work on early childhood, but perhaps she was not entirely impressed with him and agreed with a common judgement that he was vain. His opinions on women were alien: he admired her particular spirit but later endorsed the notion that 'immoderate' intellectual development harmed female grace and beauty, much as Rousseau thought.[14] Yet, possibly on Carlisle's recommendation, she visited the Westminster New Lying-in Hospital in Lambeth, which, unlike more fashionable hospitals, admitted unmarried mothers for their first child. There she spoke with an impressive midwife and mother, the matron Mrs Blenkinsop, brought in during 1792 to help reform the hospital. Sadly, she was inferior in rank to the male doctors: 'Women might certainly study the art of healing,' Wollstonecraft had written in *The Rights of Woman*, 'and be physicians as well as nurses.' She confided the secret of her state to Mrs Blenkinsop.

To others, including Everina who came to stay in February, she kept mum. The sisters had never much confided in each other and in the last years had grown far apart. Everina was on her way north. She had left her Dublin post and was going for a short spell to Etruria, the Wedgwood family home, close to Stoke-on-Trent. Possibly she was acting as a temporary companion and supervisor of the young children of Tom's brother, Josiah Wedgwood II, who had become a gentleman in Surrey but still made lengthy stays back at the old Potteries home, where he now was. The eldest child, Bessie, was only four, and the boy, Josiah, two, but it was common for educated women to take on duties in good families, to prevent what Mary had once so feared: the corruption of children by lower servants. This superior lady would supervise the children's dressing, eating and playing, although the actual physical care would be taken by menials. In addition, she would read to the ladies of the family during the morning while they sewed.[15]

With the Wedgwoods, any pedagogical position had special significance since Josiah, still a young man under thirty, supervised his children's education on Rousseauian, progressive lines. A governess must follow his system. He kept a journal of his offsprings' activities and talk, and insisted on a routine of permissiveness and encouragement, despite a sense that Bessie was already rather vain and imperious. He was at one with Wollstonecraft in dislike of provoking shame in children, since he felt it led to deception, but he went further than she in hiding the power of adulthood. A later governess hired in May 1798, Thomasin Dennis, agreed in general with the system, while tartly remarking that the idea of inducing learning with rewards directly opposed the advice of Epictetus. Sometimes she found the results in the spoilt and demanding children more than she could bear and she was dismissed the following year.[16] In his writings on his children Josiah made no mention of Everina; so she was probably always intended as a temporary presence.[17]

The Wedgwood place was perhaps found for Everina by Mary, through Godwin and Montagu, who was engaged to Sarah, sister of Josiah and Tom. To add to the connections, Mrs Josiah Wedgwood had formerly been Elizabeth (Bessie) Allen of Cresselly, whom Everina met as a child in Laugharne. A little older than her husband, she was a few years younger than Everina at an age when it mattered, so they are unlikely to have been friends. Perhaps the remote connection lent attraction to the position, although there was now little equality between the Wollstonecrafts and Allens, as Eliza's alienation in Upton revealed.[18]

During her stay in London the sisters could talk over this distant Welsh past shared with Bessie Wedgwood, but they avoided the present. Mary kept not only her pregnancy secret but even her relationship with Godwin. So she had to seek clandestine meetings as in November with Mrs Cotton. She must have seemed preoccupied and secretive to Everina, who responded with sullen reserve, far from her earlier vivacity. Listlessness was exacerbated by a heavy cold; when Godwin came she sat as silent as a tomb, dampening his spirits, then uncivilly went to bed. It was hard for anyone to be cheery. Snow had turned to incessant rain and Mary felt she could not risk going out; so she and Everina sat drearily at home.

When the weather cleared, they took tea with Godwin at Chalton Street, but Everina's cold prevented a proposed visit to Mary Hays. Fortunately, their old friend Anne Cristall also invited Everina. She had recently published a book of poems by subscription with Johnson, and both Mary and Everina had subscribed.[19] They were rather remarkable if conventional poems, as the poet Southey testified, but Wollstonecraft was not a great connoisseur of verses and did not allude to them.[20] Now Anne was precious; Mary wrote to Godwin that she had managed to get a free day through her good offices and they could dine together alone.

Mary was glad to hear that another visit was projected. The intervening evenings alone together were oppressive, but worse with outside company, for Everina's silent presence embarrassed and restrained the usual chatter. At one time she nearly persuaded Everina to attend the theatre, but Godwin's ill-timed criticism of the play dissuaded her. 'Well a little patience,' Mary exclaimed. She herself broke the monotony by taking an outing with Montagu, but mostly she felt dragged down by Everina. When the day of the next Cristall visit dawned, Everina cancelled, declaring her cold too bad.

In early March came liberation. Just before Everina went, she joined a theatre party with Mary, Godwin, Holcroft, and others, the kind of group that the more political Eliza Bishop would have relished. Then she was booked on the evening mail coach out of London. On the morning Godwin called round to say goodbye. Mary saw her sister off and, newly freed, stopped by at Johnson's. Evenings alone with Godwin stretched deliciously ahead. It had ceased to rain and little Fanny could go and fetch her mother's newspaper by herself.

Even after she went, Everina irritated. She had not even left a drawing in gratitude; her thank-you letter asked for a parcel to be sent to an illegible address and for things to be forwarded that Mary could not find – there was only some powder which she assumed her sister could not want. Worse, she left a debt to a mantua maker of £3 4s. The poor seamstress needed money for rent; Mary felt sorry for her and paid her, though she could ill afford so much. Anne's brother, young Joshua Cristall, was also a supplicant and she gave him all her ready cash. Her father remained importunate and she sent money to stop him coming to London. Everina was either not receiving wages or having to wait until the end of a quarter for pay; she too needed something, but Mary had nothing. As soon as she could get money from Johnson, she would forward a guinea, she promised, but for now she was broke.

The most worrying element was Johnson, now asking repayment of old debts.[21] Was he in difficulties or had he grown mean? He *could* be hard up, for he served as banker to Fuseli, Barlow, Wollstonecraft and others, provided mail delivery for friends, and philanthropically sustained unpaying causes like the Unitarian Society. In addition, his health was erratic and he lost clients through inattention. Yet, he is unlikely to have felt really poor since, when he died not long after, he left £60,000. Possibly he was prepared to support Wollstonecraft when alone, less so when he felt that Imlay or Godwin should have kept her. The latter was one of his authors but regularly attended his dinners only after the beginning of the liaison with Wollstonecraft; perhaps there was not complete harmony between the two men. Fuseli, to whom Johnson was devoted, often disagreed with Godwin and each judged the other overrated. When Johnson died, he left generous annuities to Fuseli and Bonnycastle, but nothing to the needy Godwin.[22]

Her own anxieties made Mary unreceptive to Everina's pleasantly chatty letter from Etruria. Her sister liked the cheerful, welcoming Wedgwoods more than any other family. Since Josiah was pedantic and domineering, Tom self-centred and vain, her enthusiasm must mainly have been due to their sisters, well educated at home and at a Manchester school, and to Josiah's wife.[23] The Wedgwood ladies had a voracious appetite for novels and Everina happily told Mary of their tastes, begging her to send books. She especially wanted Radcliffe's Gothic *Italian* but also tactfully requested her sister's *Mary, A Fiction*.

Wollstonecraft was in no mood to admire Wedgwood domestic life and she wrote back scornfully to Everina, who must have wondered quite what she had written to offend:

Your description of the females, of your happy family, makes me hug myself in the solitude of my fire side. I was really fatigued at only hearing of their animal spirits; and the contents of the dozen novels, they devour in a week, whirled round my head till it ached again. In short when you call them an amiable set you have contrive[d] to give me an idea of a party destitute of sentiment, fancy or feeling, taste is, of course, out of the question.

She had never liked other people's family bliss but, in the case of the Wedg-woods, she envied their secure wealth, so contrasting with her own poverty. Also, her habit of reading differed from most women's. They tended to cluster in domestic groups, while she read in solitude. Reading for her was more business and self-improvement than recreation – even novels were primarily for review. In this preference for solitary over communal reading, she was at odds with one of the culture's cherished visions – in which she herself had indulged when fondly imagining Imlay reading while she mended stockings. For women solitary reading was regarded as selfish, tending to erotic or radical ideas; Wollstonecraft and Hays were satirised together in a con-servative novel in which the butt, Brigetina Botherim, refuses to 'read aloud to any one'.[24]

Though scorning the cheerful practice, she sent books. She had not yet reviewed *The Italian* for the *Analytical*, so could not lend that, but they could have Mary Robinson's *Angelina*, reviewed the previous year. She had praised its aim of rebuking parents who tried to force daughters into mercenary marriages but admitted that the confused and over-complicated story 'will not greatly rouse or deeply agitate.' Still, it kept the reader's attention and the writing was elegant and correct – except for the ignorant confusion of 'laying' and 'lying'. In short, it was the kind of run-of-the-mill sentimental novel quite suitable for the Wedgwood ladies. When she *could* send *The Italian*, she advised Everina to read it alone in her room. She disapproved of Radcliffe's tendency to excite and then deflate, but she wrote with genius and any work of hers differed markedly from other books tumbling from the presses; the poetic images of *The Italian* needed savouring by the solitary reader.[25] As for her own *Mary, A Fiction*, she would send it if Everina wished; she and the Wedgwoods could laugh over it. Despite Godwin's surprising liking, she now saw the book as crude and sentimental, probably feeling towards it rather like the older Rousseau had towards *La Nouvelle Héloïse*, that it was a slightly shameful overflow of past emotional circumstances. Now she was embarrassed for anyone whose good opinion she valued to judge her on it. About the tasteless 'animal'-spirited Wedgwoods she cared not a jot.

As the pregnancy progressed Wollstonecraft dreaded its effect on her social life; in *The Wrongs of Woman* she described the fears of a pregnant unwed girl. Although she was still called Mrs Imlay, her new child could not be Imlay's, for she had made his desertion very public.[26] When she was known to be pregnant she would be shunned by respectable women, even perhaps feminists such as Hays and Eliza Fenwick. Certainly the more conventional

Alderson, Inchbald, the Twisses and 'The Siddons' would ostracise her. Theatrical people could not afford tainted acquaintances, especially Siddons, who complemented her cross-dressed roles with a much-paraded virtue in private life.

It was all especially hard, for Wollstonecraft had never written against marriage and wanted it if certain equalising conditions were met. Godwin, however, had attacked forcibly 'the most odious of all monopolies'. He had done so not to promote the kind of free love in which they had indulged but for the highest motives, as his daughter Mary Shelley was at pains to record when she described him as a 'conscientious man' whose 'sense of duty' would not 'permit him to indulge in any deviation from the laws of society' even those he regarded as unjust.[27] He *had* deviated, however, and it was not he who was pregnant. He could no longer afford his abstract opposition, Wollstonecraft thought. At the beginning of the year she had persuaded him to talk of 'children & marriage'; now she had some hopes of parting him from his principles. She must do so quickly if they were to save any shred of her reputation.

Wollstonecraft's distress touched Godwin. He considered, weighed his theory with her pain and wavered. Then he agreed to a wedding, knowing the world prejudiced against females who opposed 'the European institution of marriage'. '[T]he comfort and peace of a woman for whose comfort and peace I interest myself would be much injured if I could have prevailed on her to defy those prejudices.'[28] At the end of February, presumably with Wollstonecraft's consent, he wrote to Tom Wedgwood requesting an immediate loan of £50. It was an awkward letter since, knowing Tom was aware of his economical habits, he declared he needed money for 'another person': so embarrassed was he at his subterfuge that he dispensed with the 'concluding compliments & professions'.[29] The money came at once and paid Wollstonecraft's most pressing debts.

It was not to be an ordinary marriage: the couple would live as if the ceremony had not occurred. They would not cohabit if love declined and would not, even now, be always mewed up together in one house. As Wollstonecraft later explained to Amelia Alderson: 'it is my wish that Mr Godwin should visit and dine out as formerly, and I shall do the same; in short, I still mean to be independent, even to the cultivating sentiments and principles in my children's minds (should I have more), which he disavows.' She did not admit her advanced pregnancy.

The wedding took place on 29 March at the nearest church, the Gothic St Pancras, still picturesquely nestling in trees, a Saxon foundation reputedly the last English parish church where Catholic mass was said. Godwin recorded the event in his diary simply as 'Panc'. Only his friend Marshall attended and there was no wedding breakfast.

He tucked his marriage between reading-lists and visits to politicians and journalists; on the following Sunday, he was with Holcroft, then Johnson and William Blake; then he went to tea and the theatre alone with Elizabeth Inchbald – indeed, in one periodical he was actually being linked with her.[30] Nothing was said to these friend and so, apart from Marshall, few were aware that anything had changed. As they had kept the affair, so Godwin and Wollstonecraft aimed to keep the marriage a secret.

Why? Obviously Godwin was embarrassed about the contradiction of his theories – later Mrs Barbauld reported, '[N]umberless are the squibs that are thrown out at Mr Godwin ... and he winces not a little on receiving the usual congratulations.'[31] Mary Shelley, too, wrote that he felt 'a slight shrinking ... to avow that he had acted in contradiction to his theories'.[32] There was also the matter of their joint poverty. Godwin had never contemplated having a family, certainly not a ready-made one, and had not the resources. Wollstonecraft was chronically in debt and a series of good friends had stood between her and ruin, most notably Johnson. When she and Godwin married, this gallant behaviour must end.[33] Godwin claimed it was Wollstonecraft who wanted the secret kept, not he, and 'having settled the principal point in conformity to her interest', he might as well agree to everything else.

*'The most extraordinary married pair in existence'*

When news seeped out, Godwin's women friends were irritated at the subterfuge. The first to learn was Maria Reveley, who feared she was losing an
admirer and intimate friend. She sobbed a little, then heard of their strange
domestic arrangements, found she could continue visiting Godwin as before,
and accepted the event. She liked his new wife, which helped.[1]

Mary Hays was not shocked, already knowing the circumstances of
Wollstonecraft's earlier non-marriage. Indeed, to make her friend more of
the feminist heroine, she had urged her to resume her own name. So, when
appeasing her, Godwin playfully alluded to this:

> She bids me remind you of the earnest way in which you pressed me to prevail
> upon her to change her name, she directs me to add, that it has happened to me,
> like many other disputants, to be entrapped in my own toils: in short, that we
> found there was no way so obvious for her to drop the name of Imlay, as to assume
> the name of Godwin.[2]

Other women were more problematic. The raffish Mary Robinson, with
multiple lovers and a chequered past, could not have disapproved. She knew
what it was to suffer the sneers of women 'friends': 'I have experienced little
kindness from [women],' she wrote, 'though my bosom has often ached with
the pang inflicted by their envy, slander, and malevolence.'[3] Yet Wollstonecraft
may have thought her insufficiently loyal and saw little of her over the next
months. The failure probably sprang from Robinson's own miseries. She had
had a tempestuous relationship of fifteen years with Tarleton; now he bowed
to family pressure and told her all was over. Less than a month after the
Godwin-Wollstonecraft wedding, she fled to Bath but was taken ill on the
road: 'bed of sickness! thou to me / No keener pangs canst bring', she wrote.
She returned to London, sold her carriage, took opium against pain, and
began work on another novel: 'I am forlorn but not misanthropic ... I
shrunk, I yielded, before I learnt to exercise the virtue of resistance.' Her life
contracted to a distance between bed and couch; newspapers expected her
imminent death.[4] Yet, however explicable her retreat, Wollstonecraft
appeared hurt, and she dismissed Robinson's *Hubert de Sevrac* in the May

issue of the *Analytical* as 'imperfect', the work of a writer who thinks herself 'so happily gifted by nature, that her first thoughts will answer her purpose'. Other critics found it inferior but had something good to say; Wollstonecraft's harshness was unusual.[5]

The greatest difficulty was Elizabeth Inchbald. Without wanting him herself, she was competitive with Godwin's ladies and had not been entirely ironic when complaining to Amelia Alderson that, since the latter arrived in town, Godwin never came near her. She had not cared for Wollstonecraft and now liked her even less. She had been unaware of the nature of the relationship and of Wollstonecraft's indecorous status: the present marriage was bigamous or it declared the lack of a previous one.[6] Inchbald knew what it was to be infatuated and pursue men – she had loved John Philip Kemble and was obsessed with a Dr Warren – but she guarded her reputation. Wollstonecraft was no longer a suitable acquaintance.

Before the wedding became public knowledge, an arrangement had been made for a box at the theatre, with a group including Godwin, Wollstonecraft, Inchbald, Amelia Alderson, Maria Reveley and Eliza Fenwick. Now Inchbald made it known she wished to avoid Wollstonecraft. When she heard this, the latter remarked tartly to Alderson on female jealousy and vanity; she was glad not to be sharing a box with such a viper.

Then Godwin received a note:

> I most sincerely wish you and Mrs Godwin joy. But, assured that your joyfulness would obliterate from your memory every trifling engagement, I have entreated another person to supply your place ... If I have done wrong, when you next marry, I will act differently.[7]

He showed it to his new wife, who reconsidered her previous scorn. Inchbald was widely known and respected; an open breach could be unfortunate. She had been unwise to mock her to a close friend. So, resolving to ignore the insult, she asked Alderson to mediate. The insolent letter was 'Nonsense!' Inchbald *must* be of their party even if she herself sat in the pit. Godwin was also badgered; he persuaded the ruffled Inchbald to rescind the cancellation.

The theatre encounter answered their friends' fears. The two women met coldly, then publicly quarrelled. Everyone had heard, everyone knew. There was no reconciliation and there were to be no further meetings between them.

The insults hurt. When Wollstonecraft and Godwin reached home, she was irritable, blaming Godwin and, as usual, letting rebukes spiral out of control. She accused him of not caring enough for her happiness. Knowing how easily she sank into depression, how much she then lashed out at those who did not offer immediate and repeated comfort, the next morning Godwin wrote to stifle any incipient quarrel. 'The sole principle of conduct of which I am conscious in my behaviour to you has been in every thing to study your happiness,' he assured her. 'I found a wounded heart, &, as that heart cast itself upon me, it was my ambition to heal it.' Perhaps his obstetrical studies had taught him that a pregnant woman should be humoured. He had done the right thing: Wollstonecraft was calmed.

About Inchbald he remained resentful. Her conduct was 'base, cruel, and insulting'; she should be ashamed of such 'shuffling behaviour'. He had expected conventional people like the Twisses to follow 'mean and pitiful conduct' but not a superior person like her. Later Inchbald justified her behaviour: 'I never wished to know her: as I avoid every female acquaintance, who has no husband, I avoided her. Against my desire you made us acquainted.'[8]

Wollstonecraft continued to worry about her reputation. Writing to Alderson about Inchbald, she defended herself against what appeared fickleness in feeling. A year was short to move from a grand and publicly lamented passion into a new love affair and marriage. Such swiftness suggested sexual appetite gratified at the expense of propriety or, worse, desire for an establishment. But, she declared, she had been truly in love with Imlay and 'the wound my unsuspecting heart formerly received is not healed.' It was not for sex or advantage that she had married. No, she had wanted a father for Fanny and another name for herself, since the Imlay one was disgraced; above all, she desired a little rational company in the evenings. If she had been simply eager to marry well, she could have done a great deal better than Godwin:

> Since I have been unfortunately the object of observation, I have had it in my power, more than once, to marry very advantageously; and of course, should have been courted by those, who at least cannot accuse me of acting an interested part, though I have not, by dazzling their eyes, rendered them blind to my faults. I am proud perhaps, conscious of my own purity and integrity; and many circumstances in my life have contributed to excite in my bosom an indignant contempt for the forms of a world I should have bade a long good night to, had I not been a mother. Condemned then to toil my hour out, I wish to live as rationally as I can; had fortune or splendor been my aim in life, they have been within my reach, would I have paid the price.

The priggish letter amused Amelia Alderson, who wrote to a Norwich friend about these 'extraordinary characters': 'Heigho! what charming things would sublime theories be, if one could make one's practice keep up with them;

but I am convinced it is impossible, and am resolved to make the best of every-day nature.' Although she did not break off relations with the Godwins, she had her reservations. She might flirt with republican principles and have ached for a married man herself, but in her conduct, like Inchbald, she followed convention.[9]

Godwin too worried about the figure he was cutting. With Tom Wedgwood, whose money he had taken, the situation was especially delicate and he indulged in nifty intellectual footwork to reconcile theory and marriage:

> Some persons have found an inconsistency between my practice in this instance and my doctrines. But I cannot see it. The doctrine of my 'Political Justice' is, that an attachment in some degree permanent, between two persons of opposite sexes is right, but that marriage, as practised in European countries, is wrong. I still adhere to that opinion. Nothing but a regard for the happiness of the individual, which I had no right to injure, could have induced me to submit to an institution which I wish to see abolished, and which I would recommend to my fellow-men, never to practise, but with the greatest caution. Having done what I thought necessary for the peace and respectability of the individual, I hold myself no otherwise bound than I was before the ceremony took place.

His close male friends were the easiest to handle. Holcroft knew of some relationship but had not been warned of a wedding. When he heard the news he was hurt by his exclusion but responded felicitously:

> From my heart and soul I give you joy. I think you the most extraordinary married pair in existence. May your happiness be as pure as I firmly persuade myself it must be. I hope and expect to see you both, and very soon. If you show coldness, or refuse me, you will do injustice to a heart which, since it has really known you, never for a moment felt cold to you.
>
>    I cannot be mistaken concerning the woman you have married. It is Mrs. W. Your secrecy a little pains me. It tells me you do not yet know me.[10]

Fuseli was characteristically amused: '[T]he assertrix of female rights has given her hand to the *balancier* of political justice,' he told Roscoe.[11]

Perhaps the most welcoming because the most ignorant of circumstances was Godwin's pious mother in Norfolk. She had been saddened by her son's principled stand against marriage and was pleased at the change. She took a while to digest his surprising letter, during which time she heard some details about which Godwin had been silent – such as the existence of a stepchild. When she replied she was unaware of the imminent approach of another baby:

Your broken resolution in regard to mattrimony incourages me to hope that you will ere long embrace the Gospel, that sure word of promise to all believers, and not only you, but your other half, whose souls should be both one ... You might have been so good as told me a few more particulars about your conjugal state, as when you were married, as being a father as well as a husband; hope you will fill up your place with propriety in both relations; you are certainly transformed in a moral sense, why is it impossable in a spiritual sense, which last will make you shine with the radiance of the sun for ever.

She offered some worldly advice: 'My dears, whatever you do, do not make invitations and entertainments ... Live comfortable with one another.' She invited the couple to Norfolk, though, since she was crippled with rheumatism, they would have to fend for themselves. She was eager to mark the happy occasion at once and sent some eggs packed in sawdust bran and laid inside Godwin's sister's box; they should be turned often to keep them good. She could also dispatch by wagon a feather bed fit for a servant if they wished.[12]

Later in the summer on a visit to Norfolk, Holcroft took the parents of his son-in-law to call on Godwin's elderly mother, just then being visited by her daughter-in-law and grandchildren. Mrs Godwin was short-sighted and her daughter-in-law had not seen Godwin for a couple of years. So, when they spied two men, one spectacled and with a woman, they excitedly assumed them to be William and his famous wife Mary. The old lady stood waiting on the porch, while the children dashed forward. Then the sister-in-law addressed Holcroft tentatively, 'I think I know you, sir.' They stood in embarrassment until Holcroft's friends introduced him, when 'the change of countenance ... was visible, for though your sister could not perhaps have fully persuaded herself that my face was actually yours, yet she seemed rather to trust to her hopes than to her recollection; and these being disappointed, an immediate blank took possession of her features, and the rising joy was damped.'[13]

With no further need for secrecy Godwin and Wollstonecraft moved into a semi-circular block of newly built houses in Somers Town: 29, the Polygon. The houses were semi-detached and had three storeys: bedchambers were on the second floor, a large dining-room was on the first and a parlour on the ground. There was a balcony on the front, and porch and front door on the side; at the back was a wedge-shaped garden.[14] Open country extended nearby and there were nursery gardens to the north. It was a good place for children: Fanny planned 'to make Hay in the fields' with her new rake. The couple seemed properly married, and Godwin ceased to note his sexual relations in his diary.

Yet they retained their unconventional notions of housekeeping and Godwin took another apartment solely for himself in 17 Evesham Buildings about twenty doors down from their joint home. He was revising *Political Justice* for its third, gentler edition, and needed his space. The pair shared a bed at the Polygon but, when morning came, Godwin retreated to his apartment to study, write and be visited. He might come round during the day, but often did not appear till dinner in late afternoon. Things moved along the street between them, a second volume of a work both were reading, a bit of India rubber, a portion of last night's supper and bottles of wine.

The arrangement amused their old acquaintances. Anna Laetitia Barbauld commented: 'In order to give the connection as little as possible the appearance of such a vulgar and debasing tie as matrimony, the parties have established separate establishments, and the husband only visits his mistress like a lover when each is dressed, rooms in order, &c. And this may possibly last till they have a family, then they will probably join quietly in one menage, like other folks.'[15] For posterity the arrangement had the advantage that husband and wife communicated through notes.

It was expensive and, a fortnight after moving, Godwin once more approached Wedgwood, apprised of the marriage by Montagu. He reminded Wedgwood that he and Wollstonecraft were authors with past successes, and delicately pointed out that his wife's financial predicament derived from her 'former connection', assuming that, since the Imlay affair had been so publicly conducted, Wedgwood knew about it. Now they needed another £50 for their new life. 'This you shall afford us, if you feel perfectly assured of its propriety,' Godwin wrote airily, 'but if there be the smallest doubt in your mind, I shall be much more gratified by your obeying that doubt, than superseding it. I do not at present feel inclined to remain long in any man's debt, not even yours.'[16] Wedgwood sent the money.

In *The Rights of Woman* Wollstonecraft had replaced the sensitive voice of *Mary, A Fiction* with that of the austere reasoner. Then, in the Imlay letters she was rationalist and imaginist. Now, beside the super-rationalist Godwin, she stressed the imaginist in herself. Other women like Robinson and Hays were trying to dent the security of male reason with their claims for feminised experience.[17] She was not as definite as these – still uncomfortable at the gendered divisions – but, with Godwin she sometimes felt the representative of imagination and feeling, and he regarded her as such.[18]

Partially in this role she contributed an essay on culture and aesthetics to the April issue of the *Monthly Magazine*, a new journal founded the previous year in St Paul's Churchyard by the Leicester radical Richard Phillips and aimed in part at a Dissenting readership. Hays also wrote for it. Entitled 'On Poetry, and Our Relish for the Beauties of Nature', Wollstonecraft's essay recapitulated her perceptions in Hull and Scandinavia: sensibility promotes understanding and self-awareness but could be perverted by sensual men: 'The same sensibility, or quickness of senses, which makes a man impart delight, frequently makes a libertine of him.'[19] As in *Letters from Sweden*, so here she accepted the power of sublimity and, using a male poet beside her enthusiastic female self, felt no need to puncture its appreciation with female cares or discordant observations. Again she displayed a quasi-mystical sense of God in nature, a view quite unlike Godwin's current atheism and one which separated her from the Unitarian Dissenters with whom she had so often mixed, 'the world [which] seems to contain only the mind that formed and contemplates it'.[20] Although attenuated and attacked by Godwin, her faith in an author of life remained.

In the past, despite Fuseli's influence, she had largely believed literature should be didactic. Literary taste was now moving from this emphasis. Blair, whom she had once so admired, insisted on moral virtue as the foundation of genius and appreciation, while stressing the need for impassioned observation; the new writers emphasised imagination over observation. In her essay, Wollstonecraft did not travel all the way with this taste – literature was still less important than the truth of observation – and, for all her fashionable lip-service to poetry, she remained the devotee of prose: many young persons could string together pretty epithets to make passable poetry, but their prose showed the 'barrenness of their minds'. She stressed the need for authentic response to mankind and nature and judged the best poetry 'the transcript of immediate emotions'.[21]

A similar balance appears in fragments or aphorisms written over a long period and later printed by Godwin as *Hints*: the fine arts are irrelevant if they do not serve virtue, she wrote. '[S]ome flights of the imagination seem to reach what wisdom cannot teach' and point to an afterlife, but they still delude people in *this* life.[22] The imagination transcended, leapt over and surpassed reason; though what it *mainly* transcended was self-interest, that ground of Enlightenment thinking which Wollstonecraft had come to associate in its darkest aspect with Imlay, his speculation and commercial face.

In reiterating her belief in truth from observation and the necessity of independent thinking and self-expression, her essay, ostensibly a meditation on art, nature and the artist, formed another answer to Godwin and his incomprehension of her personal method of writing. It also summarised many of the opinions so painfully spelt out to Imlay in her final letters. She had been knocked by life, she implied, but she wanted both men to know she thought herself of consequence as a writer and a woman, however her emotions and body might sometimes let her down.

Her major work in progress remained the troublesome *Wrongs of Woman*. To pursue this she largely gave up reviewing for the *Analytical*, her last contribution appearing in May, the swipe at Mary Robinson for being too prolific. Some envy, as well as disappointment, may have driven the remark.

Given the furore that greeted Hays's outspoken *Emma Courtney* at the beginning of the year, Wollstonecraft must have worried about the reception of her book when done. By 1797, the French war was taking its toll. French invasion was feared; indeed a small French force did actually land near Fishguard in Pembrokeshire on its way to Ireland. The economy was suffering from blockades. Individuals who revealed 'French' values provoked rancour or censorship. Even though the Terror had been succeeded by the less blood-thirsty Directory, the French were still seen as morally corrupt. Indeed, in some respects the Directors were worse than the Jacobins – in private morals, for example. Robespierre had been famously abstemious, but the Directors were synonymous with licence and sexual depravity, epitomised by Madame Tallien appearing in transparent silk and no underwear. England distinguished itself from the enemy by retreating into political and social conservatism, which Burke heralded. The arch-conservative Hannah More had vast success with her first *Repository Tract*, which provided the reactionary comfort that 'God is pleased to contrive to make things more equal than we poor, ignorant, short-sighted creatures, are apt to think.' It was not a propitious moment for radical writing women like Wollstonecraft and Hays to make the unpopular points that their own country had inequities, especially in regard to women, and that one of these was the double standard of behaviour. Freer marriage and divorce had become associated with the brutal French Revolution and seemed profoundly un-English.

Mediating as a rationalist-feminist always depressed Wollstonecraft – the struggle to reform women *and* society was so uphill. When she had first met Godwin and talked of women's status in society back in 1791, she had been 'gloomy', to repeat his word; now she could not avoid being so again for she was less certain and more experienced. She had stopped raising feminist issues when reviewing fiction; yet she was now writing a book that must address them as they impinged on imagined women's lives. It was bound to be difficult for there was no precedent.

The novel would question society through characters placed in an asylum.

Insanity had been a spectacle through much of the eighteenth century, but a more humane attitude now obtained. Around 1770 the London Bedlam stopped encouraging indiscriminate sightseeing, but Wollstonecraft, Godwin and Joseph Johnson visited it in February 1797, perhaps to see an old friend or relative – possible even her brother Henry – or to provide Wollstonecraft with some background for her writing.[23] She was probably savouring material from talks with Amelia Alderson, who, as a morbid young girl, was obsessed with insanity; she had stared through the iron gates and barred windows of the Norwich Bedlam and used her pocket-money to buy the inmates nosegays. She sought those delicate love-sick women that sentimental writing, especially Cowper with his Crazy Kate and Sterne with mad Maria, had taught her to expect and was much unnerved by a singing maniac and a picturesque love-sick girl who, when approached, let out an unearthly laugh. The pair seem fused in the 'lovely maniac' of *The Wrongs of Woman*, who shatters her sentimental image with screaming mirth.[24]

Inevitably the asylum setting drew on Gothic fiction, which delighted in places of confinement. Fearing stereotypes while wanting their appeal, Wollstonecraft insisted that *her* horrors were real. Her inmates were not prettily mad but actually so. The twist in her bleak book was that the heroine, Maria, disappointed in love and in an asylum, is *not* mad but sometimes sounds like it.[25]

In this she was pointing to a real social disgrace, the easy incarceration of victims by greedy relatives. People could be admitted without a certificate of lunacy; although this had to be obtained within three days, it could be signed by a doctor, surgeon or apothecary without his having a sight of the patient, while the term 'apothecary' was so loose that almost any asylum-keeper could claim it. When imprisoned, the sane could be driven mad by being manacled, beaten, starved and tied to bedposts, left to defecate where they stood. Famous cases included a vicar incarcerated by his wife and her lover, and locked up for seven years, and Mary Daintree, dragged from her coach and rushed to the Hoxton madhouse to be straitjacketed and chained for fifteen weeks so that her nephew and his wife could inherit her property.[26] The horrors of real asylums were worse than anything Wollstonecraft was drawing: Gothic fiction did not need to be invoked for a *frisson*.

In her novel a man and two women, one a keeper, tell their tales. Into these are incorporated miserable accounts of other oppressed women. The most expansive narrator, the sentimental middle-class Maria, is the closest to Wollstonecraft in demeanour and needy childhood background, although her experience of being sold within matrimony more resembles Mary Robinson's: as a girl of fifteen Robinson had married a law clerk and lived fashionably believing him a man of means; then, disabused, had to fend off the approved advances of her husband's libertine friends. Debtors' prison followed, but in Robinson's case *à deux*. An even more pressing parallel was with Imlay's sentimental novel, *The Emigrants*, the book that had swelled her love. In a subsidiary plot, the heroine's sister Eliza is married to a degraded husband who, when ruined, proposes 'the prostitution of her person'. After the escape, Maria's hounding is closer to Godwin's portrayal of Caleb in *Caleb Williams*. And, as in the account of Scandinavia, there was the pervasive sense of *Hamlet*: Maria was now the meditative prince, now Ophelia maddened by a brutal male world. A lot of stories were pressing on the book.[27]

Maria narrates a tale of domestic betrayals. Like Eliza Bishop, she escapes from her husband's house, but Wollstonecraft rewrote history by having the absconding wife take her baby, thus risking more dramatic persecution than Eliza suffered. The baby is snatched from her mother, who is incarcerated by her brutal husband to grab her money. As an asylum-prisoner, she falls in love with a charming fellow-inmate, the male narrator, called Henry like the hero of *Mary, A Fiction* although a sexier man. After a misspent youth of extravagance and women, this Henry went to America and was drawn to the western wilds and freedom. No longer so enamoured of things American, Wollstonecraft let freedom degenerate into commercial speculation and selfishness. As in *Emma Courtney*, the romantic vulnerability of the heroine is displayed by having her first fall in love with the hero by proxy: in Hays's novel through his portrait and his mother's words, in Wollstonecraft's through his political writings and impassioned marginalia on that most corrupting of novels, Rousseau's *Nouvelle Héloïse*. The book may have helped liberate Wollstonecraft into sexual activity, but for the sensitive Maria it is romantically imprisoning – or rather it turns the cell momentarily into a bower of bliss with no exit in divine rapture as in *Mary, a Fiction*. In her own letters the author had never so clearly fetishised her romantic thraldom. Here as narrator she remains ambivalent towards Maria, who is both superior to other women and mistaken.

The hero and heroine are characteristically close to life – although Henry Darnford resembles Banastre Tarleton, Mary Robinson's faithless lover, as much as Imlay. However, the other narrator, Maria's gaoler, is a new departure: a lower-class woman named Jemima, whose 'wrongs' include prostitution, abuse and abortion. In her, gender and class starkly connect – though she is termed 'superior to her class'. It is a remarkably sympathetic account, especially in the contemporary context: Hannah More judged that a woman who lapsed from morality should *for ever* be excluded from polite society, not be reintroduced through good ladies' 'affectation of charity'.[28] For all her sympathy, however, Wollstonecraft can find no redemption for her character outside the maternal kindness of a middle-class friend or, though Jemima never quite loses her hard-won cynicism, any humanity except through aping the sensibility that defined 'woman' in society and helped bring Maria to the asylum. Jemima compares herself to beasts; at the least she remains an outsider.

Pregnant for a second time, Wollstonecraft must have felt how easy it was to become a pariah: in Jemima she showed that a woman's life could be so miserable that maternal feelings failed to develop. Yet she did not associate herself with Jemima or her depressed servant-mother. In *Letters from Sweden*, she had noticed a poor wet-nurse in Tønsberg, left to raise her own child alone. The girl had sung a sad song and Wollstonecraft had mused on the constant failure of happiness, but she had not equated herself with the abandoned mother and had hurried from the house to walk by herself.[29] So here, she is closer in circumstance to the lower-class woman who had become illegitimately pregnant than to the married heroine bearing her child in wedlock; yet there is little identification.

They are not even associated as working women. Although Jemima's activities – scrubbing, laundering, and serving – are below anything Wollstonecraft stooped to, they were occupations outside the home like her own. The middle-class Maria never considers paid work, despite criticising her sister for the 'false pride' that made her shrink 'at the name of milliner or mantua-maker as degrading to a gentlewoman'. Wollstonecraft had urged her sisters into the conventional labour market, but she herself never really came to terms with female employment in a hostile world – that is, outside her unusual literary one, unrepresented in her book. She might declare in *The Rights of Woman* that women might become 'mistress of [their] own actions', but she found it difficult to illustrate any middle-class callings. (Mary Hays had a similar problem in *Emma Courtney*: when rejected, the heroine longs for 'independence' and yet 'would not submit [to] the degradation of servitude'; so she endures increasing poverty until rescued by marriage.)

Yet it is the strength of the Jemima portrait that the identity as working woman stays as she is liberated into sensibility; the positive section of the novel unites her with Maria and her lover not on terms of equality or sentiment but as *paid* housekeeper. She also remains clear that poverty is evil; Wollstonecraft had progressed from her sentimental idealisation as she relinquished her romantic, Imlay-inspired visions.[30] The combination of the very different Jemima and Maria begins to fulfil the stated aim in the preface:

to exhibit the general 'misery and oppression, peculiar to women'; it also presents (fleetingly) a heartening, unidealised possibility of community: Maria thinks of 'Jemima's peculiar fate and her own' and is 'led to consider the oppressed state of woman.'[31] Love of Darnford had resulted in self-absorption; some romantic disillusion, together with Jemima's friendship, leads onwards to 'social pleasure' and the 'soft touches of humanity'.

*The Wrongs of Woman* is clear on the political, economic and legal ills of women, the wife's inability to own property, her lack of rights over her children when separated, the physical and financial abuse of men, together with the salve: the help women might give each other across class. Here, as in *The Rights of Woman*, Wollstonecraft could use the political language that had sounded so hollow when she tried it on Imlay in an emotional frame-work. The problem came in the treatment of sexuality and subjectivity.

In the earlier book, she wanted women, including herself, to be 'rational creatures' not victims of desire; they should share with men in a purified masculinity, interact with but not desperately need the other sex. When she put her fictional pen to paper, however, she entered romance and harked back to the despised *Mary, A Fiction*, where she had imagined a sickly, androgynous man nurturing the feminine heroine with platonic admiration. Here the men were untamed. In *The Wrongs of Woman* Maria with her 'infantine ingenuousness' once fancied her husband, and her relationship with him, though distasteful, is oddly sensual; she seems fascinated with his lolling posture, his soiled linen, stretches and uninhibited yawns, while she refers to her own 'glow', a term Wollstonecraft often used in letters to Imlay to describe sexual feeling.[32] The husband is unsuitable, of course, and Maria's experience might have taught her to eschew libertines and fantasies and become rational and independent, but without giving up her sexuality. Her sensibility need not have been eroticised passivity, transcended in love of God like Mary's in *Mary, A Fiction*, or a hybrid of sexual allure and chaste reputation like Sophie's in *Émile*, but an active attitude in harmony with rationality and desire for reciprocal pleasure; 'the libertine reveries of men' might be mastered.[33] Though it is hard to see how without contraception.

In the event, the alternative romance collapses, and external, man-made imprisonment becomes internal and woman-made. When she refuses sex with her husband's friends, Maria is acting from old-fashioned feminine 'delicacy', but this is not strong enough to make her eschew sex for long or judge with whom to indulge it. As Maria reads the romance of Rousseau and tells, then repeats her own story with yet another unsuitable if less squalid man, the asylum becomes the symbol of romance. Sex, the foundation of marriage, assumes the kind of sacredness Wollstonecraft had conveyed to

Imlay: 'As her husband she now received him.' The bosom that was once 'bursting with ... nutriment' for the baby – as Wollstonecraft's had in Le Havre after Fanny's birth – heaved again for a man. When this Henry fails through lack of imagination – like Imlay rather than the dying Henry of *Mary, A Fiction* – no further repetition is on offer, and Maria falls into suicidal depression despite knowing that she owed herself 'respect'.

If Wollstonecraft had succeeded in freeing the feelings repressed in *The Rights of Woman* – female desire, as well as need for sexual relief – she had no idea what to do with them. In literature as in life, the seemingly desirable combination of released sexuality and rationality led simply to suicide: she could not move from her own past experience. In the one slightly positive conclusion of several, Jemima saves Maria at the brink of death by urging the needs of her newly discovered child: in *The Rights of Woman*, too, only motherhood had been opposed to sexual dependence. Yet, like the damaged mother of *Mary, A Fiction*, Maria has already shown herself capable of forgetting her daughter in her swooning over a man (the child is not named, rather like Wollstonecraft's little niece Mary in so many of the letters during her sister's flight), and solitary motherhood had not saved Maria's creator from despair.[34] Was repetition in disastrous romance simply caused by gullibility in ill-educated women, as Wollstonecraft had once believed? Or by a female fascination for glamorous, corrupt men who would never have the transparency in which Maria and her creator thought they trusted? Would it be better to return to the solitary mother in *The Rights of Woman* who was praised for forgetting 'her sex', instead of following medical commonsense and natural desire into socially disruptive and emotionally damaging sexual 'fulfilment'? The ostensible subject of the book is 'the wrongs of woman'; its boldness, however, is in the way it uses its main stories and inset tales of abuse and exploitation to scrutinise women's collusion in their subjection. With a courage even beyond that in *The Rights of Woman*, it admits that for them, 'the evils they are subject to endure degrade them so far below their oppressors, as almost to justify their tyranny'. Defiant pessimism is the final effect: oppression is too huge and irrational to combat successfully.[35]

Was pessimism intended? Or is it possible that, in the calmer time with Godwin and during a second pregnancy, Wollstonecraft was reassessing her obsession with Imlay and wondering if perhaps something might be salvaged from the energy of desire, some knowledge from erotic pain beyond reason and sensibility?[36]

Perhaps at the outset she had not intended the intrusion of her unkind lover into her novel. The fictional husband was a failed financier: he should perhaps have been the main image of Imlay. But Imlay pervaded the book –

'What chance had Maria of escaping?' asks the narrator of her growing feeling for Darnford. It was the past rearing up into Wollstonecraft's God-winian present. The Dissenting rational sort of God was not much use to women in madhouses and marriages, and the desire, fatal, swooning, and deathly, that her heroine periodically experiences through a man for something transcendent and suicidal, is not unlike what Wollstonecraft expressed in *Letters from Sweden*, with its yearning for nothingness and the ineffable at one minute, its hunger for identity at another. The sensible equal relationship she was forging with Godwin must sometimes have been haunted by this imprisoning, perhaps infantile longing. Contentment and sanity would always be fragile for Wollstonecraft.

Yet despite her tendency to indulgent autobiography, it was no small achievement for Wollstonecraft to have exposed contradictions she could not resolve. Robinson and Hays, and even her old friend Helen Maria Williams, had all tried to rescue feminine passion and give it supreme value. Wollstonecraft would not take this philosophically easier if just as unpopular route, while also being less secure than she had been in her rationalist contempt for sexual and romantic passion, that excess feeling so often labelled 'feminine'. She respected strong emotion – had felt it – but would not declare it either treacherous or *supremely* valuable.

In her quandary with her novel, she wanted an outside opinion beside Godwin's.[37] She may have thought Hays too close to the problem and probably Hays expected a more simply political book from her powerful friend. Holcroft was the most appropriate critic given his experience with radical novel-writing and his interest in her work – while on vacation in Norfolk he had written to enquire: 'Pray inform me, sweet lady, in what state is your novel?'[38] But she was wary of him for personal and professional reasons, including his tie to Inchbald. She must have known that he had corrected her successful novel, *A Simple Story*. The first part in particular was well crafted and Wollstonecraft would not relish comparison. Instead, she applied to another of Godwin's friends, the volatile translator and amateur painter George Dyson, whom she had known before she left for France.

She had already flattered him by assuring him he had 'talents, or promise to have them, that are not common', so might have expected leniency. But, after reading the manuscript, he provided an unwelcome critique. He could not see that Maria, with her relative security, was in so dreadful a state and he thought her precipitate flight from her husband's house an over-reaction. Remembering her own indignant childhood and part in her sister's escape from her husband, Wollstonecraft must have been stung by the criticism.

She was even more dismayed when Dyson found her innovative presentation of Jemima vulgar. She fought back:

I have been reading your remarks and I find them a little discouraging. I mean I am not satisfied with the feelings which seem to be the result of the perusal. I was perfectly aware that some of the incidents ought to be transpossed and heightened by more harmonious shading; and I wished to avail myself of yours and Mr G[odwin]'s criticism before I began to adjust my events into a story, the outline of which I had sketched in my mind at the commencement; yet I am vexed and surprised at your not thinking the situation of Maria sufficiently important, and can only account for this want of – shall I say it? delicacy of feeling by recollecting that you are a man – For my part I cannot suppose any situation more distressing than for a woman of sensibility with an improving mind to be bound, to such a man as I have described, for life – obliged to renounce all the humanizing affections, and to avoid cultivating her taste lest her perception of grace, and refinement of sentiment should sharpen to agony the pangs of disappointment. Love, in which the imagination mingles its bewitching colouring must be fostered by delicacy – I should despise, or rather call her an ordinary woman, who could endure such a husband as I have sketched – yet you do not seem to be disgusted with him!!!

These appear to me (matrimonial despotism of heart & conduct) to be the particular wrongs of woman; because they degrade the mind. What are termed great misfortunes may more forcibly impress the mind of common readers, they have more of what might justly be termed *stage effect* but it is the delineation of finer sensations which, in my opinion, constitutes the merit of our best novels, this is what I have in view; and to shew the wrongs of different classes of women equally oppressive, though from the difference of education, necessarily various...

I am not convinced that your remarks respecting the style of Jemima's story is just; but I will reconsider it. You seem to [m]e to confound simplicity and vulgarity. Persons who have received a miscellaneous education, that is are educated by chance, and the energy of their own faculties, common display the mixture of refined and common language I have endeavoured to imitate.

However wounding to her sensitivity as an author, the criticism helped Wollstonecraft clarify her aims as well as her sense of herself as thinker, and it may be at this moment that she wrote a letter sounding like a manifesto and possibly addressed to her fellow feminist Mary Hays, in which she declared, 'Those who are bold enough to advance before the age they live in, and to throw off, by the force of their own minds, the prejudices which the maturing reason of the world will in time disavow, must learn to brave censure. We ought not to be too anxious respecting the opinion of others.' She copied out her reply to Dyson for Godwin, retaining even its errors so that he could properly judge. The retention suggests that, although she submitted to Godwin's grammatical tutelage and solicited others' opinions, she continued to revere her own self-expression – she admitted to a 'certain charm as well as sanctity about these little negligences & rudenesses that would not permit me remove them'.[39] Spontaneous style and consciousness were still conjoined.

Dyson's criticism might have influenced one of the last episodes of *The Wrongs of Woman*: Maria claims 'a divorce' citing her husband's appalling behaviour. '[C]onvinced that the subterfuges of the law were disgraceful', she states her case with the frankness on which Wollstonecraft prided herself (quite impossible in reality since women neither represented themselves nor were represented in divorce cases which were between two men, lover and husband). The judge is unsympathetic, regarding marriage as naturalising male dominance and the law as supporting it, though the latter 'might bear a little hard on a few'.[40] Knowing women to be synonymous with feeling, he heard none of her reasoning, only an appeal to feeling. The episode declares that men cannot hear what women say, whether they be a fictional hero and judge, or the real Dyson and Godwin. *The Rights of Woman* had been addressed to men and women; the narratives of the new book must appeal to female readers.

# 37

*'A husband is a convenient part of the furniture of a house'*

When Wollstonecraft wrote her first letter to Godwin as his wife, she alluded playfully to the wedding ceremony: 'Pray send me, by Mary, for my luncheon, a part of the supper you announced to me last night – as I am to be a partaker of your worldly goods – you know!' A week later, she wrote to persuade Godwin to visit Johnson, adding coyly, 'when I press any thing it is always with a true *wifish* submission to your judgment and inclination.' To friends she signed herself 'Mary Godwin'. Together the pair anticipated parenthood with pleasure, sure that their infant would be a boy, William.

Heedless of the injunction of Godwin's mother against entertaining, they gave teas and dinner parties, inviting old acquaintances like Fuseli – on one occasion he became so irritated he went home in a huff – as well as Marshall and Montagu, who also dropped in whenever they wished. Up-and-coming writers of the new Romantic generation called, eager to glimpse the notorious couple. The nineteen-year-old Hazlitt noted their easy relationship, while Coleridge saw them as uniting imagination and intellect, with Wollstonecraft's imagination dominating her husband's intellect; he liked the new Mrs Godwin's conversation but deplored her books. Despite its slight expression of superiority, Southey approved her face; she is a 'first-rate woman, sensible of her own worth, but without arrogance or affectation', he wrote. Godwin was not prepossessing: he had 'large noble eyes' but a 'most abominable nose'.[1]

His new husbandly status brought Godwin duties as well as pleasures. Since returning to England with Fanny, Wollstonecraft had had to keep up an establishment for a child. No man comprehended the extra laundry required, the warmth to be created in naturally cold rooms, the cleaning and cooking and boiling of coppers, the negotiations with pets and other infants. Godwin mocked the number of domestics she seemed to employ; yet there was always more to cope with than people to act.

Wollstonecraft liked household management no more than continuous childcare. Her lofty contempt for the 'square-elbowed family drudge' suggests she saw little virtue in the servicing of linen and listing of cupboard contents, usual domestic duties for a wife.[2] In the past Johnson and other male friends had dealt with tradespeople. Now she had married, these helpers had retired and Godwin had not taken their place. 'Mary will tell you about the state of the sink,' she wrote, 'do you know you plague me (a little) by not speaking more determinately to the Landlord.' Sometimes not even the cat behaved as it should; one day it had fits and flew up the chimney. It was so wild she had to drown it but told Fanny it had run away.

She envied Godwin in his snug bachelor digs with his housekeeper. She knew he considered domesticity a clog on genius. So did she. Why should a man's time be more important than a woman's? If he would do nothing himself, could he not send round the useful Marshall? '[M]y time appears to me, as valuable as that of any other person accustomed to employ themselves. Things of this kind are easily settled with money, I know; but I am tormented by the want of money – and feel, to say the truth, as if I was not treated with respect, owing to your desire not to be disturbed.'

Quarrels continued to erupt, but now she realised that both justified themselves at the expense of the other, without necessarily meaning much harm. She still thought some sincerity in relationships essential, but, faced with Godwin's principled frankness, was reconsidering her long-standing regard for complete transparency: 'Perfect confidence, and sincerity of action is, I am persuaded, incompatible with the present state of reason.'

One argument arose from her meeting with the restless Tom Wedgwood, now staying with his banking brother John in a fine newly-built house in Devonshire Place, Marylebone. She criticised him harshly and Godwin rebuked her for '*savage resentment, and the worst of vices*'. She objected, then wrote to apologise – and reproach – her usual manoeuvre: 'I know that respect is the shadow of wealth, and commonly obtained, when that is wanted, by a criminal compliance with the prejudice of society. Those who comply can alone tell whether they do it from benevolence or a desire to secure their own eas[e].'

However irritating she found the Wedgwoods, she knew the seductions of wealth. It allowed tasteful entertainments and outings. So, when Montagu breakfasted with her, bearing an invitation from them to join an overnight excursion, she was tempted. She loved visiting the country, even believing 'with a poor mad woman, I knew, that there is God, or something, very consolatory in the air'. She would have accepted at once had she not agreed to spend this time with Godwin's sister Hannah. Keenly she felt the difference between the two parties. It would have been pleasant indeed to go with people of substance who drove their own carriage, but her prior engagement ought to be honoured. Godwin's family was more lowly placed than her own and, except for William, none had risen from the edge of poverty. Hannah had come from East Anglia to London and was now a dressmaker, aiding her self-esteem by writing verses. Wollstonecraft may have shuddered to remember the headaches and eye-strain of the months sewing with Fanny Blood and her mother. No wonder it was with Hannah that the abstemious Godwin occasionally drank 'rum'.[3]

While in London Wedgwood had not called on Godwin as much as he ought and, though promising to take leave, had failed to do so. (The two touchy, diffident men rarely managed to meet or separate without requiring later apology; this was no exception.) Godwin wrote to complain and Wedgwood replied that he had felt unwelcome. He knew he had 'scepticism in friendship, & proneness to suspect', but was hurt when the gossipy Montagu told him Godwin found him cold. Godwin expressed 'surprise and pain' at the accusation and, for a mixture of motives, hastened to smooth matters. Both of them were 'inclined to a vicious reserve'; the remedy was to spend a few complete days together. For this reason, though he disliked wandering, he proposed to visit Tom in Etruria; there they could come to 'a mutual understanding'.[4]

But Wedgwood remained hurt. He wrote again: others, including himself, found *Godwin's* manner 'distant & cold'. He was not resentful, he thought, but admitted to having 'constitutional' moments of apathy in which he was indifferent to others.[5] He was unready for the projected 'cohabitation'; unfortunately, Godwin did not receive this letter before setting out with Basil Montagu.

On the way to Etruria the two men would visit Dr Parr in Hatton. He and Godwin enjoyed a bracing argument, each quaintly accusing the other of not properly understanding *Political Justice*. Parr's pert daughter Sarah would also be there; not best pleased to learn of Godwin's apostasy in marriage, she promised him 'the most complete roasting'. He looked forward to it, as also to his meetings *en route* with the radical novelist Robert Bage and the evolutionary poetic botanist Erasmus Darwin. It was as much worth visiting clever men as cathedrals and palaces, he thought. From Etruria he would bring back a china mug for Fanny.

He had a further undivulged reason for his excursion. He believed that absence would increase his 'value' to his wife: 'it is a refinement in voluptuousness, to submit to voluntary privations.'[6]

On her side Wollstonecraft had no objection. But now she found '[a] husband ... a convenient part of the furniture of a house, unless he be a clumsy fixture'; though he should be 'rivetted' to her heart, he need not be always at her elbow. Also she wanted news of Everina, who had heard of the marriage and was probably upset. She would be distant with Godwin but he should treat her with greater kindness than her manner deserved. He should tell her to write more to her sister. With her duties to Fanny and advanced pregnancy, there was no question of Wollstonecraft's accompanying the men. As with Imlay, she felt the distinction between male and female, the one sex footloose, the other forced to be stationary. Still she would send frequent letters through the frank of Mary Robinson's inconstant lover, Tarleton, who, as MP for Liverpool, had the right of free postage.

Godwin and Montagu planned to set out on 3 June and be away for some days – they were uncertain how many. But, on the proposed day, Montagu was tired and reluctant; when he saw the hired horse and small carriage, he was even more so. The weather was so bad that Wollstonecraft assumed the plan would be changed and she wrote Godwin a playful note, 'How glad I am that you did not go to day! I should have been very uneasy lest you should have pushed on in the teeth of the weather, laying up a store of rheumatism in your bones – and who knows what effect it might have had on future generations!!!' Godwin was not deterred, however, and, after inspiriting Montagu and making a quick visit to Wollstonecraft at the Polygon, they left London on the fourth.

The pair spent the first night at Beaconsfield and on Sunday reached Oxford, where, to cheer himself up, Montagu drank too much punch. Next day when they reached Hampton Lucy he vomited it up. Both were now in high spirits – 'Our horse has turned out admirably, & we were as gay as larks' – despite being almost drowned in a swollen brook. They breakfasted with a clergyman and met another of Dr Parr's daughters, the beautiful Catherine. Although engaged to Sarah Wedgwood, Montagu was much struck by her charms.

Godwin had expected that absence would strengthen affection – it was a bonus of his journey. With him it worked quickly. When he sat down to write, he felt especially affectionate though a little inhibited by the formality of long letter-writing after so many quick notes. He wondered what style to adopt for a travel narrative and decided on a jocular man-to-man one. He noted that at Oxford their host had described himself and Wollstonecraft as, 'the two greatest men in the world'. He had met 'a Mr Swan, & his two wives or sisters ... but they were no better than geese'. He hoped she would find this part of his letter amusing. Then he changed style:

And now, my dear love, what do you think of me? Do not you find solitude infinitely superior to the company of a husband? Will you give me leave to return to you again, when I have finished my pilgrimage, & discharged the penance of absence? Take care of yourself, my love, & take care of William. Do not you be drowned, whatever I am. I remember at every moment all the accidents to which your condition subjects you, & wish I knew of some sympathy that could inform me from moment to moment, how you do, & how you feel.

Tell Fanny something about me. Ask her where she thinks I am. Say I am a great way off, & going further & further, but that I shall turn round & come back again some day. Tell her I have not forgotten her little mug & that I shall chuse a very pretty one. Montagu said this morning about eight o'clock upon the road, Just now little Fanny is going to plungity plunge. Was he right? I love him very much. He is in such a hurry to see his chere adorable [Sarah Wedgwood], that, I believe, after all, we shall set forward this evening, & get to Etruria to-morrow.[7]

Despite the slightly tactless allusion to drowning, Wollstonecraft was delighted with the letter, which combined gallantry and domesticity, exactly what she had long sought in men. The references to Fanny were especially touching. She wrote back at once, sending her words to greet Godwin in Etruria. She was in equally high spirits, admitting for once that she was actually 'happy':

It was so kind and considerate in you to write sooner than I expected that I cannot help hoping you would be disappointed at not receiving a greeting from me on your arrival at Etruria. If your heart was in your mouth, as I felt, just now, at the sight of your hand, you may kiss or shake hands with the letter and imagine with what affection it was written – If not – stand off, profane one!

I was not quite well the day after you left me; but it is past, and I am well and tranquil, excepting the disturbance produced by Master William's joy, who took it into his head to frisk a little at being informed of your remembrance. I begin to love this little creature, and to anticipate his birth as a fresh twist to a knot, which I do not wish to untie. Men are spoilt by frankness, I believe, yet I must tell you that I love you better than I supposed I did, when I promised to love you for ever – and I will add what will gratify your benevolence, if not your heart, that on the whole I may be termed happy. You are a tender, affectionate creature; and I feel it thrilling through my frame giving and promising pleasure.

Fanny wanted to know 'what you are gone for', and endeavours to pronounce Etruria. Poor papa is her word of kindness – She has been turning your letter on all sides, and has promised to play with Bobby till I have finished my answer.

I find you can write the kind of letter a friend ought to write, and give an account of your movements. I hailed the sunshine, and moon-light and travelled with you scenting the fragrant gale – Enable me still to be your company, and I will allow you to peep over my shoulder, and see me under the shade of my green blind, thinking of you, and all I am to hear, and feel when you return – you may read my heart – if you will.

I have no information to give in return for yours. Holcroft is to dine with me on Saturday – So do not forget us when you drink your solitary glass; for nobody drinks wine at Etruria, I take for granted . . .

Her distaste for the Wedgwoods even led her to mock their temperance.

Before receiving this letter, Godwin wrote again to recount his 'adventures'. He and Montagu had been heading towards dinner at Hatton when they were accosted by an agitated Dr Parr on the road to Stratford. They should not bother visiting him at present, he said. The previous night his daughter Sarah had eloped to Gretna Green with one of his pupils, a boorish inarticulate boy of eighteen (ever since Lord Hardwicke's Marriage Act of 1753 made English marriage a slow process, couples had circumvented the law by dashing to the Scottish border for a speedy wedding). Since the young man was the son of a wealthy Welsh MP, Godwin suspected that, though he protested, the doctor was not utterly desolated. He blamed the mother and her foolish maxim 'that the wisest thing a young woman of sense could do, was to marry a fool.' Poor Sarah had found her fool.

Wollstonecraft was less sympathetic when she heard the news.[8] If Miss Parr set so little store by affection, perhaps she could find solace in status and enough money to entertain well. Her action was not entirely due to her mother's eccentricity; a corrupt system of female education which urged a girl to make a financially good match was also at fault. In the event Sarah paid for the culture's or her mother's mistake: after years of quarrels, violence, lawsuits and separations, she returned ailing to her father's house where she died at the age of thirty-seven. Dr Parr was inconsolable.

Bypassing Dr Parr's, Godwin and Montagu proceeded to Birmingham and Cannock, where Montagu unbridled their poor horse so he could eat hay freely. The result provoked another merry account:

The horse finding himself at liberty, immediately pranced off, overturned the chaise, dashed it against a post, & broke it in twenty places. It was a formidable sight, & the horse was with great difficulty stopped. We however are philosophers; so, after having amused ourselves for some time with laughing at our misadventure, we sent for a smith to splinter our carriage.[9]

Finally they reached Etruria where 'our reception appears to be cordial'. Or so he wrote to Wollstonecraft, probably fearing to fuel her dislike of Tom

Wedgwood if he told the truth. In fact Wedgwood had not wanted Godwin and the pair did their usual dance.

Godwin was 'silent stiff & reserved' with the Wedgwood family, 'occupied in observing them, and imagining them occupied about every thing but me'. Although Josiah was polite, he did not approve Godwin, whose views on marriage would 'make a foundling hospital of the world'.[10] Godwin probably felt similarly repelled. He did not even like Sally Wedgwood, Montagu's beloved, finding her fat and unworthy of him; ungallantly he reminded Wollstonecraft that marriage for anyone was a gaol sentence.[11]

Godwin felt in 'a state of warfare'. He tried to separate Tom from his family for *tête-à-têtes*. Then Tom, himself 'out of spirits', spoke of metaphysics and the sceptical Godwin, instead of arguing, fell silent and appeared dull. He knew he was behaving badly and that the 'mutual good understanding & confidence' which were the purpose of his stay were not coming about.[12] Initially, Everina would not even see him – 'I have nothing to say about her,' he remarked candidly. She has 'very mistaken notions of dignity of character', her sister concluded.

Over the next days Everina cheered up, especially when they visited the Wedgwood pottery, which she had not seen before. The outing gave Godwin a chance for private talk and he broached the subject of her tardy letter-writing. Everina replied that she was awaiting the parcel she had asked her sister to send. Godwin had no instructions about this and was silenced. Neither made more effort: they could not warm to each other, then or later.

His alienation with the Wedgwoods increased Godwin's affection for his Polygon family and, when he wrote his first letter from Etruria, he told Wollstonecraft, 'I think of you with tenderness, & shall see you again with redoubled kindness (if you will let me) for this short absence. Kiss Fanny for me; remember William; but (most of all) take care of yourself. Tell Fanny, I am safely in the land of mugs.' Then, as he had promised, he chose a mug with an F on it.[13]

He was delighted to receive Wollstonecraft's appreciative letter; absence had already done its work. He read it over four times, finding it lost 'not one grace by the repetition'. He felt to the core the happiness of the domestic life so long avoided:

You cannot imagine how happy your letter made me. No creature expresses, because no creature feels, the tender affections, so perfectly as you do: &, after all one's philosophy, it must be confessed that the knowledge, that there is some one that takes an interest in our happiness something like that which each man feels in his own, is extremely gratifying. We love, as it were, to multiply our consciousness ... even at the hazard of what Montagu described so pathetically one night upon the New Road, of opening new avenues for pain & misery to attack us.[14]

With her strong sense of associations, Wollstonecraft no doubt recalled that it was on this road that she had had her last interview with Imlay.

So enthusiastic was Godwin for the letter that he was soon berating Wollstonecraft for writing too little. (After years of scolding her sisters and lover, this was a novel reversal.) When he did not hear for several days he imagined 'sickness of the heart, a general loathing of life & of me'. He knew her depressive nature: 'Do not give place to this worst of diseases! The least I can think is, that you recollect me with less tenderness & impatience than I reflect on you.' In fact it was he who was depressed while she was visiting and being visited as usual. She had tea with Godwin's old flame Maria Reveley, who brought round her son Henry to play with Fanny. The little girl amused them all with her easy acceptance of Godwin and her extension of him to everything else: losing her toy monkey, she declared 'that it was gone into the country'. The two mothers then spent a pleasant day together, but Wollstonecraft noticed she tired easily. Otherwise she was quite well – as was baby 'William'. Everyone now knew she was pregnant; presumably her friends were restrained in calculating dates. 'What a fine thing it is to be a man!' she sighed.

Now the delayed letter which Tom Wedgwood had written to Godwin at the end of May arrived at the Polygon. Wollstonecraft knew the hand-writing and opened it. Ready to disapprove the writer, she was repulsed by tone and contents. She was hurt for Godwin and thought she might now venture some censure with impunity: 'He appears to me to be half spoilt by living with his inferiours in point of understanding, and to expect that homage to be paid to his abilities, which the world will readily pay to his fortune. I am afraid that all men are materially injured by inheriting wealth; and without knowing it, become important in their own eyes, in consequence of an advantage they contemn.' Wedgwood and she shared enquiring minds and a tendency to depression, but she could never get past the notion of him as an over-privileged youth on the model of brother Ned. She set little store by his financial favours.

The Wedgwood letter put her in the wrong mood for affectionate writing. Combined with this, she had to hurry to catch the post at Tarleton's. With such pressures she could most clearly express what was uppermost in her mind: desire to know Godwin's date and time of return. He had fallen foul of this coercing desire before; Wollstonecraft was always impatient to see and hear from those she valued and quick to feel she was being improperly treated if they failed to conform. The long months of desiring Imlay had sensitised her to the misery of waiting and confirmed her need to fix those who travelled with a firm and dated commitment to come back.

By the time Godwin left Etruria, he was on reasonably good terms with Tom Wedgwood, so the two men could resume their writing about ideas and loans when need arose. After failing to see Erasmus Darwin in Derby, he and Montagu managed a meeting with Robert Bage on the road outside Tamworth near his paper and flour mills. During a walk of six or seven miles, Bage told them his life-story: on the failure of an ironworks and in the absence of books, he dissipated his melancholy by writing a cheerful novel. He was then fifty-three and had written five more, one every two years. Godwin judged him a man 'of great intellectual refinement, attained in the bosom of rusticity'.

Leaving Tamworth, they now visited Dr Parr's, where they found the elopers. Godwin was horrified at the young man: a 'raw, country booby of eighteen, his hair about his ears, & a beard that has never deigned to submit to the stroke of the razor.' After this introduction, it is surprising to read that he stuttered and was a 'lad of very good disposition'.[15] Sarah he still regarded as a sensitive victim. To avoid sitting with this company all day, he and Montagu visited the ruins of Kenilworth, but lost their way in the fields.

Quitting Hatton they went to Coventry to see the famous Fair, a procession of trades with a woman acting Lady Godiva dressed so as 'to represent nakedness'; they arrived too late for the show. Then they went to Cambridge and their expectation of returning to London on Saturday or Sunday was changed to very late Monday. If they did not arrive by ten, Wollstonecraft should send some whisky round to Lincoln's Inn where Montagu lodged.

Encouraged by his wife's appreciation of his first letter, Godwin set off again at greater length to describe the Parrs, his meeting with Bage and his missed one with Darwin, as well as his failure to see Coventry Fair. By now Wollstonecraft was tired of his descriptions, however – thinking them more of an *aide-mémoire* than an address to her – and annoyed that he changed his return date. Darwin and Parr were worth seeing – in her *Rights of Woman* she had implicitly defended Darwin against those who felt his erotic botanizing inappropriate for women. She did not mention Bage, although she probably approved this meeting since he had enthusiastically used her feminist arguments in his recent novel *Hermsprong*. But Coventry Fair was not worth a detour. Godwin even failed to comment on what she said in *her* letters, being more concerned to tell how well *he* was thought of than assure her of his tenderness. He was becoming like Tom Wedgwood, eaten up with vanity from the homage of stupid people.

On Monday night she waited up until almost midnight. When Godwin did not appear she lashed out at him with a letter meant for his late arrival. She had cured him of some of his intellectual pride and 'icy Philosophy' she said, but feared her work undone by sycophants. His slowness was inconsiderate: did he think she was 'a stick or a stone'?

Godwin arrived home the following day to learn that short absences might increase affection, but indefinite ones did not.


Socially Wollstonecraft was troubled on two counts. First, she and Godwin had decided to carry on separate lives in society. Eighteen months or so before, she had resented the companions Imlay had kept exclusively for himself as a threat to her ideal of joint and shared sociability, but she accepted Godwin's less disruptive desire, welcoming her own continuing intimacy with her friends. Now she had been abandoned by several of her most hospitable acquaintances such as the Twisses and Sarah Siddons. (When Siddons dropped Mary Robinson, she lamented: 'one's whole life is one continual sacrifice of inclinations, which, to indulge, however laudable or innocent, would draw down the malice and reproach of ... prudent people.'[16]) The marriage had been the cause, but no doubt Wollstonecraft's growing pregnancy aided it. Bitterly her feelings burst from the novel she was struggling to write: if a woman has been

> practising insincerity, and neglecting her child to manage an intrigue, she would still have been visited and respected. If, instead of openly living with her lover, she could have condescended to call into play a thousand arts, which, degrading her own mind, might have allowed the people who were not deceived, to pretend to be so, she would have been caressed and treated like an honourable woman.[17]

In his poem 'Mary', which may have called on memories of Wollstonecraft, Blake described a woman who 'went out in Morning in plain neat attire, / And came home in Evening bespatter'd with mire' to moan 'O, why was I born with a different Face?' Wollstonecraft must occasionally have felt like this in her dealings with the world.[18]

Since the Twisses no longer invited her to their dinners, she resented Godwin's Sunday arrangement with Holcroft. Also she was a little jealous of the tie between the two men: there was no one like Holcroft in her own life. Godwin saw her point and, after his troubled homecoming, was eager to humour her. As a result, they dined together at Holcroft's the Sunday following his return.

Secondly, given their expressed theories, it was not unreasonable that some should think Godwin and Wollstonecraft free agents, able to enter other emotional relationships. A Miss Pinkerton acquired this notion.[19] Godwin's journal records his writing to her in mid-May, and between then and his trip to Etruria, her name appeared three more times.[20] Throughout the summer Wollstonecraft brooded over the growing friendship, although she mentioned the woman without rancour just after Godwin left: 'I was amused by a letter [Miss Pinkerton] wrote home. She has more in her than comes out of her mouth.'

On Godwin's return, the lady came to tea at his lodgings, and subsequently he visited her alone. She then bombarded him with letters in the manner of Mary Hays – or indeed of Wollstonecraft with Fuseli. Inviting Maria Reveley to a dinner to which Miss Pinkerton was also bidden, Wollstonecraft suggested Maria visit at another time as well to view 'one of Mr Godwin's epistles, I mean one addressed to him, from another Fair in intellectual distress', presumably a reference to Pinkerton. After one visit, Godwin wrote 'infelicité' in his journal.

By July Wollstonecraft was seriously upset by the passionate attentions and Godwin's acceptance. Their unconventional marriage should never have implied this; she would not repeat her final forbearing attitude towards Imlay's mistress. Perhaps the disturbance gave her the look of slightly resigned sadness that Opie painted in his portrait. The picture would have taken thirteen or fourteen sittings and sometimes she must have yearned to confide in her old friend.[21] But the situation had changed since her marriage, and she may have held back.

In private she was plunged into depression. It was windy and rainy, more like November than July, and she was always affected by weather. She felt suicidal again, for the affair dredged up old emotions, especially from the rejecting Imlay years. Agitatedly she wrote to Godwin in Evesham Buildings; it was as if she were writing to Imlay:

> To be frank with you, your behaviour yesterday brought on my troublesome pain. But I lay no great stress on that circumstance, because, were not my health in a more delicate state than usual, it could not be so easily affected. I am absurd to look for the affection which I have only found in my own tormented heart; and how can you blame me for tak[ing] refuge in the idea of a God, when I despair of finding sincerity on earth?
>
> I think you *wrong* – yes; with the most decided conviction I dare to say it,

having still in my mind the *unswervable* principles of justice and humanity. You judge not in your own case as in that of another. You give a softer name to folly and immorality when it flatters – yes, I must say it – your vanity, than to mistaken passion when it was extended to another – you termed Miss Hay[s]'s conduct insanity when only her own happiness was involved – I cannot forget the strength of your expressions. – and you treat with a mildness calculated to foster it, a romantic, selfishness, and pamper[ed] conceit, which will even lead the object to – I was going to say misery – but I believe her incapable of feeling it. Her want of sensibility with respect to her family first disgusted me – Then to obtrude herself on me, to see affection, and instead of feeling sympathy, to endeavour to undermined it, certainly resembles the conduct of the fictitious being, to whose dignity she aspires. Yet you, at the very moment, commenced a correspondence with her whom you had previously almost neglected – you brought me a letter without a conclusion – and you changed countenance at the reply – My old wounds bleed afresh – What did not blind confidence, and unsuspecting truth, lead me to – my very soul trembles sooner than endure the hundred[th] part of what I have suffer[ed], I could wish my poor Fanny and self asleep at the bottom of the sea.

She sent it round to Godwin immediately.

Less impressed than formerly by Wollstonecraft's suicidal self-pity and over-reaction – having also seen Everina at close quarters he probably understood the family bent – Godwin declared himself 'much hurt' by the letter, but, after rereading it later, understood her point. He calmed her down so effectively that in a few days the pair were exchanging their usual comfortable notes about meetings, invitations, visits and shared books.

Perhaps it was Miss Pinkerton who again caused Wollstonecraft's especially volatile mood later in July. Godwin always found trying her refusal to rein in her feelings; at one moment she would attack, at the next be tender and warm. He would feel calmed, then jolted by a grating remark. He must take her to task. So he sent a note to the Polygon declaring, 'I would on no account willingly do any thing to make you unhappy.' Though they might joke of his being an unemotional philosopher, he had feelings. She should not give him pain 'without a determined purpose'.[22] Wollstonecraft replied, 'You say "WITHOUT a determined purpose". Do you wish me to have one?'

Although she had gained the point about Miss Pinkerton's impropriety, Godwin did nothing about it. By August Wollstonecraft felt *she* should take the initiative before the lady began 'extorting' further visits. So she drafted a severe note expelling her from their company: 'Miss Pinkerton, I forbear to make any comments on your strange behaviour; but, unless you can determine to behave with propriety, you must excuse me for expressing a wish not to see you at our house.'

The maid, Mary, carried the note to Godwin. If he found nothing objectionable, she would take it on to Miss Pinkerton. Although convinced that Godwin would back her up, she gave him some freedom, 'If you have the slightest wish to prevent my writing at all – say so.' She added with irony, 'I shall think you actuated by humanity, though I may not coincide in opinion, with respect to the measures you take to effect your purpose.' It sounds as if Godwin had been glossing the latest visits as his efforts to rid himself of an importunate woman; despite his blushes at her name, they both blamed Miss Pinkerton alone for the intimacy.

Godwin accepted that Wollstonecraft was doing the right thing, but asked for a short delay. Unlike his wife, he tended to think about a letter before dispatching it. Then he changed 'strange behaviour' to 'incomprehensible conduct' and returned the note to be recopied and sent.

It prompted a speedy and proper reply from Miss Pinkerton to the injured wife: 'At length I am sensible of the impropriety of my conduct. Tears and communication afford me relief.'[23]

# 38

The baby was due at the end of August. Coming in the middle of tempestuous public and private events. Fanny's arrival had not allowed Wollstonecraft much time to consider issues and habits of childbirth, but she had been firm in her aim to avoid unnecessary intervention: 'the proper business of a midwife, in the instance of a natural labour, is to sit by and wait for the operations of nature, which seldom, in these affairs, demand the interposition of art.'[1]

Now that she had more opportunity to consider, she did not alter her opinion, still believing that many of the injunctions to women enfeebled them. With Fanny she had eschewed the usual habit of 'lying in' for a month after confinement and been up next day. She meant to do the same with 'William': she would be down for dinner the following afternoon, she promised.[2]

By the 1790s maternal deaths from home confinements were not common – perhaps five or six in a thousand – but enough to provoke anxiety. It had become usual for women of Wollstonecraft's class to employ men midwives in their homes, men who would, if necessary, use forceps to aid a birth rather than the hooks and crochets of the female midwife; the shift no doubt depended on women's desire to follow fashion but also answered their very real worries about themselves and the possible mutilation of their babies. Godwin favoured having a physician present, probably John Clarke of the General Lying-in Hospital, who published his work on obstetrics with Johnson. Or he might have wanted his friend Fordyce though he was not a practising midwife and was reputed to be more interested in his lectures than his patients.

Expecting a routine birth, Wollstonecraft desired only a woman. She won the argument. As Hazlitt recalled of their relationship a little before the birth, '[Wollstonecraft] seems to me to turn off Godwin's objections to something she advanced with quite a playful, easy air.'[3] She approached the time cheerfully, anticipating a repetition of Fanny's delivery.[4] She had perhaps not been as well during this pregnancy, but it was a commonplace that a mother's ill health denoted a robust foetus.

She would use as midwife Mrs Blenkinsop.[5] Given her straitened circumstances, she might have felt economical in choosing to bear her child, like the vast majority of her poorer countrywomen, with only a female helper; as Elizabeth Inchbald later remarked, 'She was attended by a woman, whether from partiality or economy I cant tell – from no affected prudery I am sure.'[6] Though certainly not prudish, Wollstonecraft *did* think that 'decency' as well as policy seemed to allot midwifery to women and she saw the earlier preference for the midwife over the male *accoucheur* as a proof of 'the former delicacy of the sex'.[7]

By late August she felt overripe, eager 'to regain my activity, and to reduce to some *shapeliness* the portly shadow, which meets my eye when I take a musing walk'.[8] This poignant description just before she began her ordeal echoed her past remarks on the shifting boundaries of the female body, the body she had so often tried to transcend. On 25 August she felt a bit unwell, but the following days were uneventful, and she and Godwin continued visiting. Mary Hays called and Godwin saw Fuseli and Inchbald, but without his wife; the breach with the latter had not been closed. On Tuesday, 29th, Wollstonecraft and Godwin walked together and in the evening read Goethe's *Werther.*

Then on Wednesday, 30 August, Wollstonecraft awoke at about five in the morning, feeling the onset of labour. When nothing much happened, Godwin left the Polygon for his separate apartment in Evesham Buildings. There, still in the morning, he was visited by a couple of friends, including Dyson. Perhaps they spoke of her new novel, not yet finished, for later he took down *Mary, A Fiction* to read again. He still liked it better than its author now did; it revealed the sensitivity of mind he so admired in *Letters from Sweden* and which he relished in his wife in her gentler moments.

Left alone but unable to concentrate, Wollstonecraft expected to see 'the animal' that day and so sent for Mrs Blenkinsop, probably through Mary. Then she dispatched another servant to Godwin asking for a newspaper. She wished she had a novel or some light book by her to while away the time and take her mind off herself. After a lifetime of despising escapist reading, at this crisis she craved it. Things were taking too long; they had been quicker in Le Havre.

By nine o'clock Mrs Blenkinsop had arrived at the Polygon. She felt the belly and vulva, possibly anointing the latter with grease as was the custom. Although midwives were notoriously dirty, she had probably washed her hands in line with the latest views on hygiene. The baby was in the right position, so there was no fear of that most worrying of conditions, a breech birth. Mrs Blenkinsop confirmed Wollstonecraft's sense that the baby would be born that day, though she apprehended a long labour.

This was an adverse sign but Wollstonecraft wrote another note to Godwin to reassure him that the midwife believed 'Every thing is in a fair way,' and that she herself remained 'very well'. Probably she wished he had stayed with her that morning, but she had got used to their separate lives and, as long as he returned regularly, she could stand his errant ways. They usually dined about three: she wanted to see him at their house before then, unless she told him otherwise.

She found it hard to stick by her intention of reading and keeping quiet. Although nothing had happened, she wrote again to Godwin: 'Mrs Blenkinsop tells me that I am in the most natural state, and can promise me a safe delivery – But that I must have a little patience.' The repetition of her mother's dying words, chilling for any later reader, was simply a matter of good midwife practice, which recommended 'patience to wait on Nature'.[9] There *was* nothing to be done.

The labour was already long. Pains accelerated slowly and it was only at two o'clock that she went up to her bedchamber. Until the late eighteenth century women had sensibly chosen to crouch, sit or kneel for birth, but midwives and obstetricians preferred them supine because the helper did not have to work on his or her knees. Wollstonecraft would probably lie down for contractions and walk around between them to help shake down the child. Unlike so many of her acquaintances, from Tom Wedgwood to Mary Robinson, she seems not to have been a great user of opium or laudanum, so she had no obvious ways of combating pain.[10]

In mid-afternoon Godwin dined with Maria Reveley and her husband. He returned to the Polygon where he had supper with John and Eliza Fenwick. Still Wollstonecraft was waiting upstairs when he left in the evening for Evesham Buildings. He returned to the Polygon at ten to be with her for the night.

At 11.20 the baby was born. It avoided entanglement in the umbilical cord which finished off so many infants and emerged alive, though puny and weak. Wollstonecraft had been in labour for eighteen hours, far longer than with Fanny.

Then they waited. She had wanted to present 'the new-born child to its father' but was delaying until her placenta was expelled.

For nearly three hours Godwin sat anxiously in the parlour below not daring to go upstairs. After two o'clock on Thursday morning he was called up to be introduced to the baby: 'Mary' not 'William'.

Then he received the alarming news that still the placenta had not come out, and the midwife 'dared not proceed any further'. Probably she had kneaded the belly to try to stimulate contractions but without success. Midwives were fearful of a woman's dying on their hands. Perhaps she had already waited too long, perhaps she should have waited longer, following her own advice of 'patience'. Most likely the latter, since if nothing had been done the placenta might have come out naturally in time or been reabsorbed into the body. Or it could simply have rotted and caused death. It was a dangerous situation and she did what she thought best.

It was standard practice in the Westminster to call in a man in difficult cases, although obstetricians were no more trained than midwives. Mrs Blenkinsop asked Godwin to fetch her senior colleague Dr Louis Poignand. Wollstonecraft had not anticipated this and probably had never met him, but she was in no position to protest. The request shook Godwin. He knew enough about obstetrics now: that a long labour was unfortunate and that the placenta should swiftly follow the baby. Later he confessed to 'despair . . . in my heart' as he set off.

When the men returned it was nearly four hours after the birth. Poignand studied his patient, then took action, reaching into the womb and pulling at the placenta with his hands. It did not come away in the hoped-for smooth mass, but broke into pieces, some of which adhered to the womb. Obstetric practice had improved in the eighteenth century but, with no theory of germs, Poignand cannot have been aware of the huge danger and damage of this breaking, especially when, as now, he repeatedly put in his hand. On finishing he felt satisfied that all had been removed. This was barely conceivable once the placenta was broken; in any case there was no way to be sure, for the results of leaving fragments in the womb would only appear three or four days later, heralded by a jet of blood and the evacuation of smelly, decaying tissue.[11]

Without anaesthetic, the manual tugging was acutely painful, resulting in great loss of blood and haemorrhaging. Wollstonecraft repeatedly fainted away; probably she screamed, most women did. Later she declared that she would have died 'but that she was determined not to leave [Godwin].' She had never before this known what bodily pain was. Godwin came to believe that it was now that the fatal infection was introduced and that Poignand's intervention was the crucial act in the tragedy.

By the afternoon, still in desperate pain, Wollstonecraft was anxious and asked for Fordyce, their physician friend, to be fetched. Poignand was irritated, there was no need for other opinions; it seemed a lack of confidence in himself. Obstetricians were touchy about their status: they knew that higher-ranking physicians saw them as trying to raise themselves above the level of ordinary surgeons. He sourly noted that 'Dr Fordyce was not particularly conversant with obstetrical cases.'

As soon as Poignand left, Godwin sent for Fordyce, who came about three o'clock. He approved the treatment both of Dr Poignand and of Mrs Blenkinsop and saw absolutely no need for alarm. Indeed, he was so impressed with the patient that, on the following day, when discussing childbirth in company, he used Wollstonecraft's case to support his own view that women should be employed as midwives. She 'had had a woman,' he told them, 'and was doing extremely well.'

Godwin remained unconvinced. He had little trust in Poignand and had watched him inflict immense pain. He stayed with Wollstonecraft the rest of the afternoon, much of the time in her bedroom, until guests, including Maria Reveley, called in the evening. Then, as time passed and appearances began to look 'favourable', his 'alarms wore off'.

The night proved quiet and he felt he could devote Friday morning to urgent business in different parts of town. He saw Mary Hays to give her a progress report, while Joseph Johnson visited Wollstonecraft at the Polygon. Fordyce called again and remained optimistic. Godwin persuaded himself that his anxiety was excessive and that, if she did not catch cold or have further accident, she should recover. He went to bed calmly.

Saturday proved less satisfactory and Sunday was alarming. While Godwin was out, travelling as far as Kensington, Wollstonecraft suffered uncontrollable fits of shivering. They signalled septicaemia, the decaying of the bits of placenta left in the womb. She was rotting internally. Godwin returned in the afternoon before dinner to learn that his wife had called for him and to see dread on all faces. Hurriedly a message was sent to his sister Hannah not to come to dine as planned and meals were henceforth set out in the parlour on the ground floor, not in the dining-room immediately under the bedroom. Godwin deeply regretted his absence and determined not to go so far again. This day, he concluded, 'finally decided on the fate of the object dearest to my heart that the universe contained'.

The progress of decay was carefully, clinically and tactfully recorded by Godwin in his diary and *Memoirs*. The actual event was undoubtedly more unpleasant for the sufferer and onlookers. Whatever her enlightened views of childbirth, she was in the hands of professionals, who, desperately fearing puerperal fever and believing one cause to be a woman's taking cold, would have kept her muffled up and sweating in an overheated room. Much of her suffering occurred at night by the light of candles that warmed the air, inevitably by now smelling of urine, blood, sweat and mortifying flesh.

In the evening Wollstonecraft had a further shivering fit lasting for as much as five minutes. Her teeth chattered and the bed shook with the trembling of her muscles. By now she would be suffering extreme thirst, while her mouth would be dry and encrusted, her belly swollen. With her body so out of control, she felt herself hovering between life and death, fearful of losing consciousness for the last time. It was devastating to watch and in the early hours of the following morning Godwin dashed off for Dr Poignand again. Surely something could be done.

When Poignand arrived and found that Fordyce had been in constant attendance, he grew testy. Godwin's surgeon friend Carlisle had also been calling each day, and Poignand must have wondered how many more men would be consulted to undermine his care. He declined to treat the patient further. Godwin did not much value him and cannot have been appalled at his going, but he did perhaps worry that they were losing the most experienced of the attendants. Now they had mainly to rely on the learned but eccentric Fordyce and the friendly Carlisle; neither had much practical knowledge.

Since Wollstonecraft seemed so poorly, it was felt best for Maria Reveley to take Fanny (and probably Marguerite) home to stay with her. Fanny was used to the kindly, even-tempered Maria, who would be a comforting presence for the child in what they must all by now have been secretly dreading. Eliza Fenwick helped Wollstonecraft's servant Mary and Godwin's housekeeper with the nursing.

The following morning, Monday, as decay continued Fordyce must have regretted his earlier optimism. Wollstonecraft had, of course, planned to breast-feed Mary, as she had Fanny. No wet-nurse had therefore been procured. But now her body was becoming so weak and contaminated that she should not give milk to a baby. As after Fanny's birth, so again, she was producing copious amounts and Fordyce told them to ease the swelling by allowing puppies to suckle her. No longer in such acute pain, Wollstonecraft took this extraordinary incident in her stride and even joked with Godwin about her grotesque appearance.

There was no longer reason to keep the baby in the house and she was dispatched to join Fanny at Maria Reveley's. No one really expected her to survive since she appeared so weakly. Eliza Fenwick moved into the Polygon and impressed Carlisle as 'the best nurse he ever saw'.[12] Truly the Godwins did not want for help. In addition to the women and the doctors, four male friends, Montagu, John Fenwick, Dyson and Marshall, had moved into the Polygon, 'to be sent at a moment's warning anywhere that should be necessary'. Despite the Godwins' indebtedness, economy was thrown to the wind.

On Tuesday afternoon, growing yet more anxious, Godwin sent for Fordyce again. This time he brought with him Dr John Clarke 'under the idea that some operation might be necessary'. In her healthy days, Wollstonecraft would not have approved a man who, although the most advanced in obstetric thinking, had attacked female midwives as 'ignorant', described the involvement of women in childbirth as a 'rooted and inveterate prejudice', and seen the pregnant woman as an animal with an obstructive will.[13] Godwin knew him to be the leading specialist on awkward deliveries; later he tortured himself by wondering whether, had he insisted on having Clarke at the outset instead of Mrs Blenkinsop and Poignand, the tragedy might have been averted.[14] 'Every skilful effort that medical knowledge of the highest class could make was exerted to save her,' wrote Eliza Fenwick. With hindsight, perhaps it would have been better if the efforts had come in another sequence or if they had not been made at all.[15]

By Wednesday, 'the day of greatest torture in the melancholy series' as Godwin wrote, Clarke saw that it was much too late for any intervention and said what the studiously optimistic Carlisle was refusing to say, that she was dying. In cases of extremity, his book suggested 'bark, wine, and other cordials in as large quantities as the stomach will bear' should be offered, and it noted that, where there had been neglect, 'no remedies will avail to avert the death of the woman.'[16] Now he told Godwin he must give her wine, as much as she would take, to help her suffer what was coming. He should administer it to her himself.[17]

Horribly aware of what the action implied – that they were simply alleviating the suffering of a dying woman – Godwin hated playing thus with life. None the less, he began giving the wine to Wollstonecraft at about four in the afternoon, continuing until seven when her situation grew graver. 'Foolishly' he asked Mary how she thought her mistress was doing. Mary replied that 'she was going as fast as possible.' He knew the dialogue absurd, but reason was no guide.

In such extremity most women had sisters or other female relatives to turn to. Wollstonecraft did not think of Eliza and Everina, but instead of her old friend from Berkshire, perhaps the nearest she had to a family friend. She wanted Mrs Cotton to come to help nurse her. Godwin duly wrote a letter but Fordyce and Clarke told him it was pointless to send it, implying that all would be over long before the lady could arrive. A little after seven, desperate to do something, Godwin dispatched Basil Montagu at full speed to find Carlisle, who was dining out of town. He should come whatever he was or wherever he was.

Although he already had two doctors visiting each day, Godwin now derived most comfort from Carlisle, and it was probably as much for himself as for his wife that he desired the soothing presence. Montagu was so speedy that he returned with the doctor after three quarters of an hour, much to Godwin's relief. Carlisle too immediately moved in and promised to stay as long as necessary. Godwin was deeply grateful: 'It was impossible to exceed his kindness and affectionate attention. It excited in every spectator a sentiment like adoration. His conduct was uniformly tender and anxious, ever upon the watch, observing every symptom, and eager to improve every favourable appearance. If skill or attention could have saved her, Mary would still live.'

On Wednesday night Godwin snatched a few hours of sleep. Towards morning the ever-optimistic Carlisle disturbed him to tell him his wife was 'surprisingly better'. Godwin hurried to her room but, having yielded to rash hope once before, now could not bear to nourish it again. He was right; by ten in the evening Carlisle changed his mind and told him that Wollstonecraft could not last long, even though, to Godwin's mind, she appeared less exhausted. He took the pessimistic report where he had refused the optimistic one.

Then they all waited. Wollstonecraft had often been lonely – in Norway, in Mitchelstown Castle, with a small baby in frozen Paris – but emphatically she was not dying alone. Or unloved. Mary Hays records, 'The attachment and regret of those who surrounded her appeared to increase every hour.'[18] The attentive Eliza Fenwick, with her during all these days, made the more general point that 'she was admired, and almost idolised, by some of the most eminent and best of human beings.'

Still she lingered on and it was only on Friday that Godwin felt she had any real sense she was dying. She did not dwell on it. Carlisle approved since he believed morbid thoughts collaborated with disease. By this time her faculties were disordered, but Godwin was keen to note that 'not one word of a religious cast fell from her lips'. Perhaps not in his hearing. Wollstonecraft had never believed in a cruel afterlife, but she had kept a residual belief in a benevolent creator. It was probably of some inner comfort now or perhaps she was too fuddled to think. One story related that, when she felt momentarily better after being given one of Carlisle's sedatives by Montagu, she exclaimed, 'I feel in heaven.' To which Godwin replied, 'I suppose, my dear, that that is a form for saying you are in less pain.'[19] But the dialogue seems too pat for truth, too clear an illustration of the supposed distinctions between the 'extraordinary' pair. Others, like Mary Hays, testified to her mental ease: 'my imagination could never have pictured to me a mind so tranquil, under affliction so great ... if her principles are to be judged of by what I saw of her death, I should say that no principles could be more conducive to calmness and consolation.'[20]

Mostly, she tried to be compliant, to take what was offered and sleep when her nurses suggested. She had been prickly in her life, but now many of her friends commented on her appreciation of them and their care. Mary Hays, who had sometimes felt her tongue, had no experience with nursing and could not offer the help of Maria Reveley and Eliza Fenwick, but she visited each day and was struck by Wollstonecraft's 'anxious fondness' for her friends and by the warm affections she had always so admired in her. But Wollstonecraft was no saint and she remained impatient with false comfort, complaining bitterly when one of the servants tried to rally her. The self-centredness of the dying was overtaking her and she did not want to be bothered with triviality.

On Saturday morning, 'seeing that every hope was extinct', Godwin tried to speak to her about the future of little Fanny and baby Mary, while somehow following Carlisle's advice about positive thinking, that he should not intrude the idea of death. She had been very ill, he pointed out, and he would have to care for the children alone for some time and needed instruction. She was too weak to 'follow any train of ideas with force or any accuracy of connection', but she caught his drift, 'I know what you are thinking of,' she told him, but she had nothing to say of her daughters. They were slipping from her sight. She retained her feeling for Godwin however: 'He is the kindest, best man in the world,' she told Eliza Fenwick.

Carlisle regarded her living on at all as quite miraculous and believed they should not absolutely give up hope. He and Godwin spoke of her good constitution and firm mind and, if only one woman in a million could recover from her present state, might it not be she? He told Godwin to get some rest and promised to let him know if there were any change during the night. So, aware that they had merely amused themselves 'in the very gulph of despair', Godwin went to bed at one o'clock on Sunday morning.

He was roused at six; at twenty to eight on Sunday, 10 September, Wollstonecraft died. Godwin recorded the time in his journal, then drew three wordless lines.

Her women friends were mobilised as scribes. Mary Hays wrote to Hugh Skeys. Her sister Eliza did not receive a letter of her own, but Godwin wanted her told that Mary had been sincerely fond of her.[21] Eliza Fenwick reported to Everina: 'No woman was ever more happy in marriage than Mrs Godwin.

Who ever endured more anguish than Mr Godwin endures?' A month later Godwin himself wrote to Mrs Cotton, 'I partook of a happiness, so much the more exquisite, as I had a short time before had no conception of it, and scarcely admitted the possibility of it.'[22]

He did not attend the funeral, which was arranged by Marshall. It took place on 15 September in St Pancras Church, where he and Wollstonecraft had recently been married. A tombstone was erected which preserved her identities as feminist and lover:

Mary Wollstonecraft Godwin,
Author of
A Vindication
Of the Rights of Woman:
Born 27 April, 1759:
Died 10 September, 1797.

Godwin was left with two little children, her debts, her manuscripts, and the memory of a 'bright ray of light that streaked across my day of life'.

# NOTES

## Chapter 1

1 *The Works of Mary Wollstonecraft* ed. Janet Todd and Marilyn Butler (London: Pickering & Chatto, 1989), 1, 124 and 132. Hereafter referred to as *Works*.

2 The will is in the Public Record Office, Kew.

3 *Parish Register, St Botolph's,* Guildhall Library.

4 *Works,* 5, 223.

5 Godwin's biography of his wife, *Memoirs of the Author of* A Vindication of the Rights of Woman (1798), in the Penguin edition, ed. Richard Holmes, 1987, pp. 205–6. Throughout this work, material on Wollstonecraft ascribed to Godwin is from the *Memoirs.*

6 Cecilia Lucy Brightwell, *Memorials of the Life of Amelia Opie* (Norwich, 1854), p. 18.

7 A few months after her birth, the *Parish Register, St Botolph's* records the death of another Mary Wollstonecraft and just before, in 1754, a Mary Wolsoncroft was christened in Clerkenwell, daughter of Thomas and Ann, to be replaced by another one in 1760. There are, too, other Wollstonecrafts bearing the family combination of names, Charles, Edward, Bland, Henry and Woodstock. Wollstonecrafts lived in London back into the seventeenth century but a larger number appear in Lancashire, from where the family probably originated. A relative with the same name as her brother Ned, Edward Bland, had been first officer on her grandfather's part-owned ship.

8 Elizabeth Ogborne, 'Biographical Notices [Royal Liberty of Havering]', *The History of Essex, from the earliest period to the present time . . . with Biographical Notices of the most distinguished and remarkable Natives* (1814), p. 161.

9 In *The Female Reader* Wollstonecraft could excerpt the passage from *The Task,* vol. I, in which this line occurs, *Works,* 4, 286.

10 There is a local tradition that the farm was the present mixed farm of Broadgate just off the road from Beverley to York, but there is no firm evidence of this.

11 *Memoirs of the Late Thomas Holcroft, written by Himself* ed. William Hazlitt (London, 1852), p. 12.

12 Henry Skrine, *Three Successive Tours in the North of England . . .* (London, 1795), p. xix.

13 In the *Memoirs* Godwin noted Edward's 'cruelty' to Mary; the hitting is mentioned in a letter from Godwin to Johnson, 11 January, 1798, Abinger MSS, Bodleian Library, Oxford, Dep.b.227/8.

14 Where not ascribed to *Works* or particular articles, quotations from Wollstonecraft come from *Collected Letters of Mary Wollstonecraft* ed. Ralph M. Wardle (Ithaca: Cornell University Press, 1979). This quotation occurs on p. 66. The quotations are mainly in chronological order except where indicated in the notes.

15 John Gregory, *A Father's Legacy to His Daughters* (Dublin 1774), pp. 25–6.

16 *York Courant,* 7 February 1775, Beverley Public Library.

17 *York Courant,* 12 February 1771.

18 *York Courant,* 8 January 1771.

19 Jacques Gélis, *History of Childbirth: Fertility, Pregnancy and Birth in Early Modern Europe* (Cambridge: Polity Press, 1991), p. 12.

20 Ivan and Elizabeth Hall, *Burton Constable Hall: A Century of Patronage* (Hull City Museum and Art Galleries, 1991), p. 25.

21 John Arden's lecture syllabus was published as *A Short account of a course of Natural and Experimental Philosophy* by J. Arden Teacher of Experimental Philosophy at Bath (Beverley, 1772).

22 Jane's letters have not been preserved while Mary's were carefully copied out by the friend who was berated for her indifference.

23 On 15 January 1799, Jane Arden, now Jane Gardiner of Beverley, wrote to Godwin: 'In the early part of our lives miss Mary Wollstonecraft and I kept up a correspondence for some years: part of those letters I have carefully preserved as valuable marks of her friendship at that time. / I have been greatly solicited by several ladies to part with them, but as she was the beloved friend of my youth I have been unwilling to do it. Yet as I think it a pity that any of the writings of such a genius should be buried in oblivion, they are at your service if you wish to publish them.' (Abinger MSS Dep.b.214/3.). Godwin chose not to do so.

24 As Gary Kelly pointed out, 'friend' had once meant a person assisting one in material, social or political interests, but, in the eighteenth century, the word had come to denote someone with mutual moral, intellectual and emotional interests to oneself, *Revolutionary Feminism: The Mind and Career of Mary Wollstonecraft* (London: Macmillan, 1992), p. 12.

25 *Lady's Magazine* X, 1779, p. 203.


## Chapter 2

1 Beverley Corporation Apprentices Register lists the indenture of apprenticeship for seven years of Henry Woodstock Wollstonecraft, son of Edward John Wollstonecraft. In *A Different Face: The Life of Mary Wollstonecraft* (New York: Harper & Row, 1975), pp. 36–8, Emily W. Sunstein first suggested that Henry went mad. It still seems the most plausible explanation, since, had he died and the 'Henry' of the letter been another man, one might have expected some mention to be made of him as a lost brother. Between 1777 and 1811 about 144 patients were concealed in the Beverley area. See J. A. R. Bickford, *The Private Lunatic Asylums of the East Riding* (East Yorkshire Local History Society, 1976), pp. 1–9.

2 *The Historical Medical Register* from 1814, East Riding Archives. In 1807 there were thirty-three assessed insane people in Hull and the East Riding, including Beverley. Three were in houses of industry, five in York Lunatic Asylum and twenty-five were unconfined, that is cared for at home or privately.

3 Andrew Marvell, 'The Rehearsal Transposed' (1672); Arthur D. Morris, *The Hoxton Madhouses* (March, Cambs., 1958), n.p.; Walter Harrison *New and Universal History, Description ... London* (London, 1776), p. 545; James Norris Brewer *London and Middlesex: or, an Historical, Commercial, and Descriptive Survey of the Metropolis of Great-Britain* (London, 1816) IV, 28.

4 15 May 1787. In the *Analytical Review* Wollstonecraft gave much space to an argument for not placing people in lunatic asylums at the first sign of insanity, *Works*, 7, 236–7.

5 In the first edition of the *Memoirs* Godwin made this tie equivalent to heterosexual romance by comparing it to the relationship of Goethe's Werther and Charlotte. Wollstonecraft, of course, takes the manly role of Werther.

6 *Works*, 5, 197–8. Rousseau condemned masturbation as unhealthy and corrupt, a facet of premature sexuality. The influential work on the subject was Tissot's *L'Onanisme* (1760).

7 Most biographers assume that this disappointment was connected with Skeys. The letter Fanny wrote from Lisbon declaring she hardly knew the man she was marrying does not quite fit this, but Wollstonecraft's later blame of him for the upsetting delays seems to do so.

8 In the mid and late eighteenth century there were several short-stay commercial people in Laugharne. See S. Lewis, *A Topographical Dictionary of Wales* 3rd ed. (London, 1844), pp. 462–

3. I am grateful to Tom Lloyd for information about the history of Laugharne and the Allens of Cresselly.

9 The name of Wollstonecraft does not occur in the lists of state annuities (NDO 2/1, 2/3, 3/29 and 3/32 in the PRO) and I have not been able to find the name in any listing of private annuities. The records from Ireland are notoriously sparse. In *The Wrongs of Woman*, which includes several autobiographical details, the heroine mentions 'the settlement made on my mother's children' which the eldest brother manages to set aside so that it can in part be used to keep the impoverished father, *Works*, I, 140. In the same book Wollstonecraft describes a kindly uncle who gives his niece affection and settles money on her. In *Mary Wollstonecraft: A Biography* (New York: Howard, McCann & Geoghegan, 1972) Eleanor Flexner speculates that Edward Bland Wollstonecraft, the cousin or uncle who served as first officer on their grandfather's part-owned ship, might be a possible source of the legacies, but, since he was not the owner of the ship and since he married Lydia Cooke in November 1761 and produced at least one daughter, this seems unlikely.

10 See lists of merchants and principal tradesmen, *Kent's Directory* for 1770s and 1780s, Guildhall microfilms 96917/5.

11 G. J. Barker-Benfield notes that, in *Mary, A Fiction*, the mother is given the 'lingering' complaint. He sees Wollstonecraft as 'at some level ... taking on her mother's illness; her attempt to argue herself out of such a lingering illness represented her father's way of treating her mother [he believed it fashionable affectation],' 'Mary Wollstonecraft's Depression and Diagnosis: The Relation Between Sensibility and Women's Susceptibility to Nervous Disorders,' *Psychohistory Review*, vol. 13, 1985, pp. 18–19.

12 *Memoirs of Mary Robinson, 'Perdita'*, ed. J. F. Molloy (London: Gibbings & Co., 1895). See Roger Lonsdale ed. *Eighteenth-Century Women Poets* (Oxford: Oxford University Press, 1989), pp. 468–70.

13 'A Supplement to Memoirs' in *Memoirs of Mary Wollstonecraft* ed. W. Clark Durant (London: Constable & Co., 1927), p. 150. George Mills Harper speculates that Fanny Blood and Mary Wollstonecraft stayed with Taylor for three months in 1782, *Notes & Queries*, IX, December 1962, 461–3. As Eleanor Flexner has noted, there does not seem time for this, *Mary Wollstonecraft*, p. 289, n. 10.

## Chapter 3

1 In later Minerva Press works, employment outside the home could help define a heroine's virtue, but, except for Frances Sheridan's *Memoirs of Sidney Biddulph* (1761), this was not usually the case in earlier fiction, which saw paid work as an unmitigated disaster. Companioning, in particular, was treated with horror, see Jane Collier's *Essay on the Art of Ingeniously Tormenting* (1753) and Sarah Fielding's *David Simple* (1744). The greatest horror was working for a parvenue, a vulgar woman below the educational and social level of the companion. In novel after novel, the companion of such a woman responds by internalising the shame and anger and by declining in health. The stereotypical nature of this trajectory can be seen from the fact that, years later, Jane Austen mocked the expectation in *Sanditon*: the heroine contemplates Clara, the companion of the dominating Lady Denham, and concludes: 'She seemed placed with her on purpose to be ill-used. Such Poverty & Dependance joined to such Beauty & Merit, seemed to leave no choice in the business.'

2 'The Witlings' (1779), *The Witlings and The Woman-Hater* ed. Peter Sabor and Geoffrey Sill (London: Pickering & Chatto, 1997), Act V, pp. 76–7.

3 *Works*, 4, 25.

4 Higher placed, Frances Burney had the opposite impression: she found Bath peculiarly unsnob-

bish. 'There is something nearer to independence from the shackles of fortuitous circumstances in the society of *Bath* than I have witnessed elsewhere,' 25 April 1816, *Journals and Letters of Fanny Burney, 1791–1840*, ed. Joyce Hemlow (Oxford University Press, 1972–84), IX, 102–3. For further description of Bath see Mark Girouard *The English Town* (New Haven: Yale University Press, 1990).

5   *The Bath Chronicle*, 26 February 1778.

6   *The Bath Chronicle*, 18 February 1779. In the 26 February issue John Arden was advertising his fourth course of lectures, declaring that he was waiting until he had twenty or more subscribers to begin; this suggests that he was not doing as well as he hoped or that he had exhausted the self-improving element of Bath. The advertisements then ceased.

7   *A Governess in the Age of Jane Austen: The Journals and Letters of Agnes Porter*, ed. Joanna Martin (London: Hambledon Press, 1998), p. 37.

8   This is probably the Edward Bland who had been first officer in the ship of which her brother had inherited a part and for whom he may have been named. *The Gentleman's Magazine*, vol. LXV, 2, for August 1795 records his death in Southampton.

9   *The Bath Chronicle*, which records the arrival of distinguished visitors to Bath, mentions the Revd Mr Waterhouse among newcomers in the 17 December 1778 issue.

10  'Amongst the many fair ones to whom the singular rector of Stukeley paid his addresses was the once-famous Mary Wollstonecraft, distinguished during the period of the French Revolution for her democratical writing ... How far the rev. gentleman sped in his wooing with this intellectual amazon we have not been able to ascertain ...' See T. Lovell, *Narrative of the Murder of the late Rev. J. Waterhouse* (1827). The letters disappeared after Waterhouse's death.

11  *The Bath Chronicle*, 22 April 1779 and 10 June. In 1780 Sophia, Harriet and Ann Lee opened a school in Bath and by the 1790s were in charge of the very successful boarding school at Belvedere House.

12  *First Hull Directory*, East Riding Archive Office, Beverley. Beverley churchwardens' accounts have John Arden as a regular but very modest contributor (PE 124/5).

13  Wollstonecraft's own lack of sartorial frivolity was due in part to her poverty, but, when she alluded to it in one letter, she crossed out the word 'purse' and substituted 'power'.

## Chapter 4

1   *Works*, 5, 222.

2   *Works*, 1, 132.

3   *Memoirs*, p. 206.

4   Godwin dates the mother's death to 1780, so exaggerating the time of Wollstonecraft's stay with Fanny Blood.

5   Bodleian Library, Abinger MSS Dep.b.210/9.

6   In *Mary Wollstonecraft: A Critical Biography* (Lincoln: University of Nebraska Press, 1951) Ralph Wardle suggests that Waterhouse might be 'Neptune', partly because of the name and partly owning to the crossings out in several letters mentioning 'Neptune'. Eleanor Flexner makes the valid point that these defaced passages occur during references to her family and may well have been made by Everina, the last surviving sister, before she handed the letters over. See Appendix B, pp. 269–70. Sunstein speculates that 'Neptune' might be the widowed Hugh Skeys, whose second marriage Wollstonecraft resented, pp. 136–7. In his edition of the letters, Wardle concludes that Neptune is not Waterhouse but one of the several Bloods actually called Neptune, of which there were three in Wollstonecraft's generation, the first of the name being a sixteenth-century sailor, see *Letters* p. 111 n. 3. The International Genealogical Index lists several. The one born in Ireland about 1750 to Mark Blood and a mother with the maiden name of O'Neill is

possibly the man. Wardle speculates that Neptune was a second cousin of Fanny and George Blood; in 1800 George married Deborah, another name that recurs in the Blood genealogy. Deborah was born about 1780, sister of a Neptune and daughter of Neptune Blood of Ballyshean and ? O'Neill.

7   J. Norris Brewer, *London and Middlesex*, IV. 111.

8   Meredith Bishop was admitted to the guild in 1775, *Worshipful Company of Shipwrights, Admissions Stamp Duty Book* 1727–1825, Guildhall Library; *Kent's Directory* . . . 1778–1788; Documents of the Commissary Court of St Katherine's Near the Tower, Guildhall Library MSS 9740/4, 9772/34; Marriage Register of St Katherine's Near the Tower, Guildhall Library.

9   *Works*, 4, 31.

## Chapter 5

1   Register of Baptisms, St Mary Magdalen, Bermondsey.

2   Austen, *Northanger Abbey, Lady Susan, and Sanditon* ed. John Davie (Oxford: Oxford University Press, 1990), p. 278. By Austen's time many novelists such as Mary Brunton and Elizabeth Hamilton praised women's earning their living but Austen remained entirely sceptical, see also *Lady Susan* and *Emma*.

3   Skeys had a brother and occasionally this man rather than Hugh might be referred to.

4   Wollstonecraft had not by this time become a devotee of Rousseau, who declared in *Discourse on Inequality* (1755) that, 'if the human mother happens to perish, her child is in great danger of perishing with her'.

5   See Lawrence Stone, *Broken Lives: Separation and Divorce in England 1669–1857* (Oxford: Oxford University Press, 1993).

6   Abinger MSS Dep.b.210/9. This is one of the few extant letters from Fanny Blood and it suggests her writing skills.

7   Carla H. Hay, 'James Burgh', *Biographical Dictionary of Modern British Radicals*, vol. I, ed. Joseph O. Baylen and Norbert J. Gossman (Brighton: Harvester, 1979), p. 73.

8   Quoted in Lionel Taylor, *A Little Corner of London (Newington Green) with its History and Tradition of a Non-Conformist Meeting House* (Lincoln: J. W. Ruddock & Sons, 1925), p. 7. See also P. W. Clayden, *The Early Life of Samuel Rogers* (London, 1887).

9   A later friend of Wollstonecraft's, Eliza Fenwick, in 1799 had six pupils between the ages of two and five; she received £8 a quarter for teaching six hours a day. Her scheme did not work because she also had her own numerous family to care for.

10  Meredith Bishop was buried in Bermondsey on 2 December 1835.

## Chapter 6

1   The problems of keeping a small school are described in *Miss Weeton's Journal of a Governess: 1807–1811* and *1811–1825*, ed. Edward Hall (Newton Abbot: David & Charles Reprints, 1969). Ellen Weeton ran a school with her mother and helped her brother Thomas Weeton train for the law, only to find herself despised as a 'schoolmistress' by his wealthier wife, who would not offer her a home. Jane Marks kept a 'Genteel Day School' in Fetter Lane, Holborn for nearly thirty years, and was driven at last to poverty by the 'failure of several of the Parents of my Boarders in their Payments'. Everina ascribed the failure of the sisters' enterprise to over-stretching and one lodger's refusal to pay the board for her three children (to William Godwin, 24 November 1797), *Shelley and his Circle*, ed. Kenneth Neill Cameron (Cambridge, Mass.: Harvard University Press, 1961) I, 45. It is worth pointing out that, at about the same time as the Wollstonecrafts were

running their school, William Godwin tried to start one intended for twelve pupils in Epsom but did not manage to attract sufficient. Edward Copeland, *Women Writing about Money: Women's Fiction in England 1790–1820* (Cambridge: Cambridge University Press, 1995), pp. 176–7 discusses the rates of pay for women companions, teachers and governesses.

2 *Works*, 5, 265–6.

3 Price resigned his pastorate in 1783 because of his wife's invalid state but he remained at the Green until 1787, revising his work and involving himself in political and religious affairs. D. O. Thomas, *The Honest Mind: The Thought and Work of Richard Price* (Oxford: Oxford University Press, 1977).

4 *An Account of the First Settlement, Laws, Forms of Government, and Police of the Cesares, A People of South America* (1764; modern Spanish edition, *Un relato de la colonización ... de los Césares*, tr. Eugenio Pereira Salas, 1963); Carl Cone, *The English Jacobins* (New York: Charles Scribner's Sons, 1968).

5 The record of this meeting exists only in Godwin's *Memoirs*. Although some admirers wanted to make much of it, in the *Athenaeum*, 2985, 16 January 1885, Alexander Napier commented that it amounted to no more than that 'Mary Wollstonecraft, then an unknown person of about four-and-twenty, was on one occasion received by Johnson with the kindness and affability which invariably characterized his intercourse with ladies'. See also 20 December 1884.

6 Dr Johnson accepted Hewlett but had no time for Dr Price; James Boswell records that in Oxford he instantly left the room when Price entered, *Life of Johnson*, ed. R. W. Chapman (Oxford University Press, 1980) p. 1248.

7 There was some speculation that George had witnessed a fraud of his landlord Palmer since the latter was accused of forgery at this time; Kegan Paul suggested that he was articled to Palmer, Charles Kegan Paul, *William Godwin, his friends and contemporaries* (London, 1876) I, 175. George does not seem to have had sufficient education for such a position. Wardle points to George's manuscript autobiography, where he claims to have been falsely charged in the paternity case, see *Letters*, pp. 91–2.

8 30 March, 1785, Abinger MSS Dep.b.210/9 (ult.)

## Chapter 7

1 See Holcroft's description of a voyage in *Memoirs*, p. 279.

2 *Works*, 6, 271.

3 *Works*, 7, 29.

4 *Mary, A Fiction, Works*, 1, 35.

5 *Memoirs*, p. 220.

6 There are sixteen lines crossed out of this letter. Possibly, since it finally came into the hands of Everina, this defacement was hers and the obliterated passage may have expressed too warm a regard for the lowly George by Mary in her miserable state.

7 I have used the words 'depressed' and 'depression' anachronistically to refer to Wollstonecraft. 'Depression' in fact became a current term only in the mid-nineteenth century when it came to be used for the lowness of spirits felt by the sick. By 1900 it had achieved its modern meaning of a general sinking of the spirits. I have used 'melancholy' and 'melancholia' also, especially when Wollstonecraft seemed in part to be celebrating her condition.

8 Frederick A. Pottle, *James Boswell: The Earlier Years 1740–1769* (London: Heinemann, 1966), p. 1.

9 This important contact seems to have lapsed later. In May 1787 Wollstonecraft described Hewlett as having thrown himself away but she still asked Everina in London to remember her to him 'in the most affectionate manner'. On 5 April 1797 Hewlett was appointed Morning Preacher at

the Foundling Hospital near Somers Town, close to where Wollstonecraft and Godwin lived, and they seem to have re-established loose contact. He was invited to her funeral but did not attend.

10 *Works*, 4, 8.

11 Letter to Gabell, 13 September 1787.

12 *Observations on the Nature of Civil Liberty, the Principles of Government, and the Justice and Policy of the War with America* (London, 1776), p. 11.

13 Editorial note, *Lady's Magazine*, May 1787. The magazine excerpted *Thoughts* on pages 227–30, 287–8 and 369–70, using copy on exterior accomplishments, dress, boarding-schools, matrimony, treatment of servants and public places.

## Chapter 8

1 The wage suggests the difference between a governess and the ordinary servants. Housemaids got on average about £4 10s, male servants twice as much. See J. Jean Hecht, *The Domestic Servant Class in Eighteenth-Century England* (London: Routledge & Kegan Paul, 1980) and Amanda Vickery, *The Gentleman's Daughter: Women's Lives in Georgian England* (New Haven: Yale University Press, 1998), p. 321, n. 27.

2 The letters of Eliza Bishop to Everina quoted in this and subsequent chapters are from Abinger MSS Dep. b. 210/7.

3 This suit remains a mystery. A Roebuck was involved in litigation with another Roebuck in 1787, but there is no record of any Wollstonecraft–Roebuck suit in the Chancery Records in PRO or in the Depositions in the Exchequer.

4 Robert Southey characterised public schools as 'nurseries' of 'tyranny and brutality', see *Life and Correspondence of the Late Robert Southey* ed. C. C. Southey (London, 1849), I, 149.

5 *The Autobiography of Arthur Young*, ed. M. Betham-Edwards (London, 1898), pp. 77–80.

## Chapter 9

1 As an adult Margaret retained some of her childhood characteristics, as the unflattering picture painted by Godwin reveals: 'Lady Mountcashel is a singular character, a democrat and a republican in all their sternness, yet with no ordinary portion either of understanding or good nature. If any of our comic writers were to fall in her company, the infallible consequence would be her being gibbetted in a play. She is uncommonly tall and brawny, with bad teeth, white eyes, and a handsome countenance. She commonly dresses, as I have seen Mrs Fenwick dressed out of poverty, with a grey gown, and no linen visible; but with gigantic arms, which she commonly folds, naked and exposed almost up to the shoulders,' quoted in Edward C. McAleer, *The Sensitive Plant: A Life of Lady Mount Cashell* (Chapel Hill: University of North Carolina Press, 1958), p. 66. For a description of Irish ascendancy life during the years when Wollstonecraft was there, see *Betsy Sheridan's Journal*, ed. William Lefanu (London: Eyre & Spottiswoode, 1960).

2 The description in *The Rights of Woman* of three vain trivial girls not allowed to read novels but left to concentrate on dress, quarrel with each other and converse with the maids in stealth probably refers to these girls. Their mother is described as a widow, 'a very good woman' of fortune and fashion but 'narrow mind', *Works*, 5, 257.

3 The governess Agnes Porter displays a different attitude. 'What a pleasure it is to spend one's days encircled by beauty, youth and innocence,' she exclaims about her life with her charges. In *The Wrongs of Woman* Wollstonecraft generalises this alienation of governesses in the large mansion: 'alone, because they had no companions with whom they could converse on equal

terms, or from whom they could expect the endearments of affection, they grew melancholy, and the sound of joy made them sad' (*Works*, 1, 141).

4    *Works*, 5, 244–5.

5    *The Bath Chronicle* advertisements 1778–9. She would also have seen such advertisements in the *York Courant*.


## Chapter 10

1    The house is still standing but the terrace has been gutted – as two plaques lament – and the street is no longer grand.

2    Conventionally, Wollstonecraft had often described her depressions in terms of harassed 'spirits' – what nerves transmit. I am suggesting not a change but rather a change in emphasis. See Robert Whytt, *Observations on the Nature, Causes, and Cure Of those Disorders which have been Commonly called Nervous Hypochondriac, or Hysteric* (Edinburgh, 1765). For a description of medical fashion, see the early chapters of Peter Melville Logan, *Nerves & Narratives: A Cultural History of Hysteria in Nineteenth-Century British Prose* (Berkeley: University of California Press, 1997).

3    Account given by Margaret King in later life, McAleer, *The Sensitive Plant*, p. 5. Dress for presentation to the vice regent in Dublin was an emotive national issue. In the 1740s some Anglo-Irish ladies tried to replace the elaborate silks and brocades of court dress with 'Irish stuff' to help poor Irish weavers. As so often in Ireland, Wollstonecraft was silent on the sort of problems which would later strike her when contemplating countries with large social differences.

4    *Journals and Letters*, pp. 85, 94 and 113.

5    Later Eliza would meet Neptune in Wales, resolve to dislike him, but discover that he found 'a corner in my heart'.

6    Miss Crosby received an annuity of £50 drawn up by Arthur Young. See *Autobiography*, p. 79.

7    Bishop Percy of Dromore was commenting on Robert King's trial in 1798, see BL add. MS 32.335 ff. 15–18. See Tomalin, p. 261. Mary King was only eight when Wollstonecraft left the Kingsboroughs, but her immoral behaviour was blamed on her governess's bad example.

8    *Works*, 4, 18 and 1, 51. In *Mary, A Fiction* she makes her heroine sing Handel to the accompaniment of a storm.

9    Although there is much vacillation in Wollstonecraft between different theories and discourses, she is self-confident in each. As Syndy McMillen Conger notes in *Mary Wollstonecraft and the Language of Sensibility* (Rutherford: Fairleigh Dickinson University Press, 1994), 'Wollstonecraft rarely acts like a prisoner of any kind of discourse, sentimental or rational' p. xiii.


## Chapter 11

1    See Jacqueline Pearson, *Women's reading in Britain 1750–1835* (Oxford: Oxford University Press, 1999), pp. 58–9. For a male satire on women's reading of novels, see Courtney Melmoth's 'The Secrets of a Circulating Library' in *Family Secrets* (1797).

2    Wollstonecraft may have felt dissatisfied with George and his many failures. Once the favoured correspondent, he was not often visited during her time in Dublin.

3    *Works*, 1, 37, 46.

4    Margaret later wrote, 'the society of my father's house was not calculated to improve my good qualities or correct my faults; and almost the only person of superior merit with whom I had been intimate in my early days was an enthusiastic female who was my governess from fourteen

to fifteen years old, for whom I felt an unbounded admiration because her mind appeared more noble & her understanding more cultivated than any others I had known – from the time she left me my chief objects were to correct those faults she had pointed out & to cultivate my understanding as much as possible,' Lady Mount Cashel's account, quoted in McAleer, *The Sensitive Plant*, p. 5.

5 The description is Blake's, see Thomas Wright, *The Life of William Blake* (Olney, 1929), I, 20. Wollstonecraft called him 'little Johnson', 12 February 1787.

6 Miss Rowden obviously took more trouble with her own daughter whom she sent for education to St Quintin's in Reading, of which she later became headmistress before setting up a lavish and successful school in Paris primarily for English pupils. The daughter was said to be 'Methodistical', so perhaps, like Eliza, Everina found her employer too pious. See Frances Ann Kemble, *Record of a Girlhood* (1878) I, 78.

## Chapter 12

1 Abinger MSS Dep.b.210/3, letter from Johnson to Godwin.

2 This sentiment formed part of Barbauld's rejection of a proposal from Maria Edgeworth to co-edit a periodical featuring literary ladies. She added, 'different sentiments and different connections separate them much more than the joint interest of their sex would unite them. Mrs. Hannah More would not write along with you or me, and we should probably hesitate at joining Miss Hays, or if she were living, Mrs Godwin' (4 Sept. 1804), Anna Letitia Le Breton, *Memoirs of Mrs Barbauld* (London, 1874), pp. 86–7. In *The Life and Death* ... (p. 235) Tomalin has speculated that Barbauld was the author of an anonymous account of Wollstonecraft in the *Monthly Visitor* (Feb./March 1798), a serious estimate of her life and views at a time when she was being much abused; ultimately it was felt that Wollstonecraft had deviated in this account 'from propriety' and that the notion of sexual equality was dangerous.

3 See also Sarah Fielding's *The Governess* (1749) and Ann Murry's *Mentoria* (1778). Fielding's Mrs Teachum has the 'commanding Eye' of so many powerful governesses, including Wollstonecraft's.

4 The fictional Mary was fourteen, the same age as Wollstonecraft's favourite, Margaret King. Presumably Margaret read the work of her charismatic governess since she assumed the name of Mrs Mason when she disgraced her family and passed as a commoner.

5 The notion that parents were not fit to educate their children also occurs in James Burgh's *An Account of ... the Cesares*, which argued that parental vices can ultimately destroy the state.

6 Wollstonecraft knew a Mrs Mason at Newington Green who may have influenced the portrait. The illustrations by Blake prepared for the second revised edition in 1791 are frequently so inappropriate for this stern work that one might suspect irony, especially since the austere vision of childhood is much at odds with Blake's own. See especially the picture of the unfortunate family saved only by Mrs Mason's benevolence. The parents sit upright and doleful, while the children lour or cower as if crying; the caption from Wollstonecraft reads 'Indeed we are very happy!' Blake does, however, catch the religious significance of Mrs Mason, who deputises for God in her pupils' lives: in his frontispiece to the second edition Mrs Mason stands Christlike in the position of a cross over two much younger, almost praying children.

7 This appears to have been so since her obituary in the *Gentleman's Magazine* (68, part 2, October 1797) describes her 'practical skill in education'. There is much to tie Mrs Mason to her author in attitude. Both have a proud austerity, the conviction that inner worth supersedes outer beauty, and the lack of care for dress except as it shows respect for others. In her Bath letters, Wollstonecraft separates herself from the aristocracy through her feeling for animals; Mrs Mason cares for snails and inhabits a sentimental world in which her care mirrors God's.

Occasionally Mrs Mason echoes Wollstonecraft's miserable feelings, though she is given proper social cause for her misery and in the last chapter Mrs Mason is described as writing down the stories to form the book Mary Wollstonecraft has herself written – a technique also used by Mme de Genlis in *Adelaide and Theodore*. However, in circumstance – without money and therefore needing to teach to support herself – Wollstonecraft is closer to another character in her work, Anna Lofty. Unlike the feeble women forced to earn a living in *Thoughts*, Anna would rather be poor and independent than a hanger-on of the great and she chooses school-teaching over a life eating the 'bitter bread' of rich relatives. But the resemblance ends with the attitude given to Anna: '[Anna] was formed to shine in the most brilliant circle – yet she relinquished it, and patiently labours to improve the children consigned to her management, and tranquillize her own mind. She succeeds in both.' After all her experiences, it seems that Wollstonecraft held to independent school-teaching over governessing and companioning, although it had to be done privately. The suffering it entailed should not be viewed by old friends: Anna fiercely 'lives alone'.

8   See the letter from Fuseli quoted in D. H. Weinglass, 'Henry Fuseli's Letter of Enquiry to Paris on Behalf of Mary Wollstonecraft's Sister Everina,' *Blake: An Illustrated Quarterly*, Spring 1988, pp. 144–6.

9   Hester Lynch Piozzi, *Anecdotes of the Late Samuel Johnson during the Last Twenty Years of His Life*, ed. (with Shaw's *Memoirs*) A. Sherbo (Oxford: Oxford University Press, 1974), p. 112. See also Bernard Mandeville's *A Treatise of the Hypochondriack and Hysterick Diseases* (1711).

10  First preface to *Elements of Medicine; or, A Translation of the Elementa Medicinae Brunonis* (1788).

11  Johnson had been a printer of medical books since his establishment as a bookseller, his earliest being John Hawkridge's *A Treatise on Fevers in General* (1764). From 1783 to 1790 he was proprietor of the *London Medical Journal*. I cannot prove Brown's specific influence on Mary Wollstonecraft but am sure of some medical input into her thinking about this time and I use Brown's name as shorthand for this.

12  The theory 'wrought a memorable change in medical opinion and practice' in Britain, as well as Europe and America, Preface by Thomas Beddoes to *The Elements of Medicine of John Brown* (1795), p. xi.

13  Bernard Mandeville had used 'hypochondriack' for melancholy in men and 'hysterick' for it in women.

14  At the same time Wollstonecraft was repulsed by degraded bodily processes and in *The Rights of Woman* was even shocked at Frenchwomen's casual mention of indigestion. *De la santé des gens de lettres* (1766) was the most influential work popularising the idea that intellectual activity could endanger health, an idea also stressed by Rousseau in *Discourse on Inequality* (1754).

## Chapter 13

1   *Works*, 7, 450. Henry Fuseli, who knew Lavater well and translated his *Aphorisms* in 1788, was critical of Holcroft's translation. Wollstonecraft's interest in Lavater's physiognomy is clearest in 'The Cave of Fancy' where the sage discerns character from the faces of shipwrecked corpses. When Lavater visited London, he met Wollstonecraft and visited a masquerade with her and Fuseli.

2   *The French Revolution, Works*, 6, 42.

3   *Works*, 2, 110.

4   Most notably in Richard Polwhele's *The Unsex'd Females* (1798), which is outraged not only at the notion of women mentioning human sexual organs but even at the idea that 'the study of the sexual system of plants' could be compatible with 'female modesty', a clear swipe at Erasmus

Darwin. In Book 4 of *Émile*, Rousseau complained that adults hide sexuality from children in a way that excites curiosity; children should be kept ignorant or spoken to frankly.

5  *Works*, 4, 55–7.

6  See for example Elizabeth Benger's *The Female Geniad* (1791), which Wollstonecraft harshly reviewed in 1792, Clara Reeve's *The Progress of Romance* (1785) and Lady Mary Walker (later Hamilton)'s *Letters from the Duchess de Crui* (1776). The earliest female works Wollstonecraft excerpted are Lady Pennington's *An Unfortunate Mother's Advice to her Absent Daughters* (1761) and Elizabeth Carter's 'Written at Midnight During a Thunder-Storm' *Poems* (1762).

7  *The Female Reader* came out under the name of 'Mr. Cresswick'. He was a popular writer on and teacher of elocution and one of Johnson's other authors. He too compiled anthologies for women and in *The Lady's Preceptor* (1792) he included passages from Wollstonecraft's writings. See Margaret Maison, 'Mary Wollstonecraft and Mr Cresswick', *Notes and Queries*, New Ser. 34, Dec. 1987, pp. 467–8. In the *Memoirs* Godwin declared Wollstonecraft's anonymity had 'a cause not worth mentioning' and then claimed it came from her desire to keep her authorship secret. For an account of the work, see Moira Ferguson, 'The Discovery of Mary Wollstonecraft's *The Female Reader*, *Signs*, 1978, 3, 4, pp. 945–50.

8  *Works*, 4, 60.

9  When she herself went to Paris after the Revolution, Wollstonecraft tried often to contact M. Laurent. She could find no trace of him and assumed that, since the nobility had frequented his shop, he had prudently stopped trading when the Revolution turned bloody.

10  Initially articles were to have been signed, as can be seen from the comment of Anna Seward, the poet and bluestocking literary commentator in Lichfield, who refused to contribute to the work: 'I approve of its being a day-light business! To have the names of its authors and compilers known, will be the great guards of its integrity', cited in Gerald P. Tyson, *Joseph Johnson: A Liberal Publisher* (Iowa City: University of Iowa Press, 1979), p. 98.

11  *Works*, 7, 19.

12  Wollstonecraft's first long review suggests that, in her initial exciting months with Johnson, she had even turned against culturally acceptable sentimental reading. *Emmeline* by Charlotte Smith, whose gloomy sonnets she had received in Ireland, was included among books that 'debauch the mind'; Smith was especially censured for allowing the theatrical contrition of a fallen woman.

13  *Memoirs*, pp. 226–7.

14  *Works*, 7, 228. Mitzi Myers argues that Wollstonecraft's reviews are 'an instructive example of a woman writer's struggle' to define her difference of view, 'Sensibility and the "Walk of Reason"': Mary Wollstonecraft's Literary Reviews as Cultural Critique,' *Sensibility in Transformation ... Essays in Honor of Jean H. Hagstrum* ed. Syndy McMillen Conger (Rutherford, N.J.: Fairleigh Dickinson University Press, 1989).

15  Abinger MSS Dep.b.210/3.

16  Dep. b. 215/5.


# Chapter 14

1  The letters describing this incident are undated, but the letter to Johnson was listed as letter XI in the series of letters printed by Godwin, suggesting that he dated it between the letter asking for a German grammar and the letter concerning Dr Johnson's *Sermons*, *Works*, 6, 359–62. Despite Godwin's placing, Wardle ascribed the incident to 1795, assuming that Wollstonecraft's 'almost hysterical reaction' suggests that the proposal was intended to make an honest woman of her after the Imlay affair. William St Clair places the incident even later, in 1797 when Wollstonecraft found herself pregnant again with Godwin's child, before he offered marriage,

*The Godwins and the Shelleys* (London: Faber & Faber, 1989), p. 170. He speculates that the 'source of perfection' mentioned in the letter might have been Godwin. Yet, if the proposition had been made during the Godwin period, it seems probable that it would have had more repercussions on the relationship. The 'source of perfection' is much more likely to be divine than human and the orthodox religious sentiments would seem to date the incident to the years before Wollstonecraft went to France, while the emphasis on poverty rather than her lone parent status suggests the same conclusion. After she returned from France Wollstonecraft was passing as married and a man is therefore unlikely to have proposed marriage; if he had been told by Johnson that she was not married, then she might have been expected to berate Johnson for this failure of confidence. Also, the abuse of Johnson seems to come from a time when they were more intimate than they were during her later life. Finally, the reference to Dr. Johnson would seem to support Godwin's placing.

2  Leigh Hunt, *Lord Byron and Some of His Contemporaries* (London, 1828), II, 34.

3  W. G. S. Dyer, *Joshua Christall* (Cambourne, 1962); quoted in Roger Lonsdale, p. 484. Joshua Cristall went on to become a distinguished watercolourist.

4  It was a general response. Boswell in his *Life of Johnson* described the sermon as 'full of rational and pious comfort to such as are depressed by ... severe affliction', p. 171.

5  This is speculation based on a blurred passage in a letter of 23 February 1792 when Wollstonecraft is asking about the Kingsborough circle, including George Ogle: 'Make some inquiries about ... the thoughtless ungrateful Lady [Mount Cashell?]' Margaret King became Lady Mount Cashell on her marriage in September 1791.

6  The identification comes from Godwin, *Memoirs*, p. 228. An American friend of Wollstonecraft in London, Mrs Mark Leavenworth, said that the child was not from the Skeyses but was 'an orphan Girl, which the dying mother of the Child an East Indian gave her to bring up, and which she is educating she says as a child of nature, aet. 11'. Quoted from *The Literary Diary of Ezra Stiles* (1901), in Tims, p. 152.

## Chapter 15

1  Alexander Gilchrist, *Life of William Blake*, 3rd ed. (London, 1863), p. 92; recollection of James Hurdis from 7 February 1792 in Thomas Wright, *William Blake*, I, 21; Leslie F. Chard, 'Joseph Johnson: Father of the Book Trade', *Bulletin of the New York Public Library*, 79, 1975, p. 63; Phyllis G. Mann, 'Death of a London Bookseller', *Keats-Shelley Memorial Bulletin*, XV, 1964, 8–11.

2  Johnson to Godwin, 12 September 1797.

3  The physical description of Fuseli occurs in William Hazlitt's 'On the Old Age of Artists', quoted by Durant in 'Supplement', p. 182.

4  Knowles, *Life and Writing of Henry Fuseli* (London, 1831), I, 59. Leigh Hunt called Fuseli a mixture of violence and pretension and his pictures a chaos of mingled genius and absurdity, *Lord Byron* . . ., II, 30–31.

5  Knowles, I, 42.

6  See Weinglass, 'Henry Fuseli's Letters . . .', p. 145: 'A young woman, who purposes to become a teacher of French in a school here and who is already somewhat familiar with the language, wishes to live in Paris for six months *En pension* with a good family. Let me know whether 15 Guineas will cover her *board* and *lodging* for this period. She is not rich –' The intermediary Fuseli mentions was probably Johnson. The letter in German is in the Zentralbibliothek, Zurich.

7  The painter Hayden, quoted in Stephen Gwynn, *Memorials of an Eighteenth-Century Painter* (London, 1898), pp. 148–9.

8  Godwin told Johnson that Wollstonecraft copied Fuseli's 'cynical cast ... impatience of contradiction, and ... propensity to satire', 11 January 1798, Dep.b. 227/8.

9   Robert Browning, 'Mary Wollstonecraft and Fuseli' in *Jocoseria*; Allan Cunningham, *The Lives of the Most Emminent British Painters, Sculptors, and Architects* (London, 1830) II, p. 281–2. As with so many of his lives Cunningham was not very scrupulous in his research on Fuseli; Wordsworth had occasion to complain when he received a copy of the life of Sir George Beaumont (letter 13 January 1834). His main source for Wollstonecraft was Godwin's *Memoirs* unkindly glossed and misinterpreted.

10  Knowles, I, 165.

11  Knowles, I, 164.

12  Knowles, I, 166. Wollstonecraft's letters to Fuseli passed into the hands of Fuseli's executor, John Knowles. Fearing their unkind use, Wollstonecraft's friend Roscoe requested them, but Knowles held on to them, declaring them 'chiefly if not entirely amatory ... for the sake of all parties [they] had better be consigned to oblivion', see D. H. Weinglass ed., *The Collected English Letters of Henry Fuseli* (NY: Kraus International Publications, 1982), p. 503. None the less and despite Godwin's plea that Knowles avoid mentioning Wollstonecraft, Knowles quoted the letters in his 1831 biography of Fuseli. In 1870 E. H. Knowles announced in *Notes and Queries* (19 November, p. 434), that the letters were now in his possession. In 1884 they were purchased by Wollstonecraft's grandson, Sir Percy Florence Shelley, who refused Elizabeth Robins Pennell permission to use them for her biography in 1885. It seems most likely that Percy Shelley and his wife Lady Jane, who survived him, burnt them as improper. See Richard Garnett, ed., *Letters about Shelley* (London: Hodder and Stoughton, 1917).

13  Wollstonecraft wrote reams of letters to Fuseli and some must have been answered, though none of his replies has survived. Fuseli had experience with amorous letters and had addressed a good many to various men and women in the past, of which this is an example, 'you slanting eye of love, you creature of roses, lilies and violets, you womanly virginity, you precious coaxer of tears, you who make me wring my hands so desperately' (quoted by Tomalin, p. 89).

14  See Aphorism 226 'The epoch of eunuchs was ever the epoch of viragoes.' In his memoirs, the artist James Northcote describes Fuseli as being 'humorously satirical' about friends behind their backs: 'He seemed to have no idea of the existence of such a quality as gratitude,' *Memorials of an Eighteenth-Century Painter*, pp. 145–6.

15  Fuseli idolised Rousseau and, when Wollstonecraft reviewed his shocking *Confessions* and excused adultery and abandonment of his children where, shortly before, she had berated Charlotte Smith for allowing an adulteress to re-enter society after despair rather than repentance, Johnson at least must have realised the strength of Fuseli's influence. *Works*, pp. 25–7 and 228–34. For the suggestion of Wollstonecraft's influence on Fuseli's art, see Peter Tomory, *The Life and Art of Henry Fuseli* (London: Thames and Hudson, 1972), pp. 177–8. The nastiest part of Browning's 'Mary Wollstonecraft and Fuseli' is the image of Wollstonecraft with 'much amiss' in her head toiling at languages and taxing her brain to attract Fuseli.

16  Knowles, I, 13. Letter to Roscoe, 1792. Women's attitude to Milton's depiction of Eve in unfallen and in fallen subservient mode became a touchstone of their wider attitudes to the place of their sex in society. In her popular didactic novel *Coelebs in Search of a Wife*, Hannah More presents a critique of those who misread the Eve sections of *Paradise Lost* as an improper portrayal of tyrannical patriarchy. Her character Charles sees Milton's Eve as the model of the 'delicately attentive wife'.

17  Whatever the status of Wollstonecraft's suspicions, Johnson was remarkably generous with his friend Fuseli. He lent him money to live on while working on his Milton project, even after he had given up the notion of printing a major edition. By 1793 two fifths of Fuseli's total income came from Johnson. Johnson's support of Fuseli continued even when in 1796 he failed to procure enough subscriptions to publish engravings of the Milton pictures. In 1797 Johnson and Roscoe and four other friends agreed to subsidise Fuseli until the project was finished. The

Milton Gallery was exhibited in 1799 at the Royal Academy Rooms, but aroused little public interest despite some critical acclaim. See Tyson, pp. 153–4.

18  14 February 1792.

19  Knowles, I, 165.

20  *The Task*, Book III.

21  *Works*, 6, 22. Wollstonecraft was prepared for the significance of the Bastille's fall since she was already using the French prison as a symbol of oppression. Mitchelstown Castle was compared to the Bastille in its effect on her, 30 October, 1786.

22  4 November 1789. To many Price's views sounded more like the republican 1640s than the Glorious Revolution.

23  *Works*, 7, 185–7.

24  In fact, although Burke took some time to write and correct *Reflections*, the style he aimed at was not far from Wollstonecraft's: 'Indulging in the freedom of epistolary intercourse, I beg leave to throw out my thoughts, and express my feelings just as they arise in my mind, with very little attention to formal method.' *Reflections on the Revolution in France*, ed. Conor Cruise O'Brien (Penguin, 1969).

25  *Works*, 5, 103.

26  The account occurs in Godwin's *Memoirs*, p. 230.

27  *Works*, 5, 30.

28  *Works*, 5, 46.

29  *Works*, 5, 52. See also Godwin, *An Enquiry concerning Political Justice* (1793), I, 83.

30  Kelly, *Revolutionary Feminism*, p. 100.

31  The letter from Wollstonecraft, together with Macaulay's reply, is reproduced in Bridget Hill's 'The Links between Mary Wollstonecraft and Catherine Macaulay: new evidence', *Women's History Review*, vol. 4, no. 2, 1995, pp. 177–92. In the Wollstonecraft letter the title has been cut out.

32  'The Life, Death, and Wonderful Achievements of Edmund Burke' (1791).

33  *GM*, 61, 151–4; April 1791, Abinger MSS Dep.b. 210/7.

34  *Analytical Review*, VIII, 1790, p. 416. Other journals made much of her sex. The reviewer in the *Critical Review* (December 1790) noticed leveling tendencies but did not at first know the author was a woman; when he did, he remarked that sex overwhelmed text: 'if she assumes the disguise of a man, she must not be surprised that she is not treated with the civility and respect that she would have received in her own person'. The *Gentleman's Magazine* (February 1791) thought the author might be a 'fictitious lady'; if not, it exclaimed, 'The *rights of men* asserted by a fair lady! The age of chivalry cannot be over, or the sexes have changed their ground.'

## Chapter 16

1  Johnson to Godwin, Abinger MSS Dep.b. 210/3.

2  In the last line of this letter 'in his' is repeated. Eliza Bishop's letters are in Dep. b. 210/7.

## Chapter 17

1  See Anna Wilson, 'Mary Wollstonecraft and the Search for the Radical Woman', *Genders*, 6, Fall 1989, p. 92.

2  *Letters on the Revolution in France and on the New Constitution Established by The National Assembly* (London and Dublin, 1791), pp. 115–16, 192, and 155.

3 *A Review of the Principal Questions of Morals* ed. D. Daiches Raphael (Oxford: Oxford University Press, 1948), pp. 177–81.

4 *Observations on … Civil Liberty*, p. 13.

5 *Works*, 5, 175. In one respect Macaulay went further than her successor. She argued that, to avoid the inhibitions and decorum insisted on for girls, the female body could be developed to the point where it was identical with the male's in force. In *The Annual Necrology for 1797–8* (1800) Mary Hays stressed Wollstonecraft's debt to Macaulay: 'It is but justice to add, that the principles of this celebrated work are to be found in Catherine Macauley's *Treatise on Education*.'

6 *Rapport sur l'instruction publique … 10, 11, et 19 de septembre 1791*. For translation see Karen Offen, 'Was Mary Wollstonecraft a Feminist? A Contextual Re-reading of *A Vindication of the Rights of Woman*, 1792–1992', *Quilting a New Canon: Stitching Women's Words*, ed. Uma Parameswaran (Black Women and Women of Colour Press, September 1996), pp. 3–24.

7 *Works*, 5, 129–30. Adam Smith, *Theory of Moral Sentiments* ed. D. D. Raphael and A. L. Macfie (Oxford: Clarendon Press, 1976). See Conger, *Mary Wollstonecraft*, pp. 114–15.

8 *Works*, 5, 217. Margaret King, Wollstonecraft's pupil in Ireland, had imbibed these views and, when she left her husband for another man, was glad to move out of the aristocracy into 'the middle rank of life for which I always sighed …', McAleer, *Sensitive Plant*, p. 8.

9 *Works*, 5, 167–9.

10 *Works*, 5, 147–62. Wollstonecraft probably never read the fragmentary sequel to *Émile*, in which Rousseau described Sophie's infidelity; she would not have been surprised at the outcome of Sophie's education.

11 One revealing incarnation of the sexual woman is allowed into *The Rights of Woman*, the prostitute, about whom Wollstonecraft must have known a good deal through Caroline Blood. As was common for the time, the character was used to suggest a need for social reform, but this was usually conveyed through a sentimental depiction of the fallen woman. Wollstonecraft argues for equality and justice, not sympathy. Her prostitute has the sincerity she was suggesting for all women, and fell because duped. Yet Wollstonecraft still keeps her prostitute within romance, unlike in her final novel.

12 *Works*, 5, 31.

13 For an overview of this kind of philosophy, see Charles Taylor, *Sources of the Self: The Making of the Modern Identity* (Cambridge: Cambridge University Press, 1989), pp. 314–15.

14 In views on marriage *The Rights of Woman* remains in the Dissenting tradition, close to James Burgh's *Thoughts on Education*. Burgh's work too insists that women be educated in reason, that they gain a 'rational, modest and cool inclination' towards marriage, and avoid belittling romantic notions acquired through novels, plays and poems, p. 55.

15 Wollstonecraft joins contemporary men in some of her views: Theodor Gottlieb von Hippel in Germany (*On the Civil Improvement of Women*, 1792) and Condorcet in France both assumed that, if women were treated as rational creatures, they would be more rather than less fitted to raise children.

16 Wollstonecraft seems to have read the poetical botanist Erasmus Darwin, whose *Loves of the Plants* made poetry out of Linnaeus's classification. Unlike many fearful commentators, she saw no problem in women talking as openly as he had done about botany, including the sexual reproduction of plants. She used his sort of imagery to describe women's minds as flowers planted in too rich a soil, flaunting useless leaves which too quickly decayed.

17 *Works*, 5, 160. At the same time she demanded male chastity, see review of *The Evils of Adultery and Prostitution*, which argued against licensed brothels, *Works*, 7, 457–9.

18 Durant, 'Supplement', pp. 218–19; Dep.c.526; *Letters of Anna Seward written between the years 1784 and 1807* (Edinburgh, 1807), III, 117. When she did read the book Grant declared it 'every way dangerous', *Letters from the Mountains*, p. 213.

19 *Henry Crabb Robinson's Diary*, ed. Thomas Sadler (London, 1972), I, 109.

20 Hannah Cowley, Advertisement to *A Day in Turkey* (Dublin, 1792); *Critical Review*, April 1792, 389–98 and June 1792, 132–41.

21 *A Vindication of the Rights of Brutes* (London, 1792), chapter 6. Thomas Taylor is the presumed author of the work, which appeared anonymously. The book also attacks Wollstonecraft's notorious remarks in the preface to *Elements of Morality* in which she had urged openness about sexual parts presumably as a cure for secret masturbation. He suggests that dogs might be the best instructors. For a later description of Taylor's character, see *Memoirs of the Late Thomas Holcroft*, p. 226. Hannah More also ridiculed the notion of rights by extending them to 'grave descants on the *rights of children*', *Strictures*, I, 146–7 and Richard Graves imagined the 'Rights of Infants' in 'Maternal Despotism', *New Oxford Book of Eighteenth-Century Verse* ed. Roger Lonsdale (Oxford, 1984), pp. 791–2. In 1797 Thomas Spence published a serious pamphlet, *The Rights of Infants* about land rights, see Alan Richardson, *Literature, Education and Romanticism: Reading as Social Practice, 1780–1832* (Cambridge: Cambridge University Press, 1994), p. 279 n. 91.

22 See James Raven, *Judging New Wealth: Popular Publishing and Responses to Commerce in England, 1750–1800* (Oxford: Clarendon Press, 1992). The estimates of sales for *The Rights of Woman* and *Coelebs* are from William St Clair's Cambridge lecture, February, 1998. See also Robert Hole's introduction to Hannah More, *Popular Propaganda, Village Politics and The Cheap Repository Tracts* (London: Pickering & Chatto, 1996) and M. G. Jones, *Hannah More* (Cambridge University Press, 1952), p. 142. *Mary Berry's Journals & Correspondence* ed. T. Lewis (London, 1865–6), II.

23 Denise Riley, *'Am I that Name?': Feminism and the Category of 'Women' in History* (London: Macmillan, 1988), p. 6.

## Chapter 18

1 *Journals and Letters*, p. 135.

2 29 March 1792. There may have been more sneering comments in the sisters' letters now lost, since Kegan Paul remarks, 'the small spite with which [the book] is discussed in their letters which still remain seems to point to envy and jealousy . . .', 'Mary Wollstonecraft: A Vindication', *Fraser's Magazine*, 17 June 1878.

3 This portrait of a woman reading, with a quill pen in the background, is in the Tate Gallery. It was engraved by Ridley for the *Monthly Mirror*, 1 Feb., 1796; yet it has never been absolutely accepted by scholars as a portrait of Wollstonecraft.

4 *The Love-Letters of Mary Hays*, ed. A. F. Wedd (London: Methuen, 1925), p. 5.

5 This was the final version – presumably the original was more effusive: 'It is observed by the sensible vindicator of female rights – "that as society is at present constituted, the little knowledge, which even women of stronger minds attain, is of too desultory a nature, and pursued in too secondary a manner to give vigour to the faculties, or clearness to the judgment." I feel the truth of this observation with a mixture of indignation and regret: and this is the only apology I shall make to the critical reader, who may be inclined to censure as unconnected, or inconclusive, any of the subsequent remarks.'

6 Hays had just published a well-received pamphlet arguing the need for public religious ceremonies. *Cursory Remarks on an Enquiry into the Expediency and Propriety of Public or Social Worship* by 'Eusebia' responded to Gilbert Wakefield's argument that there was no need for public religious ceremonies since religion was essentially private. Many people including Mrs Barbauld and Joseph Priestley had written to protest, but Hays's answer was particularly commended.

7 Johnson to Godwin, Dep.b.210/3. The second volume was supposed to cover the legal situation of

women and would have been welcomed by Johnson, who had already published the anonymous factual *Laws Respecting Women, as they Regard Their Natural Rights* (1777).

8　On 20 September 1792 the French Legislative Assembly made divorce available to women.

9　In his *Vision of Columbus* (1787) Barlow had seen a transcendent America of the future going beyond Europe and its own European past and present.

10　Knowles, I, 168. Some critics suggest that Blake's *Visions of the Daughters of Albion* with its denunciation of imaginative, erotic and social repression generalised Wollstonecraft's failure with Fuseli, see Michael Ackland, 'The Embattled Sexes: Blake's Debt to Wollstonecraft in The Four Zoas', *Blake*, 16, Winter 1982–3, pp. 172–83; Kelly, *Revolutionary Feminism*, p. 142. Blake was a friend of Fuseli's and, if he did not know Wollstonecraft well personally, would have heard the gossip.

11　John Keane, *Tom Paine: A Political Life* (London: Bloomsbury, 1995), pp. 343 and 349.

12　Many hints of horrors concern this incident, 'scènes de carnage que la pudeur se refuse à tracer', Paul Fassy, ... *Princesse de Lamballe et la prison de La Force* (Paris: Librairie du Petit Journal, 1868), p. 30. *Almanach des Honnêtes Gens* (Paris, 1793) records '... ses bourreaux profanèrent son corps par de tels excès de barbarie et de lubricité, que nous n'avons pas le courage d'en présenter le tableau.' See also Alfred Bégis, 'Le massacre de la princesse de Lamballe', *Les Amis des Livres* (Paris, 1891) and Alain Vircondelet, *La Princesse de Lamballe: 'L'Ange' de Marie-Antoinette* (Flammarion, 1995), p. 249.

## Chapter 19

1　*Works*, 7, 413.

2　*Works*, 6, 443.

3　The conjecture of Wollstonecraft's viewpoint is Richard Holmes's. I have walked round the Fillietaz house and the traffic-congested Place de la République and found the same difficulty in squaring Wollstonecraft's account with the king's route.

4　*Works*, 6, 443.

5　Johnson did not publish the 'Letter', probably because as a comment on political events it was out of date by the time he received it. There were no further letters in the series. Something of the same materialistic development in the American Revolution had been noted by both Paine and Price.

6　Cooper responded with *A Reply to Mr Burke's Invective against Mr Cooper, and Mr Watt ... on the 30th of April, 1792*, printed by Joseph Johnson in which he reiterated his republican principles and referred approvingly to Paine and Barlow. In 1833 when president of South Carolina College Cooper translated a work entitled *On Irritation and Insanity* by the French medical professor F. J. V. Broussais, which provided a detailed critique of Brown and his mentor Cullen, whose doctrines were prevailing in European schools by that time. Broussais agreed that life was kept up by excitement but he believed that Brown's theories were too abstract and that he neglected to study each part of the body in relationship to this excitement.

7　Letter from Derby dated November 13, 1797, Abinger MSS Dep.b.214/3. Johnson was replying to Godwin's request for information of Wollstonecraft during her Paris days. In *Shelley and his Circle* (I, 125) Johnson is identified as Dr William Johnson, a wealthy follower of Paine's, but Keane in *Tom Paine* reveals a discrepancy in dates which makes this identification unlikely, pp. 370 and 401.

8　*Patriote français*, 21 novembre 1792, p. 588.

9　'Premier Mémoire: nature et objet de l'instruction publique': 'L'instruction doit être la même pour les femmes et pour les hommes'. Women who were not going to carry out public functions could attend only primary classes but those with an aptitude for learning should not be prevented from continuing. Sciences were suitable for women, especially those branches that depended on minute observations, *Condorcet: cinq mémoires sur l'instruction publique*, ed. Charles Coutel and Catherine Kintzler (Paris: Flammarion, 1994), pp. 96–100.

10  *Henry Crabb Robinson's Diary*, I, 299.

11  Durant, 'Supplement', p. 251. See also Emma Rauschenbusch-Clough, *A Study of Mary Woll-stonecraft and The Rights of Woman* (London, 1898), pp. 201–2, where the German has been translated rather differently: 'intelligent' becomes 'thoughtful'. The German naturalist, Georg Forster, described Wollstonecraft at this time as 'a very pleasant woman and very forthcoming, more so than other Englishwomen', Tomalin, p. 129.

12  In all the political agitation at the end of the century in Britain there is surprisingly little about women's legal and civic exclusion. A campaigner for constitutional reform in the 1770s and 80s considered suffrage for women in *Legislative Rights of the Commonwealth Vindicated* (1776) dismissing it on the biblical and legal grounds that married women were subject to husbands. Jeremy Bentham discussed the matter in an unpublished memorandum for Mirabeau in 1788; this argued against female suffrage in the text and for it in the annotations.

13  See *Les Droits de la femme* (Paris, 1791). For a discussion of Wollstonecraft and Olympe de Gouges, see Karen Offen, 'Was Mary Wollstonecraft a Feminist?'

14  As Frank Hamel pointed out, it was primarily the vilification of the royalist press and later historians such as Carlyle and Michelet who made Théroigne into a wild Amazon, *A Woman of the Revolution: Théroigne de Méricourt* (London, 1911).

15  I. B. Johnson records that their dining parties with Paine, Wollstonecraft and the other expatri-ates sometimes included 'Mademlle. Theroigne'. See David V. Erdman, *Commerce des Lumières: John Oswald and the British in Paris. 1790–1793* (Columbia: Univ. of Missouri Press, 1986). Thomas Cooper brought the two women together in a footnote when he wrote, 'I have seldom met with views more enlarged, more just, more truly patriotic; or with political reasonings more acute, or arguments more forcible, than in the conversation of Theroigne, and the writings of Miss Wollstonecraft', *A Reply to Mr Burke's Invective*, p. 81.

16  *Letters from France* (New York: Scholars' Facsimiles & Reprints, 1975), 1792, p. 5. Williams' published letters were extremely popular. Lady East, a gentry lady from Berkshire, whom Wollstonecraft later knew, recorded her reading for the year, 1791–2; she mentions only two political works, Paine's *Rights of Man* and Williams' *Letters from France* with which she was 'much pleased', MS 'Journal' of Lady East, Jan. 1791–June 1792, Berkshire County Archive Office, D/Ex 1306.

17  Smith's letter to Joel Balow praised both his *Advice to the Privileged Orders* and *Letter to the National Convention* (November 1792). In many ways Smith was the closest in views among contemporary women writers to Wollstonecraft, but there is no evidence that they ever met. The older Smith was loaded down with legal and domestic problems and did not socialise much with London literary people. The women admired each other, however. Before she went to France, although Wollstonecraft invariably praised Smith as a poet, she gave mixed reviews to the early novels, *Emmeline* in 1788, *Ethelinde* in 1789 and *Celestina* in 1791, but a more com-plimentary one to the politically radical *Desmond* in 1792. The penultimate review of her life (1797) was an approving notice of *Marchmont*. Smith admired Wollstonecraft, was saddened by her death, and praised her in the preface to her last novel *The Young Philosopher*. In her dissertation on Charlotte Smith (UEA, 1999) Antje Blank argues that the suicide in *The Young Philosopher* may respond to Wollstonecraft's suicide described in *Memoirs* and to her depiction of herself in *Letters from Sweden*.

18  *Gentleman's Magazine*, August 1795, LXV, 2, p. 672 and February 1793. *Letters of Anna Seward*, III, 44, 203 and 208. Mrs Piozzi declared Williams had sacrificed 'her Reputation to her Spirit of Politics'.

19  *Works*, 7, 252 and 322–4. The latter review was signed 'T', not quite so sure a signature for

Wollstonecraft as the 'M' of the former. The reviewer called Williams' *Letters* 'feminine', an unusual word for Wollstonecraft to use as a compliment, but one which Williams seemed repeatedly to inspire. More commonly Wollstonecraft used 'masculine' as a term of praise for both men and women.

20 It is unclear whether Wollstonecraft met Manon Roland. I. B. Johnson said she did but Mary Hays in her obituary stated that, although Wollstonecraft admired Madame Roland, 'various accidents, which she was accustomed to mention with regret, prevented her from being introduced . . .', *Annual Necrology 1797–8*. According to a letter, Madame Roland tried to make a match in 1793 between an English 'Mademoiselle', M.W., and a Girondist deputy, Bancal des Issarts, formerly her own admirer. This 'Mademoiselle' might be Helen Maria Williams, occasionally referred to as Maria; Bancal did propose to Williams in 1796 and, close to the time of Mme Roland's writing, Williams believed that Bancal was in love with her and that she had influenced him to vote against the death sentence of the French king. Possibly, however, the reference is to Wollstonecraft since the letter mentions that the lady might stay 'three months' in Paris. The letter suggests to Bancal that he should 'love her enough to wish truly to relieve her sadness'. See *Lettres de Madame Roland* (1900). Whoever the 'Mademoiselle' in question might be, nothing came of the attempt since Bancal had to go on a diplomatic mission in March. He was taken prisoner by the Austrians and thus survived the Terror.

21 See Madeleine Schweitzer's journal, quoted in Durant 'Supplement', p. 247 and *Athenaeum*, 3011, July 11, 1885.

22 The information comes from the poet, Robert Southey: 'she had never seen any person who possessed greater abilities, or equal strength of character'. Presumably this remark was made to Southey in 1797; it was repeated thirty years later in a critical review of a work on Babeuf's ideas in the *Quarterly Review* (1831), 45, LXXXIX. By this time Southey was antagonistic to communitarian ideas and the article also attacks Robert Owen, the promoter of the cooperative movement and an admirer of Wollstonecraft.

23 *Memoirs*, p. 240.

24 *Memoirs*, p. 244.

25 24 June 1793 to Eliza.

26 13 and 24 June to Eliza. In the *Analytical Review* 1792, Appendix to vol. 12, Wollstonecraft had lengthily reviewed a work on the early Revolution and its antecedents, *An Historical Sketch of the French Revolution, from its Commencement to the Year 1792*, which she blamed for giving 'but one side of the question' – it opposed republicanism and supported constitutional monarchy, *Works*, 7, 429. Her work would seem to have been offered as a corrective.

27 Wollstonecraft seems to see her sort of history as more 'masculine' than Williams's, but it is also possible to gender history another way. While boys were urged to read history to prepare for public life, girls were supposed to benefit morally. See for example the heroine of Jane West's *The Advantages of Education: or, the History of Maria Williams* (1793), who is educated in the 'Morality of History' and learns virtue and integrity.

28 *Lectures on Rhetoric and Belles Lettres* (London, 1783), II, 288–9. For a discussion of Wollstonecraft's relationship with historical theory and early historians such as David Hume, see Jane Rendall ' "The grand causes which combine to carry mankind forward": Wollstonecraft, history and revolution', *Women's Writing* 4, 2, 1997, pp. 155–172.

29 *Works*, 6, 6.

30 There is just one quotation from Burke, 'it was not to be supposed, that the chivalrous spirit of France would be destroyed in an instant, though *swords had ceased to leap out of their scabbards* when beauty was not deified', *Works*, 6, 189. Wollstonecraft sounds a little like Madame de Genlis in her anxiety over mass action but she did not sneer at 'women of the people' taking part in debates as Genlis did (see *Memoirs*, 1822).

31 *Works*, 6, 196–206. See Natalie Z. Davis for the notion that in France and England men used

women's dress to make political protests, both to conceal themselves and to allow scope for acting as unruly women, *Society and Culture in Early Modern France* (Stanford: Stanford University Press, 1975). Wollstonecraft's sense here that women could not decently act together as a collective throws some light on the hopes of *The Rights of Woman* and its wavering sense of its readership.

32  Women were 'disposed by their organization to an over-excitation which would be deadly in public affairs', quoted in Sara Maza, *Private Lives and Public Affairs: The Causes Célèbres of Prerevolutionary France* (Berkeley: University of California Press, 1993), p. 172.

33  *Works*, 6, 147–8.

34  *Works*, 6, 328, 84–5. Versailles had been empty since 6 October when the royal family had been forced back to Paris.

35  *Works*, 6, 115 and 22. These ideas were common among some philosophical historians of the 1770s and '80s such as Blair, William Robertson, whom Wolstonecraft had excerpted for *The Female Reader*, and Alexander Jardine, whose *Letters from Barbary* she had reviewed. For a discussion of Wollstonecraft's relationship to the works of these men, see Jane Rendall, 'Wollstonecraft, History and Revolution'.

## Chapter 20

1  *Letters of Anna Seward*, III, 209.

2  The association with Paine was indeed worrying. In December 1792 he had been tried *in absentia* for propagating seditious libel and found guilty. Public opinion was being heavily controlled and, while Paine's cheap editions were being suppressed, the country was being flooded with scurrilous ballads and handbills vilifying his name. It is interesting to learn from Eliza's letters that Paine was translated into Welsh.

3  For the commoner attitude to the French king's death, see Agnes Porter's *Journals and Letters*, pp. 167–8, which quotes the Abbé Edgeworth's account of Louis's last days. Agnes Porter's reaction was, 'I never was more affected by another's distress.'

4  24 April [1793].

5  14 July 1793.

## Chapter 21

1  Dep.b.214/3. The description of Imlay comes from marginalia quoted by Wardle in *Mary Wollstonecraft*, p. 187. Apparently Imlay was awkward in his walk.

2  Quoted from an anonymous source by Anne Elwood, *Memoirs of the Literary Ladies of England from the Commencement of the Last Century* (London, 1843).

3  Joel Barlow to Ruth, Houghton Library, Harvard; quoted in Flexner, p. 181.

4  A full account of Imlay's business life, although not his personal one, occurs in Ralph Leslie Rusk, *The Adventures of Gilbert Imlay*, no. 57, Indiana University Studies, vol. X, March 1923. See also the 1998 Penguin edition of *The Emigrants* with an introduction by W. M. Verhoeven.

5  Wilkinson also appears in *The Emigrants* as the kindly General W—.

6  *British Critic*, January 1795; *Gentleman's Magazine*, April 1796.

7  From a letter of Imlay's dated 1785, Durant speculates that Imlay owned a black slave girl in Kentucky: 'I have been obliged to part with the girl that Mr. Brent brought down. If she has been lodged with you be so good as to send her to Mr. Joel Collins's in Lexington,' 'Supplement', p. 230.

8  See Frederick J. Turner, 'The Policy of France Toward the Mississippi Valley in the Period of

Washington and Adams', *American Historical Review* X, 2 January 1905, pp. 249–279.

9  *Émile*, tr. Barbara Foxley (London: Dent, 1974), p. 334.

10 For some years after its publication in French and English in 1761 *La Nouvelle Héloïse* was read by respectable women as well as the more radical such as Charlotte Smith; the very proper Frances Burney, when young, found it acceptable. After the French Revolution, however, women described in novels as reading the work tended to be flawed and liable to a sexual fall; the proper response to the book became shock and disgust. See, for example, Amelia Opie's *Adeline Mowbray* (1804). There were ten English editions between 1761 and 1800, James Warner, 'Eighteenth-century English reactions to *La Nouvelle Héloïse*,' *PMLA*, Sept. 1937, pp. 803–19.

11 *Works*, 1, 95.

12 *Works*, 6, 17.

13 Durant, 'Supplement', p. 247.

14 Wollstonecraft may have been amassing this large sum of money against the political uncertainty to come. In both cases the bills were probably ultimately drawn on Joseph Johnson. For a discussion of the bills, see *Shelley and his Circle*, I, 121–3 and 128–30.

15 Throughout her life, Wollstonecraft believed in a society of small properties. Mary in *Mary, A Fiction* throws her estate into small farms; *The Rights of Men* has a vision of 'decent farms' instead of large estates; while in *Letters from Sweden* Norway is praised for its small farms.

# Chapter 22

1  See for example, James Burgh's *Crito or, Essays on Various Subjects* (1766): 'There is no more of holiness in holy matrimony, than in an apprenticeship or partnership in trade.' I, 45.

2  *Letters from France* (1975): *Letters Containing a Sketch of the Politics of France* (1795), I, 174.

3  *Letters of Anna Seward*, III, 215, 329 and 332.

4  *Henry Crabb Robinson, Diary*, I, 300.

5  Information on Imlay's business dealings with Backman can be found in Per Nyström's *Mary Wollstonecraft's Scandinavian Journey* (Göteborg: Acta Regiae Societatis Scientiarum et Litterarum Gothoburgensis, 17, 1979). See also Durant's 'Supplement', pp. 243–4.

6  *Letters from France*, II, 157 and 163. Williams tended to find heroism in the deaths of all the people she supported and even some of those she did not, like Danton.

7  Amelia Alderson to Mrs Taylor, Brightwell, *Memorials of ... Opie*, pp. 58–9.

8  *Memoirs*, p. 244.

9  The trial of William Stone for high treason in *A Complete Collection of State Trials*, vol. XXV, ed. Thomas Jones Howell (London, 1818), 1215.

10 Wollstonecraft wrote a serial review of *Zeluco* in three parts, *Works*, 7, 168, 178 and 192.

11 Wollstonecraft later mentioned a letter from Eliza that arrived at her lodgings terribly out of date since it had travelled to France, back to Britain, then to France again. I have assumed that this is the letter.

12 When her daughter Mary Shelley summed up Wollstonecraft's life before Godwin she again quoted Milton's phrase, 'evil days'.

13 *Émile*, p. 328.

14 Dr Nicolas, *Le cri de la Nature en Faveur des Enfants Nouveau-nés* (Paris, 1775), I, 20.

15 Gélis, pp. 78–9.

## Chapter 23

1 *Works*, 6, 235. The topos of a diseased or prostituted female body standing for a state had a long history; it had been used for Rome in ancient literature, been confirmed by Milton's picture of Sin in *Paradise Lost*, and recently employed by Burke in *Reflections*.

2 *Works*, 7, 168, 178 and 192. Moore also vilified the women's march to Versailles but believed the Duke of Orléans childish rather than malevolent. He also differed from Wollstonecraft in rather admiring Marie Antoinette in adversity.

3 *Émile*, pp. 324 and 350. This line also appears in nerve theorists like Mandeville and Malebranche, who thought the reproductive activities were debilitating and that female brain nerve fibres were too sensitive to bear much intellectual thought. It was exaggerated in late eighteenth-century France in the wake of Pierre Roussel's *Système physique et moral de la femme* (1775), which saw female intellectuality as pathological.

4 John Adams kept notes as he read *The French Revolution*, many criticising Wollstonecraft's heavy use of others and her lack of knowledge of what she wrote, as well as her continued idealism in the face of horror. Yet, he also appreciated the effort: 'Her style is nervous and clear often elegant, though sometimes too verbose. With a little Experience in Public Affairs and the Reading and Reflection which would result from it, She would have produced a History without the Defects and Blemishes pointed out with too much Severity perhaps and too little Gallantry in the Notes,' Durant, 'Supplement', p. 267. The book became the least read of Wollstonecraft's works.

5 She believed that in his general work, *The Philosophy of Natural History*, Smellie should have addressed the analogy between the sexual system of plants and animals, presumably following the lead of Erasmus Darwin, *Works*, 7, 293–300. For a description of Smellie and the mechanisation of childbirth, see Andrea K. Henderson, *Romantic Identities: Varieties of Subjectivity, 1774–1830* (Cambridge: Cambridge University Press, 1996), pp. 14–16.

6 Lindsay Wilson, *Women and Medicine in the French Enlightenment: The Debate over 'Maladies des Femmes'* (Baltimore: The Johns Hopkins University Press, 1993), pp. 5–6; *Works*, 5, 253.

7 *Works*, 7, 385–6.

8 *Works*, 4, 470.

## Chapter 24

1 Johnson had pulled out of publishing this inflammatory work, which appeared with the name of J. S. Jordan on it, but the government suspected that the man was a mere convenience and, at the trial of Horne Tooke, Jordan implicated Johnson in the publishing.

2 One hopes Lady Mount Cashell found some way to reward Hardy for his bad shoes, since he was desperately poor following his trial, McAleer, *Sensitive Plant*, pp. 62–3.

3 The *Analytical Review* predictably thought it 'a production of genius' (December 1794); the *Monthly Review* found it vigorous but too 'figurative' to be clear (new series, 16, April 1795, 393–402); the *Critical Review* disliked the mingling of history and comment and accused it of 'want of grace' (16, 1796, 390–6); the *British Critic* thought the book lacked the intellectual rigour a man could have commanded and found it too novelettish; the *New Annual Register* for 1794, 221–2.

4 Helen Maria Williams was also blamed for failing to respond properly to the suffering of Marie Antoinette. *The Gentleman's Magazine* for August 1795 declared that 'Miss W. has not condescended to "heave one sigh, or set apart one tear", to the memory of the ill-fated Queen of France; nor to express one sentiment of compassion for all the evils she suffered', LXV, 2, p. 672. As inhabitants of France, Wollstonecraft and Williams would have been subjected to the

substantial erotic and obscene literature on Marie Antoinette written during the Revolution, see Lynn Hunt, *The Family Romance of the French Revolution* (London: Routledge, 1992), p. 91. Mary Robinson, *Monody to the Memory of the Late Queen of France* (London, 1793), p. 11.

5 John Haygarth, *An Inquiry How to Prevent Small-Pox* (1784). In the year of Fanny's smallpox Haygarth published a sequel with Johnson, *A Sketch of a Plan to Exterminate the Casual Small-Pox from Great Britain* (1794). He proposed fines for those who would not be inoculated or, when they caught the disease, quarantined.

6 Wollstonecraft's assertion that she loved dead characters had been anticipated in *Émile*, where the usually passive Sophie makes her own choice of a sexual object in the fictional Telemachus. Barbara Taylor has argued that Sophie is 'the focus of the extended encounter with Rousseau which runs throughout [Wollstonecraft's] writings', Introduction to *The Rights of Woman* (London: Everyman, 1992), p. xxx.

7 Although the romantic novel equated feminine beauty with virtue, Burke and many cultural critics associated it with female insipidity and described its effects on men in terms of luxury and debility; the antidote for men was exertion and labour. As so often Wollstonecraft was close to Burke when not strongly disagreeing with him. See *A Philosophical Enquiry into the Origin of Our Ideas of the Sublime and Beautiful*, ed. James T. Boulton (London: Routledge & Kegan Paul, 1958), p. 135.

8 *Reflections*, p. 194.

9 *Athenaeum*, 3011, July 11, 1885; Durant, 'Supplement', p. 247.

10 *The Autobiography of Archibald Hamilton Rowan*, (1840; ed. Williams H. Drummond, Shannon: Irish University Press, 1972), pp. 253–4, 256, and 249.

11 *Annual Necrology 1797–8*.

## Chapter 25

1 Godwin, note to Letters to Imlay XXXI, *Works*, 6, 397.

2 Nyström, pp. 23–4.

3 *Works*, 5, 223.

4 Gélis, p. 251.

5 *Works*, 5, 172. See Hester Lynch Piozzi, *Letters to and from the late Samuel Johnson* (London, 1788), I, 100.

6 Rowan had used Wollstonecraft to send a letter to his wife in Ireland dated 20 March 1795 and enclosed in one for Everina. Now Wollstonecraft was carrying back to Britain for him a watch to be given to 'G.M.' See Durant, 'Supplement', pp. 254–5.

7 Ironically after her death an unwise phrase in Godwin's *Memoirs*, that Wollstonecraft had derived 'particular gratification' from Rowan, led to the assumption in conservative periodicals like the *Anti-Jacobin Review* that the pair had been lovers.

8 *Works*, 5, 223.

9 *Works*, 5, 208.

10 When he wrote a description of his relationship with Wollstonecraft for Godwin (Abinger MSS), Johnson ended it with her journey to Paris.

## Chapter 26

1 Eliza also clearly used the botanical language of Erasmus Darwin for her mental debility. She seemed impressed with the paralleling of human and vegetable, the revelation of new sensitivities, new languors and collapses, in response to irritation and violence (Mary to Everina *c.*

23 August 1790). An example from Erasmus Darwin is the sensitive plant, the mimosa, whose leaves meet and close at night during sleep or when exposed to cold or violence. When so affected, they experience 'a numbness or paralysis consequent to too violent irritation, like the faintings of animals from pain or fatigue', *The Botanic Garden, Part II* (London: J. Johnson, 1789), p. 25.

2   Abinger MSS Dep.b.210/7; 5 November, 1793.

3   James may not have been made a lieutenant until February 1805, *Commissioned Sea Officers of the Royal Navy 1660–1815* (London, 1954), although the event is listed as 1794 in the volume for the Navy Records Society (1994). Godwin declared that he became a lieutenant shortly after his training, *Memoirs*, p. 227.

4   Mary had been similarly comforted by 'a sweet little boy' who called himself her 'son' at the Kingsboroughs.

5   30 January 1794.

6   24 May 1794. Charlotte Smith had a similar radical political vision combined with sympathy for the French emigrants she saw in England. In a letter to Joel Barlow in November 1792 she declared the revolutionaries had both 'Theory and Practice' on their side but felt that the emigrants she was actually meeting and lodging were much to be pitied. She hoped that the French Convention would 'bring about a reconciliation'. See 'The Emigrants' (1793) for an undercutting of the sentimental presentation of the clergy, distressed for loss of power and riches as well as their country.

7   22 July, 1794.

8   15 August 1794.

9   Abinger MSS Dep.b.210/7.

10   4 March, 1795.

11   Wollstonecraft wrote 'accepting', Margaret Tims suggests that this error might have been subconscious for she was so inured to sacrifice. See *Mary Wollstonecraft: A Social Pioneer* (London: Millington 1976), p. 240.

# Chapter 27

1   Tomalin's suggestion in *The Life and Death of Mary Wollstonecraft*, p. 179. It is made more likely by some of the similarities in opinion and tone between Roland's *Appeal to Impartial Posterity* (later called *Memoirs of Mme Roland*) and *Letters from Sweden*. Both authors were writing *in extremis*, Manon Roland awaiting the guillotine and Wollstonecraft poised between suicide attempts. Johnson brought out the translation of the *Appeal* in 4 vols. in 1795.

2   Abinger MSS Dep.b.210/4.

3   Wollstonecraft was more consistent in her concept of 'imagination' than in her praise of sensibility in *Mary, A Fiction*, but her expression still tended to betray her. Despite its separation from mindless sensual gratifications which so often disturbed her, this new tasteful quality was still reached by 'abandonment'.

4   Jane Arden would marry William Gardiner in June 1797; she continued school-teaching in different locations to within a few years of her death in 1840.

5   Everilda Jane Gardiner, *Recollections of a Beloved Mother* (1842). Jane remained a reader and writer however and, when she retired in the late 1830s, had a library of 2,800 books. The proscription on Byron existed in more fashionable schools too, see Mrs Rowden's Paris school as described by Frances Ann Kemble, *Record*.

6   A subscription was started for the relief of the widows and children of dead fishermen, *York Courant*, 17 February 1794.

7   The term 'elastic' was much used by proponents of nerve theory, such as Cheyne. The degree

of elasticity concerned the body's ability to transmit sense through vibrations to the brain and could be affected by environment. A pathological state was 'unelastick'. Although she had now moved once more towards a mental analysis of her states, Wollstonecraft's language was often still embedded in the theory of nerves she intermittently espoused.

## Chapter 28

1   *Works*, 6, 243–4.
2   *Works*, 6, 245.
3   *Works*, 6, 248.
4   It needs to be remembered that Godwin cut the letters to avoid informing the world of Wollstonecraft's business and probably to make them more intense; the originals have not survived.
5   *The Elements of Medicine*, I, 47–8.
6   In response to this letter Mary Jacobus argued that Wollstonecraft seems to be writing as much to keep her own love alive as to make her correspondent fall in love again. See 'In Love with a Cold Climate', *First Things: The Maternal Imaginary in Literature, Art, and Psychoanalysis* (London: Routledge, 1995), p. 67.
7   *Works*, 6, 254. Interestingly, given her earlier contempt for the Kingsboroughs and all their crew, Wollstonecraft most approved an elegant aristocratic estate outside Gothenburg where 'the hand of taste was conspicuous.' The comment reinforces the idea that France had defeated some of her middle-class puritanism.

## Chapter 29

1   *Works*, 6, 268.
2   *Works*, 6, 269.
3   *Works*, 6, 271.
4   *Works*, 6, 252. In her question Wollstonecraft seems to have been varying Hume's, 'what' is this 'I', although she did not espouse his scepticism about an afterlife. She had no Humean doubts about the unity of the secular self and was in these last years moving closer to a Kantian notion of the subject apprehending its own unity above its mental contents.
5   *Works*, 6, 280.

## Chapter 30

1   *Works*, 6, 289.
2   *Works*, 6, 295.
3   *Works*, 6, 298–9.
4   There may also be some parody of male style. Imlay and his friend in Paris no doubt wrote much of numbers and Burke in *Reflections* gave economic details, which she had avoided in her *Rights of Man*.
5   The English James Remnant had set up a bookshop in Hamburg. He returned to England in 1794 and sold German books to the English. A few years later Altona was home to her friend Rowan awaiting permission to return to Britain.
6   *Works*, 6, 340–1 and 344; the quotation is from Young's *Night Thoughts*.

7 Once before Wollstonecraft had lamented leaning on what could not support her: in her misery over Fanny Blood, she had moaned that she had 'leaned on earth'.

8 Nyström, p. 27.

## Chapter 31

1 *Memoirs*, p. 245.

2 In addition, there was the madness and melancholy described by Philippe Pinel in 1801 as a by-product of revolutions; this also sometimes led to suicide.

3 When Wollstonecraft actually contemplated Goethe's *Young Werther* when reviewing an adaptation, she both identified with the hero and lamented 'the wanderings of his distempered mind, the sad perversion of those talents which might have rendered him a useful and respectable being ... The sensations of the moment are confounded with the convictions of reason; and the distinction is only perceived by the consequences' (*Works*, 7, 71). She might have addressed these final words to herself in certain moods.

4 24 October, 1795. See Tims, p. 273. Joseph Farington lived near Wollstonecraft before she left for Scandinavia. He mentions various rumours about her in his diary. He gave the following account of her suicide: 'she took a Boat and was rowed to Putney, where going on shore & to the Bridge, she threw herself into the water. Her cloaths buoyed her up and she floated, & was taken senseless abt. 200 yards from the Bridge, and by proper applications restored to life. Her mind is now calm; she is separated from Imlay, and visits her friends as usual, & does not object to mention her attempt.' Quoted by Durant in 'Supplement'. See *The Farington Diary* ed. James Grieg (London 1923), July 13, 1793–August 24, 1802.

5 *Gentleman's Magazine*, May 1798, LXVIII, 1, p. 368.

6 Since the rescue was at Fulham where Johnson had a house, it is just possible that he sent the coach.

7 *Shelley and his Circle*, I, 144.

8 The tradition includes the seventeenth-century fictional *Portuguese Letters* and the real letters of Lady Mary Wortley Montagu. Like Wollstonecraft, the Portuguese nun comes to see her rejected love as an imaginative act, a way of understanding beyond the calculating of her lover.

9 When the Victorian Prime Minister William Gladstone read the letters in 1883, he wrote to Kegan Paul, 'It presents to me again Héloïse, not to say Dido, with the freshness which nearness gives.' Rightly he sensed that 'as far as I have read, her mental history is not fully told in the Imlay letters, and I should crave to know it all'. Quoted in 'General Introduction', *Works*, 1, 27–8.

## Chapter 32

1 In addition, the love-mad Maria created by Sterne as a focus for sentimental sympathy in his travels would inevitably affect her reader's response: her own name 'Mary' was on the title page.

2 See *The Emigrants*. Fittingly, Smith, with a large brood of children, admired *Letters from Sweden* and quoted the work in a footnote to *The Young Philosopher* (1798).

3 *Works*, 6, 321–2.

4 Abinger MSS, Dep.b.210/6.

5 *Letters of Anna Seward* V, 48. None the less Seward praised Wollstonecraft after the publication of the much vilified *Memoirs*, declaring that her virtues greatly outweighed her errors, Letter to Humphrey Repton, 13 April 1798.

6 Not everyone found her fashionable pose attractive or indeed proto-Romantic. A later visitor

to Sweden, the Frenchman Bernard de la Tocnaye, saw her as a sentimental throwback and was irritated by her emotionally charged passages. He accused her of using 'that special new vocabulary which is deemed *sentimental*, the grotesque linguistic garb adapted from Lawrence Sterne, and the new-fangled "moonlight and apparitions" style of writing ... In short, it's all modish nonsense', *Une Promenade en Suède* (1801), translated by Holmes in Introduction to *Letters from Sweden*, p. 37. It was a little unfair to isolate the lyrical nature passages from the observations and economic facts, but La Tocnaye was probably right in stressing the literary self-consciousness of the book. Wollstonecraft was rehabilitating herself as writer. The politically impartial *Monthly Mirror* also disliked Wollstonecraft's style but took more notice of her sceptical political opinions; they were, described as a jumble of contradictions.

7   A second edition appeared from Johnson in 1802. Extracts were translated into Portuguese in 1806. In 1816 when Byron's *Childe Harold* made popular the travelogue of a desolate wanderer, the moral philosopher Thomas Brown rewrote *Letters from Sweden* as the title poem of a collection, *Wanderer in Norway*, with other poems.

8   Durant, 'Supplement', pp. 306–7.

9   'Journal' of Lady East Jan. 1791–June 1792.

10  Despite their kindness, both Mrs Cotton and Sir William East may have recoiled from Godwin's publication of the intimacies of his wife's life, and his mention of them was deleted from the second edition of the *Memoirs*. Godwin remained on good terms with Mrs Cotton, however, since he called on her on 29 November, 1799, in Cookham. (Either Mrs Cotton moved a good deal within a small area or it is unclear exactly where she lived. Godwin recorded Cookham for his visit but, two years earlier, he had given her address simply as near Henley-upon-Thames. In the *Memoirs*, he declared her nearest neighbour Sir William East, who lived near Hurley, while Wardle gives her address as Sonning near Reading. *Letters*, p. 359.) Probably the Austen-East connection continued after young Gilbert's departure since the Austens had a portrait of Sir William hanging in their house at Steventon in 1801. Jane Austen's extant letters do not mention Wollstonecraft but she could not avoid knowing of her in the 1790s. She possessed a copy of Bage's *Hermsprong* which mentioned Wollstonecraft's feminist arguments favourably and she read Anne Grant's *Letters from the Mountains*, which attacked Wollstonecraft. See Claire Tomalin, *Jane Austen, A Life* (Harmondsworth: Penguin, 1998), p. 139.

11  Harriet Jump speculates that Rowan might have been the author of the posthumous defence of Wollstonecraft, *A Defence of the Character and Conduct of the Late Mary Wollstonecraft Godwin* (1803), see 'Introduction', *Lives of the Great Romantics III* (London: Pickering & Chatto, 1999), p. xix. Although he did not respond to Wollstonecraft's letters Rowan did arrange for a further publication of *Letters from Sweden*.

12  The text reads 'illness'.

13  *Love-Letters*, p. 228 and p. 6.

14  7 May, 1795 *Shelley and his Circle*, I, 139.

15  The letters date from mid-January to mid February 1796; Pforzheimer MSS, kindly supplied by Gina Luria Walker.

16  Despite her disapproval of Mary Hays's self-indulgent misery, it sounds as though Wollstonecraft was of some use to her in her obsession, for Hays wrote: 'I early one morning, in last week, accompanied by a friend (to whom a full explanation of my motives and conduct was unnecessary) call'd on the man who had been the subject of my confessions. I made my friend announce and precede me to his apartment, and notwithstanding this precaution, which I conceived delicacy required, my entrance most completely disconcerted him ... "I am come (said I smiling) to call upon you for the exercise of less than a christian duty, the forgiveness, not of an enemy, but of a friend – I have no doubt been guilty of errors, who is free?" – I held out my hand ...' *Love-Letters of Mary Hays*, p. 234.

17  *Annual Necrology 1797–8*, Elizabeth Hamilton, *Memoirs of Modern Philosophers* (London, 1800).

18  Amelia Alderson, 28 August 1796, Abinger MSS, Dep.b.210/6.

19  *Memoirs of the Late Thomas Holcroft*, p. 307.

20  See William St Clair, p. 162. The handwriting certainly looks like Holcroft's in his more formal letters to Godwin in Dep. c.511, although Holcroft's handwriting varies a good deal when he writes quickly and informally. The postmark, almost obliterated, appears to be 2 January, 1796. See review of *Anna St Ives*, *Works*, 7, 439, *The Road to Ruin*, pp. 448–9. In *Anna St. Ives*, the hero asks: 'Didst thou ever in thy life behold her without feeling unusual throbs, doubts, desires, and fears; wild, incoherent, yet deriving ecstasy from that divinity which irradiates her form and beams on every object round her? – Do! – Think me a poor, raving, lovesick blockhead!' Later he declares, '... the union of two people whose pure love, founded on an unerring conviction of mutual worth, might promise the reality of that heaven of which the world delights to dream; whose souls, both burning with the same ardour to attain and to diffuse excellence, would mingle and act with incessant energy ...' (Oxford: Oxford University Press, 1970), pp. 16 and 133–4. In *Memoirs of Modern Philosophers*, Hamilton mocked Holcroft as Mr Glib, who exclaims of 'the Goddess of Reason' (Wollstonecraft), 'faith, and a comely wench she is, that's certain.'

## Chapter 33

1  Godwin may have disapproved of the suicide attempt since he thought suicide wrong when a situation was not hopeless – he felt himself too robust 'ever to be made the suicide of my body, or the suicide of my mind', *Love-Letters of Mary Hays*, p. 232; letter to Maria Reveley, Dep.c.513.

2  Godwin adopted this outfit for receiving Amelia Alderson, see J. Menzies-Wilson and Helen Lloyd, *The Tale of a Plain Friend* (London, 1927), p. 31.

3  St Clair, p. 151.

4  St Clair, pp. 155–6, for the speculation that Godwin and Maria Reveley had a secret trip to Greenwich and that a letter from Inchbald to Godwin mentioning an attentive 'Beautiful Lady' refers to Maria Reveley.

5  Information on Godwin's movements and social encounters from this time to September 1797 comes from his manuscript diaries, vols. 6–7, Dep.e.201–2.

6  Kegan Paul, I, 73.

7  1 November 1796, Dep.b.210/6.

8  Kegan Paul, I, 16.

9  *Love-Letters of Mary Hays*, p. 10.

10  *Morning Herald*, 31 July 1783.

11  Norwich, 28 August, Dep.b.210/6.

12  In the prologue to *Every One Has His Fault* performed in 1793, Inchbald responded to *The Rights of Woman* by granting women's 'frailty' but declaring they should cultivate their minds and not be confined to 'Producing only children, pies, and tarts'. See the reviews of *The Married Man*, *Works*, 7, 166; *A Simple Story*, 7, 369–70. The latter was praised for skill but denigrated for its morality.

13  *Works*, 7, 462–3.

14  John Fenwick was made famous by Charles Lamb as the flamboyant 'borrower' Ralph Bigod in 'The Two Races of Men'.

15  *Things As They Are, or, The Adventures of Caleb Williams*, ed. Maurice Hindle (Penguin, 1988), p. 3. A review of *Robert and Adela; or, The Rights of Women Best Maintained by the Sentiments of Nature* in the September 1795 issue of the *Analytical Review* had pointed out the incompatibility of the feminism of *The Rights of Woman* and the conventional novel: 'Were the doctrines of that work to become prevalent, and the female mind universally braced up to the

tone of vigour which they are adapted to produce, where would be found women with nerves sufficiently relaxed to write, or to read, soft sentimental tales?' Quoted in Kelly, pp. 204–5.

16 Dep.b.210/6.

17 *Works*, 7, 486. Wollstonecraft's one known commission to Godwin, March 1797, was for a review of Isaac d'Israeli's *Vaurien*: 'There is a good boy, write me a review of Vaurien. I remember there is an absurd attack on a Methodist preacher, because he denied the Eternity of future punishments.' What she playfully ignored was that Godwin himself was portrayed in the book as Mr Subtile, 'the coldest blooded metaphysician of the age', while she was clearly Miss Million, who supports sex outside marriage. Godwin did the review and panned the book as malicious and sarcastic. The review appeared in the April 1798 issue of the *Analytical Review*.

18 Godwin's Diary for 3 September 1796; St Clair, p. 122; William Hazlitt, *The Spirit of the Age: or Contemporary Portraits* (London, 1825), p. 58.

19 See Lionel-D. Woodward, *Une anglaise amie de la Révolution française: Hélène-Maria Williams et ses amis* (Paris: Librairie Ancienne Honoré Champion, 1930), p. 140 Flexner, Appendix F.

20 Godwin to Mary Jane his second wife, 5 April 1805; *Memoirs*, p. 257.

21 *Works*, 1, 105.

22 Godwin's letters are published in *Godwin & Mary: Letters of William Godwin & Mary Wollstonecraft* ed. Ralph M. Wardle (Lincoln: University of Nebraska Press, 1977).

23 This appears the case from a letter quoted by Kegan Paul, I, 337.

24 *Godwin & Mary*, pp. 16–17.

25 *Godwin & Mary*, pp. 19–20.

26 *Godwin & Mary*, p. 22.


## Chapter 34

1 *Godwin & Mary*, p. 23.

2 For a full description of Godwin's diary codes, see St Clair, pp. 497–503.

3 Dep.b.210/6.

4 Dep.c.513.

5 St Clair, p. 155.

6 *Godwin & Mary*, p. 370.

7 Between August 1796 and January 1797, Godwin wrote essays on Education, Manners and Literature, published in February 1797 in *The Enquirer*. Responding to one on public versus private education, Wollstonecraft urged Godwin to reconsider and recommend day schools over boarding schools: 'Looking over some of your essays, this morning, reminds me that the one I most earnestly wished you to alter, from the most perfect conviction, was that on Public and private Education – I wanted you to recommend, Day Schools, it would obviate the evil, of being left with servants, and enable children to converse with children without clashing with the exercise of domestic affections, the foundation of virtue.' Godwin appears to have taken the hint and later added a paragraph suggesting a middle way, neither entirely private nor public, much as Wollstonecraft had proposed in *The Rights of Woman*. See *Letters*, p. 371. Godwin's essay on education is Essay VII of Part I of *The Enquirer*, entitled 'Of Public and Private Education'. As originally an Anglican rather than a Dissenter, Wollstonecraft wanted a universal state-controlled education system; other radicals such as Paine and Godwin feared the state's control.

8 Several years after Wollstonecraft's death, Mrs Cotton wrote to Godwin to say that her friend was hourly in her mind: 'I never met her fellow', 18 March 1800, Dep.b.214/3.

9 *Political Justice* 1793, VIII, ch. 6. Mark Philp noted that Godwin was changing his views *before* his relationship with Wollstonecraft. *Godwin's Political Justice* (London: Duckworth, 1986).

10  *Godwin & Mary*, p. 49.

11  *Godwin & Mary*, p. 50.

12  *Letters from Barbary, France, Spain, Portugal, etc.* (London, 1778), I, 321; *Works*, 7, 107–9 and 154–6.

13  *Godwin & Mary*, p. 56.

14  *Journals and Letters of Agnes Porter*, p. 180.

15  Dep.b.210/6. Opie seems not to have been intent on matrimony at this time however, since Joseph Farington recorded in his diary for 11 November, 'I told Opie it had been reputed that he was going to be married to Mrs Wolstencraft, but that could not be as she is already married to Mr Imlay an American. He replied that would not have been an obstacle if he had had any such intention, as Mrs Wolstencraft had herself informed him that she never was married to Imlay ...', Durant, 'Supplement', p. 312. None the less Opie might have been courting Wollstonecraft before the onset of her relationship with Godwin for in a letter written in the same month she wrote to Godwin 'Opie called this morning – But you are the man'. According to Amelia Alderson, Opie was, by spring 1797, her 'declared lover'. Brightwell, *Memorials*, p. 62.

## Chapter 35

1  The debt to Johnson seems to have been settled only after Wollstonecraft's death, when he agreed to cancel it and pay off her creditors in return for the copyright of Godwin's *Memoirs*.

2  18 December 1796, Dep.b.210/6.

3  Dep.b.210/6. A little earlier Godwin had even been ungracious about some dried apples, a speciality of Norwich, which Alderson had sent him.

4  Mostly Wollstonecraft was passing as Mrs Imlay. The item exists in a scrap book of local history compiled by Ambrose Heal of the furniture company, Heal and Sons. For about forty years Heal collected historical documents, cuttings, deeds, maps and historical items connected with St Pancras. He died in 1913 and left his collection to the borough of St Pancras. It is now in Holborn Local Studies and Archives (B iii 84). The fact that the item (which has no source) exists in the collection ties it to St Pancras; in 1800 a William Waugh was an overseer recorded in the St Pancras Vestry Minutes Index.

5  Deb.b.215/5.

6  Dep.b.228/3.

7  9 November 1795, Wedgwood Archives. For an account of Tom Wedgwood see R. B. Litchfield, *Tom Wedgwood: The First Photographer* (London: Duckworth, 1903), especially pp. 30–31.

8  In terms of the novel, the hero's revelation of love might seem a validation of the heroine's sincerity, making the point that both men and women are repressed by the social order.

9  18 December 1796, Dep.b.21. One reason for public irritation at *Emma Courtney* was the attitude to the dangerous *Nouvelle Héloïse*; the heroine is fascinated with the novel, which her father takes from her. His action prevents her from reading the final volume, which moves Julie from being a mistress into a wife – albeit an ambivalent one.

10  *Love-Letters of Mary Hays*, p. 222. For Hays, Wollstonecraft was the emblem of women's freedom and its consequences. After her death, Hays wrote a second novel, *The Victim of Prejudice*, with a heroine called Mary who stands both for Wollstonecraft and all aspiring and tragic women who glimpse but cannot attain female autonomy. The nastiest attack on *Emma Courtney* occurs in Hamilton's *Memoirs of Modern Philosophers* which caricatures Mary Hays as the ugly Bridgetina Botherim. In *The Anti-Jacobin Review*, vol. 5, 1800 Wollstonecraft is a shameless prostitute; Hays avoids her fate only by being one of those women denied 'the attractions of successful prostitutes ... their figures are too hideous to entice man'. Both Hays and Woll-

stonecraft debauch other women however. The apparent lack of sympathy between Woll-stonecraft and Barbauld was underlined by passages in *The Rights of Woman*. Although referring to her as 'of superior sense' and approving lines describing the transience of beauty, Woll-stonecraft mocked Barbauld's early poem in which she argued that women's empire is the pleasing of men. *Works*, 5, 122–3 and 125. Barbauld retaliated with 'The Rights of Woman' in which she distanced herself from Wollstonecraft's approval by reiterating that the empire of women is indeed their femininity and grace; their rights are 'sacred mysteries'. However, see chapter 12, note 2.

11  *Thoughts, Works*, 4, 47.

12  Dispensaries were charitable institutions set up to give free consultations and medicine to the poor and employ doctors to visit the sick. The first one was the London Dispensary founded in 1773. Details of the Westminster one are in the City of Westminster Archives Centre, Marylebone Cuttings 7/83–4. The useful Lady Lanesborough appears again in Godwin's diary when he makes a second woman pregnant, Mrs Clairmont in 1802. See St Clair, p. 541, note 4.

13  See Sir Herbert Croft, *The Abbey of Kilkhampton; or, Monumental Records of the Year 1980* [*sic*] (London, 1780), p. 30, where one item concerns Lady L—. In the Cambridge copy a con-temporary hand added 'Lauderdale' but in the index the name is given as L—h, so Lady Lanesborough seems intended. She is accused of treating 'with the most sovereign Contempt and Insolence, a Nobleman who, though he had fallen a Victim to her Hypocrisy, exerted Spirit enough to chastise her Offences in the very Instant that he bade adieu to Life and Infelicity'. Ignorant of her future marriage to the wealthy money-lender who had supplied her needs before her husband's death, the author saw her following her bad settlement with extravagance and ending 'in a private Receptacle . . . unpitied by those of her Creditors who had remembered —'. There was another scandalous lady in the century, Lady Luxborough, whom this would just about fit, but the date of Viscount Lanesborough's death, 1779, makes his wife the prime candidate. See also *Town and Country Magazine* XIX, 1787, p. 298. This describes a young noblewoman, separated from her husband and needing the money-lending services of K—g, a Jew springing from the dregs of the Jews. K—g left his wife and children to elope with the noble lady. John King (a Sephardi Jew of Portuguese extraction, born Jacob Rey) and his first wife Deborah were the parents of the Gothic novelist Charlotte Dacre or Rosa Matilda, who featured abandoned women in her novels, but attacked the feminism of Wollstonecraft, see *The Passions* (1811).

14  Carlisle, when elevated into Sir Anthony Carlisle, revised Mrs A. Walker's *Female Beauty, as Preserved and Improved by Regimen, Cleanliness and Dress* of 1837, in which this opinion is expressed, p. 149.

15  The very respectable governess Agnes Porter took on this role for the Talbots of Penrice in 1799, *Journals*, p. 24.

16  'Hints Respecting the Management of the Children', Wedgwood Archives, Keele University; Frank Doherty, 'The Wedgwood System of Education', *The Wedgwoodian*, 6, 8, 1983, 182–7.

17  The Wedgwood histories state that Everina was governess to Josiah II, clearly an impossibility. A letter from Charles Rochemont Aikin to the Barbaulds in May 1797 describes Everina as the governess: 'a sister of Mrs Wollstonecraft (now Mrs Godwin is she not!) . . . She has much of her sister's good sense but is more reserved.' Quoted in Tomalin, p. 235.

18  See *Memoirs*, p. 211. Godwin notes that two of the Allen girls of Laugharne later married the two eldest sons of the first Josiah Wedgwood.

19  Probably the conventional deprecating preface irritated Wollstonecraft – Anne Cristall referred to her poems as 'these light effusions of a youthful imagination'.

20  When a common friend suggested that Anne Cristall collaborate on a 'poetical novel' in the manner of the popular Gothic novelist Ann Radcliffe, the proposed novelist-collaborator was not Wollstonecraft but Hays, *Love-Letters of Mary Hays*, pp. 238–9.

21 This was not because of any diminution of regard, for he continued to 'admire and love her', letter to Godwin, probably 10 September 1797.

22 Tyson, *Joseph Johnson*, pp. 148–9; Mann, 'Death of a London Bookseller'. Legacies went to Barbauld and Maria Edgeworth too. Johnson did cancel a bond of £200 which Godwin owed him, but he intended to benefit Fanny Imlay with this action.

23 In an undated letter after Wollstonecraft's death, Everina wrote to Eliza, who was especially depressed from the failed hopes of a position: 'The whole world is ... not unfeeling ... the Wedgwoods were all good, and the Irwins tho' weak were humane' (Dep.b.210/5). For an account of Mrs Josiah Wedgwood, see *Tom Wedgwood*, p. 42.

24 Hamilton, *Memoirs of Modern Philosophers*, II, 76. Hamilton's reaction to Wollstonecraft is complex. Bridgetina is mainly based on Hays but many of her opinions are Wollstonecraft's and Godwin's. At the same time Hamilton approved some of Wollstonecraft's feminist arguments – she called her a 'sensible authoress' – but felt she carried them too far in *The Rights of Woman* and she disapproved Wollstonecraft's plea for sexual freedom. In her tale of Scottish education, *The Cottagers of Glenburnie*, she used the name of Mrs Mason for her good teacher, possibly in reference to Wollstonecraft's *Original Stories*.

25 *Works*, 6, 461 and 484–5.

26 In the *Memoirs*, Godwin insisted that Wollstonecraft made it clear she was not married to Imlay when she returned to London. In fact, although a few people knew the situation, such as Johnson, Opie, and Hays, she was mainly passing as Imlay's wife in both Paris and London. The reviewer of *Letters from Sweden* in *The British Critic* (1796, 7, 602–10) accepted that she was married; marriage and motherhood had softened her.

27 Mary Shelley's life of Godwin, fragment in Abinger MSS, quoted in Jump, *Lives*, pp. 249–50. It was not quite clear what Godwin wanted in place of marriage, but it was certainly not promiscuous 'sensual intercourse'. In the second edition of *Political Justice* (1796), he seems to advocate a sort of relative monogamy. After Wollstonecraft's death, Bishop Percy expressed the common view, that Wollstonecraft was against marriage, 'a Woman ... who professed to discharge the Marriage Duties, without submitting to the Marriage Ceremonies'. BL MS 32.335.ff.15–18.

28 Godwin to an unknown correspondent 9 May 1797, quoted in St Clair p. 173.

29 Dep.c.513.

30 *The True Briton*, 1, 2, 1797.

31 Jump, *Lives*, p. 249.

32 Abinger MSS and Kegan Paul, I, 239. Durant quotes a confirmation of this: 'Mrs Proctor told me that Godwin concealed his marriage with Mary Wollstonecraft because she was in the receipt of an annuity from 3 people!' 'Supplement', p. 315.

## Chapter 36

1 According to Mary Shelley, 'Two ladies ... shed tears when he announced his marriage: Mrs Inchbald & Mrs Reveley ... Mrs Reveley feared to lose a kind & constant friend, but, becoming intimate with Mary Wollstonecraft, she soon learned to appreciate her virtues & to love her – ... a cordial intercourse subsisted between the parties,' Jump, *Lives*, p. 250 and Kegan Paul I, 239.

2 *Love-Letters of Mary Hays*, p. 241. Names denoting marital status were important in libertarian circles: in *The Wrongs of Woman*, when Maria loses her love for her husband, she renounces the name he has given her, 'as solemnly as I took his name, I now abjure it', *Works*, 1, 152. They were even more important in conventional society. Years later when she had long been a Quaker, the elderly Amelia Alderson, now Opie, rebuked someone for addressing her as 'Mrs Amelia

Opie', thus suggesting that she had assumed the title 'Mrs' as a courtesy and was really an old maid. She was, she said proudly, the 'widow of a distinguished man', 28 February 1842, letter in Norfolk Archives, Norwich.

3 Quoted in Lonsdale, p. 469.

4 'Lines Written on a Sick Bed, 1797'. The *Oracle*, 17 October 1797; for a full description of Robinson's fifteen-year relationship with Tarleton, see Robert D. Bass, *The Green Dragoon: The Lives of Banastre Tarleton and Mary Robinson* (London: Alvin Redman, 1957).

5 *Works*, 7, 486. Bass, pp. 370–6. Later in *A Letter to the Women of England, on the Injustice of Mental Subordination*, published under the pseudonym Anne Frances Randall in 1799 (Godwin's *Memoirs* had made feminist writings dangerous for the author's reputation), Robinson echoed many of Wollstonecraft's ideas and called on her own and Wollstonecraft's experiences of desertion. After Wollstonecraft's death, Godwin was one of the few people Robinson asked to stay in her cottage.

6 According to *The British Critic* XII, 1798, Inchbald and Siddons regarded Wollstonecraft as married to Imlay.

7 Kegan Paul, I, 240.

8 Kegan Paul, I, 277–8. For an account of Elizabeth Inchbald, see James Boaden *Memoirs of Mrs. Inchbald* (London, 1833) and Roger Manvell, *Elizabeth Inchbald* (Lanham MD: University Press of America, 1987).

9 In her portrait of Adeline in *Adeline Mowbray*, Amelia (Alderson) Opie drew on Wollstonecraft to portray a young girl 'ardent in the love of virtue' corrupted into practising unwise free love by her 'new and singular opinions on the subject of moral duty'. She learns that marriage is more beneficial than 'connexions capable of being dissolved at pleasure' and dies piously. None the less the book is politically ambiguous and the conventional are ridiculed along with the radical.

10 Kegan Paul, I, 240.

11 Knowles, I, 170. The congratulations of Archibald Hamilton Rowan, came too late. He wrote to Wollstonecraft from Delaware on 15 September 1797: 'I rejoice most sincerely that you have such a companion protector & friend as I believe him to be whose name you now bear. I have been much to blame. In the more than two years that I have been in America I have written only thrice to you. You were not happy I had no right to trouble you with my dark reveries I was displeased with my past & my present conduct and undecided as to my future how could I speak comfort to so wounded a mind as yours. Now I may be allowed to croak . . .'

12 Kegan Paul, I, 237–8.

13 26 July 1797. See *Memoirs of the Late Thomas Holcroft*, pp. 311–12.

14 Heal Collection B ii, 47: Polygon in 1850.

15 'Supplement', p. 313–14.

16 The letter foreshadows many Godwin would later send to his son-in-law Percy Shelley, asking assistance for the family that had, in part, fallen into his lap and required supporting beyond his abilities.

17 Mary Robinson made a claim for specifically female feeling and poetry. See preface to *Sappho and Phaon* (London, 1796).

18 Wollstonecraft was affecting his thinking as he again revised *Political Justice*, moving it a little more towards marriage and domestic affections. The new edition would accept marriage as long as it could be terminated at any time by either party.

19 *Works*, 7, 11.

20 *Monthly Magazine*, III, April 1797, pp. 279–82. When Godwin republished the piece in *Posthumous Works*, (*Works*, 7), the changes which he himself may have made – or which may represent an original manuscript, though this seems unlikely – slightly modify the emphasis on the imagination and do not give it so dominating a role in the creation of art. They also

downplay the personal intrusions – 'to me' is removed, for example. Perhaps for Godwin one of the joys of *Letters from Sweden* as opposed to the bold *Rights of Woman* was that the speaker was always and justifiably present and did not need to intrude, as he seemed to feel Wollstonecraft did elsewhere, in what should have been objective prose. In this quotation, the *Posthumous Works* version reads 'the mind that formed and the mind that contemplates it', so ensuring that there are two minds present. See Harriet Devine Jump, '"A Kind of Witchcraft": Mary Wollstonecraft and the poetic imagination', *Women's Writing* vol. 4, 2, 1997, pp. 235–45.

21  This is the *Monthly Magazine* version; *Posthumous Works* reads 'immediate sensations'.

22  *Works*, 5, 274.

23  Roy Porter, *A Social History of Madness: Stories of the Insane* (London: Phoenix Giants, 1987), p. 31; Godwin's Diary for 6 February 1797 refers to an 'old Clothes-man' and Bedlam with Johnson and Wollstonecraft. Perhaps they were visiting a mad 'old Clothes-man'.

24  *The Task* I; Wollstonecraft excerpted the passage in her *Female Reader*. Alderson wrote, 'my feelings were . . . forcibly interested by an unseen lunatic, who had, they told me, been crossed in love, and who, in the cell opposite my window, sang song after song in a voice which I thought very charming . . . a poor girl . . . had let the dark tresses fall over her shoulders in picturesque confusion . . . [then], she uttered a screaming laugh,' *Memorials of . . . Opie*, pp. 15–17. The late eighteenth-century vogue for madwomen was also much influenced by Henry Mackenzie's *Man of Feeling* (1771), in which the hero Harley visits a bedlam and gives money to a loving madwoman.

25  In this year, 1797, Johnson published a book that also used insanity as a metaphor, in this case for the government's reactionary policies, *Thoughts on National Insanity*. Cited in Tyson, *Johnson*, p. 136.

26  See House of Commons Select Committee on Lunacy in 1827; *Hoxton Madhouses*. However Lawrence Stone argues that, although the abuse still occurred, it was increasingly difficult by the end of the eighteenth century to incarcerate wives in private asylums, see *Road to Divorce: England 1530–1987* (Oxford: Clarendon Press, 1990).

27  One other parallel worthy of note is to the story, 'Cleora, or the Misery attending Unsuitable Connections' by Elizabeth Hays (Mary Hays' sister) in *Letters and Essays* (1793) which Wollstonecraft had proof-read; this describes a cultivated virtuous country woman unhappily marrying a coarse and superficial urban merchant because she sees a patina of sensibility on him when he visits her home.

28  Hannah More, *Strictures on the Modern System of Female Education* (1799), vol. I. In some ways sympathy for a prostitute was safe at this time since, in the more conservative and reforming late 1790s, prostitution had become a civic concern. Yet Wollstonecraft was taking a risk. She was not providing the sentimental magdalen seduced by an upper-class rake, nor yet the oppressed working woman of the reformers, Mary Ann Radcliffe and Priscilla Wakefield. Vivien Jones argues that, along with novels of Hays and Inchbald, *The Wrongs of Woman* is part of a renewed politicisation of prostitution in the later 1790s, 'Placing Jemima: women writers of the 1790s and the eighteenth-century prostitution narrative', *Women's Writing* 4, 2, 1997, pp. 201–20.

29  *Works*, 6, 283.

30  Wollstonecraft may also have been reacting to Inchbald's celebration of contented rural poverty in her recent published novel *Nature and Art*.

31  *Works*, 1, 83 and 120. Cf. Clara Reeve's *The School for Widows* (1791), which, also invoking the Gothic, provides a contrasting outcome of warden and madwoman: here the commonsensical warden talks the madwoman out of insanity by reducing her fear of marauding male sexuality.

32  The fascinated horror of Wollstonecraft for slack bodies and effeminate luxurious living marks all her works, especially *The Rights of Woman* as Claudia L. Johnson has noted in *Equivocal*

*Beings: Politics, Gender, and Sentimentality in the 1790s* (Chicago: University of Chicago Press, 1995).

33  Wollstonecraft gave Maria erotic feelings, of which she should be proud. She did not believe with Freud that sexuality could be sublimated or with Rousseau that it should be repressed into erotic glamour (Jemima, too brutalised by a life of poverty and prostitution, is allowed none at all). Maria can express sexual feelings outside marriage, even as her creator can now express hers within. Yet, while celebrating sexuality, Wollstonecraft laments the false consciousness of romance that exaggerates its importance for sheltered women. When Maria writes her life for her missing daughter, it is part warning of a woman's fate, part celebration of free sexuality, which she wants for her child. People lived by fantasies and these had to be changed, but the novel gives no hint as to how. This sexual aspect of the work was inevitably a shock to the public which had only recently come to accept that in fiction women might be depicted leaving their inadequate husbands and seeking a worthy and asexual life beyond marriage, see for example Clara Reeve's *The School for Widows*.

34  Stemming from the passionate mothering of Claire's daughter by Julie and Claire in *La Nouvelle Héloïse* and perhaps appearing a solution to the long burden of infancy and child-rearing, the notion of two mothers seemed attractive to some women writers of the time, e.g. Helen Maria Williams. Yet it was always a downbeat ending, with none of the culturally acceptable euphoria of romance.

35  Within Jemima's narrative there is a successful lower-class suicide which grotesquely parallels Wollstonecraft's efforts to drown herself in the Thames: an abandoned mistress kills herself by lying in a horsetrough on a cold night.

36  The fatalism of passion is never quite admitted in the presentation of Maria, but it is clearer in the shoplady who, although her problem is couched in terms of brutal marriage laws, yet betrays the sort of co-dependence, a tendency to love beyond sense and reason, which Wollstonecraft had shown in her life.

37  Almost from the start of their relationship, Godwin and Wollstonecraft had interacted intellectually. Formerly he had had little regard for her early works, but now he read them conscientiously, sometimes mocking his wife's residual belief in a comforting God and occasionally wincing at her self-indulgent style.

38  Kegan Paul, I, 271. The most appropriate woman reader would probably have been Charlotte Smith whom Wollstonecraft did not know personally but who was addressing similar problems of unhappy marriages, especially in *Desmond*. It is possible that Smith *did* read the manuscript of *The Wrongs of Woman* after Wollstonecraft's death while Godwin was preparing it for publication. See Carrol Lee Fry, *Charlotte Smith, popular novelist* (New York: Arno Press, 1980).

39  Godwin was impressed with the defence and used part of the letter, newly punctuated, to preface his edition of the unfinished *Wrongs of Woman*.

40  In the early eighteenth century most divorces were started by women but by the late part most were instituted by men. In her plea Maria accepts the female weakness against which *The Rights of Woman* had argued: the law should not 'throw the whole weight of the [marriage] yoke on the weaker shoulders'. The notion of the 'few' was an emotive one for Wollstonecraft. Miserable in Schleswig, she had seen herself as one of the 'few' sacrificed for ideological consistency, an image again invoked in the preface to *The Wrongs of Woman*: 'surely there are a few, who will dare to advance before the improvement of the age.' In her plea for divorce with remarriage for women, Wollstonecraft had parted company with the once admired Paley, who thought an adulteress should not be allowed to remarry. For a discussion of the 'trial' see Elaine Jordan, 'Criminal Conversation; Mary Wollstonecraft's *The Wrongs of Woman*, *Women's Writing*, 4, 2, 1997, pp. 221–34.

## Chapter 37

1 Ford K. Brown, *The Life of William Godwin* London: Dent, 1926, pp. 117–8; Southey, *Life*, I, 305–306, quoted in Kegan Paul, 234. Southey had dedicated *The Triumph of Woman* to Wollstonecraft in 1795.

2 *Works*, 5, 136. She did however note that the fulfilling of domestic duties required some self-sacrifice and 'austerity of behaviour'.

3 Godwin transliterated the word into Greek characters in his journal.

4 Dep.b.215/5.

5 26 May 1797, Dep.c.507. Wollstonecraft described very similar changes in mood in herself. *Letters*, pp. 220–1.

6 *Godwin and Mary*, p. 90.

7 *Godwin and Mary*, p. 80.

8 Godwin often praised Miss Parr's 'sensibility' but Wollstonecraft did not credit it. As *The Wrongs of Woman* suggested, Wollstonecraft linked sensibility with morality, as most popular sentimental novels now tended to do. If Miss Parr had real sensibility, she could not have acted unethically.

9 *Godwin and Mary*, pp. 86–7.

10 Letter, 3 July 1800, Wedgwood Archives.

11 In fact Sally Wedgwood avoided marriage; although rather ill-looking, she was kindly, generous and rich and had many suitors, including Montagu, but in the end rejected them all. Montagu went on to marry twice more.

12 Dep.b.228/3.

13 *Godwin and Mary*, p. 88.

14 *Godwin and Mary*, p. 89.

15 *Godwin and Mary*, p. 103.

16 Quoted in Marguerite Steen, *The Lost One, a Biography of Mary (Perdita) Robinson* (London, 1937).

17 *Works*, 1, 176.

18 Blake was probably influenced in his view on sexuality and marriage by Wollstonecraft, but the poem, which dates from the early nineteenth century, is likely to have had another primary genesis. The connection sometimes made with Wollstonecraft may have resulted from the earlier error that saw Blake rather than Fuseli as the object of her love.

19 Possibly Miss Pinkerton was a distant relative of John Pinkerton, the green-bespectacled Scottish antiquarian and miscellaneous writer, famous for composing 'original' old ballads. Living out in Hampstead, he was a friend of Holcroft and other philosophical radicals, although, unlike many of his friends, he believed people were getting worse rather than better. John Pinkerton seems not to have had a sister and I cannot find a female Pinkerton born in Scotland at about the right time. John Pinkerton's main (and tenuous) connection with Mary Wollstonecraft was that he provided a source for her daughter's novel *Perkin Warbeck*.

20 Sometimes Miss Pinkerton appears as 'A', sometimes as 'N'. This might signify sisters or a single woman called variously, perhaps, Ann and Nancy.

21 Holcroft had thirteen sittings for an Opie portrait at the beginning of 1799.

22 *Godwin and Mary*, p. 115.

23 The letter is dated July 10 Saturday; Wardle notes that this cannot be correct and assumes that, in her distraught state, Miss Pinkerton miswrote the month.

## Chapter 38

1 *Memoirs*, p. 265. The debate between male obstetricians and female midwives had been raging since the seventeenth century. It was made more intense by the introduction of forceps in the 1730s. The debate resulted in many books and pamphlets in the 1790s, including one by the Queen's midwife, Margaret Steven, *Domestic Midwife* (1795). See also the more sentimental *The Pupil of Nature* (1797) by Martha Mears. Olwen Hufton points out that the vast majority of European women continued to use midwives, many of whom were highly respected, *The Prospect Before Her: A History of Women in Western Europe* (London: HarperCollins, 1995), pp. 183–4.

2 *Memoirs*, p. 265.

3 *Collected Works of William Hazlitt* ed. Waller and Glover (London, 1904), XII, p. 264.

4 Vivien Jones has given the most detailed account of this much recorded and moving death. She notes that its interest is due partly to the fact that it seemed avoidable and that there were so many candidates for blame, and partly to its huge effect on the famous daughter. 'The death of Mary Wollstonecraft *British Journal of Eighteenth Century Studies* vol. 20, no. 2, Autumn 1997, pp. 187–205. Unless where indicated, the quotations from Godwin in this chapter are from the *Memoirs*.

5 Possibly the midwife was Mary Holby Blenkinsop since, although Godwin and Wollstonecraft gave her name as Blenkinsop, the registration document is signed by Mary Holby, who declared herself present at the birth.

6 *Memoirs of Mrs. Inchbald*, II, 14. Durant, *Memoirs*, p. 324.

7 *Works*, 5, 218. Many scholars have blamed men for the rise of the male obstetrician, but Wollstonecraft saw it as primarily the result of fashionable ladies not wishing to be classed with common women. See A. Eccles, *Obstetrics and Gynaecology in Tudor and Stuart England* (London, 1982) and Adrian Wilson, *The Making of Man-Midwifery: Childbirth in England, 1660–1770* (London: UCL Press, 1995).

8 Letter reproduced by Doucet Devin Fischer & Stephen Wagner from the Pforzheimer Collection in 'Visionary Daughters of Albion: A Bicentenary Exhibition Celebrating Mary Wollstonecraft and Mary Shelley', *Bulletin of The New York Public Library* vol. 6, no. 2, Spring 1998, p. 82.

9 Alexander Hamilton, *A Treatise of Midwifery* ... (London, 1781), p. 208. See Jones 'The death of Mary Wollstonecraft', p. 200.

10 Given all its experimentation with mind-changing substances such as nitrous oxide, much favoured by Tom Wedgwood, the period seems remarkably uninterested in the control of physical pain.

11 Gélis describes the awful progress of the condition in a French woman dying about the same time as Wollstonecraft. In this case the slow decay went on for two months, pp. 242–3.

12 Godwin to Mrs Cotton, 14 September 1797, Kegan Paul, I, 280.

13 John Clarke, *Practical Essays on the Management of Pregnancy and Labour; and on the Inflammatory and Febrile Diseases of Lying-in Women* (London, 1793), published by Joseph Johnson.

14 Godwin to Holcroft, 10 September 1797, Kegan Paul, I, 275–6: 'nobody has a greater call to reproach himself, except for want of kindness and attention ... than I have.'

15 Kegan Paul, I, 281.

16 *Practical Essays* (1793), pp. 100–101.

17 It was also thought by many that wine could help replace lost blood.

18 Kegan Paul, I, 282.

19 The story was passed down in Basil Montagu's family. Godwin thought Montagu an incorrigible gossip and often inaccurate in his anecdotes. 7 December 1797, Dep.b.228/3. See Durant, 'Supplement' and Kegan Paul, 'Vindication' for a variant.

20 Kegan Paul, I, 282. After the publication of Godwin's notorious *Memoirs* much would be made

of Wollstonecraft's supposed lack of religion by hostile commentators: the Anglican clergyman Richard Polwhele in the notes to his poem *The Unsex'd Females* remarked 'the Hand of Providence is visible, in her life, her death . . .' Mary Hays valiantly tried to counter the effect of the *Memoirs* in her *Annual Necrology for 1797–8* where she insisted that Wollstonecraft 'adored the Creator in the temple of the universe . . . and . . . humbled herself before him in the still hour of recollection' and 'She believed in a being, higher, more perfect than visible nature'. This disagreement over the interpretation of Wollstonecraft's spiritual life may have been one of the sources of the coldness that grew up between Hays and Godwin immediately after Wollstonecraft's death. The anonymous *Defence of the Character and Conduct* also stressed 'Mrs Godwin's genuine piety . . . sentiments of the sublimest and purest devotion.'

21 Back in Ireland, both Eliza Bishop and Everina Wollstonecraft thought themselves handicapped in their careers by their relationship to so infamous a sister, though Hugh Skeys saw their disadvantage as due to 'their own infirmities of temper'.

22 Kegan Paul, I, 281.

# BIBLIOGRAPHY

## Primary works

(Unless indicated otherwise, works are published in London.)

*Almanach des Honnêtes Gens*. Paris, 1793.

*Analytical Review* 1788–99.

Anon, A *Defence of the Character and Conduct of the Late Mary Wollstonecraft Godwin*, 1803.

*The Anti-Jacobin Review*, 1800.

Arden, John. *A Short account of a course of Natural and Experimental Philosophy*, Beverley, 1772.

Austen, Jane. *Sanditon* in *Northanger Abbey, Lady Susan, and Sanditon*, ed. John David, Oxford: Oxford University Press, 1990.

\_\_\_\_ *Sense and Sensibility*, ed. R. W. Chapman, Oxford: Oxford University Press, 1988.

Bage, Robert. *Hermspong: or, Man as he is not. A Novel*, 1796.

*The Bath Chronicle*, 1778–1779.

Barbauld, Anna Laetitia. *The Works of Anna Laetitia Barbauld*, 1825.

Barlow, Joel. *Advice to the Privileged Orders*, 1792.

\_\_\_\_ *Letter to the National Convention*, 1792.

\_\_\_\_ *Vision of Columbus*, 1787.

Beddoes, Thomas. Preface to *The Elements of Medicine of John Brown*, 1795.

Benger, Elizabeth. *The Female Geniad*, 1791.

Berry, Mary. *Mary Berry's Journals & Correspondence*, ed. T. Lewis, London, 1865–6.

*Beverley Corporation Apprentices Register*.

Blair, Hugh. *Lectures on Rhetoric and Belles Lettres*, 1783.

Boswell, James. *Life of Johnson*, ed. R. W. Chapman, Oxford: Oxford University Press, 1980.

Brewer, James Norris. *London and Middlesex; or, an Historical, Commercial, and Descriptive Survey of the Metropolis of Great-Britain*, 1816.

Brightwell, Cecilia Lucy. *Memorials of the Life of Amelia Opie*, Norwich, 1854.

*British Critic*, 1795–8.

Brown, John. *Elements of Medicine; or, A Translation of the Elementa Medicinae Brunonis*, 1788.

Burgh, James. *An Account of the First Settlement, Laws, Forms of Government, and Police of the Cesares, A People of South America*, 1764.

\_\_\_\_ *Crito, or, Essays on Various Subjects*, 1766.

\_\_\_\_ *Thoughts on Education*, 1747.

Burke, Edmund. *A Philosophical Enquiry into the Origin of Our Ideas of the Sublime and Beautiful*, ed. James T. Boulton, London: Routledge & Kegan Paul, 1958.

\_\_\_\_ *Reflections on the Revolution in France*, ed. Conor Cruise O'Brien, Harmondsworth: Penguin, 1969.

Burney, Frances. *Journals and Letters of Fanny Burney, 1791–1840*, ed. Joyce Hemlow, Oxford University Press, 1972–84.

\_\_\_\_ *The Witlings and The Woman-Hater*, ed. Peter Sabor and Geoffrey Sill, London: Pickering & Chatto, 1997.

Carlisle, Sir Anthony. Revision of Mrs A. Walker's *Female Beauty, as Preserved and Improved by Regimen, Cleanliness and Dress*, 1837.

Carter, Elizabeth. *Poems*, 1762.

Chapone, Hester. *Letters on the Improvement of the Mind*, 1773.

Christie, Thomas. *Letters on the Revolution in France, and the New Constitution Established by the National Assembly in France*, 1791.

Clarke, John. *Practical Essays on the Management of Pregnancy and Labour; and on the Inflammatory and Febrile Diseases of Lying-in Women*, 1793.

Condorcet, Jean-Antoine de. *Condorcet: cinq mémoires sur l'instruction publique*, eds Charles Coutel and Catherine Kintzler, Paris: Flammarion, 1994.

Cooper, Thomas. *A Reply to Mr Burke's Invective against Mr Cooper, and Mr Watt . . . on the 30th of April, 1792*, 1792.

____ transl. *On Irritation and Insanity* by F. J. V. Broussais, 1833.

Cowley, Hannah. Advertisement to *A Day in Turkey*, 1792.

Cowper, William. *Poems*, 1782.

____ *The Task, a Poem*, 1785.

Cristall, Anne. *Poetical Sketches*, 1795.

*Critical Review*, 1790–96.

Croft, Sir Herbert. *The Abbey of Kilkhampton; or, Monumental Records of the Year 1980* [*sic*], 1780.

Dacre, Charlotte [Rosa Matilda]. *The Passions*, 1811.

Darwin, Erasmus. 'Loves of the Plants', *The Botanic Garden*, 1789.

____ *A Plan for the Conduct of Female Education in Boarding Schools*, 1797.

D'Israeli, Isaac. *Vaurien; or, Sketches of the Times*, 1797.

Durant, W. Clark, ed. 'A Supplement to Memoirs', *Memoirs of Mary Wollstonecraft*, London: Constable & Co., 1927.

Enfield, William. *The Speaker*, 1774.

*The Enquirer*, 1797.

Farington, Joseph. *The Farington Diary*, ed. James Grieg, London, 1923.

Fenton, Richard. *A Historical Tour Through Pembrokeshire*, 1811.

Fenwick, Eliza. *Secresy; or, The Ruin on the Rock*, 1796.

Fielding, Sarah. *The Adventures of David Simple*, 1744, 1753; London: Oxford University Press, 1969.

____ *The Governess*, 1749.

*First Hull Directory*, East Riding Archive Office.

Fordyce, John. *Sermons to Young Women*, 1766.

Fuseli, Henry. *The Collected English Letters of Henry Fuseli*, ed. D. H. Weinglass, New York: Kraus International Publications, 1982.

____ *Remarks on Rousseau*, 1767.

Gardiner, Everilda Anne. *Recollections of a Beloved Mother*, 1842.

Genlis, Stéphanie de, marchioness de Sillery. *Adelaide and Theodore; or Letters on Education* 2nd edn, London, 1785.

____ *Tales of the Castle*, transl. T. Holcroft, 1785.

____ *The Theatre of Education*, 1781.

*The Gentleman's Magazine*, 1795–98.

Godwin, William. *An Enquiry concerning Political Justice*, 1793; Oxford: Clarendon Press, 1971.

____ *Godwin & Mary: Letters of William Godwin and Mary Wollstonecraft*, ed. Ralph M. Wardle, Lawrence: University of Kansas Press, 1966.

____ *Memoirs of the Author of A Vindication of the Rights of Woman*, 1798; ed. Richard Holmes, Harmondsworth: Penguin, 1987.

____ 'Of Public and Private Education', Essay VII of Part I of *The Enquirer: Reflections on Education, Manners, and Literature*, 1797.

____ *Things As They Are, or, The Adventures of Caleb Williams*, 1794, ed. Maurice Hindle, Harmondsworth: Penguin, 1988.

Goethe, Johann Wolfgang von. *The Sorrows of Young Werther*, 1774.

Gregory, John. *A Father's Legacy to His Daughters*, 1774.

Grant, Anne MacVicar. *Letters from the Mountains*, n.d.

Hamilton, Alexander. *A Treatise of Midwifery . . .*, 1781.

Hamilton, Elizabeth. *The Cottagers of Glenburnie*, 1808.

\_\_\_\_ *Memoirs of Modern Philosophers*, 1800.

Harrison, Walter. *New and Universal History, Description . . . London*, 1776.

Hawkridge, John. *A Treatise on Fevers in General*, 1764.

Haygarth, John. *An Inquiry How to Prevent Small-Pox*, 1784.

\_\_\_\_ *A Sketch of a Plan to Exterminate the Casual Small-Pox from Great Britain*, 1794.

Hays, Mary. *Annual Necrology for 1797–8*, 1800.

\_\_\_\_ *Cursory Remarks on an Enquiry into the Expediency and Propriety of Public or Social Worship*, 1792.

\_\_\_\_ *Letters and Essays, Moral and Miscellaneous* (with Elizabeth Hays), 1793.

\_\_\_\_ *The Love-Letters of Mary Hays*, ed. A. F. Wedd, London: Methuen, 1925.

\_\_\_\_ *Memoirs of Emma Courtney*, New York: Garland Publishing, 1974.

\_\_\_\_ *Victim of Prejudice*, 1799.

Hazlitt, William. *Collected Works of William Hazlitt*, 'My First Acquaintance with Poets', *The Liberal*, 1823.

\_\_\_\_ *The Spirit of the Age: or Contemporary Portraits*, 1825.

*The Historical Medical Register*, East Riding Archives.

Holcroft, Thomas. *Anna St Ives*, 1792; Oxford: Oxford University Press, 1970.

\_\_\_\_ *Memoirs of the Late Thomas Holcroft, written by Himself*, ed. William Hazlitt, 1852.

Howell, Thomas Jones, ed. *A Complete Collection of State Trials*, 1818.

Hunt, Leigh. *Lord Byron and Some of His Contemporaries*, 1828.

Inchbald, Elizabeth. *Every One Has His Fault*, 1793.

\_\_\_\_ *Nature and Art*, 1796.

\_\_\_\_ *A Simple Story*, 1791; London: Pandora, 1987.

Imlay, Gilbert. *The Emigrants*, 1793; ed. W. M. Verhoeven, Harmondsworth: Penguin, 1998.

\_\_\_\_ *A Topographical Description of the Western Territory of North America*, 1792.

Jardine, Alexander. *Letters from Barbary, France, Spain, Portugal, etc.*, 1788.

Johnson, Samuel. *Prayers and Meditations*, 1785.

\_\_\_\_ *The Rambler*, 1750–2.

Kemble, Frances Ann. *Record of a Girlhood*, 1878.

*Kent's Directory*, 1778–81.

Knowles, John. *Life and Writing of Henry Fuseli*, 1831.

*Lady's Magazine*, 1779–87.

*Laws Respecting Women, as They Regard Their Natural Rights*, 1777.

Le Breton, Anna Letitia. *Memoirs of Mrs Barbauld*, 1874.

Locke, John. *Some Thoughts Concerning Education*, 1693.

Lovell, T. *Narrative of the Murder of the late Rev. J. Waterhouse*, 1827.

Macaulay, Catherine. *Letters on Education*, 1790.

Mackenzie, Henry. *The Man of Feeling*, 1771.

Mandeville, Bernard. *A Treatise of the Hypochondriack and Hysterick Diseases*, 1711.

Mears, Martha. *The Pupil of Nature*, 1797.

Melmoth, Courtney. 'The Secrets of a Circulating Library', *Family Secrets*, 1797.

*Monthly Magazine*, 1797.

*Monthly Review*, 1795.

Montolieu, Elisabeth de, Baroness. *Caroline of Lichtfield*, transl. T. Holcroft, 1786.

Moore, John. *A View of the Causes and Progress of the French Revolution*, 1795.

More, Hannah. *Popular Propaganda, Village Politics and The Cheap Repository Tracts*, ed. Robert Hole, London: Pickering & Chatto, 1996.

_____ *Strictures on the Modern System of Female Education*, 1799.

*New Annual Register for 1794.*

Nicolas, Pierre. *Le Cri de la Nature en faveur des enfants nouveaux nés*, Grenoble, 1775.

Ogborne, Elizabeth. 'Biographical Notices [Royal Liberty of Havering]', *The History of Essex, from the earliest period to the present time … with Biographical Notices of the most distinguished and remarkable Natives*, 1814.

Opie, Amelia. *Adeline Mowbray*, 1804.

Paine, Thomas. *The Age of Reason; Being an Investigation of True and Fabulous Theology*, Part I, Paris, 1794.

_____ *The Rights of Man*, 1791–2.

Paley, William. *Principles of Moral and Political Philosophy*, 1785.

*Parish Register, St Botolph's*, Guildhall Library.

Paul, Charles Kegan. 'Mary Wollstonecraft: A Vindication,' *Fraser's Magazine*, 17 June 1878.

_____ *William Godwin, his Friends and Contemporaries*, 1876.

Pennington, Lady. *An Unfortunate Mother's Advice to her Absent Daughters*, 1761.

Piozzi, Hester Lynch. *Anecdotes of the Late Samuel Johnson during the Last Twenty Years of His Life*, ed. A. Sherbo, Oxford: Oxford University Press, 1974.

_____ *Letters to and from the late Samuel Johnson*, 1788.

Polwhele, Richard. *The Unsex'd Females*, 1798.

Porter, Agnes. *A Governess in the Age of Jane Austen: The Journals and Letters of Agnes Porter*, ed. Joanna Martin, London: Hambledon Press, 1998.

Price, Richard. *Discourse on the Love of our Country*, 1789.

_____ *Observations on the Nature of Civil Liberty, the Principles of Government, and the Justice and Policy of the War with America*, 1776.

_____ *A Review of the Principal Questions of Morals*, ed. D. Daiches Raphael, Oxford: Oxford University Press, 1948.

Radcliffe, Ann. *The Italian*, 1797; Oxford: Oxford University Press, 1981.

Radcliffe, Mary Ann, *The Female Advocate; or, an Attempt to Recover the Rights of Women from Male Usurpation*, 1799.

Reeve, Clara. *The Progress of Romance*, Colchester, 1785.

_____ *The School for Widows*, 1791.

Robinson Henry Crabb. *Henry Crabb Robinson's Diary*, ed. Thomas Sadler, 1869.

Robinson, Mary. *Angelina*, 1796.

_____ [Anne Frances Randall] *A Letter to the Women of England, on the Injustice of Mental Subordination*, 1799.

_____ *Memoirs of Mary Robinson, 'Perdita'*, ed. J. F. Molloy, London: Gibbings & Co., 1895.

_____ *Monody to the Memory of the Late Queen of France*, 1793.

_____ *Sappho and Phaon*, 1796.

Roland, Manon, *An Appeal to Impartial Posterity*, 1795.

_____ *Memoirs of Madame Roland*, transl. Evelyn Shuckburgh, London: Barrie & Jenkins, 1989.

Roscoe, William. 'The Life, Death, and Wonderful Achievements of Edmund Burke', 1791.

Rousseau, Jean-Jacques. *The Confessions*, 1781; transl. J. M. Cohen, Harmondsworth: Penguin, 1953.

_____ *The Confessions … with The Reveries of the Solitary Walker*, Dublin, 1783.

_____ *A Discourse on Inequality*, 1755; Harmondsworth: Penguin, 1984.

_____ *Émile*, 1780; transl. Barbara Foxley, London: Dent, 1974.

_____ *Julia or the New Eloisa*, 1761; London, 1773.

Rowan, Archibald Hamilton. *The Autobiography of Archibald Hamilton Rowan*, ed. William H. Drummond, Shannon, Irish University Press, 1972.

Seward, Anna. *Letters of Anna Seward written between the years 1784 and 1807*, Edinburgh, 1807.
Sheridan, Betsy. *Betsy Sheridan's Journal*, ed. William Lefanu, London: Eyre & Spottiswoode, 1960.
Skrine, Henry. *Three Successive Tours in the North of England . . .*, 1795.
Smellie, William. *The Philosophy of Natural History*, Edinburgh, 1790.
Smith, Adam. *Theory of Moral Sentiments*, ed. D. D. Raphael and A. L. Macfie, Oxford: Clarendon Press, 1976.
Smith, Charlotte. *Desmond*, 1792.
_____ *Elegiac Sonnets, and Other Essays*, 1784.
_____ *Emmeline, or The Orphan of the Castle*, Oxford: Oxford University Press, 1971.
_____ Preface to *The Young Philosopher*, 1798.
Southey, Robert. *Life and Correspondence of the Late Robert Southey*, ed. C. C. Southey, London, 1849.
_____ *Quarterly Review*, 1831, 45, LXXXIX.
Sterne, Laurence. *The Life and Opinions of Tristram Shandy*, 1759–67.
_____ *A Sentimental Journey*, 1768.
Steven, Margaret. *Domestic Midwife*, 1795.
Stiles, Ezra. *The Literary Diary of Ezra Stiles*, ed. Franklin B. Dexter, New York, 1901.
Talleyrand-Périgord, Charles de, bishop of Autun. *Rapport sur l'instruction publique . . . 10, 11, et 19 de septembre 1791.*
[Taylor, Thomas] *A Vindication of the Rights of Brutes*, 1792.
Thomson, James. *Poems on Several Occasions*, 1750.
_____ *The Seasons*, 1730.
*Town and Country Magazine*, 1787.
Trimmer, Sarah. *Fabulous Histories, designed for the Instruction of Children*, 1786.
_____ *The Oeconomy of Charity*, 1787.
Wakefield, Priscilla. *Reflections on the Present Condition of the Female Sex*, 1798.
Weeton, Ellen. *Miss Weeton's Journal of a Governess: 1807–1811 and 1811–1825*, ed. Edward Hall, Newton Abbot: David & Charles Reprints, 1969.
West, Jane. *The Advantages of Education: or, the History of Maria Williams*, 1793.
Whytt, Robert. *Observations on the Nature, Causes, and Cure Of those Disorders which have been Commonly called Nervous Hypochondriac, or Hysteric*, Edinburgh, 1765.
Williams, Helen Maria. *Julia*, 1790.
_____ *Letters from France 1790–96*, New York: Scholars' Facsimiles & Reprints, 1975.
Wollstonecraft, Mary. *Collected Letters of Mary Wollstonecraft*, ed. Ralph M. Wardle, Ithaca: Cornell University Press, 1979.
_____ *The Works of Mary Wollstonecraft*, ed. Janet Todd and Marilyn Butler, London: Pickering & Chatto, 1989.
*Worshipful Company of Shipwrights, Admissions Stamp Duty Book* 1727–1825, Guildhall Library.
*York Courant*, 1771–6, 1792–5.
Young, Arthur. *The Autobiography of Arthur Young*, ed. M. Bentham-Edwards, 1898.
Young, Edward. *The Complaint: or Night Thoughts*, 1742–5.
_____ *Love of Fame, the Universal Passion*, 1728.

## Secondary works

Ackland, Michael. 'The Embattled Sexes: Blake's Debt to Wollstonecraft in The Four Zoas', *Blake*, 16, Winter 1982–3, pp. 172–83.
Barker-Benfield, G. J. 'Mary Wollstonecraft's Depression and Diagnosis: The Relation Between

Sensibility and Women's Susceptibility to Nervous Disorders', *Psychohistory Review*, vol. 13, 1985, pp. 18–19.

Bass, Robert D. *The Green Dragoon: The Lives of Banastre Tarleton and Mary Robinson*, London: Alvin Redman, 1957.

Bégis, Alfred. 'Le massacre de la princesse de Lamballe', *Les Amis des Livres*, Paris, 1891.

Bickford, J. A. R. *The Private Lunatic Asylums of the East Riding*, East Yorkshire Local History Society, 1976.

Boaden, James. *Memoirs of Mrs. Inchbald* (London, 1833).

Brown, Ford K. *The Life of William Godwin*, London: Dent, 1926.

Browning, Robert. *Jocoseria*, London: Smith, Elder Co., 1883.

Cameron, Kenneth Neill, ed. *Shelley and his Circle*, Cambridge, Mass.: Harvard University Press, 1961.

Chard, Leslie F. 'Joseph Johnson: Father of the Book Trade', *Bulletin of the New York Public Library*, 79, 1975.

Clayden, P. W. *The Early Life of Samuel Rogers*, London, 1887.

*Commissioned Sea Officers of the Royal Navy 1660–1815*, London, 1954.

Cone, Carl. *The English Jacobins*, New York: Charles Scribner's Sons, 1968.

Conger, Syndy McMillen. *Mary Wollstonecraft and the Language of Sensibility*, Rutherford: Fairleigh Dickinson University Press, 1994.

Copeland, Edward. *Women Writing about Money: Women's Fiction in England 1790–1820*, Cambridge: Cambridge University Press, 1995.

Davidoff, Lenore and Catherine Hall. *Family Fortunes: Men and Women of the English Middle Class, 1780–1850*, Chicago: University of Chicago Press, 1987.

Davis, Natalie Z. *Society and Culture in Early Modern France*, Stanford: Stanford University Press, 1975.

Doherty, Frank. 'The Wedgwood System of Education', *The Wedgwoodian*, 6, 8, 1983, pp. 182–7.

Dyer, W. G. S. *Joshua Christall*, Cambourne, 1962.

Eccles, A. *Obstetrics and Gynaecology in Tudor and Stuart England*, London, 1982.

Elwood, Anne. *Memoirs of the Literary Ladies of England from the Commencement of the Last Century*, London, 1843.

Erdman, David V. *Commerce des Lumières: John Oswald and the British in Paris, 1790–1793*, Columbia: University of Missouri Press, 1986.

Fassy, Paul. ... *Princesse de Lamballe et la prison de La Force*, Paris: Librarie du Petit Journal, 1868.

Ferguson, Moira. 'The Discovery of Mary Wollstonecraft's *The Female Reader*', *Signs*, 1978, 3, 4, pp. 945–50.

Fischer, Doucet Devin & Stephen Wagner, 'Visionary Daughters of Albion: A Bicentenary Exhibition Celebrating Mary Wollstonecraft and Mary Shelley', *The Bulletin of The New York Public Library*, vol. 6, no. 2, Spring 1998.

Flexner, Eleanor. *Mary Wollstonecraft: A Biography*, New York: Howard, McCann & Geoghegan, 1972.

Fry, Carrol Lee. *Charlotte Smith, Popular Novelist*, New York: Arno Press, 1980.

Garnett, Richard ed. *Letters about Shelley*, London: Hodder & Stoughton, 1917.

George, Margaret. *One Woman's 'Situation': A Study of Mary Wollstonecraft*, Urbana: University of Illinois Press, 1970.

Gélis, Jacques. *History of Childbirth: Fertility, Pregnancy and Birth and Early Modern Europe*, Cambridge: Polity Press, 1991.

Gilchrist, Alexander. *Life of William Blake*, 3rd edn, London, 1863.

Girouard, Mark. *The English Town*, New Haven: Yale University Press, 1990.

Gwynn, Stephen. *Memorials of an Eighteenth-Century Painter*, London, 1898.

Hall, Ivan and Elizabeth. *Burton Constable Hall: A Century of Patronage*, Hull City Museum and Art Galleries, 1991.

Hamel, Frank. *A Woman of the Revolution: Théroigne de Méricourt*, London, 1911.

Harper, George Mills. *Notes & Queries*, IX, December 1962.

Hay, Carla H. 'James Burgh'. *Biographical Dictionary of Modern British Radicals*, vol. I., ed. Joseph O. Baylen and Norbert J. Gossman, Brighton: Harvester, 1979.

Hecht, J. Jean. *The Domestic Servant Class in Eighteenth-Century England*, London: Routledge & Kegan Paul, 1980.

Henderson, Andrea K. *Romantic Identities: Varieties of Subjectivity, 1774–1830*, Cambridge: Cambridge University Press, 1996.

Hill, Bridget. 'The Links between Mary Wollstonecraft and Catherine Macaulay: new evidence', *Women's History Review*, vol. 4, no. 2, 1995, pp. 177–92.

Hufton, Olwen. *The Prospect Before Her: A History of Women in Western Europe*, London: HarperCollins, 1995.

Hunt, Lynn. *The Family Romance of the French Revolution*, London: Routledge, 1992.

Jacobus, Mary. *First Things: The Maternal Imaginary in Literature, Art, and Psychoanalysis*, London: Routledge, 1995.

Johnson, Claudia L. *Equivocal Beings: Politics, Gender, and Sentimentality in the 1790s*, Chicago: University of Chicago Press, 1995.

Jones, M. G. *Hannah More*, Cambridge: Cambridge University Press, 1952.

Jones, Vivien. 'The death of Mary Wollstonecraft', *British Journal of Eighteenth Century Studies*, vol. 20, no. 2, Autumn 1997, pp. 187–205.

____ 'Placing Jemima: women writers of the 1790s and the eighteenth-century prostitution narrative', *Women's Writing*, 4, 2, 1997, pp. 201–20.

Jordan, Elaine. 'Criminal Conversation: Mary Wollstonecraft's *The Wrong's of Woman*', *Women's Writing*, 4, 2, 1997, pp. 221–34.

Jump, Harriet Devine. Introduction to *Lives of the Great Romantics* III, London: Pickering & Chatto, 1999.

____ ' "A Kind of Witchcraft": Mary Wollstonecraft and the poetic imagination,' *Women's Writing*, vol. 4, 2, 1997, pp. 235–45.

Keane, John. *Tom Paine: A Political Life*, London: Bloomsbury, 1995.

Kelly, Gary. *Revolutionary Feminism: The Mind and Career of Mary Wollstonecraft*, London: Macmillan, 1992.

King-Harman, Robert Douglas. *The Kings, Earls of Kingston*, Cambridge: private printing, 1959.

Lewis, S. A. *A Topographical Dictionary of Wales*, 3rd edn London, 1844.

Litchfield, R. B. *Tom Wedgwood: The First Photographer*, London: Duckworth, 1903.

Logan, Peter Melville. *Nerves & Narratives: A Cultural History of Hysteria in Nineteenth Century British Prose*, Berkeley: University of California Press, 1997.

Lonsdale, Roger. ed. *Eighteenth-Century Women Poets*, Oxford: Oxford University Press, 1989.

Maison, Margaret. 'Mary Wollstonecraft and Mr. Cresswick', *Notes and Queries*, New Ser. 34, Dec. 1987, pp. 467–8.

Maza, Sara. *Private Lives and Public Affairs: The Causes Célèbres of Prerevolutionary France*, Berkeley: University of California Press, 1993.

Menzies-Wilson, J. and Helen Lloyd. *The Tale of a Plain Friend*, London, 1927.

McAleer, Edward C. *The Sensitive Plant: A Life of Lady Mount Cashell*, Chapel Hill: University of North Carolina Press, 1958.

Mann, Phyllis G. 'Death of a London Bookseller', *Keats-Shelley Memorial Bulletin*, XV, 1964, pp. 8–11.

Manuell, Roger. *Elizabeth Inchbald*, Lanham MD: University Press of America, 1987.

Moore, Jane. 'Wollstonecraft's Secrets', *Women's Writing*, 4, 2, 1997, pp. 247–260.

Morris, Arthur D. *The Hoxton Madhouses*, March, Cambs., 1958.

Myers, Mitzi. 'Sensibility and the "Walk of Reason": Mary Wollstonecraft's Literary Reviews as Cultural Critique', *Sensibility in Transformation ... Essays in Honor of Jean H. Hagstrum*, ed. Syndy McMillen Conger, Rutherford, N.J.: Fairleigh Dickinson University Press, 1989.

Nixon, Edna. *Mary Wollstonecraft: Her Life and Times*, London: Dent, 1971.

Nyström, Per. *Mary Wollstonecraft's Scandinavian Journey*, Göteborg: Acta Regiae Societatis Scientiarum et Litterarum Gothoburgensis, 17, 1979.

Offen, Karen. 'Was Mary Wollstonecraft a Feminist? A Contextual Re-reading of *A Vindication of the Rights of Woman*, 1792–1992', *Quilting a New Canon: Stitching Women's Words*, ed. Uma Parameswaran, Black Women and Women of Colour Press, September 1996.

Pearson, Jacqueline. *Women's Reading in Britain 1750–1835*, Oxford: Oxford University Press, 1999.

Philp, Mark. *Godwin's Political Justice*, London: Duckworth, 1986.

Pocock, J. G. A. *Virtue, Commerce, and History: Essays on Political Thought and History*, Cambridge: Cambridge University Press, 1985.

Porter, Roy. *A Social History of Madness: Stories of the Insane*, London: Phoenix Giants, 1987.

Pottle, Frederick A. *James Boswell: The Earlier Years 1740–1769*, London: Heinemann, 1966.

Rauschenbusch-Clough, Emma. *A Study of Mary Wollstonecraft and The Rights of Woman*, London, 1898.

Raven, James. *Judging New Wealth: Popular Publishing and Responses to Commerce in England, 1750–1800*, Oxford: Clarendon Press, 1992.

Rendall, Jane. ' "The grand causes which combine to carry mankind forward": Wollstonecraft, history and revolution', *Women's Writing*, 4, 2, 1997, pp. 155–72.

Richardson, Alan. *Literature, Education and Romanticism: Reading as Social Practice, 1780–1832*, Cambridge: Cambridge University Press, 1994.

Riley, Denise. *'Am I that Name?': Feminism and the Category of 'Women' in History*, London: Macmillan, 1988.

Roper, Derek. 'Mary Wollstonecraft's Reviews', *Notes and Queries*, 203, 1958, pp. 37–8.

Rusk, Ralph Leslie. *The Adventures of Gilbert Imlay*, No. 57, Indiana University Studies, vol. X, March 1923.

Sapiro, Virginia. *A Vindication of Political Virtue*, Chicago: University of Chicago Press, 1992.

St Clair, William. *The Godwins and the Shelleys*, London: Faber & Faber, 1989.

Steen, Marguerite. *The Lost One, a Biography of Mary (Perdita) Robinson*, London: Methuen, 1937.

Stone, Lawrence. *Broken Lives: Separation and Divorce in England 1669–1857*, Oxford: Oxford University Press, 1993.

____ *Road to Divorce: England 1530–1987*, Oxford: Clarendon Press, 1990.

Sunstein, Emily W. *A Different Face: The Life of Mary Wollstonecraft*, New York: Harper & Row, 1975.

____ 'Mary Wollstonecraft: Another Brother, and Corrected Dating', *Notes and Queries*, CCXX, Jan. 1975, pp. 25–6.

Taylor, Barbara. Introduction to *A Vindication of The Rights of Woman*, London: Everyman, 1992.

Taylor, Charles. *Sources of the Self: The Making of the Modern Identity*, Cambridge: Cambridge University Press, 1989.

Taylor, Lionel. *A Little Corner of London (Newington Green) with its History and Tradition of a Non-Conformist Meeting House*, Lincoln: J. W. Ruddock & Sons, 1925.

Thomas, D. O. *The Honest Mind: The Thought and Work of Richard Price*, Oxford: Oxford University Press, 1977.

Tims, Margaret. *Mary Wollstonecraft: A Social Pioneer*, London: Millington, 1976.

Todd, Janet. *The Sign of Angellica: Women, Writing and Literature 1660–1800*. London: Virago, 1989.

____ *Women's Friendship in Literature*, New York: Columbia University Press, 1980.

Tomalin, Claire, *Jane Austen, A Life*, Harmondsworth: Penguin, 1998.

_____ *The Life and Death of Mary Wollstonecraft*, London: Weidenfeld & Nicolson, 1974.

Tomory, Peter. *The Life and Art of Henry Fuseli*, London: Thames and Hudson, 1972.

Turner, Frederick J. 'The Policy of France Toward the Mississippi Valley in the Period of Washington and Adams', *American Historical Review*, X, 2 January 1905, pp. 249–79.

Ty, Eleanor. *Unsex'd Revolutionaries: Five Women Novelists of the 1790s*, Toronto: University of Toronto Press, 1993.

Tyson, Gerald P. *Joseph Johnson: A Liberal Publisher*, Iowa City: University of Iowa Press, 1979.

Vickery, Amanda. *The Gentleman's Daughter: Women's Lives in Georgian England*, New Haven: Yale University Press, 1998.

Vircondelet, Alain. *La Princess de Lamballe: 'L'Ange' de Marie-Antoinette*, Paris: Flammarion, 1995.

Wardle, Ralph. *Mary Wollstonecraft: A Critical Biography*, Lincoln Neb.: University of Nebraska Press, 1951.

Warner, James. 'Eighteenth-century English reactions to *La Nouvelle Héloïse*', *PMLA*, Sept. 1937, pp. 803–19.

Weinglass, D. H. 'Henry Fuseli's Letter of Enquiry to Paris on Behalf of Mary Wollstonecraft's Sister Everina', *Blake: An Illustrated Quarterly*, Spring 1988, pp. 144–6.

Wilson, Adrian. *The Making of Man-Midwifery: Childbirth in England, 1660–1770*, London: UCL Press, 1995.

Wilson, Anna. 'Mary Wollstonecraft and the Search for the Radical Woman', *Genders*, 6, Fall 1989.

Wilson, Lindsay. *Women and Medicine in the French Enlightenment: The Debate over 'Maladies des Femmes'*, Baltimore: The Johns Hopkins University Press, 1993.

Woodward, Lionel-D. *Une anglaise amie de la Révolution Française: Hélène-Maria Williams et ses amis*. Paris: Librairie Ancienne Honoré Champion, 1930.

Wright, Thomas. *The Life of William Blake*, Olney, 1929.

# Index

Adams, John 256, 480 n. 4

Addison, Joseph 243

Alderson, Amelia (*née* Opie) 5, 368–9, 381, 382, 383, 386, 387–8, 395, 397, 406, 408–9, 411, 417, 420, 421–2, 427, 479 n. 10, 488 n. 15, 491 n. 9

alienation/exclusion 154, 262, 288, 306, 335, 404; Eliza Bishop's feeling of 188–9, 413; Godwin's sense of 441; of loved ones 262–3; MW's sense of 16, 25, 33, 36, 43, 66

Allen, John Bartlett 24–5

Altona 346–7

America 13, 232–3, 240; War of Independence 33, 59

*Analytical Review* 138–9, 162, 168, 181, 182, 184, 232, 256, 384, 420, 426

Anker, Bernard 338

Ann (adopted daughter of MW) 151

*Annual Register* 255

Arden, Ann 34–5

Arden, Jane 60, 156; correspondence with MW 15–18, 30–1, 33, 34, 35, 40, 44; friendship with MW 14–18, 23, 32, 42, 460 n. 23; as governess 34; with school 34–5, 309

Arden, John 14–15, 20, 29–30, 35, 59, 257, 462 n. 6

aristocracy, aristocrats 13–14, 82, 87, 102, 111, 165, 200, 218, 220, 221, 243, 330, 334, 347, 369

*Aristotle's Master-piece* 398

Armstrong, John 195; *The Art of Preserving Health* 32, 103

Astell, Mary 136

Austen, Cassandra 371

Austen, George 22, 371

Austen, Jane 22, 32, 60, 371–2, 463 n. 2; *Persuasion* 360; *Sanditon* 461 n. 1; *The Watsons* 47

Babeuf, François–Noel 215, 370

Backman, Elias 240, 274, 303, 315, 318, 319, 321, 325, 338, 343, 350

Bage, Robert 437, 443; *Hermsprong* 443, 485 n. 10

Baillie, Archdeacon 94

Bancal des Issarts 477 n. 20

Barbauld, Anna Laetitia 89, 125, 136, 152, 411, 418, 424, 467 n. 2

Barlow, Joel 152, 189–91, 195, 197, 210, 217, 232, 233, 238, 240, 243, 255, 265, 475 n. 9; *Advice to the Privileged Orders* 190, 476 n. 17; *A Letter to the National Convention* 194, 210, 476 n. 17

Barlow, Ruth 189–91, 195, 208–9, 210, 217, 232, 240, 243, 250, 254, 258, 265; correspondence with MW 208–9, 258, 259, 260

Bartholomew Fair 21

Bath 28–9, 32–3, 82, 171, 335, 461 n. 4

*Bath Chronicle* 29

Behn, Aphra 136, 167

Benger, Elizabeth 468 n. 6, 496 n. 20

Bentham, Jeremy 476 n. 12

Berkshire 371–2

Bernstorf, Count 343

Berry, Mary 185

Beverley (Yorkshire) 8–12, 14, 20, 30, 35, 159, 308–9

Bishop, Elizabeth *see* Wollstonecraft, Elizabeth

Bishop, Mary Elizabeth Frances (MW's niece) 45, 49, 51, 57, 431

Bishop, Meredith 43, 45, 47–9, 50–1, 54–5, 57, 62

Blackden, Colonel 247, 251, 252

Blair, Hugh, *Letters on Rhetoric* 96, 218

Blake, William 127, 152, 153, 178, 198, 418, 467 n. 6, 474; 'Mary' 444, 494 n. 18

Blenkinsop, Mrs 412–13, 449–50, 451, 452, 454, 494 n. 5

Blood, Caroline (Fanny Blood's mother) 23, 41, 42, 73, 79, 81, 94, 95, 130, 437

Blood, Caroline (Fanny's sister) 42, 71, 130, 141, 145, 148, 473 n. 11

Blood family 45, 47–8, 71–2, 75–6, 145, 149, 462–3 n. 6

Blood, Fanny 26, 94, 102, 137, 138, 148, 149, 396; correspondence with MW 23, 30, 37; correspondence with MW's sisters 52, 53, 63–4; relationship with MW 22–4, 25, 30, 34, 47; relationship with MW's family 37–8, 52–3, 64; failing health of 41, 52, 53, 61–3, 92; timidity 42–3, 52, 53; portrayed in MW's fiction 112–113; Life: meets MW 22; aids Eliza's flight 49; joins MW and Eliza 55, 56; as teacher 58; marriage to Skeys 24, 27, 30, 42, 62, 63, 460 n. 7; moves to Lisbon 62–4; becomes pregnant 66; death of 68–9

Blood, George 42, 54, 56, 82, 86, 98, 130, 156, 157, 224, 243, 303, 464 n. 7; correspondence with MW 65–6, 69, 72, 74, 75, 76, 79, 91, 94, 96, 137, 147–8, 154, 174, 176–7; relationship with MW 73, 95, 99, 119, 145; in Newington Green 56, 62–3; in Dublin 62–3, 72; to Lisbon 66; love for Everina 99, 118, 173–4; offer of school rejected 117–18; invites Eliza to stay 300–1

Blood, Matthew 23, 42, 43, 71–2, 79, 86, 130, 134, 145, 148

Blood, Neptune 240, 462; as object of MW's interest 42, 77, 79, 94, 104; snubbed by MW 105

Bonnycastle, John 146, 152, 153, 415

Boswell, James 75; *Life of Johnson* 213

Bowyer, Robert 406

Boyse, Samuel 174

Bregantz, Mrs 146, 168, 169, 199

Brissot, Jean-Pierre 215, 216, 240, 241

*The British Critic* 233

Brontë, Charlotte 363; *Jane Eyre* 116

Brown, John 194, 265, 303, 468 n. 11, 475 n. 6; *Elements of Medicine* 131–2, 209

Browning, Robert 154

Burgh, Hannah 55–6, 60, 61, 66, 67, 71, 75, 77, 79, 82, 94, 98, 99, 124, 130, 136, 145

Burgh, James 60–1, 75, 243; *The Art of Speaking* 136; *Thoughts on Education* 76, 473 n. 14; *A Warning to Dram-Drinkers* 316

Burke, Edmund 167, 168, 178, 180, 211, 213, 218, 219, 221, 243, 263, 267–8, 291, 323, 426; *Philosophical Enquiry into . . the Sublime and Beautiful* 165, 322, 328, 481 n. 7; *Reflections on the Revolution in France* 162–3, 164–6, 335, 472 n. 24, 477 n. 30

Burney, Frances (Fanny) 28, 60, 103, 117, 291, 461–2 n. 4

Burton Constable Hall (Hull) 14

Byron, George Gordon, Lord 309, 485 n. 7

Cambon, Maria de, *Young Grandison* 134

Carlisle, Dr Anthony 399, 400, 412, 453, 455, 456

Caroline Matilda, Queen of Denmark 368

*Carysfoot* 37

Carter, Elizabeth 468 n. 6

Catholicism 70, 82

Chapone, Hester 12, 77

Cheyne, George, *The English Malady* 131, 482 n. 7; childhood: clothing in 135; being second child 4; as guide to the adult 5, 9; books for 125, 126–8, 134, 135–6; importance of control and self-control 5; and maternal neglect 83; MW's memories of 9; MW's views on 76

Christian VII, King of Denmark 368

Christie, Jane 198, 211

Christie, Rebecca 198, 210, 357, 372, 380, 381, 401, 417

Christie, Thomas 138, 149, 162, 193, 195, 198–9, 209, 210–11, 212, 213, 216, 218, 231, 236, 243–4, 357, 401

Chudleigh, Mary, Lady 177

Church, Mr 61, 66, 71

Clare, Mrs 22, 23, 52, 53, 63, 99

Clare, Revd 22, 23, 28, 60, 63

Clarke, Dr John 448, 454

Cockburn, Mrs 60, 67, 71, 81, 91

Coleridge, Samuel Taylor 234, 435

Colman, George (the Younger) 384

Condorcet, Antoine Nicolas, Marquis de 210, 215, 220, 476 n. 9

conduct-books 77, 134, 136, 185, 238, 245

Constable, William 14, 35

Cooper, Thomas 209, 216, 233, 234, 475 n. 6

Copenhagen 341, 342, 343, 350

Corday, Charlotte 220

Cotton, Mrs 196, 371, 376, 401, 454, 457, 487 n. 8

Cowley, Hannah 184

Cowper, William 7, 89, 136, 138, 159, 328, 427

Coxe, William, *Voyages and Travels* 303

Cristall, Anne 137, 148, 149, 414, 489 n. 20

Cristall, Joshua 148, 149, 158, 415

*Critical Review* 139, 184, 472 n. 34

Crosby, Miss 85, 466 n. 6

Cullen, William 131, 209, 475 n. 6

Cunningham, Allan 154, 470 n. 9

Daintree, Mary 427

Danton, Georges Jacques 215, 479 n. 6

Danvers, Sir John 33

Darwin, Erasmus 437, 443, 473 n. 16, 481 n. 1

Dawson, Sarah 28, 31, 33, 35, 36, 106

Defoe, Daniel 177, 243

Delane, Betty 41–2, 65, 72, 82, 86, 89, 102, 137–8, 145, 148

Denmark 330, 341

Dennis, Thomasin 413

Dependence 11, 31, 80, 96, 288, 374, 395

depression, *see* melancholy

Dickinson, John 347

d'Israeli, Isaac 487 n. 17

Dissenters 56, 59–61, 76, 82, 104, 125, 136, 162, 163, 166, 177, 212, 243, 425

domesticity 159–60, 161, 220–2, 238, 245, 249, 254–5, 264, 331, 393, 435–6

Dryden, John, *Marriage à la Mode* 411–12
Dublin 72, 82, 84, 94–5, 117, 118, 224, 290
Dyson, George 432–4, 449, 453

East, Gilbert 371
East, Lady 371, 476 n. 16
East, Sir William 371
Edgeworth, Maria 60, 467 n. 2, 489 n. 22
education 259–60, 463–4, 467 n.7, 487 n. 7;
    affliction and perfection 54; day-schools 12,
    83, 380, 487 n. 7; books for 10, 128–9; Dis-
    senting view of 60, 76, 125, 136; and elocution
    136; female 110, 178–83, 185, 475–6 n. 9; gender
    differences in 11–12; as improvement of
    society 136; MW's 11–12, 17–18, 20; MW's
    views on 12, 58, 76–8, 178–83; public-school
    culture 82–3; Rousseauian 102, 413; and
    setting up of schools 34–5; teaching 47;
    utopian view of 60–1
Ellefsen, Peder 258–9, 260, 264, 274, 335, 368
Enfield, Dr William 136
Eton College 82, 89

Farington, Joseph 484 n. 4, 488 n. 15
female community 24, 43, 47, 51–2, 113, 429
Fenwick, Eliza 416, 420, 450, 453, 454, 455, 456,
    463 n. 9; *Secresy* 383
Fenwick, John 383, 411, 450, 453
Fielding, Sarah 461 n. 1, 467 n. 3
Fillietaz, Aline 199, 205, 206, 208, 216
FitzGerald, Mary 89, 95, 115, 148
food and drink 33, 36, 152, 155, 216–7, 274, 316,
    322, 339
Fordyce, Dr George 152, 169, 412, 448, 452, 453,
    454
Fox, Charles James 32
Franklin, Benjamin 59
French Revolution 162–3, 164–5, 178, 195, 196,
    198, 199, 205, 210, 211–13, 215–21, 224–5, 241–2,
    244, 252, 259, 282, 291, 308–9, 343–4, 426
Frend, William 373–4, 375–6, 410
friendship: commitment to 16, 23, 76, 80, 460 n.
    24; female 18, 22–3, 32, 50, 113, 150–1, 429; and
    governessing 77, 78; in MW's fiction 108, 112–
    13, 429; romantic view of 16, 17, 18–19, 23
frivolity, MW's dislike of 32–3, 35, 82, 92–3, 155,
    397, 465 n. 2
Fuseli, Henry 168, 169, 170, 176, 184, 199, 214, 215,
    231, 232, 235, 240, 247, 273, 333, 351, 385, 394,
    415, 422, 449; and MW's letters 359, 471 ns. 13

and 17; relationship with MW 152–7, 194–5,
    196, 197–8, 200
Fuseli, Sophia 153, 154, 156, 197–8

Gabell, Ann 158–9, 160, 161, 196, 221, 238, 334
Gabell, Henry 86, 95, 108–9, 110, 118–19, 158, 160,
    161, 165, 196, 221, 238, 337
Gascoyne family 7, 25
gender: Burke's treatment of 165–6; Rousseau's
    treatment of 181–2; differences 247, 352, 428–
    32, 438; and voice 163, 255
Genlis, Stéphanie de 136, 181, 216, 219, 347; *Theo-
    dore and Adelaide* 96, 126, 467 n. 7
*Gentleman's Magazine* 138, 168, 177, 356, 472 n. 34
George III 4, 22, 36, 59, 163, 206, 368
Gladstone, William 484 n. 9
Godwin, Mrs Ann (Godwin's mother) 422–3,
    435
Godwin, Hannah 437, 452
Godwin, William 21, 23, 153, 178, 228, 263, 469–
    70 n. 1, 486–7 n. 22, 487 n. 7, 491 n. 20, 493 n.
    39; correspondence with MW 388, 389–92,
    393, 394–6, 398–9, 402–5, 438–47, 450; on
    young MW 22, 62, 74; on MW's religion 60,
    455; on MW as reviewer 139–40; on MW's
    relationship with Fuseli 156, 199; relationship
    with MW 385–92, 393–406, 407–18, 409–10,
    419–24; on MW's relationship with Imlay 236,
    240, 247, 352, 363; on MW's attempted suicide
    287, 357–8; on letters to Imlay 363; on *Letters
    from Sweden* 369, 380, 449, 491–2 n. 20; on
    *Mary, A Fiction* 113, 416, 449; on *Vindications*
    168, 177, 184, 491–2 n. 20; life: described 379–
    80, 435; attempts to set up a school 463 n. 1;
    at Johnson's dinners 152, 168; female friends
    380–1, 383, 445–7; relationship with Mary
    Hays 374–6, 445; meeting with MW 168, 378,
    379, 380; health of 400–1; marriage to MW
    417–21, 435; maintenance of separate estab-
    lishment 424; visit to Etruria 437–44; and
    MW's death 449–57; writings: *Caleb Williams*
    379, 382, 383, 384, 387, 428; *The Iron Chest* 384;
    *Memoirs* 4–5, 12, 21, 22, 24, 40, 60, 74, 108,
    111, 113, 123, 127, 139–40, 153, 156, 177, 184, 199,
    215, 236, 243, 247, 273, 286, 344, 352, 363, 369,
    386, 452, 485 n. 10, 490 n. 26; 'Of Public and
    Private Education', 487 n. 7; *Political Justice*
    379, 386, 401, 405, 410, 422, 424, 437; 'Diary'
    380, 381, 392, 393, 398–9, 400, 403, 405, 412,
    418, 423, 445, 452, 456

Gordon riots 33
Gothenburg 318, 320, 321, 324, 339, 350
Goethe, Johann Wolfgang von 354, 363; *Sorrows of Young Werther* 449, 484 n. 3
Goldsmith, Oliver 10
Gouges, Olympe de 211, 220
Grant, Anne MacVicar 184
Graux, Bishop 291, 293, 295
Gregory, Dr John 11, 136, 181, 184

Halifax, George Savile, Marquis of 136
Hall, John 134
Hamburg 343, 346–9
Hamilton, Archibald 370, 490 n. 24
Hamilton, Elizabeth 463 n. 2, 486 n. 20, 488 n. 10, 490 n. 24
Handel, George Frederick 105
happiness 159–60, 161
Hardy, Thomas 263, 264
Hartley, David 5
Hassell, J. 367
Hays, Elizabeth 193, 492 n. 27
Hays, Mary 192–4, 198, 367, 373–6, 377, 378, 379, 381, 382–3, 384, 386, 390, 396, 397, 400–1, 407, 414, 416, 419, 424, 432, 433, 449, 452, 455–6, 472 n. 5, 474 n. 6, 485 n. 16, 488 n. 10; *Letters and Essays* 193; *Memoirs of Emma Courtney* 410–11, 426, 428, 429, 488 n. 10; *Victim of Prejudice* 488 n. 10
Haywood, Eliza 136
Hazlitt, William 435, 448
Hess, Magdalena *see* Schweitzer, Madeleine
Hewitt, Marmaduke 20
Hewlett, John 61, 67, 75, 76, 77, 89, 99, 131, 152, 464–5 n. 9
Hinxman (musician) 72, 171
Hippel, Theodor Gottlieb von 473 n. 15
Holcroft, Thomas 9, 134, 228, 377–8, 380, 381, 418, 422, 423, 432, 444; *Anna St Ives* 377, 383, 486 n. 20; *The Force of Ridicule* 404
Hume, David 131, 354, 477 n. 28, 483 n. 4
Hunter, Roland 117
hypochondria 132, 194, 468

Ilchester, Lord and Lady 32
imagination/fantasy 103, 268, 322, 334, 335, 364, 395, 435, 482 n. 3; and reason 139, 268, 306–7, 364, 424, 425; male 306; in MW 424–5; in MW's fiction 112, 428; Rousseauian 307
Imlay, Fanny (Françoise) 267, 271, 283, 414, 438, 453, 456; birth 258; appearance 267, 278, 398; breast-feeding of 269, 284; MW's pride in 259, 270, 319; MW's thoughts on 326–7; relationship with Imlay 258, 269, 274, 275, 327, 331, 372; smallpox 265, 266; weaning 259–60, 277, 284; 'Lessons' for 259–60; arrangements for 281, 355; MW's irritation with 309, 269, 352; journey to Hull 304–5; teething 311; journey to and through Sweden and Norway 310, 311, 315, 318, 319–20 341; missed by MW 327, 328, 332, 335; MW's reunion with 339–40; journey to Copenhagen 341; journey to Hamburg 344, 345, 347; relationship with Godwin 394, 396, 439, 441, 442; chickenpox 397–8; education of 406; and MW's death 453, 456
Imlay, Gilbert 292, 351, 385, 387, 397, 405, 407, 478, 483; appearance 231–4; as philanderer 264–5; business affairs 258–9, 260, 264, 273–4, 278; correspondence with MW 237, 240–1, 242–3, 245–6, 247–8, 262–3, 267–8, 285–6, 312–14, 319–20, 330–1, 332–3, 336–7, 340, 342–3, 346–7, 348–9, 359, 360–2, 363–4, 372, 373; mistresses 233, 286, 353–4, 360; relationship with MW 234–8, 239–43, 244–51, 252–4, 253–4, 272, 273–7, 348–50, 489–90 n. 26; criticism of 267, 268, 320; desertion of MW 265, 276, 279–83, 286, 358; letter to Eliza 294; and MW's Scandinavian journey 303–4; and MW's suicide attempt 357; portrayed in MW's fiction 429–32; chance meetings with MW 371, 373; writings: *A Topographical Description of the Western Territory of North America* 232; *The Emigrants* 234, 314, 428
Inchbald, Elizabeth 28, 377, 380, 382, 387, 393, 404, 417, 418, 420–1, 449, 486 n. 12, 490 n. 1; *A Simple Story* 182, 432; *Nature and Art* 382
independence: Godwin's need for 379; and marriage 77; MW's need for 44, 59, 116, 129–30, 137, 157, 170, 269, 278, 334, 351, 408; MW's views on 183; and sexual love 234–5; and women 179
individual/individuality 60, 163, 354; MW's sense of 13, 19, 35–6, 139, 306, 329, 432
Ireland 4, 53, 71–2, 82, 83, 84–6, 148–9, 313

Janeway, James 379
Jardine, Alexander 367, 404, 478 n. 35
Johnson, Joseph 78, 108, 131, 136, 146, 193, 195, 216, 225, 245, 263, 373, 407, 415, 418, 427, 452, 468 n. 11, 469–70 n. 1; as publisher of MW's

works 77, 89, 96, 128–9, 369; comment on MW 194; correspondence with MW 119–20, 141, 201–2, 245; description of 116–17; evening dinners 152–3, 162, 168, 207, 208, 476; financial position 415; health of 169, 170, 176, 201, 415; need for translated books 134; relationship with MW 117, 123, 124, 125, 126, 129, 141–2, 144–5, 157, 158, 163–4, 196, 286, 415

Johnson, Samuel 10, 61, 78, 102, 103, 131, 142–3, 464; Sermon. . .for the Funeral of his Wife 149–50

Kauffman, Angelica 153
Kemble, John Philip 384, 420
King, Caroline, Lady Kingsborough 79–80, 84–5, 94, 123–4, 128; concern for MW's health 99–100; and lack of intimacy with MW 92, 100; MW's contempt/dislike for 88, 93, 100–1, 105; MW's description of 87, 92, 93; pride of 101; tense relationship with MW 100–2, 105–8, 115
King, Edward 85
King, John 412
King, Margaret, Countess of Mount Cashell 89, 91, 92, 95, 100, 115–16, 150–1, 264, 465 n. 1, 466 n. 4, 467 n. 4
King, Robert, Lord Kingsborough 79–80, 84–5, 94, 123–4, 466 n. 7; MW's contempt for 87, 88; possible sexual attentions to MW 104, 115; as possible source of money for MW 111
Kingston, Earl of 94
Knowles, John 155, 156, 158, 195, 197, 470–1 n. 12
Kvistram 324, 339

La Rochefoucauld, François, Duc de 103
Lackington, James Memoirs 367
Lacombe, Claire 211
Ladies of Llangollen 18
Ladies Monthly Museum 185
Lady's Magazine 13, 18, 77
Lane, Nicholas 26
Lanesborough, Lady 412, 489 ns. 12 and 13
Lanthénas, François 215, 385
Lara, Ben, Essay on the Injurious Custom of Mothers not suckling their own Children 257
Larvik 334–5
Laugharne 24–5, 41, 146, 157, 171, 175
Laurent, M. 137, 469 n. 9
Lavater, Johann Kaspar 136, 153, 192, 214, 242, 468 n. 1; Essays on Physiognomy 134
Le Havre 240, 242, 243, 244, 247, 249, 250, 251, 252, 253, 258, 265, 283, 350
Leigh-Perrots 371

Léon, Pauline 211
Lisbon 42, 43, 57, 62–4, 66, 70, 252, 338
Locke, John 5, 181, 255; Some Thoughts Concerning Education 76
London 6–7, 155, 160, 163, 283–6, 334, 352–3, 384, 427
Louis XVI 206, 209, 217

Macaulay, Catherine 167, 168, 179, 192, 214, 218, 246, 472 n. 5
madness 491–2; and female hysteria 45; in fiction 427–34; in Hamlet 104; MW's fear of 46; possibility of in MW's brother 21–2; treatment of 21–2, 427; and vivacity 103
Mandeville, Bernard de 468 n. 13, 480 n. 3
Manley, Delarivier 167
Marat, Jean Paul 215, 219, 220, 266
Marguerite (MW's maid) 270, 281, 282, 304, 305, 310, 311, 315, 316, 318, 319, 323, 325, 341, 344, 347, 387, 391, 392, 397, 453
Maria and Margaretha 350
Marie Antoinette 166, 168, 199, 219, 368, 480 n. 4
Marks, Jane 463
marriage 47, 50, 77, 80, 476 n. 12; conjugal relations in 45–6; or the contemplative life 70; equated with tyranny 11; in fiction 234; Godwin's views on 417, 422, 441; MW rejects proposal of 144–5; in MW's fiction 114, 430; MW's reason for 421–2; MW's views on 5, 22, 31, 35, 43–4, 47, 61, 77, 79, 80, 144, 192, 200, 239, 417, 490–1 n. 2; power in 44; separation/divorce 50, 51, 57, 434, 493 n. 40
Marriage Act (1753) 440
Marshall, James 380, 395, 418, 435, 453, 456
Marshall, John 15
Martin, Sir Mortdant 30
masochism 313
maternal role: Lady Kingsborough's attitude towards 88, 91–2; MW's assumption of 11, 40, 50, 92, 108, 146, 267; MW's comments on 39; MW's reaction to first child 257–8, 259–60, 270–1; MW's views on 246–7
melancholy 183, 483; female 75, 77; in MW 30, 31–2, 33, 34, 44, 65, 66–7, 71, 72, 73–5, 83, 89–91, 92, 94, 96–7, 99–100, 104, 108, 138, 142–3, 159, 238, 274, 277–8, 280–2, 307–8, 321, 337, 338–9, 341–3, 403–4, 407, 411, 464 n. 7, 466 n. 2; in MW's sisters 51, 53, 75, 96, 169; reflected in women's conduct-books 77; religious and secular 75; in Wollstonecraft family 21, 74–5, 171, 446

melodrama/activity, MW's need for 46–7, 51, 54, 72, 74, 104, 281, 282, 303, 307, 317, 362, 384
Mesmer, Franz Anton 257
Methodist 10
Milton, John 157, 158, 180, 181, 238, 246; *Il Penseroso* 112; *Paradise Lost* 112, 159, 396, 471
mind/body relationship: Brown's holistic sense of 131; as interdependent 134; MW's interest in 72, 92, 108, 132–3; MW's views on 277, 331, 332; and sexual difference 186, 256
Minerva Press 461 n. 1
Mirabeau, Honoré Gabriel de Riquetti, Comte de 238
Mitchell, John 337
Mitchelstown Castle (County Cork) 86, 87–8, 471 n. 21
Montagu, Basil 385, 396, 401, 413, 414, 435, 440, 441, 443, 453, 455
Montagu, Elizabeth 126
Montagu, Lady Mary Wortley 484 n. 8
*Monthly Magazine* 424
*Monthly Review* 139
Montolieu, Baroness de, *Caroline de Lichtfield* 96, 111
Moore, Dr John 212, 244; *View of the Causes and Progress of the French Revolution* 255, 480 n. 2
Moore, Mary 95, 106
morality 262; for children 134, 135–6; female 179; imposed on women 246; MW as moralist 65–6, 82, 83, 84, 96, 97, 110, 136; and women 428–9
More, Hannah 27, 60, 291, 367, 428, 467; *Coelebs in Search of a Wife* 185; *Repository Tracts* 185, 426; *Strictures on the Modern System of Education* 185
Moser, Mary 153
Mounsell, David 290

Necker, Jacques, *Of the Importance of Religious Opinion* 134–5
nerves, theory of 131–2, 482–3 n. 7
Newington Green 56–7, 58, 59, 61, 67, 80–1, 94, 98–9, 126, 136, 146, 152, 162, 166, 179, 208, 212, 243, 313
Nordberg, Christoffer 274, 303, 324, 325
Norway 325–6, 328, 330, 348

Ogle, Elizabeth 95, 106
Ogle, George 89, 102, 103, 153; pays court to MW 106–8, 115

Opie, Amelia, *see* Alderson, Amelia
Opie, John 191–2, 385, 396, 401, 406, 487
Orléans, Lois-Philippe-Joseph, Duke of 219, 480 n. 2
Oslo 328, 341, 350

pain 219, 248, 332, 333, 337, 495 n. 10
Paine, Thomas 152, 177, 185, 210, 214, 215, 216, 237, 244, 265, 329–30, 379, 478 n. 2; *The Age of Reason* 330; *Rights of Man* 164, 168, 178, 185, 194, 207, 263
Paley, William 110, 172, 493 n. 40
Palm, Etta 211
parents: affection of 331; affection and neglect from 4–5, 39, 50, 83; MW's attitude towards own 4–5, 11, 25, 38, 39, 41, 99, 142; bonding with children 4, 257–8, 275, 342; in MW's fiction 111–2, 127, 128; MW's views on 286; maternal influence on MW 11, 27, 39–40, 74–5; paternal influence on MW 5, 8, 26–7, 39, 40–1, 67, 74–5, 111, 158, 171, 232, 247; surrogate 4, 5, 67, 126, 142, 151; tyranny of 5, 8, 11, 14, 39, 75
Paris 195, 199, 250, 334, 370, 384; MW in 205–22, 237, 266
Parr, Dr Samuel 380, 437, 440, 443
Parr, Sarah 380, 382, 437, 440, 443
patience 40, 46, 48, 65, 74, 136, 141, 149, 158, 400, 450
Pembroke 291, 292, 297, 300
Pennington, Sarah, Lady 77, 468 n. 6
Phillips, Richard 425
physicians 20, 99–100, 256–7, 412, 448–456
piety: in MW's fiction 126–7, 136–7; MW's sense of 10, 30, 31, 33, 53–4, 66, 72, 75, 83, 102, 133, 149, 150, 219, 310, 455
Pindar, Peter *see* Wolcot, John
Pinkerton, Miss 444–7, 494 n. 19
Pitt, William (the Younger) 59, 217, 263
Poignand, Dr Louis 451–2, 453
Polwhele, Richard 468 n. 4, 496 n. 20
Polygon, the (London) 423–4, 441, 442, 449, 450, 452, 453
Porter, Agnes 31, 32, 42, 102, 188, 465 n. 3
power/control: equated with love 11; in marriage 44; in relationships 5; MW's bid for 11, 49, 55; MW's longing for 18–19
Prescott, Rachel 184
Price, Dr Richard 59–61, 67, 77, 79, 81, 99, 119, 152, 162, 163, 165, 166, 178, 209, 464 n. 3

Priestley, Joseph 59, 474 n. 6

Primrose Street (Spitalfields) 6, 7, 24, 25, 146, 157, 189, 292

Prior, John 79, 82, 83, 84, 124

Prior, Mrs 79, 83, 84, 85, 94, 124

prostitute/prostitution 130, 165, 428, 473 n. 11, 492 n. 28

public speaking 136–7

Radcliffe, Ann, *The Italian* 415, 416

rank/status: female 426; MW's attitude to upper orders 87; MW's awareness of 29, 82, 84, 85, 88, 101, 139, 409; in MW's fiction 128, 428, 429

reason/rationality 35, 46, 49, 128, 152, 162, 163, 180, 208, 218, 221, 247, 400, 436; and emotion/ sensibility 48, 76, 82, 97, 107, 112, 113, 125, 132, 176, 182–3, 186, 201, 202, 236, 241, 261, 271, 282, 304, 313, 342, 363, 364, 383, 394, 431, 483 n. 4; and imagination 139, 268, 306–7, 364, 424, 425; and religion 31, 54, 60, 135, 149, 150, 164–165, 176; and suicide 354, 355

Rees, Mr 172, 173

Reeve, Clara 468 n. 6; 492 ns. 31 and 33

religion 30, 54, 59–60, 149–150, 165, 180, 329–30, 425, 426, 436, 455, 474 n. 6, 495–6 n. 20

Reveley, Maria 381, 388, 397, 419, 442, 450, 452, 453, 456, 486 ns. 1 and 4, 491 n. 1

Richardson, Samuel 60; *Clarissa* 112, 157, 235; *Pamela* 18, 235; *Sir Charles Grandison* 134

rights 59, 163, 165, 177, 179–180, 182, 185, 186, 210, 211, 247, 268, 329, 402, 430

Robespierre, Maximilien 215, 216, 219, 242, 263, 265, 266, 426

Robinson, Mary 27, 264, 381–2, 405, 406, 410, 419, 424, 426, 427–8, 432, 438, 450, 490 n. 4, 491 n. 17; *Angelina* 416; *Hubert de Sevrac* 419–20; *Letter to the Women of England* 491 n. 5; 'Stanzas Written between Dover and Calais' 382

Roebuck, Mr 26, 81, 91, 94, 98, 111, 147, 189, 465 n. 3

Rogers, Samuel 56

Roland, Jean-Marie 215

Roland, Manon 214, 215, 216, 241–2, 477 n. 20, 482 n. 1

Roscoe, William 158, 167, 175, 177, 189, 197, 199–200, 236

Rouget de l'Isle, Claude-Joseph 271

Rousseau, Jean-Jacques 183–4, 194–5, 220, 233, 246, 256, 306–7, 314, 382, 412, 463 n. 4, 471 n.

15; *Confessions* 140, 307; *Émile* 102, 107, 111, 112, 127, 181–2, 430, 481 n. 6; *La Nouvelle Héloïse* 235, 416, 428, 488 n. 9, 493 n. 33; *Reveries of the Solitary Walker* 307, 314, 368, 389

Rowan, Archibald Hamilton 271–2, 273, 283–4, 285, 370, 373, 385, 481, 485 n. 11, 491 n. 11

Rowe, Elizabeth 136

Royal Humane Society 356

Russell, Thomas 284

St Paul's Churchyard 116, 123, 138, 146, 160, 425

St Pierre, Jacques, *Paul and Virginia* 239

Salzmann, Christian 155, 183, 184; *Elements of Morality, for the Use of Children* 135–6

Schlabrendorf, Gustav, Graf von 210–11, 231, 236, 239, 240, 266, 371, 373

Schweitzer, Johann Carl 214

Schweitzer, Madeleine (Magdalena Hess of Zurich) 153, 214–15, 217, 271, 344

self, MW's sense of 32, 33, 34, 36, 41, 51–2, 53, 74, 107, 109, 136, 161, 162, 317, 320–1, 328–9, 368, 425–6, 433–4

self-pity 38, 40, 48, 74, 75, 92, 97, 140, 360

sensibility/sensitivity 74, 86, 110, 134, 135, 140, 151, 163, 166, 182, 241, 268, 271, 327, 337, 364, 430, 482 n 3; and imagination 307; and reason 48, 76, 82, 97, 107, 112, 113, 125, 132, 176, 182–3, 186, 201, 202, 236, 241, 261, 271, 282, 304, 313, 342, 363, 364, 383, 394, 431, 484 n. 4; associated with women 125, 180; cult of 102–3; female 125, 374, 429; gendered view of 183; in literary style 15–16, 163, 176, 424; in MW's fiction 112, 114–15, 125, 427; in MW 19, 26, 68, 102–4, 138, 146, 192, 328, 433, 442–3; male 106, 108, 163, 425

servants 63, 84, 88, 322, 344, 413

Seward, Anna 18, 184, 212, 213, 224, 239, 369, 469 n. 10

sex 154, 393, 398–400, 401–2, 403, 421, 468 n. 4, 473 ns. 16 and 21 ; curbing of 183; demystification of 183; difference 180, 181–3, 195, 256; equality 186–7, 193, 211, 313, 432, 467 n. 2; MW's allusions to 23, 46; MW's attitude towards 154, 156, 253, 275, 430, 493 n. 33; MW's encounters with/reactions to 104, 107, 115, 234–8, 284, 351–2; in MW's fiction 111–12, 113–14, 135, 429–31; relationships 342, 351–2, 373; repression of 103–4, 183–4, 375, 493 n. 33

Shakespeare, William 154, 246, 303; *Hamlet* 103–4, 154, 241, 341; *King Lear* 154; *Macbeth* 154

Shelley, Mary Wollstonecraft 417, 450, 453, 456, 490 n. 1
Shelley, Percy Bysshe, *Queen Mab* 185
Shelley, Percy Florence 471 n. 12
Siddons, Sarah 384, 417, 444
Skeys, Hugh 35, 456, 496 n. 21; in Ireland 95; in Lisbon 57, 66; involvement with Meredith Bishop 48, 54–5; relationship and marriage to Fanny Blood 24, 27, 30, 42, 62, 63; relationship with MW 54, 69–70, 70, 71, 74, 81, 98; remarriage of 138, 151
slavery 233
Smellie, William 256, 480 n. 5
Smith, Adam 180
Smith, Charlotte 89, 367, 384, 471 n. 15, 476, 482 n. 6, 493 n. 38; *Desmond* 212, 493 n. 38; *Elegiac Sonnets* 75, 317
Smollett, Tobias 10
Snell, Hannah 14, 22, 212
Southey, Robert 370, 435, 464 n. 4, 477 n. 22
Staël, Anne-Louise-Germaine de 60
Sterne, Laurence 140, 241, 314, 427
Stone, John Hurford 213, 218, 243, 252, 265, 385

Talleyrand-Périgord, Charles-Maurice de 155, 179–80, 214, 385
Tallien, Jean Lambert 263
Tallien, Thérèse 426
Tarleton, Banastre 381, 382, 419, 428, 438, 491 n. 4
Tasker, Mr 170–1
Tavistock, Lady 131, 180
Taylor, Thomas 27, 70, 185; *Vindication of the Rights of Brutes* 185, 473 n. 21
Théroigne de Méricourt, Anne-Josèphe 211, 219, 220
Thomson, James, *Seasons* 112
Thrale, Hester (*née* Piozzi) 280, 367
*The Times* 356, 357
Tønsberg 325, 328–30, 334, 335, 337, 338, 429
Tooke, John Horne 7, 59, 152, 228, 263–4, 401, 407, 480 n. 1
Trimmer, Sarah 126, 246; *Oeconomy of Charity* 127
Turner, Thomas 149
Twiss, Francis 385, 417, 421, 444

Ungar, A. J. 274, 303, 325
Unitarianism 60

Upton Castle (Pembrokeshire) 170–1, 224, 290, 291, 293, 346, 413

Walpole, Horace 168, 246
Waterhouse, Joshua 33–4, 35, 42, 77, 231, 462 n. 6
Wedgwood, Elizabeth [Bessie Allen] 413, 414
Wedgwood, John 436
Wedgwood, Josiah II 413, 441
Wedgwood, Sarah 441, 494 n. 11
Wedgwood, Thomas 409–10, 413, 422, 424, 436–7, 442, 443, 450
Weeton, Ellen 463 n. 1
West, Jane, *The Gossip's Story* 384, 477 n. 27
wet-nursing/breast-feeding 4, 45, 69, 257–8
Wheatcroft, John 252, 258, 350
White's Hotel (Paris) 210, 212, 216, 244
Wilkes, John 7, 263
Williams, Helen Maria 212–14, 215, 216, 217, 218, 219, 220, 224, 239, 240, 243–4, 252, 264, 265, 317, 371, 385, 432, 477 n. 20, 480 n. 4; *Julia* 213; *Letters from France* 212, 217, 218, 219, 241–2, 252, 264, 371
Willis, Francis 22
Windsor Castle 13–14
Wolcot, Dr John (Peter Pindar) 191, 377
Wollstonecraft, Charles (brother) 37, 47, 91, 137; and America 189–91, 195, 245, 289, 290–1, 292–3, 370, 407; and sisters 191, 290–1, 292–3, 295–6, 298, 299, 302; character 37, 130, 195, 196–7, 245, 266–7, 291; as correspondent 137, 157, 188–9, 245, 266–7, 290, 292–3, 298, 385, 407; financial affairs 141, 174–5, 292; in Ireland 147, 148–9; in Laugharne 41, 169, 172, 174; MW's attitude towards 124–5, 130, 141, 147–9, 157, 174–5, 189; with brother 47, 91, 147, 174
Wollstonecraft, Edward Bland (Ned) (brother) 25, 37, 47, 124, 125, 146–7; and grandfather 3; and parents 5, 11; relationship with sisters 41, 49, 51, 53, 55, 83–4, 90, 97–8, 99; life: articled 20; marriage of 26; at marriage of Eliza 43; Bishop appeals to 51; takes over family finances 40–1; and 'Roebuck' money 81, 91, 98–9, 147, 189
Wollstonecraft, Edward (grandfather) 6, 7; will of 3
Wollstonecraft, Edward John (father) 3, 4, 6, 45, 146–7, 171, 189, 243; agrees to Eliza's marriage 43; attitude to wife 38–9; becomes gentleman farmer 7–8; as father–tyrant 5, 8, 11, 14, 75; financial affairs 40, 146, 157, 172, 415; frequent

trips to London 24, 25; health of 289; influence on MW 5, 8, 26–7, 39, 40–1,67, 74–5, 111, 158, 171, 232, 247; in MW's writings 111–2, 171; marriage to Lydia 40–1; moves back to London 20, 25; moves to Laugharne 24–5, 41; moves to Yorkshire 8–9; settles in Beverley 9–11; visits Eliza at Upton 173

Wollstonecraft, Elizabeth (aunt) 3

Wollstonecraft, Elizabeth (Eliza bishop) (sister) 6, 37, 38, 137, 154, 171, 295, 456; and America 292–3, 294, 295; and Fanny Blood 37–8, 45, 62, 63–4; and Ireland 91, 301–2; and money 51, 157, 174, 199, 227, 228, 288–9, 292, 297–301; as companion and teacher 58, 79, 80, 81, 120, 129, 146; as governess 170–3, 293–4, 295; attitude of MW towards 66, 67, 81, 170, 288; attitude to MW 38, 188–9, 195–6, 199, 206, 228, 289–290, 385; depression 45–6, 244–5, 288–9, 290; marriage and separation 43–4, 46–7, 49–57; obsession with France 223–30, 253, 288, 289, 295–7; political views 146, 224–5, 226, 228, 291–2

Wollstonecraft, Elizabeth (mother) 4–5, 6, 37, 45; character 5, 11, 14, 75; illness and death 38–40; in MW's fiction 18, 40, 111

Wollstonecraft, Everina (sister) 6, 22, 25, 37, 38, 47, 56, 63–4, 289, 290, 292, 437–8, 456; annuity of 111; as governess 79, 160, 161, 174, 224, 413, 415–16, 489 n. 17; as reader 415–6; as teacher 58, 111, 117, 169; as translator 146; correspondence with MW 49–50, 89–90, 91, 96, 97–8, 124, 160, 161, 190–1, 195, 201, 205–6, 267, 288, 292, 293, 385, 414–6; illnesses of 38,137, 169, 189; in Paris 129, 134–5, 137, 141, 146, 154; in brother's household 80, 83–4, 90, 97–8, 99; relationship with George Blood 99, 173–4; relationship with Godwin 414, 437–8, 441, 446; relationship with MW 48, 66, 67, 169–70, 413–14

Wollstonecraft family: declining fortunes of 8–9, 25–6, 29, 37; dependence on each other 289; fictionalised by MW 111–15, 134; MW's correspondence with 38, 46, 47, 49–50, 81–2, 83–4, 88, 91–2, 95–8, 102, 103–4, 110, 129; MW's management of 146–9, 174–5, 189–90, 191; MW's moralizing attitude towards 65–6, 82, 83, 84, 96, 97, 110; MW's relationship with 21, 27, 38, 41, 62, 64, 66, 67, 73, 117–18, 129–30, 158–9; MW's responsibility for 66, 73, 79, 91, 98, 99, 119, 124, 141, 146, 169–70, 174–5, 195–6, 288

Wollstonecraft, Henry Woodstock (brother) 6, 427; apprenticed 20; uncertain fate of 21–2

Wollstonecraft, James (brother) 7, 37, 146, 169, 170, 171, 174, 197, 225–6, 253, 267, 289, 290, 296, 299, 385, 482 n. 3

Wollstonecraft, Lydia (step-mother) 40–1, 91, 172

Wollstonecraft, Mary: and nature 7, 317–18, 322, 323, 324, 326, 328–9, 330, 331–2, 436; and mortality 281–2, 329, 339, 355, 370, 384; and theatre and art 384–5, 404, 414, 420; appearance 28, 142, 155, 376–7; as reader 10, 12–14, 18, 90, 95, 96, 103, 112, 131, 235, 245, 415; as reviewer 138–41, 149–50, 154, 157, 195, 213, 382, 383–4, 419–20, 426, 468, 469, 477–8; as translator 134–6, 239; attitude to Amelia Alderson 382, 409; attitude to the Kingsboroughs 87–8, 93; attitude to Mary Hays 193–4, 376; attitude to Neptune Blood 42, 79, 94, 95, 105; attitude to own writing 18, 23, 128–9, 150, 359–60, 362–3, 433–34; attitude to Wedgwood 436, 442; character 11, 15, 17–19, 41, 42, 49, 55, 75, 101–2, 106, 141, 145, 161, 235, 309, 344, 358; concern for reputation 416–17, 421–2; austerity/stoicism of 35–6, 48, 61, 79, 92–3, 101, 137, 147, 155, 163, 194, 235, 322, 324, 332, 334, 339; financial affairs 26, 51–2, 54, 55, 58, 70, 71, 72, 78, 79–80, 81, 94, 111, 131, 141, 157, 170, 199, 223–4, 227, 228, 236, 281, 372–3, 408–11, 415, 424, 461 n. 9, 479 n. 14; health of 205, 208, 248, 250, 251, 265, 277, 279, 282, 318, 321, 323, 331, 340, 403, 404, 407, 411–12; literary activities 78, 110, 111, 117, 119–20, 123–9, 340–1; relationship with Fanny Blood 22–4, 25, 41–3, 69, 80; relationship with the Bloods 41–3, 73; relationship with the Clares 22, 23, 53; relationship with Hannah Burgh 55–6, 60, 61, 66, 67, 71, 75, 77, 79, 82, 94, 98, 99, 124, 130, 136, 145; relationship with Fuseli 152–7, 169, 170, 196, 196–7, 197–8, 200, 201; relationship with Gilbert Imlay 234–8, 239–43, 244–51, 252–4, 258, 260–2, 267–8, 272, 273–7, 313, 320, 335, 348–50, 351–2, 357, 358–9, 371, 373, 489–90 n. 26; relationship with Godwin 381, 385–92, 393–406, 407–18, 419–24, 445–7; life: birth and christening 4; ignored by grandfather 3; early years 6; memories of childhood 9; education of 14, 15; as Londoner 6–7, 123, 334; determines to leave home 26, 27; as lady's companion 28–9, 35, 36; nurses mother 39–

Wollstonecraft, Mary – cont'd

40; failed romances 33–4, 35, 42, 79, 115; romantic leanings 44, 61, 64, 65, 79, 103–4; as 'Princess' 42, 63, 73, 99, 137; removes Eliza from her family 46–7, 49–57, 66–7; sets up school 55–6, 58, 62, 63, 66–7, 71, 77, 79, 463 n. 1; as pedagogue 58; journey to Lisbon 68, 70; and death of Fanny Blood 68–9, 73–4, 83; and the French ship 70–1; at Eton 82–3; journey to Ireland 82–6; as governess 79–81, 82, 83, 87–8, 89–93, 102; dismissed as governess 116, 124; moves to London 123; use of humour in writings 140–1; in Warminster 158–62; oppressed by domesticity 159–62; views on governessing 183; takes title of 'Mrs' 188; pregnancy of 242, 246–51, 256, 407, 408, 411–13, 414, 416–17, 438; suicidal thoughts 254–7, 286–7, 304, 319, 329, 339, 340, 484 n. 4, 486 n. 1; birth of Fanny 256–60; as mother 261, 265, 267, 268, 269, 270, 272, 284; plans sequel to French Revolution history 263; flirtations with men 271–2, 273; journey through Scandinavia 303–4, 308, 309–13, 315–24, 325–33, 334–50; portrait painted 155, 474; possible autobiography 359; and anonymous love-letter 377–8; marriage to Godwin 417–21; reactions to her marriage 419–21; visit to Bedlam 427; abandoned by friends 444; birth of Mary 449–50; death 450–6, 495 ns. 4 and 7; correspondence: adolescent/adult similarities in 15; with Fanny Blood 23, 63, 64; with George Blood 65–6, 69, 72, 74, 75, 76, 79, 91, 94, 96, 137, 147–8, 174, 176–7; with Gilbert Imlay 237, 240–1, 242–3, 245–6, 247–8, 262–3, 267–8, 312–14, 269–71, 274–7, 278–82, 305, 311, 319–20, 323, 327, 329, 330–1, 332–3, 336–7, 340, 342–3, 346–7, 348–9, 359, 360–2, 363–4, 372, 373; with sisters 38, 46, 47, 49–50, 81–2, 83–4, 88, 91–2, 95–8, 102, 103–4, 110, 129, 137, 158, 160, 195, 205–6, 229–30, 244–5, 253–4, 265, 267, 288–9, 297–8, 300–1, 415–16; with Jane Arden 15–18, 30–1, 34, 35, 44; with Joseph Johnson 119–20, 141, 201–2, 245; with Ruth Barlow 208–9, 258, 259, 260; with William Godwin 388, 389–92, 393, 394–6, 398–9, 402–3, 404, 405, 438–47, 450; writings: 'The Cave of Fancy' 125, 182; The Female Reader 136–7, 154, 491; Hints 425; An Historical and Moral View of the . . French Revolution 217–22, 236, 245, 251, 252, 255, 256, 263, 264, 282, 341, 359, 369, 480 ns. 1 and 4; 'Letter on the Character of the French Nation' 207–8; Letters from Sweden 69, 367–70, 372–3, 377, 384, 385, 394, 425, 429, 432, 449, 484 n. 6; Mary, A Fiction 18, 61, 68, 111–15, 125, 126, 137, 140, 150, 151, 154, 156, 166, 182, 211, 268, 309, 311, 314, 328, 329, 364, 415, 416, 424, 428, 431, 449, 461 n. 11; 'On Poetry, and Our Relish for the Beauties of Nature' 425; Original Stories 126–9, 134, 135, 151, 166, 177, 178, 193, 245, 467–8 n. 7; Thoughts on the Education of Daughters 76–8, 82, 83, 108, 115, 351, 468 n. 7; A Vindication of the Rights of Men 164–8, 176–7, 178, 207, 212, 218, 220–1, 243, 244, 246, 255, 472 n. 34; A Vindication of the Rights of Woman 177–87, 188, 194, 195, 212, 214, 215, 218, 220, 235, 236, 241, 246, 247, 248–9, 250, 255, 256, 276, 279, 279–80, 282, 313, 317, 330, 335, 351, 356, 368, 369, 371, 382–3, 395, 401, 405, 424, 429, 431, 434, 443, 465 n. 3, 468 n. 14, 473 n. 11, 486 n. 12, 489 n. 24, 492–3 n. 32; The Wrongs of Woman 18, 395, 426, 427–34, 461, 465–6 n. 3, 493 n. 33

women: and childbirth 256; cultural construction of 157; cultural corruption of 176; cultural misery of 76–7; dependence of 408; and fashion 32–3, 135, 155, 255, 404–5; freedoms for 220; gendered duties 404; male talk of 180–1, 182; and melancholy 75, 77; MW's defence of 46–7, 55, 62; MW's portrayal of 'the wrongs of' 427–32; MW's views on education of 76–7; as psychologically identical with men 180; as rational 183, 430–1; and reading 10, 416; in revolutionary Paris 211–14; rights of 178–180; and romantic love 280; and sexual equality 186–7; as slave and victim 383; society's treatment of 165–6; status of 426; weakness of 3, 180

women's fiction 182, 480; reviewed by MW 139, 157, 213, 382, 383

Wordsworth, William 152

work, women's 28, 165, 180, 183, 404, 429, 461 n. 1, 463 n. 1, 465 n. 3

Wulfsberg, Jacob 325, 328, 332, 350

York Courant 8, 13, 21, 242

Young, Arthur 85

Young, Edward, Night Thoughts 112